THE
TRUMP
IMPEACHMENT
ORDEAL

GEOFFREY KEANE

The Trump Impeachment Ordeal

This book is written to provide information and motivation to readers. Its purpose is not to render any type of psychological, legal, or professional advice of any kind. The content is the sole opinion and expression of the author, and not necessarily that of the publisher.

Printed in the United States of America.

ISBN   978-1-951913-64-9   (Paperback)
ISBN   978-1-951913-65-6   (Digital)

Lettra Press books may be ordered through booksellers or by contacting:

Lettra Press LLC
30 N Gould St. Suite 4753
Sheridan, WY 82801
1 307-200-3414 | info@lettrapress.com
www.lettrapress.com

Contents

Members of the House Intelligence Committee:

(Democratic) Majority Leader:
Adam Schiff- Chairman of these proceedings

(Republican) Minority Leader:
(Ranking Member) Devin Nunez

(13 Democrats and 9 Republicans)

Democratic Committee members:

Eric Swalwell, Julian Castro, Jim Himes, Ms. Sewell,
Mr. Carson, Ms. Speier, Mr. Quigley, Mr. Heck, Mr. Welch,
Mr. Maloney, Ms. Demmings, and Mr. Krishnamoorthi

Republican Committee Members:

Mr. Ratcliffe, Mr. Jordan, Mr. Turner, Dr. Wenstrup,
Mr. Stewart, Ms. Stefanik, Mr, Conanway, and Mr. Hurd

Members of the House Judiciary Committee:

(24 Democrats, and 17 Republicans)

(Democratic) Majority Leader:
Jerrold Nadler- Chairman of these proceedings

(Republican) Minority Leader:
(Ranking Member) Doug Collins

Democratic Committee members:
Ms. Scanlon, Ms. Lofgren, Ms. Jackson-Lee, Mr. Cohen, Mr. Deutch, Mr. Richmond, Mr. Cicillene, Mr. Lieu, Mr. Johnson, Ms. Bass, Mr. Jeffries, Eric Swalwell, Mr. Raskin, Ms. Jayapal, Mr. Correa, Mr. Neguse, Mr. Stanton, Ms Mucarsel-Powell, Val Demmings, Ms. Garcia, Ms. McBath, Ms. Dean, Ms. Escobar

Republican Committee Members:
Mr. Sensenbrenner, Mr. Chabot, Mr. Buck, Mr. Gohmert, Mr. Jordan, Mr. Ratcliffe, Mr. Roby, Mr. Johnson, Mr. McClintock, Mr. Reschenthaler, Mr. Armstrong, Mr. Gaetz, Mr. Biggs, Ms. Lesko, Mr. Cline, Mr. Steube

Introduction

The following is my summary of the valid, pertinent facts, and points made by the Intelligence Committee during this public presentation phase of the Trump Impeachment Inquiry; along with the Republicans' attempted defense tactics and representations. It is moreover a transcription of the hearings, with my commentary.

The public hearing process was unduly longwinded, with much repetition of the information probably most pertinent for the public to learn of; but even much worse, the Republicans were able to repeat contentions and false statements that Democratic Intelligence Committee members, especially often Adam Schiff, had subsequently illuminated clearly to us all, as being "smoke and mirrors" illusory statements, or representations otherwise insignificant to the issue at hand.

My main reason for undertaking this commentary and report, in addition to stating more concisely the Democrats' case, is to take <u>out</u> of this report, the many times' repeated Republicans' statements and contentions (which I will recount in detail the first time one of their points is being made) that were subsequently again stated or contended, despite the fact they had been rendered pointless arguments, for clearly-defined reasons.

In addition, I will attempt to fact-check the statements and contentions; particularly of Devin Nunez, the Republican Minority leader, each time he had his 5-minute opening statement at each hearing, just after Adam Schiff's opening statement. There were six hearings altogether, where Schiff and Nunez gave 5-minute opening statements;

and I will make every effort to avoid duplicate restatements of the same information; and especially, I will omit Nunez's duplicate statements and contentions that (there is clear evidence) either are without basis, or those which have no bearing on the matter; and I believe there are a multitude of these.

I think this whole process would have been much more effective if Adam Schiff had simply written up a long report, read this as a statement at the beginning, (even if it took a couple of hours), laying out what has ultimately become exposed, of greater significance, and why it would lead to impeachment. It would have been much more effective, in my view, if Adam Schiff had indeed read a two-hour-long summary of all that has been discovered, and then merely had the witnesses comment on their involvement, substantiating in their testimony, that what Adam Schiff is describing is in accord with their own witness, and their own understanding regarding this whole scenario.

I think that unfortunately, this process took many more hours than it needed to, as well as giving ample opportunity for Republicans to make repeated false contentions (which of course, can be hypnotizing to less-sophisticated souls, perhaps), and there was way too much opportunity for Republicans to repeatedly promote a narrative that is in large part either untrue, or otherwise insignificant, in terms of it being any reasonable defense, against what Trump had commanded all of these people in his administration to do, under the coordinating influence of Rudy Giuliani, as Trump ongoingly hatched this odious scheme.

Therefore, my objective here is to condense the message (that the House Intelligence Committee had intended to give to the American public), into its more essential elements. However, I am thinking that it would be most helpful, to first procure a transcript, of the entirety of the six hearings; and my plan is then, to mine through it, and create a much shorter document containing what I can determine as the most essential elements which the public should probably come to understand. In addition to replaying my DVR recordings in order to create this transcript, I have watched the lion's share of the impeachment hearings live, and I can also add my own perspective to this report, based on what I have learned in recent years, from reading the New York Times, daily, and also watching cable news pretty avidly.

I trust that this could be helpful to those, who either could not afford to sit through all of these hearings, or were otherwise confused, or perhaps just became disinterested in the whole matter, because there were severely-conflicting contentions and points of view being strongly voiced. I hope to cut through many of the bull-slinging, and lay out the simple truth.

You know, this "everyone was in the loop" concept; and all of the testimony showing that there were quite a few top-level officials with knowledge of the scheme, indicates to me that perhaps, this was a scheme that was not only endorsed by the President and Rudy Giuliani; but it would make sense that several other top officials and Republican Congressmen might well have endorsed this plot, so that they could all keep their jobs, and keep getting their agenda moved forward; to the detriment of the common man, nevertheless.

Later in the book, I will write about the Judiciary committee hearings, as well; and then I will subsequently write briefly about the impeachment trial.

I have written out a pretty thorough transcription of the first several Intelligence Committee hearings; so that some readers could skim through, and realize that there was a lot of repetition of similar revelations of the scheme that President Trump is being impeached for having carried through with, over a period of the better part of a whole year; each witness explaining their experiences, and basically corroborating each other's stories along the way.

However, following the Vindeman/Williams hearing, I started to get away from a complete transcription of the hearings; instead transcribing only the opening statements, in some cases; and otherwise mainly trying to capture the highlights, and the most significant testimony and questioning.

I would encourage any American citizen to look through this book, to hear about, and come to understand what has been happening in government, during the Trump administration; because only voters, en mass, can foil this conservative movement, which continues to fulfill the objectives of the rich, special interests, and Republican politicians, working in concert to have everything go their way, to the detriment of the common man.

Putting an end to this injustice is only possible, to the extent that American citizens, as a whole, stop being falsely convinced that what is being purported by the conservative media, and Internet disinformation campaigns, is best for this country. It is not; if we, as a people, want to give ourselves an opportunity to run successful small businesses, and earn a more comfortable living; and at the same time, achieve our objectives of getting away from fossil fuel; otherwise converting to clean energy which effectively reverses global warming, so that our legacy will be to leave the future generations with other than an uninhabitable planet, it is imperative that we begin to open our eyes to the treachery being levied against us by those who simply intend to make a lot of money off of pushing oil and gas, and rolling back regulations that hurt us in many ways; especially including deregulation of the financial markets; some of which led to the crash of 2008; but it could get much worse. I sure hope we can all wise up!

I can assert, that my portrayal of the hearings, along my own added commentary, does significantly capture, and characterize, the true nature and substance of what is testified to, related to the matters at hand.

Let me just remind any nit-picky potential-readers, that if there are occasional inaccuracies in my transcription, in a small number of instances, due to my own misinterpretation; or if I have accidentally misrepresented a stray few portrayals, by witnesses or committee members, this does not invalidate the work; in which I have made every effort to recount the happenings at these hearings; as well as additional information I have been exposed to, via newspaper articles, and Cable news channels. So, without ado, let me begin illuminating the whole picture, as objectively as I can:

Intelligence Committee hearing #1- Taylor and Kent

The first hearing was for Bill Taylor and George Kent to testify and answer questions. William Taylor is the newly-appointed ambassador to Ukraine, since Ambassador Yovanovitch was recalled last spring; as one strategy of President Trump's Ukraine scheme. George Kent is the Deputy Assistant Secretary of State for Eastern Europe and the caucuses. he has served for 27 years as a nonpartisan official, under five Presidents; both Republicans and Democrats. He oversees US policy on Ukraine, at the State Department. He has decades of experience in Ukrainian foreign-policy.

The first hearing begins with Adam Schiff's opening statement, after the swearing-in process.

In Adam Schiff's opening statement, he says that in 2014, Russia invaded Ukraine "to reverse Ukraine's embracement of the West," meaning that Ukraine was remodeling itself, in like manner to the US and other Western democracies; and at the same time, Russia's hostile acts were being carried out, in order to fulfill Putin's desire to rebuild a Russian Empire.

Since 2014, roughly 14,000 Ukrainians died battling Russian forces in this conflict. Volodymyr Zelensky was elected in April of 2019. Zelensky was actually a former comedian, and played the role of Ukrainian President, in a Ukrainian TV series. In reality, he had no political background at all; but this was perhaps one of the main reasons that Ukrainians were quick to elect him in a landslide victory; because, for generations, mainstream politicians within the government of Ukraine have been quite corrupt; perhaps largely as a result of corrupt Russian influence, most notably. Russia has taken advantage of huge oil and gas profit windfalls to put itself at the center of Ukrainian politics in a very corrupt, financially-influential manner.

Schiff asks, "Did President Trump seek to exploit our ally's vulnerability and invite Ukraine's interference in our election? -And did Trump condition official acts such as a White House meeting, and Congressionally-appropriated military assistance of $391 million, on condition that the Ukrainian government announce the opening of an investigation into Joe Biden (his chief rival in the upcoming election), and his son Hunter, who served on the board of Burisma, a historically-corrupt large natural gas company in Ukraine at the same time; (Hunter also having had no prior experience that would indicate he would be an especially advantageous pick for such a position, except that he was the son of the Vice President; so this could curry some favor, perhaps). At the time of Hunter's appointment to the board of Burisma, his father, Vice President Joe Biden was at the heart of a legitimate campaign to root out long-standing corruption in Ukraine. (During this time period in 2015, the Ukraine's government was in the middle of a regime change.)

Joe Biden had worked in concert with official diplomatic mandates consistent with the official policies of the State Department, along with the Ambassador and the US Embassy in Ukraine, working in coordination with a clearly-designated official strategy; in a valiant effort to work with Ukraine and help them to finally become a democracy without corruption. (This also involved fighting off a plethora of Russian corrupt influence into Ukraine's highest positions in government).

The opening of these investigations, that Trump was calling for, while withholding crucial support (in a few different forms) to Ukraine, (until Zelensky in particular was to "knuckle under" to pressure, and publicly-announce that these investigations were underway), was obviously intended to hurt the credibility of vice-President Biden (now running against Trump in 2020) by suggesting that Biden himself was corrupt. Joe Biden was, and still is now the front runner in the Democratic Party; so, in other words Trump wanted to dig up dirt to make his most likely opponent appear very much corrupt; giving Trump great advantage in his re-election efforts.

Adam Schiff then adds that, if the President has done these things, it is Congress's place to determine whether these actions were indeed "incompatible" with the office of the presidency of the United States. Schiff also explains that, how this situation resolves, will likely have much potential to set a precedent in the US, as to whether Presidential corruption, and using the office of the President for such odious personal objectives is something that will be tolerated, in the case of future Presidents; (or more plainly, will the country now be allowed to effectively become under authoritarian rule, perhaps?)

Schiff explains that sometime earlier this year, Rudy Giuliani began a campaign of pressuring the new Zelensky administration that had just been elected in March in Ukraine; pressuring them into announcing an investigation into Burisma, the largest natural gas company in Ukraine; and specifically into possible corrupt dealings in connection with the Bidens; and in addition, Trump also was asking Zelensky to renew efforts to investigate his contention that the "meddling in the 2016 election" had been initiated by Ukraine, and not Russia.

Schiff explains that the US intelligence agencies have very thoroughly investigated this notion, and have determined unequivocally that it was a Russian campaign of influence and disinformation, which was responsible for the massively overwhelming campaign of corrupt influence, into the 2016 election. As we know, many falsehoods were foisted on the American people, in this Russian Internet and other media disinformation campaign. Real people's identities were stolen so that Russians could use these fake bots as mouthpieces for propaganda. This company Crowdstrike had first discovered that Russia was behind the effort that greatly aided Trump in winning the election; but now, Trump and Rudy Giuliani wanted to promote the (debunked) theory that the election meddling effort came from Ukraine, and not Russia.

(Although Schiff doesn't mention the following, in his opening statement, I think it's important to emphasize that it's been determined that it was actually Russian intelligence agents who initially started this rumor that it was Ukraine and not Russia that meddled in the 2016 Presidential election in the US. Of course, Russia's great motivation for doing this, is because the US levied huge sanctions against Russia, as punishment for having carried out this huge disinformation and propaganda campaign; and if the Russians could be absolved of this, and the Ukrainians blamed instead, then sanctions placed on Russia could possibly be lifted. These sanctions on Russia are very crippling to Russia's economy; Russian companies are prohibited from doing business or having any financial involvement with the United States, which is largest economy in the world; and this has really hurt them badly; so they were desperate to get the sanctions lifted, and they saw spreading this rumor as perhaps paving the way to do it!)

Also, at this same time earlier in the year, in March and April, Marie Yovanovitch, the US Ambassador to Ukraine who has been there for years, was subjected to a smear campaign initiated by Rudy Giuliani (at Trump's direction), in conjunction with Rudy's affiliation with the corrupt head prosecutor in Ukraine. They circulated rumors that Ms. Yovanovitch was corrupt, by drumming up a false narrative, and making false public statements; which turned out to be pretty effective; as she was subsequently removed from service, and brought back to the United States in mid-April.

This timing is important, because this scheme, that the intelligence committee is trying to enlighten us on, involved getting her out of the way so that they could bring in other people, as substitutes, to negotiate Trump's odious demands for these investigations. Schiff also points out that one of the main people involved in this scheme is Gordon Sondland, who had no diplomatic experience at all. He merely had donated $1 million dollars to Trump's Super-Pac; and Sondland had also made other donations to other US politicians, who were subsequently instrumental in getting Marie Yovanovitch removed from her Ambassadorship in Ukraine.

As a thank you for Sondland's large donation to him, and realizing that Sondland would be an ideal patsy to undertake this scheme, Trump appointed Sondland Ambassador to the European Union; and in this capacity, (with the EU also in a position of support to Ukraine in fighting off the Russians), as Ambassador to the EU, Sondland would reasonably be expected to have regular contact with the Ukrainian government. But it seems pretty clear, Sondland, having no background in the area of international diplomacy, that Trump had likely satisfied himself that Sondland would do whatever he asked; whether it was part of historic, ongoing US policy in recent years between the US and Ukraine, or not. Sondland wouldn't even know the difference, for that matter.

Republicans point out that after Marie Yovanovitch was removed, she was subsequently replaced by Bill Taylor, who it turns out is somebody who was equally formidable, in terms of having many years of foreign service for the US, including three years as Ambassador to Ukraine from 2006 to 2009. We learned that Taylor is of high integrity, and he is very familiar with US foreign policy relating to Ukraine; so, in this respect he was certainly an appropriate appointment as a replacement Ambassador in Ukraine.

However, it turns out that there was a much-exploited time gap, by Trump and Giuliani, between when Yovanovitch was removed, up until Taylor was installed in that position; and had subsequently started to become wise to this apparently-counterproductive scheme.

Although Marie Yovanovitch was removed on May 20th, and Taylor had arrived in Ukraine on June 17th, the smear campaign against Yovanovitch significantly impeded her good ability to see through, and deal effectively with this scheme, and its corrupt actors; she was pretty badly hampered; mentally and emotionally; as a result of having suffered a significant undermining of her credibility, which had been widely broadcast, by early spring.

Then too, although Taylor had arrived in June, he initially was fine with the efforts of Sondland and Volker, coordinated by Giuliani, because at first, their efforts appeared to support initiatives in-keeping with stated Ukraine policy.

However, within a couple of months, Taylor started to see evidence that Sondland, working through Giuliani, was apparently complicit with a scheme that was going against stated US policy for Ukraine; and it was quite corrupt in nature.

But it was during this 3 or 4-month time frame, while there was no potent acting Ambassador to Ukraine from the US, that the scheme which the intelligence committee is now exposing to our public knowledge, was most-forcefully carried out, by a handful of Trump appointees and top officials in the US, as instructed by Trump, according to corroborated testimony.

Bill Taylor testified that, fairly soon after he did get over there to Ukraine in June, he began to see what was being attempted, vis-a-vis this unofficial corrupt scheme, and he contacted George Kent who was Deputy Assistant Secretary for European and Eurasian affairs; as Kent was Bill Taylor's immediate supervisor. Taylor told Kent he had discovered that Trump was putting pressure on the new Ukrainian President Zelensky, to fulfill political favors for Trump that would help him win reelection in 2020, (by designing derogatory characterizations of his chief rival, Joe Biden.)

Chief of Staff Mick Mulvaney was the top US official carrying out Trump's orders to suspend release of $391 million of Congressionally-appropriated support for Ukraine; much needed for continued strong defense against ongoing Russian aggression on Ukraine's eastern border.

However, this hold on the release of the aid then became a national security issue; which became a concern for Dr. Fiona Hill, the National Security Council Senior Director, after she attended a meeting on May 23rd, involving two top advisors to President Zelensky, John Bolton, the National Security Advisor, and Gordon Sondland, among a few others. John Bolton abruptly ended this meeting, once Gordon Sondland had expressed to the Ukrainian officials who were visiting at the White House, that the Ukrainian government would have to open up investigations into Burisma and the Bidens, in order to become invited to the White House for a coveted meeting with President Trump. (We should understand that what has been going on between Russia and Ukraine is that, in 2014, there was a huge uprising of Ukrainian citizens who desperately wanted to get rid of the corrupt people in their government. The movement was known as the "Revolution of Dignity," and it culminated in the expulsion of corrupt Ukrainian officials (whom the Russian government had either installed, or bribed to cooperate. Historically, Ukraine's corrupt leadership basically bribed or threatened others in government, exerting great influence on Ukraine to continue corrupt initiatives, often centered around oil and gas drilling, and profits from distribution, arranged unfairly to benefit Russia, at the expense of the Ukrainian people).

Once this Ukrainian uprising had made an impact, forcing Russian actors to flee back to Moscow, it was shortly after that, when Russia invaded Crimea and took control over this territory on the Eastern end of the country, also nearest to Russia. This act violated the worldwide agreement made after World War II; a pact that countries would no longer expand their boundaries by military force; and this has been in place for nearly 70 years. But then suddenly in 2014, Russia violated that agreement, when it annexed Crimea, on the easternmost end of Ukraine territory.

Russia didn't stop there, though. They have continually been making efforts to move further into Ukraine, claiming more territory for mother Russia. So, with the annexation of Crimea, this was the point at which the US, in concert with the European Union, became allies of Ukraine; funding and otherwise supporting Ukraine's military expansion, as well as the training of many newly-enlisted soldiers, to defend against ongoing Russian aggression; keeping up a sustained effort, not only as far as offering military support, but also diplomatically.

Up until early 2019, US Presidents have consistently demonstrated strong support for Ukraine's objectives to newly become a democracy; in highly-publicized White House meetings, and through the coordinated efforts of a vast network of diplomatic support, at US Embassy in Ukraine; fighting fiercely to resist Russia's "Hot War" attack on Ukraine.

Therefore, suspending our US support, for any reason, can easily give Russia the message that this is a time to push the envelope, and be more aggressive in their efforts to capture further territory, to be claimed by Russia. Support from the US, as the most significant military power in the world, is a great catalyst for Ukraine's effective resistance, not only militarily, but also in rooting out Russian corrupt influence; whereas, suspending this US support, even temporarily, gives Russia much greater leverage to negotiate Ukraine's further sacrifice of territory, in its ultimate attempt to end this war; which has already killed 14,000 Ukrainians, to date since 2014.

It should also be noted that our support of Ukraine, and the EU's support (European Union countries) as well, are being put forth in order to bring serious consequences to Russia, for trying to capture more territory, through occupation and military action. If Russia succeeds in expanding further into Ukraine, once again exerting corrupt influence on people in the Ukrainian government, this gives Russia a signal that it's okay for them to bring military action against other countries too; in order to capture more territory, and take more governing control over people in other countries.

So, in this respect, what Russia is doing; if left unchecked; can actually be seen as a national security risk for the US, too. If we fail to keep enough consistent pressure on Russia, perhaps it could be that coastal states in the US, will become Russia's next attempted conquest.

However, under President Trump's direction, his newly-appointed Ambassador to the EU, Gordon Sondland, working in concert with Mick Mulvaney (White House Chief of Staff), Rick Perry (Energy Secretary), Rudy Giuliani, and a few others, this group was engaged in a continuing campaign to pressure the new Ukrainian President Zelensky into making Joe Biden appear as corrupt, so he would cease to be a significant threat to Trump's re-election efforts.

In addition to the demand that Zelensky announce these investigations, as a condition of getting a White House meeting as a show of greater US support for the new Ukrainian government; in mid-July, in a videoconference call to foreign service officers in Ukraine, the OMB (the US Office of Management and Budget) announced that the $391 million in aid that Ukraine was to receive, was being put on hold. Staff members were told that the directive had come from Mick Mulvaney, but it was also reported that President Trump had ordered the hold. No explanation was offered, as to why; and this was quite the mystery, at the time.

Adam Schiff points out we have recently learned that every official associated with our National Security efforts to Ukraine, as well as all of our Foreign Service staff and leaders in our Embassy in Ukraine, were unanimously in support of providing that congressionally appropriated aid immediately, as was supposed to have already been provided to Ukraine by mid-year.

The above-mentioned videoconference call took place on July 18th, and then a week later, on July 25th, President Trump had his infamous call to President Zelensky. On this call, right after Zelensky said that they were ready to purchase more Javelin antitank missiles, (which are key to Ukraine's staving off the Russian invasion), right after President Zelensky indicated that they were anxious to receive more Javelin missiles, President Trump basically said, "Well, we need you to do us a favor, though…" and then he talked about really wanting these investigations into Burisma and the Bidens; and that he also wanted the newly-installed President Zelensky to investigate the Crowdstrike server conspiracy theory, which has already been debunked, of course.

Yet, as we learned from several witnesses' testimony, none of this dialogue was any part of what had been more-widely discussed with staff, in preparation for the call. Apparently, a call between the US President, and another country's President is always very thoroughly and meticulously prepared for. In a call such as this one, what almost invariably transpires is the President's recitation of what our policy objectives are, toward that foreign country; and the President would have concentrated on becoming briefed on the most current policy positions, with respect to the other foreign country; in order to at least touch on this subject, during the call.

In the case of US policy towards Ukraine, heavy emphasis has been placed on rooting out corruption in their government; and in fact, according to multiple witnesses' testimony, Ukraine has really come a long way on that scale, with help from the US foreign service presence, and top US officials such as Vice President Joe Biden, whom during the Obama administration, was very instrumental in pressuring the new Ukraine government, (post "revolution of dignity") to follow through on ousting many corrupt officials at the top. Several were removed while

Biden was Vice President, particularly due to his 2015 efforts, where he traveled to Ukraine pretty extensively.

Part of what the Democratic intelligence committee finds so objectionable about all of this, is that it has come to our attention, disclosed during closed-door depositions; before the public hearings that are now going on; that in advance of this July 25th phone call, Gordon Sondland, along with Kurt Volker (Special Envoy to Ukraine), and Rick Perry, Energy Secretary (the three, dubbed as the "Three Amigos,"), working in concert with Rudy Giuliani, had been pressing Ukrainian officials and the new President Zelensky to very publicly announce the opening of investigations that would personally help Trump get reelected, and they were not in any way consistent with stated US Foreign Policy.

Actually, I should temper this contention a bit; we find out that it appears Kurt Volker was not even aware, much less complicit with Trump's scheme; Rudy Giuliani artfully kept Volker in the dark, while still utilizing Volker's influence as leverage. I should also mention that Gordon Sondland feigns innocence during these proceedings; but as you will see, this is doubtful to the more astute onlooker. We don't hear that much about Rick Perry, but what we do hear sounds suspect.

In addition to the investigations of the Bidens, the three amigos (however complicitly), along with Giuliani were forcing it upon the Ukrainian government to cook up the contended scenario that Ukraine was really the country that meddled in our 2016 election; and as I mentioned, if this narrative could be given any credence, it may well clear the path to the lifting of US sanctions on Russia; which Putin is desperate to bring about. (And I will take this opportunity to mention, it seems that all along, ever since Trump's campaigning for President, and also related to much of what Trump has said and done since he's been in office, it all seems to very much promote, and be in accord with things that Russia would derive great benefit from. So, touting this false narrative of "Ukraine election meddling" is just another example of this.

In other words, here Trump seems to be in favor of promoting a narrative that potentially would ultimately incline the US Congress to lift sanctions on Russia which are very crippling to them.

After this infamous July 25th call, between Trump and Zelensky, a number of designated officials and their assistants, listening in on that call, made reports to higher officials and top lawyers within the State Department. Multiple reports were made through several different official channels, that the call was highly irregular, and that there were serious concerns over issues of national security, if this was the way that Presidential calls could be conducted.

The State Department then reported this information to the White House (Meaning the Justice Department under Bill Barr). Apparently, it was of such concern to several people at the top, and they didn't want Trump to get in trouble, so they moved the transcript of that call to a server that only very few top people in government could have access to. In other words, they wanted to hide, or bury the record of that call, so what Trump had said could not leak out, and cause a scandal).

In subsequent weeks Bill Taylor, the new Ambassador to Ukraine, continued to correspond with Gordon Sondland, Ambassador to the EU; and at one point, Taylor texted Sondland, "Are we now saying that security assistance, and a White House meeting are conditioned on investigations?" (This is where the "No quid pro quo" phrase originates; because once Sondland received this text, he apparently spoke with Trump right away; who told him to tell Taylor not to text about this anymore, let's just talk on the phone; and I believe that Trump also asked Sondland to make sure that part of his text response contended that there is "no quid pro quo" being demanded; -even though there really was, of course; they just didn't want anyone saying that, for obvious reasons).

It is not completely clear at what point Zelensky became aware that the security assistance too, was being held until he made the announcements of opening Trump's demanded investigations; but we will hear of text exchanges in August, showing Andre Yermak's knowledge of this, and indicating Zelensky's apprehension to get involved in US politics in this manner.

As Bill Taylor testified, soon after their private text exchange, Sondland informed Taylor that, not only was announcing the investigations a condition of the White House meeting, but that release of the $391 million in aid money was also conditional on announcements of these two investigations Trump was demanding. Sondland's exact words to Taylor were that, "Everything is conditional on the announcements of the investigations."

We are now a little way into Adam Schiff's opening explanation of the overall scheme. I have taken the liberty to summarize the beginnings of it above, adding in my own perspective.

Intelligence Committee hearing #1- Kent and Taylor

Adam Schiff here makes reference to White House Chief of Staff Mick Mulvaney's press conference announcement, which had taken place a few weeks earlier (in late October?), that yeah, we do that stuff all the time, quid pro quo's; it's business as usual, just get over it! {Mulvaney seems to consider that we should come to expect political influence in foreign policy! This is a well-documented no-no!}

Schiff continues, Republicans have argued that, "What's the big deal? The aid money was released!" but Adam Schiff points out that sure, it was eventually, but it was only released after a whistleblower had come forward to report these irregularities; and then again, really only once Congress found out the nature of the whistleblower complaint about Trump's abuse of office, and had begun to ask questions about what was going on, here?

The intelligence Committee opened an investigation into the matter, and then it was a couple of days after that, that the aid was released; in other words, once Trump had basically been caught for carrying out this odious scheme.

Adam Schiff now points out that, although several people who have given depositions so far; government officials and diplomats that have come forward, despite Trump having ordered everybody in government not to cooperate in any manner with this impeachment investigation; and although several officials have also testified that a White House meeting with President Zelensky would be key to demonstrating US strong support in the face of Russian aggression; still even now, in November as these impeachment hearings are underway, the President has not had the long-sought White House meeting with Zelensky; that's pretty odious in itself, I think.

The President has instructed the State Department, and anybody who is given subpoenas, to not cooperate in any way with this investigation, which is obviously an obstruction campaign; and obstruction, we can be sure, will be one item in the articles of impeachment that become drafted up subsequent to these hearings.

Schiff also points out that Trump has threatened that any who do cooperate in this investigation, given his prohibition, should be seen as traitors, and treated as traitors! That constitutes a very strong threat, because as we know, the penalty for being a traitor is death! Yet I ask, how might it be traitorous, to simply point out corruption going on, within a democracy?!

Adam Schiff also points out that if Trump is able to get away with "nixing" any investigation into Presidential wrongdoing, as he and his Attorney General have been trying to contend Trump is immune from, as a sitting President, then this will have constituted a significant alteration in the separate powers concept of government; and he suggests this is not at all what the founders had intended.

Schiff asks pointedly that, if indeed the President has done what it appears he has, in this pretty odious scheme that has come to light, must we indeed get over it? (as Mick Mulvaney suggested in his recent press conference)

Schiff asks, is this what Americans should now expect from their President? He quotes one of the founders at the time the Constitution was written, "The separation of powers separates ambition from ambition." In other words, three forces are designed to make equally-significant and protective determinations; congressional power to appropriate funds, pass laws, and hold the President accountable for any possible wrongdoing; as separate and equal to Presidential leadership (Executive) power; as also separate and equal to the Judicial power of the Supreme Court; so that we avoid ever becoming a monarchy, like the Framers of the Constitution had intended.

In a monarchy, the ruler has the exclusive power and ability to command every important government initiative and action; whereas, in our democracy, there are three co-equal branches of government having combined influence over the positions and initiatives the government will take. Prescriptively, the President, heading the executive division, must leave some categories of decisions to the congressional division, such as determining appropriations of funding for government initiatives; and the Judiciary, being the Supreme Court, must be given the power to determine what is lawful and constitutional, in its ultimate judgment.

Our governmental structure was determined over 200 years ago, and things have changed and developed a lot since then. Unfortunately, rich and powerful individuals, large companies, and special interest groups, such as the NRA, have figured out how to become effectively self-serving, to the detriment of most ordinary citizens, and we have been loath to bring things back under our control, as a people; so this current situation may be an important crossroads, as far as determining the fate of the common man in this country going forward; absent a full-blown revolution. -And even then, this might be effectively thwarted by a powerful-enough self-serving governmental force; and we actually do seem to be moving in that direction.

If this kind of underhanded scheming in the highest executive office of government stands undeterred, then I would say that the reign of our democracy is in serious jeopardy. My hope is that many of us will realize this, and either the Republican-majority Senate will have to vote to remove Trump, or perhaps risk certain defeat (Republicans becoming the minority party in the Senate), in the next election. Either way, if we can either elect a new President, or at least get Mitch McConnell out of our way, by electing a Democratic majority in the Senate in 2020; if these proceedings could pave the way for one of these alone, I think we could consider this impeachment effort to have been worthwhile. We just can't have both Trump and McConnell still at the helm, once the votes have been counted next November. That would be the nightmare of all nightmares!

Back to my impeachment hearing summary:

So next, it was Devin Nunez' turn to give an opening statement on behalf of the Republican minority of the House Intelligence Committee; and he starts off by claiming that the Mueller investigation was unsuccessful as far as Mueller ever finding conclusive evidence of conspiracy. (I need to point out that there was enough wrongdoing to uncover, that the investigation went on for 2-1/2 years; and everyone besides the untouchable President, who nonetheless, factually was complicit, has since been convicted of serious related crimes.)

Next, Nunez claims that Mueller's address to the nation was a pitiful finale of a three-year long investigation; claiming that the media is corrupt (I say, really? Dozens of prominent news publications and thousands of reporters across America all have it wrong? -And only Fox news has the true story, to the opposite effect?) -But Nunez claims that it was merely partisan bureaucrats trying to overturn the 2016 election results. He says that Mueller's address of his findings constituted an implosion of the Russia hoax (I must point out that Mueller describes hundreds of pages of much evidence of Trump's apparent complicity in a crooked subverted effort to steal the election; however, due to those who lied to protect Trump staying in office mainly, there wasn't enough direct evidence for Mueller to declare this, in definitive criminal terms.)

Nunez claims that the Democrats have denounced any Republican whoever shook hands with a Russian (No, just politicians who did dirty things after multiple meetings, phone calls and emails with known corrupt Russians).

He claims that Democrats then turned on a dime to make a new claim that the real malfeasance is Republicans dealings with Ukraine. (There was no turning; Trump was so dirty in the Russia investigation, that his newly-hired Attorney General had to hold back the results, and tell outright lies about what was uncovered, meanwhile. This Ukraine scheme is yet another dirty thing Trump has done, which has also come to light, in addition.)

Nunez says Democrats claimed that they had evidence of collusion and that's why they went through with the Mueller investigation (yet, the investigation was opened by Trump's own appointee; not democrats), and he claims that the Steele Dossier had fabricated Trump-Russian collusion. (The Steele Dossier "A 35-page collection of Steele's memos" while investigating suspicious activities between Trump and the Russian government in 2016, was put together by the former British agent, who was actually hired by an opposition research firm funded by the conservative website, "The Washington Free Beacon." It was funded on behalf of competing Republican candidates of Trump, to "out" him as a corrupt actor unfit for office; but when Trump surprisingly got the nomination, Republicans scrapped the idea of this exposure, and instead concentrated on opposition research into Hillary Clinton.) Nunez claims that the Democrats tried to obtain nude photos of Trump to smear him (I couldn't think of a better mark to smear, but it was Steele who uncovered contentions that hidden footage of Trump being peed on by Russian call-girls was allegedly being used to bribe him to cooperate with the Russian agenda.)

Nunez also claimed that Democrats put forth a false story to CNN, claiming that Donald Trump Junior was colluding with WikiLeaks (Trump Junior had in fact met with Russians in the Trump Tower that summer; an undeniable fact.) and Nunez says that Democrats were just hurling preposterous accusations at their political opponents. (They are preposterous; but they are also mostly true!)

Nunez suggests that Democrats should not be taken at face value when they trot out these new allegations, and he claims that the Democrats are merely having a scorched earth war with Trump, and that this is a carefully-orchestrated media smear campaign. (Really? Somehow involving coordination of hundreds of long-trusted news sources all across America, yet only rebutted by Fox and Breitbart?), and he contends that Democrats are pushing into this impeachment initiative without the support of a single Republican. (This, of course, is true in every case of a vote in congress these days; all Democrats vote one way, and all Republicans vote the opposite way; Nunez voicing this, is simply being deliberately deceptive; and here we begin to see that Republican committee members intend to be very deceptive at these hearings; because there certainly is no defense, otherwise!)

Nunez accuses the Democrats of having these closed-door depositions in a cult-like atmosphere, claiming that Democratic House Intelligence

Committee members have then released a flood of misleading, and one-sided leaks (What other side is there, besides stating the facts of the matter? -And the closed-door hearings were to <u>prevent</u> leaks of details testified to, so that other witnesses could not possibly listen to, and coordinate their own testimony in some false manner. The <u>general gist</u> of the testimony, was all that was provided to major news sources.)

Nunez then claims that Democrats on the Intelligence Committee had released transcripts in a highly selective manner violating their own guidelines. (We are moving to multiple deceptions in the same sentence now; the depositions only had to be private because the Justice Department under Bill Barr would not even begin to investigate the reported wrongdoing. Normally, a Grand Jury would be convened to hold these private sessions to interview witnesses; and then once separate testimony was collected and assembled into a report given to Congress, "open public hearings" would be the first phase of Congressional proceedings. -But in this case, the Intelligence Committee had to conduct the private sessions first; because Bill Barr wouldn't. Also, all of the Republican House Intelligence Committee members had been allowed to attend these sessions; and most of them had indeed.

Nunez claims that Democrats deleted the name of Alexandra Chalupa repeatedly; her name was redacted from the transcripts of the Steele Dossier. Alexandra Chalupa was a contractor with the Democratic National Committee who supposedly worked to collect dirt on the Trump campaign. (Hardly an unfair tactic, even if it is true, since the Republicans have done this kind of thing in spades.)

Nunez claims that the Democratic majority members of the House Intelligence Committee rejected the Republican House member requests, to include other witnesses (we can be sure that if allowed, they would have packed the sessions with witnesses that would try to call down the character of the valid witnesses, and push an entirely different and false narrative. In fact, the one witness they requested who did testify said things like, that some of these decorated Foreign Service diplomats testifying, had been considered untrustworthy; when one such official had to read his last review aloud, which basically stated he was very exemplary.)

Nunez went on and on; Democrats rejected most of the Republican's witness requests resulting in a horrifically one-sided process (Yes, it's one sided; the side of true and pertinent testimony) where the crucial witnesses are denied a platform if their testimony does not support the Democrats absurd accusations. (Anyone who has observed the stellar character of these witnesses in action in these hearings, for hours at a time, noting their position which puts them right in the middle of what has been going on, could not possibly consider these accusations the least bit absurd.)

Nunez contends that notably, Democrats are trying to impeach the President for inquiring about Hunter Biden's activities; so, it is unfair if they refuse Republicans' requests to hear from Biden himself. (He has a lot of nerve, to complain about witnesses who have very little direct bearing on the matter; when their party with Trump at the top, will not even provide a single piece of paper to the Congress, as they are supposed to, upon request; much less defying every subpoena for any lawyer or official in the Trump administration to come before Congress; which has never happened before on this level.

Nunez contends that the whistleblower has a bias against Trump (Yet, all of these witnesses coming forward are very evidently nonpartisan, most having served in both, Democratic and Republican administrations, for a couple of decades).

He contends that Democrats have been calling for Trump's impeachment ever since just after the 2016 election. (Yes, because Russian meddling and Trump campaign interaction with Russian operatives had been discovered by then).

Nunez claims, at this hearing, that Adam Schiff had read out a fictitious account of the phone call between President Trump and President Zelensky on July 25th, at a prior hearing. (Adam Schiff had read out the same transcript of the call that has been read out by dozens of news reporting sources in the past couple of month; I recognized it word for word), he claims that Democrats found the real conversation insufficient for the impeachment narrative, and so they made up a new one. (Wait, who is being completely absurd here?!)

Nunez goes on to contend that the Democrats on the committee had direct discussions with the whistleblower, before the whistleblower's complaint was submitted to the inspector general. (They didn't even know the nature of the complaint until it was finally given over to them, despite Bill Barr's refusal to even make Congress aware of its existence.)

Nunez claims that the Democrats had said they would have the whistleblower testify in these proceedings, and then they changed their mind (if so, it was to protect this individual from certain smears and ruin, and even possibly being rubbed out, maybe).

(This is interesting; this is the beginnings of the unfolding in these hearings, of a psychological strategy involving accusing the other side, of doing things that only your side has actually done).

Nunez claims that Democrats hid things from the Republicans and then lied about them to the American people on national television. He contends that Democrats have a history of accusing Republicans of the things that Democrats themselves are subvertedly committing; Democrats accused Trump of colluding with Russia when they themselves were colluding with Russia, as Nunez contends, by funding and spreading this Steele Dossier (we already know this is false), and now they accuse Trump of malfeasance in Ukraine when they, the Democrats themselves are culpable. The Democrats cooperated in Ukrainian election meddling and they defend Hunter Biden's securing of a lavish position on the Burisma board (Actually, several witnesses testified that this was a concern, even that it could merely appear as a conflict of interest; but they also knew that Vice President Biden was involved in a legitimate well-coordinated US Foreign Service effort to root out the rampant corruption still existing within the Ukrainian government in 2015).

Nunez points out that Burisma was a corrupt company, perhaps even all the while his father Joe Biden served as Vice President. (Burisma's corruption, we later learn in the hearings, was chiefly at the hands of the President of that company).

(God; when is Nunez finally wrapping up this ridiculous rant?), Now he's saying that despite this hypocrisy the Democrats are going through their impeachment sham. He calls Democrats hypocrites, and he says that we should not hold any hearings at all, until the Republicans get answers to three critical questions: Number one, what is the full extent of the Democrats' coordination with the whistleblower (only the whistleblower's lawyer has been in contact with Congress), what is the full extent of Ukraine's election meddling against the Trump campaign? (This theory has been debunked by Steele's investigation, and then again by Mueller's two-and-a-half year-long subsequent investigation, by the US Foreign Service Council, by the FBI, etc...)

Three; why did Burisma hire Hunter Biden? what did he do for them, and did hunter Biden's position affect any government actions under the Obama administration? (This is not germane to Trump's abuse of power being discussed here), Nunez claims this will be a televised theatrical performance.

Then, he sarcastically congratulates Bill Taylor and George Kent having passed the Democrats' star witness chamber auditions, held for the last two weeks in the basement of the capital. He then accuses these fine upstanding Foreign Service officers of being willing to participate in an inauthentic drama; but the main performance, the Russia hoax has ended. (Yes, with a 400+ page damning report).

He finally concludes by contending that the Democrats, with this proceeding, have done immense damage, what the politicized bureaucracy has done to American's faith in government. He contends that these administration employees (witnesses) are charged with implementing the policy set by our President (Trump had actually approved a current policy drawn up by his advisors, based on historic continuing integral strategies; none of which he was able to bring up during any of his conversations with Ukrainians, apparently), and that elements of the civil service have decided that they, and not the President, are really in charge. (They are indeed charged with carrying out current Ukraine Foreign Policy, which hasn't changed in recent years; and these witnesses were objecting to the fact that Trump's scheme was seriously getting in the way of accomplishing their worthy objectives).

Nunez claims that Trump was merely acting on concerns over how much foreign aid was given, and for what purposes; and that he was concerned mainly about foreign corruption (It comes out that Trump never mentions any corruption besides in connection with the Bidens and Burisma; hardly a noteworthy campaign against corruption. Also, the aid money he was holding up would partially be going toward efforts to resist Russian organized crime from infiltrating into the Ukrainian government once again). Nunez was insinuating that Trump was genuinely concerned about foreign corruption, when he held up the release of the congressionally appropriated aid. (There is no real evidence of this).

Then he claims that the Democrats' campaign here, is based merely on second, third, and fourth-hand information, rumors and innuendo. (It comes out, that first hand witnesses do actually come to testify, despite Trump's absolute prohibition for anyone in government to say one word, in order to protect himself).

Nunez then insinuates that he doesn't think it's an outrage for President to fire an Ambassador, because the President has full authority to do so. (Yes, but to do so for no good reason, and to first orchestrate a smear campaign against an exemplary 30-year veteran Foreign Service officer?!) Nunez claims that Trump is deeply concerned over Ukrainian meddling in our election; (in other words advancing Russia's narrative, Trump once again continuing to do things and express himself in ways that promote the accomplishment of Russian objectives).

Finally, and most preposterously, Nunez claims that, despite the dissatisfaction with President Trump's Ukraine policy, he says that in any event, Trump did release the aid. (Yes, after eventual complaints to congress started a slew of questioning about what was going on), the President approved the supply of weapons to Ukraine; and he points out that the Obama administration would not authorize Javelin missiles. (It seems to be his one half-way worthy point, perhaps.)

Nunez claims that only because of the Democrats initiatives and representations to the public, this (exclusively) has disrupted the faith of Americans, in the FBI, the State Department, and now the Foreign Service. (And everybody is fine with Trump and the Republicans' complete obstruction of being able to question anyone within the administration about these serious charges? -Also, Trump repeatedly recites how he trusts the word of others, such as Putin's explanations, over the intelligence services' assessments; doesn't this cause exactly what Nunez is complaining about?)

Because of Democrats, he claims, the Department of Justice has lost the confidence of millions of Americans, who believe their vote should count for something. (Quite apparently, Trump making somehow-believable, impossible promises while campaigning; in conjunction with a massive Russian disinformation campaign, cleverly aimed to trick unwitting Americans into making sure their votes would crookedly count for a narcissistic lunatic, and his Republican lawmaker Mob protectors).

Nunez finally bellows his last refrain; It will take years, if not decades, to restore faith in these institutions (I suppose he infers that Republicans within the Trump administration have done nothing that might contribute to any loss of faith in these government agencies; what a laugh!), he says this spectacle which is doing great damage to the country is nothing more than an impeachment process in search of a crime. (end of Devin Nunez's opening statement) (We've already found the crime; now we are just telling the American people about it publicly.)

By the way, it is important to note that the reason why Nunez and the Republicans, in solidarity, are so fiercely fighting Trump getting in any trouble; is because they don't care about any wrongdoing, as long as their Republican corrupt initiatives, trading favors for money perhaps mostly, making Republican Congressional decisions and acts that special interest groups like the NRA are willing to pay up considerably for, and legislation designed to inure to the benefit of big donors and special interest groups; of course, at the expense of, and detriment to, the common man in the US.

Adam Schiff now recites descriptive background, on today's witnesses, at this first hearing:

Bill Taylor is a graduate of West Point, he served as a soldier in the Vietnam war, he was awarded a bronze Star, and the air medal for valor, as well. He worked at the Department of Energy, and as an advisor to the US Ambassador to NATO. He served in Afghanistan and Iraq, and he worked on the Middle East peace process. Taylor was nominated as Ambassador to Ukraine in 2006 by President Bush. Obama appointed him to be special coordinator for Middle East transitions. Mike Pompeo had asked Taylor to return to Kyiv, as acting Ukrainian Ambassador, in June of 2019.

George Kent served as Deputy Chief of Mission in Kyiv. Kent joined the Foreign Service in 1992, and he has long overseen anticorruption initiatives, and further initiatives to strengthen the rule of law in foreign democracies.

The witnesses are sworn in and then, before Adam Schiff begins, Miss Stefano (a Republican committee member) interjects, beginning a concerted effort to try and heckle him, and throw him off, it appears. She asks when the committee is going to respond to Republicans' requests for nine additional witnesses, and Schiff tells her that three of those witnesses are scheduled to testify next week and so she asks, how about the other six? She further tasks Adam Schiff to refrain from stopping witnesses from asking questions, as he did in the closed-door depositions; and Schiff points out that the only time that he had intervened was to protect that the whistleblower did not get outed, as a few of these questions were obviously asked specifically to reveal this. (I should explain that there is a significant concern about retaliation, because of Trump's recent threats; and prudently Schiff must deter that from happening. Schiff explains that this was the only time he had stopped witnesses from answering a few of Republican committee members' questions).

Then, Mr. Conaway (another Republican) further heckles the process suggesting that there should be a closed-door hearing, so that they can ask questions of the whistleblower; (but of course, that would be outing the whistleblower which obviously Adam Schiff is going to protect against; so Schiff suspends the motion to have a closed-door interrogation of the whistleblower until after these hearings; and he says that at that point, the committee can consider it. They then complain that it wouldn't be right if it will be only Adam Schiff's decision. Schiff assures them it won't be).

Jim Jordan (the biggest cheese Republican in the committee, perhaps), then interjects to contend that Schiff is the only one who knows the identity of the whistleblower; to which Schiff responds that that is not true; he does not know the identity of the whistleblower. (as the contact with Congress has exclusively been made by the whistleblower's lawyer only).

George Kent is then recognized for his opening statement. {I will quote, comment, and summarize}: Kent is the Deputy Assistant Secretary of State for Eastern Europe and the caucuses. he has served for 27 years as a nonpartisan official, under five Presidents; both Republicans and Democrats. He oversees US policy on Ukraine, at the State Department. He has decades of experience in Ukrainian foreign-policy.

He offers that he appears under subpoena, merely as a fact witness. He begins with explanation of key principles of why he's appearing today. His principal public service has been in the pursuit of our national interests, in the place of Ukraine. Kent offers that, over the past five years, the US has supported Ukraine in its fight for the cause of freedom, and the rebirth of a country free from Russian dominion, and the warped legacy of Soviet institutions and post-Soviet behavior.

He explains that when you are confronting corruption, you get some pushback; and that when his actions are hitting home against corrupt officials, and they indicate this, it merely means that he's doing his job! -And he takes strong exception to the collusion of US political actors working in concert with corrupt divisions of Ukrainian government, to smear Ambassador Yovanovitch, and get her removed from her Ambassador post in Ukraine.

This campaign against Yovanovitch, Kent says, undermines US and Ukrainian national interests, and damages our bilateral relationship. He goes on to explain that, following World War II, there was the creation of a worldwide order, protected by the collective security provided by NATO. Western Europe has been able to thrive for decades. Europe's security and prosperity, he explains, contributes to our own security and prosperity in the US. He says that the Trump administration's national security strategy, in other words, not Trump's personal strategy, but the ongoing strategy of the foreign service division of government, which was explained to Trump, and Trump had earlier approved, is what Kent has been working to implement.

There is a global strategic challenge now before us, being that there's corrupt actors such as Russia and China; the US must compete for positive influence, as opposed to authoritarian rule. In 2014, when the Ukrainians had this "revolution of dignity," it forced the Russian element in Ukraine government to fully withdraw, and go back to Moscow; and then subsequently, in retaliation, Russia invaded Ukraine and occupied 7% of its territory; Crimea, an area about the size of Texas.

Congress has appropriated $1.5 billion to Ukraine in the past five years for training and assistance in their fight against Russia. Kent explains that having US forces fighting on the front lines of this Russian aggression in Ukraine, also gives the US valuable insight into the latest tactics of Russian aggression.

Kent also explains that the elections this year swept out most of the corrupt powers that were embedded in the Ukrainian government. Zelensky was a young 41; and that now, the average age of his Ukrainian Cabinet is now 39. The Ukrainian Parliament also has an average young age, of 41.

Kent explains that, only once Ukraine is free from corruption in government, is there an opportunity for foreign investors such as the US to do business with Ukraine in a way that everybody profits, in a just manner; whereas, acting inconsistently with the rule of law comes at great peril. Kent suggests that we cannot allow our resolve to falter or waiver; that too much is at stake; not just for Ukraine, and for the future of European security in general; but it is also in the national interest of the United States. Broadly defined, US-Ukraine policy is intricately involved with going after corruption. We assist Ukraine as they investigate, prosecute, and judge alleged criminal activities with appropriate institutional mechanisms.

Kent then says he does not recommend that a foreign country, the United States in this case, ask other countries to selectively engage in politically-associated investigations against opponents of those in governmental power, because such actions undermine the rule of law, regardless of the country. He offers that Burisma's main most-corrupt actor was the President of the company; and although in 2014, there was a concerted effort to bring him to judgment, and a case against him was being prosecuted; but then suddenly the case went away; and Kent says that he suspects the prosecutors working on the case were bribed into closing that case; they were paid-off to drop the case, in other words.

Pertaining to these impeachment hearings, in February of 2015, Kent had raised concerns with his superiors, about Hunter Biden being on the board of Burisma; he pointed out that this could (at least) create a perception of a conflict of interest for Joe Biden. Kent tells us that he has also consistently advocated reinstituting a scuttled investigation of Zlochevsky, Burisma's founder, as well as holding the corrupt prosecutors who closed the case, to account.

In 2018 and 2019, he became aware of Rudy Giuliani's initiatives to interject himself into foreign affairs with President Zelensky, including his two henchmen Lev Parnas and Igor Fruman, who ran a campaign to smear Ambassador Yovanovitch. Also involved with this scheme were (former President) Petra Poroshenko, and (former Prosecutor General) Viktor Shokin, who was known as a very corrupt head prosecutor in Ukraine. These individuals were acting in concert with Rudy Giuliani, peddling false information and contentions, in order to extract revenge against those who expose their misconduct; including US foreign service officials and Ukrainian officials fighting corruption.

These efforts led to the ousting of Marie Yovanovitch, and hampered US efforts to establish rapport with the new Zelensky administration in Ukraine; and it became clear to Kent in August, that Giuliani's efforts to gin up dirt on the Bidens were now infecting US engagement with Ukraine.

Then he explained that in the US, Congress and the Executive branch work together to put some conditionality on the appropriation of funding for a foreign country's assistance initiatives. He says that the State Department has collected all of his notes and records pertaining to September 25th, (and we can be sure that Kent was locked out of access to any notes or communications in any way related to Ukraine over the entire year). Learning that Kent was to testify before the Intelligence Committee, all of these (rounded-up) communications were then kept from him, so that he must rely solely on his recollections, as he testifies. (Thanks, Mr. Trump! Hide your dirty dealings from the American people!)

Bill Taylor then gives his opening statement, and he starts out by saying that even though he's here to testify, that he's not here to take one side or the other; or to advocate for the outcome of these proceedings. Taylor started as a cadet at West Point 50 years ago, and he has since worked in Afghanistan, Iraq, Jerusalem and Ukraine. He served in the Obama and Bush administrations, and he actually had recently come out of retirement, in order to become acting Ambassador in Kyiv, in June.

Like George Kent, Taylor is nonpartisan, and has been appointed by both Democratic and Republican Presidents. He asserts that it is clearly in our national security interest to deter further Russian aggression. {He was the one that wrote that infamous text to Gordon Sondland, emphasizing that the withholding of security assistance, in exchange for (exacting help from President Zelensky) with (Trump's) domestic political campaign is crazy!} Taylor says that he still believes that. He testified, that on May 28th, he met with Secretary of State Mike Pompeo, who had asked him to rejoin the State Department, and return to Kyiv. He offers that it was, and is, a critical time for US-Ukraine relations.

Taylor had previously served as Ambassador to Ukraine for the three years, from 2006 to 2009; and he asserts that he has also remained engaged with the US embassy in Ukraine, during the past 10 years, as well.

In 2013, Vladimir Putin was so threatened by the prospect of Ukraine joining the European Union, that Putin tried to bribe the Ukrainian President; and this is what triggered a mass uprising which resulted in that Ukrainian leader later fleeing back to Russia, where he came from.

In February of 2014, when Russia occupied Crimea, they erroneously claimed that 97% of Crimean citizens had voted in favor of having Russia take over; (just as one example of the kind of disinformation that fuels Russia's initiatives). Taylor explains that once this Russia-installed Ukrainian leader was forced to flee back to Moscow, this is when the

Ukrainian government newly began a great campaign to build an army, to counter this Russian aggression; and our US assistance demonstrates our commitment, to resist aggression and defend freedom. Taylor says that he was pleased when the Trump administration sent in Javelin antitank missiles, and enacted stronger sanctions on Russia. (of course, those increased Russian sanctions were the consequence given to Russia by the US, for the Russian meddling in our 2016 election), but even so, Bill Taylor says he appreciated the stronger sanctions (no matter why they were initiated).

We learn that, in order to break through Taylor's initial hesitation to take the post, as requested; an apprehension due to his knowledge of the recent wavering support of US diplomats in Ukraine; Secretary of State Pompeo had pledged his assurance to Taylor, that the US would be continuing their strong support of Ukraine; and Pompeo also had pledged that he would support Taylor personally, in defending that policy.

With that understanding, Taylor had finally agreed, on June 2nd, to go back to Kyiv, and serve as acting ambassador. Taylor arrived in Kyiv on June 17th, carrying a letter from President Trump, congratulating Zelensky on his parliamentary election success, and inviting Zelensky to come to the White House for a meeting with Trump.

Zelensky installed his reformist minister appointees, and began supporting long-stalled anticorruption legislation. He opened a high anticorruption court. Zelensky also managed, with the help of his new Parliament, to change the Ukrainian Constitution, under which absolute immunity was to be removed, in the case of any government official who might be acting corruptly. This basically covers the extent of what we learned from Adam Schiff's (and his Lead Counsel, Mr. Goldman's) 45-minute questioning segment; of Taylor and Kent.

The following is a bit of my own commentary:

If you are one of those who are continually inclined to believe it, when FOX News, or even the President tells you that the media is merely fake news, and Fox is the only source of true reporting, you may want to consider how likely it would be that many dozens of different newspapers and cable news sources, across the country, are all in a national conspiracy to flood the country with propaganda and false representations. Isn't it a pretty ridiculous idea that thousands of reporters, who don't even know each other, are somehow coordinated in this malevolent mass effort?! -Or wouldn't it be a lot more likely, that thousands of news sources in agreement of what is true and significant to be reporting on an ongoing basis, these are the sources that we would be better off listening to in a believable spirit; and the only news sources contending otherwise, Fox, and Breitbart, and a handful of other sources negating all of what everyone else is reporting as truth, is much more likely the propaganda-generators; doesn't that really make the most sense?!!

Just as an aside, a front-page article in the New York Times today (11/24/19) quoted Trump as saying "We had a tremendous week with the hoax. That worked out really incredibly well." What does he possibly mean?! -That he was pleased and impressed with how effectively Republican Intelligence Committee members were able to lie and deceive, and repeat falsehoods over and over again, enough, so that a base of unwitting bystanders who have been blindly supporting Trump were likely hypnotized into avoiding absorbing the damning information that Adam Schiff and other Democrats were putting forth; backed by credible witness testimony?

Because if it is not that, then we must certainly be dealing with a real Mr. McGoo here! In just what universe could what I have just finished describing so far in this summary, regarding what was revealed at these hearings, could be, the slightest-bit-reasonably judged as a mere hoax?!

Yet, here is a man who appears so psychologically damaged, that with his having been merely used as a puppet for greedy Conservatives, big business, and Russia, Trump has probably not done one good thing (for the common man in America) since he's been in office; or if anything his administration did, that proved helpful; such as was pointed out that Javelin missiles, of great effectiveness, were first provided under the

Trump administration; I'd bet you dollars to donuts that the assessment and decision-making process leading to this, probably all went down while he was out playing golf, or something; and that if he had anything at all to do with it, it would have only have been his being later talked-into moving ahead with this initiative.

-But despite his odiousness and ineptitude, I get the sense that he honestly feels like he is the most able person for the job of being President, that there ever was; and that he considers that he is beyond anyone else's intelligence (one quote of Trump's is (me) "in my infinite wisdom"); so it is evident that he is continually rather pleased with himself, no matter how dirty and damaging his words or actions are at any moment. In my view, Trump obviously has no idea what a lunatic he is; and that the only reason he has a following, is that a US President is-to-be-believed and trusted; so perhaps, roughly half the folks do this blindly; with the help of many of Trump's lies, his strong voicing of denial, coupled with the disinformation initiatives of the right wing media.

It's complicated, but there are many forces acting on what gets decided and who becomes allowed to do what, at the highest levels of government. However, we can be pretty certain that when rich powerful people, and their business entities, are enabled to arrange for governmental decisions to go "their way," they will surely benefit, and the economy will reflect business successes.

However, in the process of "fixing" arrangements greatly in their favor, the rich and powerful tend to diminish benefits and available opportunities for the common man; rendering the population of the country somewhat poor and troubled; while economic indices are, regardless, looking rather robust.

This is an oversimplification, of course; but the principal is valid. The <u>degree</u> to which some of us may have found limited opportunity, or have otherwise come to benefit or not, from aspects of their personal situation and circumstances, would be the only variable. (i.e.- not too bad, bad, or terrible!)

Then, beyond this fate, there are the further variables contributing to your comparative success, such as your relative degree of intelligence compared to others, how well you have become educated, and what skills and facility you might have developed, etc...

But if we look at the well-being of the common man, from (the combination of) these standpoints, and judge our personal ability to be successful in our endeavors; working within the current governmental structure in the US; it is plain to see that, just in terms of achieving financial success alone, the average American doesn't look too successful.

The average household income, for the lion's share of the population, is in the $30,000 per year range. Being that the median income is around $50,000 per year; and this means half of households are making more, and half are making less than this amount of annual income; then, for the half that is earning less than $50,000 per year, the average of earnings in those thirty-million households is more like around $15,000 per year. (To support a household!)

Yet, even as an individual with no dependents, it costs well over $30,000 per year, just to pay rent on an apartment, make auto loan payments, pay for car insurance, pay for cell phone service, pay your utility costs, and pay for inexpensive food, and gas for your car, for example.

The Trump administration has effectively hidden these relative-household-income figures from the common man. In recent years, we have no longer had the ability to obtain government charts showing household income, in the same format as in years past. You can't do any meaningful analysis and comparison with past time periods, when the averaged figures for each of five "fifths" of household income levels, are all you can see in the charts of the most recent years.

In fact, you can't even see the charts you used to work with, because all you get, when you look them up on the Government website, is a message that these charts are not available anymore!

If we were to vote-in a Bernie Sanders, for example, who could then (ideally) take away rich people's legislative and tax advantages, and bring back regulations which are pretty necessary, like clean air and water, heavy taxes (paid by the <u>sellers</u>) on fossil fuel, and regulation of wall street (broker-dealers, insurance companies, banks, and ratings agencies) that would prevent another crash like in 2008 (because many of these entities were basically "self-dealing"); we are now being told that rich companies will leave the US. This actually won't hurt the common man in this country. Right now, all the extra money is in rich people's pockets, and it isn't doing anything good for us common folk making up the vast majority of the US population, anyway.

-And if the rich were to leave the country, along with their crookedly-advantaged political "bought-decisions" (through lobbying efforts and campaign donations), then the rules would actually become a lot more-fair, potentially, for all of us. Our economic opportunities would likely flourish, it seems, given this type of financial and political governing atmosphere. Let's "vote-in" someone who might expel the rich and greedy, or otherwise force them to pay their fair share if they want to stay in America; that is my suggestion.

Anyway; back to my summary of the impeachment hearings:

We resume at the point where it is time for the 45-minute questioning of the witnesses (George Kent and Bill Taylor), now by the Republican Minority leader, Devin Nunez, and his staff lawyer, Steve Castor; and then there will be 5-minute rounds of questioning of the witnesses, by alternating Democrat and Republican Intelligence Committee members.

At this, Devin Nunez's first opportunity, to speak at length within this set of hearings, he starts off by accusing Democrats of trying to "invent a narrative." He says the facts that (Democrats) need, do not exist. {this is the first time that Nunez argues that the Ukrainians did not even know, at the time of the July 25th call, that a hold had been placed on the Ukraine security assistance. However, this really isn't any object; because what is important, is that Zelensky did ask to buy more Javelin missiles, on this call; to which Trump made his famous reply of, "but we would like you to do us a favor, though..." -And later, we find out that the Ukrainian leadership did know about the hold; probably for at least a month before the hold was released; but certainly for a period of at least 10 days, officially speaking.}

Also, there were a number of US officials and their assistants, in the White House, at the Pentagon, at the Office of Management and Budget, as well as several key US Foreign Service agents, who knew that the money was intended to be released on July 1st, and the phone call took place on July 25th. -And should we really doubt, that since there were an ample number of US Government actors who did have knowledge that this financial aid was being inexplicably held up; {some of the witnesses testifying here knew of this hold-up of the aid, as early as at the beginning of July; and several other witnesses tell us they had first found out about the hold on July 18th, so is Nunez really going to contend that no one; out of these dozens of US Government personnel, might likely have cracked, and let this information slip from their lips; to any Ukrainian official? This is not too likely, in my view.

How could any reasonable soul think it was unlikely that at least a few US contacts had indicated this, in response to eager Ukrainian officials voicing great concern, at some point in mid-to-late July? -being that all of $391 million was being eagerly awaited?}

Next, Nunez suggests that, holds on foreign aid assistance money are somewhat common for a President to put into effect; {but we later find out that it is uncommon, and generally improper, to hold up aid that has been appropriated by Congress. By design, Congress is given the "power of the purse," related to US funding of any measure or initiative. We also later learn that there was never any reason given for the hold; which is obviously why the Committee members were merely left to deduce that release of the hold was indeed conditioned upon Zelensky's very public announcement of these supposed "investigations" being underway.}

Next, Nunez claims that security assistance was released to Ukraine, despite the fact that none of these things that were asked of them by President Trump to do, were ultimately done. -But as I said before, the hold was lifted only after the whistleblower came forward, and Congress started asking questions; which was a few days before the hold was suddenly and inexplicably released; in other words, because Trump had gotten caught, and he knew he now needed to release the aid ASAP, if he had any chance of casting some doubt that might at least partly mitigate his guilt, and enable him to effectively cover some of it up.

Nunez claims, that the Democrats accusing Trump of asking Zelensky to dig up dirt on his political rivals, is supported by "zero evidence." He says that once again, the Democrats simply made it up. {We will hear over a dozen witnesses corroborate basically all of the Democrats' claims}. Then he asks us to consider questions about possibly why President Trump may want to elicit answers of Zelensky, to questions about Ukraine meddling in the 2016 election. {of which our intelligence sources assure us that instead, it was Russia who meddled in the 2016 election}.

Next, Nunez contends that it is the Republicans' view, that Ukraine was the country that did the 2016 meddling in the election, and therefore President Trump would have a perfectly good reason to find out what happened. {but of course, Trump was just trying to spin-out an alternate narrative, that supporters who are perhaps hypnotized by Trump's lies, might potentially buy; as they made their way to the polls next November}.

Furthermore, Nunez claims that the meddling that occurred was against Trump, and so therefore he had good reason for sending his personal attorney, Rudy Giuliani, to make inquiries about it. {The meddling was not against Trump, and it was not Ukrainians, of course.} An article that Nunez is now quoting, cites three Ukrainian officials reporting that the Ukrainian Embassy was exclusively supporting Hillary Clinton's candidacy. This article reported that the US embassy in Ukraine had meetings with Hillary, while only criticizing Trump.

Sergei Lutsenko, a member of the Ukrainian Parliament, had said this article was accusing a former Trump campaign official {Paul Manafort, I assume} of being corrupt, in an effort to undermine Trump's candidacy. {Manafort was, in fact, judged to be corrupt, of course; and he is now sitting in prison. I should also mention that Lutsenko was apparently involved in funding the "Free Beacon" conservative website's hiring of Christopher Steele, who investigated what Russia had on Trump, to potentially make him act as their puppet; and it was he who wrote the steel dossiers; as reported by the political opposition research firm "Fusion GPS." i.e.- he was obviously a <u>Republican</u> who didn't approve of Trump}.

Nunez claims this was on behalf of the Clinton campaign and the Democratic National Committee; {but I just learned that it was a group of competing Republican Presidential candidates, who were behind the hiring of Christopher Steel, in order to try and expose the dirty truth about Trump's unfitness for office, due to Russian leverage over him that they had heard about; in order to take him out of the competition among rival Republican candidates}.

Nunez then twists Taylor's statement about him feeling upset that Ambassador Yovanovitch was smeared; Nunez says that he interpreted that Taylor had said he was upset about Ukrainian election meddling! {Talk about "preposterous?!"} Taylor later clarifies that he was mainly upset that Trump made a statement, while campaigning in 2016, that he might think it would be okay for Russia to keep Crimea {without having to suffer any consequences for having attacked and occupied it unlawfully, I suppose}; and that he also considered it was possible that most Crimean citizens wanted to go back to Russian rule; as was being contended by Putin. Taylor says that this statement is extremely inflammatory, and undoubtedly very upsetting for many Ukrainians to have heard. {These types of statements are also counter to (the US and Europe's) foreign policy objectives regarding Ukraine.}

Nunez says that while some government officials objected to what President Trump was doing in Ukraine; they had no idea what legitimate concerns he might have had. {Flash preview, we never hear of Trump having voiced any concerns about Ukrainian corruption; in any of the hearings; other than related to Burisma and the Bidens}.

Nunez says that in this case, it was numerous interferences in our 2016 election, to oppose Trump's campaign; in support Hillary Clinton; {which we already know is bull}.

Next, Nunez passes the baton to Mr. Castor, his staff lawyer; who informs us that Ukraine's former Prime Minister, as well as the Interior Minister at the time (in 2016), blocked any endorsement of Trump. Therefore, Trump was concerned that several people within the Ukrainian government did not support him; and that some elements of the Ukrainian government were not in favor of him, did not support him, and were out to get him.

{Kent could neither confirm or deny any of this}. Schiff at this point says that questions, whether from majority or minority members, containing "facts not in evidence," {i.e.- regarding contended evidence that has not been established as factual, in the minds of all committee members here}, should not be asked of a witness; but actually, he soon clarified that he meant that witnesses need not indicate affirmation of such (possibly disputable) contentions.

More theatrics by Republicans: At this point Mr. Ratcliffe, {a constantly-heckling Republican Intelligence Committee member}, says that he had sat through Adam Schiff's 45-minute session, and had an objection to every question that Mr. Goldman (Schiff's staff lawyer) had asked! Schiff says that he was instructing the witness not to answer questions in this category; (and not instructing the committee members asking questions); pointing out that witnesses should not presume that questions from any committee member, that may posit "facts not in evidence" are correct.

Castor reads to us, that Lutsenko was a former (Ukrainian) investigative journalist, and now a member of the Ukrainian Parliament. Castor refers to when, after the Mueller Report came out, Bill Barr appointed Connecticut US Attorney Durham, to investigate the (so-called suspect) beginnings of the Mueller investigation; and some concerns over possible Ukraine meddling; and he offers that Durham's administrative review has now turned into a criminal probe. {Knowing Barr, this is probably some trumped-up claim out of thin air; Barr has no credibility; he has amply demonstrated this, in my view}.

US attorney Durham is the person who was hired by Bill Barr to do this investigation; and Castor asks if it seems reasonable to ask the Ukrainians to cooperate with Durham's investigation. Taylor says that Ukrainian-American relations will pretty-certainly be responsive to these kinds of requests.

Castor continues, contending that he thinks it is official and appropriate to ask the Ukrainian President to talk with Bill Barr about matters mutually pertaining to the Ukrainian government and the

US Justice Department. Castor claims, that's the way to deal with an issue with the Ukrainian President; it's appropriate for the US Attorney General, the Justice Department and the Prosecutor General of Ukraine to cooperate, and exchange information. {But, assuming we are discussing the topic of corruption here, I should point out that, what will continually be established throughout these hearings, is that Trump only ever expressed concerns of corruption related to Burisma and the Bidens; despite the fact he was counseled, by staff, to address broad corruption, a number of times}.

Castor then asks Taylor how come he was not involved in preparation for the July 25ᵗʰ call? Kent says, sir we work for the Department of State; the Embassy actually oversees the preparation for a Presidential call, along with the staff of the national Security Council. Normally, if there is enough additional time, National Security staff can solicit a memo to the President, by one of us; and this was not asked of us, in the case of the July 25ᵗʰ call preparations.

Castor then says Zelensky had won the election on July 21ˢᵗ (he must have been referring to Ukraine's parliamentary elections, after having won the Presidential election in April) and Kent says that foreign service staff, along with himself, had indeed recommended a congratulatory call from President Trump to Zelensky; {because apparently, at one point, the call wasn't going to happen after all}; Taylor was not privy to a transcript of the July 25ᵗʰ call; whereas he had seen the readout, that the <u>Ukrainians</u> had put out after the call, roughly one week after the call. But in addition, Taylor had heard from Mr. Morrison, of the National Security Council, about the July 25ᵗʰ call.

On the other hand, George Kent says that, on July 26ᵗʰ, the day after the call, he had been sent a partial readout on the July 25ᵗʰ call (the US readout); but the limited information he got wasn't detailed enough to be upsetting to him, at that point.

Regarding what came out in the Ukrainian newspapers, just after the call, Taylor explains that this statement made by the Ukrainians was, at as it is typically, a very short concise statement; to hit the highlights, and it doesn't go into detail about the call. The Ukrainian statement said that there are issues to be pursued, in order to improve relations between our two countries; and Taylor says he had found that a bit mystifying and unusual, in such a customary standard procedure.

Taylor then said that Tim Morrison had also briefed him, before the end of July, about the call; saying that it could've gone better, and that Rudy Giuliani's name was mentioned; and Taylor mentions that this was a concern, for him. {The mentioning of non-official private individuals is not appropriate in such a congratulatory call, I assume}.

Castor points to a statement that Zelensky made, inferring that he was very much looking forward to meeting "America's Mayor" (Giuliani) {of course, Zelensky knowing the strong connection between Trump and Giuliani, who he was directing Zelensky to confer with; and given Zelensky was desperate for a show of US support, of course Zelensky would have said anything favorable probably, to usher this along}.

Then, Castor turns to George Kent and says, corruption is endemic in Ukraine, right? -And of course, the answer is yes. Kent says, the courts, and the prosecutors' narratives; historically, there have been problems with all of the prosecutors in Ukraine; (that is) up until the new set of prosecutors were appointed by President Zelensky, in the last few months.

Castor concedes that supposedly Zelensky is the real deal, he is committed to rooting out corruption, prosecuting the bad guys. One element of the corruption, Kent agrees, is oligarchs, committing virtual theft of the "rights to certain energy licenses."

At this, Castor seizes the opportunity to again bring up Burisma {as if corruption in this company was any more concerning than dozens of other companies Trump never mentioned}. He says, Zlochevsky has a storied history of corruption. {Zlochevsky was Minister of Energy from 2010 to 2012, under the pro-Russian government, and he abused his regulatory authority, to give natural gas exploration licenses to entities that he himself controlled. i.e.- self-dealing and self-enriching}.

Castor asks, just how was he dealt with, in the spring of 2014, once Zelensky took over? Kent says the new government, after the revolution of dignity, turned to partners in the US and the UK to try to recover tens of billions of dollars in stolen assets. The first case pursued was that of Zlochevsky; as the case was already open in the UK against him; and the Brits worked together with the US and the Ukrainians, to develop more information. $23 million of Zlochevsky's assets were initially frozen, until someone in the general prosecutor's office in Ukraine shut the case down. Zlochevsky then issued a letter to his lawyer, and that money went "Poof." Kent's assumption is that they paid a bribe to make the case go away.

Kent continues, Mr. Zlochevsky spent time in Monaco, and in Moscow, after he fled Ukraine; but because US taxpayer dollars were used in an effort to try and recover that money, the US Foreign Service has a fiduciary responsibility (to keep following through), and they continue to press Ukrainian officials for answers, to why corrupt prosecutors had closed the case; and up until this point, they have not received a satisfactory answer. Kent says he would love to see the Ukraine prosecutor's office find out who the corrupt prosecutor was, who evidently had taken the bribe, and subsequently closed the case.

Castor again turns to the subject of Burisma; and Kent says that Burisma is the largest natural gas company in Ukraine, and that its reputation is mixed. (not entirely corrupt, in other words). Castor was beating around the bush, but he was basically trying to suggest that it would be a legitimate reason for Trump to bring up the topic of Burisma, in the July 25th phone call; {but later it becomes well-established by the witnesses, that in fact, Trump was merely heading in some personal, rogue direction, which had nothing to do with US efforts to help fight corruption in Ukraine}.

Then Castor starts asking about the new appointments that the President of Burisma made to the Board of that company, {but this was all of roughly 5 years before Zelensky assumed the Presidency}; and Kent answers that Zlochevsky (Burisma's President) invited a series of new people to be on the board of Burisma in 2014; most notably, the former President of Poland. Zlochevsky also invited Americans to be on the board, and Hunter Biden was one of them.

When Castor asked about his knowledge of the extent of Biden's trips to Ukraine, Kent offers that Joe Biden's first visit to Ukraine, as Vice President, was with (former President) Poroshenko, of the old regime; and then five more visits were made in 2015, with the new Poroshenko regime in Ukraine, which came into being after the revolution of dignity; which started in February of 2014.

Next, Castor tries to suggest that it was inappropriate for Biden to have told the new Ukrainian government back then, that the US was not going to come through with (an earlier-promised) $1 billion in loan guarantees {which would enable the Ukrainian government, at the time, to borrow a lot more money for its various initiatives}, contending that Biden inappropriately threatened, that if they don't fire (the corrupt Prosecutor General), they will lose the billion-dollars in loan guarantees the US was offering to sponsor. Biden had apparently said this in a speech, at the Council on Foreign Relations conference, in January of 2014.

Kent responds that, to the best of his knowledge, Biden made six visits while he was Vice President. Castor heckles that Biden claims that he's made 13 visits to Ukraine altogether; and Kent says he doesn't have any particular reason to doubt that. {He could have visited before or after he was Vice President, for example}. Then Castor asks, did the State Department ever express any concerns to the Vice President's office, (to the effect of) "was the Vice President, engaging in Ukraine currently" {at that time} presenting any issues? Kent says no, the Vice President's role was critically important; it was "top cover," to help us pursue our policy agenda.

Castor then brings up this irregular channel of diplomacy, that these Foreign Service witnesses now coming forward, were objecting to. Castor says, in fairness this irregular channel of diplomacy is not as outlandish as it could be... (Kent laughs, yes, I suppose I could agree with that); a big smile comes over his face. {of course, almost anything terrible that happens to you, can have been worse. i.e.- this is like when a lawyer for the guy that smashed into your car and broke both of your legs, says it could have been worse; you could have been paralyzed, or killed instantly. Some consolation this is!}

Castor brings up Ambassador Volker, who was a former Senate-confirmed Ambassador of NATO, and a long-standing free-agent diplomat. Taylor confirms that he's known Ambassador Volker for years. Castor continues, (he is) a man of unquestionable integrity;

someone with incredible knowledge of the region. Then Castor argues that Gordon Sondland was a Senate-confirmed Ambassador to the EU; Castor inferring that it certainly doesn't seem outlandish for Sondland to be engaged pursuant to Pompeo's direction... (Taylor responds that actually, it's a little bit unusual for the US Ambassador to the EU to play a role in Ukraine policy).

Castor says, it might be irregular, but it's certainly not outlandish. {yet, one of the most significant discoveries that the Intelligence Committee is exposing to the public, within these hearings, is that, what Sondland was engaging in, under Trump's direction, appears extremely outlandish, of course}.

Castor continues, Energy Secretary Perry is the third member of the irregular channel; a Senate-confirmed official with experience in energy markets. He was pursuing some liquefied natural gas projects; so, Castor contends that Perry being involved in Ukraine seems perfectly acceptable. Taylor says yes. {What is not revealed here is that, with the Republican majority in the Senate, of which all Republicans invariably will vote unanimously, to either affirm or oppose whatever is being voted on; such as a confirmation like Sondland's; it is the case that, all of the Democratic Senators could have opposed Sondland's certainly-inappropriate background and inexperience for the position, and still he would be confirmed, due to a Republican Majority in the Senate}.

Castor then asks, when did this become problematic? Taylor says that he arrived in Kyiv in mid-September; and by late September, a couple of phone calls (Taylor gets corrected; he means in mid-June (June 17th), and Taylor had already made a couple of phone calls by the end of June, once Taylor had begun to hear references to investigations, as something that would have to happen in order for Zelensky to get his White House meeting with President Trump. Taylor explains that for a while during this time period in June, both channels, the irregular and the regular diplomatic channel, were in alignment; and because they both wanted a meeting to occur between President Trump and President Zelensky, there wasn't an issue.

Taylor explains that he became concerned when the irregular channel (began) going against the overall direction and purposes of the regular channel. Taylor says that he was concerned about Rudy Giuliani's statements and involvement in Ukraine policy. When Castor asks, Taylor states that he had never talked with Rudy Giuliani at any point during the year.

Castor says that according to the record, Taylor had an August 25th phone call to Ulricht Brechtbuhl, and earlier, also a July 10th phone call with Brechtbuhl; and then Taylor sent a cable to the (Secretary of State) on July 29th, expressing his concerns.

Taylor points out that he also had raised his concerns with George Kent, and he had mentioned to Kent that it was odd, that the July 25th phone call did not include the normal staff, who would be listening in on such a call. Even Ambassador Sondland's staff was not on the call {yes, obviously because he wanted to avoid them hearing how Trump was intending to pressure Zelensky into announcing investigations, during that July 25th call}; but this had struck Taylor as unusual; and when he consulted with Kent, Kent then suggested that he make a note of it, which Taylor said he did. That call to Kent was apparently a July 28th call.

Taylor says that Giuliani's pursuit of these investigations was a concern for him. Castor then says, that in his deposition, Kurt Volker testified that he had only spoken to Giuliani once. (Taylor says he is aware of that.) They also had (only) one breakfast together, with Zlochevsky. {Castor was inferring that perhaps there wasn't enough contact between Giuliani and Volker, for them to have been conspiring; and as I mentioned, we later learn that Giuliani had kept Volker in the dark about the quid pro quo; but let's suppose that Volker had spoken a lot to Sondland, for example; and Sondland spoken a lot to Giuliani maybe. Have you heard of the game of "telephone?" Do you see how this would fit into a possible cover-up strategy here?)

This concluded the 45-minute initial Committee-party-leader-and-lead-counsel's questioning, and it now moves to five-minute rounds of questioning; and it goes, Democratic intelligence committee member five minutes, and then Republican intelligence committee member five minutes, back and forth.

The Majority leader running these proceedings always has the first 5 minutes, just after the 45-minute questioning by the Republicans' counsel; and this is the point, within each of the nine separate hearings, where Adam Schiff had often effectively debunked the Republican-uttered insinuations and claims, that either were false, twisted out of context, or had no bearing on the case.

So now, Schiff is speaking for the first five minutes; and then it goes to Devin Nunez for five minutes. Then after that, each of the other committee members get to ask their questions for 5 minutes each.

Schiff starts out asking about the questions regarding Burisma that they've just been discussing. Schiff brings up the testimony about Zlochevsky; an oligarch who was self-dealing as Minister of Energy and Ecology, under (corrupt) President Yanukovych; and clarifies that the time frame here was from 2010 to 2012, and during that time, licenses for exploration of oil and gas were administered, often in a corrupt manner, by Zlochevsky, the Minister of Energy and Ecology. Schiff points out that this was approximately seven years before the phone call on July 25th. Hunter Biden had joined the board in 2014, and Schiff points out that there wasn't any discussion in Trump's phone call with Zelensky about this oligarch Zlochevsky, {who, long before the time that Hunter was elected to Burisma's board, had been self-dealing, right?}

(Kent says no), and there is no discussion, during that July 25th phone call, of the corrupt acts of awarding contracts to oneself, back to the 2012 and 2014 timeframe? (Kent says no) Schiff continues, (in the July 25th call) what the President brings up is Crowdstrike, the server, and the Bidens. (Kent says, I see that here, yes.) There was no discussion on that call of setting up an anticorruption court, or of looking into corruption among oligarchs, or companies, in general... Schiff then reminds us, that the President's comments were focused on two things: 2016 election meddling, and the investigations into the Bidens...

Then Schiff brings up this July 26th phone call, when Gordon Sondland had called President Trump from an outdoor restaurant in Kyiv; saying that because Trump was talking loudly, and the volume on the phone was up, a couple of the Foreign Service agents accompanying him at lunch had overheard Trump specifically asking whether Zelensky was going to go forward with announcing the investigations; and then, after that phone call had ended, one of the agents (David Holmes) had asked Sondland, what does the President think about Ukraine? -And Sondland's answer was that the President was more interested in the Bidens; {no discussion of Zlochevsky's corruption, or about things that happened seven years ago… Schiff had just demonstrated that Castor's questioning really had no significant bearing on the issue; he was merely lost in a questioning strategy that was actually asking about a time period long before any of the issues being discussed at these hearings occurred. i.e.- trying to take the focus off of what the President had done just recently, this year.}

{I think it is also important to understand that, as far as all of these questions being asked by Mr. Castor, as the point person; the Republican committee members knew, that what was being exposed by the Democrats in the Committee here, was very serious and damning about the President's statements and actions; of whom they are yet, desperate to have continue to enable everything to go their way, no matter how unjust it may be to the common man; so these Republican Committee members inevitably would have had to work feverishly, in the days before the first hearing; ostensibly spending long, tedious hours discussing what possible strategic questioning, might dilute the impact of all they knew there was to be revealed within these hearings; -So, this was their best shot?!}

Back to my impeachment hearing summary:

Schiff then refers to Taylor's testimony, where he had said that Trump wanted Zelensky in a "public box," meaning that private statements, or private promises to look into these investigations, were not enough. Zelensky had to get on TV, to go public in some way…

Next, Schiff discusses how Taylor had also testified that after subsequently telling Taylor about this call that Sondland and Trump were on together (on July 26th), Taylor had asked Sondland to "push back" on that demand from Trump, that he pressure Zelensky for announcements of investigations; and so Schiff noted, that Taylor certainly understood, by then, that this was the <u>President's</u> demand, and not Gordon Sondland's...

Taylor explains, he considered that Sondland obviously had good access to President Trump; and so he sought to impress this upon Sondland; that to put pressure on another country's President (such as Zelensky) is not a good idea, from either leader's standpoint; and so Taylor had asked Sondland to try and make that point to President Trump, since Sondland seemed to have direct access to the President.

Then Schiff points out how Taylor had testified that he was still concerned, that even after the aid had been released on September 11th, it seemed Zelensky was continuing to feel obligated to make those public announcements; and he thought this would be a bad idea. So, when there was some indication that this still might be happening; in the form of an upcoming interview with CNN, in New York, that President Zelensky had finally given-in and scheduled; Taylor wanted to try and make sure that the investigation announcements didn't ultimately happen; so he addressed it with Mr. Doniluk, the National Security Advisor to Zelensky; who intimated to Taylor that Zelensky was indeed concerned, because he did not want to be used as some corrupt tool of American politics.

So at this point, Schiff verbally emphasizes that Zelensky did not want to go on TV and make these announcements of investigations; that he thought this would mire him in US politics; and Schiff says again, so Zelensky and his advisers knew that it was a bad idea to interfere in other nations' elections. (Taylor affirms).

Schiff says, so it appeared that Zelensky, you see, in fact <u>did</u> feel compelled to (go through with) the CNN announcement of investigations, during the time when the aid was being withheld. (and even after, because his White House meeting had still not yet occurred).

With that, Adam Schiff recognizes Devin Nunez for seven minutes, as he had gone over the 5-minute time allotment himself, having had the floor for seven minutes.

Nunez calls it the "mother of conspiracy theories" that the President of the United States would want a country that he doesn't even like, that he doesn't want to give foreign aid to; to have the Ukrainians start an investigation into the Bidens! -And then he yields to Jim Jordan; {and this is a strategy that the Republicans used throughout; where they yield their time to the most effectively-aggressive Republican Committee members to badger the witnesses).

Jordan starts in, the aid was held up on July 18th, and was delivered on September 11th; and in the 55 days that the aid was delayed, Taylor met with Zelensky three times. Taylor says that the Ukrainians were (potentially) not aware of the hold, until an August 29th Politico article revealed this publicly.

Jordan then declares that Taylor's testimony was false, in terms of his having developed a "clear understanding" that the hold on the aid would not be released, until the investigations were announced, (at any time before the July 25th phone call); and that if the Ukrainians didn't even know the hold had been placed on the aid, until the August 29th Politico article came out, then Taylor's testimony was wrong!

Taylor then explained that his clear understanding came from his interactions with Gordon Sondland, subsequent to the July 25th call by President Trump to Zelensky; and that a couple of weeks later, Sondland had reported to him that he had just spoken to Mr. Yermak, who is Zelensky's top advisor; and told him that; although this was (supposedly) not a quid pro quo; if President Zelensky did not "clear things up in public," then the US and Ukraine would be "at a stalemate."

Taylor said this was one point, where he had developed a clear understanding about the conditionality of the aid; and then Taylor further offers, that Sondland had also intimated to him, (this was in August), that he recognized it was a mistake to have told the Ukrainians, that only the meeting with Trump in the Oval Office was being held up, pending the (opening of) the investigations; (Sondland at the time) lamenting that he now had to face explaining to Yermak and Zelensky that, in addition to the quid pro quo for the White House meeting, the aid money was also not to be released, unless and until a public announcement of the investigations took place. Taylor quoted Sondland's exact words, that "everything" was conditional on the announcement of Ukrainian investigations being underway.

{Let me interject here, that the above is clear evidence that President Zelensky had knowledge that "everything" -the aid, and the coveted White House meeting, was conditional on the announcement of the investigations that Trump was demanding. President Zelensky knew this, and had indicated to some of the officials testifying at these hearings, at least by some point in early August, that he felt cornered with such pressure, that he had finally made arrangements to go on CNN and make an announcement; and he had indicated to his top advisor, Andre Yermak, as well; that US domestic politics was not something he would ever have wanted to become involved in.}

So at this point, Jordan rambles on quickly, and still continues to rant about how there were three meetings that Taylor was in with Zelensky, since the aid was held up; and nothing was discussed in those meetings about the aid... {but this is ridiculous because, as Taylor had just explained to him, Gordon Sondland had only let on to Taylor about the candid discussion of the demanded quid pro quo, that he had had with the Ukrainians just prior to Trump and Zelensky's July 25th phone call, the day after that phone call, on July 26th.

Ignoring the significance of what Taylor had just established, regarding exactly where his certainty had come from, Jordan sarcastically reads a very complex statement (that Sondland had issued to amend his initial testimony), about who told who, when; and he tries to insinuate that nobody could have a clear understanding, because of that sentence. {This was all just a ridiculous, phony brow-beating act, of course. This convoluted explanation had been concocted by Sondland, once he had heard of others' testimony since his first deposition, where he had said "I don't recall" to just about every question; and he was obviously worried about getting nailed for giving falsified answers, if he didn't come forward and amend his testimony.}

Jordan now forcefully chides Taylor, trying to contend that Taylor had not really had a clear understanding, about the conditionality; and then Jordan chides further, that Taylor is supposedly the star witness, (I guess because he was the first to testify along with Kent at these hearings). Jordan says, I've seen church prayer chains that were easier to understand than this! {of course, this is just a bunch of echoing nonsense, trying to drown out the significant truth.}

So in response, Taylor says that he made it clear at the beginning, that he's not here to advocate for one side or the other; that he's here in response to a subpoena; and Taylor offers further, that the statement Jordan had been reading was something that Gordon Sondland had submitted, when he amended his original testimony to the committee (he initially had testified that he could not remember; but that after talking further with his staff and others, he had since remembered things more clearly); and Taylor offered that Sondland's memory corresponds to the way that he too understands that things went.

So, next it goes to Jim Himes; {who is without a doubt the most powerful Democratic committee member, in terms of his command, and his ability to cut through the (bullshit smoke and mirrors) tactics of the Republicans, thus far.}

Himes starts off by expressing outrage, at the way Republicans are badgering these fine veteran Foreign Service agents. He says that, despite the very strong allegations of the President's misconduct, the Republicans don't engage in discussion of this specifically, nor do they defend that conduct; but rather they spin theories about black ledgers, and Steele dossiers; and revelations that certain Ukrainians might be upset; when a Presidential candidate had suggested that perhaps he would let the Russians keep Crimea. -Or we get the attack, so epitomized by Devin Nunez in his opening statement; He attacked Democrats, he attacked the media, and most disgustingly, he attacked the extraordinary men and women of the State Department and the FBI.

Next, Himes sums up what the Republicans' narrative is so far; that Ukraine is a long-established corrupt country, and that President Trump was just acting in a long line of tradition, of formidably trying to address corruption in Ukraine...

Himes then turns to George Kent; repeating that Kent has worked on anticorruption and the rule of law for much of his 27-year career, since 1994, and that Kent has specialized in looking into corruption, and upholding the rule of law, as his major emphasis. So, at this point, Himes asks Kent to just take a minute, and clarify what "a real anticorruption effort" looks like, in terms of its structure and components.

Kent responds that it starts with law enforcement, stating further that a new government will often need a specialized anticorruption agency. In Ukraine, that agency was the National Anticorruption Bureau (NABU). Another governmental body is tasked with reviewing asset declarations for (the unusually wealthy); and (in Ukraine) this is called the National Anticorruption Prevention Council; and then the US State Department has helped Ukraine to establish a Special Corruption Prosecutor, and a High Court on Anticorruption; and Kent explains that our efforts were to try to create investigators, prosecutors, and courts with integrity; that couldn't be bought; that would be focused on high-level corruption.

Himes says, what I'm hearing here, is a very comprehensive effort. -And then he goes to reading Trump's own words, on this phone call, "There's a lot of talk about (corrupt Burisma and) Biden's son; and that (his father, Vice President) Biden stopped the prosecution; and a lot of people want to find out about that; so whatever you can do with the Attorney General (Bill Barr) would be great. So, if you could look into that, it sounds horrible to me."

Then Himes asks Kent, when you hear these words, do you consider that the President is engaging in a thoughtful and well-calibrated anticorruption program? Kent {manages somehow not to smile, at the ridiculousness of anyone trying to equate the two}, and he says sternly, "I do not."

Then, Himes points out that the Republicans made a big deal out of the fact that Vice President Biden encouraged the Ukrainians to fire a corrupt prosecutor, and he quotes Rand Paul, (over the weekend, having said) that "They are impeaching Trump for the very same thing that Biden did."

Himes then asks Kent if he thinks that is correct? -that what the President did on this phone call, was the exact same thing that Biden did, related to (the corrupt prosecutor) Victor Shokin? -and (how about) what President Trump was talking about in this phone call? -were they exactly the same thing? (he asks Taylor and Kent).

Kent says, I do not think that they are the same thing. What Biden requested of former President Poroshenko was the removal of a corrupt prosecutor general, Victor Shokin; who had undermined a program of assistance, that we had spent US taxpayer money on trying to (help) build an independent investigator unit (in Ukraine), to go after corrupt prosecutors; and there was a case called (Donovan?) in which Shokin destroyed the entire ecosystem of what we were trying to create; (shutting down) the new investigators, the judges who issued the warrants, the law enforcement that had obtained warrants to do wiretapping; <u>everybody</u>, in order to protect his former driver, who Shokin had made a prosecutor. That's what Joe Biden was asking; to remove this corrupt prosecutor.

Himes points out that Joe Biden was participating in an established, whole government effort, to address corruption in Ukraine. Kent says yes, that's correct. Then he asks Kent, as you look at this situation with Trump and Giuliani and Sondland, etc..., in your opinion, was this a comprehensive, and whole government effort into fighting corruption in Ukraine? (Kent says, I would not say so).

Himes says, President Trump wasn't trying to end corruption in Ukraine; (but that he thinks) President Trump was trying to "<u>aim</u> corruption" at Vice President Biden, in the 2020 election!

So then, the Republicans' next five minutes segment of questioning, which was supposed to be Mr. Conaway's time; Conaway yields his time to Ratcliffe, who is another extreme attacker, in terms of his nasty tactics, twisted statements and contentions, and other hardline tactics, to badger the witnesses. (He was right up there with Jordan, in that category).

Ratcliffe starts right in on Kent and Taylor: If nobody knows that the money is being withheld, as a condition of anything, then there could be no quid pro quo, right? (So, Taylor does agree that on the July 25ᵗʰ phone call, the Ukrainians didn't know that the aid had been withheld). {Taylor is alluding to the fact that it hasn't yet been established, with complete certainty, that the Ukrainians knew about the hold on the aid, at the time of the phone call; but this might likely become more firmly-established, with the revelation of further testimony and evidence, perhaps}.

Of course, that was Ratcliffe's point; that Taylor doesn't know anything definitive, that would enable him to effectively dispute this contention, at this time. Ratcliffe then mentions, that on October 10th, President Zelensky had a "marathon news day" with reporters, and that Zelensky had said, over and over again, that he was not aware of a military aid hold, during the July 25th call. {Yet, we find out that Trump had first ordered the hold on July 25th, and that the planned hold was announced to Foreign Service staff on July 18th}. Ratcliffe further references, that Zelensky had said there was no conversation, in that July 25th call, about arms, or blocking of arms. The military assistance to Ukraine was blocked prior to the conversation on July 25th, but this issue was not discussed during that phone call. (and he rants on) about Zelensky not having disputed Trump's claims that there was "no quid pro quo," contending that there were no conditions, and no pressure to investigate Burisma; that there was no corruption of any kind during that July 25th call, in Zelensky's reported statements on October 10th!

Then Ratcliffe proceeds to tell an out-and-out lie, that there was no condition of investigations into the Bidens, or the Burisma company; Zelensky was never pressured, and there were no conditions being imposed; emphasizing that this is what Zelensky had officially said! {but we discover a little bit further into these impeachment hearings, testimony that Zelensky and his top advisor really <u>did</u> know, and that they really were upset about being pressured. In fact, just minutes before, Taylor gave testimony to the fact that they were made aware of it, and they had intimated, at least within text exhanges with the Three Amigos in August, that they were upset about these important shows of US support being conditioned on investigations into Trump's rival Presidential candidate}.

So then, Ratcliffe denies that there is any impeachable conduct; because of the public statements which Zelensky had made, characterizing that there was no pressure. {but these statements were undoubtedly made because Zelensky desperately wanted to maintain an amicable relationship with the Trump administration; and, had he told the truth, and said that he did feel pressure; this might well derail the US aid, and other needed US support that Ukraine is continually looking to the US for; this year especially. i.e.- Zelensky was probably once again, feeling "Trump-Administration pressure" which had inclined him to make sacrifices to his integrity, and bow to his understanding of further insinuations being made by US actors complicit in the scheme; if not outright Trump-Administration instructions; that he was to deny knowing, what pretty-clearly he really <u>had</u> known}.

Ratcliffe then contends, that if they impeach President Trump for a quid pro quo, then they have to call Zelensky a liar, in order to do this; {of course, Democrats merely have to acknowledge that Zelensky would reasonably say this because he was under pressure, to do the things that the Trump Administration would have the Ukrainians do, in order to continue receiving valued support from the US}.

Intelligently, Ms. Sewell, who was next to have five minutes to question the witnesses, yields her time back to Adam Schiff. Schiff points out, that other witnesses' testimony had confirmed that Ukraine had in fact found out that the aid was being withheld, when it became public knowledge; once the Politico article came out, (on August 29th), and by this time, that the Ukrainians certainly would have found out.

Schiff continues, they also knew what President Trump wanted from them; these investigations, right?! (and Taylor says, yes) {the point being that the aid was released on September 11th, without any mention that it would be, beforehand; so, this means that, at very least, the Ukrainians unquestionably knew the aid was being withheld, for at least 10 days; between when the August 29th Politico article had declared this; and September 11th, when the aid finally was released; and during this interval, the "three amigos" had continued their strong push for Zelensky to make these bogus and damaging public announcements of investigations, on Trump's behalf, right?)

Schiff continues, and didn't Ambassador Sondland inform Mr. Yermak, President Zelensky's top advisor, of what they wanted? (Taylor nods, and Schiff continues), Ukraine finds out about the hold; you're not able to give them a reason for the hold, they know the President wants these investigations; and then they are told, in Warsaw, by Ambassador

Sondland, essentially, "You're not getting the aid unless you do these investigations."

Taylor says, that's correct. The Ukrainians were told on September 1st {During a Warsaw meeting between US officials and Zelensky}, about the hold; so at least between the time the politico article came out on September 1st, (sorry; at several points during these hearings, dates are quoted inaccurately; but I observe that, whenever it's critical for a given argument, clarifications are being made; here it was just 3 days off (article date: August 29th), and not important to the argument), Taylor says, and when the hold was finally released, on September 11th, for those 10 days at least, the Ukrainian government had strong reason to believe that the aid was being conditioned on their public announcement of investigations, that yet, they really didn't want to be involved in.

{The significance of Adam Schiff pointing this out, is to emphasize that, so far, the Republicans have been focused on defending Trump's contended innocence related to the July 25th phone call; whereas, we should all realize that Trump is not being impeached, merely for any transgressions solely-related to that fateful call; we should also be turning our attention to Trump's further transgressions throughout the year, as well.}

Then, Ms. Sewell picks up, and she wants to discuss a May 23rd meeting at the White House in the Oval Office, when the President met with those who had gone to Ukraine, for Zelensky's May 10th inauguration ceremony.

Kent had earlier testified that, in preparation for arranging a US delegation to attend Zelensky's inauguration, {as was his responsibility}, he had proposed a list of names of certain officials that he recommended should appropriately attend. Ms. Sewell then asked Kent, if Gordon Sondland, the Ambassador to the EU, was one of the names that he had submitted; and Kent says no. {She was just pointing out that an Ambassador to another country would not typically attend an inauguration ceremony, in a country where they are not the Ambassador}.

Next Ms. Sewell refers to Kent's testimony that Sondland had also used his "connections" with Mick Mulvaney (White House Chief of Staff), to secure this Oval office meeting; and she says, it seems that this Oval Office meeting was a pivotal turning point in US-Ukraine policy, in the minds of certain individuals, right? (Kent nods). She asks, "Coming out of that (May 23rd) meeting, who was given responsibility, Mr. Kent, for the Ukraine policy? Kent answers that he had never seen any document that changed the nature of the (ongoing) policy, at any point this year. {Formal policy changes must be documented, of course. Unfortunately, as merely a fact witness, Kent could not directly comment; but Ms. Sewell was alluding to Trump's directive to his "back-channel" diplomats, Sondland, Perry, and Volker; to embark on what was really Trump's most important initiative to undertake, in Ukraine).

Ms. Sewell then brings up Kent's earlier testimony, that Energy Secretary Perry and Ambassador Sondland both "Felt that they had a mandate, to take the lead on Ukraine policy."

Kent then points out, that their "feeling" doesn't mean that they actually had been delegated that responsibility. {Kent nevertheless explains that it was his understanding, that the three amigos, being (Special Envoy to Ukraine) Kurt Volker, (the Trump-appointed Ambassador to the EU) Gordon Sondland, and (Energy Secretary) Rick Perry were the ones put in charge of Ukraine policy during last summer; and Kent adds that, what (former mayor) Giuliani's exploits were, in Ukraine, in January, this Kent considers to have been a different phase, than what happened in the summertime. Sewell asks if it is normal for a private individual to take an active role in foreign diplomacy, as Giuliani did?

Kent says that he did not find this particular engagement normal, no. Then Taylor says he came to see, that Giuliani had a large influence on the "irregular" channel (of Ukraine Foreign Policy- being carried out by the three amigos, and Lev Parnas); but, Taylor continues, it is not unusual for people outside the government to be asked to give opinions, in order to help form certain policies, on US Government aid given to a foreign country. (He adds this caveat), However, it is indeed unusual to have a person get put into a channel that goes <u>contrary</u> to the existing, regular channel of US policy, related to that country.

So, the next Republican, Mr. Turner, chides Taylor and Kent over their affirmation that neither one of them has ever spoken to President Trump, and he says that he finds it amazing that the two "star witnesses," the first witnesses called in an impeachment hearing about President Trump, have never even spoken with President Trump before.

{But of course, the only reason why this was indeed the best Democrats could do, is because Trump has refused to cooperate; and he has refused to allow anyone else either, to cooperate, in any way, with Congress's investigation. Those officials who do regularly speak with Trump; people such as Rick Perry, John Bolton, and Secretary of State Mike Pompeo, have all been muted, as a cover-up.}

This all-day hearing with Taylor and Kent, was broken up into two parts; and we resume here, at the beginning of the afternoon session. These two were questioned for an entire day; whereas, most other witnesses will either just be questioned during a morning, or an afternoon session. My DVR recording missed the very beginnings of this session; so, we are coming in, a little way into the session:

At this point, Republican Committee member Mr. Turner is talking about NATO Ambassador Kurt Volker, {who was appointed as Special Envoy to Ukraine, originally once Russia had begun a protracted hot war with Ukraine; he is quite a legitimate diplomat. Volker has been charged with helping in ongoing negotiations between Ukraine and Russia; he had, at one time, been the US ambassador to Russia, I believe. We later find out that apparently, Volker was effectively kept in the dark about the "quid pro quo" scheme; Giuliani had been pretty clever in his efforts to hide Trump's true underhanded motives and his pressure campaign from Volker; {an upstanding career professional}, even as Volker was yet, made well-aware that US Foreign Service agents were facing a challenge, to bring together Presidents Trump and Zelensky; the Foreign Service's goal being to demonstrate strong US support, in Ukraine's fighting off of Russian military advances.}

Anyway, Turner is confirming that George Kent would agree, that Ambassador Volker is a very exemplary diplomat, with extensive knowledge into foreign relations in Europe; and Taylor does agree. Turner asks whether he has any evidence that Volker had lied in his deposition, or that he had perjured himself with that testimony.

Taylor says, I believe Kurt Volker has served the US very well; and George Kent says, I believe that Kurt Volker's testimony ran over 400 pages; and I don't have it in front of me, so I can't really tell if I might think that he would have perjured himself by anything he said... {Kent agrees that he certainly has no evidence that Volker had lied or perjured himself, in the related testimony he gave; but I consider it as further evidence that Trump's scheme must have been pretty intricate and disturbing to Volker, if he wrote a 400-page document about it!}

Then, Turner asks Taylor and Kent, have either one of you ever walked into a meeting with the President, with a belief or an idea (a certain impression), and then found out that you were wrong? Taylor says, (re: discovering that you had the wrong impression sometimes) I learn something at every meeting.

Next, Turner talks about the sixth amendment; that it doesn't allow hearsay as evidence; {but the sixth amendment pertains to a courtroom trial; which this is not}. Turner asks Taylor if he may have been mistaken about some of what he thought he understood; (pertaining to his impressions, or understandings of what had gone on) in his (having heard of) communications, during the earlier part of the year, regarding Trump's "back-channel" campaign to influence President Zelensky to announce investigations of the Bidens, and Burisma.

Taylor says, I'm here to tell you what I know; I'm going to tell you everything that I do know... {Turner is trying to suggest that what Taylor heard or believed he knew, could actually be incorrect, or mistaken, heard incorrectly}. Taylor says, people make mistakes... Turner yields to Jordan, who asks Taylor, were you wrong when you said you had a clear understanding, that President Zelensky had to commit to investigations of Biden; before the aid got released? -because the aid did get released; and Zelensky didn't commit to the investigations... {we find out later, that Zelensky had indeed let on that he was planning to go on CNN, and make a public announcement of opened investigations of the Bidens, and Burisma; and only because he knew he had to!}.

Jordan goes on to contend that what Taylor had heard, did not happen. Taylor says, the other thing that went on while that assistance was on hold, is that we shook the confidence of a close partner (Ukraine) (related to) our reliability...

Schiff then interrupts, and says that Turner's time has expired. Schiff continues, taking the opportunity to follow up on some questions regarding the public statements that President Zelensky had made, in the news, after the scandal came to light. When Zelensky was asked, were you pressured? (etc.) He turns to Kent, and says, the Ukrainians are pretty sophisticated, are they not? (Kent agrees) -Perhaps you would agree that if President Zelensky contradicted Mr. Trump, and said, "Of course I felt pressured..." they were holding up $400 million in military assistance; Ukraine had people dying every day! If Zelensky were to contradict President Trump directly, he (undoubtedly) is sophisticated enough to know that they may pay a very heavy price...

(Kent says, that's a fair assessment.) Schiff continues, -and beyond what he has to worry about Trump doing, if he were to say that he had felt pressured, President Zelensky also has to worry about how he is perceived domestically, right, Mr. Taylor? (Taylor says, President Zelensky is very sensitive to the Ukrainian people, who indeed are very attentive to US-Ukraine politics). -So, if Zelensky were to say, "I had to capitulate and agree to these investigations; and I was ready to go on CNN until the aid got restored;" that would obviously be hurtful to them back home, would it not? (Taylor and Kent agree). Schiff continues, Zelensky cannot afford to be deferring to any foreign leader; he is very confident in his own ability; and he knows that the Ukrainian people expect him to be clear, and to defend Ukrainian interests. (Then, Schiff yields to Mr. Carson)

Carson starts asking questions about the extent to which Kent knew what was going on, in real time; which he contends was basically limited to what had unfolded in the media; but to Kent's understanding; then-Prosecutor-General Yuriy Lutsenko met Rudy Giuliani in New York, on private business, last January; then they had a second meeting in

February; and through the good offices of the former mayor of the new of New York; (Lutsenko was interviewed by) John Solomon, of whom was, at that time, writing stories for The Hill publication; this was in early March; and the (written) campaign (to smear Yovanovitch) was launched on March 20th.

Carson says, a corrupt Ukrainian prosecutor gave an interview to a reporter in the United States, and made claims that the Ambassador provided officials with a "do not prosecute" list… Sir, do you have any reason to believe this is true? (Kent says, I have every reason to believe that it's __not__ true; Yuriy Lutsenko was a politician of long-standing, and Minister of the Interior after the Orange Revolution. The US embassy had good relations with Lutsenko for years. He was imprisoned by (former Ukrainian President) Victor Yanukovych. {It has been a very common practice of corrupt leaders, such as Yanukovych, to slander and bring false charges against anyone in government that would not be complicit in the leader's corrupt schemes}. After Lutsenko came out of prison, he was elected Majority Leader of then-President Poroshenko's party; and then he became Prosecutor General, in 2016. Kent says, every US Government official in Ukraine is dedicated to helping Ukrainians overcome corruption; which they have actually made a number of important steps toward, since 2014).

So, Carson asks Kent, you and your superiors had asked Marie Yovanovitch to stay on, in Ukraine? Kent says, that's correct; I asked her to extend until the end of this year, to get through the election cycle in Ukraine; and then, Undersecretary David Hale asked her to stay on until 2020. at this point Kent coins this phrase that "you can't promote principled anticorruption action, without Pissing off corrupt people…" (and he gets a laugh). Carson says, some of those people in Ukraine helped Giuliani's smear campaign, did they not? (they did). -So, ultimately that smear campaign enabled President Trump to remove her, is that right Mr. Kent?

(Kent says, Rudy Giuliani's smear campaign was ubiquitous on Fox News, and on the Internet…) So, Carson asks Kent if he, in his entire career, has ever known of an Ambassador who got smeared and removed, like Marie Yovanovitch did? (-and Kent says, I have not).

Carson yields back; and the floor goes to Dr. Wenstrup; who then yields to Mr. Stewart.

Stewart starts in on the fact that the Obama administration did not provide lethal weapons; although Obama was asked by people on the ground in Ukraine to provide them. He emphasizes, "Yet, Trump did provide lethal weapons;" notably, Javelin missiles. Stewart makes the point, that the reason Obama did not provide lethal weapons is because he was afraid that this might provoke Russia; but Stewart says, Russia had already invaded Ukraine! -Why was he worried about upsetting them?

Then, Stewart suggests that a lot of Ukrainian lives could have been saved, if Obama had taken the Foreign Service's recommendation to provide lethal weapons…

{Stewart points out that Taylor had said, in his written statement, that the Trump administration had provided a substantial improvement in military support; so, Stewart nitpicks that when Taylor said that he was concerned about the wavering of the long-standing US support relationship with Ukraine, Carson says, it wasn't "long-standing," because Obama had not been providing lethal weapons; that only began with the Trump administration.}

Taylor replies, the "long-standing" part, that I'm referring to (in my statement), is economic support; political support; and financial support; (as well as) increasing military support.

Stewart then suggests that Obama purposely did not provide weapons to Ukraine, because he wanted then-President Medvedev of Russia, to be able to have a more successful attack on Ukraine. {How ridiculous! Later, we find out that it was actually <u>before</u> Russia had invaded Crimea, that Obama had let on that he was afraid of inflaming Russia; had the US provided lethal weapons to Ukraine. These Republicans should really learn the background behind what they are basing their silly arguments on; perhaps it might be less embarrassing for them, in the long run}.

Stewart yields to Ratcliffe; who starts another baseless rant, chiding that there was, no pressure, no demands, no conditions; nothing corrupt;

{Let me interject, all four of those contentions are patently false; hasn't he been listening to what is being disclosed about Trump's behavior?!}

Stewart continues, nothing on the call; that's what we heard President Zelensky say. {But of course, the hole in this argument, is that President Zelensky would naturally have been inclined to deny being pressured, when he was later interviewed on the news; for at least a few very important reasons}.

Stewart raves on, you have to ask what President Zelensky had to do, in order to get the aid. The answer is nothing… {this, of course, is a ridiculous rant; because we will hear much testimony revealing that, for three months, Trump and the operatives in his back-channel of crooked diplomacy were trying various tactics, to muscle Zelensky into announcing that Ukraine has opened these investigations; and then once the subversive plot was discovered; (i.e.- Trump got caught out); then he release the aid quickly, out of fear and guilt; so it is totally irrelevant whether Zelensky ultimately had to do anything, or not; in order to get the aid.

Of course, right from the start of his presidency, Zelensky was never supposed to have to "do anything" (except to avoid keeping on the old, or appointing new corrupt officials, perhaps), in order to get the aid; it had been congressionally approved; and it had, specifically because the Zelensky' administration was determined to be non-corrupt; and serious about fighting any corruption related to Ukraine's government, and businesses.

Ms. Speier is now recognized; she thanks them both for their true heroic efforts; "today, and throughout your career." She reads Kent's testimony, that in mid-August, Giuliani's efforts to gin up politically motivated investigations were now infecting US engagement with Ukraine; leveraging President Zelensky's desire for a White House meeting. Ms. Speier asks Kent, did you, at that time, write a memo documenting your concerns, that there was an effort underway, to pressure Ukraine to open an investigation, to benefit President Trump?

Kent answers, yes ma'am; I wrote a memo to the file on August 16th; but we don't have access to that memo… {Kent says that he has not been able to have access to any records, pursuant to Trump's orders that nobody within government cooperate with the investigation}. Ms. Speier further emphasizes, we have not received one single piece of paper from the State Department, relative to this investigation.

Ms. Speier says, Ukraine has been of importance to us, for several reasons; including the United States' commitment to our goal, to continue to support sovereignty of nations. Meanwhile, Russia is violently attacking people in Ukraine, in the Donbas area; so, the withholding of military aid, does it weaken Ukraine?

Kent says, well, I think it sends the wrong signal; and it did, for a short period of time; but now the funds have been released; and they are in the process of heading for Ukraine. (it is later explained that it can take months for military shipments to actually arrive; once funds are released). Ms. Speier asks, doesn't it embolden Russia, when there was no aid being sent to Ukraine? Kent says, I think the signal, that there is controversy between Ukraine in the US; and the signal that there is controversy in question about the US support of Ukraine; this sends a signal to Vladimir Putin, and he can leverage that; as he seeks to negotiate, not only with Ukraine; but other countries.

Speier refers to Kent's testimony, that a White House meeting, for Zelensky, would boost his ability to negotiate for a peaceful settlement, with Vladimir Putin, and Russia in general. Taylor says, it is certainly true that US support for President Zelensky, in his negotiations with Russians, is very important; and will enable him to get a better agreement; with that support from the United States; both, in terms of the military assistance, but also from the political assistance that we can provide.

Speier asserts, Zelensky has not yet had that White House meeting, has he? (no) (Speier quips that she thinks it's interesting, that Soviet-born Lev Parnas was able to get a meeting with President Trump at the White House, during a number of Trump's campaign events; and that he had contributed $325,000 to the President's super PAC); so maybe it's a requirement that you give money to the President's PAC, in order to order to get a meeting (with the President) at the White House…

Speier now is asking Taylor about what investigations are being opened currently, in Ukraine; (Basically, they can't say) Taylor says that the new Prosecutor General, whom Zelensky has appointed, is in the process of opening investigations. It is not specified, what investigations he has undertaken…

Speier yields to back to Adam Schiff; who says, my colleagues were referencing the (hot-microphone) discussion between President Obama, and some Foreign Service people, regarding military weapons for Ukraine. That was (actually) in 2012; yet my Republican colleagues are trying to claim, that when President Obama was saying that he was afraid that supplying lethal weapons to Ukraine might incite Russia to become more aggressive; when my Republican colleague was inferring that this was a stupid thing for Obama to say, because they had already invaded and annexed Crimea by that point; {but Schiff sets the record straight, that this concern of Obama's was expressed during a phone call, in 2012; two years before Ukraine was actually invaded by Russia}. Schiff yields to Mr. Stewart.

Stewart starts off with a sarcastic, "Welcome to year four, of the ongoing impeachment of President Trump; I'm sorry you got dragged into this." {This apparently was a concocted line that a few Republican committee members had strategized that they would accost the witnesses with). "After the secret hearings, and the leaks, it comes down to one thing; in the transcript that the President has released; of this phone call; one sentence of this phone call, is what this entire impeachment process is centered around. If you have to amplify, and exaggerate this President, then you've got a problem. The American people, lied to, again and again; first we heard quid pro quo, then extortion and bribery; then cover up, and obstruction." {-And then he bewilderingly contends that} "There is zero evidence of obstruction, and zero evidence of a cover-up;" {which is a completely ridiculous statement!}

Stewart then says, "The Democrats' description of the phone call was so outrageously inaccurate, that it had to be a parody; but none of this matters; it comes down to this: We appreciate your insight, and your opinion; but all you can do is give your opinion of this one phone call," he says, "There's dozens and dozens of countries around the world that are steeped in corruption; would you agree?"

Taylor cleverly responds, "Every country has corruption, including this one…" {it gets a laugh- because, of course, that's what this whole hearing is about; Trump's corruption!}

So, then Stewart goes back to this contention, about Biden having demanded that a specific prosecutor be removed; where the Vice President of the United States shows up and demands that a specific prosecutor be fired and gives them a six-hour time limit to do that. He asks Taylor and Kent, are you aware of that (kind of thing) ever happening? -And he pontificates that, out of dozens of nations and many years, that this has only happened one time! {Well, actually I would doubt that; considering there are over 300 countries in the world; with over 200 years of governmental history each}.

Then Stewart asks Kent and Taylor whether somebody running for the office of President, as a candidate, should be able to be investigated? {-sure, any candidate should be able to be investigated; however, only for "just cause," of course. The manner in which it was being suggested to open investigation of Biden was very corrupt underhanded; and a non-corrupt President Zelensky was being seriously pressured, to engage in some kind of corrupt conspiracy, to help Trump's reelection by falsely hurting Biden's reputation}.

Next, Stewart quotes from the 2019 NDA manual, that the availability of funds, under assistance to Ukraine; has to be certified; for the purposes of decreasing corruption; yes; are you surprised that there would be questions about corruption? An increase in Ukraine aid would be discussed; and actually, it would be discussed; the possible holding of this aid; until it's established that the corruption has been eliminated, or addressed. (Kent responds, the certification, in that case, is done by the Secretary of Defense upon advice of his staff, in consultation with the interagency community. We were fully supportive of the conditionality.) {Ukraine had met conditions to qualify for the aid}; and the Secretary of Defense (too) had already certified that "conditionality had been met."}

(Stewart yields back)

So, the floor goes to Mr. Quigley; who first seeks to verify when the certification was validated. (Kent basically responds that the DOD did say that they {had obtained} the certification, probably in July, he thought). Quigley says, it's actually kind of amazing how much we have been able to determine about what happened, {considering} this {blanket} directive from the President, to not cooperate in any manner. Quigley says to Kent and Taylor, were you both asked not to participate in this hearing, by the State Department? (Kent says, I received a letter directing me not to appear; but once the (House Intelligence Committee) issued a legal subpoena, I was under obligation to appear.) Taylor says he was told by the State Department: don't appear, under the circumstances; and just like Kent, Taylor decided that the circumstances were different, once he had received a legal subpoena from Congress; that is why he is here.

Quigley notes, but besides yourselves, we were not able to hear testimony from (those such as) Chief of Staff Mick Mulvaney, John Eisenberg, Michael Ellis, John Bolton; and more than a dozen other witnesses! So, he says, I suspect that if (my Republican colleagues) have a problem with hearsay, (let me say) you would have a lot more direct testimony, and direct evidence, if you weren't (patently) blocking that ability; (as well as blocking the transfer of any and all related documents, notes and emails), we would have a lot more documents that my colleagues would consider legitimate; that have not been turned over (to Congress), by the State Department, or any other agency; is that correct, gentleman?

Quigley confirms that none of the documents that (Taylor and Kent might have wanted to turn over) were ever turned-over to the committee, right? (Kent and Taylor both affirmed). Quigley then asks if they were involved in getting President Zelensky to announce these investigations? -and Kent says I was not; and I would not; if I were asked to do so. Taylor says, no sir, I was not involved.

Quigley then reads a text, between Kurt Volker and Andre Yermak, on August 10th. Volker texts: I agree with your approach; but iron out the statement, and we will use that statement to get a date set, and let the press go forward with it...

Then, at 5:42, Yermak responds: Once we have a date, we will call for a press briefing, announcing the upcoming visit, and outlining a vision for a reboot of the US-Ukraine relationship; including among other things, (announcing) Burisma and the election meddling investigations. Once we have the date, we will announce the investigations into Burisma and the election meddling...

{One frictional theme that persists throughout the summer, is that Trump insisted that Zelensky first make the announcements, and then he would set a date for the White House meeting; whereas, Zelensky kept insisting that the White House meeting be scheduled first, and then he would make the announcements.}

Kent says that he first heard about this plot to get Zelensky to announce investigations, when Bill Taylor had called him, on August 16th; and Kent says he memorialized his concerns "in a note to the file" after that phone conversation.

Quigley next establishes that it was only in the back-channel (through the three amigo's and Giuliani), that this initiative to get Zelensky to announce investigations was being put forward. (they both affirm)

Quigley closes by saying that countless people have been convicted on hearsay, because the courts have routinely allowed it, and created needed exceptions, to allow it. Hearsay can even be much better evidence than direct evidence, as we have learned, in painful instances; and it can certainly be valid.

Next, Ms. Stefanik is recognized; she starts off by saying the most important thing to consider is that the aid was released, and no investigations into Biden were undertaken. {-but of course, that's irrelevant, because the only reason why this is so, is because Trump got caught out, on his fiendish plot; so he suddenly dropped everything and released the aid}.

{It is very unfair, that Republican Committee members are allowed to make these false statements over and over again. What if they were interrupted by the Chairman, and had to pay a whopping fine, if they didn't cease to utter the debunked falsehood?!}

Stefanik goes on a rant about corruption in Ukraine, in general; and she talks about how George Kent was involved in investigating Burisma in 2015 and 2016; (and of course, this has no bearing on the matter at hand).

Next, the floor goes to Mr. Swalwell, who clarifies that, while Kent and Taylor are not direct witnesses who have spoken with Trump; they are, however, witnesses to the shakedown scheme that others participated in, who did speak with President Trump. Swalwell says, John Bolton and Mick Mulvaney spoke directly to Trump; but unlike you (Kent and Taylor), they have refused to honor the request to be a part of these proceedings. However, we do know how Ambassador Bolton feels about the hold-up of the aid. (Bolton had characterized it as being like a "Drug deal," that thugs might be arranging). Mulvaney (even) said, at a press conference: To be clear, (a reporter, I assume is saying, at this press conference), what you've just described, is a quid pro quo; (the conditioning of the White House meeting, upon Zelensky's public announcement of the so-called "opened" investigations); (for that matter), funding will (also) not flow, unless an investigation into the Democratic server happens, as well; "We do that, all the time, with foreign policy," (Mulvaney had said publicly). Swalwell asks, do we do this all the time, really?

Taylor says, we condition assistance on issues that will <u>improve</u> our foreign policy; <u>serve</u> our foreign policy; and ensure that taxpayers' money is well spent. Those are the conditions coming from Congress; (or they are based on standing) policy decisions; to make sure the taxpayers' money is well spent; or that the receiving country takes actions in our national interests.

Swalwell says to Taylor, we know you already wrote, in a text to Sondland, that conditioning aid in a scheme like this is crazy! Can we also agree that it's just wrong?! (yes) -Why is it wrong? (Taylor responds, our holding up, of security assistance, that would go to a country that is fighting aggression from Russia; for no good positive policy-reason, or substantive reason, or national security reason, is wrong).

Swalwell continues, Mulvaney, in that same press conference said, if you read the news reports and you believe them; McKinley said he was really upset with the political influence in foreign policy; that was one of the reasons he was so upset about this; and I have news for everybody; get over it! There's going to be political influence in foreign policy!

Swalwell asks, Ambassador Taylor, should we get over it?

(Taylor says, if we're talking about political influence, meaning attempts to get information that is solely useful for political campaigns; if that's what you're talking about, we should not be doing that!)

Swalwell then refers again to Mulvaney's statement, "I was involved in the process by which the money was held up temporarily; okay? There were three issues for that; corruption of the country; whether or not other countries are participating in the support of Ukraine; and whether or not they were cooperating with an ongoing investigation, with our Department of Justice… {Oh; so now the DOJ has corruptly opened an investigation into Trump's chief rival in the upcoming 2020 election?!}

Swalwell asks, Mr. Kent, were you aware of any formal Department of Justice cooperation request made to the Ukrainians? (Kent says, I think you have to refer that question to the Department of Justice-Fiona Hill could probably answer that). Lastly, Swalwell asks, Mr. Kent, are you a "never Trumper?" and Kent says, I am a career professional who serves whatever President is duly elected, and carries out the foreign policies at present in the United States; and I've done this for 27 years; for three Republican Presidents, and for two Democratic Presidents. Taylor says he is also not a "never Trumper."

Swalwell yields back, and the floor goes to Mr. Hurd. After a few courtesies, he quotes, as the fabled foreign service officer Ambassador Ryan Crocker says; "Because we have palms and wingtips on the ground, (being diplomats), that prevents us from the need for having boots on the ground." (meaning military presence). Hurd continues, foreign service is an important role in our national security; and I thank you and your colleagues. Next, he establishes that Ukraine received $200 million of security assistance in 2017; and Ukrainians got aid, including security assistance, in 2018, as well. Then, he wants to talk about Javelins, that they were not able to purchase in previous administrations. Next, Hurd asks Kent and Taylor when the first time it was, that they got calls from Ukrainian officials with concern about the withholding of the aid? Taylor says, on August 29th; Kent says, I first found out when the September 1 politico article came out.

Hurd then asks, would you find it surprising if Ukrainian officials in fact did know about the aid being held up, but they did not contact you? (Taylor basically says he can't speak to that.) Hurd continues, there's a lot of talk about Rudy Giuliani; and who he was, and wasn't meeting with; do you know which Ukrainian officials was he was meeting with, over the last couple of years? (Neither of the two have anything to say). Have you had any Ukrainian officials call you after meeting with Rudy Giuliani; concerned about the context of that conversation?

Taylor says, yes; Mr. Yermak has expressed concern about his interactions with Mr. Giuliani; there were meetings, and also phone calls (between Taylor and Yermak) in August.

Hurd then asks Kent, have you seen whatever this anticorruption statement we had wanted Ukrainians to make? Kent says, are you referring to the statement that was being negotiated between Kurt Volker, Gordon Sondland, and Andre Yermak? (Hurd says yes) Kent says, that was not an anticorruption statement; are you referring to the back-and-forth, and "Whats App" (communications) that were shared with Rudy Giuliani? -because Giuliani said (the proposed statement, as written) was not be acceptable, if it did not mention Biden, Burisma, and the 2016 election meddling investigations. Kent explains that, in fact, (because of that), no statement was ever issued to the Ukraine government, as a result of those efforts.

A bit later, in response to Hurd's question regarding what US businesses are concerned with, in terms of corruption; pertaining to their business dealings with any foreign country; Taylor tells us that businessmen are particularly concerned with the possible level of corruption within the foreign country's judicial system.

Shortly thereafter, Hurd yields back; and the floor goes to Mr. Castro. Castro says, listening to all the evidence, and all I've heard so far in this investigation, it seems to me that the President of the United States either committed extortion, bribery of foreign official, or attempted extortion and bribery of an official. When President Trump got President Zelensky on the phone, on July 25th, He was talking to a desperate man, who was, and is, very interested in US support (in terms of military) assistance, and political support. What would have happened if the aid had gotten cut off, Ambassadors? What would happen to Zelensky's career, and what would happen to Ukraine, if the assistance had been cut off?

Taylor answers, he would have been much weaker in his negotiations with the Russians; he would've been much weaker on the battlefield. The Russians may have taken this as an invitation; the Russians always look for vulnerability, and they know the United States has supported Ukraine. If the Russians determine, or suspect that this support is less than usual; or not there; they will likely pounce... (They could have) taken every advantage.

Castro says, so he had a desperate man on the phone and he asked for a favor; and it sounds like; begrudgingly; Zelensky may have agreed to do that favor, and investigate the Bidens, and Burisma; is that right?

Taylor nods, Zelensky does say, in the transcript, that he will pursue the investigations... Castro says, so we know that Trump asked for a favor; to help his political career; and it appears as though President Trump... do we know <u>why</u> it didn't actually happen? -why was there no announcement, in front of CNN; about the investigations?... Kent says, because we determined, as was discussed here; on September 11th, just before any CNN interview, the hold was released.

Castro asks, is it possible that the hold on the aid was released because the whistleblower turned in this complaint? (and Taylor humbly says he couldn't say) -So, we have a President, who the other side has claimed, or defended the President by saying the aid went through; and that there was never any investigation; but the President attempted to get those things done; and it looks like there was an initial agreement by the President of Ukraine to actually do those things. (So, Castor asks) Ambassadors, is attempted murder a crime? (certainly) Attempted robbery? (neither of us is a lawyer, but I think we can say yes) is attempted extortion and bribery a crime? (they didn't answer; but I think it is). Castor then contends that if there is no consequence, (if the Senate acquits), then it's a green light to do it again, right? (Kent says, "On principle; regardless of the country; whether it's Ukraine, the US, or any country; the facts of law, (in other words), <u>a criminal nexus, should draw investigations by law enforcement;</u> it is not the role of politicians to be involved in directing judicial systems; of their own country, or other countries). Castro yields back, and the floor goes to Mr. Ratcliffe.

Ratcliffe first turns attention to George Kent, to quote a passage from Kent's deposition; he quotes Kent as saying, "Every Ambassador serves at the pleasure of the President; and everyone knows this; that is without question, and everybody understands that." Ratcliffe wants to drive home that a President clearly as the prerogative to choose Ambassadors. Ratcliffe refers to something that a Democratic committee member had said; it's an abuse of power to remove an Ambassador for political reasons because you don't like what they're doing…

Kent clarifies, the President has the right to have Ambassadors serve at his pleasure. {Ratcliffe takes this to mean that we are trying to impeach Trump for doing what is within his constitutional rights; in other words, we shouldn't impeach a President for executing his constitutional authority, is what Ratcliffe is suggesting}. Kent declines to weigh in on this idea; he says, (I'm here to answer your questions; your {Committee members'} obligation is to is to consider the evidence before you…)

Ratcliffe asks, when did Marie Yovanovitch get recalled from Ukraine? Kent says, I believe on or around April 24th; (the President had the constitutional authority to remove Yovanovitch which is true; nobody is disputing that. What is objectionable, is the way in which he did it; a President does not have the constitutional authority to ruin a stellar Foreign Service officer's reputation without cause). Ratcliffe asks, since Yovanovitch was removed in April, and the call was in July… {he's asking Kent whether he has any idea why Yovanovitch is being called to testify? (in lieu of this?)} (Kent says, I'm here is a fact witness, under subpoena. That is a question that you should ask your Democratic colleagues.)

So next, Ratcliffe claims that both, Presidents Trump and Zelensky, have said that there was no pressure, and no quid pro quo… (Taylor affirms we have not unquestionably established that President Zelensky knew that the security assistance was on hold, as of July 25th); so,

Ratcliffe asks, do you have an explanation of why; within days of that phone call; when no quid pro quo was even possible; a person who later became the whistleblower (supposedly) walked into Chairman Schiff's office, to discuss the outlines of the (supposedly forthcoming) complaint? {I'm paraphrasing a little, here. Ratcliffe is asking this of Taylor, but he's really just taking the opportunity to mouth the scenario that he's trying to sell to the American public}.

Next, he says, a colloquy is a way for legislators to clarify important issues for the public... {Ratcliffe tries to engage in a colloquy with Adam Schiff; but Adam Schiff, as moderator, says, you will direct your questions only to Ambassadors Taylor and Kent...} Ratcliffe sarcastically says, when are House Republicans going to find out, what House Democrats already know; the details of the contact between Adam Schiff and the whistleblower; what they met about, etc...

At this point, Swalwell asks to make a point of order; and says, the gentleman is questioning the chair; which is not permitted, under the resolution applicable to the hearing, and under the rules of this committee. Efforts to undermine lawful whistleblowing is moreover contrary to law; nor is it the practice of this committee; and I would also like to... Adam Schiff interrupts, and asks both Swalwell and Ratcliffe to suspend; and Schiff instead asks Ratcliffe to continue his questioning; that "The ball is in your court..." Schiff says, Mr. Ratcliffe, your time is dwindling; I suggest that you use it... (so Ratcliffe yields back, and Mr. Heck now has the floor).

(Heck starts out), Some people have suggested, the real reason that President Trump's special campaign on Burisma, was to root out corruption in Ukraine. I've gone back and read the memorandum of the call; two or three times, actually; and I don't recall a single instance where the President had ever used the word "corruption," or the word "corrupt." (Heck asks Kent if he recalls this to be correct). Kent says, it's a matter of record... and Mr. Heck says, yes, and it is in the matter of record, that Trump did not mention the word corrupt, or corruption; on the July 25th phone call {either}; so the Republicans' argument, that Trump was concerned about corruption, doesn't really hold water; does it, Mr. Kent? (Kent affirms this)

-Was it not true, that rather than fighting corruption, in general, in Ukraine; wasn't it true that President Trump; what he did, (merely amounts to) unceremoniously recalling and removing Ambassador Yovanovitch from her post, in Ukraine? (Kent says, the President has the right to recall (an Ambassador); it remains a matter of (what is best, to carry out the) policy of the United States, towards Ukraine; to help them overcome the legacy of corruption; by creating new institutions; -and much of what we've been discussing today, this should have gone through the regular channel; it was a request against US policy, that would've undermined the rule of law, and our long-standing policy goals in Ukraine; as in other countries).

Heck establishes for the record, from Kent, that what Trump was asking for on the July 25th call, was not part of (our long-standing foreign policy towards Ukraine). Heck says, you also testified on October 15th, in your deposition, about fundamental reforms, necessary for Ukraine to fight corruption, and to transform the country; and you cited the importance of reforming certain institutions; notably the Security Service, and the Prosecutor General's office. Heck asks, was investigating President Trump's political opponent a part of those necessary reforms? (no, they weren't) Heck continues, in fact, historically, isn't it true that the major problem in Ukraine has been its use of prosecutors, <u>precisely</u> to investigate political opponents?! {i.e.- to slander them and render them noncompetitive}

(Kent responds, that's a legacy I dare suggest, from the Soviet era prosecutors, like the KGB.) {Heck now is quoting Kent} "instruments of oppression." (Kent adds, I said that I believe it's true, for as long as I can remember; US foreign policy has been predicated on advancing principled interest in democratic values; notably freedom of speech, press, assembly, religion, free fair and open elections, and the rule of law.)

Heck asks, Mr. Kent when American leaders ask for a government to investigate their potential rivals, doesn't that make it harder for us to advocate on behalf of those democratic values {that Kent had just listed off}? (Kent says, I believe it makes it more difficult for our diplomats overseas to carry out our policy goals. It is an issue of credibility; they hear their diplomats on the ground saying one thing, and they hear the US leader saying something else.)

Heck asks, Ambassador Taylor, would you agree with that? (Taylor says, yes I would; our credibility is based on respect for the United States; and if we damage that respect, it makes it more difficult for us to do our job.) Heck says, anyone looking at the facts, can see that it was an abuse of power, and can see that what happened was an abuse of power. Anyone looking at the facts, could see that what happened was unethical; anyone who looking at the facts, can see that what went on was just plain wrong.

Heck yields back; and it goes to Jordan, who says, 55 days; 55 days, between July 18th and September 11th, there was a delay in sending hard-earned tax dollars from the American people, to Ukraine; one of the most corrupt countries on the planet... {Jordan is trying to claim that the July 25th phone call was about claiming a "time out" from sending aid to Ukraine; because of corruption; and yet this was finally a new administration in Ukraine that, for once, very clearly to all of our Foreign Service workers, was not corrupt; this is what we are finding out, through these hearings}.

Jordan says that President Trump has done more already, for Ukraine, than Obama did; {yet, it should be noted that Obama was in office in 2014, during the revolution of dignity in Ukraine; and during the Russian invasion of Crimea; and Obama was the one who put together a coalition of several countries, to help Ukraine; Obama took the initiative to be the lead negotiator, putting together multi-country support for Ukraine; militarily, politically, and financially; for Ukraine to repel Russia's attack. So, Trump simply inherited that; and threw some money at it; big deal!}

So then, Jordan claims that Trump was saying, let's just see if the new President Zelensky is legit? {yeah, like Trump isn't!} -so Jordan claims that during the 55 days while the aid was being held, that Trump was talking with five top administration officials; Bolton, Mulvaney, and Pence, etc... and it took them that 55 days, for these administration officials to report back to Trump, that Zelensky is legit; {but I don't even think those officials are in the position to make that judgment;

this is done by diplomats stationed in Ukraine. In any event, it probably doesn't take 55 days to determine whether somebody is corrupt or not- it only took one phone call to show that Trump was very corrupt!}

Jordan says, no matter how many witnesses come in, this will not change that the call shows no linkage between dollars, and an investigation into Burisma and the Bidens. Both Presidents said there was no linkage; no pressure; no pushing; the Ukrainians didn't even know the aid had been with withheld; at the time of the phone call; and most importantly, the Ukrainians didn't take any specific action in order to get the money released. {Damn, that these Republicans can keep restating these immaterial contentions; when it is being clearly demonstrated by all of these witnesses, that the Ukrainians did feel pressure and they did know that release of the money was being conditioned on announcements}.

Then, Jordan says, there's one witness that they won't bring forward; and that's the whistleblower… {but in fact, the whistleblower wasn't a witness either; apparently, he was just a CIA agent, who heard from people who <u>could</u> be called, as direct witnesses; except that Trump has shut everybody down.} Obtusely, Jordan once again claims that Chairman Schiff knows who the whistleblower is; {but of course, the intelligence committee has only spoken with the whistleblower's lawyer}.

Jordan goes on this rant, but it's all the same bullshit we hear, over and over again; he says this is a sad day; {and I suppose and it is pretty sad, that we have a President that is so corrupt!} Jordan accuses Democrats of launching initiatives against President Trump for no reason; {but the fact is, there were 400 pages of reasons, in the Mueller report, why the investigation needed to happen!} Jordan claims that the facts <u>support</u> this President- {Ha! That's ridiculous!} -and that this process is unfair, and it's a sham! {Mr. Jordan; you should read the testimony, and stop defending this lawless maniac of a President}.

Jordan yields back; and it goes to Mr. Welch. Welch jokes that he'd be happy to have the number one witness come in to testify; President Trump! He can take a seat right there (he points to the witness stand; it gets a laugh).

Welch says, the question here is not a dispute about the enormous power that the President has; the question is whether, in this case, it was an abuse of that power. The President can fire an Ambassador, for any reason whatsoever; the President can change his policy; as (Trump) did, when he opened the door for Turkey to go in, and invade Kurdistan; despite opposition from many of his own senior advisors. The President could change his position on Ukraine; but is there a limit; there is, because our Constitution says no one is above the law; and that limit, is that one cannot; even as President; use the public trust of the high office, for personal gain.

Welch continues, the law prohibits any one of us, here on the dais; from seeking foreign assistance, in (the process of) our campaigns. The question before us, is whether the abuse of power by the President was for the benefit of advancing his political campaign in 2020; and by the way, if the President wants to attack Joe Biden and his son; by all means, he's free to do it; all fair and square, in campaigns. He is just not free, to change our foreign policy unless he gets his way; to assist him in his campaign; that line he cannot cross!

Now, you (Taylor and Kent) have been very clear about what our continuous foreign policy was; -and Ambassador Taylor, just very quickly describe, why is (how is it, that) withholding aid, interferes with achieving our national security goals? (Taylor says, one of our national security goals is to resolve conflicts in Europe. There is one (country right now in Europe) in major conflict (with Russia; the world's enemy). It is fighting a war that our national security goals are in support of, in Ukraine; and in support of a broader strategic approach to Europe... and to have our support, as we facilitate Ukraine's negotiations with Russia, for an end to this war).

Welch says, we had 70 years of peace, after World War II; and what the Russians have done; in attacking Ukraine (going on now, and since 2014), threatens each and every one of us, up here, and the constituents that we represent. On July 24th, Director Mueller testified about his investigation, and he established, beyond doubt, that it was the Russians who interfered in our (2016) election. He expressed the fear that this would be "the new normal."

On July 25th, according to the readout of the President's campaign, he asked the Ukrainians to investigate Ukrainian interference in our election; that has been repudiated (by Mueller's report, and by all other US intelligence sources) and yet, on July 26th, as I understand it, this person who reported (to Taylor), (having overheard the loud cell-phone call, between Sondland and Trump, speaking from an outdoor terrace, at a restaurant in Kyiv), they overheard the President, saying again, that he wanted (he was eagerly awaiting the announcements of) investigations in Ukraine; so this is the question: The new normal that director Mueller feared; is there a new normal that you fear? -that a President; any President; can use congressionally approved foreign aid as a lever to gain personal advantage, and something that is in <u>his</u> interest, but not the public interest? (Taylor says, that should not be the case.)

Welch yields back, and at this point Ms. Stefanik makes a motion to enter into the record, the transcript of the July 20th phone call, between Trump and Zelensky. She says, you (Democrats, I assume) have mischaracterized the call... Schiff interrupts her, to say, the gentlewoman will suspend; by unanimous consent; we would be happy to enter the call record, into the record.

Schiff then announces, Mr. Maloney is recognized. Upon being asked, Taylor says he graduated in 1969; the height of the Vietnam war; and that he was number five in his class, at West Point; out of 800 classmates.

Maloney comments, in the top 1% of your class, at West Point; you probably got your pick of assignments; yet, you picked the infantry... (Taylor says, yes I did.) Maloney continues, so, you were a rifle company commander. Taylor goes on to tell us that he served in Vietnam; he saw combat; he got commendations; badges, a bronze Star, and an Air Medal of Valor. Maloney says, let's talk about July 26th, in Ukraine; you go to the front, you're on the bridge, and are looking over on the front line of the Russian soldiers; do you recall what the Commander said to you there? (Taylor says yes...) Maloney tells us, the commander there; the Ukrainian commander thanked you for the American military assistance; that (yet) you knew was being withheld, at that moment...

Taylor says, that's correct... that made me feel badly, because it was clear that that commander counted on the US; it was clear that he had confidence in the US; and it was clear that he was appreciative of the abilities that he was given, by that (US military) assistance; but (he was also appreciative of) the reassurance that the US was supporting Ukraine.

Maloney says, one month later, on August 28th, you're in Ukraine, with John Bolton; and he conveyed his (own) concern about the withholding of the military assistance; what he said to you, (Bolton said that he too was concerned), (is that) he advised you to express that; in a very special way; to the Secretary of State. Now, (keep in mind); Bolton is the national security advisor; he works directly with the President; but he tells you, Mr. Taylor, to bring it up with the Secretary of State...

(When asked, Taylor says he's never sent a cable like that in his entire career. This was the only time in his 50 years of service.)

So, (in other words), the National Security Advisor, who can tell it to the President himself; and he shares your concern; says that you, Taylor; serving in Ukraine, should cable the Secretary of State directly... -and you do, don't you? (Taylor says, yes I did) Maloney asks, what did the cable say? (Well, it was about the security assistance) Taylor tells us that he wrote: At this particular time, (the aid) is important, for our national security; and we should support (the Ukrainians' war efforts); so, not to provide aid (at this critical time), that would be would be folly!

Maloney asks, did you get an answer? (not directly) -Kent says, I was on vacation when this cable was sent, but I submitted it to Secretary Pompeo... Maloney asks, what did Pompeo do with it? Kent says, I honestly can't say...

Maloney then brings up September 1st, and asks if Kent recalls a meeting, between VP Pence, and Zelensky, in which, right off the bat, the President of Ukraine raises the issue of security assistance; and the Vice President; according to intelligence; says, I'll talk to the President, tonight, about that; I'll make a call. Maloney then asks Kent, do you know if the Vice President made that call? (he doesn't). Can you tell us anything about the Vice President's role in this? (Can you tell us) if he ever raises issues anywhere within the administration, to push for the release of the aid? Taylor answers, I can't say. Kent says, to my understanding, the Vice President was an advocate for the release of the assistance.

Maloney yields back, and the floor now goes to Val Demmings. First, one of the Republican committee members asks to enter a certain Politico news article into the record; and Schiff says it will be entered, without objection. Ms. Demmings starts out by sarcastically asking, -the President's right to remove an Ambassador, does that come with the right to do a smear campaign on the Ambassador, (executed) by the President? (Kent soberly says that, basically, he has the right to do it; so far as his Presidential constitutional authority extends).

Ms. Demmings says, the committee has uncovered a web of "shadow-diplomacy;" engaged in, and executed by several State Department officials, and the President's personal attorney, Rudy Giuliani; and ultimately directed by President Trump. We have heard several ways of describing this shady "shadow-diplomacy" back-channel…

Next, she quotes Taylor as having said this was a highly irregular channel of policymaking; and she identifies the President's men, involved with the scheme; the "three amigos," and Giuliani… (Taylor says, yes ma'am; that's correct).

Ms. Demmings now brings up how Taylor had expressed that he was particularly concerned, once the irregular channel began to go against official US policy and interests. (Kent and Taylor both affirm that Giuliani was not working on official US foreign policy). (When asked, Kent says, I believe he was looking to dig up dirt against a potential rival in the next election cycle). (Taylor says, I agree with Mr. Kent). (Then Kent says, all federal employees are subject to the Hatch act; interactions are supposed to be promoting policy; and (foreign policy should not involve any) partisan politics). (Taylor says, I agree.) Taylor explains that, while there can be communication outside of the normal channels of foreign policy initiatives, any such discussions must ultimately be channeled back together; with the major emphasis that the (stated) foreign policy (should be) being carried out.

Ms. Demmings then brings up a phone call that took place shortly after Taylor arrived in June, in Ukraine; in which Ambassador Sondland asked State Department officials not to listen in, on a July 20th call he planned to have with President Zelensky. She asks, did you find that unusual? (Taylor says, I did.) Demmings asks, what was the impact of Ambassador Sondland making that request? (Taylor answers, the impact was that it was not recorded). Demmings asks, (is this commonly done?) (Taylor says, normally, State Department employees in the operation centers would've been there transcribing and taking notes. Taylor adds, that is the norm; but it's not (entirely) unusual to not have a recording).

Demmings then notes that the State Department is holding Taylor's records of notes and communications; despite the duly authorized subpoena from the intelligence committee. (Kent says, I turned all of my records in, to the State Department, because whatever we do is considered a federal record; not a personal record; but no; the State Department isn't turning over anything to this investigation).

Ms. Demmings yields back; and one of the Republican committee members asked to enter a New York Times op-ed article (something about the Obama administration) into the record; and Schiff says, you can enter it into the record without objection.

The floor next goes to Mr. Krishnamoorthi, and he starts off saying that (it has been contended that) Ukrainians didn't feel any pressure to comply with any of President Trump's request for investigations... In fact, Ambassador Taylor, in your deposition, you stated that, due to the hold that President Trump placed on aid to Ukraine, Ukrainians became "desperate." (Taylor says, in August, they did not (unquestionably) know (about the hold), as far as I know; but at the end of August, the article came out, and the (Ukrainian) minister of defense, for example, came to me in desperation; to figure out why the assistance was being held. He thought that perhaps if he went to Washington, to talk to the Secretary of Defense, he would find out why; and he could then give whatever answer was necessary, in order to have that assistance released).

Krishnamoorthi says, my colleagues on the other side of the aisle, claim that President Zelensky never felt any pressure, at any time; and yet later on, in September, he finally relented; in a conversation with Gordon Sondland, according to your deposition; in which he had (ultimately) agreed to make a statement on CNN; isn't that right?

Taylor says, he had planned to make a statement on CNN, yes sir. Krishnamoorthi continues, my colleagues also say that the hold on US security assistance was lifted on September 11th, without any investigations happening, on the part of the Ukrainians; and therefore everything ended up fine, in the end; however, Mr. Kent, as you know, the House Intelligence, Foreign Affairs, and Oversight Committees began this current investigation, leading to these proceedings today; on September 9th; in fact it was only two days after this particular set of committees began their investigations, that the Trump Administration eventually released the military aid; is that correct?

(Kent says, yes that's correct.) Krishnamoorthi then points out that Taylor had used the word "concerned" 16 times altogether, in his earlier testimony; "concern" that aid was being conditioned on political investigations; "concern" that irregular channels of diplomacy were being used to conduct our foreign policy; can you rule out the possibility that these irregular channels of the policy are (perhaps) being used in other countries where we conduct foreign policy? (Taylor says, I've not heard of any other separate channels that have this kind of influence; that is, the "Giuliani" kind of guidance; but I can't rule it out). (Kent says, no sir; I have no basis to make a determination).

Krishnamoorthi jokingly says, you don't think that the July 25th call was perfect, do you? (Kent says, I believe that call was cause for concern). (Taylor says, I agree). Krishnamoorthi continues, and what was the cause for concern? (Taylor says, the discussion of the previous Ambassador was cause for concern...)

Next, Krishnamoorthi notes Ambassador Taylor's background in infantry, and says, Ambassador Taylor, I want to draw on your experience, finally; as a West Point cadet, and as an infantry commander in Vietnam, in a battlefield situation. Is a commanding officer allowed to hold up action, placing his troops at risk, until somebody provides a personal benefit? (Taylor says no) -Is that because, if commanding officers did that it would be betraying their responsibilities to the nation? -and (if a commander had done this, and then they were subsequently found out), could that person be subject to discipline? Could that type of conduct trigger a court-martial? (Taylor affirms this.)

Krishnamoorthi yields back; and next, Jordan asks for unanimous consent to enter in to the record, Mick Mulvaney's statement; where he said there was no quid pro quo. {Let me interject; to say that's kind of funny, because it was Mulvaney, a little later, who at a press conference, admitted that yes, in fact there was a quid pro quo; and this kind of stuff happens all the time; and we need to get over it, or in other words, he insinuated that we need to get used to the President playing dirty politics}.

Finally, it is time for Schiff and Nunez to give their closing statements. Nunez goes first, and he starts by saying, I want to reiterate what I said earlier; {then he goes through his three things that he thinks we should find out before we move forward with any hearings}; (Sir, we are already moving forward; too late!), but he says (just a tiny piece of) the exact same spiel that he had said at the beginning; nothing new, in other words:

"We really should stop holding these hearings until we get the answer to three important topics; (how do you get the answer to a topic?!) the first being the full extent of the Democrats' coordination with the whistleblower; who the whistleblower coordinated with; second; the full extent of Ukraine's election meddling against the Trump campaign; and third, why did Burisma hire Hunter Biden, and what did he do for them; and did his position affect any US Government actions under the Obama administration? You (Democratic committee members) are not allowing those witnesses to appear before the committee; which I think is a problem; so we'll expect hopefully you will allow us to bring in the whistleblower, the folks that he spoke to; and also numerous Democratic operatives who worked with Ukraine to meddle in the election; with that I yield back." {Every word of that was bullshit, of course}.

Nunez yields back, and now Adam Schiff cordially says, I want to thank the witnesses for their testimony today, and for their decades of service to this country; and I want to exemplify so many courageous men and women who serve in our diplomatic corps; serving our military; who represent the United States so well, around the world. I appreciate how, today, you endeavored to stay "out of the fray;" to relay what you heard, and what you saw; without commentary, as it should be. You were both compelled to appear, and we are grateful that you answered the lawful subpoenas that you both received,

The story that you have shared with us today, with your experiences, I think is a deeply troubling one; it is a story of a dedicated Ambassador; somebody who served with great distinction; Ambassador Yovanovitch was the subject of a vicious smear campaign, (starting) at the beginning of the year. It is the story, that once this Ambassador was pushed out of the way, the creation of an irregular channel which you described, went all the way from the President, through Mick Mulvaney, to Ambassador Sondland, through Ambassador Volker, to Rudy Giuliani.

Over time, it became apparent; this was not serving US interests, but running deeply contrary to US interests. It was, in fact, conditioning a White House meeting that the President of Ukraine; who desperately sought to establish himself as a new President of Ukraine; and to demonstrate with friend and foe alike, that he had a relationship with his most powerful patron; the United States of America; and President Trump conditioned $400 million of bipartisan taxpayer-funded military support for a nation at war, on the front lines of Russian expansionism; the suspension of providing this aid which was not in the US interests, or in Ukraine's; or (in the interest of) our national security; in any way shape or form.

You described a situation in which, those in the service of the President, made clear to the Ukrainians that they need to publicly announce, that Ukraine had opened these investigations; and they weren't going to get that meeting, and they sure weren't going to get that military assistance otherwise!

I would point out; this may not have come to your attention; but it certainly came to our attention; that on September 9th, the Inspector General informed our committee that the Director of National Intelligence was withholding a whistleblower complaint; in violation of the statute. By that point, on September 9th, that complaint had made its way to the White House. At some point, the White House also learned that the Congress now inevitably would learn about the complaint. It was less than 48 hours later that the military aid would be released.

Over the days to come, we will hear from other dedicated public servants, about other aspects of this inviting of foreign interference into our election; to condition a White House meeting, and military aid, on the performance of political favors for the President's reelection campaign. We will hear from other witnesses.

I appreciate members of both sides of the aisle who I think participated today in a serious way, and in a civil way. This is as it should be. There is no shortage of strong feelings about what this means to the country. At the end of the day, you have to decide, based on the evidence, whether we are prepared to accept, in the President of the United States, a situation where a President, for his own personal or political benefit, can condition military aid, or any other official act; in order to get help in their election; whether this be diplomatic meetings, or any other performance of official act, in order to get help in their reelection; and whether we will need to accept, in this President, or any future President, the idea that the President of the United States can invite a foreign country to intervene in our foreign affairs. These are decisions that we will have to make; when we decide whether this President should be impeached. -But I wanted to thank you again; and to conclude by saying that I can't let it go unanswered; Republican committee members have made the statement, repeatedly, that I've met with the whistleblower, and otherwise know who the whistleblower is; this was false, the first time they said it; and it was still false, the next 40 times they said it; and it will always have been false! This concludes this portion of the hearing; the witnesses are excused.

(Thinking back on Nunez's closing statement, it seems that he was rendered somewhat speechless, by the end of this hearing; as he only offered one paragraph of speech, in his closing argument; whereas, Adam Schiff; looking only at the camera and not reading from anything, fit in 2 pages, typed, of "off-the-top-of-his-head" wording, into his very cogent closing statement.)

A bit of commentary:

{I must interject, that I've only been working on this transcription project for less than a week; and I've already had to stop once, earlier, to write about an article which had revealed some pertinent information, related to this impeachment process. Now I've just read another New York Times article in today's paper (Monday, November 25th), having a bit more of the back story laid out, concerning this concerted effort, on Trump and Giuliani's part, to dig up dirt on Trump's chief rival in the 2020 election, Joe Biden.

We didn't know this before, but this article brings to light the fact that Trump and Giuliani had also been working on trying to get investigations announced, and to dig up dirt on Joe Biden, much earlier on, than when Zelensky became elected as President of Ukraine.

Zelensky's predecessor was Petra Poroshenko; and by April of this year, Poroshenko was indeed already poised to announce investigations into Biden and Burisma; but then on April 21st, Zelensky beat Poroshenko in the election, foiling Trump and Giuliani's plan. Now, they would have to try and get the newly-elected President Zelensky to make these desperately-sought announcements of investigations.

At this time, Trump and Giuliani must have had reason to believe that Zelensky would not cooperate with them as willingly as Poroshenko; who was known for being corrupt; so they realized that they would have to find a way to put some pressure on Zelensky. It seems that one obvious way they knew they could put pressure on Zelensky, was that they knew Ukraine needed to have continued US support for their war against Russian invaders; hence, the strategy of withholding a White House meeting for Zelensky, that would show strong US support was continuing.

So, the new strategy involved Giuliani attempting to influence Zelensky's greatest (financial) patron, a Mr. Kolomoisky, (who is an oligarch in Ukraine; however, his record, as far the possibility of his supporting of Russia's agenda), is that instead, he was actually supporting (financially), the backing of Ukrainian militias, against Russian attackers, in recent years).

Now in addition to Kolomoiski, we do already know that Giuliani was working with Dmitri Firtash, another oligarch; but Firtash is considered to have direct linkage to Russian government operations.

On the other hand, Kolomoiski doesn't appear to be as easily pushed into becoming involved in this scheme of Trump and Giuliani's. In fact, today's New York Times article reports that when Giuliani went to see Kolomoiski; (and he did this under the auspices of discussing the marketing of liquefied natural gas); Kolomoiski realized, almost right away in the meeting, that Giuliani's real purpose of meeting with him was to try and get Kolomoiski to help arrange a meeting, between Giuliani and Ukrainian President Zelensky; and at this point, Kolomoiski threw Giuliani out of his office; stating something to the effect, that he did not want to get involved with this scheme, to give Trump some political advantage in his upcoming domestic elections.

Getting back to Firtash, he was-to-prove much more useful to Giuliani, in that he was already under indictment, for bribery and other serious charges, and was facing extradition from Vienna, to the US, to face these charges. He is a very rich oligarch, and we can be sure he used his riches in the process of finding ways to put off this extradition, which he has successfully accomplished, for at least a few years now. However, it seems that Firtash would likely be understandably worried, that he would indeed eventually become extradited to the US; and when Giuliani approached him knowing this, Firtash turned out to be a good mark, to exact funding for Giuliani's mission of bringing down Trump's rival opponents; in exchange for Giuliani's promise to try and get the US Justice Department to drop the case against him.

Firtash has claimed that he did not participate in financing the scheme to dig up dirt on Joe Biden; but it turns out that Giuliani had recommended, that if Firtash wanted his help to get off of these US charges, he would perhaps be best off hiring a team of two lawyers, that Giuliani had claimed, could be instrumental in helping to resolve Firtash's problems in the US. Now it comes out, that Firtash paid over $1 million, in a four-month contract, to retain these two new lawyers that Giuliani had basically instructed him to hire.

Do you see the sneakiness in always trying to cover their ass, in terms of hiding their underhanded scheming? -Rather than Firtash directly funding an effort to dig up dirt on Biden, he did so indirectly instead; by paying these lawyers, who likely funneled some of this money back into funding Giuliani's scheme to dig up dirt.

Incidentally, Giuliani and these two lawyers were ultimately successful in doing as they had promised, namely getting a meeting with Bill Barr at the Justice Department, ostensibly to discuss "calling off the dogs" on Firtash.

(In case you are asking yourself, why would Giuliani need money in this effort? Well, certainly to fund travel expenses for the different people that he had working with him, on this scheme; and it also seems likely that some money would be needed to pay bribes, for credible-appearing Ukrainian reporters, and possibly a few (bribe-able) government officials in Ukraine, to become willing to put out lies about Joe Biden that would cast him falsely as corrupt.)

There is more to this story; more related to Lev Parnas in particular; (he is one of Giuliani's (Russian-born, but US citizen) henchmen, one who was recently arrested for making illegal campaign donations, that perhaps likely had pretty-directly helped to fund necessary bribes of US officials having the authority to unseat Ambassador Yovanovitch, in this scheme as well). There is also some lack of clarity, as to where Parnas got these funds that he was donating; hundreds of thousands of dollars! -when he was apparently generating very little income himself.

Since he has direct ties to Russian oligarchs; or at least to Firtash, who is a Ukrainian oligarch very much tied to Russian operatives; it is suspected that Russian money was funneled through Lev Parnas, to make these donations to US politicians, for leveraging purposes; to an official, in the case I just described; who did subsequently facilitate the removal of Ambassador Yovanovitch; likely in order that Trump's scheme of getting the Ukrainian government to cast aspersions on Joe Biden could be carried out, without her being in the way.

I am just pointing all of this out, to further illustrate the degree of what lengths that Trump and Giuliani have apparently been willing to go to, in order to eliminate Joe Biden from remaining as Trump's greatest competition in the 2020 election; and I also wanted to point out that it appears Russian money had perhaps likely funded Yovanovitch being pulled out of her Ambassador position in a Ukraine; which could further give us reason to believe that Trump and Giuliani were somehow connected to Russians helping in this effort to discredit Joe Biden; as this would perhaps greatly increase Trump's chances of becoming reelected.

It really appears to be quite a bunch of dirty scheming, the effects, as seen by Trump and Russians alike, to be fairly essential insurance, against Trump failing to be reelected, doesn't it? -And once again, we could view this as a tie between Trump and Russia's underhanded campaigns, first to put, and then to keep Trump in office, as President. I can't help but consider that the Russians appear to be ardent supporters of Trump; and vice-versa! -even as I try to remain as objective as possible here.}

Intelligence Committee hearing #2- Marie Yovanovitch

In the second hearing, the sole witness is Marie Yovanovitch. Adam Schiff makes his opening statement:

In April of 2019, Ambassador to Ukraine Marie Yovanovitch was in Kyiv, when she was called by a State Department official and told to get on the next plane back to Washington. Upon her return to Washington DC, she was informed by her superiors that, although she had done nothing wrong, she could no longer serve as Ambassador to Ukraine, because she did not have the confidence of the President.

It was a stunning turn of events for this highly-regarded career diplomat, who had done such a remarkable job fighting corruption in Ukraine, that a short time earlier, she had actually been asked to extend her term in Ukraine. Marie Yovanovitch has been in the Foreign Service for 33 years, and served much of that time in the former Soviet Union. Her parents had fled Stalin, and later Hitler, before fleeing to the United States. She is an exemplary officer, who was widely praised and respected by her colleagues. She is known as an anticorruption champion, whose tour in Kyiv was viewed as very successful.

Ambassador Mike McKinley, who had served with her in the foreign service for several decades, stated that from the earliest days of her career in the US Foreign Service, she was excellent; serious; and committed. McKinley said he certainly remembers her as being one of those people who seemed to be "destined for greater things."

Ambassador Bill Taylor, who was her successor as acting Ambassador of Ukraine, described her as very frank. She was very direct; she made points very clearly, and she was indeed tough on corruption; and she even named names (of corrupt people she was targeting), and sometimes that is controversial out there, (it takes unusual courage) but she's a strong person; and she made those charges.

in her time in Kyiv, Ambassador Yovanovitch was tough on corruption; too tough on corruption, for some. -And her stands made her an enemy; because as George Kent said on Wednesday, you can't promote principled anticorruption action, without pissing off corrupt people. Ambassador Yovanovitch did have the resolve to stand up to corrupt Ukrainians; like the corrupt former prosecutor, Yuriy Lutsenko; but (Yovanovitch also pissed off) certain (corrupt) Americans like Rudy Giuliani, President Trump's personal attorney, (along with) two individuals now indicted, who worked with (Giuliani), Igor Fruman and Lev Parnas. Last summer those individuals; joined by Lutsenko, and empowering others that would come to include President Trump's son, Don Junior; promoted a smear campaign (smearing Yovanovitch), which was based on false allegations.

(Once the false smear statements had become publicly broadcast), there was an effort to "push back;" to obtain a statement of support from Secretary of State Mike Pompeo, but (efforts to get Pompeo to defend her honor) failed; and it became known later that there was concern among higher-ups at the State Department, who might have been in a position to release a supportive statement, that President Trump might have a contradictory response anyway.

(Schiff then points out that Trump and some others, have argued that a President as the ability to remove or nominate any Ambassador that he wants; that they serve at the pleasure of the President.) -And that is true; the question before us is not whether President Trump could recall an Ambassador with a stellar reputation for fighting corruption in Ukraine, but rather, why would he want to?

Why did Rudy Giuliani want her gone, and why did Donald Trump? -And why would Donald Trump instruct that a new team be put in place; the three amigos (Secretary Perry, Ambassador Volker, and Ambassador Sondland) to work with the same man, Rudy Giuliani; who played such a central role in the smear campaign against Ambassador

Yovanovitch? Rudy Giuliani has made no secret of his desire to get Ukraine to open investigations into the Bidens, as well as (an already debunked) conspiracy theory of Ukrainian interference into the 2016 election.

(Schiff continues), as Giuliani said in one interview, in 2016, "We are not meddling in an election, we're meddling in an investigation; which we have a right to do…"

More recently, Rudy told CNN's Chris Cuomo, "Of course, I did!" when asked if he had pressed Ukraine to investigate Joe Biden; and he has never been shy about who he is doing this work for; for his client, the President. One powerful ally whom Giuliani had in Ukraine, to promote these political investigations, was the corrupt Prosecutor General Yuriy Lutsenko; and one powerful adversary that Lutsenko had, was US Ambassador Marie Yovanovitch. Now, it is no coincidence that, in the now infamous July 25th phone call to the new Ukrainian President Zelensky, President Trump brings up this corrupt prosecutor, and praises him; against all evidence. Trump claimed (during this call) that this former Prosecutor General was very good, "and he was shut down; and that's really unfair." But, as far as the woman known for fighting corruption, his own former Ambassador Yovanovitch, a woman mercilessly smeared, and removed from her post; the President does nothing but disparage her; or worse, threaten her, that "She's going to go through some things," the President declared in that call.

That tells you a lot about the President's priorities; and indicates his intentions, in getting rid of Ambassador Yovanovitch; to help set the stage for an irregular channel, that could pursue the two investigations that mattered so much to the President; the 2016 conspiracy theory, and most importantly, an investigation into the 2020 political opponent he feared most, Joe Biden. (Obviously, Trump figured that Zelensky was corrupt like him; and would therefore be upset that the "shutting-down" of such a good partner in crime as Lutsenko could be, to a corrupt leader like Zelensky's predecessor. He obviously figured Lutsenko's removal would feel like a loss to Zelensky; Trump obviously didn't even know that the (new President) Zelensky had ordered the firing of Lutsenko).

(Schiff continues), and his scheme might have worked, but for the fact that the man who would succeed Ambassador Yovanovitch, who we heard from on Wednesday; Acting Ambassador Bill Taylor; would eventually discover the effort to press Ukraine into conducting these investigations, and would push back.

-But for the fact also, that someone blew the whistle. (the whistleblower complaint really made all of Trump's scheming blaringly come-to-light).

Ambassador Yovanovitch was serving our nation's interest, in fighting corruption in Ukraine; but she was considered an obstacle to the furtherance of the President's personal and political agenda. For that, she was smeared and cast aside. (Trump mistakenly figured he needed a reason to recall her, so he invented a fake one; and now Trump insists that he doesn't need a reason to do such things; yet if he really believed that, he wouldn't have invented a fake one, would he?)

The powers of the presidency are immense; but they are not absolute; and they cannot be used for corrupt purposes.

The American people expect their President to use the authority they grant him, in the service of the nation; not to destroy others in order to advance his own personal, or political interests.

(Now it goes to Devin Nunez, to make his opening statement:)

He starts by saying it's unfortunate that we will have to engage in these day-long TVs spectacles, instead of solving the problems we were all sent to Washington to address. {Oh really? Exposing an odious scheme carried out by some of the highest officials in the land, which was evidently-destructive to our mission of support to a struggling Ukraine; and one that very unfairly smeared a 33-year-veteran Foreign Service champion in the process; this is merely a useless TV spectacle?!}

Then Nunez talks about some trade agreement with Canada and Mexico, ready for approval; a deal that will create jobs {Here we are, three years into Trump's presidency; and Trump hasn't even finalized his trading arrangements with our two closest neighbor countries yet?!}

{I do have to acknowledge that a week later I have just read a NY Times article about this new trade agreement that seductively contains elements that Democrats have been arguing for, for years; however, it also requires things like that big pharma companies will be enabled to maintain high prices on drugs traded, under this deal. So, do Democrats take the concessions thrown their way and vote the deal in; or maybe should they give Moscow Mitch a taste of his own medicine and vote no; just on principal, because Republicans are being so uncooperative?}

Then, Nunez goes on about how Congress has not yet approved funding for the government which expires next week {Get real; the Republicans always push it to the absolute last minute; before ever agreeing to anything even halfway reasonable, as far as compromising with Democrats; in order to strike a deal that further funds Trump-sponsored Republican spending initiatives; which, of course, require us to go further into debt, as a nation, in order to benefit the rich and powerful; and not the common man. Nunez is crying because he can't borrow any more money to throw around, I suppose}.

-And he plays to the heartstrings of right-wingers, insinuating that Democrats are blocking funding for men and women in the service. {But the reason we are having these hearings is that Trump blocked $391 million in funding, for our troop initiatives in Ukraine; to only become released once the Ukrainian leadership had carried out a specific corrupt deed for Trump}.

Nunez says that the Democrats have been perpetually running a campaign to topple our President. {Yes, we knew Trump was corrupt, from the very start of his presidency, of course. Why should it be any surprise, that we would make sustained efforts to oust such a phony and a lunatic?}

Nunez notes that five Democrats on the Committee had already voted to impeach Trump, before the Trump-Zelensky phone call ever occurred (yes, that is because the Mueller investigation implicated Trump, and members of his campaign enormously, in a 420-page severely-damning report), and Nunez continues, that Democrats have been trying to oust Trump since he got elected {yes, again, because of all that was turned up in the Mueller Report; of which his Russia pretty strong evidence of collusion had been indicated, as far back as half-a-year before the 2016 election}.

Nunez asserts that the phone call is just unfairly being used as an excuse for the Democrats to fulfill their Watergate fantasies. {No, apparently Trump is much dirtier than Nixon ever was}. He says the American people are seeing a farce; hours of hearsay, second, third, and fourth-hand testimony {Even this testimony is evidently still valid; and it is only because Trump has used his Presidential powers to prohibit anyone who interacts with him directly, to testify).

Nunez claims this is all rumors; then he says it's a problem to try and overthrow a President based on this. {Yes exactly; that is why the President is playing dirty pool, and not allowing any first-hand testimony to come out!}

Nunez argues that this is what their case relies on; {and of course, he says this in order to try and delegitimize the claims being made, including by the whistleblower; as we know that hearsay is typically not regarded as solid evidence}; and he criticizes that the Democrats don't have much direct evidence. {Of course, we know that there can be no direct evidence, if the President has forbidden everybody in his administration to say one word, or give one document over to Congress}. He says Republicans are used to what Americans are seeing "for the first time," that he considers absurd. {Oh really? What about Democrats' similar posture, taken after the Mueller report came out?}

Nunez says that Democrats haven't done anything in the last three years besides exploring conspiracy theories. {Of course, many of us are aware that, just in the last year alone, the Democratic-Majority-led Congress has put, over 100 bills on Mitch McConnell's desk; and I don't think McConnel has even brought a one of them to the floor, for a vote- he just blocks the House's every effort. So, in other words, they are doing their job in drawing up legislation, but Mitch McConnell has blocked every initiative; i.e.- he's the one not doing his job!}

Then Nunez says something about nude photos (we already talked about the footage of Trump being peed on by Russian prostitutes, contended to exist by an investigator hired, in 2016, to explore Trump's Russian engagements).

Next, Nunez accuses Democrats of cooperating with some Ukraine scheme {this theory was debunked; Ukraine election meddling didn't really happen}. He talks about Alexandra Chalupa, a contractor for the Democratic National Committee, hired to supposedly dig up dirt on the Trump campaign. Nunez says that Alexandra was, at the same time, simultaneously working on behalf of Ukraine and the DNC, and the Clinton campaign; in an effort to (I suppose he means falsely) influence US Government officials. {I don't believe any of this bull}.

He mentions that the Russia investigation, is now being investigated itself, by Bill Barr, {A cagey defensive move, that Trump and his complicit corrupt protector Bill Barr can fiendishly get underway only because Barr is head of the Justice Department, the only source this initiative could be gone forward within}.

Nunez accuses Democrats of being blind to these blaring signs of corruption {Ha! The Democrats who are bringing these serious charges against Trump, are blind to corruption?! -That's a laugh}. Then he spews something about Hunter Biden; followed by launching the put-down of (so-called) Democratic media hacks {Which I suppose he means, is every news source except for Fox, Breitbart, and a smaller number of other conservative news sources}.

Then he repeats his diatribe of 3 questions, that we have already heard at yesterday's hearing; {I suppose he has to do something to fill up his time slot; since there is no defense, for what Trump has done here}. He states the neatly-written-out verbiage exactly like the day before. Then he claims that Democrats had initially vowed that they would not go into an impeachment effort without bipartisan support {That's right; it's become the corruption fighters against the complicit actors with their corrupt President, who are so secretly scared of losing their ability to keep pushing-through, their self-serving agenda, contrary to the interests of the common man in this country, that they are acting with false bluster, as their only means of trying to dispel this serious confrontation}.

Nunez raves on, saying that Democrats have an ever-growing list of broken promises and destructive deceptions. {Once again, we see this defense of accusing the other side, of doing what only your side is doing malevolently}; then he reads a transcript of Trump's congratulatory call to Zelensky (on July 20th).

On this call, interestingly, Trump claims that he "knows many people in Ukraine." {Out of one side of his mouth, Trump is saying that he has lots of friends in Ukraine; while out of the other side of his mouth, Trump claims that the people of Ukraine were out to get him; whatever is convenient at the moment, I suppose}. On this July 20th call, Trump had said, "We're making tremendous progress in the US;" (and he adds something about the economy). He claims that Zelensky had said that Trump was a "great example;" Zelensky supposedly says to Trump, you are a great example for our new managers; {probably mere strategy; i.e.- Pander to the narcissistic lunatic, who somehow became placed in the White House!}, and then Zelensky invites Trump to the inauguration.

Trump indicates that he may not come himself; but that the US will send a great representative, at a minimum; someone at a very, very high level, will be there at your inauguration, Trump says. (Rick Perry, the Energy Secretary, is not a particularly high-level official, of course}.

Then he brags that he used to own "Miss Universe," and he compliments that Ukraine was always very well represented. {as if, how a couple of vanity-conscious, usually-not-too-bright Ukrainian beauty-queen-contestants had conducted themselves in a Miss Universe pageant, is any indication of what the Ukrainian people are like}.

Then Trump supposedly said, "When you're settled in and ready, I'd like to invite you to the White House. We have a lot of things to talk about." {Just two actually, as it turns out; Burisma and the Bidens}. Trump says, we are with you all the way. Zelensky then says that he will practice, so that he can conduct his visit entirely in English, when he comes. {This was the very first call; a week before the infamous July 25th phone call, for which the President is being impeached}.

Nunez concludes by saying he feels great, that he's read this into the record. {I don't know why}.

Then, just after Schiff takes back the floor, to begin the testimony section of the hearing, the Republicans started heckling him, to throw him off; as they have no defense otherwise, of course. Some woman, the lone woman the Republicans would ever have on a committee, I assume, starts the round of heckling, which is ultimately unsuccessful.

Nunez yields back his time, and Schiff wants to say a few words about this call record, that Nunez had just read into the record; but Republican Committee members snapped at Schiff like a pack of Jackals. -And after the heckling stops; which Adam Schiff is very effective at shutting these hecklers down; they were basically restating exactly the same objections as they had voiced, to of no avail, at the first hearing. {The Republicans did a lot of that; saying the same things over and over again; whether they were true or not; and whether or not they might have had any bearing on the crux of the matter at hand}; but anyway, next, Nunez states that, although we have some <u>notes</u> from the July 25th call, we don't have a complete transcript of it; {insinuating that, without the full word-for-word transcript, nothing being testified-to today, about what had been said in that phone call, was the least bit valid; so in other words, if as President, you engage in corrupt practices, but then you simply effectively hide all definitive evidence, this will render any proceedings against you invalid; yeah, sure}.

Schiff doesn't even address this stupidity; instead, he takes the opportunity to cordially (but sarcastically) say, "Thanks, Mr. President for releasing that transcript;" (and adds that) I would now ask the President to release the thousands of other records that he has instructed the State Department not to release, including Ambassador Taylor's notes and memos, and Undersecretary Kent's; and documents from the Office of Management and Budget, as to why the military aid was withheld.

(Schiff had to, once again, hit is gavel down, and say the gentleman is not recognized, when Jordan tried to interrupt again, for like the 20th heckling time). Schiff says, the gentleman will suspend. Schiff continues, We would ask the President to stop obstructing the impeachment inquiry in this manner; (and he reiterates, that while we are grateful that he has released a single document), Trump has, nonetheless, obstructed witnesses and their testimony, and the production of thousands of other records (which the Intelligence Committee has been asking for, for many months); and finally I would say this, Mr. President: I hope you explain to the country today, why, after this call, and while the Vice

President was making plans to attend the inauguration, you instructed the Vice President not to attend?

(The other main Republican heckler, besides Jim Jordan, is Miss Stefanik (I was just now able to see her name tag).

(Here is a bit of my commentary, as an aside):

{To digress, I suppose it is plain to see that; when I write about the Republicans continuing to repeat the same false, or otherwise meaningless contentions; it fuels an escalating anger within me; and I find it easier to start losing my objectivity, to some extent. Perhaps, this provides an interesting insight into the psychology of Republican lawmakers; this purposeful creating of strong partisanship, as a key ingredient in their strategy; being a strategy of basically, screw you, we won't cooperate; we won't admit to anything you say we have done wrong; and we will consistently object to your narrative, no matter how factual and sensible your keen observations and arguments are. We are going to spin bullshit; and spin the same bullshit over and over. We are banking on a large faction of the country continuing to be on our side; because being contrarian in this manner is cool and fun, for quite a number of people perhaps. (i.e.- The interviewer (George Papadopoulos) says to Trump, "We have just heard (the top official on foreign involvement in our elections) tell us, that what you have done, in asking officials in another country to dig up dirt on your political opponent is absolutely illegal!" -And Trump's cool response, "Oh yeah? -well the guy is wrong," said with a wry smile.

It would seem that, in this fight, the Democrats are going to have to embrace coolness, as a part of their strategy, as well. That will be a creative challenge; because sober judgment doesn't sound very cool. But on the other hand, a cut-up who does something nasty and destructive while everybody laughs, will almost invariably, still be punished in a suffering way himself. That's sort of cool; being the one who can creatively meet out justice, in order to bring "wildness" back to "reasonable;" and "falsely inconsequential" back to "properly consequential," for a bad actor, when they try and get away with being glibly destructive.

Adam Schiff has been kind of cool; he sure comes across as intelligent, and in control over his environment; I'm not sure Jerry Nadler can pull that off; perhaps he seems a bit too easily riled-up. (As it turns out, he did just fine, in moderating the Judiciary Committee hearings).

One thing Democrats have in their favor, is that Republicans really don't like these proceedings; and they appear to make nasty fools of themselves much of the time; but more opportunistically, Trump has done so many nasty, sick things since he's been in office, that Democrats could spend months and months pointing them all out in a long series of public hearings.

(As of a couple of weeks later, I have to tell you that I was quite disappointed when only two articles of impeachment were brought against Trump; and then the hearings and debates were over within about two weeks! I'm afraid I don't quite understand what sensible rationale there could be, behind that.) The Mueller report findings are 400 pages long; that could be a month by itself. Then, there is all of the good protections and regulations that Obama put into effect, which Trump routinely and irresponsibly reversed; dozens and dozens of terrible reversals! This could be another couple of months of hearings, just to reasonably explain to Americans just how damaging all of this has been, to our health and well-being.

Then, there is climate change; there are so many facts of the matter which Trump obviously doesn't give a damn about. Sure, he and his senior cronies won't be alive to see the terrible consequences of Trump's cavalier disregarding of how much quicker the world will go down the road to extreme hardship and ruin; as climate change reversal initiatives are denigrated and thwarted; all of which Trump's lead has perhaps chiefly caused, and continues to cause.

Anyway, I started out saying that it makes me come unglued too easily, to have to write, a number of times, about the same stupid, repeated phrases that have no bearing on the issue, in many cases; so from this point on, I'm just going to have to try and avoid even mentioning these heckling repeats any further. It undoubtedly means that Devin Nunez' ridiculous rants, from now on, in this hearing-substantive transcript, will perhaps become a mere few sentences, that could have been spoken in under a minute; even though he may have actually been jawboning for seven, at times.

{Here, I am interrupting my Intelligence Committee impeachment transcription, in order to make a few comments on the first <u>Judiciary</u> Committee hearing last Wednesday; where we heard from four distinguished law professors. (However, I saw a short segment illustrating how Mr. Turley had attempted a bogus defense, during the trial of the last impeached official, in 2010; and his arguments here also appear to be based on some complex form of spin.)

First, we heard from three experts, that what Trump has done is a classic case of what the Framers of the Constitution had in mind to intervene in, when they designed an impeachment mechanism. It is literally inarguable, that Trump acted with malevolent intent; to scheme and falsely smear our Ukrainian Ambassador; in order to claim a reason to recall her, to get her out of the way; so that his corrupt back-channel of rogue diplomats were enabled to lean on the new President Zelensky, and make him take a corrupt action in order to get anything of good value for the Ukrainian people, from the US. Then, after 45 minutes of hearing sound reasoning behind these legitimate arguments, it became time for the deterrent circus of the right, to argue ridiculous stances; although those of us who are perhaps less-adept, and less-well-informed, could perhaps easily fall for some of their claims and contentions. I will try to explain why some of their points of contention are mere theatrics:

The Minority counsel, at the Judiciary committee's first impeachment hearing, (John Turley) seems to be staking his argument on two bogus claims: One is the claim that there are no fact witnesses that have testified, as first-hand witnesses of the President's statements and conduct. (If I could have spoken to this, in the moment; I would say something like):-If counsel is suggesting, that if a President engages in corrupt conduct, and then subsequently, we are to assume that it constitutes legitimate use of executive privilege, for him to block everyone (having any potential to implicate him, as far as our hearing from those having regular contact with the President on daily matters), from giving testimony, or from giving over any documentation, related to Congress's investigation of this corruption; if counsel thinks this deceitful strategy should be deemed to offer protection from reasonable judgment relating to the crimes the President is trying to cover up, then he takes falsely for granted, that those with integrity on this committee could not see through that hollow argument!

Turley's second bogus argument is that in past impeachments, there was bipartisan agreement, that what the President had done was indeed a crime; and he now contends that, without this level of agreement among all committee members, impeachment proceedings can somehow be declared illegitimate.

Once again, Turley is insinuating that if the President and his own political party supporting him are complicit in committing and covering up a bribe, for example; then subsequently, the confrontation and consequences for having committed this wrongdoing are to be escaped, simply by having every complicit actor deny they think it's a crime, to do what the President has done; and once again, counsel vastly underestimates the ability of an integral body of judgment, such as the Democratic majority within the Judiciary Committee, to be able to see through this sham claim.

Another bogus claim being made by Minority leader Collins, and his counsel, is that Congress is usurping its power by refusing to go through the courts, like Trump and Barr are trying to orchestrate. Although it is true, that obtaining the Supreme Court's judgment would definitely be binding in these matters; the (Framers of the Constitution) couldn't have predicted how seriously the Republican party could effectively "pack the court," by pulling maneuvers, such as refusing to hold confirmation hearings on a Democratic President's Supreme Court Judge nominee, for example; (holding the spot open for the next Republican President to fill the seat), in violation of enduring, set-forth structure; nor could the Framers have foreseen how the cagey procedure of pulling maneuvers to progressively drag things out, further and further in court, has increasingly lengthened the time frame, before ultimate judgment is rendered; after multiple appeals, and other delay tactics are maximized by a corrupt Republican body. It can take 3 years, in some cases; We can't wait for that!

Minority's arguments are all basically on the grounds that Congress is not following procedural guidelines; which would render the impeachment effort illegitimate; regardless of whether serious wrongdoing was committed; as long as those in the President's corner disagree with the accusing party's assessments. That's a ridiculous argument!

Additionally, the Republican minority is claiming that obstructing Congress's investigation into Presidential wrongdoing (i.e.- the President ordering all government personnel to defy any document request, or Congressional subpoena of a witness, to testify) can't really be "legitimately considered to definitely amount to obstruction," until it has played itself out, in delays within the courts, for years, in order to get a final, (Republican-packed) Supreme Court ruling, undoubtedly in favor of the party that had packed the court (in this case, the Republicans).

No, of course we cannot tolerate these unending delays; we must act very soon, in order to ensure that Trump doesn't take any further opportunity to fix the election results, in like manner to what he has already encouraged and initiated, through his corrupt actions and schemes, so far this year alone.

And there can be no grounds for claiming executive privilege here! That is for when the President might be doing something covert, for the good of the nation; and not while taking action that plainly subverts our national interests!

Turley contending that, as a basis for impeachment, there must be a concrete body of law legitimating that, in fact, crimes have been committed; this assertion negates the broader definition of "impeachable offenses," defined, within the Constitution, as not necessarily having to constitute illegal actions on the part of the President. The idea of impeachment, I should think is more of a consensus, among us all, that the President acted abominably. Maybe that judgment could have even been overstated in the past; certainly with respect to Bill Clinton; (because what does a personal sexual indiscretion have to do with the hundreds of fine decisions and actions Clinton put forth, in his admirable service of protecting and promoting the nation's interests, during the time he was President?)

So, I'm just saying, that if Republicans can claim Bill Clinton's behavior qualified him to become subject to impeachment; what we have here is 10 times worse even, than Watergate! -And I dare the Senate not to remove Trump; I think that, by the time the Democrats are through with their exposure of how much against the common man, that these Republican representatives have been throwing-in with Trump, many of those nasty Republican Senators will probably never get re-elected! (i.e.- they will be brought to change their tune, or they will not be re-elected; and I think we can be pretty certain, re-election is more important to them- but maybe not...)

Turley tries to suggest that bribery must consist of someone being given money in exchange for being granted a favor or a privilege; but it occurs to me that the essence of bribery is a seduction. In other words, someone comes to you, and asks you to do something for them, that you wouldn't normally be inclined to do for them; but the fact that they are offering you money in exchange, is seductive; and you begin to flirt with the idea of granting the briber something otherwise seen as perhaps out of the question; from a standpoint of integrity.

So, before we go any further, we should consider that Trump has taken unusual license to be unwilling to do customary things always done by every other President; such as granting a White House meeting for a new President of Ukraine, as a show of undaunted US support against Russian aggression in Ukraine, for example.

So, in a weak position, as the newly elected President of Ukraine; even if you are not normally the least bit susceptible to being talked into doing something corrupt; if the US President indicates that he may even delay a White House meeting indefinitely otherwise, this would seduce you into considering doing the corrupt thing that the US President is demanding.

Since money merely represents value; whether it be the purchasing power of to own a car, or a piano, or a painting, for example; and the White House meeting with the US President is a thing of great value for a new Ukrainian President Zelensky; it can be readily seen that Trump was seductively using his official action (versus a potential-inaction), to grant or deny this thing of value; which was unmistakably hinged upon

Zelensky doing the corrupt thing that Trump was putting pressure on him to do.

This might be the equivalent of offering your kid brother an ice cream cone later, if he will tell your mother that your older sister, (whom you want to get back at, because she revealed something awful you did), was picking on him (so she will get in trouble); only this is a much more serious offense indeed! No money was exchanged, but clearly this constitutes a bribe, because of the seductive incentive.}

(Back to my Intelligence Committee Impeachment Hearing summary:)

Adam Schiff continues: Today, we are joined by Marie Yovanovitch. She was born in Canada, to parents who had fled the Soviet Union and the Nazis. She emigrated to Connecticut at the age of three, became a naturalized US citizen at 18, and entered the US Foreign Service in 1986. She has served as US Ambassador three times, been nominated by Presidents of both parties, (George Bush nominated her to be Ambassador to the (Kurus?) Republic where she served from 2005 to 2008; President Obama then nominated her to be Ambassador of Armenia. She served there from 2008 to 2011; then she was appointed US Ambassador to Ukraine by President Obama in 2016; where she served until last summer.

Marie Yovanovitch has held other senior positions at the State Department, including in the Bureau of European and Eurasian affairs. She served as Dean, at the Foreign Service Institute; and taught national security strategy at the Defense University. She also previously has served in US embassies in Kyiv, Ottawa, Moscow, London, and Mogadishu, Somalia. She has received multiple honors from the department for her diplomatic work; including the Presidential distinguished service award, and the Secretary (of State's) diplomacy and human rights award. Schiff says that this committee, and Congress will not tolerate any reprisal, or threat of reprisal, or attempt to retaliate against any US Government official testifying before Congress. Then he swears in the witness.

Marie starts out (reading her written opening statement), saying that she has devoted 33 years of her life; the majority of her life, to serving this country (that all of us love). She says that she has always implemented the foreign policy designated by the Government and the President. She says she has gratitude for all that she has gotten out of being an American citizen; and she says that her late parents did not have the fortune to come of age in a free society. Her father fled the Soviet Union before ultimately finding refuge in the United States; and that her mother's family escaped the USSR, after the Bolshevik Revolution, and grew up stateless in Nazi Germany, before eventually making her way to the United States.

Marie says that her parents' history, and hers, gives her great gratitude for the United States, and empathy for others like the Ukrainian people, who want to be free. She joined the Foreign Service during the Reagan Administration, and has subsequently served three other Republican Presidents, as well as two Democratic Presidents. She has served as Ambassador three times; twice under George Bush, and once by Barack Obama. She says that, contrary to the perception that diplomats lead a life of throwing parties for rich people, she says that, for her, it has not always been easy. She has moved 13 times, and served in seven different countries; five of them hardship posts. Her first tour was Mogadishu, Somalia; as a civil war was grinding on. The military took over policing functions in a particularly brutal way; basic services disappeared, etc…

At her next post, she was there when the embassy was attacked, and sprayed with gunfire. She later served in Moscow. In 1993, she says she was once caught in crossfire, between Presidential and parliamentary forces; and that it took three tries (and she was without a helmet or body armor), to make it to a vehicle to leave the embassy. Lastly, Yovanovitch served, from August 2016 to May 2019, as Ambassador to Ukraine.

Yovanovitch informs us that, while serving in Ukraine, she went to the front line 10 times, during their "hot war" with Russia, sometimes hearing the artillery all around her. Throughout, she was working to embrace US policy, and to see how US assistance dollars were being put to use. She has carried out US policy, as fully embraced by Democrats and Republicans alike; to help Ukraine become an independent Democratic state.

She claims that a secure, Democratic, and free Ukraine serves not just the Ukrainian people, but the American people as well. That is why it was our policy to help the Ukrainians to achieve their objectives; they match our objectives.

Yovanovitch emphasizes that the US is the most powerful country in the world; in large part, because of our values; and our values have made possible the network of alliances and partnerships that buttress our own strength. Ukraine, having an enormous landmass, and a large population, has the potential to be a significant partner for the United States. {By the way, I forget if I mentioned this before, but in his testimony, George Kent said that Crimea, at the eastern end of Ukraine, has a land mass of roughly the same size as the state of Texas. We can see that this is a huge landmass, that the Russians have taken over. Can you imagine how the US would respond, if the Mexicans took over Texas?}

Marie goes on to say that, while the US sees the potential of Ukraine, Russia sees the risk that a free Ukraine would pose, to their corrupt expansionist efforts; and she says that accordingly, Ukraine is now a battleground for a great power competition, for the control of territory; in a hybrid war (military force, along with cyber/political-influence), to control Ukraine's leadership. The US has provided security assistance since the onset of the war, in 2014; and (earlier on), the Trump administration had actually strengthened our policy, by approving the provision of Javelin (antitank) missiles.

Marie submits that supporting Ukraine is the right thing to do; and if Russia prevails, and Ukraine falls to Russian dominion, we can expect to see other attempts by Russia to expand its territory and its influence. Ukraine's economy, as a struggling democracy, also poses a challenge, battling the Soviet legacy of corruption; which has pervaded Ukraine's government, in the past; and that corruption makes Ukraine's leaders ever-vulnerable to Russia; and the Ukraine people understand this. That is why they launched the Revolution of Dignity, in 2014; demanding to be a part of Europe; demanding to live under the rule of law.

Ukrainians wanted the law to apply equally to all people, whether the individual in question is the President, or a common citizen. It is a question of fairness and dignity. There is a coincidence of interest; corrupt leaders are inherently less trustworthy, as well and being dishonest.

Independent Ukrainian leadership makes the US-Ukrainian partnership more reliable, and more valuable to the United States. A level playing field in this strategically-located country, bordering four other NATO allies, creates an environment in which US businesses can more easily trade, invest in, and mutually-profit from. Corruption is also a security issue, it is in our own national security interests, to help Ukraine transform into a country where the rule of law governs, and corruption is held in check. it remains a top US priority, to help Ukraine fight corruption; and significant progress has been made, since the 2014 Revolution of Dignity.

Unfortunately, the past couple of months have underlined, that not all Ukrainians embrace our anticorruption work; plus, it was not surprising that when our anticorruption efforts got in the way of a desire for profit or power, Ukrainians who preferred to play by the old corrupt rules, sought to remove her.

She says that it continues to amaze her, that they (corrupt Ukrainian officials) found Americans willing to partner; and working together, they apparently succeeded in orchestrating the removal of the US Ambassador. {Actually, it's worse, because it wasn't Ukrainians finding American officials willing to partner with them; it was American officials, instead seeking out Ukrainian officials, to help them carry out their malevolent American plot}. She asks, how is it, that foreign corrupt interests can manipulate our government?! Which country's interests are served, when the very type of corrupt behavior that we've been criticizing past Ukrainians of, is allowed (and encouraged by the US) to prevail?

She says, such conduct undermines our efforts, and widens the playing field for autocrats like Putin. Our leadership depends on the power of our example; and on the consistency of our leadership. Both have now been open to question...

Next, she wants to briefly address some issues that she anticipates being questioned about in this hearing. She starts by clarifying, that she arrived in Ukraine on August 22, 2016, and she left Ukraine permanently on May 20, 2019. She then summarizes some of the events that preceded her involvement in Ukraine; such as the release of the "black ledger," showing payments to Paul Manafort; who subsequently resigned from the Trump campaign. -And she also wasn't there to see the departure, from office, of the former Prosecutor General, Victor Shokin.

Next, Yovanovitch talks about events taking place after she returned on May 20th. She starts out with stating that she was not involved in, nor did she have any idea what was even said in that July 25th call, until the (partial) transcript was released, months later; and that she didn't know of any delay of the release of the $391 million in aid, either. (The determination that the aid would be put on hold, was not made until July 1st).

Next, she talks about what she did while she was in Ukraine. First, the allegation, that she had disseminated a do-not-prosecute list (suggesting that she tried to protect corrupt officials from being prosecuted), is a fabrication. Mr. Lutsenko, the former Prosecutor General who made that allegation, has since acknowledged that the list never existed.

Yovanovitch emphasizes that she merely advocated the US position; that the rule of law should prevail, in Ukrainian Law Enforcement; and that all Judges should stop wielding their power selectively, as a political weapon; and start behaving consistently according to the rule of law.

She also denies that she ever said that President Trump's orders should be denied, (as this was one thing she had been accused of); she says that such statements would be inconsistent with her training as a Foreign Service Officer. In her role as Ambassador to Ukraine, the Obama administration did not ask her to help the Clinton campaign, or to harm the Trump campaign; nor would she have taken such steps, if they had; that partisanship of this type, is not compatible with her role, as a career Foreign Service officer.

She offers that she has never met Hunter Biden, nor had any correspondence with him; but she says she has met Joe Biden, several times over the course of their many years of mutual government service; and that nobody had ever raised the issue of either Burisma, or Hunter Biden, with her personally.

She says that she only ever had three conversations with Rudy Giuliani; and she says she did not understand Giuliani's motives for attacking her {I'm sure she does now, though}, and she acknowledges that she doesn't know why he offered the allegations that he made, {but I think we can see pretty clearly now that Giuliani needed to get her out of the way so they could scheme in some underhanded way without being intervened in}.

Yovanovitch says Giuliani should've known that the claims of these corrupt Ukrainian officials were suspect, coming as they reportedly did from individuals with questionable motives. {Even by now perhaps, it appears as though she hasn't developed the full realization, that Giuliani had ostensibly put these corrupt Ukrainian officials up to broadcasting these lies). -And she had no reason to believe that her political and financial ambitions would be stymied by our (hijacked) anticorruption policy in Ukraine; (especially) after just recently having been asked, by the Undersecretary of State for Political Affairs, in early March, to extend her tour until 2020.

Marie says, (in March), a smear campaign against me entered a new public phase in the United States. In the wake of the negative press statements, a State Department official had now suggested an earlier departure; and we agreed upon July 2019. {She then tells us that, just weeks later, in April, that she was to come back to Washington, from Ukraine, "On the next plane."}

At the time she departed, Ukraine had just completed game-changing elections; it was insensitive. Much was at stake for the United States, and these times called for "all the experience and expertise we could muster."

When Yovanovitch returned to the US, Deputy Secretary of State Sullivan met with her, and told her that there had been a concerted campaign against her; and that the President no longer wished her to serve as Ambassador to Ukraine; and that in fact, the President had been pushing for her removal since the previous summer {of 2018}.

As Mr. Sullivan recently recounted during his Senate confirmation hearing, neither he, nor anyone else explained, or sought to justify the President's concerns about her; nor did anyone else in the department justify her departure by suggesting that she had done something wrong.

Sullivan had said that Yovanovitch had served capably and admirably; although then and now, she has always understood that she serves at the pleasure of the President.

Yovanovitch says she still finds it difficult to comprehend that foreign and private interests were able to undermine US interests, in this way. She explains that the State Department fully understood, that the allegations against her were false; still they didn't protect her. She contends that when a chief representative is knee-capped, (as Yovanovitch was indeed), it basically limits our effectiveness at safeguarding the vital National Security interests of the United States.

Our Ukraine policy has now been thrown into disarray, she states; and the rest of the world has learned how easy it is to remove an Ambassador, when they're not giving what the current government leader wants, {even if that President's documented policy is being forthrightly carried out}.

She points out that other Ambassadors might be harboring fear that the State Department won't support them either, in a difficult period like the one she just went through; even as they implement stated US policy, and protect and defend US interests.

Yovanovitch wanted to address that, at her deposition, she expressed grave concerns about the degradation of the Foreign Service, over the past couple of years; and the failure of State Department leadership to push back, as foreign and corrupt influence has apparently hijacked our Ukraine policy; and says she's also upset that her department leaders have declined to say, that what went on against her was wrong. She says foreign service officials are being denigrated and undermined; the institution is also being degraded; and this will soon cause real harm, if it hasn't already.

Yovanovitch argues that "We are the pointy end of the Spear," and if we lose our edge, then the US will have to use other tools, even more than it does today; those other tools are blunter, more expensive, and not universally effective. These attacks are leading to a crisis in the State Department. As the policy process is visibly unraveling; leadership vacancies go unfilled; and senior, and mid-level officers ponder an uncertain future. She contends that the State Department is being "hollowed out, from within," during a competitive and complex time on the world stage. This is not a time to undercut our diplomats!

It is the responsibility of the department's leaders, to stand up for the institution, and for the individuals who make that institution still today, the most effective diplomatic force in the world. Foreign Service agents answer the call to duty; and not only they, but their whole families too, must make sacrifices in order to do this important work.

To sum up, Yovanovitch mentions that she takes the same oath as everybody in the room (all of the Committee members; but of course, there is some doubt about whether some of those heckling Congressman are actually <u>upholding</u> that oath, on a day-to-day basis). Then she recites the oath: To support and defend the Constitution of the United States, against all enemies, foreign and domestic; and to bare true faith and allegiance to the same…

So, this concludes her statement, and now Adam Schiff has 45 minutes, for he and his lead counsel to be the first questioners of Marie Yovanovitch:

Adam Schiff's first question to Marie Yovanovitch is: is fighting corruption in Ukraine a top priority? Is it a key element of US policy? -and one in which she places the highest priority? (and she says yes; that it's important, because corruption was undermining the integrity of the governmental system in Ukraine. Countries that have leaders that are honest and trustworthy make better partners for us; countries that have a level playing field for US businesses, make it easier for our companies to do business there; to trade, and to profit in those countries; and what has been happening since the Soviet Union dissolved, and this is a Soviet legacy; corrupt influences were undermining, not only the government, but the economy of Ukraine. We see enormous potential with Ukraine and would like to have a more trustworthy partner there.)

Schiff says, "You are a champion of anticorruption efforts in Ukraine... (Yovanovitch says yes). Then, Schiff refers to Kent's statement about, if you fight corruption, then you are going to piss off corrupt people; and she says yes; then Schiff asks her about people that she angered, while fighting corruption; and she acknowledges that (Yes, Yuriy Lutsenko, the corrupt Prosecutor General was one of those). Schiff continues, and how about Victor Shokin, his predecessor?

"Yes," she says, "Apparently so; although I've never met him.

Schiff asks her if she knew that at some point, both Yuriy Lutsenko and Viktor Shokin were in touch with Rudy Giuliani, in this effort; and that Giuliani tried to overturn the decision that you participated in, to deny Viktor Shokin a travel visa?

Yovanovitch says yes; that was what she was told. Then she affirmed that it was Lutsenko, among others, who coordinated with Giuliani to pedal false accusations against her, as well as the Bidens.

Schiff adds that these smears were also amplified by the President's son, Donald Trump Junior; as well as by certain hosts on Fox news. (Yes, that is the case). Schiff asks, in the face of this smear campaign did colleagues at the State Department try to get it try to get a statement of support for you, from Secretary Pompeo? (Yes).

Schiff continues, were they successful? (no) Didn't you come to learn that they couldn't issue such a statement because they feared that it would be undercut by the President? (yes) Then Schiff points out that Marie was rushed out of the country on the very day of Zelensky's inauguration; the day that the new irregular channel began working on Zelensky, to get him to do President Trump's bidding? (yes). Then, Schiff comments that the inauguration was attended by the infamous "three amigos;" (Ambassador to the EU, Sondland, the Special Envoy Kurt Volker, and Rick Perry, Trump's appointed Energy Secretary.)

Schiff says that three days later, Trump, in a meeting with these three, designated them to coordinate Ukraine policy with Rudy Giuliani. Schiff then reminds us that Rudy Giuliani had also been recommended by the President. In the July 25th phone call, Trump had instructed Zelensky coordinate with Giuliani, in the context of the two investigations he was requiring Ukraine to sponsor. Then Schiff says, referring to those two corrupt prosecutors that ran the smear campaign against (Yovanovitch), that on this July 25th phone call, President Trump praised these corrupt prosecutors; Trump had said that they were treated very unfairly. Schiff emphasizes that Trump thought that "they" were treated unfairly; not "you" he says to Marie.

Schiff rhetorically asks, what message does that send to your colleagues in US Embassy? Do you have concern about the message that this sends to our foreign service people who are still in Ukraine? -Representing the United States; when a well-respected Ambassador can be smeared and pulled out of her post with the participation and acquiescence of the President of the United States? (Yes; for those in the embassy, but also more broadly in the entire State Department). Schiff asks, is it fair to say that other people serving in your capacity around the world might be thinking to themselves, that, "If I serve in the capacity of confronting corruption, this could happen to me!" (and she says yes, this is a fair statement).

At this point, Daniel Goldman takes over: On April 24th, at 10 o'clock at night, you received a telephone call from the Director General at the State Department; this was three days after Zelensky's election; and the call that Minority leader Nunez had just read into the record; the congratulatory call. (yes)

Goldman asks Yovanovitch, at the time of this call what were you doing? (She says that she was hosting an event for a formerly-assassinated anticorruption activist in Ukraine. She says that the State Department had given this courageous activist the "Woman of Courage" award from Ukraine; and also that at the Worldwide Courage event, in Washington DC., Secretary Pompeo had singled her out, for her work in fighting corruption in the south of Ukraine. She was later attacked by acid and she died from that attack several months later. She died a very painful death; so, they thought it was important that justice be done; for her and for others who fight corruption in Ukraine.

At this event (that Yovanovitch was hosting when she got that late night phone call, indicating that her good name was being unjustly smeared), we had decided that, since she had passed on, we would give the "Woman of Courage" award to her father, who was still mourning her death).

Goldman asks her if the person was ever caught, who through the acid? (Although some of the lower echelon people involved did get caught; the upper-echelon people who ordered the throwing the acid, however, have not). So Goldman asks her again about the State Department call she had received at ten o'clock that night, and Yovanovitch says that she had been told that there was great concern about her, on the "seventh floor," (which is where the Director General's office is at the State Department; and Goldman clarifies that Yovanovitch is referring to the leadership of the State Department, in general.)

Yovanovitch was told that they were worried, and they just wanted to give Marie a heads up about this. When she asked what it was about? The director said that she didn't know what was up and that she would try to find out more and call her back by midnight. So, Marie got a call, a couple of hours later, at 1 o'clock in the morning; telling her that there was great concern "up the street." I guess that means at the White House; and she needed to get on a plane and come home right away!

At the time, Marie had asked if these concerns were over her physical security; and the Director General had said no; she didn't think that it was about her physical security; but that she needed to come home right away. Yovanovitch had argued that this is extremely irregular; and it was also bewildering, as no reason had been given! -but she did get on the next plane home.

Goldman referred to the fact that she had been offered an extension to her post, because they were very pleased with her performance; which is just another reason why it was ridiculous for her to be recalled early. The Undersecretary for Foreign Affairs asked her if she would extend for another year, departing in July of 2020. That request was made in early March.

Goldman asked if anybody ever had expressed concerns about her performance? (no) After she came back, a couple of days later she met with the Deputy Secretary of State, who told her that she had done nothing wrong; but that there was a concerted campaign against her.

Goldman asks if she believes her removal was related to the false allegations being put out there, by some members of the press; Fox-News-type press; that were working with Rudy Giuliani on the smear campaign in Ukraine? -Lutsenko, the prosecutor general, working with Mr. Shokin, his predecessor? (yes)

Goldman then points out that Zelensky had indicated that he would not be keeping-on the corrupt prosecutor, Lutsenko, after the election. Then he refers to Yovanovitch's earlier testimony, that Lutsenko had a reputation for being corrupt.

Yovanovitch offers that the buzzword phrase, apparently, is that, as a State Department worker, when your boss says, "The President has lost confidence in you," it's a terrible thing to hear. Yovanovitch lets us know her thoughts at the time, she said to herself, I guess I have to go, then; but no reason was offered.

Goldman asked if she had any indication that the State Department had lost confidence in her? (no) The meeting (you had once you had reported-in, after returning to DC) was with Deputy Secretary Sullivan, a couple of days after that. Do you understand who Pompeo was trying to protect you from, when you were told that secretary Pompeo was making some effort to protect you?

Marie says it was her understanding that the President wanted her to leave; and there was some discussion over that, over the prior months. She says, that made her feel terrible; after 33 years of service; this is not the way she wanted her career to end.

Goldman refers to her testimony that it sets a dangerous precedent to do what happened to her. Yovanovitch had asked Sullivan how he was going to explain to people in the State Department, the press, and the public; to Ukrainians? because everybody is watching! She says the attacks on her in Ukraine had been very public; if people see that, knowing that she has worked very hard on anticorruption efforts; if people see that she can be pulled out of her position by corrupt people, what does that mean for our policy? Do we still have that policy when other actors in other countries see that private interests, foreign interests, can come together and get a US Ambassador removed? What's going to stop them from doing that, in the future, in other countries? (This was her argument to Deputy Secretary Sullivan).

Sullivan had said these were good questions, and that he would get back to her. Yovanovitch had testified that she had another meeting with Sullivan the following day, but that it was really more to see how she was doing, under this stress, and he had offered that if there was anything he could do; but he did not address the issues that she had brought up, the day before.

Goldman then asked her, in your 33 years of service, to the United States, as Ambassador, have you ever heard of another Ambassador being recalled with no reason given; based on allegations that yet the State Department knew to be false? (no) Goldman reminds us that the first time Yovanovitch had seen the call record of the July 25 call, was when it was publicly released, at the end of September.

In other words, Marie had no idea that the President had made reference to her in that call, until reading it at the end of the September. She says she was shocked and devastated, to learn that she was the subject of the President's call, in this way; she was shocked and devastated that she would be spoken about, between two Presidents, in such a manner. Trump had said that she was bad news, and that she would be "going through some things." She said that someone watching Marie initially reading this, said that the color had drained out of her face!

{I once again have to interrupt this effort, this time to comment on the current Judiciary Committee meeting where they will come to a House vote whether to impeach Trump in some matter of hours. What really stood out in the back-and-forth between Democrats and Republicans on the Committee, was when one Republican listed what he believed were Trump's greatest accomplishments; and they were really a list of all of Trump's worst ills visited on the nation; but this representative had no clue! He said that standing up to China, in terms of their dumping steel at low prices into the US, is such a great thing… (but really, what is wrong with providing US manufacturers with such a widely-used resource, cheaply enough to allow US companies to maximize profit on sales of their manufactured goods; and it also allows

US manufacturers to be more competitively priced, bolstering export of US-made products to other countries around the world?)

He says that Trump has reigned-in China's intellectual property theft of US-developed technology; but Chinese businessmen have certainly maintained the ability to fly over to the US and learn firsthand of new technology and innovation; and the Chinese have also had the continuing ability to correspond, and make deals with US companies, over the internet. Tariffs have probably not affected that exchange. So how has Trump's trade war accomplished anything of value on that front?

For all the hoopla, we only import 18% of all we import, from China. Our economy has done well because we still get 82% of our imports elsewhere.

Farming was not mentioned in this list, but not only has the trade war with China put thousands of farms out of business; but Trump's generous farm subsidies are mainly going into the pockets of the largest farms, corruptly. We know that a lot of people are able to find jobs; but where are the statistics showing how many Americans have been put out of a job due to the extreme measures Trump has taken in his battle with China? -and nothing has changed about China's resolve to keep the fight going as long as we'd like. In my view, Trump's trade war has done very little good; yet it has certainly been costly, in terms of the many different types of hardships and financial loss being experienced by the common man in the US.

But I was truly able to see the shortsighted, disregarding underlying motive and rationale behind what these Republican politicians are always pushing for; as this guy continued to read his list. He said he was particularly proud that Trump had cut regulations; and he explained that there is a direct relationship between robust economic climate, and cutting regulations.

Sir, the two should have nothing to do with each other. You do whatever you can fairly do, to earn money; but regardless of anything else, regulations are not some optional consideration, when they don't impinge on your ability to maximize you profits at any expense! Regulations are put in place to protect the public, from things like water pollution; to keep order; and to keep unscrupulous souls from taking unfair advantage of the American people.

When, in the George W. Bush administration, there were no regulations regarding banks and brokers; who would, because of this, create investments out of risky mortgages which had unscrupulously and deceptively been given triple A ratings; this eventually caused a financial crash of huge proportions; the middle class especially got cleaned out, when their packaged mortgage-loan-investments, girded only by the mortgage holder's ability to make payments on time; was purposely set up to fail; there was no way that a store clerk could ongoingly afford to pay down a $200,000 home loan; but these kinds of worker classes were qualifying for mortgage loans!

The investors in these packaged loans could buy insurance that would supposedly cover any losses to the investor due to loan defaults; but little did the public know that the premium paid for this insurance would only cover a small fraction of the overall loss, once these bogus lending practices soon led to a massive number of loan payment defaults.

This meant that mortgage insurance companies would be stuck with a bill they couldn't begin to pay. Foreign investors holding these US packaged mortgage loans also couldn't get a fraction of what they were owed, under their contracted terms with the mortgage insurer. If it weren't for the artful way in which President Obama was able to bring us through the worst of this crisis, providing funding to AIG; by far, the largest US mortgage insurance company; the whole world was due to experience the tremendous hardship that the US was to experience, in the coming years; in terms of fallout.

Obama was then smart enough to realize the importance of creating regulations for the financial markets, reigning in banks and broker-dealers' unconstrained ability to literally collapse the whole economy, in the process of maximizing their profits, at everyone else's expense!

Under Obama's new regulations, banks were now required to meet standards, in terms of having adequate reserves, in case of loan future default of payments on what they were lending; broker-dealers, such as Goldman Sachs and Merrill-Lynch, were forced to pay multi-billion-dollar fines; and now had to seek approval for any new type of investment it sought to introduce into the marketplace. (Regulatory agencies would now first assess the risk that any newly-proposed type of investment instrument would likely pose, prior to any approval.)

The Trump administration canceled all of this regulatory protection! Sure, some tycoons are making money off of this now; but now, another real estate investment crash can happen again, too!

Trump trashed the clean water act, the clean air act, and many, many other important environmental protections. It was all for money; and what happens to any of us doesn't matter a lick, to them. Poison us, make our planet uninhabitable for those in future generations. What do these guys care? They are all going to be dead in ten or fifteen years, right?

Yet, this Republican Committee member was bragging about how great it was, that Trump trashed all of these regulations! He bragged about how what Trump has been doing, is unearthing all of this natural gas in the US; petrochemicals, he said with a glean in his eye. He doesn't even begin to get, that we have to stop using gas and oil; and invest in renewable energy; and cut way back on pollution. This isn't just a preference! It is what the world must do in order to save itself; but beyond that, working in this direction will also create a lot of jobs, while we develop this capability to provide for ourselves, without using fossil fuel.

The whole reason why we haven't yet begun going down the path toward this much-more worthy way of life, is, of course, that production and sales of oil and gas, is making certain large companies incredible sums of money; and corrupt government actors around the world are complicit in oil producers' schemes to continue being allowed to dredge up and sell fossil fuel.

The US Government could ban all drilling and severely cut back the country's use of fossil fuels; through things like levying huge taxes on oil and gas sellers (Exxon, Shell, Sunoco, etc...); which would also create price increases which would incline people to find other ways of generating energy, from which instead, consumers could receive a large tax credit, for having switched away from using so much oil and gas.

It is in our power to do; just not while a corrupt, short-sighted lunatic is President!

(A few hours later, I write:)

I must say, I am very impressed at the earful I have gotten, listening to much of what has been being argued by all of the members of the Judiciary Committee, being televised today, as I am yet writing about the Intelligence Committee hearings. It will be my next step, in this writing project, to transcribe, and write commentary based on review of my DVR recording of these hearings. What was really impressive is that I heard dozens, and dozens of repeated entreaties by Democratic Committee members, that Republican colleagues turn their main focus on the President's wrongdoing; explaining in countless illustrious terms, how malevolent and dangerous to us all, that a President who would cheat, to fix his assurance of re-election; holding the Ukrainians over a barrel for hundreds of millions of taxpayer dollars, for President Trump's personal benefit; ruthlessly smearing a 30-year veteran Foreign Service officer known for her exemplary action in corruption-fighting; measuring all of this bewilderingly crooked Presidential behavior, by referring to the basis of the Framers of the Constitution; as far as what impeachment was designed to protect the population against; just on and on.

These great (Democratic) representatives have restored my faith in the ideals of a forthright high-level US politician. Listening to the entreaties of these worthy Democratic members of the Judiciary Committee, fills me with the strong sense of their solid integrity; that they are of good character; that they are intelligent, and well-informed.

I am impressed that they will fight for 12 hours straight, debunking the Republican's witty, but shallow contentions, and denunciations of the impeachment process, that yet, every Democratic Judiciary Committee member knows damned well is quite timely and appropriate; and they know that impeachment has never been more fitting.

It heartens me to hear all of this great oratory on the principals of democracy; it certainly heightens my own conviction, in terms of what I think the response should be to Trump's blasphemous casting aside of the historical boundaries, acting way beyond the limits of acceptable Presidential behavior which; in the case of all Presidents before Trump, have symbolized the behavioral underpinnings that have always girded American democracy.}

At the end of this final Judiciary Committee debate, Chairman Nadler pulled a surprise punch; he adjourned the hearing until tomorrow morning, for the vote. {Those damned Republican naysayers were counting on being able to enter their reprehensible "no" vote, and be done with having to suffer the pains of their conscience any further; but no, Mr. Nadler will perhaps make their tyranny ring in their own ears all night long! Just maybe; one of them might decide that it's just too much for him; his conscience bids him vote yes. (Yeah; fat chance)

So, Collins, the Minority leader, was really put out, that he wasn't consulted, in Nadler's making this decision. It was almost as if he thought it entirely unfair that he should have to come back for another day, on the matter. (After all, it's only impeachment; done every hundred years, or so, right? The issue pretty obviously isn't all that important, in Collins's view).

(Back to my Intelligence Committee impeachment hearing summary:)

Next, Goldman refers to the transcript of the July 25th phone call where Trump says, concerning the former Ambassador from the United States, "That woman is bad news; and the people she was dealing with in Ukraine were bad news; so I just wanted to let you know that..." but the people that she was dealing with in Ukraine were at the Embassy, and she was fighting corruption in a manner consistent with ongoing policy, set forth in writing; which she has been doing for years; so it seems Trump had it exactly backwards.

Goldman asks Yovanovitch how she felt, when she first read the call notes released in September? (She says she felt threatened). Goldman asks, "How so?" (She says, it kind of felt like a big threat).

So, Goldman reads the part in the July 25th call record where Trump says, "I heard you had a prosecutor who is very good and he was shut down, and that's really unfair; a lot of people are talking about that;

the way they shut your very good prosecutor down; and you had some very bad people involved."

Later in the call, Trump says, "I heard the prosecutor was treated very badly and he was a very fair prosecutor; so good luck with everything…" Of course, these are both excerpts that show how odious the President's thinking is. You know, that the corrupt prosecutor that smeared Yovanovitch, and did many other corrupt things; that curiously, he was a very good guy it was really unfair that he got shut down; Trump called him a very good prosecutor; and very bad people were involved in shutting him down.

{My understanding is that it was Zelensky that kicked Lutsenko out, and hired somebody else who wouldn't act corruptly, going forward. Trump had Zelensky figured wrong; and this phone conversation also indicates that Trump probably has the impression that every country's leader aspires to surrounding themselves with corrupt actors, who will be unquestionably loyal to their leader, no matter what they are ordered to do; and Trump probably expects that this is what leadership constitutes; that fairly or unfairly, there is one top dog; and the country is his oyster; tough shit for anyone that should happen to get trampled as he has his way, as mercilessly as he pleases. We need to show Trump; and everyone else, that this is not the way that the modern world works anymore!)

Goldman asks Yovanovitch to acknowledge that the prosecutor being discussed, Lutsenko, was very corrupt. Then he asks Marie, how did she feel, when Trump described the corrupt prosecutor? (It was disappointing to realize early on that Lutsenko was acting corruptly, considering that there was an interagency consensus, when Lutsenko had first come into office, (on a ticket of promising to clean up corruption). We were all very hopeful that he would actually do the things that he supposedly set out to do, including reforming the inspector general's office; but that did not materialize).

Goldman refers to the fact that she testified she knew that Giuliani and the corrupt prosecutor Lutsenko were in regular contact with each other in 2018 and early 2019. Marie had testified she was told by Ukrainian officials that Giuliani and Lutsenko were planning to "do things" to her; although she didn't know just what, until the smear campaign happened. Goldman asked her who else was involved? So, in addition to Lutsenko and Shokin, she refers to Lev Parness, and Igor Fruman; who have recently been indicted (basically for donating Russian money illegally, to US politicians that were then persuaded to remove Yovanovitch).

Goldman says that in March, there were a series of articles that came out in "The Hill" publication, that were based on allegations in part from Lutsenko, the corrupt prosecutor general. To summarize three categories of attacks against her, they claim that she had badmouthed the President; and had given the prosecutor general a "do not prosecute list." (To protect certain criminals from being brought to justice, supposedly). Another article included allegations of Ukrainian interference into the 2016 election; and a third category was allegations concerning Burisma, and the Bidens. (Yovanovitch says yes, that's accurate)

Goldman continues, Then, these articles were promoted by others associated with the President of the United States, and by those around mayor Giuliani. (yes, she says) Goldman shows a tweet from Trump, the day that one of those articles was published. John Solomon was the author of the articles he says as Russian collusion story fades, Ukrainian plot to help Clinton emerges. it's on Sean Hannity at Fox News. Four days later, Donald Trump Junior tweets, "We need more at Richard Grinnell's the Ambassador to Germany; and less of these jokers as Ambassadors." It is a retweet of one of John Solomon's articles with the headlines: "Calls grow, to remove Obama's US Ambassador to Ukraine." This was March 24th.

Goldman asks Yovanovitch if she was aware of these articles, at the time; and she said she was; and that she was worried. It was most concerning that these attacks were being repeated by the President himself! (and his son) Goldman points out that these articles received primetime attention on Fox News; and that the first article against her was in the form of an interview with Lutsenko.

At this point early on, The State Department came out, the following day, with a very strong statement saying that these allegations were fabrications. When Goldman asks, Yovanovitch offers that there were no others in the State Department that had ever expressed concerns about her, that she was ever aware of. People thought it was ridiculous; so Marie had complained, after these tweets, that unless the State Department came out pretty strongly against this, it would be hard for her to continue having authority in Ukraine.

So, that following weekend, there was an email discussion, involving a number of State Department people, about what could be done? Then, the Undersecretary for Political Affairs called her on Sunday. On that call, Marie had said that it's very important that the Secretary himself come out and be supportive; because otherwise, "it's hard for me to be the kind of representative that you need here." and the Undersecretary said he would talk to the Secretary. (this was David Hale the Undersecretary for Political Affairs, who was the number three person at the State Department)

Goldman asked, did he indicate to you that he is in support of such a statement of support for you? (Marie points out that, just the fact Hale was wanting to speak to the Secretary, to ask for his support, must mean that he was in support of it, of course!) Goldman continues, Marie's general understanding was that she did have the full support of the State Department; and she acknowledges is that in her 33 years of service, that she's never heard any complaints about her work, or serious concerns about her job performance.

Yovanovitch then acknowledges that a statement of support never was issued. Goldman asked her if she ever learned why not? -and she said that she had been told there was "a concern on the seventh floor," that if the statement was issued; whether by the State Department or by the Secretary personally, it could be undermined; that the President might issue a tweet contradicting that.

So Goldman summarizes, you are one of the most senior diplomats in the State Department; you been there for 33; years you've won numerous awards; you been appointed Ambassador three times, by both Republican and Democratic Presidents; yet the State Department would not issue a statement in support of you against false allegations, because they were concerned about a tweet from the President of the United States?! (she says yes that's my understanding).

Then Adam Schiff joins in, to say, "The President is attacking you on twitter, right now, as you are testifying!" Schiff reads the present tweet: Everywhere Marie Yovanovitch went, turned out bad. She started off in Somalia; how did that work out? (Yovanovitch responds that she actually thinks that, over the years, concerning where she has served, that she and others like her have actually helped to make things better, in those foreign countries, and for the US. Marie goes on to say that there are huge challenges in Ukraine; including the one we are discussing today; being corruption. Marie says that they've made a lot of progress since 2014; part of that credit goes to the United States; and a part of it to her, as well.

Schiff brings up the point that she's here testifying today, notwithstanding that she had testified earlier, that the President implicitly threatened her, in that call record; (He addresses Yovanovitch) and now the President, in real time, is attacking you! What effect do you think that has on other witnesses, who might have been meaning to come forward and express their evidence of his wrongdoing? (and she says it's very intimidating). Schiff says, it is designed to intimidate, is it not?! (she humbly says that she can't speak to what the President is trying to do, but she says the effect is intimidating).

At this point Adam Schiff sternly says some of us here take witness intimidation very, very seriously. Then he gives the floor back to Mr. Goldman. At this point, Goldman says that he's going to finish up by referring back to the July 25th phone call; and he reads more of Trump's devious, underhanded dialogue, of which Trump has several times referred to as a (perfect) call!

(My thoughts- Can you pull the wool over the eyes of a nation? I suppose we are about to find out; because that is certainly what the Republicans involved in this public hearing process have been trying to do.

It is the equivalent of the Democrats saying, "It's raining." -and the Republicans say, "No, it's not!" -and then the Democrats say, "Look at yourself, you are wet with rain that is falling on you right this second!" -and Republicans say back, "It's not raining, and we are not wet!" -as the rain is dripping from the speaker's nose. -But these are Republican leaders; and they know that leaders are to be believed. Somehow, we have to get people in the public to touch their sleeve, and feel how wet it is!

We need to just keep on shedding light on what the President is doing; and what he has done; its terribleness will speak for itself!

It is also clear to me that the Democrats in the Intelligence and Judiciary Committees have to do what I am basically doing here; which is to address each point the Republicans make; right as it is being made; whenever creatively possible. For example, wouldn't it be better to change the structure of the hearings, such that Republicans speak first, instead of Democrats; because then Democrats could address their worst bogus statements and contentions right away.

It appears that currently, under the rules of these hearings, there is no opportunity for rebuttal over what the last people just said. Democrats could start by summarizing how there have been quite a number of accusations that have been made by those who have testified so far; and for the next 5 minutes, they can respond to any of these; but we would ask you to confine your discussion and comments to the subject at hand; or in other words, arguments for why President Trump should be impeached, or not; and not to instead be talking about trade agreements, or raising the debt ceiling, for example.)

Anyway, back to my impeachment hearing summary:

Goldman's first question to Yovanovitch was, how do you think that President Zelensky, the newly-elected President of Ukraine, would interpret such a sentence as, "… but I need you to do us a favor, though…"

(The US relationship with Ukraine is the single most important relationship for them; so I think they would try to "lean in" on such a request, and see what they could do).

Goldman asks, is it fair to say that the new President of Ukraine, who is so dependent on the United States, would do just about anything in his power, to please the President of the United States? (If he could; I'm sure there are limits, but yeah, we are an important relationship, on the security side, and on the political side; and one of the most important relationships that the President of Ukraine has to (protect and nurture), is to try and make sure that the relationship with the US is rock solid).

Goldman asked her if she's familiar with this theory about Ukraine meddling in our 2016 elections? she says there have been rumors out there about things like that, but there is nothing hard, at least nothing that I was aware of. Goldman asks, there was nothing based in fact to support these allegations? (Marie says that's correct). So, Goldman asks, and who was it, that is responsible for interfering in the 2016 elections? Marie says that the US intelligence community has concluded that it was Russia.

Goldman asks if Yovanovitch is aware that this theory of Ukraine meddling in 2016 was originally the theory of Putin? that In February of 2017, Vladimir Putin himself promoted this theory of Ukrainian interference in the 2016 election. (Marie admits that maybe she heard that once; but she's not familiar with it now). Goldman then shows her a press statement that Putin made, (to Victor Orban?) in a joint press conference; the statement says that "During the Presidential campaign in the United States, the Ukrainian government adopted a unilateral position in favor of one candidate more than the other; and that certain oligarchs, certainly with the approval of the political leadership in Ukraine, funded this candidate, or female candidate, to be precise" {In other words, indicating Hillary Clinton was the one that was being helped by meddling- this is bogus}.

Goldman asks Marie how would it be in Vladimir Putin's interest to promote this theory of Ukrainian interference in our 2016 elections? And she responds that Putin must have been aware of the concerns, in the US, about Russian meddling in the 2016 election; and what the potential was for Russia to be in danger of being punished; so its chief intelligence officer might likely create a narrative, an alternative narrative, that would resolve his own wrongdoing.

Goldman asks, "And when he talks about the support of an oligarch and the Ukrainian government, there's also a reference in the July 25 call to a wealthy Ukrainian; is it your understanding that the statement made; what Vladimir Putin is saying here in his statement in February

2017, is it similar to what President Trump says on the July 25th phone call, related to the 2016 election? (she says maybe).

Goldman then shows her another exhibit from the call, which reads, "There's a lot of talk about Biden's son; that Biden stopped the prosecution, and a lot of people want to find out about that; so whatever you can do with Attorney General Barr would be great. Biden went around bragging that he stopped the prosecution so if you can look into it; it sounds horrible to me!"

Goldman asked Yovanovitch if she's familiar with these allegations related to Vice President Biden, and she says yes. Goldman asks if she knows whether Biden went around bragging, that he had stopped the prosecution? (-and Marie says no; in fact when Biden acted to remove the corrupt former prosecutor of Ukraine, he did so as part of the official United States policy, that was endorsed, and it was the policy of a number of other international stakeholders; other countries, and financial institutions). Goldman says, in fact, if you were to remove a corrupt prosecutor-general, who is not prosecuting enough corruption, could Vice President Biden then be increasing the chances that corrupt companies in Ukraine would be investigated? isn't that right? -and that could include Burisma, right? (she says yes)

Goldman states for us that, at the time of this phone call, Joe Biden was Trump's chief rival for the 2020 election; and then he asks her if it's her understanding, that President Trump's request to have Vice President Biden investigated, was that part of the official US policy, as you knew it? She responds that, I should say that, at the time of this phone call, I had already departed Ukraine; but it certainly would not have been the policy, when I left in May.

Goldman asks, were these potential investigations part of the anticorruption platform that you engaged in, in Ukraine, for the last three years? (Marie says no) -And these investigations; did they appear to you to benefit the President's personal and political interests, rather than national interests?" (she says, well, they certainly could. Goldman returns to the allegations made within the article in "The Hill" in March, promoted by Rudy Giuliani, the President's lawyer; were those two allegations similar to the two allegations that the President sought to investigate? (Marie says yes); so ultimately, Goldman continues, in the phone call, the July 25th phone call with President Zelensky, the President of the United States endorsed the false allegations, against you and the Bidens; is that right? (she says yes; and Goldman yields back).

{At this point, there is an intermission in the hearing; as there has been in every hearing so far. These last for over and hour usually, as I remember. Much of the time is filled with commentary on what has happened so far in the hearing; but on this break, for example, additionally there was coverage of Roger Stone having just become convicted on all 7 counts, of lying to Congress. But there are also a lot of commercials crammed into these intermissions; I would say that roughly a third of the hour and a half break today consisted of 8-minute barrages of commercials; as is pretty usual for cable news coverage in general. I will not be covering these commentary sessions, as part of the hearing coverage (on CNN or MSNBC); instead I will be adding in my own commentary, as we go along!}

After the long break, now it goes to Devin Nunez (minority House Intelligence Committee spokesman), to have his 45 minutes of questioning time, for he and Castor, Nunez's chosen counsel. Nunez wants to submit, for the record, Senator Grassley's letter to the Department of Justice dated July 20, 2017. He then makes a second sarcastic comment, about Yovanovitch supposedly having graduated from being down in the secret deposition meetings; then he emphasizes that she does not have any firsthand knowledge regarding the phone call.

Nunez says, I assume that you know who Senator Grassley is, (she says yes) Castor asks her if she believes that Senator Grassley is a serious and credible elected official? She says, I have no reason to think otherwise. Castor continues, were you involved in the call, or in preparations for the call? (no) she says I was not involved in deliberations about the military support for Ukraine, {as President Trump supposedly reviewed the commitment of the new President Zelensky's confrontation of corruption.} Nor did Yovanovitch know anything about the pause in military assistance to Ukraine, or the pause in military sales to Ukraine, as the Trump administration reviewed newly-elected President Zelensky's commitment to corruption reforms.

Castor then asked if she was involved in any meetings with Trump; (she says no) -and Castor emphasizes that she hasn't talked to Trump or Mick Mulvaney; so now he asks, why is she here today? then Nunez says he thinks a hearing on this issue would be more appropriate for the subcommittee on human affairs, instead of an impeachment hearing, and he claimed that Yovanovitch is not a material fact witness.

Then, Nunez tries to give Ms. Stefanik the floor, but Schiff asks her to suspend; and he asserts that under the rules of the impeachment hearing process, this 45 minute time-slot is reserved solely for the Minority leader and his counsel to speak with the witness; and that the other committee members will have 5-minute rounds each, to question the witness afterward.

Castor thanks Marie for service, and acknowledges that she spent 33 long years in the Foreign Service; and then he sarcastically comments that this is a television studio performance; and he seemed to feel put out, that they had to sit through eight hours of her testimony in the closed-door session; he had missed his train. (Gee, we're sorry that the President had done such terrible things that it took eight hours to talk about them in that one hearing alone!)

Castor confirms that she spent the last three years in Ukraine as Ambassador; and that nobody disputes that the President can select the envoy and yet she understands that her return coincided with the inauguration of President Zelensky. Next, Castor asks, after you return, the Deputy secretary John Sullivan asked you what you wanted to do next; is that correct? (yes, that's correct); and then you met with Ambassador general Perez, to identify a meaningful new assignment? (yes). Castor informs us: and she now serves at Georgetown University, as a fellow. Castor asks her if this is a rewarding position? (and she admits that she's very grateful to have become in this situation when in this position after all that happened to her this spring).

(Castor here is insinuating that Yovanovitch was treated reasonably; in that she was recalled from Ukraine, but then put at another satisfactory post. (but again this negates the fact that it was very dirty, what happened; very underhanded; what she was subjected to, with this smear campaign). Castor once again says you don't have a lot of direct facts and information. (and once again I say, that's because the President has blocked the testimony of all those administration officials who normally would be the fact witnesses, at such a hearing; and whose truthful testimony pretty-undoubtedly would have implicated Trump in a very direct way otherwise.

All of the things that Castor asks her, over the next five minutes after that are mostly the exact same things that Nunez just asked her; wastefully; but as far as new information we learned, Yovanovitch said that she had heard about the July 25th phone call from Deputy Assistant Director George Kent. Kent had explained to Yovanovitch that President Trump asked President Zelensky to help him out; which Kent had understood to be in announcing these investigations; but Marie claimed that Zelensky had said he's putting in a new prosecutor general; an independent individual (someone who did not have any corrupt ties). Castor then asked her if she believes that President Trump was trying to weaponize her, in this scheme; and she objectively says that she doesn't really know what the President's motives were. Castor asks her if she believes that her removal was part of a plot, to do things counter to US interests? Marie responded that these two individuals who were working with Rudy Giuliani, Lev Parnas and Igor Fruman, who have recently been indicted in Southern District of New York, had indicated that they wanted to change out the Ambassador; and they must've had some reason for that.

Castor then asked if maybe they just wanted to put in a different kind of Ambassador, to achieve their objectives? Marie answered that she doesn't know what other reason there would be, and that she herself understands the long-standing policy, which has not been changed this year; and she has been conducting it admirably, herself. So, next Castor asks her if Taylor is the kind of guy who would go along with corrupt investigations? (and she says no it was a good pick for the post), and she added that acting Ambassador Taylor is of the highest integrity. Castor says that in her testimony about Giuliani having this concerted campaign against her, when it first came to her attention in January and February, at some point, she had testified that the Ukrainian Minister alerted you to this campaign? Yes, her memory was that he had a conversation with Marie in February 2019. Castor asks if she remembers what he related to her. Marie answers yes, he said that Lutsenko was working with mayor Giuliani through these two individuals (Parnas and Fruman), and that they basically want to remove me from my post; and that they were working on that. Marie offered that she didn't know why; she didn't understand that at all; she had never met Parnas or Fruman, so it was unclear to her, why they were interested in doing this.

Castor asks if she was especially influential in implementing policies that stymied their interests? or were you advocating for some sort of an environmental policies that would be adverse to them? she says I think that the general idea was that I was the US Ambassador at the US Embassy in Ukraine; and one of the most important functions in this capacity is to facilitate US business abroad. Trade and commerce are one of those responsibilities, but everything has to be aboveboard, on a level playing field, and so forth; but at the Embassy, we obviously advocate for US businesses. These two individuals Parnas and Fruman, in hindsight, what we learned later is that they were looking to open up a new energy company, exporting liquefied natural gas to Ukraine; yet they never actually came to the embassy; which is unusual; because that would usually be the first stop, to come to the US Embassy, to see how they could provide assistance.

Castor clarifies that he's wondering if she was aware of Parnas and Fruman being stymied or frustrated with trying to contact the embassy, and do business with their blessing? She says that she never met them; that she had only heard of those two, for the first time, in February 2019. she asked her team, the commercial representatives who might more-usually meet with American businessmen; and she said that no one had heard from them; so all she could conclude was that it was the general US policies that she was working to implement, that might've been a concern to them. Castor stupidly asks her if she ever tried to reach out to Lutsenko, and ask him why he was conducting this smear campaign against her? (-and why didn't she do that?) She answers, I don't know that there would be any purpose to it; as you can't negotiate with the corrupt person who is trying to ruin you! He clearly had, I would say, an animus for doing this…" She offered that she had been told that Lutsenko was working with Americans; so she says that she reached out to the American side, to try and find out what was going on.

Castor asked Yovanovitch when it was that she had first realized Lutsenko was an adversary; and she reiterated February 29th; and she says "adversary" would be a strong word. We, at the embassy, are visiting key people from the State Department and other agencies; we were pushing the Ukrainians like Lutsenko, to do what they said they were going to do. When Mr. Lutsenko first took office, he said that he was going to clean up the corruption; make reforms, bring justice to the people who died in the MyDon incident, in 2016; and in 2014 after the Revolutionary war; and he pledged that he was going to prosecute cases, and to repatriate the approximately $40 billion it's believe that former President Yanukovich and his cronies fled the country with; and he didn't do any of that! -And we kept on trying to encourage him to do the right thing…

Castor asked her, when she contacted the State Department in late March; was that Undersecretary Hill? Yovanovitch responded that she had contacted the State Department about the concerns that she had, much earlier than that. She says it was an ongoing discussion. Whereas, Castor makes it sound very formal, she says, we had many ways of going back and forth with Washington. On phone calls, or DDC's we would have this discussion; and if I can amplify my answer, we had discussions because we were concerned that Ukrainian policymakers, or Ukrainian leaders, were hearing that I was going to be leaving; that there was maybe somebody else waiting in the wings; and that undermines not only my position, but our US position. The Ukrainians didn't know what to think. We need to be out there all the time, firing on all cylinders, in order to promote our national security interests.

Castor says, so it was a concern… (yes, sir) He then asks her, when did she first gain the sense that this contrary initiative and smear campaign was seriously affecting her ability to do her job well? and she says well when they started asking me if I was going to be leaving. By then, she knew that this was upsetting the embassy's normal operations. (she said this was in February or March).

Castor asked her if she undertook any efforts to push back on this, with the State Department, the public uncertainty among Ukrainians. She answered that this situation has nothing to with that distraction; our policy remains the same; and we should focus on our job; yes, we had discussions at the State Department about this, Yovanovitch says that she reached out to the European Bureau and she mentions that Dr. Fiona Hill was also aware of this situation going on; at the NSC; and that she had other discussions with more senior people, as well.

(By the way, I don't see how any of this has any bearing on the fact that Marie Yovanovitch was smeared by Rudy Giuliani and his team, working with Lutsenko and other corrupt people like Lev Parnas and Igor Fruman. How she reported this, and when, etc... is of no real relevance. What is relevant is the fact that she got smeared. She talked about what was happening to her; what was so unfair about it, and that there were others in the State Department, that were talking about this, and being upset about it. So, that's the real crux of the matter.

Castor had asked her if she pushed back, while this was going on; but why does that even matter? A month earlier, she had just been asked to stay on for another year; just around the time when this was all starting to brew up, with Giuliani. Her superior had understanding of what was transpiring. He had knowledge of it; and he said yeah, don't worry; I know that there's nothing legitimate about these claims; so he still asked her to stay on for another year. That was in early March.

But then she says, once it became a public political story here in the United States, it became a different picture; because by then, the State Department had come to feel as though it wasn't manageable anymore, and the more prudent thing would be to come back in July. She says that she had subsequently learned from Deputy Secretary Sullivan that the State Department was apparently aware of this plot since the summer of 2018.

So, then Castor goes on to the ridiculous notion that since corruption has been endemic for years in Ukraine, that this somehow legitimizes Trump's asking, the way he did, for investigations into this narrow band of corruption, on that July 25th phone call. Of course, those were only about Burisma and the Bidens; and not about corruption in general. Yovanovitch points out that talking about fighting corruption in Ukraine, with Ukrainians, is something that you couldn't do in Russia, for example; because you would probably be imprisoned or killed for saying anything against what the top leaders were doing.

Castor then asks, are oligarchs a big part of the corruption problem in Ukraine? She answers affirmatively, offering that most of the money in Ukraine is in the hands of six oligarchs; and they also have political power, and control over the media. Castor asks, have these oligarchs acquired, much of what they acquired, improperly, according to US standards? (and she says yes), and Castor asks her about the head of Burisma, Mr. Zlochevsky. Castor mentions that George Kent had said, the other day in his testimony, that Zlochevsky was investigated for stealing millions and millions of dollars; some of which had been supplied by the US and Great Britain; and it comes out that this is why it was initially a British investigation, that the US joined in on; to try and get the money back. That was one of Mr. Kent's initiatives; and he said that a bribe was paid to the prosecutor; and so Zlochevsky was let off the hook. This was in 2014, Castor asks her if this is something that she's familiar with? Yovanovitch answers that she heard about it; this was before her arrival, and her understanding is that the US money Castor was referring to, was the (US taxpayer) money that that we use to fund an FBI team that began working with the Ukrainian Prosecutor General's office, to do the investigation of Burisma; and Mr. Kent testified that this bribe was paid, and the case went away.

So, Castor asks her, during her term in the Ukraine as Ambassador, has Burisma been further investigated? Yovanovitch says that the US was actually welcoming the nomination of Lutsenko, as Prosecutor General, because he had claimed that he was going to clean corruption up. That, in fact, is not what happened. She explains that politicians, investigators, prosecutors, and judges are used as tools against your political adversaries. Regarding Burisma and Zlochevsky, in August of 2016, when she first arrived, her understanding was that the case was sort of on a "pause;" that it wasn't an active case; but that it also was not a "fully closed" case either; and that was the way, for those in power in Ukraine, to keep a little hook into Burisma, and in Mr. Zlochevsky.

Castor continues to inquire into Burisma; as if that really has any bearing on what happened to her! Corruption within Burisma is one of dozens of large-scale corruption operations that need to be investigated intervened with, an stopped for good; and Castor's beating of the drum about Burisma, is just looking for any kind of a straw they can grab onto, to try and take some of the awfulness off, of what President Trump has done, of course. Castor goes into what Hunter Biden's role was, at Burisma; and I suppose it is pretty obvious that Hunter Biden's getting hired to be on the board, must have had something to do with the fact that Joe Biden was Vice President, at the time; but whether there was any corruption that Hunter Biden participated in, as a board member, is questionable.

Marie says that the Bidens, and Burisma was not a focus of what she did in 2016. She tells us, once again, that during her Senate confirmation preparation, there was a question about that; and a select answer; and this is the only reason she knew about the Bidens' involvement, at all; she remembers that when there was a meeting between prior President Poroschenko, and Trump, that Trump had said a friend of his had told him that Ukraine was the most corrupt country in the world. (-and of course, this is even more telling about Trump's real immediate concerns, as being the investigations merely of the Bidens; because he did not mention this great degree of corruption that he might've been concerned about related to Ukraine, at all, on the July 25th phone call. Marie goes on to say that President Trump had not impressed upon them, at the embassy, any of these great concerns, while she was Ambassador there.

Castor then asked her if there were murmurings about anything against candidate Trump, in 2016? -and Marie says actually, there were not. We didn't really see it that way. Then Castor contends that someone at Politico was trying to work with the Ukrainian embassy in Washington DC, to trade information, and share leads. Yovanovitch says that she had seen the article he is talking about; and that she did not have any further information about that.

Castor says that if what Mr. Looper told Vogel was accurate, then wouldn't you want to investigate this? (so, she says that this article was put out in the United States, making it a United States issue; and that she was in Ukraine, and she had figured that if it was an issue, then Government officials in the United States would investigate that; not her.

Mr. Looper apparently worked for the US Embassy in Ukraine; but Marie said that she's never spoke to him. Castor asks her if she's ever heard of the role that this investigative journalist played, in publicizing the Manafort "Black Ledger?" (yes, she says) Castor continues, and he publicized some information in a pretty grand way; in August of 2016; and it coincided with Manafort leaving the Trump campaign... Was there anything about that issue that concerns you?

Yovanovitch says she certainly noticed it, because she was about a week from arriving in Ukraine, as Ambassador; and she realized that she was looking at this from an American perspective. From a Ukrainian perspective, she thinks that what this investigative journalist, and others who were looking into the "Black Ledger" were most concerned about, was not actually Mr. Manafort; but former President Poroschenko, and his political party; and the amount of money that they allegedly stole, and where it went, and so forth. I think there is a difference in perspective, depending on which country that you're in.

Castor then asked her if she thinks it's reasonable for (then) candidate Trump to have concluded that there were elements in Ukraine against him? At that point, Yovanovitch says that this investigative journalist got a hold of the black ledgers, and he published them as journalists do; and she's not of the opinion that this would indicate anything directly against Mr. Trump, in terms of a of some effort to knock him out of the running as President. Castor quips, well, it certainly did begin some inquiry into what Manafort's ties were to Russia; and it caused him to leave the Trump campaign... She says, that might've been the effect here in the United States; and it was certainly of interest to reporters in the United States, that Manafort was (prior President) Yanukovitch's political advisor!

Castor suggests that maybe some of what Lushenko, that investigative reporter, printed in the article about the "Black Ledger" was not all correct; it was doctored! (she says I wasn't aware of that). Castor refers to when Ambassador Jolly wrote an op-ed in the Hill, taking issue with (then candidate) Trump; and asks her, were you aware of that, when it occurred? (yes) He continues, and did you have some communications with the Ambassador, to express concerns? (no) How frequently did you communicate with Ambassador Jolly? (Yovanovitch was in a different post, in a different country). She said, I didn't see him or talk to him very often.

Castor says, you can see, given the subject matter of that op-ed; there were sensitivities. Can you see how just a simple effect of the Ukrainian Ambassador to the US, writing this article, might create the impression that there are elements of the Ukrainian establishment that were advocating against (then candidate) Trump? Marie said that her recollection of that article, was that Ambassador Jolly was critical of the policy position that candidate Trump had, with regard to Crimea; and Trump's view that perhaps Crimea should be considered part of Russia; that's a tremendously sensitive issue, to Ukrainians!

Castor asks, were you aware that the Ukrainian ministry wrote of such candid things on social media platforms? (she answers that she is aware of it, because of the previous deposition she heard from another official; but she says she doesn't recall being aware of it at the time. Castor contends that the minister is one of the more influential individuals in Ukraine; he asks her, is that correct?

He is, she says; he spanned both the Poroschenko and the Zelensky administrations, yes. Castor says, looking back, in hindsight, you see how a very influential person in Ukraine was advocating against then candidate Trump? This minister said some really nasty things about Trump! Yovanovitch's comical response was that, well, sometimes that happens on social media… (it gets a laugh) If you are you asking me whether it's appropriate? Probably not; but I would say that Minister Belockov, as well as others, have been have been in (previous) President Poroschenko's administration, as well as in Zielinski's. He has been a good partner the United States; he's a very practical man, and we were looking for partners in getting the job done.

(Castor keeps hammering at this idea that there was some unfair campaign against (then candidate) Trump; but we all know that lots of people had come to realize that Trump was dirty; and also that Ukraine was trying to break away from Russia; and if Russia was basically backing Trump, and Ukraine was not under Russian influence anymore, then it would only be natural to have occurred, right?)

Yovanovitch says that those elements of written expression don't seem to be any kind of a plan, or a plot, encompassing Ukrainian corruption working against (then candidate) Trump. We all know that in public life, people are critical; and that does not necessarily mean that a government is undermining a campaign, or interfering in an election. I would just emphasize again, that our own intelligence community in the U.S. has conclusively determined that those who interfered in the election were in Russia.

Castor then turns his attention to Ambassador Kurt Volker, who has been a colleague of Yovanovitch for many years. It is established that he is an honorable man, and a legitimate diplomat. Then Castor asks, you wouldn't have any reason to suspect that Kurt Volker was doing anything counter to US interests, would you? Yovanovitch says, I think that he tried to do what he thought was right. (Even though Volker did seem to have a little involvement on the fringes, with this scheme, he certainly was not one of the three amigos or anything), Castor then goes to the topic of the held-up aid; and asks Yovanovitch why is it important that Javelin missiles were made available, (which had not been made available in the Obama administration, it has been pointed out), and she explains that they are tank busters, so if the war with Russia all of the sudden accelerated, in some way; and tanks were to come over the horizon, Javelin missiles are very serious weapons to deter that; and also the symbolism is important; that the United States is providing Javelins to the Ukrainians fighting this war with Ukraine's Russian adversary.

Castor then asks Yovanovitch if she thinks that the provision of the Javelins were effective? -and she, answers yes, as they were certainly a very symbolic sign of the U.S.'s strong support of Ukraine, against this Russian invasion; but then she adds, referring back to Trump's actions and initiatives earlier this year, that perhaps it has now become questionable, as to whether or not our security assistance is going to continue to be there for Ukraine; (due to these kinds of suspect actions of the Trump administration), that undermine this strong message of (consistent) U.S. support.

Castor then reminds us that the aid money was ultimately released; but of course, that's irrelevant; because it only went through once Trump got caught with his pants down, doing this scheme). Are we giving Ukraine enough money? he stupidly asks; and she says well, one can always use additional funding; that said, I think that the Congress has been very generous in advocating for security assistance and other assistance to Ukraine. (This concludes Castor's 45 minutes and now the five-minute rounds begin, and Adam Schiff recognizes himself first.)

Schiff starts out saying he wanted to address some of the prior questioning by Nunez and Castor: he starts out by saying some of these questions seem to suggest that hearing your testimony is irrelevant; and why are you even here? Isn't this just some small matter, that should have been referred to HR? -So, I want to bring our attention to somebody who thought that you were very important to this whole plot or scheme; that is the President of the United States! There was one Ambassador discussed, on the July 25th call; and that was you, Ambassador Yovanovitch; and I want to refer back to how you were brought up in that conversation: The President brings up this prosecutor that is very good, and was shut down; and that was really unfair... and Schiff says, that was a likely reference to Lutsenko the corrupt prosecutor... (Yovanovitch says she believes that is the case) Schiff continues, so immediately after the President brings up this corrupt foreign prosecutor, only one American Ambassador is brought up, in the call. After praising this corrupt prosecutor, he then asks Zelensky to get in touch with Rudy Giuliani, who ran the smear campaign against you; and then the President brings you up. He obviously thought you were relevant to this! What's even more telling, is that immediately after he brings you up, and says, "The woman is bad news," he says there's a lot of talk about Biden's son (etc…), so in summary, Schiff says, he praises the corrupt prosecutor; attacks you; and then he goes right to the investigation of the Bidens. He connects you somehow with this prosecutor that you are at odds with, and his desire to see this investigation of Biden go forth, does he not?

Yovanovitch responds, again; you're absolutely right; that is the thought progression. (Schiff continues) Since you were pushed out of the way, ultimately Ambassador Taylor got appointed, who is a national hero; and the kind of person that would not further Giuliani's aims; and we could all agree that Ambassador Taylor is a remarkable public servant. -But what if the President could put somebody else in place, who wasn't a career diplomat; say, a substantial donor to his inauguration; with no diplomatic experience at all; somebody's who's portfolio (territory) doesn't even include Ukraine, was to be appointed, as Ambassador to the EU; might not that person be willing to work with Rudy Giuliani, to pursue these investigations? That's exactly what happened, wasn't it? (she says yes)

My colleagues say that they ultimately released the aid money; but are you aware, Ambassador Yovanovitch, that this security assistance was not released until after a whistleblower complaint made its way to the White House; and then not even until Congress announced it was doing investigation? Schiff then says, just to clarify, for the public; there were two calls; one was on April 20th; it was a perfunctory congratulatory call; as versus the problematic call on July 25th; and one of reasons we are here, is to bring out what happened between April and July; but there was a readout, put out by the White House at the time that the April 20th congratulatory call was made; and the White House readout said that the President had discussed, with Zelensky, helping Ukraine root-out corruption. Now, that, in fact, doesn't appear anywhere in that call readout; so, Schiff then asks Yovanovitch, why would the President have (orally contended) this statement, that he mentioned to Zelensky; that he brought up rooting out corruption? -if that wasn't actually said in the call? (Yovanovitch humbly responds, I don't have visibility into that.)

Schiff then yields to Nunez, Minority leader (of the House Intelligence Committee), as it is time to begin 5-minute rounds of questioning of Yovanovitch; alternatingly from first, a Republican committee member, then from a Democratic committee member.

Nunez immediately yields to Ms. Stefanik, who thanks Yovanovitch for her 30 years of public service, and for hosting numerous bipartisan delegations, at the U.S. Embassy in Ukraine; of which she said that she (Stefanik) herself had attended one of those delegations. She says she wants to us ask about three key themes: Appointment of Ambassadors, corruption in Ukraine, and the third being aid to Ukraine. Stefanik brings up Yovanovitch's previous testimony, that in her practice exam questions, just before going before the Senate, for her confirmation hearing, she reiterates that the questions about Burisma were specific; relating to Hunter Biden. Stefanik's question to Yovanovitch was, what can you tell us about what was told to you about Hunter Biden being on the board of Burisma? (Stefanik explains that, for the sake of the American public, she wants to emphasize that President Obama was so concerned about corruption within Burisma; and Hunter Biden's role at Burisma, that the Obama administration had raised it themselves; while prepping this wonderful Ambassador-nominee, before her confirmation.) -But let me interject that, of course, the Obama administration naturally would have addressed this issue, because Joe Biden was Vice President at the time; and after a period of time of VP Biden working within Ukraine, (it later comes out that) an increasing number of US officials were finding out that Biden's son was serving on Burisma's board; and so there were murmurings, that this might cause, at least a perception of, something possibly improper; but that doesn't mean that there <u>was</u> anything improper going on. In fact, Biden was ardently fighting corruption (as an integral part of the legitimate overall Foreign Service campaign) all throughout his term, there in Ukraine; and it could just as easily have been that Biden believed he could get a handle on more of "the inside," as to what was happening, in terms of corruption within this Burisma company, by having somebody as close as his son implanted on the board there. Yet, Stefanik obnoxiously insinuates that it's so significant for the Republicans to inquire into Burisma's corruption, in connection with the Bidens; and that this was somehow way more important, than the fact that Trump was hatching this dirty campaign to smear and remove Ambassador Yovanovitch, in order to strong-arm the new President of Ukraine to make public announcements which would badly hurt Trump's chief rival for the upcoming Presidential election, in 2020).

Next, it is Jim Himes's turn. He says, those of us sitting up there today are supposed to be dispassionate, and judicial, and measured; but he says I'm angry and I'm angry since I learned about your (summary and unexplained) dismissal; after a lifetime of excellent and faithful service to this country; and I'm angry that a woman whose family fled communism and Nazism, and who has served this country beautifully for 33 years; not in Paris, or Rome; but in dangerous places like Mogadishu Somalia, and Kiev. Himes says, I'm angry that a woman like you would not just be dismissed, but also humiliated by a smear campaign; humiliated and attacked by the President of the United States! -and he says, I'm not just angry for you; I'm angry for every single foreign service officer; for every military officer; for every intelligence officer, who right now may believe that a lifetime of service and sacrifice might be ignored by the President of the United States; or worse yet, attacked, using language that would embarrass a mob boss! Now, it's the President's defense, as it is emerging from my Republican colleagues today, that this is all okay; because, as the President put it in his tweet, this morning, that it is a U.S. President's absolute right to appoint Ambassadors. I'm a little troubled by the idea of an "absolute right," because that doesn't feel to me like the system of government we have here. I think that how, and why, we exercise our powers and rights, matters.

He then asks Yovanovitch, when you are Ambassador somewhere, do you think you have the right to ask the intelligence committee, or the CIA, or anyone in the embassy, what operations they are engaged in? (she says we talk about these things collaboratively; there are some things that, in short, yes.) Himes continues, So, you have the right to ask the intelligence agency in your embassy what they are doing? Why do you think you have the right to do that? why might you do that?

Yovanovitch answers, because sometimes operations have political consequences. Himes says, right; so the performance of your duties in the interest of the United States gives you the right to ask very sensitive questions of our intelligence community, in your embassy; so, what if instead, you went to a dinner that night, and had handed over that information to a Russian agent; for $10,000 dollars; would that be an appropriate exercise? What if instead of working through the issues, as you just described, you went to dinner and sold your information to a Russian agent for $10,000; would that be an appropriate exercise of your right? (no, it would not) What would happen to you, if you did that? (I can't even begin to imagine; I imagine I would be pulled out of post…) So, this is not about an Ambassador's right; a police officer has the right to pull people over; but if a police officer pulls over his ex-wife, because he's angry; that's probably not right! -and Himes continues, (as a Congressional member of the House) I am charged to cast my vote today; but if instead of casting my votes according to what my constituents want, I cast a vote in an opposite manner, because I was bribed? -That's a severe abuse of power… (she agrees) -so Himes says, the question is why, after your exemplary performance as Ambassador to Ukraine; that you should be removed by the President? -because I think we just agreed that it's not in the national interest… that's a problem Ambassador; if you had remained Ambassador to Ukraine, would you have recommended to the President of the United States, that he ask the new Ukrainian President to investigate Crowdstrike, or the server? (no)

Himes continues, I would repeat once again, as Ms. Yovanovitch has recounted to us; the US intelligence agencies have unanimously concluded that it was the Russians, who interfered in our 2016 elections. -So, Ambassador, had you not been summarily dismissed, would you have supported a 3- month delay in congressionally-mandated military aid to Ukraine? (she says no) -And would you have recommended to President Trump, that he ask the new President of Ukraine to (quote) "find out about Biden's son?" (she says no) Himes then yields back the balance of his time, and it goes to Mr. Conaway.

Conaway wants to read into the record, a part of Nancy Pelosi's "Dear Colleagues" letter, dated September 23rd. He quotes: …We also believe that we will establish a path for the whistleblower to speak directly to the house, and to the Senate… Conaway says he looks forward to the committee honoring that statement from the speaker. (but of course that statement was made before threats were made by the President, that he would convict the whistleblower of treason; of which the penalty is death; and this would obviously not be the least bit fair, for somebody coming forth to point out corrupt and improper actions in government, that are going on currently). Conaway then says he wants to focus on what has happened since Yovanovitch was removed. (as if that's of any bearing on the matter). Conaway asks her a little about her fellowship teaching position at Georgetown University; he says Georgetown is fertile ground for future Foreign Service agents to come out of; and next, he tries to suggest that Yovanovitch was doing a better service to the country by working with the (potential) future foreign service agents. (again, just a diversionary tactic, having nothing to do with the issue at hand, of the President acting in deleterious ways).

Yovanovitch responds that she has only been teaching one class, at Georgetown; and that there are a total of only 14 students in her class.

Conaway tries to insinuate that she hasn't suffered anything, in terms of disregard, or ill regard of her, as a person; such as people not sitting with her in the lunchroom; (and she says that no, people over here recognize the odious smear campaign against me; yet by the President of the United States himself; but they are very sympathetic and supportive.

Conaway yields to Jordan, who reads into to the record, sections of a few other memos and articles, suggesting that the whistleblower is expected to testify; one from USA today; another article of September 29, 2019, where Schiff confirms tentative agreement for the whistleblower to testify before the House intelligence committee; one article from CNN on September 29th; and one article dated September 29, 2019 in the Huffington Post; saying Schiff panel will hear from whistleblower. (all of these things he just read are all reflecting the thinking on the subject, as of one particular day, September 29th; and again, this was before Trump's threats of pronouncing the whistleblower as having committed treason).

Next, Ms. Sewell is recognized, and she wants to emphasize Yovanovitch's background, where she had referred to her parents, in her opening statement; reiterating that they didn't get to experience freedom and democracy in America; that they had come from totalitarian regimes, and that this had an effect on her desire to be in the Foreign Service, in the United States. Sewell goes on to state Yovanovitch's credentials; and that she also had studied and learned how to speak Russian.

Sewell asks how all of this has affected her, on a personal level; and how it has affected her family? Yovanovitch answers, it's been a very difficult time; because the President does have the right to choose every Ambassador, to every country in the world; but does the President have the right to malign people's character? Sewell contends that this is against decorum, and decency; and she points out that all President Trump would've had to do is say that he wants different Ambassador. (and this speaks to the point that President Trump, in his crooked thinking, thought it would be better to smear her; and therefore, create a situation, where other officials would see good reason to get rid of her; but he never realized, that in the process of concocting a corrupt Smear campaign against Yovanovitch, that he might well be implicated himself, the fool!

In response to Conaway's insinuations that nothing about this conspiracy, and her removal, has tarnished her reputation here in the United States, Sewell rebuts that this has maligned Marie's reputation; and perhaps has also had a chilling effect on Foreign Service agents around the world, in general; and especially on the morale within the Foreign Service.

Yovanovitch adds, I think it has, exactly had a chilling effect, not only on those working at the Embassy in Kiev, but throughout the State Department; because people don't know whether their efforts to pursue our stated policy are going to be supported; and that is a dangerous place to be. Sewell asks her to explain why it's important for Foreign Service agents to be nonpartisan. She says, because our work is essentially nonpartisan; and she refers to one of our historic forefathers having said that "Politics should stop at the water's edge;" and that she thinks that it's good that Senator Vanderberg, a Republican Senator who partnered with President Truman, coining the phrase, that politics should stop at the water's edge. She says, I think that's exactly right, because while obviously the competition of ideas, in a democracy; having different parties, and different individuals; is hugely important; but at the end of the day, what we're dealing with in other countries it needs to be what's right; it needs to be about what is right for the United States interests; and whether a person works for the CIA, the State Department, or the military, we've got to be nonpartisan; and think about what's right for the United States.

Next, the floor goes to Mr. Turner, who starts off, Ambassador, I want to say that I have great respect for what you do; as he discloses that he serves on the armed services committee, the intelligence committee. He says, I've worked with the native parliamentary assembly, including being its President; and I (understand the) complexity of what you do. I know you have little access to decision-makers; little resources; but you have a great deal of responsibility. It is a complex task, and I will take this from just the concept of one-dimensional Ukraine, being corrupt; to the other issues that you have to deal with, as Ukrainian Ambassador. You had to deal with more than just the bilateral relationship with Ukraine, for example. You had to deal with the OSC Budapest agreement; and the denuclearization of Ukraine; the issues of its territorial integrity of the signatories; correct the organization for the security and cooperation for the Budapest agreement; under which Ukraine gave up its nuclear weapons; and I believe they had its territorial integrity guaranteed by the United States, and Russia. (Marie says, yes)

Ukraine is an aspiring NATO country; and of course, you have the Bucharest Summit; where the US, and the NATO allies made a statement that they would get membership; that too, would have been in your portfolio, right Ambassador? Yovanovitch responds, yes, certainly; Ukraine has aspirations to NATO membership.

Turner continues, and it's also consistent with US policy that the US supports Ukraine joining the EU, and have a great deal of interest and desire for joining the EU, correct? (yes) -and they just had a summit in Ukraine, in July; where they talked about the associate agreement on economic integration, between Ukraine and the EU; and they also had a discussion about the illegal annexation of Crimea; and the blocking, by Russia, of the Ukrainian sailors that came out of the Sea of Asimov, who were captured; those all would have been issues in your portfolio; and they would, if it's consistent with what US interests are, correct?

Yovanovitch responds, yes; we work closely with our EU parties. Turner continues on, and you'd also have to work with France, and Germany; and you might have different ideas with the investors to Ukraine; some of them have different ideas about these issues, he says. You have to work with NGOs (nongovernment organizations) on illegal human trafficking, building democratic institutions, and HIV-AIDS... (yes, she says) -and you've spoken at several NGOs while you were Ambassador to Ukraine... So, he gets to the crux of the matter; saying that the Ambassador to the EU would have overlapping interests, within their portfolio. Ambassador Sondland would have had, in his portfolio, relations with aspiring nations to the EU, would he not? (yes) -And Ambassador Sondland would have had Ukraine in his portfolio; because they are an aspiring nation and he is the Ambassador to the EU, correct? (yes) (Turner tries to muscle through, to cut off her answer; as he can tell that she obviously doesn't like the direction that he's going in; the scope of Sondland's role is being taken out of context). Next, Turner quickly tries to yield to Dr. Wenstrup; -and Adam Schiff intervened; announcing that Ambassador Yovanovitch will be allowed to finish answering the question. So, this Republican committee member gets very obnoxious, and says, "No, not on my time, you will!" -but Schiff says no, Mr. Wenstrup is not; the gentleman is not recognized! Ambassador Yovanovitch will finish answering the question.

Marie completes her answer, I would say that all EU Ambassadors deal with other countries, including aspiring countries; but it is unusual to name the US Ambassador to the EU, to be responsible for all aspects of Ukraine.

Turner weakly states, it's still in his (Sondland's) portfolio. Then he goes on to attack from another direction. He starts out confirming that Yovanovitch knew Mr. Holbrook; (who was also an esteemed Ambassador). Then he relays that a member of John Kerry's Presidential campaign, in 2004; an adviser to Kerry; traveled to Ukraine; and met with the US Ambassador to Ukraine, in July of 2004. He asks Yovanovitch, would you have taken that meeting, if a member of John

Kerry's campaign had traveled to Ukraine? (Yovanovitch answers, that would depend upon the purpose of the meeting.) -Well, the meeting did occur, with John Holbrook. (Holbrook was a private citizen, at the time, though). He traveled to Ukraine and met with US Ambassadors; he met with Ukrainian officials; and he also was working on HIV-AIDS which is something at the Clinton administration was working on. {his point is that there was a private-citizen's meeting with the Ambassador, and the government of Ukraine} -and she says, well, we meet with private individuals all the time. {and the other thing that was being left out, was that this private citizen went to the legitimate Ambassador to Ukraine, from the US; and did not go through back-channels, with other-than the Ambassador to Ukraine. Rudy Giuliani, as Yovanovitch has testified, never spoke with her; he never approached her on any legitimate basis at all. Giuliani's operations were also underhanded, and counter to US policy on fighting corruption, of course}.

His time had now expired, and the floor went to Mr. Carson; who says, returning to the topic of corruption, we heard evidence that you were successful at efforts to address corruption, on Wednesday; and testifying about your very sterling career. (He refers to George Kent's statement, that you can't promote principled anticorruption efforts actions, without pissing off corrupt people!) -and it seems that Yovanovitch's effort to reform the very powerful corrupt prosecutor in Ukraine, did exactly that. Then he asked Yovanovitch, what concerned you about this prosecutor, when you were Ambassador to Ukraine? She says, what concerned us, was that there didn't seem to be any progress, toward the three overall objectives that Lutsenko had (initially) laid out. The first thing was in reforming the prosecutor general's office; it's a very powerful office, and it has authority not only to conduct investigations, along with an FBI-like function; but also, it has authority to go after prosecution; so, very wide powers. It was sort of a Soviet legacy, that there just wasn't a lot of progress; in that although there was a lot of progress in handling personnel issues, how the structure should be organized, and who should have important jobs within the Ukrainian government; because some of the people who were currently holding those jobs, were considered to be corrupt themselves. Secondly, the issue that was tremendously important to the Ukrainian people, was bringing justice to the over 100 people who died during the revolution of dignity, in 2014. Nobody has been held accountable for that; and thirdly, Ukraine needs all of the money that it has; and there is a strong belief that former President Yanukovich, and those around him, made off with over $40 billion! This is a huge amount of money; in Ukraine, only 1 billion has been repatriated. Lutsenko was the head of that office; and he was corrupt, Yovanovitch answers.

Carson followed up, so you believed he was corrupt; and you got the driving sense that he was involved in orchestrating some of the attacks against you... (I do) -which ultimately led to your removal, right? (yes) -but it wasn't just him; these allegations were picked up and spread by Mr. Giuliani, and Donald Trump, were they not? (yes) -so let me get this straight; you were effective at fighting corruption in Ukraine; fighting corruption was important to national security in the United States, and in Europe, for that matter. Ultimately you were removed from your post, by the President of the United States. So, in your opinion, let me ask you, why is it important to have a nonpartisan career; as a member of the Foreign Service?

Yovanovitch answers, I think it's important to have nonpartisan Foreign Service officers, as what we do is inherently nonpartisan. It is about our national security interest; it is not about what's good, for a particular party; it has to be about the greater interest of our security; and in, frankly, what is an increasingly dangerous world. Next, Carson asks her to describe briefly, what broad US policies she has sought to advance, in her 33 years of service; and specifically, he adds, in post-Soviet states, like Ukraine? She says, that's a broad question, but I think that certainly in my time in Russia, Armenia, etc..., all of these countries are very different; as is Ukraine; but I think that establishing positive constructive relations, to the extent that we can, with those countries, is really important; and that our three basic areas of focus are security, economic growth, and political integrity.

Carson yields back, and the floor goes to Mr. Stewart; who starts off saying that he appreciates Yovanovitch's service. He relays that, at the time he was called into service, to deploy for Iraq, (as a doctor), he had appointments scheduled with his patients, and other things he was in the middle of; so, he understands that shocking feeling, that can come with abrupt changes, like that. Stewart disclosed that he had served in the Iraq war, in 2005 and 2006, and he says that he can relate to her position; because when he was in Iraq, he saw that the people of Iraq were very concerned about corruption; and he says that unfortunately, today there is still corruption over in Iraq; but he says, as you might imagine, I take an interest in military strategies for those with boots on the ground; including you and Mr. Volker, and Mr. Taylor.

Stewart refers to Yovanovitch's earlier testimony, that we all found it very important that this administration was providing lethal weapons (she is referring to the Javelin missiles) to Ukraine. He also mentions that Yovanovitch had said that the US has been generous, in increasing aid to Ukraine; and he reiterates that Yovanovitch had responded yes, when she was asked whether she advocated for that. -And he makes note that she had also suggested the provision of Javelins during the Obama administration; so, Stewart is saying that although Obama could have provided Javelins, and she and others had advocated this; Obama had decided not to provide them.

Then Stewart contends that Trump vetted those countries that receive aid; and it is provided consistent with your interagency recommendations; and that of your colleagues. (and he asks her), -without Javelins, didn't the Russians have much greater military options, and flexibility? (Then, before Stewart goes to yield back his remaining time, Yovanovitch asks if she can just add, that although the President has a right to recall an Ambassador, she asks, why did he have to smear me?! (and of course, we addressed that a little earlier; and I also wanted to point out that these questions that Stewart was asking, once again, have nothing to do with the issue at hand; which is that the President put together a subverted scheme, in which Yovanovitch was gotten out of the way in a very nastily-unfair way; but even more importantly, Trump's campaign was to put pressure on Zelensky to make announcements that would seriously hurt his most likely competitor in the upcoming 2020 Presidential election; and in order to do this, he was willing to interrupt the strong US support that we have always deemed important to give to

Ukraine, since 2014, when Russia invaded Crimea. -And now, because of that sudden reversal of US consistent timely support, perhaps the world wonders whether the US is still to be thought of as a reliable ally; and also, Russia now has reason to think that maybe the US won't stand in their way so much, as they plunder their way further into Ukraine).

The floor next goes to Ms. Speier. She points out that Yovanovitch was unanimously confirmed by Republicans and Democrats in the Senate; and that the smear campaign began in the summer of 2018… Yovanovitch says, I didn't know it began that early; so with respect to Secretary of State Pompeo, Yovanovitch says, he did keep her in place in Ukraine, as long as he could. When asked whether she thought that Pompeo had done anything to protect her? (no) -So, in 2018, the President was already making noises that he wanted you out of there; and that, as early as April of 2018, Mr. Parnas was at a fundraiser for the President; and he had recommended that you be removed; and then subsequently, in May of 2018, he was pictured at a White House dinner with the President. -And then later in May, Parnas made a contribution of $325,000 dollars, illegally, to the President's reelection campaign… Then, Speier asked, does that help you understand why this smear campaign was underway? (Yovanovitch says yes) Ms. Speier then reads Yovanovitch's testimony, about how she was bewildered, that this smear campaign could have actually been enabled to be successfully conducted against her; and Ms. Speier says that while she was listening to this testimony the other day, she couldn't help thinking of how all the other Foreign Service people might be saying to themselves, that taking responsibility to act according to stated foreign policy isn't enough; as a Foreign Service agent; but you also have to be aware that maybe the President has a back channel, supporting alternate interests, that he is proposing, that is diametrically opposed to our stated foreign policy. Can you expand on that, please?

So, Yovanovitch says, I think it's important, whoever's messages are being represented; including the President's; that the Ambassador to the country in question, speaks with full authority, on behalf of the President, or the foreign policy establishment; and if there are others that are also helping within responsibilities; for example Kurt Volker, with his mission to bring peace to the Donbas, (a region of northern Syria); it is important that we all speak with one voice. It's all about our common security interest; it's not about personal gain, or commercial gain; but about national security.

-But in this case, Ms. Speier continues, the three amigos were more interested in getting an investigation, than in promoting an anticorruption effort in Ukraine; is that correct? (that appears to be the case.) -In April of 2019, you said that you had spoken to a minister in Ukraine that warned that when it came to Rudy Giuliani, you need to watch your back... Yovanovitch says, the Prime Minister was also saying that the rumors were that Rudy Giuliani was planning to have me removed. Ms. Speier concludes, her questioning, let me just say in closing, that you have endured an orchestrated character assassination; that it was hatched over a year and a half ago, and that it was laced with enormous campaign contributions to the President's reelection campaign. You deserve more from the American people, and you deserve more from Congress, in supporting you.

Next, Mr. Stewart is recognized. He starts off by making a sarcastic comment, welcome to year four, of the impeachment efforts; -sorry you got dragged into this, he says. He continues, the Russia collusion allegations are outrageous. (Let me add, so was the horrendous scope of the Russian disinformation scheme, of course). We now know that these allegations are nonsense (he falsely claims), despite some congressmen's secret ideas; but now, in year four, we have apparently moved on to Ukraine, and the "quid pro quo." (Yesterday, Schiff had contended that the President might be removed from office for bribery); so, Stewart asks Yovanovitch if she has any information about the President accepting bribes? (she says no) -and do you have any knowledge that the President was involved in any of illegal activity at all? (she says no)

(but if she was more on the ball, she would say something like, how <u>could</u> we possibly establish definitive proof, beyond a reasonable doubt, of President Trump's guilt, unless Trump is forced to stop blocking the people who do have direct daily contact with the President surrounding such matters, from any related testimony; or from providing any written information at all, relating to the hold on the aid; or the President's subverted little plot?)

Stewart thinks that the American people think this impeachment effort is unfair; maybe there is some percentage of Republicans who have continued to have blind allegiance; probably only because they give credence to the words that come out of the mouth of a President; no matter how false or crooked they may be. Stewart thinks that the public support for impeachment is going to be less after the hearings, than it was before. He says the American people are going to able to see the evidence and make their own determination. (but the very point is that they're not able to see the evidence, because Trump is hiding the evidence; and forbidding those who have the evidence, from coming forward with it. Clearly, the American people will not get to see the evidence; they will only get to see what seems very obvious about Trump's motives, and his subverted actions; in the course of trying to ensure his reelection.

Stewart tries to suggest that it was quite appropriate for Trump to be addressing corruption in Ukraine through this back channel; and Yovanovitch offers that that she thinks it is appropriate for a President to direct people to enhance our fighting of corruption, in foreign countries. She continues, However, provided it's in coordination with our national strategy; but what I would say is that we have a process for doing that; it's called the Mutual Legal Assistance Treaty. We have one with Ukraine; and generally, it goes from our Department of Justice to the Ministry of Justice, in the country of interest.

Mr. Turner tries to obnoxiously read something else into the record, but their time has expired; so now the floor should go to a Democrat; so, Schiff hits his gavel, and says, "Time has expired!" (Schiff then says that he will recognize Turner later; but meanwhile, Mr. Quigley, you are recognized.

Quigley starts off with a bit of levity; "It's like a Hallmark movie; you ended up in Georgetown; it's all okay!" He continues, it wasn't in your preference to be defamed by the President of the United States; including today, was it? Of course not; it wasn't your preference to be ousted, at seemingly the pinnacle of your career, was it? You wanted to finish your extended career, correct? What did you want to do after that?

Yovanovitch answers, I wasn't sure. So, Quigley says, teaching a class to 14 people at a university is not a Hallmark ending to the movie; but the ending of a really bad TV show, brought you by someone who knows a lot about that… (obviously referring to Trump's zany reality show series, "The Apprentice"). Quigley continues, you got some advice from Ambassador Sondland, about what to do, at that time, correct? (yes I did; I went to Sondland because I knew this was (so purely political); and the State Department was not in a position to manage the issue; (so she assumed, since Sondland was a political appointee; and he had just been in Ukraine, to visit with some of his EU colleagues; she reached out to him for advice when this was no longer confined locally, to Lutsenko, strictly in Ukraine; but it had become more of an American issue at hand; because US politicians and pundits were repeating those allegations. So, since Sondland was Trump's appointee, and was in close contact with Trump, she asked him for advice. (-and what was his advice?) Well; he suggested that I needed to go big, or go home! {Of course, he could have left out the "big," because he was only very much involved in a campaign to make her go home}.

Intelligence Committee hearing #3-
Vindeman and Williams

Adam Schiff starts by saying that this hearing will be conducted in the same fashion as last week's hearings. I will make an opening statement, and then ranking member Nunez will have the opportunity to make an opening statement; then we will turn to our witnesses for their opening statements; and then the questions will follow.

Last week, we heard from three experienced diplomats testifying about President Trump's scheme to condition official acts, such a White House meeting, and hundreds of millions of dollars of US military aid to fight the Russians, on a deliverable by the newly-elected Ukrainian President Zelensky; to open politically motivated investigations that Trump believed would help his re-election campaign. One of those investigations involved the Bidens, and the other involved the discredited theory that Ukraine was responsible for interfering in our 2016 election.

As Ambassador Sondland would later tell foreign service officer David Holmes, immediately after speaking to the President; that Trump did not give an (expletive) about Ukraine. He cares about big stuff that benefits the President, like the Biden investigation that Giuliani was pushing; to press a foreign leader to announce investigations into his political rival.

President Trump put his own personal and political interests above those of the nation. He undermined our military, and diplomatic support, for a key ally; and undercut US anticorruption efforts in Ukraine. How could our diplomats urge Ukraine to refrain from political investigations of its own citizens; if the President of United

States were to engage in precisely the same kind of corrupt political investigations of one of our own citizens?!

At the White House, career professionals became concerned that President Trump, through an irregular channel, that involved Chief of Staff, Mick Mulvaney, Ambassador Gordon Sondland, and Rudy Giuliani, was pushing a policy in Ukraine against, at odds with, our national interests. This morning, we will hear from two National Security officials who became aware of those efforts. Lieutenant Colonel Alex Vindeman, whose family fled oppression in the Soviet Union when he was a toddler, is a career Army officer, who served in Iraq. Colonel Vindeman was awarded a Purple Heart, and he is an expert on Russia and Ukraine; who has worked at the highest levels of the Pentagon. In July of 2018, he was detailed to the White House; in part, to coordinate policy on Ukraine. Jennifer Williams is a career foreign service officer who is currently detailed to the office of the Vice President; and responsible for Europe and Eurasia. Following his initial and congratulatory phone call with Ukrainian President Zelensky, on April 21st, President Trump asked Vice President Pence to represent him, at Zelensky's upcoming inauguration Ms. Williams was working on logistics for the trip. Pence would be a coveted attendee; second in significance, only to the President; and would have sent an important signal of support, to the new Ukrainian President. In early May however, Rudy Giuliani had been planning to go to Ukraine, to pursue the President's interest, in having the Bidens investigated. Giuliani had to call off the trip, after it became public. Among others, Giuliani blamed people around Zelensky, for having to cancel; and claimed that they were antagonistic to Trump.

Three days later, President Trump called off the Vice President's attendance at Zelensky's inauguration. Instead, a lower-level delegation was named; Energy Secretary Perry, Ambassadors Sondland and Volker; the three amigos; with Senator Ron Johnson, and Colonel Vindeman also would attend.

After returning from the inauguration, several members of the delegation briefed Mr. Trump on their encouraging first interactions with President Zelensky. They urged Trump to meet with the new

Ukrainian President. Trump instead criticized Ukraine, and instructed them to "work with Rudy." A few weeks later, on July 10th, Ambassador Sondland met, at the White House, with a group of US and Ukrainian officials; including Colonel Vindeman; and Gordon Sondland informed the group that, according to Chief of Staff Mulvaney, the White House meeting for Zelensky with President Trump, would only happen if Ukraine undertook certain investigations. National security advisor, John Bolton, abruptly ended the meeting, and said afterwards, that he would not be part of whatever "drug deal" that "Sondland and Mulvaney are cooking up."

At that point, Sondland brought the Ukrainian delegation downstairs to another part of the White House, and was more explicit, according to witnesses. Ukraine needed to investigate the Bidens, and Burisma, if they are to get a White House meeting with President Trump.

After this discussion, of which Colonel Vindeman witnesses, he went to the National Security Council's top lawyer, to report the matter; and he was told he could return in the future, with any more concerns. He would soon find the need to do so. A week later, on July 18th, a representative of the Office of Management and Budget announced a videoconference call with Mulvaney. At Trump's direction, he was freezing near the nearly $400 million in military assistance to Ukraine, which was appropriated by Congress, and enjoyed the support of the entirety of, the US National Security establishment.

In one week after that, President Trump would have the now-infamous July 25th phone call with Volodymyr Zelensky. During this call, Trump complained that the US relationship with Ukraine had not been reciprocal. Later in the call, Zelensky thanks Trump for his support, in the area of defense; and says that Ukraine is ready to purchase more Javelin missiles; an anti-tank weapon that was one of the most effective deterrents of Russian further advances into Ukraine territory.

Trump's response was, "I would like you to do us a favor, though. Trump then requested that Zelensky announce investigations into a discredited 2016 conspiracy theory; and even more ominously, to look into the Bidens. Neither was part of the official preparatory material for the call; but they were in Donald Trump's personal interests; and in the interests of his 2020 reelection campaign; and curiously, the Ukrainian President knew about both in advance; because Sondland, and others, had been pressing Ukraine for weeks, about announcing the opening of Ukrainian investigations into the 2016 election, Burisma, and the Bidens.

Both Colonel Vindeman, and Ms. Williams, were on the July 25th call; and they have testified, that due to the unequal bargaining position of the two leaders, and Ukraine's dependency on the US, the favor Trump asked of Zelensky was really a demand.

After the call, multiple individuals, including Colonel Vindeman, were concerned enough to reported to the national Security Council's top lawyer, John Eisenberg. It was the second time in two weeks, that Vindeman had raised concerns with the NSC lawyers.

For her part, Williams also believed that asking Zelensky to undertake these political investigations was inappropriate; and she thought it might explain something else she had become aware of; the otherwise inexplicable hold, on US military assistance to Ukraine. Both Colonel Vindeman and Ms. Williams, also took note of the explicit use of the word Burisma, by Zelensky. In fact, the word was then conspicuously left out of the record of the call; now also locked away in an ultra-secure server. They believed that President Zelensky must have been prepped for the call, in order to be able to make the connection between Biden, and Burisma. In fact, other witnesses have now confirmed this.

In the weeks that followed the July 25th call, Colonel Vindeman continued to push for a release of the military aid, to Ukraine; and he struggled to learn why it was being withheld.

More disturbing, word of the hold had reached Ukrainian government officials, prior to its becoming public, in an August 29th Politico news article.

By mid-August, Ukrainian Deputy Ambassador has been why the US was holding the aid all, and although Colonel Vindeman didn't have an answer, Sondland made it explicit to Ukrainian officials, at a meeting in Warsaw, that they needed to publicly commit to these two investigations, if they hoped to get the aid.

Ms. Williams; we also saw the President's tweet about you, on Sunday afternoon; and the insults he hurled at Ambassador Yovanovitch, last Friday. You are here today, and the American people are grateful.

Colonel Vindeman, you've seen far more-scurrilous attacks on your character, and watched as certain personalities on Fox have questioned your loyalty. I know that you have shed blood for America, and we owe you an immense debt of gratitude. I hope no one on this committee will become part of those vicious attacks.

Today's witnesses, like those who testified last week, are here because they were subpoenaed to be here; not because they are for, or against impeachment. That question is for Congress to decide; and not the fact witnesses. The President abused his power, and invited foreign interference into our elections. If he sought the condition, extort, or coerce our private ally, into conducting investigations; to aid in his reelection campaign; and did so by withholding official acts, or hundreds of millions of dollars, of needed military aid, it will be up to us to decide, whether those acts are compatible with the office of the presidency.

Chairman Schiff now recognizes Devin Nunez for his opening remarks:

He says, (and I warn you, it is a bogus statement): I'd like to address a few brief words to the American people watching at home. If you were watching the hearings last week, you may have noticed a disconnect between what you actually saw, and the mainstream media accounts describing when you saw three diplomats who disliked President Trump's Ukraine policy, discussing second hand, and third hand conversations about their objections to get with the Trump policy. Meanwhile, they admitted they had not talked to the President about these matters, and they were unable to identify any crime or impeachable offense the President committed. What you read in the paper were reports of shocking, damning testimony, which fully supports the Democrats accusations. These accounts have a familiar ring; it's because this is the same preposterous report the media offered, for three years, on the Russian hoax.

{Nunez goes on the contend, that the media has cast President Trump and everyone around him as Russian agents; it's actually not bad way to characterize the group of complicit actors in Trump's campaign; and there certainly are a lot of Russian operatives in Trump's orbit; such as Paul Manafort, Lev Parnas, and Igor Fruman; and then there's Jared Kushner who met with Russians during the campaign; and Trump himself who lied about the Moscow Tower building project that was still moving along, after claiming he was no longer pursuing it.

Next, Nunez claims that a bunch of headlines were false. One of them is that Trump campaign aides had repeated contacts with Russian intelligence; and that was true, according to Buzzfeed. President Trump directed his attorney to lie to Congress, about the Moscow tower project. Nunez says that was false; but we later find out that it was actually true. Then, Nunez accuses the media of being puppets of the Democratic Party. How ridiculous! The "media" that Nunez is referring to, consists of dozens of independent companies, employing hundreds of thousands of reporters, across the country, who are just simply reporting the facts of what's truly evident, about what's going on. How could all of these people possibly coordinate?}

Nunez claims that the American public has lost confidence in the press because of their so-called biased misreporting on the Russia hoax. I would say that, through the conglomerate of news exposure, the American public were enabled to understand all of the odious goings-on, connected with the Trump campaign; as well as learning of definitive foreign involvement and an unprecedented degree of influence, coordinated at very high levels of Russian government.

Here he goes again, with us three questions; and his oft-repeated refrain: Whistleblower, whistleblower, whistleblower!

{but we know, of course, that this hearing has nothing to do with the whistleblower, except that he was the first person to bring news of Trump's crooked scheme to Congress's attention; but he might as well not even exist, in light of the fact that there are so many other witnesses coming forward, and telling this horrid story; about who were supposed to be trusting as the leader of the highest office in the land!}

Nunez suggests that the Democrats have put the whistleblower in their own witness protection plan. {Yes, that's exactly what has happened, because we don't want people with that kind of integrity risking their neck, in order to clue the American public in, on this terrible corruption going on, right under her noses; in the highest office of the land. We certainly want to protect people like this whistleblower; if we didn't, what would happen next time? The whistleblower may to themselves, maybe I won't say anything, because I know what happened to the last whistleblower.}

Then, Nunez goes on about the supposed Ukrainian election meddling; that our intelligence sources say didn't really happen. blah blah blah. {look up John Solomon; Nunez talks about him having written reports that the Democrats don't like. He says that media is slandering and libeling him. Apparently, he ran some of his stories in "The Hill" publication, and liberals are very upset about the fact that Solomon had gathered some evidence of import; contending that 2017 Ukrainian efforts to sabotage Trump backfired.

Nunez complains that Hunter Biden was offered a job at Burisma, for which he had no background, training, or apparent qualifications for; but let's not forget that being the President's son; or the Vice President's son; perks come your way, sometimes. For example, there is flagrant nepotism in Trump's own family; his son Eric Trump, his daughter Ivanka, and her husband Jared Kushner; none of these relatives had any background in politics or government. Yet, they are not only hired in a job that's high-paying, with no basis for this; but they are charged with responsibilities for the United States government's actions around the world! That's pretty scary! It is way beyond any privilege that Biden's son ever had.

Nunez suggests that the Democrats have put the whistleblower in their own witness protection plan. {Yes, that's exactly what has happened, because we don't want people with that kind of integrity risking their neck, in order to clue the American public in, on this terrible corruption going on, right under her noses; in the highest office of the land. We certainly want to protect people like this whistleblower; if we didn't, what would happen next time? The whistleblower may to themselves, maybe I won't say anything, because I know what happened to the last whistleblower.}

Then, Nunez goes on about the supposed Ukrainian election meddling; that our intelligence sources say didn't really happen. blah blah blah. {look up John Solomon; Nunez talks about him having written reports that the Democrats don't like. He says that media is slandering and libeling him. Apparently, he ran some of his stories in "The Hill" publication, and liberals are very upset about the fact that Solomon had gathered some evidence of import; contending that 2017 Ukrainian efforts to sabotage Trump backfired.

Nunez complains that Hunter Biden was offered a job at Burisma, for which he had no background, training, or apparent qualifications for; but let's not forget that being the President's son; or the Vice President's son; perks come your way, sometimes. For example, there is flagrant nepotism in Trump's own family; his son Eric Trump, his daughter Ivanka, and her husband Jared Kushner; none of these relatives had any background in politics or government. Yet, they are not only hired in a job that's high-paying, with no basis for this; but they are charged with responsibilities for the United States government's actions around the world! That's pretty scary! It is way beyond any privilege that Biden's son ever had.

Then, Nunez goes into this idea that Democrats are switching their story, because they are now, at this point, calling what President Trump did "bribery," and Republicans have found out that the reason why they have used this word now, is because Democrats did some polling, and realized that people don't know what a "quid pro quo" is, in general in this country; and bribery is very easy to understand.

-But the fact is, what Trump has engaged in, could be called all of those things: a quid pro, bribery, extortion; it's all-of-the-above!

Nunez claims that Hunter Biden was paid $83,000 a month but I heard it was 50,000 a month. Nunez tries to claim that what Joe Biden did, as Vice President, in threatening for the US to not go through, with offering loan guarantees promised, enabling Ukraine to potentially borrow a lot more money, that it needed to build the fledgling democracy; unless they removed their corrupt Prosecutor General; but as we've already determined, Biden was working in concert with stated foreign policy, and in coordination with US officials, in the embassy in Kyiv; and what he was doing, was truly fighting corruption; not trying to Trump up some dirt, falsely accusing Joe Biden of corruption.

Nunez says Americans have realized how to recognize fake news when they see it. {but of course, that is so untrue; otherwise we wouldn't have this maniac Trump in the White House!}

Now, it's time for the opening statements of Alex Vindeman and Jennifer Williams. Vindeman goes first. Adam Schiff starts off with an introduction: Lieutenant Colonel Alexandra Vindeman is an active-duty military officer, who joined the Army after college, and serve multiple tours overseas; serving in South Korea, Germany, and Iraq. He was stationed in Iraq, at the time of heavy fighting, and was awarded a Purple Heart, after being wounded by roadside bomb.

Since 2008, Colonel Vindeman has served as a Foreign Service officer, specializing in Eurasia, serving both at home, and in US embassies in Ukraine, and Russia. He served as a political medical military affairs officer for Russia; for the Joint Chiefs of Staff. He joined the Trump administration in July of 2018, when he was asked serve on the National Security Council.

Jennifer Williams began her career in government service in 2005, shortly after graduating from college; when she joined the Department of Homeland Security as a political appointee during the George W. Bush administration. After working as a field representative on the 2004 Bush Cheney Presidential campaign, she joined the Foreign Service the following year; completing tours in Jamaica, Beirut, and in Lebanon; prior to joining the office of the Vice President, to serve at the US Embassy in London, as a Public Affairs officer.

In April 2019, Ms. Williams was detailed to the office of the Vice President Mike Pence, where she serves as a special advisor, on his foreign-policy team; covering Europe; and on his foreign-policy team covering European, and Russian policy issues. In that capacity, she keeps Vice President Pence aware of policy issues in Europe and Russia; and prepares him for foreign-policy engagements, and meetings with foreign leaders.

Two final points, before witnesses are sworn in: First; If first witness depositions, as part of this inquiry, were unclassified in nature, then all open hearings will also be held at the unclassified level. Any classified information that we touch on, will be addressed separately. Second, Congress will not tolerate any reprisal, threat of reprisal, or attempt to retaliate against any US Government official for testifying in front of Congress; including any of you, or any of your colleagues. If you will both please rise... (Schiff then swears them in.)

Ms. Williams is first recognized for her opening statement:

I appear today pursuant to a subpoena, and I am prepared to answer your questions to the best of my ability. I have had the privilege of working as a Foreign Service officer, for nearly 14 years; working for three different Presidential administrations; two Republican, and one Democratic. I joined the State Department in 2006, after serving at the Department of Homeland Security, for Undersecretary Michael Chertoff. It is with great pride and conviction, that I swore an oath, to uphold and defend the Constitution; administered by a personal hero of mine; former Secretary of State Condoleezza Rice.

As a career officer, I am committed to serving the American people, and advancing American interests abroad; in support of the President's foreign policy objectives. I've been inspired, encouraging that journey, made by the thousands of other dedicated public servants, who I'm proud to call colleagues, across the Foreign Service, Civil Service, Military, and Federal Law Enforcement agencies.

I've served overseas tours in Kingston, Jamaica, Beirut. Lebanon, and London, and the United Kingdom; and I've worked to implement military assistance programs, to serve millions of victims of the Syrian conflict; and I served as an advisor in the Middle East, to the Deputy Secretary of State.

This spring, it was the greatest honor of my career, to be asked to serve as a Special Advisor to the Vice President for Europe and

Russia. Over the past eight months, I've been privileged to work with the dedicated and capable men and women of the office of the Vice President, to advance the administration's agenda.

I've also worked closely with talented and committed colleagues at the national Security Council, State Department, the Department of Defense, and other agencies, to advance and promote US foreign policy objectives.

In this capacity, I have advised and prepared the Vice President, for engagement related to Ukraine. As you are aware, on November 7th, I appeared before the committee, for a closed-door deposition; pursuant to a subpoena. I would like to take this opportunity to briefly summarize my recollection of some of the events I expect the committee may asked me, about on April 21st.

Volodymyr Zelensky won the Ukrainian Presidential election on April 23rd, and the Vice President called to congratulate President-elect Zelensky. During the call; which I participated in; the Vice President accepted an invitation to attend President-elect Zelensky's upcoming inauguration; providing that the scheduling worked out. The Vice President had only a narrow window of availability, at the end of May; and the Ukrainian Parliament would not meet, to set a date for the inauguration, until after May 14th.

As a result, we did not expect to know whether the Vice President could attend, until May 14th, and we would need to make trip preparations. On May 13th, the assistant to the Vice President's Chief of Staff, called to inform me that President Trump had decided that the Vice President would not attend Zelensky's inauguration in Ukraine. She did not provide any further explanation.

I relayed that instruction to others involved in planning the potential trip. I also informed the NSC that Vice President would not be attending; so that it could identify a head of the delegation to represent the United States, at President-elect Zelensky's inauguration.

On July 3rd, I learned that the Office of Management and Budget, at President Trump's orders, had placed a hold on a tranche of security assistance designated for Ukraine. According to the information I had received, OMB was reviewing whether the funding was aligned with the administration's priorities. I subsequently attended meetings of the policy coordination committee, where the hold on the Ukrainian assistance was discussed.

During those meetings, representatives of the State Department, and the Defense Department, had advocated that the hold should be lifted; but OMB representatives reported that the White House Chief of Staff had directed that the hold should remain in place.

On September 11th, I learned that the Hold, on security assistance for Ukraine, had been released. I've never learned what prompted that decision. On July 25th, along with some of my colleagues, I listened to the call between President Trump and President Zelensky; the content of which has since been publicly reported. Prior to July 25th, I had participated in roughly a dozen other Presidential phone calls.

During my closed-door deposition, members of the committee asked about my personal views, and whether I had any concerns about the July 25th call. As I testified then, I found the July 25th phone call unusual; because in contrast to other phone calls I had observed, it involved discussion of what appeared to be a domestic political matter.

After the July 25th call, I provided an update, in the Vice President's daily briefing book, indicating that President Trump had a call that day with President Zelensky. A hard copy of the memorandum transcribing the call, was also included in the book. I do not know whether the Vice President reviewed my update, or the transcript. I did not discuss the July 25 call with the Vice President, or with any of my colleagues in the office of the Vice President, or the NSC.

On August 29th, I learned that the Vice President would be traveling to Poland, to meet with President Zelensky, on September 1st. At the September 1st meeting, which I attended, President Zelensky asked the Vice President about news articles, reporting the hold on the US security assistance to Ukraine.

The Vice President responded that Ukraine had the United States unwavering support, and he promised to relate the conversation to President Trump that night. During the September 1st meeting, neither the Vice President, or President Zelensky mentioned the specific investigations discussed, during the July 25th phone call.

Thank you again, for the opportunity to provide a statement; and I would be happy to answer any questions.

Colonel Vindeman then reads his statement: I've dedicated my entire professional life to United States of America. For more than two decades, it's been my honor to serve as an officer in the United States Army. As an infantry officer, I served multiple overseas tours, including South Korea, and Germany; and I was deployed to Iraq, for combat operations.

Since 2008, I've been a Foreign Service officer, specializing in European and Eurasian political and military affairs, I served in the United States. I served in 1996, in Ukraine, and in Moscow, Russia.

In Washington DC, I was a Political Military Affairs officer for Russia the Chairman of the Joint Chiefs of Staff in Moscow Russia in Washington DC I was up political military affairs officer for Russia Chairman of the Joint Chiefs of Staff, where I countered Russian aggression in Russian. I was asked to serve at the White House National Security Council at the NSC.

I am the principal National Security Advisor on Ukraine, and other countries. My role at the NSC is to develop core aims, implement policy, and manage the full range of diplomatic informational military and Economic National Security issues, for the countries in my portfolio.

The committee has heard from many of my colleagues, about the strategic importance of Ukraine, as a bulwark against Russian aggression. It is important to note that our country's policy of supporting Ukraine sovereignty, and territorial integrity, promoting Ukraine prosperity, and instituting a free and democratic Ukraine; as a counter to Russian aggression; has been a consistent bipartisan foreign policy objective; and strategy across various administrations; both Democratic and Republican; and President Zelensky's election, in April of 2019, created an unprecedented opportunity to realize our strategic objectives.

In the spring of 2019, I became aware of two destructive actors, primarily Ukraine's then-prosecutor Yuriy Lutsenko, and Mayor Rudy Giuliani; the President's personal attorney; promoting false narratives that undermine the United States Ukraine policy.

The NSC, and its interagency partners, including the State Department, were growing increasingly concerned about the impact that such information was having on our country's ability to achieve our national security objectives. On April 21st, 2019, Volodymyr Zelensky was elected President of Ukraine, in a landslide victory; on a unity, anti-reform, and anticorruption platform.

President Trump called President Zelensky on April 21st, to congratulate him on his victory. I was a staff officer who produced call materials, and I was one of the staff officers who listened in on the call. The call was positive, and President Trump expressed his desire to work with President Zelensky, and he extended an invitation to visit the White House.

In May, I attended the inauguration of President Zelensky, as part of the Presidential delegation led by Secretary Perry. Following this meeting, the members of the delegation offered President Trump a debriefing session followed by positive assessment of the President Zelensky and his team. After this debriefing, President Trump sent a congratulatory letter to Presidents Zelensky, and extended another invitation to visit the White House.

On July 10th, Ambassador Sondland took, then Ukraine's National Security advisor, who had visited Washington for a meeting with National Security Advisor John Bolton; and Sondland and secretary Rick Perry also attended that meeting. I also attended, along with Dr. Hill.

We fully anticipated that the Ukrainians would raise the issue of the meeting between the Presidents. Ambassador Bolton cut the meeting short, when Ambassador Sondland started to speak about the requirement, that Ukraine deliver specific investigations, in order to secure the meeting with President Trump.

Following this meeting, there was a short debriefing; during which Ambassador Sondland emphasized the importance of Ukraine delivering the two investigations; the into the 2016 election interference, and the Bidens.

I stated to Ambassador Sondland, that this is inappropriate, and has nothing to do with national security. Dr. Hill also asserted that

Sondland's comments weren't proper. Following the meeting, Dr. Hill and I agreed to report the incident to the NSC's lead counsel, Mr. John Eisenberg.

On July 21st, President Zelensky won a parliamentary election, in another landslide victory. The NSC proposed that President Trump call President Zelensky, to congratulate him. On July to 25th, the call occurred. I listened in on the call, in the situation room; with White House colleagues. I was concerned by the call; what I heard was inappropriate. I reported my concerns to Mr. Eisenberg; that it is improper for the President of the United States to demand that a foreign government investigate a US citizen, and a political opponent.

It was also clear that, if the President pursued investigations into the 2016 election, Burisma, and the Bidens, it will be interpreted as a partisan play. This would undoubtedly result in Ukraine losing bipartisan support; undermining US national security, and advancing Russia's strategic objectives in the region.

I want to emphasize to the committee, that when I reported my concerns on July 10th, related to Ambassador Sondland, and the July 25th call between the Presidents, I did so, out of a sense of duty. I privately reported my concerns in official channels; in the proper authority and chain of command. My intent was to raise concerns because they had significant national security implications for our country.

I never thought that I would be sitting here testifying for this committee, and the American public, about my actions; when I reported my concerns, my only thought was to act properly, and to carry out my duty.

Following each of my reports to Mr. Eisenberg, I immediately returned to work, to advance the President's, and our country's foreign policy objectives. I'm focused on what I've done throughout my military career, promoting America's national security interests.

I want take a moment to recognize the character of my colleagues, scheduled to appear before this committee. I want to state that the character attacks on these distinguished, and honorable public servants, is reprehensible. It is natural to disagree; and to engage in serious debate;

this is a custom our country since the time of our founding fathers; but we are better than personal attacks.

The uniform that I wear today is that of the United States Army. The many members of our whole volunteer force, are made up a patchwork of people, from all ethnicities, regions, and socioeconomic backgrounds, who come together under a common oath, to protect and defend the Constitution of the United States of America. We do not serve any political party; we serve the nation.

I am humbled to come before you today, as one of many. We serve the most distinguished and able military force in the world. The Army is the only profession I have ever known. As a young man, I wanted to spend my life serving this nation, that gave my family refuge from authoritarian oppression.

For the last 20 years, it has been an honor to represent, and protect my country. Next month will mark 40 years, since my family arrived in the United States; and as refugees, when my father was 47 years old, he left behind his entire life, and the only home he had ever known, to start over in the United States; so that his three sons could have better and safer lives.

His courageous decision inspired a deep sense of gratitude in my brothers and myself, and instilled in us, a sense of duty and service. All three of us have served, or are currently serving in the military. My little brother sits behind me here today. Our collective military service is a special part of our family's history, and a storied America. I also recognize that my simple act of appearing here today; just like the courage of my colleagues; who also have testified for this committee; would not be tolerated in many places around the world. In Russia, my actively expressing concerns, in the chain of command; in an official private channel; would have severe personal and professional repercussions; and offering public testimony involving the President would surely cost me my life.

I'm grateful for my father's decision; back 40 years ago; and for the privilege of being an American citizen, and a public servant; where I can live free of fear for my own, and my family's safety.

Dad, my sitting here today at the US Capitol, talking to our elected officials, is proof that you made the right decision 40 years ago; to leave the Soviet Union, and come to the United States of America; to lead a better life for our family. Do not worry; I will be fine for telling the truth. {Trump, the tyrant, fired him, and his brother; the vindictive so and so!} (Addressing the Intelligence Committee members) Thank you again for your consideration; I'll be happy to answer your questions.

At this point, it goes to Majority leader Schiff (who is also the Chairman at these proceedings), (and his counsel, Mr. Goldman's) combined time to have 45 minutes, to engage in questioning of the witnesses:

Schiff starts off by saying, before we get into the substance of your testimony, Ms. Williams, I want to ask you about a phone call, between Vice President Pence, and President Zelensky, on September 18th. Were you on that call? (I was) -And did you take notes of the call? (yes) -Is there something about the call, that you think may be relevant to our investigation? {at this point, her lawyer speaks up and encourages her to respond, I refuse to discuss this, with the committee. Williams' attorney says, the office of the Vice President has taken the position that the September 18th call is classified; and as a result, he refers the committee to the public record; which includes Ms. Williams November 7th testimony which has been publicly released, as well as a public readout of that call, which has previously been issued by the White House. Beyond that, given the position of the Vice President's office on classification, I've advised Ms. Williams not to answer any further questions about that call, in an unclassified setting.

Schiff says, I want to ask you, in this setting, Ms. Williams, if you think of something relevant to our inquiry, in that call; whether, if so, you'd be willing to make a classified submission to the committee?

Williams responds, I would also refer to my testimony, that I gave at the closed-door session; and I'm very happy to appear for a classified setting discussion, as well.

Schiff says, it may not be necessary for you to appear, if you were to submit information in writing, to the committee. Williams says, I'd be happy to do so.

Colonel Vindeman, if I could turn your attention to the April 21st call. This is the first call, between President Trump and President Zelensky. Did you prepare talking points, for the President to use during that call? (Yes, I did) -And do those talking points include rooting out corruption in Ukraine? (yes) -And was that something that President was supposed to raise, in his conversation with President Zelensky? (yes) -Those were the recommended talking points that were cleared through the NSC staff, for the President? (yes) -Did you listen in on the call? (Yes, I did.) -The White House has not released the record of that call. Did President Trump ever mention corruption, in the April 21st call? (To the best of my recollection, he did not.) -On that April 21st call, President Trump told President Zelensky that he would send a high-level US delegation to the inauguration.

Ms. Williams, was it your understanding, that President wanted the Vice President to attend President Zelensky's inauguration? (Yes, that was my understanding.) -And, did the President tell the Vice President, subsequently, that he should not attend the inauguration? (I was informed, by the Vice President's Chief of Staff's office, that the President had told the Vice President not to attend, but I did not witness that conversation.) -And am I correct, that you learned this on May 13th, is that right? (that's correct) -Am I also correct, that the inauguration date had not been set, as of May13th? (that is correct.) -Do know what accounted for the President's decision to instruct the Vice President not to attend? (I did not.)

Colonel Vindeman, you were a member of the delegation to the inauguration, on May 20th? is that correct? (Yes Chairman) -During that trip, did you have an opportunity to offer any vice to President Zelensky (Yes; during a bilateral meeting in which the delegation was meeting with President Zelensky and his team, I offered two pieces of advice; to be particularly cautious, with regards to Ukraine, towards Russia, and its desire to provoke Ukraine; and the second one was to stay out of US domestic politics.) -Why did you feel it was necessary to advise President Zelensky to stay out of domestic politics? (In the April timeframe, it became clear that there were actors, non-governmental actors, that were promoting the idea of the investigations into 2016 Ukrainian interference in the 2016 US election; and it was consistent with US policy, to advise any country; all the countries in my portfolio, and any country in the world, to not participate in US domestic politics; so I was passing the same advice consistent with US policy.) -And if I can return to the hold, on security assistance, which I think you both testified you learned about in early July, am I correct? (yes) You told us, in your interviews, that neither of you were provided with a reason for the hold, on security assistance to Ukraine?

Williams answers, (My understanding was that OMB was reviewing the assistance, to make sure that it was in line with administration priorities; but it was not made more specific than that.)

Colonel Vindeman, is that consistent with your understanding? (yes) -Is it consistent with administration policy? Colonel Vindeman, you attended a meeting in John Bolton's office on July 10th, where Ambassador Sondland interjected, to respond to question by senior Ukrainian officials, about a White House visit; what did he say, at the time? (To the best of my recollection, Ambassador Sondland said that in order to get at a White House meeting, the Ukrainians would have to provide a deliverable; which was investigations; specific investigations.) -And what was Ambassador Bolton's response, or reaction to that comment? (We had not completed all of the agenda items; we still had time for the meeting, and Ambassador Bolton abruptly ended the meeting.) -Did you report this incident to the national Security Council? (yes, I did) -Based on Ambassador Sondland's remark, at the July 10 meeting, was it your clear understanding, that the Ukrainians understood, they would have to commit to investigations that President Trump wanted, in order to get the White House meeting? (It may not have been entirely clear at that moment. Certainly, Ambassador Sondland was at this meeting, and he had stated that it this was, as per his conversation with Chief of Staff, Mick Mulvaney; but the connection to the President wasn't clear, at that point.) -But the import of what Ambassador Sondland said, in that meeting, was that there was an agreement with Mick Mulvaney, that Zelensky would get the meeting only if they would undertake these investigations? (yes)

About two weeks after that July 10th meeting, President Trump and President Zelensky had their second call; the now-infamous July 25th call. -Colonel, and what was your real-time reaction, during the call? (Chairman, without hesitation, I knew that I had to report this to the White House counsel. I had concerns, and it was my duty to report my concerns, to the proper people in the chain of command.) -And what was of concern? (As I said in my statement, it was improper for the President to demand an investigation into a political opponent; especially of a foreign power; where there might be, at best, a dubious belief, that this would be a completely impartial investigation; and this would have significant implications, if it became public knowledge; and it would be perceived; that policy that would undermine our Ukraine policy; and undermine our national security.)

Colonel, you would describe this as a demand, instead of a favor, that the President asked; what is it, about the relationship between the President of the United States in the President of Ukraine, that leads you to conclude, that when the President of the United States asks a favor like this, it is really a demand? (In the culture I come from; the military culture; when a senior officer asks you to do something; even if it's unpleasant; it's not to be taken as a request; it is taken as in order. In this case, there was a power disparity between the two leaders. My impression was that in order to get the White House meeting, President Zelensky would have to deliver these investigations.

-Ms. Williams, I think you described your reaction, in your deposition, as you listened to the call; that you found it unusual, and inappropriate; but I was struck by something else; based on your deposition; that shed some light on possible other motivations possibility behind the security assistance hold; what did you mean by that? (Mr. Chairman, I was asked by the poster test for how I felt about the call; and reflecting on what I was thinking in that moment, was the first time I had heard internally the President referenced particular investigations, that previously I had only heard about through Mr. Giuliani's press interviews, and press reporting; so, in that moment, it was not clear whether there was a direct connection, or linkage, between the ongoing hold on security assistance, and what the President may be asking President Zelensky to be undertaking, in regards to these investigations; so it was noteworthy in that call record. I did not have enough information to draw conclusions; but it raises questions, of weather the two were related. It was the first I heard of any requests of Ukraine, which were that specific in nature; so it was noteworthy to me, in that regard.)

-Both of you recall President Zelensky, in that conversation, raising the issue of mentioning Burisma; do you not? (both say that's correct) -And yet the word Burisma appears nowhere in the call record that was released to the public; is that right? (that's correct) -Do you know why that's the case? {Williams answers} (I do not; I was not involved in the production of that transcript.) {Vindeman answers} (I attributed that to the fact that, when this transcript was being produced, we may have not caught the word Burisma; and so when it was not in the transcript that was released, I thought it's not a significant omission.) -Colonel, you pointed out the fact that that word was used? (yes) -And yet it was not included (subsequently), in the record released to the public... (That's right; I'd say it's an oversight; (maybe, maybe not!) the folks that produce these transcripts do the best they can; and they just didn't catch the word; and it was my responsibility to then make sure the transcript was as accurate as possible; that's why I attempted to do, by putting that word back, in my notes.)

Schiff says, earlier in your testimony, Colonel, you said you found it striking, that Zelensky would bring up Burisma; that it indicated to you, that he had been prepped for the call; to expect this issue to come up. What led you to that conclusion? (It seemed unlikely that he would be familiar with a single company, in the context of a call that was on the broader bilateral relationship; and it seemed to me, like he was in the either tracking this issue, because it was in the press; or he was otherwise prepped.)

Schiff then turns over questioning to Daniel Goldman, his Democratic Counsel:

Thank you, Mr. Chairman, good morning to both of you. On July 25th, at 9am, you both were sitting in the situation room; and you were preparing for a long-awaited phone call, between President Trump and President Zelensky that occurred. Colonel Vindeman, in advance of this phone call, did you prepare talking points, as you did for the April 21st call? (Yes, I did) -What were those talking points based upon? (So, this is not in the public record, and I can't comment too deeply; but one of the areas that we have consistently talked about in public, is cooperation on supporting reform agenda, anticorruption efforts, and helping President Zelensky implement his plans to end Russia's war against Ukraine.

Goldman says, in other words the talking points are based on official US policy... (correct) -And is there a process to determine official US policy? (Yes; that is my job; to coordinate US politics. -So, throughout the proceeding, you hear that I've been on staff; I had undertaken an effort to make sure we had a coherent US policy.) -As you listened to the call, did you observe whether President Trump was following the talking points based on the official US policy? (Counsel, the President could choose to use the talking points, or not; he's the President; but they were not consistent with what I provided.) -Let's take a look at a couple of excerpts from this call; and right after President Zelensky thanked President Trump for the United States support in the area of defense, President Trump asked President Zelensky for a favor; and then he raises this theory of Ukrainian interference in the 2016 election. He says, in the highlighted portion; "I would like you to do us a favor though; because our country has been through a lot, and Ukraine knows a lot about it. I would like you to find out what happened with this whole situation with Ukraine; they say crowd strike. I guess you have one of your wealthy people; the server; they say Ukraine has it..." -Now, Colonel Vindeman, was this statement based on the official talking points that you had prepared? (no) -And was the statement related to the 2016 Ukraine interference in the election, part of the official US policy? (No, it was not.) -At the time of this July 25th call, were you aware of the theory, that Ukraine had interfered in the 2016 US election? (I was) Were you aware of any credible evidence to support this theory? (I'm not)

-Are you also aware that Vladimir Putin had promoted this theory of Ukrainian interference in the 2016 election? (I'm well-aware of that.) -Ultimately, which country did US intelligence services determine to have interfered in the 2016 election? (It is the consensus of the entire intelligence community, that the Russians interfered in the elections in 2016.)

-Let's look at another excerpt of this call, where President Trump asked President Zelensky to investigate his political opponent, former Vice President Joe Biden. Here, President Trump says, "The other thing, there is a lot of talk about Biden's son; that Biden stopped the prosecution, and a lot of people want to find out about that; so whatever you can do with the Attorney General, would be great. Biden went around bragging that he stopped the prosecution; so if you can look into it, it sounds horrible to me," he said.

Colonel Vindeman, included in your talking points, was the request to investigate a political opponent consistent with US policy? (It was not consistent with the policy, as I understood it.) -Now, are you aware of any credible evidence to support this notion, that Vice President Biden did something wrong, or against US policy, with regard to Ukraine? (I am not)

-Ms. Williams, are you familiar with any credible evidence to support this theory, against Vice President Biden? (No, I'm not.) -Ms. Williams, prior to the July 25th call, approximately how many calls between the President of the United States and foreign leaders had you listened to? (I would say, roughly a dozen.) -Have you heard of any such calls as this? (As I testified before, I believe what I found unusual or different about this call, was the President's reference to specific investigations. That struck me as different than other calls I had listened to.)

-You testified that you thought it was political in nature; why did you think that? (I thought that the references to specific investigations, such as of former Vice President Biden and his son, struck me as political in nature; given that former Vice President is a political opponent of the President.) -And so, you thought they could potentially be designed to assist in President Trump's reelection effort? (I can't speak to what the

President's motivation was, in referencing that; I just noted that that reference to the Bidens sounded political to me.

-Colonel Vindeman, you said, in your deposition, that it doesn't take a rocket scientist to see the political benefits of the President's demands. For those of us who are not rocket scientists, can you explain what you meant by that? (So, my understanding is that it was the connection to investigate into a political opponent, that was improper; I made that connection as soon as the President brought up the Biden investigation.) Colonel Vindeman, you testified that President Trump's request for a favor from President Zelensky would be considered as a demand, to Presidents Zelensky. After this call, did you ever hear from Ukrainians, either in the United States, or Ukraine, about any pressure that they felt, to do these investigations that President Trump had demanded of them? (Not that I can recall.)

-Did you have any discussions with officials at the embassy; the Ukrainian embassy here in Washington DC? (Yes, I did.) -Did you discuss, at all, the demand for investigations, with them? (I did not.) -Did you discuss, at any point, your concerns about the hold on the security assistance? (To the best of my recollection, in the August time frame, the Ukrainian embassy started to become aware of the hold on security assistance; and they were asking if I had any comment on that; or if I could substantiate that.) -And that was before it became public; is that right? (yes) -And what did you respond? (I believe I said that... I don't recall, frankly; I don't recall what I said; but I believe it may have been something along the lines of a not aware of it.)

-You testified, that one of your concerns about the request for investigations, related to US domestic politics; was it that Ukraine may lose bipartisan support? (yes) -Why was that a concern of yours? (Ukraine is in a war, with Russia; and the security assistance that we provide Ukraine is significant. Absent that security assistance; and maybe even more importantly, a signal of US support, of Ukrainian sovereignty, and territorial integrity, it would likely encourage Russia to pursue... to eventually escalate and pursue and further aggression; further undermining Ukraine sovereignty, European security, and US security.) -So, in other words, Ukraine is heavily dependent on United

States support; both diplomatically and financially; and also militarily? (correct) What languages do you speak? (Russian, Ukrainian, and a little bit of English!) (he gets a laugh)

-Do you recall what language that President Zelensky spoke, on this July 25th phone call? (I know he made a valiant effort to speak English; he had been practicing up his English; but he also spoke Ukrainian.)

I want to look at a third excerpt from the July 25th call; and Chairman Schiff addressed this with you, in his questioning. You see, in the highlighted portion, that says specifically to the company that you mentioned in this issue is that the portion of the call record that you corrected; and you thought President Zelensky actually said Burisma… (correct) -And you testified earlier, that he referred to that when President Trump mentioned the Bidens; but that Zelensky referred to the company, "Burisma," it sounded to you, like he was prepped, or prepared for this call; is that right? (that is correct) -I want to go to the next slide, if we could; which is actually a text message; this is from Ambassador Kurt Volker, to Andre Yermak, who is a senior advisor to President Zelensky. -Now this text, this is less than half-an-hour before the call, on July 25th, and since neither of you were on it, I'll read it: "good lunch; thanks; heard from White House; assuming President Z convinces Trump he will investigate, get to the bottom of what happened in 2016, we will nail down date for a visit to Washington, good luck; see you tomorrow, Kurt"

Was this the sort of thing that you're referring to, when you say that it sounded like Presidents Zelensky was "prepped" for this call? (This would be consistent, yes.) -Now, turning to the fourth excerpt from the July 25th call; where Ukraine's President Zelensky links the White House meeting, to the investigations that President Trump requests; President Zelensky says, "I also wanted to thank you for your invitation to visit the United States; specifically, Washington DC. On the other hand, I also wanted to ensure you that we would be very serious about the case, and will work on the investigation…" -And when President Zelensky says, "On the other hand…" isn't that is acknowledging a linkage, between the White House visit that he mentions in the first sentence, and the investigations that he mentions in the second sentence?

(It could be taken that way; I'm not sure if I it seems like a reasonable conclusion.) -And if that is the case, that would be consistent with the text message that Ambassador Volker sent to and Andre Yermak, right before the call; is that right? (seemingly so) -Now, you testified, in your deposition, that a White House visit; and the White House visit is very important to President Zelensky... Why? -is that the show of support for Ukraine? President's Zelensky is still a brand-new President; frankly, a new politician on the Ukrainian political scene; looking to establish his bona fides as a regional, and even a world leader. He would want to have a meeting with the United States; the most powerful country in the world; and Ukraine's most significant benefactor; in order to be able to implement his agenda. It would provide him with some additional legitimately at home? (yes)

-So, just to summarize, this July 25th call, between the Presidents of the United States and Ukraine, President Trump demanded a favor of President Zelensky; to conduct investigations, and that, to both of your knowledge, work for President Trump's political interests; and not the national interest; and in return for his promise of the much desired White House meeting for President's Zelensky. Colonel Vindeman, is that an accurate summary of the excerpts we just looked at? (yes) (Ms. Williams also says yes.)

_-Colonel Vindeman, you immediately reported this call to the NSC lawyers; why did you do that? (At this point, I'd already been tracking this, initially, what I described as an alternative narrative; a false narrative; and I was certainly aware of the fact that it was starting to really gain traction; the fact that in the July 20 10th call ended up pronounced by public official. Ambassador Sondland alerted me to this. Subsequent to that report, I was invited to follow up with any of the concerns, with Mr. Eisenberg.) -When you say, alternative, false narratives; are you referring to the two false investigations at President Trump referred to, in the call? (yes) -Now, at some point, you also discuss how the written summary of the call record should be handled, with the NSC lawyers; there was a discussion in the legal shop on the best way to manage the transcript? (yes) -What did you understand they concluded? (My understanding is that this was viewed as a sensitive transcript; and to avoid leaks. In order to preserve the integrity of the transcript, it should be segregated to a smaller group of folks.)

-So, to preserve the integrity of this transcript; what did that mean? (I'm not sure; it seems like a legal term, and I am not an attorney; I didn't take it as anything nefarious; I just understood that they wanted to keep it to a smaller group.) -If there was real interest in preserving the integrity of this transcript, don't you think they would have accepted your correction? Isn't that a reason it should have been included? (Not necessarily; the way these edits occur, they go through, like everything else, an approval process. I made my contribution; it was cleared by Mr. Morrison; and when I returned it, sometimes that does happen; there are administrative errors. I first saw the transcript about the two substantive items, and I attempted to include them; I didn't see that as nefarious. I said okay; no big deal.) -These might be meaningful. But it's no big deal. -You said there were two substantive issues; what was the other one? (There was a reference to, on page four; the top paragraph; you can look into it... There are videos; the recordings; the set of ellipses should have said that.) -There are recordings... Did you ultimately learn where the call record was put? (I understood that it was being segregated, to a separate secure system.)

-Why would it be put on a separate secure system? (This is definitely not unprecedented; but at times, if you want to limit access to a smaller group of folks, you put it on the secure system, to ensure that a smaller group of people would have access to the secure system.) -Can't you also limit access to it? -on the regular system? (You could do that; but my recollection was that the decision was made, frankly, on the fly. After the fact, I then conveyed my concerns to Mr. Eisenberg. Mr. Ellis came in and heard our conversation; and when it was mentioned that it was sensitive, the decision to segregate to this other system, was on the fly.) -But it was your understanding that it was not a mistake, to put it on the highly classified system; is that right? (yes) -Was it intended to be on the highly classified system, by the lawyers? -or was it a mistake that it was put there?

Vindeman says, I think it was intended to prevent leaks, and to limit its access.) -You testified, both of you, about an April 21st call, a little earlier; and Colonel Vindeman, you indicated that you did include in your talking points, the idea of Ukraine rooting out corruption; but that President Trump did not mention corruption. I want to go to the White House readout, from the April 21st call; and I'm not going to read the whole thing; but you see the highlighted portions part, says "root out corruption," at the end of this readout. It was false; is that right?

(Maybe; that's; it's not entirely accurate; but I'm not sure if I would describe it is false. It was consistent with US policy, that these items are for use as messaging tools; so, a statement that goes out, in addition to a reading of the meeting itself; is also a messaging platform to indicate what is important with regards to US policy.) -So, it is a part of US official policy, that Ukraine should root out corruption; even if President Trump did not mention it, in the April 21st phone call. (Certainly) -And he also didn't mention it, in the July 25th phone call; is that right? (Correct) -So, even though it was included in his talking points for the April 21st call; and presumably, even though you can't talk about it; for the July 25th call, it was not included in what he said; right? (Correct; he doesn't mention in either call.) -So, when the President says now, that he held up security assistance because he was concerned about rooting out corruption in Ukraine; that concern was not expressed, in the two phone conversations that he had with President Zelensky, earlier this year; is that right? (correct)

Ms. Williams, you testified earlier, that after this April 21st call, President Trump asked the Vice President to attend President Zelensky's inauguration? (That's correct) -And that on May 13th, you were just informed by the Chief of Staff's office, that the Vice President will not be going; at the request of the President; is that right? (That is what I was informed, yes.) -And you didn't know what had changed, from April 21st to May 13th, is that right? (No, not in terms of that decision.)

-Colonel Vindeman, since you are a little bit more familiar, perhaps, than Ms. Williams, who has a broader portfolio, I want to ask you if you are aware of the following things, that happened, from April 21st to May 13th; were you aware that Ambassador Yovanovitch was abruptly recalled from Ukraine, in that time frame? (yes) -Were you aware, that

President Trump; as of when he announced she was being recalled… Prior to her removal? (I think I found out at the end of April)

-So, you learned about it after April 24th, is that right? (correct) -And are you aware that President Trump had a telephone call with President Putin, during this time? (In early May, I was) -And were you aware that Rudy Giuliani had planned a trip, to go to Ukraine to pressure the Ukrainians to initiate the two investigations that President Trump mentioned on the July 25th call, during this time period? (I was aware that he was traveling there, and that he had been promoting the idea of these investigations.)

-I want to move, now, to the July 10th meeting that you referenced. Colonel, what exactly did Ambassador Sondland say, when the Ukrainian officials raised the idea of a White House meeting? (As I recall, he referred to two specific investigations that Ukrainians would have to deliver, in order to get this meeting.) -The White House meeting? (yes) -What happened to the broader meeting, after he made that reference? (Ambassador Bolton abruptly ended the meeting.) -He abruptly ended the meeting… Did you have any conversations with Ambassador Bolton, about this meeting? (No, I did not.)

-Then, you followed Ambassador Sondland to the ward room for a follow-up meeting? (There was a photo opportunity, that we leveraged, in order to demonstrate US support.) -So, the White House visit would demonstrate US support for Ukraine? (Yes; the visiting Ukrainians, with the National Security Advisors, we had our pictures taken, out on the White House lawn; and then, after that, we went down to a short post-meeting debrief; where the investigations, the specific investigations that Ambassador Sondland referenced in the larger meeting, were also discussed, in the ward room; restating what Ambassador Sondland had said. Mr. Sondland referred to investigations into the Bidens, and Burisma, and the election interference in 2016.)

-How did you respond, (I said that the request to conduct these investigations was inappropriate, and had nothing to do with national security policy.) -Was Ambassador Volker in this meeting, as well? (I don't recall; I believe he was there, for at least a portion of the time; I don't know if he was there for the whole meeting.) -Was this statement made in front of the Ukrainian officials? (I believe there was some discussion, prior to the Ukrainians leaving, When it was apparent that there was some discord between senior folks, Ambassador Sondland and other White House staff, including myself, were asked to step out; but I don't recall if they were there for the entire discussion.) -Senior White House staff; did that include Fiona Hill; your immediate supervisor the time? (yes) -You also reported this incident to the NSC lawyers, is that right? (correct) -And what was their response? (John Eisenberg, he took notes while I was talking; and he said he would look into it.)

-Why did you report this meeting, and this conversation, to the NSC lawyers? (Because it was inappropriate.) -And following the meeting had a short post-meeting discussion with Dr. Hill? (I had a short conversation with Dr. Hill; we discussed the idea of needing to report this.) -So, am I correct, Colonel, that at least, no later than that July 10th meeting, the Ukrainians had understood, or at least heard, that the oval office meeting, that they so desperately wanted, was conditioned on these specific investigations into Burisma and the 2016 election?

(That was the first time I was aware of the Ukrainians being approached directly, by a government official; and directly linking the White House meeting to the investigations.)

-Ms. Williams, you testified, in your opening statement, that you attended the September 1st meeting, between Vice President Pence and President Zelensky, in Warsaw; is that right? (That's correct.) -What was the first thing that President Zelensky asked Vice President Pence about, in that meeting? (President Zelensky asked the Vice President about the status of security assistance for Ukraine, because he had seen the politico article, and other news reporting, that the security assistance was being held.) -And you testified in your deposition, that in this conversation; that President Zelensky emphasized military assistance, or security assistance was not just important to assist Ukraine in fighting the war against Russia; but that it was also symbolic in nature. What did you understand him to mean by that? (President Zelensky explained that, equally with the military and financial assistance; that it was the physical value of the assistance; but that it was the symbolic nature of that assistance that really was the show of US support for Ukraine, and for Ukraine's sovereignty, and territorial integrity; and I think he was stressing that to the Vice President, to really underscore the need for the security assistance to be released.)

-And if the United States was withholding the security assistance, was it also true then, that Russia would see that as a sign of a weakening US support for Ukraine, and take advantage of that? (I believe that's what President Zelensky was indicating; that any signal, or sign, that US support was wavering, would be construed by Russia as, potentially an opportunity for them, to strengthen its own hand in Ukraine.) -Did the Vice President provide a reason for the hold on security assistance, to the Ukrainian President, in that meeting? (The Vice President did not specifically discuss the reason behind the hold; but he did reassure President Zelensky of the strongest US unwavering support for Ukraine; and they talked about the need for European countries to step up and provide more assistance to Ukraine as well.) -Vice President Pence said he would report back to President Trump? And that means, to your knowledge, the Vice President conveyed to Presidents Zelensky that he would follow up with President Trump, that evening; and convey to President Trump what he had heard from President Zelensky, with regard to his efforts to implement reforms in Ukraine... (I am not aware if the Vice President spoke to President Trump that evening; I was a privy to the conversation.) -Are you also aware that the security assistance wasn't lifted, for another 10 days after this meeting? (that's correct) -And am I correct, that you didn't learn the reason why the hold was lifted? (that's correct)

-Colonel Vindeman, you didn't learn the reason why the hold was lifted either, is that right? (correct) -Colonel Vindeman, are you aware that the committees launched an investigation into Ukraine matters, on September 9th, two days before the hold was lifted? (I am aware of that.) -And on September 10th, the intelligence committee requested the whistleblower complaint, from the Department of National Intelligence? Are you aware of that? (I don't believe I was aware of that.) -Were you aware, that the White House was aware of this whistleblower complaint, prior to that day? (The first I heard of the whistleblower complaint, was,

I believe, when the news broke; I was only aware of the committees investigating the hold on the security assistance.) so is it accurate to say, Colonel Vindeman, that whatever the reason that was provided, for the hold; including the administrative policies, which would support the hold; is that right? -to your understanding? (I didn't understand the question.) Would the administrative policies of President Trump support the security assistance? -is that your understanding? (The interagency policy was to support security assistance for Ukraine.) I yield back.

Adam Schiff now recognizes ranking member Nunez for 45 minutes.

I want to just establish a few basic facts about Burisma and the Bidens directs this to Ms. Williams and she says it's one of my water countries in my portfolio I would not say an extraordinary amount of time but certainly Vice President engaged in Ukraine policy quite a bit in my eight months and it's in your portfolio that's correct first off were you aware September 2015 he asked about an investigation in 2015 of slot Zlochevsky were you aware no I'm not aware she says you know of anti-Trump effort by Ukrainian Nunez asked her about Kent mentioning that he had concerns that it might look improper that Biden's son was hired on the board of Burisma and Williams says that she only knows that from having read the testimony he asked her questions about Burisma and Hunter Biden has nothing to do with what's going on Nunez asked about Williams knowing anything about a meeting that went on in 2015 after just after Biden did just after Joe Biden had forced the firing of the prosecutor general she says no I was not working on Ukraine policy at that time

{It's clear, that he's not really questioning her, about the scheme, or the White House meeting, or the hold on security assistance to Ukraine; he is just using the time to promote an insignificant narrative, that the corruption within Burisma might have warranted special attention; but this is not about 2015 anyway; it's about 2019, and Trump's bad behavior.

Next, Nunez asks Vindeman the same questions; so in other words, he is using the venue, not to question the witnesses, as he was supposed to be doing; but to be able to say these dubiously-factual, impertinent contentions again; it doesn't mean any more than it did when he said it to Ms. Williams; what he is talking about is meaningless to this these proceedings.

Then, Nunez goes into a thing about the Democrats and their various confrontations of Trump Russia etc., and now, regarding these impeachment proceedings, he claims to have seen classified information reported in the press; but that's not true; at least IO seriously doubt that. Surprisingly, he acknowledges that Williams and Vindeman are the first witnesses who have firsthand knowledge of the call for July 25th call. He asks Ms. Williams (he is only asking about the time frame).

-Between July 25th, and September 25th, did you discuss that July 25th phone call, or any matters associated, with any members of the press? (no) -The New York Times, the Washington Post, Politico, CNN, or any other media outlet?

{There is no reason she would not be within her rights, to talk a little about what was being revealed in the news, about the contended scheme, that was reverberating through the media by August 29th. It would be her risk to take, that she wouldn't say anything classified, by accident; as is always the case, for an administration employee. Nunez is just trying to assert false authority; as a show for less-informed US citizens watching the hearing.}

Williams answers, (no, I did not) She also says she didn't encourage or discuss the matter with anyone else, nor did she encourage anyone to go to the press. Then he asks the same of Vindeman, who also answers "no" to those questions.

-Ms. Williams, did you discuss the July 25th phone call with anyone outside the White House? (no) -During your time at the NSC, have you ever accessed any of your colleagues' computers, without their prior authorization, or approval? (I have not; just to clarify, I am in the office of the price Vice President, not the NSC; but no, I have not.)

Nunez asks Vindeman the same questions.

{Instead of concentrating on the matter at hand, Nunez is publicly investigating whether the witnesses are following the guidelines of their employment; and trying to make it seem like he is a powerful authority figure, within these proceedings; but to anyone with knowledge of what has transpired within the Trump administration; warranting these hearings; he is just making himself look like a puffed-up jerk.

It's seems pretty clear that, as a result of his performance during these House intelligence committee hearings, Devin Nunez will go down in history as a nonsense-pontificating jerk, who, it later comes out, actually took part in the effort to get the Ukrainian government to dig up dirt, or at least to announce that they are doing investigations into the Bidens; so it will appear that they suspected Joe Biden and Hunter Biden were acting corruptly in Ukraine.}

Vindeman responds, (Yes, I did discuss the call; my core function is to coordinate US Government policy; interagency policy; and I spoke to two individuals, with regards to providing some sort of readout for the call.) Were either of these, individuals who were not in the White House, and not cleared US Government officials, with appropriate need to know? What agencies were these officials with? (At the Department of State; Deputy Assistant, George Kent; who is responsible for the portfolio of Eastern Europe, including Ukraine; and an individual from the office of the intelligence community.)

Nunez says, which agency; the intelligence community has 17 different agencies… Schiff interjects, "We don't want to use these proceedings to reveal the identity of the whistleblower; we want to make sure that there is no effort to out the whistleblower, through these proceedings. If the witness has a good faith belief that this may reveal the identity of the whistleblower, that is not the purpose we are here for; and I want to advise you to answer accordingly.

So, Nunez says, Mr. Vindeman, you testified… and then Vindeman interrupts him, to say, "Lieutenant Colonel Vindeman, please." Nunez nods, and continues, you testified, in your deposition, that you did not know who the whistleblower was. (I do not know who the whistleblower is.) -How is it possible for you to name these people? (Per the advice my counsel, I was advised not to answer specific questions about members of the intelligence committee. I've been advise not to disclose which departments of the intelligence committee community that I am referring to; but I can offer any specifics on who I have spoken to, inside the intelligence community; I can offer that these are properly cleared individuals, who were properly cleared individuals, with a need to know.)

Vindeman's counsel interrupts, when Nunez starts to press, that if he's not going to answer the questions, he just needs to say, "I plead the fifth." So, at this point, Vindeman's counsel interjects, to say, "We are following the rules of the committee, of what we will share, with regard to this issue; and this does not call for an answer that is invoking the fifth, We are following the ruling of the chair... Nunez asks, "What ruling is that?"

At this point, Adam Schiff interjects, and says, "The whistleblower has the right to anonymity, and these proceedings will not be used to "out" the whistleblower..."

Vindeman's lawyer resumes, "And I've advised my client accordingly; and he's been following the ruling of the chair; if there's an alternative, and you want to work something out with the chair, that's up to you."

Nunez then yields to Castor, who begins:

Ms. Williams, the call transcript; as published on September 25th is it accurate? -will you attest to that? (It looks substantively correct) Vindeman agrees.

Nunez starts asking some questions about Burisma. Vindeman says, I had it in my notes; I know that President Trump did use the word Burisma, in that July 25th call.

Castor points out that, in her deposition Williams also had the word Burisma, that was used by both Presidents. (that's correct) Castor tries to suggest that, with regard to Vindeman's assertion that Trump's request was really to be interpreted as a demand, Castor says that Trump's words were ambiguous. {but this is just a technicality, of course; the only reason why it is ambiguous, is because Trump couldn't directly say, "I'm demanding that you do this," so he used the type of characterization that a mob boss would say. A mob boss wouldn't say, I want you to kill so-and-so; he would say, "I hope that you will just take care of the matter, for me." Well, Trump was saying, "I would like to do me a favor, though..." Gee, if you could look into Burisma for me, that would be great... it certainly was quite obvious, to the people listening in on the call, that he was pressing President Zelensky to make these announcements of investigations, that would be very damaging to his chief political opponent.}

Castor asks Vindeman about whether these transcripts that got circulated around? (no) Vindeman says that the transcript got circulated around for comment and editing suggestions, as usual; but that the transcript was stored in a different server than usual. Castor alludes to Tim Morrison, suggesting that he was worried about the transcript leaking out; and that Vindeman had agreed with him, that it needs to be; because if the transcript was leaked out, both he and Mr. Morrison agreed, that it needed to be protected.

Vindeman's counsel interrupts, "Just a correction, it was Mr. Eisenberg, not Mr. Morrison. Vindeman says, "I can say for myself, that there were concerns about leaks, that seemed valid, and it was particularly critical, that this was sensitive…"

{Castor asks if Vindeman was looking to question the attorney's judgment on this; but stupidly, Castor's pointing out that the NSC's lead lawyer, Eisenberg, was afraid of this transcript getting out, because it had a lot of damning information in it; President Trump's wording.}

Castor then asks Williams, since she was contending that she had concerns about this July 25th call, whether she had discussed any concerns about the call with anyone else; and she answers that her supervisor was in on the call too; so there was no reason for her to discuss it with him she; that didn't discuss the call with anyone else. Lieutenant General Kellogg was her immediate supervisor; and they did not discuss the call afterward. Williams says that she ensured that the Vice President had access to the transcript of the July 25 call; and, with regards to whether a transcript of the July 25th call was included in Vice President Pence's briefing material, in advance of the September 1st trip to Warsaw, Williams offers, that the phone call transcript of an earlier phone call (in this case on July 25th), would not normally be part of a briefing for the September 1st Warsaw meeting, between Pence and Zelensky.

-What else was there, in the briefing material, in preparing for this Warsaw meeting? (The news about the hold had broken, two days before; so, they were a lot more focused on what Zelensky would bring up, about the security assistance hold for that meeting.)

Nunez goes to the topic of long-standing corruption in Ukraine. {They keep beating this dead horse; that a hold on the security assistance might be warranted because of Ukraine's long-standing corruption; but it's pointed out, that Trump had given security assistance in 2017 and 2018; and he hadn't brought these matters up then... -and he had mentioned corruption in his phone calls, only in the context of asking Zelensky to investigate Burisma in the Bidens. So, Castor's questions, in this regard, are totally irrelevant.}

Castor suggests, that because President Trump has mentioned being skeptical about giving aid to foreign countries, that this would be a legitimate reason for the hold. (But again, President Trump has not enacted any broad policy changes regarding foreign aid, and he would have had to sign off on keeping foreign aid policies as they were; unless he made any changes; but it's clear that he had not made any changes to US policy. -And we later learn that, as part of US policy, countries receiving aid are vetted, in terms of being able to demonstrate that they have either rooted out corruption in government, or are addressing problems of corruption sufficiently; and Ukraine had passed that standard, according to the intelligence committees, the Foreign Service agencies, and the National Security Council.

Castor then brings up burden-sharing, with our allies; the European Union has apparently provided over $15 billion to Ukraine; so although the EU consists of 28 member countries altogether, the US has only provided, I think, something in the neighborhood of well under $5 billion, since 2014 since; but again, this had not been an issue that President Trump had ever raised with Gordon Sondland; according to his testimony; Sondland was the Ambassador to the EU during this time period.}

Now, Castor perhaps is trying to suggest that Vindeman could legitimately pass judgment on whether Hunter Biden was qualified to join Burisma's board; {but, just as Trump considered that his daughter Ivanka, and her husband Jared Kushner, and his son Eric, were qualified to run the country, with him; I don't see how Hunter Biden being hired because his father was Vice President; so that could be helpful to Burisma's visibility and connections, perhaps; if nothing else; that would seem to qualify him as a board member, in itself.

Castor alludes to the fact that normally, the Vice President and the President are not both out of the country, at the same time; but there is really no reason why they both had to be traveling at that time, necessarily. Trump could have more-appropriately gone to President Zelensky's inauguration; and then on to Japan; while leaving Vice President Pence at home in Washington.

Was there some special reason why Trump had to go to Japan, specifically on the date of Zelensky's inauguration? -or was this merely orchestrated by him, so that the three amigos could more effectively pressure Zelensky, if there was no one higher up in US Government there to distract from that paramount goal? (We learn that President Zelensky's inauguration took place on May 20th). At this point, Castor's time has expired.

Next, it is time for the committee members to have their 5 minutes each, to ask questions of the witnesses. Adam Schiff, as Majority leader, goes first:

I want to ask you both about some of the questions that you were asked, by my colleagues, in the minority. First, I would like to ask you, Ms. Williams and Colonel Vindeman, you were asked a series of questions by the ranking member at the outset; were you aware of the fact that, within this recitation of information about the Burisma the Bidens, is it fair to say that you have no firsthand knowledge of the matters that were asked about, in those questions? (that's correct)

Ms. Williams, you were also asked a series of questions about the Vice President scheduled; whether he could have made the inauguration, or was the President traveling, or the trip to Canada... Let's be clear about something, you were aware that the Vice President was instructed by the President, not to go, before you even knew the date of the inauguration; is that correct? (Yes, that's correct.) -So, at the time he was told not to go, there was no calculation about where the President might be; because the dates hadn't even been set, yet... (That's right;

they had not been set, so we were weighing different scenarios, of when the inauguration might fall.) -I think you said, originally, that the President told Vice President Pence to go; and then you received instruction that the President no longer wanted him to go; were you aware, in the interim between being told to go, and then not to go, that Rudy Giuliani had to abort a trip he was going to make to Ukraine? (I had seen that, in the press.) -And did you say that you had seen, in the press, word that Rudy Giuliani blaming the people around Zelensky, for having to cancel his trip? (I'd read that in the press reporting, yes.) -And did you read the press reporting too, that Giuliani wanted to go to Ukraine, to meddle in an investigation? (Yes, I did read that.) -And that it occurred prior to the President canceling the Vice President's trip to the inauguration? (Yes, I believe that was around August 10th, or so.

Colonel Vindeman, you were asked, by the Minority counsel, about the President's words, on the July 25th call; and whether the President's words were ambiguous… Was there any ambiguity about the President's use of the word Biden? (There was not.) -It was pretty clear, that the President wanted Zelensky to commit to investigating the Bidens; was it not? (That is correct.) -That is one of the favors that you thought should be properly characterized as a demand? (That is correct.) -There's no ambiguity about that. (In my mind, there was none.)

-It's also true, is it not; that these two investigations that the President asked Zelensky for; into 2016, and into the Bidens; were precisely the two investigations that Rudy Giuliani was calling for, publicly? (That is correct.) So, when people suggest that, maybe Rudy Giuliani was acting on his own, and maybe he was a freelancer, or whatever; the President referred to exactly the same two investigations as Rudy Giuliani was pushing on, is that correct? (Yes, that's correct.)

-Ms. Williams, you were asked about the meeting that the Vice President had with Zelensky, in September; in which the Ukrainians voiced their concern about the hold on the security assistance; is that right? (That's right.) -You were asked about whether that meeting between the Vice President Zelensky, if the Ukrainians had brought up the Bidens and Burisma; and you said they did not bring that up. Now, that bilateral meeting, it was a large meeting, that involved two or three dozen people, wasn't it? (it was) -So, in the context of this meeting, with two or three dozen people, the Vice President didn't bring up those investigations, correct? (No, he did not bring it up.) -He is never brought up those investigations; but were you aware, that immediately after that meeting broke up, Ambassador Sondland has said that he went over to Mr. Yermak, one of the top advisors to Zelensky, and he told Yermak, that if they wanted the military aid, they were going to have to do these investigations, or words to that effect? (I was not aware of any meetings that that Ambassador Sondland had, following the meeting.)

-So, at the big public meeting, it didn't come up; and you can't speak to the private meeting that was held immediately thereafter, correct? (Vice President Pence moved on with his schedule, immediately after his meeting with President Zelensky.)

-Colonel Vindeman, I want to go back to that July 10th meeting with Ambassador Bolton; and the one in the ward room, following on its heels; were you aware that Ambassador Bolton instructed your superior, Dr. Hill; he had said to go talk to the lawyers, after that meeting? (I learned, that shortly after she was finished speaking with Mr. Bolton, she did have a meeting with him, and that's what was expressed.) -Now, you thought you should go talk to the lawyers on your own; correct? (That is my recollection, yes.) -But Bolton also felt that Dr. Hill should talk to the lawyers, because of his concern over this "drug deal," that Sondland and Mulvaney were cooking up? (That's right.) -It is my understanding, that in fact, this drug deal, as Bolton called, it involved this conditioning of the White House meeting, on these investigations that Sondland brought up; is that right? (That is my understanding.) -That in fact, this same conditioning, the same issue of wanting these political investigations, and tying it to the White House meeting, this came up in the July 25th call; did it not? (That is correct.) -So, the very same issue that Bolton said to go talk to the lawyers about, the very same issue that prompted you to go talk to the lawyers about, ends up coming up in that call with the President? (That is correct.) -And it was that conversation, that once again, led you back to the lawyer's office? (That is correct.) I now yield to the ranking member; who also gets seven minutes, equal time; since Schiff went over by 2 minutes.

Nunez starts off saying that, earlier, he had questioned Ms. Williams about whether she had ever accessed anyone else's computer system, at the NSC (or the White House), without authorization; or without their knowledge. (Williams says, no, and Vindeman says, no.)

Nunez then yields to Jordan. Jordan goes to what Tim Morrison had written in his deposition about Vindeman, "I had concerns about Lieutenant Colonel Vindeman's judgment." {Morrison was Vindeman's former boss.} Morrison had said, "Among the sessions I had with Dr. Hill, on the transition, was our team's strength, as well as weaknesses; and Fiona and others had raised concern about Alex's judgment..." {Mr. Morrison was asked by Mr. Castor, did anyone bring any concerns to you, that Colonel Vindeman may have leaked something -and Morrison had replied, "Yes."

So, Jordon asks, "So, your boss had concerns about your judgment; and he said that Fiona Hill did; and her colleagues had concerns about your judgment; and your colleagues said that they were concerned, that you might have leaked some information; any reason why you think these people would have those impressions?"

{At this point Vindeman reads Dr. Hill's own words, as she had attested to, in her last evaluation; dated middle of July; right before she left.}

Vindeman reads, Alex is a top 1% military officer, and the best Army officer I ever work with, in my 15 years of government service. He is brilliant, unflappable, and exercises excellent judgment. He was exemplary, during numerous visits...

{And so forth, and so on; but I think you get the idea. The date of that review was July 13th, earlier this year.} Vindeman continues, so, Mr. Jordan, I would say that, I can't say why Mr. Morrison questioned my judgment; but we only recently started working together. He wasn't there very long; and we were just trying to figure out our relationship; we came from different cultures.

So, Jordan says, you never leaked information? (I never did, and never would; that is preposterous!)

Jordan points out, that only three of the individuals that we deposed were on the call July 25th call, between President Trump and President Zelensky; Vindeman, Williams, and Mr. Morrison.

Jordan the tries to go after trying to "out" the whistleblower again. He asks, how many other people, besides George Kent, had you communicated with? (Mr. Jordan, on the call readout, certainly after the first call, there were half a dozen people; those were people with proper clearance, and the need to know. In this case, because of the sensitivity of the call; and Mr. Eisenberg told me not to speak to anybody else. I only talked with, outside the NSC, two individuals; George Kent, and one other person. Mr. Jordan called out, "Point of order; I would ask you to enforce the rule with regard to disclosure with regard to the intelligence…

It's a good thing that Schiff interjects, to say, as indicated before, this committee will not be used "out" the whistleblower. Jordan argues that he doesn't understand why this is outing the whistleblower; "because you have said you don't know who the whistleblower is? Jordan further argues, "The witness has testified, in his deposition, that he doesn't know who the whistleblower is… No one believes you…

Chairman Schiff responds, Mr. Jordan, this is your time for questioning; and your question should be addressed to the witnesses, and not anyone else.

So, Jordan continues, Mr. Morrison tells us, in his deposition, he said he was not concerned about the call itself; there was nothing illegal, or improper about the call; but he was concerned about the call contents leaking. He said he was concerned how it would play out, in a polarized Washington, how the contents would be used in Washington's political process. Mr. Morrison was right…

Vindeman's lawyer asked for a page, and there is a brief pause. {Jordan thinks that it foils these contentions, the fact that Trump released the transcripts of the call; and actually, it was just a summary of the transcript that was released; it wasn't the actual transcript.}

Jordan claims, the two individuals on the call, had said no pressure etc… Jordan then yields back.

Now it is Jim Himes' turn. Himes says, Ms. Williams, you joined the Foreign Service in 2006? (correct) -Prior to becoming a nonpartisan career official, you worked as a field representative for the Bush-Cheney campaign, in 2004; and you held a political appointment in 2014, to Secretary Chertoff; is that correct? (yes)

Now, as a Foreign Service officer, you served three Presidents; two Republicans, and one Democrat... -In your current position, your detail is to advise the Vice President, inform him of policy, towards Europe and Russia; and on Sunday, the President personally targeted you, in a tweet. This is after he targeted Ambassador Yovanovitch during her hearing testimony.

I would like to show, and review, what he said this week: "tell Jennifer Williams, whoever that is, to read both transcripts of the Presidential calls, and see the just-released statement from Ukraine; and she should meet with the other never-Trumpers, who I don't know, and mostly never heard of; and work out a better Presidential attack."

-Ms. Williams, are you engaged in a Presidential attack? (no, sir.) -Ms. Williams, are you never-Trumper? (I'm not sure I know what the official definition of that is; but no, I would not describe myself that way.) -Did that tweet make an impression on you, when you read it? (Yes, it certainly surprised me. I was not expecting to be called out, by name; it surprised me.) -It looks a lot like witness intimidation, and witness tampering, and effectively trying get you to shape your testimony, today.

Himes then asks, Lieutenant Colonel, you had previously testified that you have dedicated your entire professional life, to the United States of America. Colonel, above your left breast, you are wearing a device, which is a Springfield musket, on a blue field. What is that device? (It's a combat infantryman's badge.)

-You have to be serving a fighting unit, in combat, under fire, to earn that... (yes) -And you are also wearing a purple heart; can you tell us, in 20 or 30 seconds, why you are wearing that? (In 2014, in the ramp-up, to probably the largest urban operation in decades, outside of Falluja, we were conducting a reconnaissance patrol, in conjunction with the

Marines; and my vehicle was struck by an improvised explosive device (IED), that penetrated the truck's armor.

-Were you injured? (I was.) -The day after you appeared for your deposition, President Trump, he calls you a never-Trumper; would you call yourself a never-Trumper? Vindeman says, representative, I call myself a never-partisan!

Colonel Vindeman, in your military career, you served under four Presidents; two Republicans, two Democrats; have you ever wavered, from the oath you took; to support and defend the Constitution; never to have any political motivations? (no.)

Colonel Vindeman, multiple right-wing conspiracy theorists, including Rudy Giuliani, have accused you of harboring loyalty towards Ukraine. They make these accusations, based only on the fact that your family, like many American families, immigrated to the United States. They have accused you of espionage, and dual loyalties. Republican committee members sitting in this room, this morning; for three minutes, were asking you about the offer to make you Minister of Defense, in Ukraine; and that it may have come close to Brooke's Brothers suit, and a parliamentary language, that was designed exclusively to give the right-wing media and opening, to question your loyalties; and I want people to understand what that was all about. It's a kind of attack you say, when you're defending the indefensible! It's what you say, when it's not enough to attack the media, the way the ranking member may; but it's what you stoop to, when the indefensible ability of your case requires that you attack a man, who is wearing a Springfield rifle, on a field of blue; above a Purple Heart. Sir, I thank you for your service, and I yield back the balance of my time.

The floor now goes to Mr. Conaway:

Conaway yields to Mr. Ratcliffe, who tells us, at a press conference last Thursday, Nancy Pelosi said President Trump committed the impeachable offense of bribery; as evidenced in his July 25th call transcript, with President Zelensky. In concert with that, multiple Democratic Committee members gave TV and radio interviews, over this past week, discussing how the President's conduct supported him committing bribery; all of which struck me as rather odd; because, for the longest time, they were calling it a quid pro quo… {so Conaway is going on about what you call it; but really, it's all of the above, isn't it? -Coercion, extortion, bribery, and of course, quid pro quo.

Ratcliffe points out, that none of the witnesses have used the word bribery; but once again; you could call it anything you want; a piece of it would still stink the same!

Next, he puts a stack of printouts of the transcripts, from the House hearings, that have been released; he dramatizes out, "Six weeks of witness interviews in this impeachment inquiry; hundreds of hours of testimony; thousands of questions asked, and answers given; 3500 pages of testimony in the transcripts…

{In a way, he's right; the two articles of impeachment, were extremely limited, in my view, compared to how many articles of impeachment would encompass all of President Trump's impeachable behavior; but those two articles of impeachment are not for bribery; they are for Trump's abuse of office, and obstruction of Congress.

Ratcliff contends that the Democrats have barred lawyers from the White House, in these proceedings; {but I believe the fact is, that Trump would not let any lawyers from the White House, become involved in these proceedings. Ratcliffe contends that the accusation of the Democrats during these proceedings, keeps changing; but it's really not; it's only broadening the definition and description of what has been happening, at the hands of Trump. -But it's still all the same; bribery, extortion, coercion, quid pro quo, it comes under all of those headings.}

Ratcliffe says, he thinks that Pelosi's promise of evidence of bribery is invisible; and he yields back. Next, it goes to Ms. Sewell.

Ms. Sewel starts by asking, Colonel Vindeman, as part of your policy portfolio at a White House, you maintain a relationship with Ukrainian officials; do you not? (That is correct.) -You explained, earlier in your testimony, that your job at the White House, was to coordinate US-Ukraine policy, is that right? (It is to create US policy, vis-à-vis Ukraine, correct.) -You testified, that in the spring of this year, these officials and Ukrainian officials began asking your advice, on how to respond to Mr. Giuliani's advances; is that correct? (That is correct.) What did you understand they meant, by Mr. Giuliani's advances? (I understood that to mean, both as public commentary symbolically, and calling for investigations.) -And it took 2016, Burisma, and Hunter Biden as well, as his direct overtures to the government of Ukraine directly, and through proxies; and as you understand it, whose authority do you think Giuliani was acting under? (The Ukrainian officials who I spoke to, understood that Mr. Giuliani was telling them to investigate about President Biden's son, and the 2016 conspiracy theories, and others.) -Did you understand, Colonel Vindeman, that Mr. Giuliani's campaign to influence the Ukrainians was clear to the Ukrainians; as being the investigation of the Bidens, and the 2016 election, and Burisma? (Yes; to be clear, I think, referring to debunking, that it was Russian interference, that it was not Ukrainian interference, and it wasn't official US foreign policy, to push investigations into the Bidens; that is not any part of what I was involved in.)

Ms. Sewell asks Ms. Williams whether she thinks it also is not part of US foreign policy. (Obviously, anticorruption is a big part of the policy. I was not in a position, to determine whether these particular investigations were part of that.)

-Is it true that President Trump directed the Ukrainian President, on the call on July 25th, to work with Mr. Giuliani on these investigations? (That's correct) -In fact, Mr. Giuliani has made no secret of the fact that he is acting on behalf of President Trump, as Mr. Giuliani told the New York Times. Let me put this up on the screen; he told them, "My only client is the President of the United States; he is the one I have the obligation to; to tell him what happens." She added, that President Trump had said, the investigations would be very, very helpful to my campaign; and may turn out to be helpful to my government."

-Is it fair to say, that the Ukrainian officials, that you are, on a daily basis, in contact; with given your portfolio; were concerned about Mr. Giuliani's advances? (Yes, they were.) -Is it your assessment, that they understand the political nature of what Mr. Giuliani was asking? Williams says (I believe they did understand, that it was affecting US domestic policy.) Vindeman says, (I'm not sure what they frankly understood; I think they understood the implications.) -You testified earlier, that you warned the Ukrainians not to get involved in US domestic policy, is that right?

Vindeman answers, (I counseled them, yes.) -In fact, you testified that you felt like it was important that you are espousing, not just what you thought; but the tradition and policy of the United States; to say that it is what I knew for a fact of the US policy and why you think it's important for foreign governments not to get involved with political affairs of the nation -like United States

the first thought that comes to mind, is of how the Russian interference in 2016, the impact that had, on internal politics; and the consequences it had for Russia itself. This administration enforced sanctions; heavy sanctions against Russia; for their introverts that would not be in US policy.) -Is it normal, for a private citizen, and not a US Government official, to get involved in foreign policy and foreign affairs, like Mr. Giuliani has done? (I don't know if I have the experience to say that; but it certainly wasn't helpful; it didn't help advance US national security interests.) Ms. Sewell yields back; and it now goes to Mr. Turner.

Turner goes back to Vindeman's disclosure, in his opening statement, that he was the principal advisor to the President on military affairs. Vindeman explains, (Although I'm advisor to the President, I have certainly spent much more time advising the Ambassador, that President.)

{Turner nitpicks that, in his statement Vindeman said that he was the principal advisor; but Vindeman backed out of the assertion, explaining to us, "That was my job description, technically; and furthermore, that wording was in my draft; but not in the transcript that I ultimately submitted to congress; I'm saying that what I read into the record this morning didn't say that.)

-Because you know Ukraine, you know that we work for allies, in multilateral relationships; and you know that Ukraine is an aspiring member of the EU? Vindeman and Williams both say (correct)

Turner goes on to say, "You both know that we have offices in the EU, and NATO; you would agree that Ambassador Sondland would be responsible for advancing at the EU and NATO agendas? Williams offers, (I would say that certainly, in terms of the specific relationship between NATO and Ukraine, that falls to Ambassador Hutchinson.) Well, the EU and Ukraine falls to Ambassador Sondland... Williams responds, (obviously, we have Ambassador in Ukraine as well.) Vindeman agrees with Williams

-And Lieutenant Colonel, you said in your written statement, that mayor Giuliani promoted false information that undermined United States-Ukraine policy... (Just to be clear, I said false narrative in my deposition, and my testimony.)

{Vindeman verifies that although he has never spoken with Rudy Giuliani, he has seen and heard Giuliani's comments on TV. Turner points out that he's never met with the President of the United States, and therefore has never advised the President of the United States; but Vindeman clarifies, (I did advise him indirectly; I made all of the preparations for his calls.)

Turner nitpicks that even though Vindeman said that, following the inauguration, the members of that delegation reported to Trump in a meeting; yet, Vindeman himself, wasn't in meeting.

Vindeman clarifies that his policy level is sub-policy... The Deputy Assistant Secretary coordinates with, and chair those meetings.

Turner asks, "Does anybody need your approval to formulate Ukraine policy?" Vindeman answers, (according to the policy signed by the President, policy should be coordinated by the NSC.)

-Ms. Williams, do you have any evidence that anybody who has testified, has perjured themselves? (she says, no; Vindeman says, not that I'm aware of.)

Turner yields back; and now it goes to Mr. Carson, who yields to Chairman Schiff. -I want to make one point clear, for folks that are watching the hearing, today. Bribery does involve the conditioning of an official act, for something of value. An "official act" may be a White House meeting; or maybe the $400 million in military aid. Something of value to the President, might include investigations of his political rival. The reason we don't ask witnesses, that are fact witnesses, to make the judgment about whether the crime of bribery has been committed; or whether, more significantly, what the founders had in mind, when they itemized bribery, or high crimes and misdemeanors; is that, as members of Congress, it will be our job, to understand whether the impeachable act of bribery has occurred; that is why we don't ask those questions. For one thing, you're not also aware of the other facts that (become gathered within) this investigation.

Schiff yields back to Carson, who goes to the July 10ᵗʰ meeting at the White House, with the Ambassador Bolton. -In that meeting, when the Ukrainian's asked about when they would get their oval office meeting, Ambassador Sondland replied that they need to quote "speak about Ukraine delivering specific investigations, in order to secure a meeting with the President; is that correct? (yes)

Colonel Vindeman, did you later learn why Ambassador Bolton cut the meeting short? (I didn't; after Ambassador Bolton ended that meeting, some of the people in that meeting attended a follow-up meeting in a different room in the White House, call the wardroom... (That's correct) -Mr. Sondland was there with the senior Ukrainian officials, is that correct? (yes) -Did the NSC lawyers tell you come to them directly, if you had any concerns, after reporting to them about the July 10ᵗʰ meeting? (I believe the words were something to the effect of, if you have any other concerns feel free to come back.)

-This follow-up meeting, so then, Ambassador Sondland left no ambiguity about what specific investigations he was requesting... He made clear, that he was requesting an investigation of Vice President Joe Biden's son; was that clear? (That is correct.) -And he stated he was asking for these requests, in coordination with White House Chief of Staff Mulvaney? (Correct, sir; that is what I heard him say.)

-Colonel, in your career, you had never before witnessed an American official request that a foreign government investigate a US citizen, who is related to the President's political opponent... (I have not) -And Colonel, you immediately reported your concern about this, is that correct? (That is correct.) -What exactly happened? After you reported it, you said that it was inappropriate and had nothing to do with national security policy; did you also raise concern that day, with White House lawyers? (I did.) What did you tell them? (I reported the same thing; the content of the conversation with Ambassador Sondland.

At that point, I was aware that Fiona Hill had also had a conversation with Ambassador Bolton; so I just relayed what I had what I experienced to the NSC legal counsel, -As we are now aware, Ambassador Bolton was addressing his own concerns, and he had instructed Dr. Fiona Hill, your supervisor, to also meet with the same White House lawyers; to tell them what happened. I agree that there is no question, that Ambassador Sondland was proposing a transaction to Ukrainian officials, trading White House meetings for specific investigations; with the full awareness of the President's Chief of Staff, and White House attorneys. As National Security Advisor, in my view that's appalling! I yield back to the Chairman.

Schiff points out, as well, that when the matter does go to the judiciary committee, the White House counsel will have the opportunity to make a submission to the Judiciary Committee. The floor now goes to Mr. Stuart:

-Colonel Vindeman, you were to directly report to Dr. Hill; and to then to Tim Morrison they were your seniors, correct? (that's correct) -When you had concerns about the July 25th call, between the two Presidents, why didn't you go to Mr. Morrison about it? (Vindeman had gone to John Eisenberg, the lead counsel) since he was in your chain of command; and…. Adam Schiff interjects, "Let him answer the question." Vindeman finishes, (I reported to John Eisenberg; I attempted to report to Mr. Morrison, but he didn't avail himself; at that point, I was told… (Stuart blurts in again) Schiff intervenes, "Please allow the witness to finish answering…"

{Stewart is nitpicking a point; that Vindeman had complained to the lead counsel, John Eisenberg, instead of Tim Morrison, who was indeed Vindeman's next up in the chain of command. {Of course, Vindeman had gone to speak to Eisenberg on July 10th, after the Wardroom meeting; and he was counseled to return if he had any further concerns about this; but Stuart just wants to try and call Vindeman down, because he hadn't worked completely within his mandate, to report up to the next in the chain of command. -But Vindeman knew he was witnessing very inappropriate and alarming words and actions here! -And at the time right, after the July 25th call, what the hell difference does it make?! Vindeman said that he couldn't reach Tim Morrison; Tim wasn't available to him, at the moment; and this was upsetting, so he felt he needed to go to Eisenberg.}

Next, Stuart points to the fact that, in Vindeman's testimony, he had made the assertion of, "I would say first of all, I'm the director for Ukraine; I'm responsible for Ukraine; I'm the most knowledgeable, and I advise the National Security Council, and the White House…" So, Stewart asks, are you the only one, in the entire universe of our government, who can advise, on Ukraine? -Couldn't Ambassador Sondland, or Ms. Williams, also advise on Ukraine? It's on her portfolio…"

Vindeman says, it's not typically what would happen; it would be; frankly, it would be Ambassador Bolton…) -Other people can decide, besides you; your testimony… (I understand the nuances surrounding these issues. I, in my judgment, expressed concerns within the chain of command, which I think, to me, as a military officer, is a completely appropriate exercise of the chain of command. I forwarded my concerns to the… no {Stewart is now pointing out that, according to Morrison, Eisenberg never spoke to Morrison about it; and that Morrison also said he didn't know about Vindeman's having gone directly to Eisenberg; until preparing for these hearings. -But that only points out that this administration's head doesn't know what its tail doing! Why isn't there any protocol for a lead counsel to report to the high up officials, such as Tim Morrison; when a complaint reaches him about a very inappropriate call, where yet, the President of the United States is coercing and extorting favors, from another foreign official, to deliver things that will exclusively benefit the President personally; and not the country?!

Well then, Stewart is heckling further; because then the men had said that a request made in a power differential of the US President to the newly elected Ukrainian President really is a lot like an order given is a lot like a request that a military commander asks a soldier to do and that both are really orders or demands even though they may be voiced as a request.

So, Stewart is trying to pick at Vindeman's explaining this; and he sarcastically asks whether Vindeman in his revisions to the July 25th call record, which was omitting words like Burisma, was one of Vindeman's edits that he suggested, replacing "Do us a favor, though" with the word demand?! (ha, ha) Mr. Stewart, this is not a joke!

Stewart yields back now it's time for Ms. Speier, who starts off: Colonel Vindeman, wasn't it the case, that Mr. Eisenberg, the attorney had said to you, after the July 10th meeting, that you should come to him, if you have any other concerns; you said... (That is correct.) -So, it's not going outside the chain of command, to go to the lawyer speak to the lawyer know he is a senior between the two serving

-Our colleagues, on the other side of the aisle, have been complaining about other witnesses having only secondhand information; and in both of your cases, you have first-hand information because you were on that July 25th phone call, is that correct? Both say yes) -Colonel, you, in your comments today, said, "I wanted to state that these vile character attacks, on these distinguished, and honorable public servants, is reprehensible..." -Would you like to expand on those comments, Colonel Vindeman? (Ma'am, I think they stand on their own; I don't think it's necessary to expand on them.) -So, in both of your situations, since you've given depositions; since those depositions have been made public, have you seen your experience, in your respective jobs, change? -or have you been treated any differently, since the report on July 25th?

Vindeman offers, "As I stated, I did notice I was being excluded from several meetings that would have been appropriate for my position; so in some respects, there have been reprisals... I'm not sure I could make that judgment..."

-In preparation for the July 25th phone call, is it standard for the National Security Council to provide talking points? (That's correct) -Yes; because the words of the President carry incredible weight; is that not correct? (That is correct.) -So, it's important to ensure that everyone has carefully considered the implications of what the President might say, to a foreign leader? (That is correct.)

-And you are the national Security Council's director, for Ukraine; did you participate in preparing the talking points for the President's call? (I did; I prepare them.) -So, you prepare that; they are then reviewed, and edited, by multiple single officers at the NSC and the White House; is that correct? (That is correct.)

-Did the talking points for the President, contain any discussion of investigations into the 2016 election the Bidens or Burisma? (They did not.) -Are you aware of any written product from the National Security Council, suggesting that investigations into the 2016 election the Bidens or Burisma are part of the official policy of the United States? (No, I'm not.)

Ms. Speier wanted to make sure that it was on the record, that it would never be appropriate for a President; in a call between another country's leader; to ask that foreign leader to open a political investigation.

Vindeman adds, "There are proper procedures in which to do that; certainly, the President is well within his right to do that; it is not something the NSC, certainly directory at the NSC would do. We are prohibited from being involved in any transaction between the Department of Justice, and a foreign power; to ensure that there is no perception of manipulation from the White House.

Mr. Stewart now has the floor:

Stewart heckles in, because he corrected one of the earlier Republican committee members, who had addressed him as "Mr. Vindeman," instead of Lieutenant Colonel Vindeman. So, he explains that he just didn't think that it was quite proper; when he's there in full dress uniform; and besides, it's pretty obvious that Republicans are trying to denigrate the witnesses; so personally, I think that it was appropriate, and a smart thing for Vindeman to do; is to, in effect say, "Call me what I am; a Lieutenant Colonel! Vindeman points out that the attacks on twitter, and in the right-wing media, have been denigrating his character; and so, he felt it important to stand up for himself.

Stewart goes on to mince words, about the word "favor," in Trump's phone call; obviously trying to make it as innocuous as possible; but as Vindeman pointed out; in a power differential such as that; a request for a favor is an order.

Next, Stewart is trying to say, that since neither President has been in the military, that negates the idea that the request is an order; but what

Vindeman was pointing out, is that when there is a power differential, certainly one, as great as there is between the US and Ukraine; where we are Ukraine's largest benefactor; giving them hundreds of millions every year; along with our show of support; the symbolic support that US provides to Ukraine while they're fighting Russia is even more important; it has been argued; so Vindeman was saying that the President saying "do me a favor" to the new President Zelensky, was like a military commander saying, "Will you do me a favor, and drive me over to my meeting," to a soldier in his command.

Stewart questions Vindeman's having made that judgment, to which Vindeman replies, "I've made that judgment, and I stick by that judgment." at which point Stewart says he says, "I gotta tell you, I think it's nonsense," he says, "I was in the military; and I could distinguish between a favor and an order; and so could my subordinates; and I think President Zelensky could too…" {but this still does not change the fact that a soldier should aptly interpret any favor or request asked of them by their commanding officer, the military mandate is that this should be considered as an order; and any favor, that the President of the most powerful country in the world, asks of a very dependent new President of a foreign country fighting Russian opposition, badly needing US help; damned well better consider it as an order, as well!

Zelensky did, in fact, tell Ambassador Taylor, that he already had an interview scheduled with CNN, and he was going to make the desired announcements then; until President Trump's plan got foiled.}

Vindeman says, "The context of this call, consistent with (what he had heard at) the July 10th meeting with Bolton, and with the reporting that was going on; including the President's personal attorney; made it clear, that this was not simply a request."

Stewart argues, that it is not clear; so now, he goes back to how Joe Biden put pressure on Ukraine to fire their corrupt Prosecutor General, in 2015; ranting about how nobody ever in the world, before Biden, had put pressure on a country to fire a corrupt prosecutor… {This has nothing to do with what is going on.} Stewart's time is expired thank God for that.

Now the floor goes to Mr. Quigley:

-Colonel, it's one thing, to ask somebody a favor, like, go pick up my dry cleaning; and it is another, when the commander-in-chief of the most powerful army in the world, asks and ally, who is in a vulnerable position, to do him a favor; is it not? (Vindeman agrees.)

I want to go back to the military assistance, if I could. Ms. Williams, when did you first learn that the security assistance was being held up; the nearly $400 million? (It was referenced on July 3rd.) -And were you aware of any additional; or did you attend any additional meetings, in which that military assistance, being withheld, was discussed? (I did; I attended meetings on July 23rd, and July 26th, where the assistance hold was discussed; and maybe also on the 31st.)

-At that point, did anyone provide a specific reason for the hold, in those meetings? (The OMB reported that the hold was being ordered by the White House Chief of Staff, Mick Mulvaney.) -And did they give reasons, beyond that, that the aid was being withheld by the White House Chief of Staff? (Not specifically; the reason given was that there was an ongoing review, as to whether the funding was still in line with administration priorities.) -Did anyone, in any of those meetings, or in any other subsequent discussion you had, discuss the legality of the withholding the withholding of the aid? (There were discussions, in the July 31st meeting; and possibly prior as well; in terms of Defense Department, and State Department officials looking into how they would handle a situation, in which earmarked funding from Congress, that was designated for Ukraine, would be resolved, if the funding continued to be held; as we approached the end of the fiscal year.) -In your witness, did anyone in the NSC support the withholding of the assistance? (no)

-Colonel, when did you first learn the security assistance was being withheld? (On, or about July 3rd.) -What exactly had you learn, from the State Department, that prompted you to draft a notice on July 3rd? (On, or about July 1st, I became aware of inquiries into the security assistance funding, in general, from the State Department, and the DOD; I believe it was around that date, that OMB put a hold on congressional notification.) -Had you had any earlier indications of this, prior to these general inquiries; and how the funds were being spent? -things of that nature? (Nothing specific.) -Did anyone in the National security community support the withholding the aid? (no) -No one from National Security? (no) -No one from the State Department? (correct) -No one from the Department of Defense? (correct)

-Did anyone raise the legality of withholding? (Yes, it was raised on several occasions.) -Who raised concerns? (So, PCC was, again, where I convene; at my level. There was a July 23rd PCC meeting, that was conducted by Mr. Morrison.)

-Were questions raised, as to the legality of the hold, over the subsequent weeks? (The issue was analyzed; and during the July 26th deputies meeting; so, these were all the departments and agencies; there was an opinion rendered, that it was legal to put the hold on.) -That's interesting; we've been hearing that OMB staff was very concerned that they were taking part in something illegal, if they were to continue the hold; but meanwhile, somewhere around the end of July, the Trump administration; without a legal opinion; which is obviously tailor-made for this administration, and never been used before; that it was legal to withhold this aid, that was appropriated by Congress.

Quigley yields back; and the floor goes to Ms. Stefanik. She says, millions of people have been watching the hysteria of the media… {it's actually the hysteria of the Trump administration that's causing the media to report} They beat the drum again. Ukraine received the aid; and there was no investigation…

{so she goes on about Ukraine corruption, in general; of which this issue has nothing to do with Trump's untoward scheme; and during her rant, she beats the drum about Burisma; referring to the fact that when Obama was President, that in 2014, Burisma was the first company that was investigated; when the US became involved. Again, this has nothing to do with what Trump said, in 2019; and it is not even just what Trump said in 2019; it is what he did; how he commanded all of the people he commanded. This whole scheme that he put together, and managed, and saw through; until it was found out, and foiled, just before the end of the fiscal year; when the funding would expire otherwise.

Well, Stefanik contends that we need to call Hunter Biden to testify at these hearings; but again, this has nothing at all to do with what Trump was leaning on Zelensky to do. In at least one of the past hearings, we heard it explained that Ukraine had passed all of the vetting, for whether the new government was indeed, either non-corrupt; or it was addressing corruption, effectively enough so that they would be deemed worthy of receiving the aid, that has been appropriated; and it was established that they had indeed been deemed deserving of the funds.

So, whatever Stefanik is saying, has no bearing on these matters.

Stefanik, once again points out, that Vindeman had testified that he was director, and he was responsible for Ukraine; and the authority for the National Security Council, and the White House; she wanted to clarify that he reports Tim Morrison. Vindeman responds, (In my advisory capacity; just to clarify; I advise up the chain of command; that is what I do. The chain of command is, Tim Morrison, up to Ambassador John Bolton. the national security advisor to the President of the United States.) -You agree, that the President sets the policy... (Absolutely)

Stefanik says my time has expired. Next, it goes to Mr. Swalwell; who says, Colonel Vindeman, I think the following question; that my colleague from New York didn't ask you, but is relevant; for everybody at home; is it true, that the Department of Defense had already certified, that the anticorruption requirements had been met, when the hold was put on by the President? (That is correct.)

Swalwell sarcastically says that Mr. Jordan said that the President did something none of us expected, when he released the call transcript. -Colonel Vindeman, you listened to the call... Ms. Williams you also listened to the call; is that right? (yes). -Ms. Williams, a lot of other people listened to that call. You read the transcript. How many others listened to that call? (I can't characterize how many; I believe there were 4, 5, or 6 of us in the listening room, at the time.)

-And the transcript was distributed to others; so, the President is asking for us Democrats to give him a gold star, because he released a summary of the transcript, of a call that a number of people listened to. There is a difference, of course, between this, and say, his one-on-one meeting in Helsinki with Putin; where he took the notes from the interpreter, so none of us could see.

-The point being, the President had no choice but to release the call transcript; everyone seems to characterize what exactly, legally, all of this means. Mr. Ratcliffe then points out that no one had used the term "bribery," in any of their depositions… He says, suppose you have a shooting victim; the police respond, after the victim is doing little better; and they ask the victim, tell us what happened; the victim says, well; he shot into the car, and the bullets hit me in the shoulder, and in the back of my neck. Miraculously, I survived; but I can identify the person who pulled the trigger…

The Policeman says, okay, you were shot; you know who it is; but shucks, you didn't tell us that this was an attempted murder! So, we have to let the person go…

Is that how it works in our justice system?! Unless less victims or witnesses have identified the legal theories that the case alleges, we just let people off?!

-Ms. Williams, Vice President Pence was described as a voracious reader of his intelligence readout book; and after President Trump's April 21st call, with President Zelensky, you put a transcript of the call in the Vice President's reading book; and in the Vice President's call to President Zelensky, two days later; and then you told us in a deposition, that he stuck pretty faithfully to what Trump had said in his April 21st call… (I believe his remarks were consistent; but he also spoke on other issues; as well including anticorruption.) -And you would describe the Vice President as someone who would make follow-up calls to world leaders, after the President had done so; is that right? (He has, on occasion; it's not a normal practice; it depends on the situation.) -In that case, he stuck to President Trump's talking points? (I would say, that I provided him talking points, for the call, which included on President Zelensky's inauguration; which President Trump didn't really discuss with us; but the Vice President also discussed other issues with President Zelensky, as well.) t

-The President sets the policy, in the United States, is that right? (yes) -So, after the July 25th call, you put a copy of the transcript into

Vice President Pence's reading book... Then, fast-forward to September 1st; Vice President Trump meets with President Zelensky, is that right? (That's right.) -You're there... (yes) -And President Zelensky meets with Vice President Pence; they talk about a lot of things, but you will agree, that Vice President Pence did not bring up the Bidens; is that correct? (correct) -He did not bring up the investigations; one reasonable explanation is that, although Vice President Pence will do a lot of things for Trump, but he was not willing to bring up investigations of the Bidens, because he thought it was wrong... (I'm not in a position to speculate, but we had discussed those issues.) Swalwell yields back, and it goes to Mr. Hurd:

Hurd asks Williams if she had participated in, or collected any information, over her many conversations, about potential information collected from Ukrainians on the Bidens; to be used for political gain. (she says no, I did not participate, or overhear any conversations along those lines.)

Colonel Vindeman, all of us would agree that you probably made the right move, in coming here. Part of the responsibilities, is developing talking points, for principals... (That's correct.) -I'm assuming you also do that for your direct supervisor, Mr. Morrison... (Mr. Morrison has left the position, some time ago.) -But you prepare talking points for the supervisors? (Frankly, at that level, they don't take talking points; they have expertise; the talking points are more intended for the national security advisor; although Ambassador Bolton doesn't require that expertise either.)

-I'm just trying to establish, does the President always use talking points? (no) -Is President Trump known to stick to the script? Is it odd that he didn't use talking points? (no) -When Zelensky was sworn in, on May 20th; you were part of the delegation... and when Zelensky won the parliamentary election on July 21st; that was when you warned them against getting involved with US domestic politics... (correct) -Then Ambassador Sondland traveled to Ukraine in late August, August 27th; did he take you with him? (he didn't)

-We know, from other witnesses, that he was there; he met with President Zelensky and his staff to talk about (the Ukrainians' progress);

because one of the things that President Zelensky did, during that time, was to change the Ukrainian Constitution, to remove absolute immunity from deputies; from some of their parliamentarians; because it had been a source of corruption, for a number of years. Were you aware of this important change? (yes)

Hurd is pointing out, that there were some anticorruption steps taking place, during this time. Vindeman had earlier testified, that he didn't think there were; but as Hurd reminds him of each of these; like the one about parliament we just discussed; and the establishment of a high anticorruption court, that also took place during that time period.

Vindeman says that he was aware of this; but that he had only met Zelensky during the inauguration trip; with the delegation; never one-on-one with him. There were a lot of people in the room. but Hurd says, yet, you still were able to advise the Ukrainians to watch out for the Russians… (yes)

Hurd then yields back, and the floor goes to Mr. Castro.

Castro quotes the part of the July 25th phone call, where Trump was asking about Crowdstrike, the server; that somebody in Ukraine supposedly had; and then he asserts that this was a defunct conspiracy theory; and that Trump's former homeland security advisor, Thomas Bossert, had called the President's assertion of the Ukrainians intervening in the 2016 election, not only a conspiracy theory; but completely debunked. Castro asks Vindeman, are you aware of any evidence to support the interference of Ukraine, in the 2016 US elections? (Congressman, I'm not; and furthermore, I think this is a Russian narrative, that the President has promoted.)

{it is once again hammered home, that all of our intelligence agencies have determined, that it is the Russians that meddled in the 2016 election.}

Castro says, it's kind of odd, that Trump is promoting a conspiracy theory that helps Russia in two ways: First, it ignores and undermines, but it is not inconsistent, to me; that President Trump would be giving credence to a conspiracy theory about Ukraine, that helps Russia; really, in at least two ways: First, it ignores, and frankly undermines, the assessment of the US intelligence community; and it seeks to weaken

Ukraine, depending upon the United States for support, in order to fight against Russian aggression. Also, for the United States, it hurts our national security, and emboldens Russia.

I want to look at what President Trump was doing on his call, instead of pushing back against Russian aggression. He was pressuring the President of Ukraine to do his political work; Trump's political work; that "there's a lot of talk about Biden's son..." Castor sarcastically says.

-Colonel Vindeman, when you hear those words of President Trump's, on that July 25th phone call, do you hear a well-coordinated, well calibrated foreign policy being carried out? (I do not.) -In fact, it sounds like President Trump was encouraging President Zelensky, to encourage the same kind of behavior; behavior that is merely leading to President Trump's own political benefit; the kind of behavior that we discourage foreign leaders from undertaking, in their own countries. Discouraging the undertaking of politically motivated investigations is, in fact, a major part of official US anticorruption policy... (That is correct.) -And are you aware of any evidence that Vice President Biden improperly interfered in an investigation of his family members? (I am not.)

-These are false narratives; that, it should be said; are damaging to our country; that poison our politics, and distract from the truth... -and pressing another country to engage in corruption is antithetical to who we are, as a nation... ...the Ukrainian judiciary is imperfect, at the moment; and their reliance on US support could conceivably cause them to tip the scales of justice, in favor of finding (an innocent) US citizen guilty; if they thought they needed to do that. So, they could "trump up" whatever false charges that they wanted to, in a corrupt system like that; they could! -And Ukraine is making progress certainly; more broadly; but it is still possible for the state to become involved in judicial processes, and drive them... Castro yields back.

The floor now goes to Mr. Ratcliffe:

Ratcliffe is trying to get Williams to say that she doesn't consider what Trump was saying to Zelensky was a demand. She says, "I don't believe I'm in a position, to characterize it further than the President did; in terms of asking for a favor; I'll just refer you back to the transcript itself...)

-Colonel Vindeman, you testified to this; explain to us why it was a demand, in your mind... {Ratcliffe tries to suggest that Williams wasn't concerned, and therefore didn't report anything she thought was improper, to anyone; whereas, Vindeman had considered it a demand; and he thought that it was improper, and he reported it; but Williams had said, "I made the call transcript available to my superiors..." so, in fact, she really did report it; it's just that the reporting was of the actual wording.

First, Ratcliffe is trying to make some muddled argument that Williams and Vindeman can't make any agreement, as to what happened on the call; but clearly they both are saying the same thing about what happened on the call; and they appear to have done what was appropriate, for each of them to do; in their respective situations.}

Ratcliffe says, "If two people disagree, whether it was, or wasn't a demand... {but that's not really the case; Ms. Williams said that she didn't feel qualified to make that judgment call herself; but of course, she wouldn't be here at these hearings if she didn't think that it was highly inappropriate.}

Ratcliffe yields back; and it goes to Mr. Jordan.

Jordan goes back to this idea of, why didn't Vindeman contact Morrison, instead of Eisner; the lead NSC lawyer? Vindeman asserts that when he made his earlier complaint to Eisner, that Eisner had told him that he could come back with any further complaints. Vindeman explains that it was an extremely busy week; and that he was working extremely long days, that week; they had three important meetings, back to back; and that all of them had required a lot of preparation. He said that he did manage to make contact with two people in the interagency; and he had also tried to make contact with Mr. Morrison.

Vindeman says, "That didn't happen, before I received instructions from John Eisenberg, not to talk to anybody else, any further... Vindeman asserted that his core function is coordination; and that he had spoken only to appropriate people within the agency; and that then;

circling back around; Mr. Eisenberg had come back around to him, and told Vindeman not to talk to anyone, any further, about this situation.

Jordan heckles, "Why didn't you go to your direct report?" etc...

So, next, now Jordan's trying one more time, to get Vindeman to give him information about who else he contacted about his concerns regarding the July 25th call; because perhaps, this could lead the Republicans toward discovering who the whistleblower is; because, between the time that Vindeman had first talked to Eisenberg, and the time that Eisenberg came back around to tell him not to talk about it to anybody else, Vindeman disclosed that he had talked to somebody else in the intelligence community (in the CIA, perhaps); but he can't say; he was advised, by his lawyer, not to say.

Jordan's trying to browbeat him. "You talked to your brother! (Vindeman never said this), you talked to the lawyer (Eisenberg), you talked to George Kent; and you talked to the one guy that Adam Schiff won't let you talk about..."

Jordan is trying to twist his words; implying that Vindeman had blabbed to a bunch of others, even though Eisner had told him not to speak to anyone about it; but Vindeman says, "No; that's incorrect; like I said, there was a time gap between when I first talked to Eisner, and the time that Eisner came back and told me not to tell anybody else; and it was during that time period, that I had told a few other people, that were appropriate for me to tell about it..."

Jordan's time expires; so now it goes to Mr. Heck:

Heck goes back to the July 10th meeting, where Bolton ended the meeting abruptly, because Sondland had said that in order to get the White House meeting, that the Ukrainians would have to make these announcements of investigations. Heck asks Vindeman, how long did it take you, to report to Eisenberg? (Within a couple hours of that meeting, I reported to Eisenberg.)

-How did Eisenberg react? (He was cool and collected; he took notes; and said he would look into it.) -And did he not also tell you to feel free to come back, if you had any additional concern? -Did you report that Ambassador Sondland had told you that, this request to the Ukrainians, had been coordinated by Acting Chief of Staff, Mick

Mulvaney? (I did.) -And what was his reaction? (He said he'll follow-up, or look into it.)

Heck quotes Vindeman's earlier testimony, that there was no doubt, that on that July 25th phone call to President Zelensky, President Trump asked for investigations into the 2016 election, and Vice President Biden's son; in return for a White House meeting.

-Within an hour of that call, you reported that to Mr. Eisenberg; did you not? (Yes, this was the suggestion; it was less of a suggestion; more of an instruction…) Did you tell Eisner, that President Trump had asked President Zelensky to speak to Mr. Giuliani? (yes) {although we can't be entirely sure, it kind of sounds like Vindeman was instrumental in the voicing of the complaint, that perhaps eventually became the information that the whistleblower was so upset about, that they decided to make his complaint.}

Heck continues, "I will have to say, I find it a rich, but an incredibly painful irony, that within a week of the President, contrary to all advice of the senior military officials, he pardons those who were convicted of war crimes; which was widely decried in the military community; but within the week of him doing that, he is engaged in an effort against allies on his behalf; including some here today; to demean your record of service, and the sacrifice, and the contribution you have made. Indeed, Sir, less than 20 minutes ago, the White House officially quoted, out of context, the comments referring to earlier questioning, about the discourse in your judgment… I can only conclude, Sir, that what we thought was just the President; as the subject of our deliberations in this inquiry; it isn't sufficient to capture what's happening here. Indeed, the subject of this inquiry, is what is paramount to our Constitution, and the very values upon which it is based. I want to say thank you for your service; thank you doesn't cut it; but please know however, that it comes from the bottom of my heart; and I know, from the bottoms of the hearts of countless other Americans. Thank you for your service; I yield back.

Unfortunately, it goes, once again, to the inappropriately-abrasive Mr. Jordan: Jordan says, last Sunday Nancy Pelosi called Trump an imposter. Jordan says, the Democrats have never accepted the will of the American people; in terms of Trump having been voted in... {but the truth of the matter is that he lost, by measure of the popular vote; in spite of the fact that he had this hugely-effective disinformation campaign, that Russia was waging all over the Internet; posing as real US citizens; and then saying things that were lies; fabrications that were yet, very convincing to many; and that's why people voted for Trump; because they didn't realize what a sham he was.

We should evolve, and listen to Christopher Steele. Instead, Jordan says, the American people decided to elect Trump on November 8, 2016... {but that's really not true, because he lost the popular vote and many people in the states where he won electoral votes are perhaps, also relatively unsophisticated folks, who were more easily influenced by Russian disinformation campaigns, over the Internet, and through other right wing media sources, such as Fox's six channels; barking out all this bullshit; that's what made people vote for Trump.}

Jordan says, Democrats are contending, that if they don't impeach President Trump, then he will win reelection... {but in fact, that's not really the reason why they elected to impeach him; the Democrats that I heard talking about, having changed over, from not wanting to impeach him because of those very political considerations; to deciding that they did want to impeach him, was because, even though there was a risk of how this might play out politically, they realized that they had a constitutional duty, to impeach a President as lawless as Trump was being, continually, and repeatedly.}

Jordan says the attacks of impeachment started before Zelensky's inauguration; which is true; but that's because there was a 420-page damning report, and a two-and-a-half year-long investigation by Robert Mueller, that showed a hell of a lot of impeachable behavior.}

Jordan says the Russia the collusion investigation started in July of 2016; when the FBI initially opened the investigation, of the Trump Russia collusion; shortly thereafter hiring Robert Mueller, as special counsel; and he alludes to the significant expense of the investigation; but that's just another argument, that Trump has cost this country so much, in so many ways; and then on top of that, we had to spend millions, on a lengthy investigation into so much wrongdoing; and that only covers what Trump and his people had done, before he ever even set foot into office!}

Jordan says, they (Democrats) got nothing… {but they didn't get nothing; they had 420 pages of damning disclosures, and 10 citings of President Trump's obstruction, on top of it!

Jordan is just browbeating away; because, as complicit with this cover-up and denial as he is; Jordan is not interested in confronting Trump's abuse of power, or in any kind of justice, in the matter. He just wants Trump to be at the helm; so they can use him, for the puppet that he's been, for the Republicans to be able to continue forwarding their crooked agenda.

Contrary to what Jordan is spewing, the facts are not on the President's side, in any way, shape or form! Mr. Jordan says, "It's an unfair process…" {Of course, it is even more unfair that these Republican committee members are just protecting a President who is nothing but a lunatic, and a crook!}

Jordan yields back, and it goes to Mr. Welch:

Welch goes back to Adam Schiff's opening statement: "The question before us is this: is it improper, for the President of the United States to demand that a foreign government investigate a United States citizen, and political opponent."

Welch says, "Very well stated. I just listened to Mr. Jordan, as you did as well; and I heard his criticisms of process; nothing really happened; and people are out to get the President… I didn't hear the answer to the question; as to whether it's proper for the President the United States to demand a foreign government to investigate a US citizen, and political opponent; and today, I haven't heard any one of my Republican colleagues address that question, in open display; and I think we have asked questions to go to this.

The facts that have come out during this process, is that we had two Ukraine policies; one was bipartisan, and long-standing; and that was to assist Ukraine, which freed itself from the domination of Russia; to fight corruption, and to resist Russian aggression; is that a fair statement? …to give folks a reminder of the extent of corruption, by way of the legacy of Russia; is it your understanding, that when the prior President Mr. Yanukovich, fled to Russia; into the arms of the Kremlin, he took with him $30-$40 billion of Ukraine's money... and is it your understanding that powerless, but motivated Ukrainians, rose up in protest to this incredible graft; and that abuse by the President... (That is correct.) --That was in May; the revolution of dignity... (correct) -Right; and young people went into that square in downtown Kyiv, and demonstrated for months; and 106 young people died; and other people died; that was between February 18, 2014 and February 20th, including people who were shot by snipers, from the rooftops of buildings... to shoot into that square, and kill, murder, and slaughter those young people; is that your understanding?

(And Ukraine has made a lot of progress since then; in part, due to US support; I thank) my Republican colleagues for a lot of bipartisan work, from your side. Thank you; but our whole commitment was to get rid of corruption; and to stop that Russian aggression; is that correct? (yes) -And that amounts to some of the key pillars; and then Giuliani and Sondland it appears they were involved in foreign policy that was not about that; it was about investigations into Trump's political opponent... (correct)

-We know that if we say, President Trump, if you want to investigate Joe Biden, and Hunter Biden; go ahead; and do it do it hard, do it rough; do it dirty; But don't do it by asking a foreign leader to help you in your campaign...

-My goal in these hearings is to do two things; one is to get an answer to Colonel Vindeman's question; and the second, coming out of this, is for us to let Congress to return to Ukraine policy... for the restoration of democracy, and Ukraine's resistance of Russian aggression. I yield back.

The floor now goes to Mr. Maloney:

Maloney addresses Vindeman and Williams, I've been listening to my Republican colleagues; and they've said just about everything, but contradict any of the substantive testimony that you've given. You may have noticed a lot of complaints, a lot of insinuations, and a lot of suggestions; maybe that the service is somehow not to be trusted; that you are to be questioned about whether you want to become wealthy;

because of some half-baked job offer that the Ukrainians made to you; which you, of course, dutifully reported.

and I guess Mr. Castor's implying that that you would accept a payoff, to become a wealthy, corrupt Ukrainian official, which they've done many times, in the history of Ukraine. They tried to say that you've overstated the importance of your job; as an advisor on the National Security Council, responsible for directing Ukrainian policy; we heard them air out some allegations, with no basis in truth; but they just want to get them out there, and hope maybe that some of those strands of spaghetti will stick on the wall; to keep throwing.

We even had a member of the committee question why you would wear the dress your dress uniform today; even though that dress uniform includes a breastplate that has a combat infantry badge, and a Purple Heart medal. It seems like, if anybody gets to wear uniform, it's somebody who's got a breastplate with those combinations on it.

-So, let's do it again... (to Ms. Williams) -You heard the call with your own ears; not secondhand... your words were that you heard what Trump said on the call... about investigating the Bidens... your words were that it was unusual and inappropriate (yes)

-And Colonel Vindeman, you were at the July 10th White House meeting, where you heard Ambassador Sondland say that... a White House meeting is conditioned, on investigations that you thought were merely political; and you went to the NSC counsel, and you reported it, right? (correct) -And then later, you were on the White House call; you heard it with your own ears; not secondhand; not from somebody else; not hearsay; you heard the President's voice on the call...

Vindeman says, "I did." -And you heard him again, talk about conditioning these investigations; just like you heard in that July 10th meeting from Ambassador Sondland... When you heard Trump say that, what was the first thought in your mind? (Frankly, I couldn't believe what I was hearing; it was probably an element of shock; maybe in certain regards, my worst fear of how our Ukraine policy could play out, was playing out; how this was likely to have significant implications for US national security.) -And you immediately reported it; why? (Because that was my duty.)

Maloney then asks Vindeman to read the second to the last paragraph of his written statement: "That my sitting here today, in the US capital, talking to our elected officials; this is proof (Dad), that you made the right decision, 40 years ago, to leave the Soviet Union, and come to the United States of America; in search of a better life for our family. Do not worry, I will be fine, for telling the truth…"

-Did you realize, when you came forward, out of a sense of duty; that you were putting yourself in direct opposition to the most powerful person in the world? -Did you realize that, Sir? (I knew I was assuming a lot of risk.)

-I was struck by that phrase, "Do not worry," addressing your dad; is he a warrior? (He did serve in the military; it was a different military then.) -And he worried that you were putting yourself up against the President of the United States? Was you father deeply worried about it because, in his context, it was the ultimate risk? -And yet, you had confidence that you can do that; and tell your dad not to worry… (Congressman; because this is America; it is a country I have served and defended; that all of my brothers have served; and here; Right Matters! (Vindeman gets a hand from the audience)

It now goes to Ms. Demmings: She starts out saying that there are no words to express our gratitude to you… (she's addressing Lieutenant Colonel Vindeman) for what you have done for our nation; and amazingly, what you are still willing to do for our nation… It is vitally important that the American people understand how President Trump's unethical demand, that Ukraine deliver politically motivated investigations, in exchange for military assistance; that created a security risk for the United States of America's national interest, and our national security. The President was not playing a political game, by holding up military aid; in meetings with Ukraine; threatening the hundreds of millions of dollars of military assistance, that Congress had appropriate.

-It has a real-life consequence for Ukraine; and for the USA… In your deposition, Colonel Vindeman, you testified, and I quote, "A strong, independent Ukraine is critical to our security interests…" -Could you please explain, why a strong and independent Ukraine is so critical; and why it is so vital to US interests?

Vindeman says, we sometimes refer to Ukraine as our front-line state; it's on the front line of Europe. It is actually described to me, that the Ukrainians that they consider themselves as a barrier between Russia and Europe; and what I've heard them describe, is a need for US support, in their service role; in order to protect European and Western security.

Lieutenant Colonel, this is not just a theoretical conflict between Ukraine and Russia; you've already said this morning, that Russia is actively trying to expand into Ukraine; that Ukraine is in a hot war with Russia right now; is that correct?

Vindeman says, it's stable; but it's still hot war.) -Isn't it true, that even though the security assistance was eventually delivered to Ukraine, the fact that it was delayed; just that fact, could signal to Russia that the bond between Ukraine, and the US was weakening?

Vindeman says, that was the concern, of myself, and my colleagues.) -And was the risk of, even the appearance, that the US Ukraine bond is shaky; that it could embolden Russia, to act with more aggression, would you say? (That's correct. I believe that was my testimony.)

-Just last month, during an interview, President Putin joked about interfering in our elections; and I guess that's what we have become to Russia; and as President, I think he felt emboldened by the President's reckless actions; bold attempts to hold critical military aid from Ukraine; and President Trump's effort to blame Ukraine not Russia for election meddling; Ms. Williams, and Lieutenant Colonel, I can only say that every American, regardless of our politics, should be critically concerned about that; and let me just say this; yes, we do trust the American people; but you know what? -The American people trust us too, as members of Congress; to support, protect, and defend the Constitution of the United States, against all enemies, foreign and domestic; and we intend to do just that!

Ms. Demmings yields back; and the floor goes to Mr. Krishnamoorthi:

He says, Colonel Vindeman, I'm concerned that your loyalties are in question not just because you bring forward efforts of wrongdoing against the President of the United States; but because you're an immigrant. Recently, a Fox News host thinks that because you were born in the Soviet Union, emigrated with your family, your allegiance tends somehow to go with Ukraine; I find this statement reprehensible; because it appears that your immigrant status is just being used against you.

-Lieutenant Colonel, I came to this country when I was three months old; your had family fled the old Soviet Union, and moved to America, when you were just 3 ½ years old, right? (correct) -I understand your father work multiple jobs, while also learning English, right? (correct) -Your father stressed the importance of embracing what it means to be an American, correct? (That is correct.) -All your childhood memories relate to being an American... (correct) -You, and your family, faced difficult times during your childhood, correct? (yes) -I can relate; that's my story too; but your father went on to become an engineer, right? -He reestablished himself in his former profession; in the United States; I can relate; I got a BS in engineering.

Vindeman jokes, regarding his father, "Some people claim that he practices the BS part, now..." (he gets a laugh) -Your father never stopped working hard, to build his American dream, did he? (He did not.) I believe that you, Lieutenant Colonel, and your father have achieved the American dream; and so did your family.

-From one immigrant American, to another American; I want to say to you, that you and your family represent the very best of America. I assume that you are as proud to be an American, as I am, correct? (yes)

Next up is Ms. Demmings:

-Sir, I want to turn your attention to Yuriy Lutsenko; you called him a destructive actor, in your opening statement, correct? (yes) Mr. Lutsenko, the former Prosecutor General, in Ukraine, has made various claims about various Americans, right? (correct) -You are unaware of any factual basis for his accusations of against Ambassador Yovanovitch, right? (correct) -He also was a source for an article by John Solomon, in the Hill, right? (That is correct.)

-And you said, the key elements of that article, as well as his accusations, are false... (correct) -Lutsenko is not a credible source, correct? (correct) -Sir, the other side claims that there was absolutely no pressure, on the July 25th phone call; I think that's what we heard earlier, right? (I believe so.) -And you have termed what President Trump asked, in terms of investigations on the phone call, as a demand, right? (correct) -You pointed out the large power disparity between President Trump, on the one hand, and President Zelensky, on the other, right? (yes) -There was pressure, on that phone call, right? -The Ukrainians subsequently found out, {that in order to get their meeting with President Trump, and their security assistance, they needed to announce the investigations}; so the pressure was brought to bear on them, right? (I believe so.)

-Sir, Colonel Vindeman, last week, we heard a decorated military veteran, namely Ambassador Bill Taylor, come before us. -You interacted regularly with Ambassador Taylor, and you know him to be a man of integrity; and he's a patriotic American; is that right? (A superb individual.) -I asked Ambassador Taylor a series of questions, based on his experience as an infantry commander. I asked him quote, is an officer allowed to hold up an action, placing his troop as at risk until someone provides a personal benefit? Ambassador Taylor responded, no.

Colonel Vindeman, and do you agree with that? (I do.) -I then asked Ambassador Taylor, is that because they would be betraying the responsibilities of the nation? _and Ambassador Taylor responded, yes. Sir, Colonel Vindeman, and you agree with that? (I do.) -I then asked Ambassador Taylor if that type of conduct would trigger a court-martial, and Taylor said yes. Do you agree with that?

Vindeman says, "I do." Ms. Demmings yields back; and now it is time for closing statements:

Mr. Nunez goes for first, as Minority leader. He says:

I'm glad this circus is over, and Democrats are no closer to impeachment than they were three years ago. {I guess that turned out to be bullshit, as they did impeach Trump, within a week after the he says that.} Nunez continues his rant; the Democrats are poisoning Americans; we sat here all day without any evidence {he must have wax in his ears or something; I heard a lot of evidence!} That said, he only had spoken for like, 30 seconds. What a relief!

Now, it's Adam Schiff's turn: He thanks both of them for their time, and their testimony today. He says, I wanted to address briefly, some of the evidence you Presented, as well as others, thus far in these impeachment hearings. First of all, I want to join my colleagues in thanking you, Colonel Vindeman, for your military service; and I should tell you, that notwithstanding all of the questions you got, on why didn't you go talk to your supervisor; why didn't you go talk to Mr. Morrison?

When you go to the National Security Council's lead lawyer, is there something wrong with that?! Are you aware, that we asked Mr. Morrison whether he went to the national security lawyer, right after the call; and he said that he did? We also asked him if he had a problem with you not going to him first. If you had gone to your supervisor, to complain; and then he went directly to the same lawyer; so, I don't see why they are giving you a hard time...

The President may attack you; and others on the right ring TV might attack you; and have. I thought you should know, and you know already, that this is what the former Chairman of the joint Chief of Staff said, "Lieutenant Colonel Vindeman is a professional, a patriotic and loyal officer. He has made an extraordinary contribution to the security of our nation; in both peacetime and war.

I'm sure your dad is proud to hear that my colleagues have tried to make the arguments today you heard of before; that the President was just interested in fighting corruption; that's our goal; fighting corruption in Ukraine; this terribly corrupt country... The problem, of course, is that is that there is no evidence of the President trying to fight corruption; the evidence all points in the other direction!

All the evidence points to the President inviting Ukraine to participate in the corrupt action of investigating a US political opponent of Trump's. Ambassador Yovanovitch was known as a strong fighter of corruption; so, what does the President do? He recalls her from her post; and Ambassador Yovanovitch, in fact, was at a meeting, celebrating other anticorruption fighters; including a woman who had acid thrown in her face; on the day she was told to get on the next plane back to Washington.

You prepared talking points for the President's session with Zelensky; he was supposed to talk about rooting out corruption; if this

President has such a deep concern about corruption in Ukraine; surely, he would've brought that up in the call. Of course, we now know, that he did not.

We then see Rudy Giuliani, not fighting corruption, but asking for investigations of the Bidens. My colleagues say that maybe he was acting on his own; even though he says he is acting as the President's lawyer; that the two investigations that Rudy Giuliani wanted, come up in the meeting you participated in on July 10th, at the White House with Ambassador Bolton. Gordon Sondland brings up Bidens, Burisma, and 2016; and says that if you Ukrainians want a meeting with the White House, you have to do these investigations.

Now, Republicans would say that Ambassador Sondland was acting on his own; but that doesn't work either, because we have the call record from July 25th. The President was forced to release the call record, in which the President doesn't bring up corruption; he doesn't say, how are those anticorruption courts going? -or great work! What does the President say? I want you to investigate the Bidens, and this debunked theory, which was advanced by Vladimir Putin; but it also helps me in my reelection; so much for fighting corruption… The message to Ukraine; the real message to Ukraine; our US policy message is: Don't engage in political investigations. The message from the President was the exact opposite; to engage in political investigations; and do it for my reelection.

-And it's also made clear, that if they want a White House meeting; if they want 400 million and US aid, this is what they have to do. The only lament I hear from my colleagues, is that it wasn't successful; they got caught. They didn't get the political investigations, and they still had to release the money. They still haven't had the White House meeting; but they had to release the money.

The whistleblower blew the whistle; the whistleblower the President wants to punish; because Congress announced it was doing investigations, very soon thereafter. The President was forced to lift the hold on the aid.

They argue well, this makes it okay; that it was a failed effort to bribe Ukraine; a failed effort to extort Ukraine. It doesn't make it better; it's no less odious because it was discovered, and it was stopped.

And we have courageous people like yourselves, who come forward to report things, and do what they should do; they have the sense as you put it Colonel, of duty; of duty not to the person of the President; to the Presidency, and to the country and we thank you for it.

At the end of the day, I think this all comes back to something we heard from another career foreign service officer just last Friday (David Holmes); in a conversation he overheard with the President; at a restaurant in Ukraine, in which the President; not Rudy Giuliani; not anyone else; the President of the United States wanted to know, are they going to do these investigations?

This was the day after the July 25th call; are they going to do the investigations? and Ambassador Sondland said yes, they are going to do it; and what does Gordon Sondland relate to that foreign service officer? -after he hangs up from the call? The President doesn't give an (expletive) about Ukraine; he only cares about the big things, that help his personal interests.

That's all you need to know; and it isn't just about Ukraine, of course; Ukraine is fighting our fight, against the Russians; against their expansionism. That's our fight; so that's why we're supporting Ukraine; for the military aid that the President may not care about, but we do we care about the defense of our allies; and we care about our Constitution. We are adjourned.

Intelligence Committee hearing #4-
Volker and Morrison

This second session, on the same day that Lieutenant Colonel Vindeman and Jennifer Williams' had testified; was an afternoon hearing, with testimony and questioning of Ambassador Kurt Volker, the State Department Special Envoy to Ukraine (the Special Representative for Ukrainian Negotiations), and Tim Morrison, the former Senior Director at the National Security Council (former National Security Council advisor).

Adam Schiff starts off: This afternoon we will hear from two witnesses requested by the minority. I appreciate the minority's request for these two important witnesses, as well as Secretary David Hale, who we will hear from tomorrow. As you heard from other witnesses, when Joe Biden had considered entering the race for the presidency, in early 2019, the President's personal lawyer, Rudy Giuliani, began a campaign to weaken Vice President Biden's candidacy, by pushing Ukraine to investigate him, and his son. In order to clear away any obstacles to this, President Trump ordered the recall of Marie Yovanovitch, the American Ambassador to Ukraine, even as she was over in Ukraine pushing anticorruption efforts. President Trump also canceled Vice President Mike pence's participation in the inauguration of President Zelensky on May 20th. Instead, he sent a delegation headed by Energy Secretary Rick Perry, Ambassador Kurt Volker, and Gordon Sondland; the "three amigos." These three returned from Kyiv, and briefed President Trump on their encouraging first interactions with the new Ukrainian administration, in the hopes that President Trump would agree to an early meeting with the Ukrainian President.

Their hopes were soon diminished however, when Trump pushed back. According to testimony, Mr. Volker believed President Trump was skeptical; and he had always said, that's not what I hear; all I hear, you know he's got some terrible people around him. President Trump also said that Ukraine tried to take him down. He told the three amigos, to talk to Rudy; and they did. One of those conversations took place a week before the July 25th phone call, between President Trump and President Zelensky. Ambassador Volker had breakfast with Rudy Giuliani, at the Trump Hotel; and Mr. Volker has testified that he pushed back on Giuliani's accusation against Joe Biden. On July 22nd, just days before Trump would talk to President Zelensky, Ambassador Volker had a telephone conference with Rudy Giuliani and Andre Yermak; who is the top advisor to President Zelensky, so that Giuliani could be introduced to Yermak. Then, on July 25th, the same day as the call between Presidents Trump and Zelensky, just before the call took place, Ambassador Volker sent a text message to Yermak saying, quote heard from the White House; assuming President Z convinces Trump he will investigate/get to the bottom of what happened in 2016, we will nail down a date for a visit in Washington. Good luck!

Later that day, Donald Trump would have the now infamous phone call with President Zelensky, in which he responded to Ukraine's appreciation for US defense support, and a request by President Zelensky, to buy more Javelin anti-tank missiles, by saying that "I would like you to do us a favor, though…" and the favor involved two investigations Giuliani had been pushing for; into the Bidens and the 2016 election interference; a debunked conspiracy theory, nonetheless. Ambassador Volker was on the call. When asked what it reflected, he testified that no leader of the United States should ask a foreign leader to help interfere in the US election.

Among us today, listening in on the 25th call, is Tim Morrison; who had taken over as Senior Director for European affairs at the NSC, only days before. He had been briefed by his predecessor, Fiona Hill, about the irregular second channel, that was operating in parallel to the official one. Lieutenant Colonel Vindeman, and Miss Williams; from whom we heard this morning; just like them, Mr. Morrison emerged from the call, troubled. He was concerned enough about what he heard on that July 25th call, that he went to see the NSC legal advisor, soon after it ended.

Lieutenant Colonel Vindeman feared that the President had broken the law potentially; but Mr. Morrison said his concern was that the call could be damaging, if the transcript were leaked. Soon after this discussion with lawyers at the NSC, the call record was hidden away, on a secure server used to store highly classified intelligence; where it remained until late September, when the call record was publicly released. Following the July 25th call Ambassador Volker worked with the new Ukrainian President's close advisor, Andre Yermak, to develop a statement that would satisfy Giuliani; but when Yermak sent over a draft that still failed to include the specific words Burisma, and the 2016 election interference investigation announcements, Giuliani said that the statement would lack credibility.

Ambassador Volker then added both Burisma, and 2016, to the draft statement. Volker and Morrison, by late July, were aware that the security assistance had been cut off; at the direction of President Trump and acting White House Chief of Staff, Mick Mulvaney. As the Ukrainians became aware of the suspension of security assistance; and negotiations over the scheduling of the White House meeting between Trump and Zelensky dragged on; pressure increased, and the pretense that there was no linkage, soon dropped away. Mr. Morrison had accompanied Vice President Pence to Warsaw, on September 1st, where Pence and Zelensky met; and Zelensky had indeed raised the issue of the suspended security assistance. Following that meeting, Ambassador Sondland has testified that he approached Mr. Yermak, to tell him that he believed that what could help move the aid, was if the Ukrainian Prosecutor General would go to the microphone, and announced that he was opening these investigations.

On September 7th, Ambassador Sondland had a telephone call with President Trump, and asked him what he wanted from Ukraine? According to Mr. Morrison, Gordon Sondland had told him that

President Trump insisted there was no quid pro quo; but that President Zelensky must personally announce the opening of the investigations; that he should want to do it; and Trump also said that if President Zelensky didn't agree to make a public statement about the investigations, the US and Ukraine would be at a stalemate; obviously meaning that Ukraine would not be receiving its much-needed security assistance. Mr. Morrison had a sinking feeling after the call, as he realized that what was being asked, was now being directed at President Zelensky himself, and not merely at the Prosecutor General; as had been relayed to a senior aide in Warsaw on September 1st. So, President Trump had claimed that there was no quid pro quo, his insistence that Zelensky himself must publicly announce the investigations, or they'd be at a stalemate, made clear that, at least two official acts; the White House meeting, and $400 million in military aid; was conditioned upon receiving what Trump wanted; investigations to help his campaign.

As the efforts to secure the investigations continued for several more days, what appeared to abruptly end it, was soon after three committees of Congress announced investigations into the Trump/Giuliani Ukraine scheme. Only then was the aid released.

I now recognize ranking member Nunez for his opening remarks.

Nunez starts out, welcome back to today's circus act. {The way I figure it, he just can't have absolutely no idea that this is a very serious offense against the country, that President Trump has just blithely seen fit to plot and go forward with, at the peril of US support for Ukraine fighting Russia; he must be the one giving the circus act! He can't possibly not know that; so everything that he's saying therefore it's just bull; that it's a spin, so that people watching, who are not sophisticated enough to understand that Republicans are only backing Trump, and defending against this confrontation by the Democrats merely because, with Trump at the helm, these Republican lawmakers get their agenda forwarded; even if Trump is a narcissistic maniac!}

(At this point, I have to interrupt the transcription, for a bit of an aside):

Trump has rubberstamped just about every last little bit of the conservative agenda; which it seems, is mostly is against the interests of the common man in this country; if you look more closely. -Things like taking away our tax deductions for mortgage interest; taking away women's rights to choose among their reproductive options; nixing initiatives to develop clean energy resources, and instead, subsidizing and promoting drilling for oil and fracking for natural gas; bringing back coal mining and readily allowing the pollution that comes with it; rolling back dozens of regulations like water pollution standards for businesses dumping pollutants and contaminating the waters that we need to live in, and around; approving dozens of harmful chemicals by the EPA, and abolishing chemical polluting standards, including re-allowing pesticide spraying that causes kids brain damage; relaxing new standards put in place after the horizon Gulf oil spill, so it could much more easily happen again; relaxing banking standards put in place after the 2008 investment crash, so that now the same crisis could much more easily happen again; repeal of the time-and-a-half pay for overtime rule; I could go on and on; you get the picture...

-And promoting this agenda not only satisfies Republican lawmakers, but it enriches them, in ways that we perhaps can't see too easily, as ordinary citizen; but (un)rest assured, there are rewards for Senators, who, as part of the Senate majority party currently banding together; to act in solidarity, one hundred percent against their (only reasonable) Democratic colleagues on the other side of the aisle.

-And in the process of Republicans' passing of toxic bills, such as reversal of increased fuel emissions standards and tax cuts for the rich; I wouldn't be surprised if they also were getting secretive kickbacks, in one form or another; maybe from well-paid lobbyists, lobbying sitting Senators to pass certain bills and laws that give a tremendous advantage to big businesses, while hurting the rest of us; and pandering to special interest groups like the NRA, obviously providing some incentive to Republican lawmakers, for things like killing gun control legislation, for example. -But since there's no visible proof of these various forms of kickbacks and masked enrichment of Senators, that's readily available to the public; and since Facebook is influenced by big money, to refuse to weed out disinformation ads, Republicans elect and protect a crook like Trump; and it will go on perpetually until the electorate wises up, I suppose.

So, when Nunez comes up with all of these bullshit contentions, about how what the Democrats are doing is not justified, and such, he is simply protecting Republican lawmakers' ability to have their unfair agenda executed, against the interests of the common man; ever continuing to be put forth; as long as the Republican majority exists in the Senate. Our only hope, at least for the short term, is that much of what I am alluding to will become somewhat clear to most Americans, by the time of the upcoming November election. We had better have been able to get rid of Trump by then; or before!

Anyway, back to my impeachment hearing summary:

Then, Nunez says that impeachment is the purview of the Judiciary Committee; not the intelligence committee. {but the Justice Department, under Bill Barr, would not investigate and look into this wrongdoing on the President's part, once the whistleblower complaint came out; so the House's intelligence committee was left to gather intelligence, on their own; regarding this scheme, and the people involved, and their advisors and assistants, who had some knowledge of what was going on, were upset by it, and felt they had a duty to come forward and testify before Congress; despite Trump's across-the-board prohibition.

The intelligence committee was left to do this investigation; William Barr would not open an investigation because he's protecting Trump, and has been complicit in participating in this outrageous obstruction of Congress; this complete stonewalling of Congress; decrying that all witnesses and all documentation will be withheld from Congress}.

Nunez continues; {Has the media really spent three years representing Trump as a Russian agent, as Nunez now suggests?! I don't think so; I think that what the media has been saying is that, it is oddly coincidental, that most of the statements and attempted actions on Trump's part, as President, have inured to the benefit of Russia; and it certainly could appear to many of us, that Trump is complicit with Russian leadership objectives; and in aiding Vladimir Putin in particular.

Trump has had many phone calls with Putin; some of these private; he met with Putin in Helsinki, and told the world of his belief that Putin did not interfere in the election; and that he believes Putin, over his own intelligence agencies; which have all said that, in fact, it was Russia that embarked on this huge far-reaching campaign of disinformation; all across the Internet and the airwaves of conservative media; that greatly helped Trump gain a lot more votes than he would have gotten otherwise.

So, when Nunez says, (as he has several times already, during the course of these hearings), that Trump was "duly elected," this is very disputable, of course).

Nunez now says that Democrats are trying to "discover" the truth; but the fact of the matter is, that Democrats discovered the truth a couple of months ago; and they have merely achieved verification, and corroboration, in the form of the testimony of multiple officials who are all saying the same thing about what Trump did. These hearings are now to explain it to the American people; but of course, Nunez is desperate to twist attention away from that!

Nunez says Democrats don't seem to understand that the President alone has the prerogative to set foreign policy, {but the truth is that Trump had already approved the official foreign-policy; basically the same foreign policy that Trump signs off on every year; which of course, is very similar to foreign-policy that has always been carried out, toward Ukraine, at least since 2014.

So, Trump was actually going forward with an alternate scheme, that yet, goes against his own stated foreign policy; which he had personally approved. I believe he has to approve it every year; although would be interesting to discover when the last time it was that he signed off on the current stated foreign policy that is being routinely carried out, by Foreign Service officers in Ukraine. Wouldn't it be interesting, if he had signed off on it, in January; and then later in that same month, he started this campaign to smear Yovanovitch; which was the first step in pressuring Zelensky.

A bit of history; it was Poroshenko, the previous Ukrainian President, who had originally committed to announcing the opening of these investigations, that Trump wanted; and that was the plan; until he suddenly got defeated in the spring election, by Zelensky, in mid-plan. Poroshenko was actually widely-expected to remain as President; it was a real upset, that Zelensky had instead won the election in April, in a landslide victory, yet! It was surprising especially since Zelensky had never even been in politics before! -He had merely played a convincing role, in a TV series in Ukraine; the role of the country's President. Had Poroshenko stayed in power, Marie Yovanovitch still would have needed to be gotten out of the way; but it was a major complication, when Zelensky took over instead, because Trump knew Zelensky wouldn't be as easily goaded into making bogus announcements, so a pressure campaign to lean on him, had to be hatched now}.

As I listen further, I have to agree that Nunez does have a point; that whenever we hear from the witnesses, it is usually something we are hearing for the second or third time, at this point; and it would have been much better if repetition of these messages wasn't quite so pervasive; and instead, the hearing format was a considerably-more-concise process, for the public.

Nunez talks again about corruption in Burisma; hardly germane here. Then, Nunez has the nerve to say that the July 25th Presidential phone call boiled down to an "unremarkable" conversation. On the contrary, I would say that, since we are hearing from several officials who thought that the conversation was remarkable enough that they had to go to their superiors, including the top lawyer in the administration, to complain about it; out of their "sense of duty" to report Presidential misconduct; only an idiot would not think it unremarkable. (I am not saying Nunez is an idiot; rather that he knows damned well that this scheme is remarkably crooked; he just needs to try and hide that fact, in order to keep getting his Republican benefits, at the expense of the common man in this country.

Nunez feigns concern, that if we if Democrats say that Zelensky was indeed feeling a lot of pressure, then necessarily that means we are, at the same time, "offendingly" accusing Zelensky of lying; and he thinks that this is such a terrible thing for Democrats to do. However, isn't it more terrible if Zelensky is lying because he's afraid to be honest; and the Trump administration has basically terrorized him into falling in line, and saying anything the Trump administration wants him to, in order to ensure continuing support from the US?

Nunez says that the Democrats have accused Trump of blackmailing President Zelensky, even though he didn't even know the aid was being withheld; but the facts are, as we've already determined in prior hearings, that President Zelensky did in fact know, at very least, 10 days before the aid was ultimately released; that he was being asked (Vindeman explains it was being "demanded" of him), to announce these investigations, if he wanted help from the US to continue. Nunez finally yields back, after all his bullshit.

Now it is time for Volker and Morrison to give their opening statements:

Adam Schiff starts by making a short introduction describing the two witnesses' positions, and their background: We are joined this afternoon by Ambassador Kurt Volker and Mr. Timothy Morrison. Ambassador Volker has served in the Foreign Service for nearly 30 years, working on European and Eurasian political and security issues; under five different Presidential administrations. During the George W. Bush administration, he served as acting director of European and Eurasian affairs, at the National Security Council. He was Deputy Assistant Secretary of State for European and Eurasian affairs. In July of 2017, Ambassador Volker was appointed to be the US special representative to Ukraine negotiations, until he resigned in September.

It's a pleasure to welcome Tim Morrison back to the legislative branch, where he served almost 2 decades as a Republican staffer. He is a professional staff member who represented Mark (?) of Minnesota, and Senator John Kyle, of Arizona; but later, Mr. Morrison served as long-time Policy Director for the Republican staff, of the House armed services committee. in July of 2018, Mr. Morrison joined the national Security Council as Senior Director for Countering Weapons of Mass

Destruction. Following the departure of Dr. Fiona Hill in July 2019, Mr. Morrison assumed the position of Senior Director for Russia…

The witnesses are sworn in, and then they read their opening statements:

(Tim Morrison goes first) Chairman Schiff, Ranking member Nunez, and members of the committee; I'm here for you today, under subpoena, to answer questions about my time as Senior Director for European affairs, at the White House, and The National Security Council; to provide you the most complete and accurate information I can assist with. Whether the conduct, that is the subject of this inquiry, merits impeachment; is a question for the US House of Representatives. I am here only to provide factual information, based upon my knowledge and recollection of events.

I will not waste time restating the details of what I stated in my deposition on October 31st, but I will highlight the following points: First, as I previously stated I do not know who the whistleblower is; nor do I intend to speculate as to who the individual may be. Second, I have great respect for my colleagues in the NSC and the rest of the interagency. I'm not here today to question their character, or integrity. My recollections and judgments are my own. My colleagues' recollections of conversations and interactions may differ from mine; but I do not view those differences as the result of an untoward purpose. Third, I continue to believe Ukraine is on the front lines of the strategic competition between the West, and Vladimir Putin's Russia. Russia is a failing power, but it is still a dangerous one. US aid to Ukraine, is for the United States to aid the Ukrainian people, so they can fight Russia, over there; so we don't have to fight a war, ourselves.

Support for Ukraine's territorial integrity and their sovereignty has been a bipartisan objective, since Russia's military invasion in 2014; and it must continue to be. As I stated during my deposition, I feared, at the time of the call on July 25th, how its disclosure would play out in Washington's political climate. My fears have been realized. I understand the gravity of these proceedings, but I beg you not to lose sight of the military conflict underway in eastern Ukraine today, the ongoing illegal occupation of Crimea, and the importance of reforming Ukraine's politics and economy.

Every day that the focus of discussion involving Ukraine is centered on these proceedings, is a day when we're not focused on the interests of Ukraine, United States, and the western goals we share. Finally, I concluded my service at the National Security Council, the day after I last appeared for you. I left the NSC completely of my own volition; I felt no pressure to resign, nor have I feared any retaliation. I made this career choice sometime before I decided to testify on October 31ˢᵗ. I am prepared to answer your questions, to the best of my ability.

Next, Kurt Volker gives his opening statement:

Thank you very much for the opportunity to provide this testimony today. As you know, I was the first person to come forward to testify, as part of this inquiry. I'm here today voluntarily, and I remain committed to cooperating fully and completely with this committee. All I can do is provide the facts, as I understood them at the time. I did this on October 3ʳᵈ, in private, and I'm doing so again today. Like many others who have testified at this inquiry, I am a career foreign policy professional. I began my career as an as an intelligence analyst for Northern Europe, for the Central Intelligence Agency, in 1986; before joining the State Department in 1988. I served in diplomatic posts primarily focused on European political and security issues, for over 20 years; under Presidents Ronald Reagan, George HW Bush, Bill Clinton, George W. Bush, and Barack Obama. My last three positions before leaving the Senior Foreign Service in 2009; where I was director for NATO and West European Affairs at the National Security Council, Principal Deputy Secretary of State for European Affairs, at the State Department; and finally, as US Ambassador to NATO, in the spring of 2017. Then-Secretary-of-State Tillerson asked if I would come back to government service, as US Special Representative for Ukraine Negotiations. I did this on a part-time voluntary basis, with no salary paid by the US taxpayer; simply because I believed it was important to serve our country in this way.

I believed I could steer US policy, and provide direction. For over two years as US special representative for Ukraine negotiations, by seeing my singular focus, I was advancing the foreign policy and national security interests of the United States. In particular, that meant pushing back on Russian aggression, and supporting the development of a strong, resilient, Democratic, and prosperous Ukraine; one that overcomes the legacy of corruption, and becomes integrated into a wider transatlantic community. This is critically important for US national security. If we can stop, and reverse rapid aggression in Ukraine, we can prevent elsewhere. If Ukraine, the cradle of civilization; predating Moscow; succeeds as a freedom-loving, prosperous, and secure democracy, this gives us an enormous hope that Russia may one day change; and there could be a better life for the Russian people; overcoming this current play of totalitarianism, corruption, and aggression toward neighbors; and threats to NATO, and the United States.

The stakes for the United States, for a successful Ukraine, could not be higher. At no time was I aware of, or took part in an effort in order to urge Ukraine to investigate former Vice President Biden. As you know, from the extensive real-time documentation I have provided, Vice President Biden was not a topic of our discussions. I was not on the July 25th phone call, between President Trump and President Zelensky. I was not made aware of a reference to Vice President Biden, or his son, by President Trump. I was not made aware of a reference to Burisma, until the transcript of that call was released on September 25th. From July 2017, to September 27, 2019, I was lead diplomat, dealing with Russia's war in Ukraine.

My role was not some irregular channel, but the official channel. I reported directly to Secretary of State Tillerson, and Secretary Pompeo. I kept the National Security Advisor, and the Secretary of Defense well-informed of my efforts, and worked personally with Ambassador Yovanovitch, Assistant Secretary Wes Mitchell, and his successor; and also with Senior Director Hill, and her successor, Acting Secretary Phil Rieger; as well as Deputy Assistant Secretary George Kent. I also worked with Deputy Assistant Secretary of Defense Laura Cooper, and NSC Director Alex Vindeman; and many, many others. I've known many of them for several years, in a team effort, until Ambassador Yovanovitch left Kyiv.

I identified and recommended Bill Taylor to Secretary Pompeo, so we would still have a strong, seasoned professional on the ground. For two years, before the events at the heart of this investigation took place, I was a Senior US diplomat, enlisting in the conflict zone; meeting with victims of Russia's aggression, and urging the increase of US security assistance, including legal defensive weapons. Working with Ukrainian President Poroshenko; and then with his successor, President Zelensky; and their teams.

I worked with France, and Germany, and Normandy, pressing for support from NATO, the EU, and OSCE. I supported the OSCE Special Monitoring Mission, engaging in negotiations with Russian officials. At the time I took the position, in the summer of 2017, there were major complicated questions swirling in public debate about the direction of US policy toward Ukraine. When the administration levied sanctions against Russia, it was some kind of grand bargain with Russian, in which we traded recognition of Russia's seizure of Russian territory for some other deal in Syria, or elsewhere within the administration. When the administration recognized Russia's claimed annexation of Crimea, this has just become another frozen conflict. There were also a vast number of vacancies in key diplomatic positions; so, no one was really representing the United States, in the negotiating process about ending the war in eastern Ukraine.

During over two years of my tenure, as Special Envoy Representative, we fundamentally turned US policy around. US policy toward Ukraine was strong, consistent, and enjoyed support across the administration; bipartisan support in Congress, and support among our allies in Ukraine. We changed the language, however, used to describe Russia's aggression. I was the administration's most knowledgeable figure, highlighting Russia's invasion and occupation of parts of Ukraine; calling out Russia's responsibility to end this war. This is a war where, 13 times, I visited the war zone; three times meeting with soldiers and civilians alike; always bringing media with me, to try to raise the public visibility of Russia's aggression, and the humanitarian impact on the lives of citizens of the Donbas.

We coordinated closely with our European allies, and Canada; gaining a united front against Russian aggression; and for Ukraine's democracy reform, sovereignty, and territorial integrity. Ukraine policy is perhaps the one area where the US and its European allies had been in lockstep. This coordination helped to strengthen US sanctions against Russia, and to maintain EU sanctions as well; along with those in the administration that strongly advocated for defensive arms in Ukraine. I advocated for increasing US security assistance to Ukraine, and urged other countries to follow suit. My team and I drafted the Pompeo declaration of July 25th, in 2018; in which the Secretary clearly and definitively laid out the US policy, of nonrecognition of Russia's claimed annexation of Crimea.

I engaged with other allies of Ukraine, with Russia and Ukraine, and engaged in negotiations to implement the Minsk agreements; holding a firm line on insisting on the withdrawal of Russian forces, the dismantling of the so-called People's Republic, and restoring Ukrainian sovereignty, and territorial integrity.

Together with others in the administration, we kept US policy steady, through Presidential and parliamentary elections in Ukraine; and worked hard to strengthen the US-Ukraine bilateral relationship, under the new President and government; helping shepherd-in a peaceful transmission of power in Ukraine.

In short, just two years ago, most observers would have said the time is on Russia's side. By 2019 when I departed, we turned the tables, and time was now on Ukraine's side. It's a tragedy for the United States, and Ukraine, that our efforts in this area; which were bearing fruit; have now been thrown into disarray.

One of the critical aspects of my role as US special representative; as the most senior US official appointed to work solely on the Ukraine portfolio, I needed to step forward to provide leadership. If we needed to adopt a policy position, I made the case for it; if anyone needed to speak out publicly, I would do it. When we failed to get a timely statement about Russia's illegal attack on Ukraine's neighbor and seizure of Ukraine, I sent a tweet about it; in order to get them to act. I knew it was my job to try and fix it; that was my perspective.

When I learned, in May of 2019, that we had a significant problem, which was impeding our ability to strengthen support for Ukraine's new President, and his effort to wrap up Ukraine's fight against corruption and his implementation of new reforms, I found myself faced with a choice, to be aware of the problem and endure; or to accept that it was my responsibility to try and fix it. I tried to fix it. The problem was that, despite the unanimous positive assessment and recommendations of those of us who were part of the US Special Delegation that attended the inauguration of President Zelensky, President Trump was receiving a different narrative about Ukraine and President Zelensky. That narrative was filled with accusations from Ukraine's then-Prosecutor General; and conveyed to the President by former mayor Giuliani. As I previously told this committee, I became aware of the negative effect this was having on our policy efforts.

Fourteen of us were present at President Zelensky's inauguration. Then, shortly afterward, back in Washington, this group met with President Trump, on May 23rd. We stressed our finding, that President Zelensky represented the best chance for getting Ukraine out of the mire of corruption; and we urged him to invite President Zelensky to the White House.

The President was very skeptical, given Ukraine's history of corruption; that's understandable. He said that Ukraine was a corrupt country, full of terrible people. He said, "They tried to take me down." In the course of that conversation, he referenced conversations with mayor Giuliani. It was clear to me, that despite the positive news and recommendations at that meeting, made by this official delegation, about the new President, President Trump had a deeply-rooted negative view of Ukraine; rooted in the past. He was receiving other information, from other sources; including mayor Giuliani; that was more negative; causing him to retain this negative view. Within a few days, on May 29th,

President Trump signed a congratulatory letter to President Zelensky, which included an invitation for the President To visit him at the White House. However, four weeks passed, and we could not nail down a date.

I came to believe that the President's long-held negative view toward Ukraine was causing hesitation in actually scheduling a meeting. Much as we had seen in our Oval Office discussion, after weeks of reassuring Ukrainians that it was just due to scheduling issues, I decided to tell President Zelensky that we had a problem with the information reaching President Trump, by mayor Giuliani. I did so in a bilateral meeting, at a conference on Ukrainian economic reform; in Toronto on July 2nd, 2019; where I led the US delegation. I suggested that he call President Trump directly, in order to renew their personal relationship, and to assure President Trump that he was committed to investigating, and fighting corruption; things on which President Zelensky had based his Presidential campaign. I was convinced that getting the two Presidents to talk with each other, would overcome the negative perception of Ukraine, that President Trump still harbored. President Zelensky's senior aide, Andre Yermak, approached me several days later, to ask to be connected to mayor Giuliani.

I agreed to make that connection. I did so, with the desire that the new Ukrainian leadership wanted to convince those like Rudy Giuliani, who believed such a negative narrative about Ukraine, that times have changed; that under President Zelensky, Ukraine is worthy of US support. Ukrainians believed that if they could get their own narrative across, in a way that convinced mayor Giuliani that they were serious about fighting corruption, and corruption reform, then mayor Giuliani would convey that assessment to President Trump; thus, correcting the previous negative narrative. That made sense to me, and I tried to be helpful. I made clear to Ukraine, that mayor Giuliani was a private citizen; the President's personal lawyer; and he was not representing the US Government. Likewise, in my conversations with mayor Giuliani, I never considered him to be speaking on the President's behalf, or giving instruction, rather the information flow being the other way around; from Ukraine to mayor Giuliani; in hopes that this would clear up the information reaching President Trump.

On July 10th, after hearing from Mr. Yermak, I wrote to mayor Giuliani, and proceeded to get together; and finally, on July 19th, we met for breakfast, for a longer discussion. At that meeting, I told Mr. Giuliani that, in my view, the Prosecutor General, with whom he had been speaking; Mr. Lutsenko; was not credible; he was acting in a self-serving capacity. To my surprise, mayor Giuliani said that he had already come to that conclusion. Mr. Giuliani also mentioned all the accusations about Vice President Biden; and about interference in the 2016 election. He stressed that all he wanted, was to see that Ukraine would investigate what happened in the past; and apply its own laws concerning the allegations.

I stressed that no one in the new team governing Ukraine, had anything to do with anything that may have happened in 2016. They were making television shows, at the time! I also said that it was not credible to me, that Vice President Biden would have been influenced, in any way, by financial or personal matters, in carrying out his duties as Vice President. A different issue is whether some individual Ukrainians may have attempted to influence the 2016 election; or thought they could buy influence; that was at least plausible, given Ukraine's reputation for corruption. -But the accusation that Vice President Biden had acted inappropriately, did not seem at all credible to me. After that meeting, I connected mayor Giuliani and Mr. Yermak; by text, and later by phone. They met, in person, on August 2nd, and I had conversations with them, following that meeting; which I did not attend.

Mr. Giuliani said that he had stressed the importance of Ukraine conducting investigations into what had happened in the past; and Mr. Yermak told Mr. Giuliani that he had stressed the importance of his government's program to root out corruption, and implement reforms; and that they would be conducting investigations, as part of this this process.

Mr. Giuliani had said he believed the Ukrainian President needed to make a statement about fighting corruption; and that he had discussed this with Mr. Yermak. I said that I did not think that would be a problem, since it is the government's position, anyway.

I followed up with President Zelensky, and he said that indeed, he would be prepared to make a statement; he said it would reference Burisma and 2016, in a wider context of bilateral relationships and rooting out corruption. Anyway, there was no mention of Vice President Biden. Rather than referencing Burisma and the 2016 election interference, it was clear to me that Mr. Yermak was only talking about whether and Ukrainians had acted inappropriately. At this time, I was focused on our goal of getting President Zelensky and President Trump to meet with each other; and I believed that their doing so would overcome the chronically-negative view that President Trump had, toward Ukraine. I was seeking to solve the problem that I saw, when we had met with President Trump in the Oval Office, on May 23rd. As a professional diplomat, I was comfortable exploring whether there was a statement Ukraine could make about its own attention to investigating possible corruption, that would be helpful in convincing Mr. Giuliani to convey to President Trump, what would be a positive assessment of the new leadership in Ukraine. on August 16th, Mr. Yermak shared… (Unfortunately, this is where my DVR recording cuts off).

Intelligence Committee hearing #5- Gordon Sondland

Adam Schiff gives his opening statement:

This morning, we will hear from Gordon Sondland, the American Ambassador to the European Union. We are here today as part of the House of Representatives impeachment inquiry, because President Donald Trump sought to condition military aid to Ukraine, and an Oval Office meeting with the new Ukrainian President, Volodymyr Zelensky; in exchange for politically-motivated investigations that Trump believed would help his reelection campaign. The first investigation was of a discredited conspiracy theory, that Ukraine, and not Russia, was responsible for interfering in the 2016 election. The second investigation that Trump had demanded, was into the political rival he apparently feared most, Joe Biden.

Trump sought to weaken Biden, and to refute the fact that his own election campaign in 2016 had been helped by a Russian hacking and dumping operation; and a Russian social media campaign conducted by Vladimir Putin to help Trump.

Trump's scheme to undermine military and diplomatic support for a key ally, and undercut anticorruption efforts in Ukraine. Trump put his personal political interests above those of the United States. As Ambassador Sondland would later tell career Foreign Service officer, David Holmes, immediately after speaking to Trump from the patio of a restaurant in Kyiv, President Trump did not give an (expletive) about Ukraine; he cares about big stuff, that benefits him; like opening the investigations that Rudy Giuliani was pushing. Ambassador Sondland was a skilled negotiator; but in trying to satisfy a directive from the President, he found himself increasingly embroiled in an effort to press the new Ukrainian President, that deviated starkly from the norm; in terms of policy, and process.

In February, Ambassador Sondland traveled to Ukraine, on his first official trip to that country. In Kyiv, he met with the US Ambassador to Ukraine Marie Yovanovitch; and found her to be an excellent diplomat with deep command of Ukrainian internal dynamics. On April 21st, Zelensky was elected President to Ukraine, and spoke to President Trump; who congratulated him, and said he would look into attending Zelensky's inauguration; or he would send someone at a very high-level. Between the time of that call, and May 20th, Trump's attitude {apparently had changed} towards Ukraine.

On May 13th, the President ordered Vice President Mike Pence not to attend Zelensky's inauguration; but instead he opted to dispatch "The three amigos," Energy Secretary Rick Perry, Ambassador Sondland, and Ambassador Kurt Volker, the special representative to Ukraine negotiations. After returning from the inauguration, members of the delegation returned, and met with Trump in the Oval office. When they returned from the trip, they had a meeting the Oval Office, where they briefed President Trump on their encouraging first interactions with the new Ukrainian administration. They urged the President To meet with so Zelensky, but the President's reaction was decidedly hot. The President's order was clear, however: Talk with Rudy. During this meeting, Ambassador Sondland first became aware that Giuliani and the President were only interested in the specific two investigations.

"This whole thing was a sort of a continuum," Sondland testified at his disposition. Starting at the May 23rd meeting, and ending up at the end of the line, when the transcript of the call came out. It was a continuum; and he would explain that it became more insidious over time. The three amigos were disappointed with Trump's directive to engage Giuliani, but they pressed ahead. Ambassador Sondland testified that, we could abandon the goal of President Zelensky getting the White House meeting; which the group had deemed crucial for

US-Ukraine relations; or we could do as President Trump directed, and meet with Giuliani, to address the President's concerns. We chose the latter path. In the coming weeks, Ambassador Sondland got more clearly involved in Ukraine policy making, starting with the June 4th US mission to the EU; Independence Day in Brussels. One month earlier, Secretary Perry, the State Department Counselor, and Sondland met with President Zelensky. Sondland met with Presidents Zelensky, whom Sondland had invited personally, on the margins of the event.

On June 10th, Secretary Perry organized a conference call with, who was then-National Security Advisor John Bolton, Sondland, Volker, and others. At the end of the call, according to Sondland, they all felt very comfortable with the strategy moving forward. Together, they would assist Ambassador Bill Taylor, the new acting Ambassador, and discuss Trump's desire for Rudy Giuliani to be somehow involved. At the end of the call, Sondland tells us, they all felt very comfortable that the strategy was moving forward.

Two weeks later, on June 27th, Ambassador Sondland called Taylor, to say that Zelensky needed to make clear to President Trump, that he was not standing in the way of investigations. On July 10th, Ambassador Sondland and other US officials in the White House, met with a group of US and Ukrainian officials also participating in the meeting. Ambassador Sondland invoked Acting Chief of Staff Mulvaney, announcing that the White House meeting, sought by the Ukrainian President, would happen only if Ukraine undertook certain investigations. Bolton abruptly ended the meeting, upon hearing this. Undeterred, Sondland brought the Ukrainian delegation downstairs, to another part of the White House, and was more explicit. According to witnesses, Ukraine was to investigate the Bidens, Burisma, and the 2016 election interference; if they wanted to get a meeting, at all. Following this meeting in July, Bolton said that he would not take part in whatever drug deal Sondland and Mulvaney were cooking up.

Sondland continued to press for a meeting. He, and others, were willing to settle for phone call; as an intermediate step. on July 21st, Taylor told Sondland, that (quote) President Zelensky is sensitive about Ukraine being taken seriously; not merely as an instrument of

Washington domestic politics. Sondland responded, absolutely; but we need to get a conversation started, and a relationship built, irrespective of the pretext; so that Zelensky and Trump could meet, and all of this will be fixed. On July 25th, the date of the Trump- Zelensky call, Volker had lunch in Kyiv, with a senior aide to Ukrainian President Zelensky; and Volker later texted Taylor, to say that he had heard from the White House; and that assuming President Z convinces Trump he will investigate, get to the bottom of what happened in 2016, we will nail down a date for a visit in Washington. Good luck!

Ambassador Sondland had spoken to President Trump, a few minutes before the call was placed; but he was not on the call. During that now-infamous call with President Zelensky, when the Ukrainian President expressed appreciation for US military defense support, then requesting to buy more Javelin anti-tank missiles, Trump's response was, I would like you to do us a favor, though... Trump asked Zelensky to investigate the discredited 2016 conspiracy theory; and even more ominously, to look into the Bidens. Neither had been part of the official preparatory material for the call; but they were in Donald Trump's personal interests; in the interest of his reelection campaign; and the Ukrainian President knew about both, because of Ambassadors Volker and Sondland's efforts to make them aware of what the President was demanding.

Around this time, Ambassador Sondland became aware of the suspension of the security assistance to Ukraine; which had been announced on a secure conference call on July 18th, telling Foreign Service staff it was extremely odd that, nobody involved in making or implementing policy toward Ukraine, knew why the aid had been put on hold. During all of this, Sondland would participate in conference calls, and text messages, with Volker and Giuliani; and he said that the gist of every call was, what was going to go into the press statement. In an August 9th text message with Volker, Sondland stated, I think POTUS really wants the deliverable; which was, according to Sondland, a public statement that President Trump wanted to see, or hear, before the White House meeting would happen.

On September 1st, Ambassador Sondland participated in Vice President Pence's bilateral meeting with Zelensky, during which Zelensky raises the issue of the suspended security assistance. Following that meeting, Sondland approached a senior Ukrainian official, telling him, I believe what could help move the aid, is if Ukraine's Prosecutor General (publicly) announced he was opening the Burisma investigation. Sondland told Taylor that he had made a mistake, by telling Ukrainians that the White House meeting for Zelensky in the Oval Office; this was all that hinged on the public announcement of investigations; in fact, everything was dependent on these demanded announcements; including the security assistance!

But even an announcement made by the Prosecutor General would not satisfy President Trump. On September 7th, Sondland spoke to the President; and he told Tim Morrison and Bill Taylor about the call, shortly thereafter. The President said that, although this was not a quid pro quo to President Zelensky; if he did not clear things up in public, "Then the US and Ukraine would be at a stalemate."

Sondland told Taylor, that Trump is a businessman; and when a businessman is about to write a check, to someone who owes him something, he asks as the person to pay up, before signing the check. The check, in this case, was the US military assistance to Ukraine; and Ukraine had to pay up for this, with investigations.

Throughout early September, Volker and Sondland sought to close the deal; an agreement that Zelensky would announce these investigations. After Taylor texted Sondland, on September 9th, "I think it's crazy to withhold security assistance for help with a political campaign!

Sixteen days later, the transcript of the July 25th call was made public; the American people want to know the truth, about how our President Tried to take advantage of a vulnerable ally. Now it's up to Congress to determine what response is appropriate. If the President abused his power, by inviting foreign interference into our elections; if he sought to condition, coerce, or extort a private ally into conducting investigations, to help his election campaign; and did so by withholding official acts; a White House meeting, or hundreds of millions of dollars of military aid; it will be up to us, to decide whether those actions are compatible with the office of the presidency.

Finally, I would like to say a word about the President, and secretary Pompeo's obstruction of this investigation. We have not received a single document from the State Department; and as Ambassador Sondland's opening statement today will make clear, those documents bear directly on this investigation, and on this impeachment inquiry. I think we now know, based on a sample of the documents attached to Ambassador Sondland's statement; that the knowledge of this scheme was far and wide; and included, among others, Secretary of State Pompeo as well as the Vice President. We can see why secretary Pompeo and President Trump have made such a concerted, and across-the-board effort to obstruct this investigation, and this impeachment inquiry; and I will just say this: They do so at their own peril. I remind the President That article 3 of the impeachment articles drafted against President Nixon, was his refusal to obey the subpoenas of Congress. With that, I recognize ranking member Nunez, for any remarks he wishes to make.

Nunez starts out by obnoxiously making another effort to get the Intelligence Committee to subpoena Hunter Biden and the whistleblower. (Never going to happen; and it has no bearing on the matter at hand). He asks Democrats to concur with a subpoena; but how do you concur with a subpoena?! Huh! That's all he has to say; nice! that's all Nunez said, and now Adam Schiff starts to announce some background about Ambassador Sondland, in preparation for Sondland to read his opening statement:

Gordon Sondland is the US representative to the European Union, with the rank of Ambassador. Before joining the State Department Ambassador Sondland was the founder and CEO of Providence hotels -the national owner and operator of these full-service hotels. Also, prior to his Government service, Ambassador Sondland was engaged in charitable enterprises...

Schiff swears-in Sondland, and Sondland then reads his opening statement:

First, let me offer my thanks to the men and women of the US Department of State, who have committed their professional lives to support the foreign policy work of the United States. in particular, I want to thank my staff at the US mission in Europe. Their dedication and hard work are often performed without public acclaim, or recognition. They serve as a shining example of true public service; and I am personally grateful to work beside you each and every day. it is my honor to serve as US Ambassador to the European Union. the US mission to the EU is a direct link between the United States and the European Union; as members of America's longest standing allies; one of the largest economic blocs in the world. Every day, I work to support a strong, united, peaceful union. Strengthening our ties with Europe serves both American and European goals, as we together promote political stability and economic prosperity around the world.

Before I begin my substantive testimony, let me share some of my personal background. My parents fled Europe during the Holocaust; escaping the atrocities at that time. My parents left Germany for Uruguay, and then in 1953, they emigrated to Seattle, Washington; where I was born and raised. Like so many immigrants, my family was eager for freedom, and hungry for opportunity; to raise my sister and me to be humble, and hard-working, and patriotic. I am forever grateful for the sacrifices they made on our behalf. Public service has always been important to me. As a lifelong Republican, I've contributed to initiatives of both Republican and Democratic administrations. In 2003, I served as a member of the transition team for Oregon Governor Ted Landau's governorship. He also appointed me to serve on various statewide boards. In 2007, President George W. Bush appointed me as a member of the commission on White House fellows. I worked with President Bush on charitable events, for his foundations, and military service initiative; and I also worked briefly with former VP Joe Biden's office, in connection with the Vice President's nationwide anticancer initiative at a local hospital; and of course, the highest honor in my public life is when President Trump asked me to service the as US Ambassador to the European Union. The Senate confirmed me as an Ambassador; from a bipartisan voice vote, over the phone; and

I assumed the role in Brussels on July 9, 2018. Although today is my first public on Ukraine matters, this is not my first time cooperating with this committee. As you know, I've already provided 10 hours of deposition testimony; and I did so, despite directions from the White House and the State Department, that I refuse to appear; as many others have done. I agreed to testify because I respect the gravity of the moment, and I believe I have an obligation to account fully for my role in these events. I also want to acknowledge that this process has been challenging, and in many respects, less than fair. I have not had access to all of my phone records, State Department emails, and many many other State Department documents; and I was told that I could not work with my EU staff, to pull together the rough files of information.

Having access to the State Department materials would have been very helpful to me, at trying to reconstruct with whom I spoke with, and when, and what was said. As Ambassador, I've had hundreds of meetings, and calls with individuals. I'm not a note, or a memo writer; I never have been. My job requires that I speak with heads of state, senior government officials, members of the cabinet, and the President. Almost each and every day, I am talking with foreign leaders. This might be memorable to some people, but this is my job; I do it all the time. My lawyers and I made multiple requests, from the State Department, and the White House, for these materials. Yet these materials were not provided to me; and they've also refused to share these materials with this committee. These documents are not classified; and in fairness, they should be made available. In the absence of these materials, my memory admittedly has not been perfect; and I have no doubt that, were there an open and orderly process of allowing me to read the statements of my records and materials, it would have made this process a lot more transparent.

I don't intend to repeat my prior opening statement, or to summarize my 10 hours of previous deposition testimony; however, a few critical points have been obscured by the noise over the last few days and weeks; and I'm worried that the bigger picture is being ignored; so let me make a few key points. First, Secretary Perry, and Ambassador Volker and I, worked with Mr. Rudy Giuliani on Ukraine matters; at the direction of the President of the United States. We did not want to work with Mr. Giuliani; simply put, we were playing the hand we were dealt. We all understood that if we refuse to work with Mr. Giuliani, we would lose a very important opportunity to cement relations between the United States, and Ukraine. So, we followed the President's orders. Second, although we disagreed with the need to involve Mr. Giuliani; at the time we did not believe that his role was improper. As I previously testified, if I had known all of Mr. Giuliani's dealings, and his associations with individuals; some who are now under criminal indictment; I personally would not have acquiesced to this participation. Still, given what we knew at the time, what we were asked to do, did not appear to be wrong. Third, let me say that, precisely because we did not know we were engaging in improper behavior, we made every effort to ensure that the relevant decision-makers at the national Security Council and the State Department knew important details of our efforts. The suggestion that we were engaged in some irregular or rogue diplomacy is absolutely false. I have now identified certain State Department emails and messages, that provide contemporaneous support for my view. These emails show that the leadership of the State Department, the national Security Council, and the White House, all were informed about the Ukraine efforts; from May 23, 2019 until the security aide was released on September 11, 2019. I will quote from some of those messages with you shortly. As I testified previously, Mr. Giuliani's requests were a quid pro quo, for arranging a White House visit for President Zelensky.

Mr. Giuliani demanded that Ukraine make a public statement, announcing the investigations of the 2016 election, the DNC server, and Burisma. Mr. Giuliani was expressing the desires of the President of the United States; and we knew these investigations were important to the President. Fifth, in July and August of 2019, we learned that the White House had also suspended security aid to Ukraine. I was adamantly opposed to any suspension of aid, as the Ukrainians needed those funds to fight against Russian aggression. I tried diligently, to ask why the aid was suspended, but I never received a clear answer. I still haven't, to this day. In the absence of any credible explanation for the suspension of aid, I later came to believe that the resumption of security aid would not occur until there was a public statement from Ukraine, committing to the investigations of the 2016 elections and Burisma.

Mr. Giuliani had demanded that I share concerns of any potential issues regarding the security aid, with Senator Ron Johnson; and I also shared my concerns with Ukrainians. Finally, at all times, I was acting in good faith, as a Presidential appointee. I followed the directions of the President. We worked with Mr. Giuliani, because the President directed us to do so; we had no desire to set any conditions on the Ukrainians. Indeed, my own personal view, which I shared repeatedly with others, was that the White House security assistance should have proceeded without preconditions of any kind. We were working to overcome the problems; given the facts as they existed. Our only interests, and my only interest, was to advance long-standing US policy and to support Ukraine's fragile democracy.

Now let me provide additional detail. Specifically, about Ukraine, my involvement, right from my very first days as Ambassador to the EU; which was starting back in July 2018; Ukraine has featured prominently, in my broader portfolio. Ukraine's political and economic development are critical to the long-standing, and long-lasting stability of Europe. Moreover, the conflict in eastern Ukraine and Crimea remains one of the most significant security crises, for Europe, and for the United States. Our efforts to counterbalance an aggressive Russia, depend in substantial part, on a strong Ukraine.

On April 21, 2019, Volodymyr Zelensky was elected President of Ukraine, in an historic reelection. With the express support of secretary Pompeo, I attended President Zelensky's inauguration on May 20th, as part of the US delegation, which was led by Energy Secretary Rick Perry. The US delegation Also Included Senator Johnson, Ukraine Special Envoy Volker, and Lieutenant Colonel Alex Vindeman, of the national Security Council. My attendance at President Zelensky's inauguration was not my first involvement with Ukraine. As I testified previously, just four days after assuming my post, as Ambassador, in July 2018, I received an official delegation from the government of then-Ukraine-President Petra Poroshenko. The meeting took place at the US mission in Brussels; and was prearranged by my staff. I've had several meetings since then, in Brussels. Later in February 2019, I worked with US Ambassador Marie Yovanovitch to make my first official visit to Ukraine; which was a U.S. Navy visit, to the strategic Black Seaport of Odessa. The reason I raise these Ukraine activities; the meetings in Brussels, in Brussels and Odessa, is that Ukraine has been a part of my portfolio, since my very first day as a US Ambassador. Any claim that I somehow muscled my way into the Ukraine relationship, is simply false.

During the Zelensky inauguration, on May 20th, the US delegation developed a very positive view of Ukraine government we were impressed by President Zelensky's desire to promote a stronger relationship with the United States. We admired his commitment to reform, and we were excited about the possibility of Ukraine making the changes necessary to support a greater Western economic investment; and we were excited that Ukraine might, after years and years of lip service, finally get serious about addressing its own well-known corruption problems. With enthusiasm, we returned to the White House on May 23rd, to brief President Trump. We advised the President of the strategic importance of Ukraine, and the value of strengthening the relationship with President Zelensky. To support this reform, we asked the White House for two things; first, a working phone call, between Presidents Trump and Zelensky; and second, an Oval Office visit. We argued that both were vital to cementing the US Ukraine relationship, and demonstrating support for Ukraine, in the face of Russian aggression; and advancing broader US foreign policy.

Unfortunately, President Trump was skeptical. He expressed concerns that the Ukrainian government was not serious about reform; and he even mentioned that Ukraine tried to take him down, in the last election. In response to our persistent efforts in that meeting; to change his views; President Trump directed us to "Talk with Rudy…" We understood that "talking with Rudy" meant talking with Mr. Rudy Giuliani, the President's personal lawyer. Let me say again, we weren't happy with the President's direction, to talk with Rudy. We did not want to involve Mr. Giuliani. I believed then, as I do now, that the men and women of the State Department; not the President's personal lawyer; should take responsibility for Ukraine matters.

Nonetheless, based on the President's direction, we were faced with a choice; we could abandon the effort to schedule a White House visit, between Presidents Trump and Zelensky; of which (this meeting) was unquestionably in our foreign policy interests; or we could do as President Trump had directed, and talk with Rudy. We chose the latter course; not because we would like to; but because it was the only constructive path open to us. Over the course of the next several months, Secretary Perry, Ambassador Volker, and I were in communication with Mr. Giuliani. Secretary Perry volunteered to make the initial calls with Mr. Giuliani, given their prior relationship. Ambassador Volker made several of the early calls, and he generally informed us of what was discussed. I first communicated with Mr. Giuliani in early August. Several months later, Mr. Giuliani emphasized that the President wanted a public statement from President Zelensky, committing Ukraine to look into corruption issues. Mr. Giuliani specifically mentioned the 2016 election, including the DNC server, and Burisma, as two topics of importance to the President. We kept the leadership of the State Department, and the NSC informed of our activities; and that included communications with Secretary of State Pompeo's counselor, Ulricht Brechtbuhl, his executive secretary, Lisa Kenna, and also communications with Ambassador Bolton, Dr. Hill, Mr. Morrison, and their staff at the NSC. They knew what we were doing, and why. On July 10, 2019, senior Ukrainian National Security officials met with Ambassador Bolton, Ambassador Volker, Dr. Hill, Secretary Perry, myself, and several others, in Washington DC. During that meeting, we all discussed the importance of the two action items identified earlier on; one, a working phone call; and two, a White House meeting between Presidents Trump and Zelensky. From my perspective, the July 10th meeting was a positive step toward accomplishing our shared goals. While I am now aware of accounts of the meeting, from Dr. Hill, and Lieutenant Colonel Vindeman, their recollection of those events, simply don't square with my own; or with those of Ambassador Volker, or Secretary Perry. I recall mentioning the prerequisite of investigations, before any White House call, or meeting;

but I do not recall any yelling or screaming, or abrupt terminations; as they have said.

After the meeting, Ambassador Bolton walked outside with our group, and we all took some great pictures together, outside on the White House lawn. More importantly, those recollections of protest do not square with the documentary record of our interactions, with the NSC. In the days and weeks that followed, we kept the NSC apprised of our efforts; including specifically, our efforts to secure a public statement from the Ukrainians that would satisfy President Trump's concerns. For example, on July 13th; and this is three days after that July 10th meeting; I emailed Tim Morrison, who had just taken over Dr. Hill's post, as the NSC Eurasia Director; and I met him that day, for the first time. I wrote to Mr. Morrison with these words: The call between Zelensky on 7/21; which was the parliamentary elections in Ukraine; the sole purpose of the call is for Zelensky to give POTUS assurances, that there is a new sheriff in town, fighting corruption and ending unbundling, moving forward; and I emphasized that any hampered investigations will be allowed to move forward, transparently. The goal was for POTUS to invite, to the Oval Office, Volker, Perry, and Bolton; and I strongly recommended it. Mr. Morrison acknowledged, and said thank you; and specifically noted that he was tracking these issues. Again, there was no secret, regarding moving forward; and the discussion of investigations moreover. I reviewed other State Department documents; some of which are not currently in the public domain; detailing Mr. Giuliani's efforts. For example, on July 10th, the very same day that Ambassador Volker, Secretary Perry, and I were meeting with Ukrainian officials in Washington, Ambassador Taylor received a communication, that Mr. Giuliani was still talking with Ukrainian prosecutor Yuriy Lutsenko, trading What's App messages, with Ambassador Volker and I. Ambassador Taylor wrote to us, as follows: Just had a meeting with Andre and (the Dean?), referring to Ukraine foreign minister ? Taylor said the Ukrainians were "Very concerned about what Lutsenko told them," that according to Rudy Giuliani, the Zelensky/POTUS meeting will not happen.

Volker responded, "Good grief! Let's tell the team to let official US Government representatives speak for the US! -That Lutsenko has his own self- interest here..." Taylor confirmed that he had communicated that message to the Ukrainians, and he added that he had briefed Ulricht this afternoon; referring to State Department Counselor Ulricht Brechtbuhl; I briefed Ulricht this afternoon, on this...

Again, everyone was in the loop. Three things are critical about this What's App exchange; while the Ukrainians were in Washington, at the White House, Mr. Giuliani was communicating with Ukrainians, without our knowledge. Ambassador Taylor, Ambassador Volker, and I, were all surprised by this. Second, Mr. Giuliani was communicating with a reportedly corrupt Ukraine prosecutor Lutsenko; and discussing whether the Trump/Zelensky meeting was going to happen; Again, without our knowledge; and third, with this alarming news, Ambassador Taylor briefed Ulricht Brechtbuhl, counselor to Secretary of State Pompeo; and even as late as September 24th of this year, secretary Pompeo was directing Kurt Volker to speak with Mr. Giuliani.

Kurt Volker told me in he spoke with Rudy Giuliani further, per guidance from the State Department's official designatee for the sector; look, we tried our best to fix the problem. We are keeping the State Department and the NSC closely apprised of the challenges we face. On July 25th, Presidents Trump and Zelensky had their official call; I was not on the call, and I don't think I was invited to be on the call. In fact, I first read the transcript on September 25th, the day it was publicly released.

All I had heard, at that time, was that the call had gone well. Looking back, I find it very odd, that neither I, nor Ambassador Taylor, nor Ambassador Volker, ever received a detailed readout of that call, with the Bidens referenced in it.

Now, there are people that say there were concerns about the call; nobody shared any at all with me; at the time; which frankly would have been very helpful to know. On July 26th, Ambassador Taylor, Ambassador Volker, and I were all in Kyiv, to meet with President Zelensky. The timing of that trip; immediately after the call between Presidents Trump and Zelensky; was entirely coincidental. This meeting had been scheduled well before the date, that the White House had finally placed the call. During RTF meeting, I do not recall President Zelensky discussing the substance of the July 25th call with President Trump; nor did he express any request to investigate former Vice President Biden; which we all later learned was discussed on that July 25th call; and this is consistent with the reported comments, from Ambassadors Volker and Taylor. After the meeting, I also met with Zelensky's Senior Aide, Andre Yermak. I don't recall the specifics of our conversation, but I believe the issue of investigations was probably part of that agenda. Our meeting also on July 26th, shortly after RTF meetings, I spoke by phone by with President Trump at the White House.

I shared certain call dates and times with my attorneys; and it has been confirmed, that this call lasted five minutes. I remember I was at a restaurant in Kyiv; and I have no reason to doubt that this conversation included the subject of investigations. Again, given Mr. Giuliani's demand that President Zelensky make a public statement about the investigations, I knew that these investigations were important to President Trump. We did not discuss any classified information.

Other witnesses have recently shared their recollection of overhearing this call. For the most part, I have no reason to doubt their accounts. It's true, that the President speaks loudly at times; and it's also true, that I think we primarily discussed, I think we primarily discussed "ASAP Rocky;" it's true, that the President likes to use colorful language. Anyone who has met with him, for any reasonable amount of time would know that; but I cannot remember precisely the details. Again, the White House has not allowed me to see any readouts of that call; and the July 26th call did not strike me as significant, at the time. Actually, I would have been more surprised if President Trump had not mentioned investigations; particularly, given what we are hearing from Mr. Giuliani, about the President's concerns.

However, I have no recollection of discussing Vice President Biden, or his son, on that call; or after the call. I know that members of this committee frequently frame these complicated issues in the form of one simple question; was there a quid pro quo? As I testified previously, with regard to the requested White House meeting; the answer is yes.

Mr. Giuliani had conveyed, to Secretary Perry, Ambassador Volker, and others, that President Trump wanted a public statement from President Zelensky, committing to investigations of Burisma, and the 2016 election. Mr. Giuliani expressed those requests directly to the Ukrainians; and Mr. Giuliani also expressed those requests directly to us. We all understood that these were prerequisites, for the White House meeting. The White House call reflected President Trump's desires, and requirements.

Within my State Department emails, there is a July 19th email. This email was sent to secretary Pompeo, Secretary Perry, Brian McCormick, who is Secretary Perry's Chief of Staff, at the time. Ms. Kenna, who was the executive secretary for Secretary Pompeo, Chief of Staff Mulvaney, and Mr. Mulvaney's Senior Advisor, Rob Blair; a lot of senior officials. Here is my exact quote from that email: I talked to Zelensky just now; he is prepared to receive POTUS's call, and will assure him that he intends to run a fully transparent investigation; and will turn over every stone. He will greatly appreciate a call, prior to Sunday; so that he can put out some media about a friendly and productive call; no details, prior to the Ukraine election on Sunday. Chief of Staff Mulvaney responded by asking the NSC to set it up, for tomorrow. Everyone was in the loop; it was no secret; everyone was informed, via email, on July 19th, days before the Presidential call.

As I communicated to the team, I told President Zelensky in advance, that assurances to run a fully transparent investigation, and turn over every stone, were necessary in this call with President Trump. On July 19th, in a What's App message between Ambassador Taylor, Ambassador Volker, and me; Ambassador Volker wrote: Had breakfast with Rudy this morning; Volker and Giuliani teeing up call with Yermak Monday; you must have helped... Most important is for President Zelensky to say that he will open investigations, and address any specific personnel issues; if there are any. Mr. Yermak said at that same meeting, once we have a date (for the White House meeting), we will call for a press briefing, announcing the upcoming visit, and outlining a vision for the reboot of the US-Ukraine relationship; including, among other things, Burisma, and election meddling investigations.

This is from Mr. Yermak, to me the following day August 11th; and this is critical; I sent an email to counselor Brechtbuhl, and Lisa Kenna; as she was frequently used as the pathway to secretary Pompeo; and sometimes, he preferred to receive his emails through her. She would print them out, and put them in front of him.

(Sondland is asked to read one of his emails, up on the screen) -With the subject Ukraine, I wrote: Mike (referring to Mike Pompeo), Kurt and I negotiated a statement from Zelensky to be delivered for our review in a day or two. contents will hopefully make the Boss happy enough (meaning President Trump) to authorize an invitation. Zelensky plans to have a big press conference on the openness subject, including specifics, next week. (all of which referred to opening the 2016 and Burisma investigations.) Thank you.

Ms. Kenna replied, Gordon, I will pass it on to the secretary; thank you again... Everyone was in the loop. Curiously; and this was very interesting to me; on August 26th, shortly before his visit to Kyiv, Ambassador Bolton's office requested, from me, Mr. Giuliani's contact information. I sent Ambassador Bolton the information directly; but they requested Mr. Giuliani's contact information from me. (It's interesting that they didn't already have Giuliani's contact information.)

I was first informed that the White House was withholding security aid to Ukraine; during a conversation with Ambassador Taylor on July 18th; however, as I testified before, I was never able to obtain a clear answer, regarding the specific reason for the hold. Whether it was bureaucratic in nature, which often happens; or reflected some other concern in the interagency process; I had never participated in any of the subsequent DOD, or DOS review meetings; so I can't speak to what was discussed in those meetings. Nonetheless, before the September 1st Warsaw meeting, the Ukrainians had become aware that the security funds had yet to be dispersed. In the absence of any credible explanation for the hold, I came to the conclusion that the aid, like the White House visit, was jeopardized.

In preparation for the September 1st Warsaw meeting, I asked Secretary Pompeo whether a face-to-face conversation between Trump and Zelensky would help to break the logjam. This was when President Trump was still intending to travel to Warsaw. Specifically, on August 22nd, I emailed secretary Pompeo directly; copying secretary Kenna. I wrote, this is my email to secretary Pompeo: Should we block time in Warsaw, for a short pull-aside, for POTUS to meet Zelensky? I would ask Zelensky to look him in the eye, and tell him that, once Ukraine's new justice folks are in place, in mid-September, Zelensky easily should be able to move forward publicly, and with confidence, on those issues of importance to POTUS in the US. Hopefully, that will help break the logjam.

The secretary replied, yes. I followed up the next day, asking again, for 10 or 15 minutes on the Warsaw schedule, for this. I said, I would like to know when it's locked; so I can tell Zelensky, and brief him. Executive Secretary Kenna replied, I will try, for sure.

Moreover, given my concerns about the security aid, I have no reason to dispute any portion of Senator Johnson's recent letter, in which he recalls a conversation that he and I had, on August 30th; that if Ukraine did something to demonstrate a serious intention to fight corruption; and specifically addressing Burisma, and the 2016 election meddling; then the military aid would be lifted.

There was a September 1st meeting with President Zelensky, in Warsaw. Unfortunately, President Trump's attendance at the Warsaw meeting was canceled, due to hurricane Gregory. Vice President Pence attended instead. I mentioned to Vice President Pence, before the meeting with Ukrainians, that I had concerns that the delay of the aid had (also) become tied to the investigations. I recall mentioning that, before the Zelensky meeting. During the actual meeting, President Zelensky raised the issue of the security assistance directly with Vice President Pence; and the Vice President said he would speak to President Trump about it.

Based on my previous communications with secretary Pompeo, I felt comfortable sharing my concerns with Mr. Yermak. It was a very brief conversation, that happened in a few seconds. I told Mr. Yermak that I believed that the resumption of US aid would likely not occur, until Ukraine took some kind of action on the public statement that we had been discussing for many weeks. As my other State Department colleagues have testified, this security aid was critical to Ukraine's defense, and should not have been delayed. I expressed this view to many, during this period; but my goal, at the time, was to do what was necessary to get the aid released; to break the logjam. I believed that the public statement we had been discussing for weeks, was essential to advancing that goal.

You know, I really regret that the Ukrainians were placed in this predicament. I do not regret doing what I could, to try and break the logjam, and solve the problem. I mentioned at the outset, that throughout these events, we kept the State Department leadership and others apprised of what we were doing. The State Department was fully supportive of our engagement in Ukraine efforts, and was aware that the commitment to investigations was among the issues we were pursuing. To provide just two examples, on June 5th, the day after US/EU mission had hosted our Independence Day, which we did a month early, acting Assistant Secretary Phil Rieger sent an email to me, to Secretary Perry, and others, forwarding some positive media coverage of President Zelensky's attendance at our event. Mr. Rieger wrote, and I quote: This headline underscores the importance, and timeliness, of Zelensky's visit to Brussels, and the critical, perhaps historic role of the dinner and engagement that Gordon coordinated. Thank you for your participation, and dedication to this effort.

Months later, on September 3rd, I sent secretary Pompeo an email, to express my appreciation for his joining the series of meetings in Brussels. Following the Warsaw trip, I wrote Mike, thanks for schlepping to Europe. I think it was really important, and the chemistry seems to be promising. I really appreciate it... Secretary Pompeo replied the next day, on Wednesday, September 4th, All good; you're doing great work; keep banging away!

State Department leadership expressed total support for our efforts to engage the new Ukrainian administration. -Look, I've never doubted the strategic value of strengthening our alliance with Ukraine; and at all times, our efforts were in good faith, and fully transparent; and those tasked with overseeing our efforts were reported, and approved; and not once do I recall encountering an objection. It remains an honor to serve the people of the United States, as the United States Ambassador to the European Union. I look forward to answering the committee's questions thank you.

Sondland's questioning now begins:

Adam Schiff starts the first 45-minute session; for himself, and his majority Counsel, Mr. Goldman. Ambassador Sondland, there's a lot of new material in your opening statement, for us to get through; but I want to start with a few top questions before passing it over to Mr. Goldman. In your deposition, you testified that you found yourself on a continuum, that became more insidious, over time. Can you describe what you meant by this continuum of insidiousness?

Well Chairman, when we met at the Oval Office, I believe on May 23rd, the request was very generic; for an investigation of corruption, in a very vanilla sense; and dealing with some oligarch problems in Ukraine. -And as time went on, more specific items got added to the menu, including Burisma, and the 2016 election meddling, specifically; the DNC server, specifically; and over this continuum it became more and more difficult to secure the White House meeting, because more conditions were being placed on the White House meeting.

Then, of course, on July 25th, while you were not privy to the call, another condition was added; that there be an investigation of the Bidens... I was not privy to the call, and I did not know the condition, of investigating the Bidens, was a condition. (correct) You saw that in the call record, right? It was not any record I received; but yes, I did see it on September 25th, when the call record became public. -And this continuum, the continuum begins on May 23rd, with the President's instruction to "talk to Rudy."(correct) -And you understood this direction by President Trump, that you needed to satisfy the concerns that Rudy Giuliani would express to you, about what the President wanted in Ukraine. (Sondland clarifies) not just me; but the entire group of us, Ambassador Volker, Secretary Perry, and myself.

In your opening statement, you confirmed that there was a quid pro quo, between the White House meeting, and the investigations into Burisma, and the 2016 election meddling, that Giuliani was publicly promoting; is that correct? (yes) -In fact, you say that other senior officials at the State Department, and the Chief of Staff's office, including Mick Mulvaney, and Secretary Pompeo were aware of this quid pro quo; that in order to get the White House meeting, there were going to have to be these investigations that the President wanted? (yes) -And those, again, were investigations into 2016 and Burisma/ the Bidens? (Yes, into the 2016 elections and Burisma; the Bidens had not come up.) -But you would ultimately learn that Burisma did come up? (of course) -But you would ultimately learn about Burisma and the Bidens, when you saw the call record? (of course; today, I know everything; but I didn't know at the time…) -But on July 26th, you confirmed that you did indeed have a conversation with President Trump, from a restaurant in Kyiv; and you have no reason to doubt Mr. Holmes' account of your conversation with the President, do you? (The only part that Mr. Holmes recounted that I took exception with, was that I do not recall mentioning the Bidens; that did not enter my mind; it was Burisma, and the 2016 elections.) -You have no reason to believe that Mr. Holmes would make that up? That's what he recalled you saying… (I don't recall saying it; I never recall saying the Bidens.) -But the rest of Mr. Holmes recollection is consistent with your own, right? (I can't testify as to what Mr. Holmes might, or might not have heard, through the phone; I don't know how he herd the conversation.) -Are you familiar with his testimony? (yes) -And the only exception you take us to the mention of the Bidens… and I think you said, in your testimony this morning, that not only is it correct that the President brought up investigations, on the phone with you, the day after the July 25th call, but you would have been surprised if he had not brought that up? (yes, because I had been hearing about it, from Rudy, and Rudy was getting it from the President; so, it seemed logical.)

Mr. Holmes also testified that you told him, President Trump doesn't care about Ukraine; he only cares about "big stuff," that relates to him personally… I take it from your comment, that you don't dispute, that in your conversation, he made that clear in the May 23rd meeting; that he was not particularly fond of Ukraine… (We had a lot of heavy lifting to do, to get them to engage.) -You don't dispute that part of Mr. Holmes recollection, do you? (no)

In August, when you worked with Rudy Giuliani, and a top Ukraine aide, to draft a public statement, for President Zelensky to issue, that included the announcement of investigations into Burisma; you understood that was required by President Trump, before he would grant a White House meeting to President Zelensky? (that's correct) -And the Ukrainians understood that as well? (I believe they did.) -And you informed Secretary Pompeo about that statement, as well? (I did.) Later in August, you told Secretary Pompeo that President Zelensky would be prepared to tell President Trump, that his new justice officials would be able to announce investigations of matters of interest, to the President; which could break the logjam? (yes) -When you say matters of interest to the President, you mean the investigations that President Trump wanted, right? (yes) -And that involved 2016, and Burisma; or the Bidens, 2016, and Burisma… -And when you're talking about "breaking the logjam," (I was talking about the logjam, that generically, nothing was moving.) -And based on the context of that email, it was not the first time you would discuss these investigations with secretary Pompeo, was it? (no)

-He was aware of the connection that you were making, between investigations, and the White House meeting; and the security assistance… -Did he ever take issue with you, and say no, that connection is very wrong? (not that I recall) -You mentioned that you also had a conversation with Vice President Pence, before his meeting with President Zelensky in Warsaw; and that you raised the concern you had, as well; that security assistance was being withheld because of the President's desire to get President Zelensky to pursue these political investigations… What did you say to the Vice President?

(I was in a briefing with several people, and I just spoke up, and I said it appears that everything is stalled, until this statement gets made; something to that effect; and that's what I believed to be the case; based on the work that the three of us had been doing. The Vice President nodded, like he had heard what I said; that was pretty much it, as I recall.)

-You understood that the Ukrainians had raised the issue of the security assistance, with Vice President, at this meeting? (I didn't know what they were going to raise, but they did, in fact, raise it.) -It had gone public, by that point, that there was a hold on the security assistance, right? (Yes; but I didn't know if they were going to raise the issue; I didn't get a pre-brief from the Ukrainians.) -You certainly were concerned about the hold on the security assistance, were you not? -You were concerned obviously, and you wanted to bring it up, with the Vice President because you wanted to help prepare the Vice President for the meeting; by letting him know what you thought was responsible for the hold on the security assistance? (yes) Do you recall anything else that the Vice President said, other than nodding his head when you made the comment? (I don't have read out of that meeting, so I can't recount it.) -It was immediately after this meeting, between Vice President Pence, and President Zelensky, that you went to speak with Andre Yermak; and you told him, similarly, that in order to release the military assistance, they were going to have to publicly announce the investigations?

(Yes; but it really wasn't a meeting; everybody got up, after the bilateral meeting, between President Zelensky and Vice President Pence; and people did what they normally do; they get up, mill around, shake hands; and I don't know if I went over to Yermak, or he came over to me; but he said, what's going on here? -and I said, "I don't know; it might all be tied together now; I have no idea." I was presuming that the aid was conditional too; but it was a very short conversation.)

-In that short conversation, as you would later relate to Mr. Morrison, and Ambassador Taylor, you informed Mr. Yermak that they would need to announce these investigations, in order to get the aid? (Well, Mr. Yermak was already working on the statement about those investigations.) -And you confirmed to him that he needed to get it done, in order to get the military aid? (I likely did.)

-Mr. Morrison, and Ambassador Taylor also related a conversation that you had with the President, following the Warsaw meeting, in which the President related to you, that there was "no quid pro quo," but that nevertheless; unless Zelensky went to the mic and announce these investigations, there would be a "stalemate" over the aid, is that correct? (that's correct) -And that was an accurate reflection of your discussion with the President? (Well, that email was not artfully written; I'm the first to admit… What I was trying to convey to Ambassador Taylor, after his frantic emails to me, and to others; about the security assistance, which by the way, I agreed with him; I thought that it was a very bad idea to hold that money. I finally called the President, I believe it was on the night of September 9th, but I can't find the records, and they will not provide them; but I believe I just asked President Trump an open question, Mr. Chairman; "What do you want from Ukraine? I keep hearing all these different ideas, and theories; and this and that; what do you want?! -and it was a very short, abrupt conversation; he was not in a good mood; and he just said, I want nothing! I want no quid pro quo; tell Zelensky to do the right thing! -something to that effect. -So, I typed out a text to Ambassador Taylor. My reason for telling him this, was not to defend what the President was saying; and not to opine whether the President was being truthful or untruthful; but simply to relate that I got as far as I could go; and this is the final word, that I heard from the President of the United States! If you're still concerned, Ambassador Taylor, please get a hold of Secretary Pompeo, and maybe he can help.)

(Schiff wants explanation, not a quote of Sondland's texts) -I'm not asking about your text messages; I'm asking about your conversations with Mr. Morrison, and Ambassador Taylor, after you spoke with the President; either on that call, or another call… Sondland says, (I'm confused Mr. Chairman; which conversation with Mr. Morrison, or Mr. Taylor?)

(Schiff clarifies) Mr. Morrison testified that that you related a conversation you had with the President, in which the President

Told you, "no quid pro quo," but President Zelensky must go to the microphone and announce these investigations; and that he should want to... Similarly, you told Ambassador Taylor, that while the President said no quid pro quo; unless Zelensky announces these investigations, they would be at a stalemate over the military assistance... Do you have any reason to question those conversations, that Mr. Morrison, and Ambassador Taylor took notes about? (Well, I think it's tied to my text, Mr. Chairman; because in my text I think I said something to the effect that he wants Zelensky to do what he ran on; pledges of transparency, etc... which is my clumsy way of saying, that he wanted these announcements to be made.

(Schiff obviously suspects that Sondland is trying to slip out of saying anything committal, and this is frustrating; but he forges on, in search of Sondland's affirmations of what others had testified; he says to Sondland,) Again; I'm not asking you about your text messages; I'm asking you about what you related to Ambassador Taylor and Mr. Morrison, about your conversation with the President... Do you have any reason to question their recollection of what you were told? (All I can say, is that I expressed what I told what the President had told me, in that text; and if I had relayed anything other than this, in that text, I don't recall.)

-Do you have any reason to question what Ambassador Taylor or Mr. Morrison, what they wrote in her deposition, about the conversation? (Sondland asks, could you kindly repeat what they wrote?) Schiff responds that he will let Mr. Goldman go through that with him; and he continues, -But let me get to the very the topline; Ambassador Sondland, you testified that the White House meeting, that President Zelensky desperately wanted, and that was very important to President Zelensky, was it not? (absolutely) -You testified that, the meeting conditioned; it was a quid pro quo, for what the President wanted; which was the two investigations; wasn't that what President Trump greatly valued, and he was quite insistent upon? (I don't want to characterize whether they were of value, or not, to the President. Again; through Mr. Giuliani, we were led to believe, that's what he wanted.)

-You said that Mr. Giuliani was acting at the President's behest; when the President says, "Talk to my personal lawyer, Rudy Giuliani," we followed his direction; and so, the official acts which that meeting was being conditioned on; the performance of these things, that the President wanted, was expressed, both directly, and through his lawyer, Rudy Giuliani. (Sondland says, Through Giuliani; only as expressed through Rudy Giuliani.)

{I now start to ask myself, is Sondland engaging in some futile effort to try and disconnect the President from his having been directly involved, and indeed guilty of directing this entire scheme and initiative? -or is Sondland just weird; and being so careful to cover his ass, so protectively, that, whether he helps the investigation and the questioning process, that doesn't really matter to him?}

(Schiff continues,)

-And you also testified that it became your clear understanding, that the military assistance was also being withheld; pending Zelensky announcing these investigations, correct? (That was my personal presumption, based on the facts, at the time; nothing was moving.) -And in fact, you had a discussion with Secretary of State Pompeo, in which you said the logjam over the aid, could be lifted, if Zelensky would announce these investigations, right? (I did not; I don't recall saying the logjam over the aid; I recall saying the logjam.)

(Schiff presses him a bit) -That's what you meant, right? (I meant that whatever was holding up the meeting; whatever was holding up our deal with Ukraine, I was trying to break that logjam... I was presuming...) -Here's what you said, in your earlier testimony; on page 18; "but my goal of the time was to do what was necessary, to get the aid released; to break the logjam..." -That is your testimony, right? (yes) -So the military aid, is also an official act, am I right? (yes) -This is not President Trump's personal bank account; he's writing a check from, this is $400 million of taxpayer money, is it not? (absolutely) -And there was a logjam, in which the President would not write that US check, you believed; until Ukraine announced these two investigations, that the President wanted, correct? (That was my belief.)

Schiff now gives the questioning over to Mr. Goldman:

Mr. Goldman says, In your opening statement, Ambassador Sondland, you detailed the benefits that you have gained, from obtaining some additional documents, over the past few weeks; is that right? -in terms of refreshing your recollection; because reviewing these documents has helped you to remember events that we are asking about; is that correct? (yes, correct) -Because you acknowledge, of course, that when you can place a document, and a date, and a context, it helps to jog your memory... (that's correct) -So, you would agree that, for people unlike yourself, that take notes; that that is very helpful to their own recollection? (Sondland astutely asks, are you saying, people who take notes will have a better recollection, or people that don't take notes? (it gets a laugh) -But you would agree, that people who do take contemporaneous notes, generally are more able to remember things; than the people who don't... (Some, yes)

-There are additional documents that you have been unable to obtain; and I think you said in your opening statement, that the State Department prevented you and your staff from trying to gather more documents... (Certain documents, yes) -Which documents? (Documents that I didn't have immediate access to.) -And who, at the State Department, prevented you from doing that? (You would have to ask my counselor- he was dealing with that.) -But certainly, based on the additional memory that you have gained, over the past two weeks; from reading the testimony of others, based on their notes; and reviewing your own documents; you have remembered a lot more than you did, when you were deposed; am I right?

(That's correct) -And one of the things that you now remember, is a discussion that you had with President Trump on July 26th, at a restaurant in Kyiv, right? (What triggered my memory, was someone's reference to "ASAP Rocky," which was, I believe, the primary purpose of the phone call.) -Certainly; so that's one way of memory works; you were sitting at a restaurant with David Holmes, in Kyiv... (I think I took the whole team out to lunch, after the meeting, yes.) -And it was a one-on-one meeting, that you had with Andre Yermak? (Again; trying to reconstruct a very busy day, without the benefit of any documentation; I had a meeting, and I went to the meeting; and I'm not disputing that.) -You sat outside the door, and you didn't let them in? (I have no control over who goes into a meeting, in Ukraine; that was the Ukrainians, that wouldn't let him in.) -And you also met with President Zelensky and others, that day? (That's correct.) -And you called President Trump from your cell phone, from the restaurant; is that right? -And this is not a secure line, was it not? -How can you be sure that a foreign government may not be listening to your phone call with the President of the United States? (I have unclassified conversations all the time, from land lines that are unsecured; and cell phones; if the topic is not classified, it's up to the President, to decide what's classified, and what's not classified.) He was aware that it was an open line, as well... and you don't recall the specifics of holding your phone far away from your ear, as Mr. Holmes testified? -But you have no reason to question his recollection about that, do you? (It seems a little strange, because I generally hold the phone close to my ear.) -But he claims to have overheard part of the conversation... (I won't dispute what he did, or didn't hear.) -And Holmes also testified that you confirmed to President Trump that you were in Ukraine, at the time; and that President Zelensky quote "loves your ass." Do you recall saying that? (It sounds like something I would say; that's how President Trump and I communicate; a lot of four-letter words; three letters, in this case.) (it gets a laugh)

Holmes then said that he heard President Trump ask, quote "Is he (Zelensky) going to do the investigations? -And you told Trump that he's going to do it; and then you added that, "President Zelensky will do anything that you ask!" -Do you recall that? (I probably said something to that effect; because I remember, in the meeting with President Zelensky, he was very willing to work with the United States, and he was being very amicable; and so I was putting it in Trump speak; by saying he "loves your ass," or whatever; he had said that he would really work with us, on a whole host of issues.) -He was not only willing, he was very eager? (That's fair.) -Because Ukraine depends on the United States, as its most significant ally… (Absolutely.) -So, just so we understand; you are in Kyiv, the day after President Trump spoke to Presidents Zelensky on the phone, and you now know, from reading the call record, that in that phone call, he requested a favor of President Zelensky to do investigations, related to the Bidens, and the 2016 election, right? (I do now know that, yes.) -You met with President Zelensky, on the day after that phone call; and then you had a conversation with President Trump, from your cell phone; from the restaurant Terrace; and he asked you whether President Zelensky will do the investigations… -and you responded that he's going to do them; or that Presidents Zelensky will do anything you ask him to do; is that an accurate representation of what you had said? (It might've been words to that effect; I don't remember my exact response.) -But you don't have any reason to dispute Mr. Holmes recollection, is that right? (I won't dispute it; but again; I don't recall.)

-After you hung up with the President, Mr. Holmes testified about a conversation, that you and he had, where Mr. Holmes said that you told him that the President does not care about Ukraine; but the President had used more- colorful language; the four-letter words that you just referenced; -do you recall saying that, to Mr. Holmes? (Again; I don't recall my exact words; but clearly, the President; beginning on May 23rd, we met with him in the Oval Office; and he was not a big fan (of Ukraine), but he was a big fan of the investigations… (Apparently so.) -In fact, Mr. Holmes said that you had said that Trump only cares about the quote, "Big stuff, that benefits himself; is that something that you would have said, at the time? (I don't think I would've said that; I would've honestly said that he was not a big fan of Ukraine; -and that he wants the investigations that we had been talking about, for quite some time, to move forward; that's what I would've said; because that's the facts.)

Mr. Holmes also remembers that you told him; giving an example of the big stuff; the Biden investigation, that Rudy Giuliani was pushing; do you recall that? (I recall Burisma, but not "Bidens.") -But you recall, at least, referring to one investigation that Rudy Giuliani was pushing; is that something likely for you to have said? (yes) -Now, even if you don't recall specifically mentioning the Biden investigation, to David Holmes, we know that it certainly was on President Trump's mind; because, just the day before, in his call with President Zelensky, he mentioned, specifically, the Biden investigation; and I want to show you that excerpt from the call, on July 25th. "The other thing, there's a lot of talk about Biden's son; that Biden stopped the prosecution, and a lot of people want to find out about that; so whatever you can do with the Attorney General would be great. Biden went around bragging that he had stopped the prosecution; so if you can look into it, it sounds horrible to me."

Presidents Zelensky then responds with reference to the company that he is referring to; and two witnesses yesterday, said that when Presidents Zelensky actually said the company he said "Burisma;" -so you would agree that, regardless of whether <u>you</u> knew about the connection to the Bidens; at the very least you now know that that's what President Trump wanted, at the time; do the Burisma investigation, he says… (I now know a lot more.) -Of course, at the time you weren't aware; but you now are aware of the President's desire, along with Rudy Giuliani's, to do these investigations, including the 2016 election interference investigation; is that right? (That is correct.) -And you said that President Trump had directed you, and the others, to talk to Rudy Giuliani; from the Oval Office, within your May 23rd meeting? (If we wanted to get anything done with Ukraine, it was apparent to us that we needed to talk to Rudy.) -You understood that Mr. Giuliani spoke for the President? (That's correct.) -And in fact, President Trump also made that clear to President Zelensky; in that same July 25th phone call; he said that Mr. Giuliani is a highly-respected man; he was the mayor of New York City; a great mayor; and I will ask him to call you, along with the Attorney General; Rudy very much knows what's happening, and he is very capable… -And after this, President Trump then mentions Mr. Giuliani twice more, in that call. Now, as to Giuliani; by this point, you understood that, in order to get that White House meeting that you wanted President Zelensky to have; Zelensky desperately wanted to have that; Ukraine would have to initiate these two investigations, is that right? (Well, they would have to <u>announce</u> that they were going to.) -Because Giuliani and President Trump didn't actually care if they did them, right? (I never heard, Mr. Goldman, anyone say that the investigations had to start, or be completed; the only thing I heard from Mr. Giuliani, or otherwise, was that these investigations had to be announced publicly, in some form or another.) -And you, of course, recognized that there would be political benefits, to a public announcement; as opposed to a private announcement... (The way it was explained to me, the way it was expressed to me, was that the Ukrainians had a long history of committing to things, privately, and then never following through; so President Trump, presumably, again; communicated to Mr. Giuliani that he wanted the Ukrainians to go on record publicly, that they were going to do these investigations; that's the reason that was given to me.)

-But you never heard anyone say that they really wanted them to do the investigations? (I didn't hear that.) Nor did you find that out in any other way either... -Now, your July 26th call with the President was not the only time that you spoke to the President, surrounding that Ukraine trip, was it? (I believe I spoke with him before his call.) -So that would be on July 25th? (Yeah, I think I was flying to Ukraine, and I spoke with him, if I recall correctly, just before I got on the plane.) -So, that's two private telephone calls, with President Trump; in the span of two days? (That's correct.)

-You have direct access, then, to President Trump, correct? (I had occasional access, when he chose to take my call; sometimes he wouldn't.) -He certainly took your call twice, as a related to Ukraine, on these two days; is that right? (yes) -Now, the morning of July 25th, you texted and Ambassador Volker, we can bring up the next text exchange; at 7:54 AM you said, call ASAP... Volker did not respond to you, for another hour and a half. Then, he texted, Gordon, got your message, had a great lunch with Yermak, and passed your message on to him; he will see you tomorrow; I think everything is in place... Then, in about a half-hour before the phone call, he wrote, Heard from White House; assuming President Z convinces Trump he will investigate, get to the bottom of what happened in 2016, we will nail down a date for a visit to Washington. good luck, see you tomorrow... -Was this message that you passed on to Yermak, the message that you left for Kurt Volker on that email; that he referenced? (You know, I don't remember Mr. Goldman; it very well could've been.) You don't have any reason to think it wasn't, right? (Again; I honestly don't remember; but seems logical to me.) -And Ambassador Volker testified that he did get that message from you... -do you have any reason to doubt that? (It's fair, to say that.)

-This is the message that you received from President Trump, that morning... (Again; if I testified to that, you would have to refresh my memory, but yes, I would have received this message from President Trump; that sequence certainly makes sense, does it not? (Right.) -You talked to President Trump, you left a message for Kurt Volker, he sent this text message to Andre Yermak, to prepare Presidents Zelensky, and then President Trump had a phone call, where President Zelensky spoke very similarly to what was in this text message; is that right? (yes) -And you would agree, that the message expressed here, was that President Zelensky needs to convince Trump that he will do the investigations; in order to nail down a date for a visit to Washington DC? (That's correct.)

-Now, to move ahead in time, to the end of August; or early September, when you came to believe, you testified, that it wasn't just a White House meeting, that was contingent on the announcement of these investigations, that the President wanted; but the security assistance, as well... -You testified that, in the absence of any credible explanation for the hold on the security assistance, you came to the conclusion that, like the White House visit, the aid was conditioned on the investigations, that President Trump wanted; isn't that what you said in your opening statement? (yes)

-So, let me break this down with you; at this time, you, and many top officials, knew that coveted White House meeting for President Zelensky, was conditioned on these investigations, right? -The announcement of the investigations...

(Sondland clarifies, that includes Secretary Mike Pompeo, Chief of Staff Mick Mulvaney, and many others) Goldman continues, -And you testified that this was a quid pro quo... (yes)

-And, at this point, by the end of August, you knew that the aid had been held up, for at least six weeks; is that correct? (I believe I found out through, Ambassador Taylor, that the aid had been held up, around July 18th, is when I heard originally.) -And even though you searched for reasons, you were never given a credible explanation, as to why? (That's right.) -And no one you spoke to, thought that the aid should be held up; to your knowledge; is that right? (I never heard anyone advocate for holding the aid.) -And now, by this point, at the end of August, it went public; and the Ukrainians knew about it; is that right? (I believe there were some press reports presuming this; or who knows, but I think, at that point, it became common knowledge that everything might be tied together.) -In fact, President Zelensky brought it up, at the September 1st meeting; with Vice President Pence, is that correct? (I don't know if he brought it up specifically.) -But he asked where the aid was at? (I think it was more that he asked; and again; I have a very vague recollection, as I don't have a readout of the bilateral meeting; but I think he basically asked, why don't I have my check? essentially.) -And you understood that the Ukrainians received no credible explanation? (I certainly wasn't given one.)

-Was this kind of a 2+2 = 4 conclusion that you reached? (Pretty much.) -It was the only logical conclusion to you, given all these factors, that the aid was also a part of this quid pro quo? (yes)

Now, I want to go back to the conversation that you had with Vice President Pence, right before that meeting in Warsaw; and you indicated that you said to him that you are concerned that the delay in aid was tied to the issue of the investigations, is that right? (I don't know exactly what I said to him; this was a briefing attended by many people, and I wasn't invited until at the very last minute; I wasn't scheduled to be there; but I think I spoke up at some point, late in the meeting, and said that, at least, it like it looks like everything is being held up, until these statements get made; and that's my personal belief.) -And Vice President Pence just nodded? (Again; I don't recall any exchange, or whether he asked any questions; I think it was sort of a duly-noted gesture.)

Goldman clarifies, Pence didn't say, "Gordon, what are you talking about?" He didn't say, "what investigations?" (no) -After this meeting; in this "aside" that you had, with Mr. Yermak, is where you relayed your belief, that they needed to announce these investigations, prior to the aid being released; is that right?

(I said, I didn't know exactly why; but this could be a reason.) -And obviously, you had been speaking with Mr. Yermak for quite a while, about the public announcement of these investigations, right? (We had all been working toward that end.) -So, you indicated to him, that in addition to the White House meeting, the security aid was now also involved in the conditioning... (I said it could've been involved, yes.)

-And I want to show you another text exchange, that you had on September 1st, where Ambassador Taylor says to you, "Are we now saying that the security assistance, and the White House meeting, are conditioned on investigations? -And you responded, "Call me." -Ambassador Taylor recalls that he did call you; and you did have a conversation; and in that conversation, you told Ambassador Taylor, that the announcement of these investigations by President Zelensky, needed to be publicly, and that that announcement was a condition of, or this would ultimately release the aid; do you recall that conversation with Ambassador Taylor? (Again; my conversations with Ambassador Taylor, and with Senator Johnson, were only based on my personal belief; as you put it, 2+2 = 4.) -In his testimony, Ambassador Taylor says, that you had said that President Trump had told you, that he wanted President Zelensky to state it publicly, as of September 1st; do you have any reason to doubt Ambassador Taylor's testimony, which he said was based on his meticulous, contemporaneous notes? (President Trump never told me directly, that the aid was conditioned on the announcements; the only thing we heard directly from Giuliani, was that investigations of Burisma, and the 2016 elections, were a condition of the White House meeting; the aid was my own personal guess; based again, on your analogy of 2+2 = 4.)

-So, you didn't talk to President Trump? -when Ambassador Taylor says that, that's what you told him; isn't that your testimony, right? (My testimony is, I never heard, spoken by President Trump, that the aid was conditioned on the announcement of election meddling investigations.) -So, you never heard the specific words? (I never heard those words.)

-Let's move ahead; because you had another conversation, a little bit later; that Tim Morrison, and Ambassador Taylor recounted similarly; in your first conversation, Ambassador Taylor says; and you also testified under oath, that you said that President Trump wanted Zelensky in a "public Boss." (Yes, that goes back to my earlier comment, that again; coming from the Giuliani source; because we did not discuss specifically, with President Trump, that he wanted whatever commitments that Ukraine made to be public, so they would be on the public record; so they could be held more accountable.)

-Ambassador Taylor also testified, that you told him that you had made a mistake, in telling the Ukrainians, that only the White House meeting was conditioned on the announcements of the investigations; and that, in fact, everything was conditional now, on the announcements. (My reference to a "mistake" was that I thought that merely a statement made by the new Ukrainian prosecutor, that these investigations would be started up again, or commenced, would be sufficient, to satisfy President Trump; as I recall. My mistake was that, if someone came back to Volker otherwise, and said "No; it's not going to do!" If the prosecutor makes the statements. The President wants to hear it from Zelensky, directly. That's the mistake I think I made.)

-Do you have any reason to question Ambassador Taylor's testimony; based on his contemporaneous notes? (I'm not going to question it; I just can't tell you what I believe I was referring to.) -Let me show you another text exchange, which may help refresh your recollection. On September 8th, you sent a text to (Volker and Taylor), "Just had multiple conversations with Zelensky, and POTUS; let's talk.

September 8th at 11:20 in the morning, Ambassador Taylor responds immediately, "Now is fine with me." -Then, we can go to the next exchange, 15 minutes later; Ambassador Taylor says 20 minutes later, "Gordon and I just spoke; I can brief you, if you and Gordon don't connect... -And the nightmare, is that, if they give the interview, and then don't get security assistance; Russians love it, (and I quit!) -That's what Taylor had said, an hour later... -When he first asked, you would agree, that this text message, after you had spoken earlier with Ambassador Taylor; that he is linking the security assistance to this interview; this public announcement by President Zelensky, right? (Absolutely.) -And in fact, Ambassador Taylor testified that you did have a conversation with him at that point, and that you had told him; just as your text message indicates; that you did just have a conversation with President Trump, prior to that text message; does that help to refresh your recollection? -That you did speak with President Trump... (Again; I don't recall President Trump ever talking to me about security assistance; what this tells me, refreshing my memory, is that by September 8th, it was abundantly clear to everyone, that there was, there was a leak; and that we were discussing the chicken-and-egg issue, of should the Ukrainians go out on a limb, and make the statement that President Trump wanted them to make; and then they still don't get their White House visit and their aid! That would be really bad for our credibility. I think that's what he was referring to.) -So, you do acknowledge that you spoke to President Trump; as you indicated in that text... (If I said I did; I did.) -And then, after that conversation, you were still under the impression that the aid was contingent on the public announcements? (I did not get that, from President Trump; but I was under that impression; absolutely.)

-And afterward, you still thought that the aid was conditioned on the public announcement of the investigations; after speaking to President Trump? (By September 8th, I was absolutely convinced it was.)

-And President Trump did not dissuade you of that, in the conversation that you acknowledge you had with him? (I don't ever recall that, because that would have changed my entire calculus; if President Trump had told me directly.)

Ambassador Sondland, I'm asking; you still believed that the security assistance was conditioned on the investigations; after you spoke to President Trump? Yes, or no? (From a timeframe standpoint; yes.) -Now, Ambassador Taylor also testified, and also Mr. Morrison; they both testified, that you told them President Trump said there was no quid pro quo; but you also referenced, in that text message, and they have slight variations, as to what you told them; but you said then to Ambassador Taylor, that President Zelensky himself, and not the prosecutor general, needed to clear things up in public; or there would be a "stalemate."

-And Mr. Morrison recounted something similar. You don't have any reason to doubt that both of their similar recollections, of conversations they had with you, do you, Ambassador Sondland? (Let me break that down, Mr. Goldman; that text, as I said about the no quid pro quo, was my effort to respond to Ambassador Taylor's concerns. Taylor could not go to President Trump; but apparently, Ambassador Taylor had access to secretary Pompeo; so I made a phone call to Ambassador Taylor; I told him that I had said to the President, "What do you want?" -and President Trump had responded with what I put in the text; and then I strongly encouraged Ambassador Taylor to take it up with the Secretary; and he responded, "I agree." As far as the other part of your question, relating to whether or not the prosecutor could make the statement, or Zelensky would have to make a statement; I don't recall who told me what; whether it was Rudy Giuliani or President Trump; but I was told that it has to be Zelensky making the announcement; it can't be the prosecutor. Wherever I got the information from, I relayed that to, I believe, Ambassador Taylor and Mr. Morrison.)

-But as of September 9th, you understood, did you not? -that President Trump; either himself, or through his agents, required that President Zelensky make public announcements of these investigations that President Trump cared about; in order to get, both the White House meeting, and release of the security assistance; is that right? (I believe that is correct.)

This concludes Schiff and Goldman's 45 minutes; and now it goes to Devin Nunez and Steve Castor; but that they will take a five-minute break, first.

{Since Sondland is obviously not exactly exuberantly trying to strengthen the case against Trump, with his answers, it's pretty clear that he is basically, only there because he had received a Subpoena from Congress; and he knows he is a key witness. I believe that his, was the first closed-door deposition in the basement of the Intelligence Committee chambers; and Trump may not even have, by then, issued the directive, that no one come forward, or give over any documentation.

In Sondland's first deposition, if you remember, he answered that he could not recall; on almost every question of significance. Then after others had come forward and spilled the beans more, Sondland had to save face; and also in order to avert a possible perjury charge later perhaps, so he felt compelled to come back before the Intelligence Committee, a second time, to amend his testimony; claiming that the recent testimony that others were giving, had refreshed his memory. That could be a little dubious, maybe. Nevertheless, Schiff and Goldman did eventually succeed in getting Sondland to admit to, what amounted to a fairly damning degree of testimony against Trump.}

Devin Nunez starts of the minority's questioning:

I'm not going to transcribe his whole opening statement; which I consider to be pretty much entirely a bunch of nonsense, that has nothing to do with the charges against the dopey, crooked, President Trump. I will just listen to it again, and make comments as we go. He says that Democrats have been unwilling to accept that their operatives were engaged in a subversive campaign to dig up dirt on Trump during the 2016 election campaign. All of this bullshit has nothing to do with the fact that Trump did what he did; and regardless of what others might have done to speak out against Trump in 2016, it doesn't even matter if Trump is upset with Ukraine, and thinks people in Ukraine unfairly expressed disapproval.

Doing what Trump masterminded and saw through, in terms of a nasty campaign to smear and remove a stellar, long-time dedicated Foreign Service worker; and even much worse; this was all to clear the way for an unimpeded pressure campaign, using the withholding of Congressionally-approved taxpayer-funded military aid, and other needed, and well-deserved, demonstrations of US support; which was merely in the US and Ukraine's best interest; in order to force the new Ukrainian regime to falsely cast, and render impotent as a contender against him, the one whom Trump had perceived of as his most-likely nominee to run against him in the 2020 Presidential election.

As a US President, you can't do this! This is way below board; it is precisely what the Framers of the US Constitution sought to guard against and punish.

Nunez, like usual, is not really asking questions of the witness, to invoke enlightening testimony; he's asking if he is aware of this crap that he is spewing about a single company's past corruption, related to a time period that is years before the planning and events being confronted, as the basis for these hearings.

Of course, Sondland doesn't know any of this contended bullshit about Ukraine in 2015 or whatever; he wasn't even appointed by Trump as Ambassador to the EU until 2018.

Nunez is now talking about the infamous "Black ledger," which became an issue in 2016 during the last Presidential campaign period. Next, Nunez reads back a part of recent testimony referring to the May 23rd Oval Office meeting of the three amigos, and Trump, He quotes what President Trump said; that he didn't like Ukrainians; and Trump's quoted statement, that (certain Ukrainians) "They tried to take him down;" this has nothing to do what's going on now, of course; there is no rationalization that would make it the least bit warranted to pull off the odious, underhanded scheme he undertook all year long.

Next, Nunez is claiming that Rudy Giuliani was trying to find out who it was that was so-called hurting Trump; obviously he thinks unfairly so; Nunez says that Republican committee members had wanted subpoena DNC operatives; but again, that's just about the 2016 tactics that went on between political campaigns. It did not in any way constitute what Trump was doing; which was leaning heavily on the vulnerable Ukraine government, to do some political favors, merely of personal benefit to Trump.

Now he goes on, once again, about the whistleblower; Nunez is asking Sondland whether he knows of any drug deal; referring to John Bolton's May 23rd characterization of the dirty dealings Trump and Giuliani were up to, as of last spring. Bolton had obviously termed what was happening, a "drug deal" as a joke. s

Nunez says that the "quid pro quo" was at a very low level. Yeah; all they wanted was a statement that would ruin Joe Biden; that's very low-level; I see.

Nunez says to Sondland, you knew nothing about military aid being withheld; as of July 25th; and Sondland contradicts, I knew about the hold on the aid, as of July 18th, when Ambassador Taylor told me.

{Why is Nunez discussing that which <u>wasn't</u> discussed, on that July 25th call? The aid was not discussed until later, as an added afterthought, to increase the pressure on Zelensky to make the desperately-sought announcements that would have perhaps clinched his reelection}.

Sondland says that the Ukrainians hadn't known about the aid at that point, perhaps; however, the 2016 election-meddling investigation, and the Burisma investigation, we knew about these, much earlier. They think Hunter Biden would have something to do with this, simply because they were pissed that Biden's son was able to make $50,000 a month, in this position at Burisma; but that's what apparently goes along with being "the Vice President's son" sometimes. Look at how monumentally that Trump's son, and his daughter, are able to not only cash in on, but also be undeservedly placed in a position of prominent leadership, as well; is this unfair and unjust? Sure; but as Mulvaney would say; get over it; it's just what happens in a case like this.

Nunez is now talking about someone who was an Ambassador in Ukraine, in 2015; still, nothing is said that has any bearing on the matter. He tells us that Hunter Biden made $3 million altogether from Burisma; that's interesting; but so what?!

To all of these little pieces of information Nunez is trumpeting, Sondland is confirming that he "did not know that;" to all the stuff Nunez is saying. Nunez is just using this opportunity to be a mouthpiece, the hearings are his latest venue to mouth all of these insubstantial things about Burisma, or Ukraine, related to past years, having nothing to do with the matter at hand.

Now Nunez is talking about how they dirtied up the Trump campaign. Well obviously, they didn't dirty it up very much; because that idiot one half the vote, across the entire country; Jesus! (even though this was greatly "Trumped-up" due to the expansive disinformation that his pal Putin orchestrated in order to ensure Trump would get into office.)

Finally, he gives over Questioning to Mr. Castor. Upon Castor's first line of questioning, Sondland tells us that his first contact with Giuliani started had actually started pretty late in the process; on August 1st apparently. (I don't know if we shouldn't doubt that; since he had been placed in Ukraine quite a while beforehand, in 2018; and with so many people now coming forward to disclose that they long-understood the gist of what Trump was trying to ultimately force Ukraine into accomplishing for him, it seems rather doubtful that Sondland was quite so unaware himself; especially given that he was one of the main point people being controlled like a puppet, by Trump and Giuliani. I'm figuring that Trump has probably put Sondland up to trying to portray a scenario that would cast doubt on his complicit plot; in that Trump obviously still has leverage over Sondland, who intends to go on being the Ambassador to the EU; with Trump's blessing.)

Sondland says that he and Volker had already begun conversations with the Ukrainians prior to that; over the course of the summer. Castor asked how did you know that Giuliani was expressing the desires of the President; when the President says talk to my personal attorney, and Giuliani asked certain demands?

Sondland says, we assumed that it came from the President, the three of us; our conclusion was that if we did not talk to Rudy, that nothing would move forward. Volker and others were talking to Giuliani earlier in the year. Stupidly for their side, Castor states that Marie Yovanovitch was a "brilliant" Ambassador." {Their side; the Republican side; is standing behind the President who smeared her and had her removed!}

Castor lauds Kurt Volker, as an outstanding Foreign Service officer, citing his long, impressive record; Sondland agrees with Castor's characterization of Volker. Next, Castor contends that Volker didn't have any knowledge of these preconditions; meaning the quid pro quo that Ukraine would have to make announcements that would ruin the reputation of Trump's chief rival, in order to receive official US acts of support. I assume that the "conditions" Castor is next referring to are that the "three amigos" had to work things out with Rudy, and take direction from him.

Castor then walked Sondland through his recollection of the related conversations that he had had with President Trump; and so, he is now alluding to what was said between them on July 25th, when Sondland was speaking to Trump from his jet, bound for Ukraine.

Then, he skips ahead, to their interactions in early September. (Of course, anything said after September 1; at which point it is firmly established that the Ukrainians had full knowledge of all three conditions which must be met, in order to get their nevertheless deserved, US support; anything after September 1st, and before September 11th, when the conditions were called off due to Trump's plot being foiled, is immaterial.)

Sondland says he may have spoken to the President on September 6th, as well September 9th; but he doesn't have his records to verify that. Sondland then alludes to his September 9th phone conversation, where he had asked Trump the open question, of "What do you want?" (regarding the Ukraine situation); where Trump had replied, "I want nothing!" -But of course, in that same conversation, Trump had later said that he <u>wants</u> Zelensky to <u>want</u> to go to the press, and announce these investigations.

The aid was paused for 55 days; Castor says there was a political news article on August 28th, where this had come out. Then, Castor nitpicks that, in the absence of explanation, Sondland had testified that he had presumed that the aid was also conditional on the announcements being made first.

Castor wants to make sure to establish, that this was merely Sondland's speculation. Sondland then alludes to the 2+2 = 4 idea that Goldman had discussed with him just minutes beforehand. Sondland replies that, the aid wasn't being released, and we weren't getting anywhere with the Ukrainians; so, it could also be seen as a reasonable and logical deduction that the aid was also being conditioned.

When Castor then asked about Vice President Pence's meeting with Zelensky, Sondland began talking about the September 1st meeting in Warsaw; we are told that he was given a "green light," by Pompeo, to brief President Zelensky beforehand, about what he should express to Pence, regarding Zelensky making the demanded announcements, in order to get the aid released. Castor asked him when his email to Pompeo, to ask for his blessing to do so; and Sondland says, on August 22nd. Castor is pointing out that, in Sondland's exchange with Pompeo, before this Warsaw meeting, there wasn't anything specifically said about the Bidens or Burisma; that only the word "investigation," had appeared within the texts; but I think it's pretty clear that everybody knew by then, what was in the offing; and especially since we just heard from Lev Parnas, in an interview on MSNBC, him telling us that everybody was in the loop, and working toward this goal of forcing the Ukrainians into making ruinous announcements, to Joe Biden; to be necessarily made by President Zelensky. Apparently, this was a scheme that even Attorney General Bill Barr was involved in, we find out!

In response to Castor's trying to obscure the fact that, certainly by September 1st, the Ukrainians knew the full extent of the conditions involved in the quid pro quo, Sondland says the statement they were all working on for the Ukrainians to put forth publicly, would have indeed mentioned the 2016 election meddling, and the Burisma investigations.

Castor is now saying, Ambassador Volker had once said, that if there were Ukrainians, who had engaged violations of Ukrainian law, then the Prosecutor General within the new administration, ought to investigate that. (Yeah, so what?) Sondland says, we just talked in general terms, about investigating Burisma, in the beginning. Sondland doesn't recall the exact date, but at some point, there was a connection between Burisma and the Bidens; that he knew that investigations of the Bidens were associated with the demands on Zelensky to make announcements of investigations underway; but later it becomes clear, that Giuliani was trying to keep that quiet; he had never even mentioned the name "Biden" to Volker, at all.

Castor is now saying that Senator Johnson called President Trump, when Sondland had told him, at the end of August, about the hold on the aid.

Johnson had called the President on August 31st. Senator Johnson had made a statement to the Intelligence Committee; and in that statement, he writes, I asked the President whether there was some kind of arrangement, where Ukraine would take some action, and then the hold be lifted? -And without hesitation, (Johnson reports), President Trump immediately denied that such a demand existed; (but of course, Trump would certainly say that to someone in Johnson's position. Trump had also said, "No quid pro quo!" -but he was indeed asking for a quid pro quo!

Castor says that Senator Johnson had characterized Trump's response to his question, about whether the Ukrainians had to do something, that would then get the aid released; Johnson had reported that Trump sounded angry, vehement, and adamant!

Well, but hasn't Trump been outwardly angry, vehement, and adamant, ever since his fiendish plot got found out, and he started experiencing a shit-storm of confrontation about this?

-And also, what Castor was talking about, only underscores that Trump will say one thing to one person who is complicit, in this scheme; and then he'll deny it to the next person who is not complicit; which was the case with Senator Johnson, right?! Johnson wasn't complicit in the scheme; so, Trump couldn't very well say, "Yes, that's true."

Next, Castor stupidly posits to Sondland, there isn't <u>that</u> many documents that you are missing, is there? in terms of your communications with the President... Sondland says, (it's true that) I haven't had that many communications with the President... (but what is stupid, is that Castor is bringing further attention to the fact that we won't be granted access to these important, potentially revealing records; purely because Trump has obstructed this investigation. Castor is trying to say, well, you're telling me that you don't clearly recall some of the material conversations that you had with the President; how can we consider your testimony as legitimate? (but of course, well if there really were no material conversations that the President might worry about being revealed to Congress, then why hasn't Sondland been enabled to access those records, and bring them into these hearings?)

Castor then stupidly asks, and are there any other fact witnesses that could help us get to the bottom of the hold, on the aid? (you idiot, of course is; like 10 of them, surrounding President Trump; that talk with him every day! Trump has barred every one of them from testifying; you can't use this as a defense against having verifiable evidence; if all of it is prohibited from the proceedings, by the very defendant at the trial, himself!)

Sondland offers that Brian McCormick, the Chief of Staff for Energy Secretary Perry, would be helpful. Next, Castor tells us that, on August 31st, the President writes Senator Johnson, and says, "Ron, I'm reviewing the situation of the aid now, and you'll probably like my decision…" so Castor is saying that the President is signaling to Johnson, that he was perhaps soon to lift the hold on the aid. Sondland says, it sounds like it…" (you know, what's interesting is that Trump has had to play this whole game, throughout the 55 days that the aid was held; and even months before that, regarding the investigation-announcing strong-arming. Strategically. Trump knew that he couldn't let on to anyone; but the people involved in the scheme; that he was even holding the aid, or strong-arming Zelensky secretly and underhandedly; so when he wrote to Johnson; after Johnson had basically complained, are you serious?! -that the Ukrainians have to do something in order for you to release the aid?!

-And so first Trump vehemently denies that; over the phone; -and then he writes Johnson a letter saying he'd be happy to know of Trumps pending decision, "I'm thinking about releasing the aid…" (but Trump didn't release the aid; that letter was sent on August 1st, and the aid did not get released to the 11th; and then again, only because Trump's plot got foiled; so he could no longer hold the aid, any further!)

Castor asks Sondland if, by that point, he had thought that the aid was going to be soon released; and Sondland smartly responded that, he never got any answer to this question, of why the aid was put on hold in the first place! -So, no. Sondland says he doesn't know if it was the politico article of August 28th, that triggered the Ukrainians' knowledge about the aid being held, or if it was before that; it might've been told to them by Giuliani, or someone else that knew about it.

He emphasizes that he, Sondland, knew about the hold on the aid since July18th, though. Sondland says, there were a lot of conversations going on, by a lot of people, with the Ukrainians. {and this is what I had rhetorically asked, earlier on; is it really possible that, with dozens of State Department, and Office of Management and Budget personnel, and a number of US administration officials, as well; who mostly had known that the aid was being withheld, since mid-July; is it really conceivable that, absolutely no one leaked a word, or a hint, to a single Ukrainian; not anybody for 55 whole days? -when the Ukrainians were anticipating the arrival of $400 million, that yet was vexingly still not coming to them? I really find that very hard to believe.}

Next, Castor comes out with the argument, that President Trump was not a fan of giving aid to any country; and so that would be a reason why he would put a hold on this aid; (but that's a stupid argument, because although there may be many other countries that, it wouldn't be critical to the US, whether we gave them aid in a timely fashion; but with Ukraine, they are fighting off Russia, nefariously expanding their territory by using military force; which no country has done for 44 years; since a pact was made among nations, since World War II; that, and what Russia is doing is dead against democracy; that the US supposedly stands for so fiercely; so, if the aid to <u>any</u> country should be questioned; it should most definitely be a country in Ukraine's situation, of course.

Castor's argument is that Trump was concerned about the EU countries, not putting as much money toward Ukraine, as perhaps they should. That, still would not be a reason, not to seamlessly fund the "hot war" going on between a democracy and Russia, under an authoritarian rule; having expanded into Ukraine's sovereign territory.

Now, Castor is talking about the July 10th meeting, in Ambassador Bolton's office, involving Volker Mr. Doniluk, and Mr. Yermak; which has been the subject of some controversy. Ambassador Volker had yesterday testified that it wasn't until the end of the meeting, when Mr. Doniluk was going through some detailed information, about some of the plans he had; that Ambassador Volker said that Sondland had mentioned something about the demanded investigations. Sondland says, again; I'm not going to dispute what Ambassador Volker is saying; but I know that, (at the time of this meeting), the desire to have the

2016 election DNC server, and Burisma investigations announced by Zelensky, were already being discussed.

Sondland adds that even though by that date, I had not yet had any direct contact with Giuliani (not until July 20th), through Ambassador Volker, I knew what Giuliani basically had wanted. I probably mentioned that the announcements need to be made first, to Ukraine staff members present; in order to move the process forward; that seemed to me, conventional wisdom; at the time. He also adds that he remembers nothing but silence, as being the immediate reaction to his comments. Sondland says, I don't recall people storming out, or anything; that would have been very memorable…

Castor, next is asking about the phrase "drug deal" (you know, which was Bolton's joke, to allude to the dirty dealing that was going on over this Ukraine matter; but Castor is, I suppose, trying to use "drug deal" in a literal sense; and he gets Sondland to say that he was shocked when that phrase "drug deal" came out. -But apparently, the fact of the matter is that, that's what Bolton had actually characterized what was going on as likened to a "drug deal;" and Republicans can deny that all they want; but it was a very apt characterization, in the viewpoint of many people looking at this nasty scheme, of course.

Sondland's recollection is that, at this point in the meeting, Ambassador Bolton had said that he had another meeting to attend; and that's how the meeting got disbanded. (but I've been at meetings before; or I've been in the middle of a conversation with somebody who says something totally outlandish; or there's some bullshit going on in the three-way conversation between me and two other people, where the two other people are being ridiculous; and at these kinds of moments, I've certainly said, "Oh look, I'm late for a meeting; I gotta go…" -so, I'm sure that's what Bolton was doing; it <u>indeed</u> an abrupt end to the meeting; he was just strategic enough about it, to end it graciously; but it still was an abrupt end.)

So now, Castor is saying, well after that meeting, you all went out and had a nice smiling picture on the White House lawn; on a nice sunny day, right? (but again, in positions like this; I mean, if you consider that President Trump, as the President of the United

States, had a hold over everybody in his administration; and we know that he just "cans" people instantly; for very little reason; Trump is so hotheaded, impulsive, impetuous, and explosive.

People who have been long-time politicians, and held government posts of great import, they don't want to get summarily canned; and so this is what has happened in the Trump administration. Trump seems to vacillate between canning officials, at the drop of the hat; as they have some amount of integrity, and stand up to Trump's ridiculousness; or the rest of the staffers become totally complicit with Trump, like we are finding out, in these hearings.

Then, perhaps there is a third category of officials, like Bolton, who wanted to keep his job, and was willing to look the other way a bit; but he couldn't stomach being part of a "drug deal," so to speak; so he would end the meeting; but then agree to go out on the lawn, and have his picture taken with them, for show.

Sondland says that that discussion in the basement in the wardroom, that took place just after this meeting had broken up, and they had their pictures taken; was mainly about whether Trump's phone call to President Zelensky should be before the parliamentary elections, or just after them?

In a July 10th meeting, Volker, Perry, and Sondland had thought that it would help Zelensky in the parliamentary election, if President Trump spoke with him beforehand, because it would give President Zelensky more credibility, and ultimately, he might do much better with his people, in the parliamentary elections.

However, others had pushed back, and said no; it's not appropriate to do it before; it should be done after. Ultimately, it was indeed done afterward. Sondland discloses that, all he ever knew about, was Burisma; and he did not even know that that there was connection between Burisma, and the Bidens; (so perhaps, this is how Giuliani kept them in the dark he only gave each of the three amigos, enough information that, this is what they need to get Zelensky to do; just get him to make these announcements. They kept this pressure campaign on for over two months.)

Interestingly, Sondland really looks cross-eyed; after answering that; (he seemed quite unsure if he should have responded to this effect, you could tell, in my view.) This was Sondland's aftershock, after answering affirmatively, when Castor asks, "To be clear; you didn't ever understand that the Ukrainians were to investigate any US people...?" (Sondland says no; and then his face suddenly gets really screwed up; as if he was saying to himself, "What the hell did I just answer?!"

He's probably thinking to himself, yeah, I knew it was about Joe Biden...

(Sondland has this real guilty look on his face)

So next, Castor is picking up on this idea, that the investigations were never started, where they? (yeah, that's only because they never even needed to actually be started; they just needed to be announced; and also, because the plot was discovered and foiled, before Trump could exact those long-sought announcements that he wanted. I'm thinking that, had Trump's scheme <u>not</u> been foiled, it seems the pressure <u>really</u> would've been on; because the aid would not pass to Ukraine if it had not passed by the end of the fiscal year, which is September 30th; so those last few weeks of September would've been a real pressure cooker for the Ukrainians; Zelensky would've been in a cold sweat all night!

Now, Castor is contending Trump's suppose-ed deep-rooted concerned about corruption in Ukraine; but Trump certainly isn't concerned enough about corruption, even to correct his own corruption! The Trump administration may even be about as corrupt as Ukraine ever was, right?!

Sondland tells us, that when he was appointed as Ambassador to the EU, by President Trump, that Ukraine was included as part of his portfolio; but what really made Ukraine a more prominent part of his focus and activities, is the fact that there was no Ambassador in Ukraine, at that time. (as of May, in other words. By that point, Marie Yovanovitch had successfully been whisked away; so now Sondland was appointed as the "substitute Ambassador." This is what he was informing us.

Sondland says that he, Perry, and Volker had impressed it upon Zelensky and his new administration, that this was a time where they needed all the support that they could get, from the US; and their course of action was cleared; by both John Bolton, and Mick Mulvaney; so Sondland contends that he considers what he was doing, was above board, on that basis.

Sondland's pride is hurt; (at least he makes it appear that way); when Castor refers to his work, as being part of an irregular back-channel of diplomacy; he asserts that he had assumed; since he knew he was doing the bidding of the President of the United States; that his role was completely above-board and legitimate; (and in most cases, this would have been true, of course; but not when the President happens to be a lawless, dirty, underhanded guy like Trump; who, only by grave accident of far too many people believing he could make, any of what he had promised, of value, come to pass).

Castor is now asking Sondland whether Ambassador Taylor had ever accused Sondland of being involved in a back channel? -And Sondland says no. (However, we already know that Ambassador Taylor had testified he had no problem with what Volker, and Perry, and Sondland were doing; in terms of trying to usher connections and cooperation between the new Zelensky government, and President Trump; but what Taylor had told us, was that, at some point, this back-channel; or the "irregular" channel, as he termed it, started going against stated foreign policy; as it normally becomes carried out, in Ukraine; or at least, as it has been, since 2014; once the prior Russian leadership figure was forced out of the country.

Castor contends that there were something like 200 text messages, that went on, between Ambassadors Taylor, Volker, and Sondland, during the early August timeframe. Sondland says, I think Ambassador Taylor started in late June (June 17th, I checked), and I think we began communicating, fairly shortly thereafter. Sondland says, at first, Ambassador Taylor was not concerned; in fact, he was appreciative of our cooperation, and our interactive work with him; but as time went on, his text messages became a lot more frantic; that's when everybody else, also had very little visibility, as to why the aid was suspended.

Castor now asks, did you resolve things, in your September 9th call, to President Trump? (well, September 9, of course, was several days after the whistleblower complaint was known to exist; and I think, one day after the whistleblower complaint was finally brought to Congress, and they saw the substance of it; which was quite alarming! -So, whatever Castor thinks that Sondland's conversation with Trump, on September 9th might have accomplished, I believe it was already accomplished, by the fact that Congress was intervening, and had begun a serious investigation into this wrongdoing.

Castor characterizes it, that Sondland had asked Taylor to call him, after one of Taylor's texts, because perhaps Sondland had thought, why should we text, when we can talk about these things on the phone, correct? (and of course, that's not at all, why Sondland asks Taylor to call him, instead of texting; it's because what Taylor is saying, in these texts, is very incriminating; things like, "Are we supposed to now condition aid, on announcement of investigations into the President's political rival?"

Castor artfully prompts Sondland to dispute that he was working in an irregular channel; and Sondland does indeed complain, that he was involved with certain officials in the administration; but the fact of the matter, is that those particular Domestic US administration officials are not normally involved, to any extent, in a Foreign Service initiative that's being carried out, on a day-to-day basis, in some foreign country.

That kind of policy is a written policy; that is merely reviewed and updated once a year, perhaps; but it's a stated policy, and there is a whole foreign Embassy of people who are to carry that policy out; certainly, including the country's Ambassador, at the top, who coordinates this. In this case, the Ambassador (Yovanovitch) was purposely pulled out, so that these irregular people; people such as Sondland, the Ambassador to the EU, (and not to the Ukraine specifically). Taylor had testified that it was unusual for the Ambassador of another country, to be a principal actor, (hot in the middle of) Ukraine's affairs.

Sondland is now trying to claim that that there were no bad vibes, at any time, over this; that nobody complained about it; nobody identified it as an irregular channel; not before these hearings began; but none of that really matters. What matters, is that dirty stuff was going on; and even though they may not have known it at the time, (which I think I dispute- Giuliani certainly knew, and Trump, coordinating with him, certainly knew that what was going on was a dirty scheme, in smearing a 30-year veteran foreign service officer, who had scores of commendations, and a brilliant record; as well as a following of many who thought the world of her integrity, and the value of her service. Yeah; smear her, and remove her; after ruining her reputation; and then put pressure on the new President; when Ukraine is so vulnerable, that they simply cannot fight a powerful and malevolent Russia, without wholehearted US support.

-And then President Trump says, I need you also to smear my opponent, so that I can guarantee my reelection; that is dirty, dirty stuff.

Sondland says, everyone's hair was on fire; but nobody decided to talk to us! (and I rest my case! Exactly! Nobody was going to say "Boo," because the thug at the top was orchestrating this; and everybody just wanted to keep their job.

Castor brings up the point, that on Sondland's first round of depositions, he said "I can't recall, I can't recall, I can't recall…" for two pages of the transcript! Castor is trying to say that, very busy people in high positions can't remember these things; this is understandable; and Sondland says, yes; I'm dealing with the European Union, 28 member countries; and even a few other countries that are not in the European Union; that yet, are part of my mandate. To that, add the White House leadership; there's a lot of stuff to juggle; and as I said in my opening statement; a phone call from the President of the United States; well for most people; they get a call like that, maybe once in a lifetime; so the call might be very memorable.

-But, Sondland continues, I'm doing that all day long; and I'm not saying that, in a way of being braggadocio; but as part of my routine every day; I talk to many high-level people; so all of these calls and meetings, with all of these important people, tend to blend together; until I have something where someone can show me what we discussed; what the subject was; and then, all of a sudden, it comes back to me. (so, this is, again, a great argument for the necessity of being able to access your records, as a State Department employee; in an inquiry such as this one. It is totally unfair, and totally dirty, that Trump has prohibited the reasonable allowance of people to look at their notes, and review their documentation; when being asked about what happened during this time period.

So, next Castor contends that Sondland's testimony, where he can't remember a lot of stuff and he has no notes, and no references; Castor calls it the "trifecta of unreliability." (isn't that true; that's exactly what Trump has made certain to orchestrate).

Sondland says, what I'm trying to do, today, is to use the limited information that I have, to be as forthcoming as possible, with you, and the rest of the committee; and as these recollections have been refreshed by subsequent testimony, and some texts and emails that I've now had access to, I think I filled in a lot of blanks.

Castor says, there is a lot of speculation; merely your guesses. Castor argues that the evidence here, ought to be pretty darn good; if it's for an impeachment trial, right? (the stupid idiot is just making the case that yes, absolutely, there needs to be an unquestionable record, and not mere speculation; and once again, Mr. Trump has seen to it that that is not can happen).

Castor's time has finally expired; so now they will move to a 2nd staff round, of 30 minutes each. (The second round of questioning is provided for, because Sondland's key testimony, like Yovanovitch's, was an all day affair).

Adam Schiff starts out: Mr. Sondland, I just have a few questions; before I turn it back to Mr. Goldman. You testified, in response to my colleagues in the minority, something along the lines of, a lot of people did not make the connection between Burisma, and Biden. I don't think a lot of people would have had real difficulty understanding that; Tim Morrison testified that, I think it took him all of a few-second Google search, to find out that this was obviously the significance of investigating Burisma; is because it involves the Bidens. -Are you saying, that during all this time, you never made the connection between Burisma and the Bidens? -You just thought that the President, and Rudy Giuliani, were interested in this one particular Ukraine company; and you didn't wonder or ask why? (Again; my role, Mr. Chairman, was just to get the meeting.) Schiff presses him, -Are you saying, that for months and months; notwithstanding everything originally said on TV, and all the discussion from Rudy Giuliani; that you never put Burisma together with the Bidens? (No, I wasn't paying attention to what Mr. Giuliani was saying.) I kind of doubt that. Schiff presses further,

Ambassador Volker testified yesterday to a similar "epiphany," for lack of a better word; this is what he said. "In hindsight, I now understand that others saw; and I should have seen that connection differently; had I done so, I would have raised my own objections." -Is that your view, as well? (yes)

Schiff continues, -Let me ask you this; Ambassador Taylor testified yesterday to a similar effect; (Taylor had said) "In hindsight, I now understand that others thought of the idea of investigating Burisma, as equivalent to an investigation of former Vice President Biden. Yet, I saw them as very different; the former being unremarkable, and the latter being unacceptable. I understand that I should have seen that connection differently; had I done so; I would have raised my own objections."

Schiff then asks, -Ambassador Sondland, is that your point of view as well? (yes) Schiff continues, I think they asked the question with a bit of an incorrect premise; my colleagues in minority; about Fiona Hill, referring to the "drug deal" between you and Mr. Mulvaney. Ambassador Bolton had made the comment that he didn't want to be part of any "drug deal" that Ambassador Sondland and Mulvaney were cooking up; no one thinks that they're talking about a literal drug deal here; or drug cocktail. The import, I think, Ambassador, is quite clear; that he believed that this quid pro quo you had described, in the meeting; that the Ukrainians would have to announce the investigations, in order to get the meeting; was not something he wanted to be a part of.

-What I want to ask you about is; he makes reference to that drug deal, cooked up by you and Mulvaney; so Ambassador Sondland, when asked about it, you testified that Mulvaney was aware of this quid pro quo; of this condition, that the Ukrainians had to make these public announcements of these investigations, in order to get the White House meeting, am I right? -A lot of people knew about it; including Mick

Mulvaney, and Secretary of State Pompeo? (correct) -Now, have you seen the acting Chief of Staff's televised press conference, in which he acknowledged that the military aid was withheld, in part because of a desire to get that 2016 investigation you talk about? (I don't think I saw it live; but I did see it) -So, you saw him acknowledge publicly, what you are confirming too; that Mr. Mulvaney understood that 2+2 = 4; is that right? (Well, again; I didn't know that the aid was conclusively tied; I was presuming he was in a position…) Schiff interrupts, and presses him; just say yes, or no… {and Sondland says, yes.}

-We do appreciate your efforts to refresh your recollection; and we share your frustration, in not having the documents to help guide this investigation; so, we do appreciate your efforts. One of the documents that you provided to us, goes back to a conversation that you and the Chairman were having, about Mr. Mulvaney. You had been trying for some time, before the July 25th call, to set up that call; is that right? (yes) -Are these the only responses you received, to this email? -No one wrote back to you, and said, what you talking about? -in terms of these investigations, and turning over every stone? (No, there was a chain; and I don't know if it's part of this email chain; but there was a subsequent email, where I believe Ambassador Bolton pushed back, and said he did not want a call to President Zelensky made by President Trump, until after the parliamentary elections.)

You were asked by Mr. Castor, if there were any other key witnesses, who might be able to help, in our investigation; and you mentioned Brian McCormick, right? He is Chief of Staff, for Secretary Perry… -You are aware that we subpoenaed him, were you not? (I was aware of that.) -And that he refused to come and testify? (yes, I did read that.) -Are you also aware that Robert Blair was subpoenaed, and he refused to come testify? -And Secretary Perry was asked to come and testify, and he refused, as well?

-Secretary Pompeo was a key witness, that would be able to provide some additional information on this inquiry? -This was not the first time that you indicated, that Mr. Mulvaney heard about these investigations into Burisma, and the 2016 election meddling, is that right? (I don't know what Mr. Mulvaney heard, or didn't hear; I think there's been a huge amount of exaggeration over my contact with Mr. Mulvaney. It was actually quite limited.)

-Well, he certainly indicated a familiarity with what you're talking about, in this July 19th email… (Yes, I think Mr. Mulvaney was in the May 23rd briefing with President Trump; I don't remember, because there were people sitting behind us, that were coming and going. We were sitting in front of President Trump's desk.) -And you said that you don't have any recollection of referencing Mr. Mulvaney, in July 10th meeting, in Ambassador Bolton's office, is that right? (I don't recall.)

-So, when both Fiona Hill and Colonel Vindeman testified, in response to a question from Ukrainian officials, at that July 10th meeting about scheduling a White House visit, that you said you had spoken with Mr. Mulvaney, and your understanding was that it will be scheduled, after they announce these investigations; do you have any reason to dispute that characterization? (no)

The floor now goes to Mr. Goldman:

Goldman says, we share your frustration, in not having the documents to guide this investigation. I want to ask you about the conversation that you and the Chairman were just having, about Mr. Mulvaney. You had been trying, for some time, before the July 25th call, to set up that call; is that right? -to set up the call between Presidents Zelensky and Trump… (yes) -I want to show you an email, that you referenced in your opening statement. This is a July 19th email, from you, Ambassador Sondland. Who is "the group," {that you had sent this email to?} (Robert Blair, Lisa Kenna, Brian McCormick, Mick Mulvaney, and Mike Pompeo.)

-Robert Blair, I believe, is the Deputy Chief of Staff, or an advisor to the Chief of Staff Mick Mulvaney. Lisa Kenna is the Executive Secretary for Secretary Pompeo. Brian McCormick is the Chief of Staff for Secretary Perry. (yes) -Will you read what you wrote, on July 19th, to this group?

Sondland reads, Zelensky is prepared to receive POTUS call; will ensure him that he intends to run a fully transparent investigation; he will turn over every stone. He would greatly appreciate a call by Sunday, so he can put out some media about a friendly and productive call; no details; prior to Ukraine election on Sunday- {Sunday was July 21ˢᵗ, the day of the parliamentary elections in Ukraine}.

Goldman continues, when you say Zelensky will assure him that he intends to run a fully transparent investigation, and will turn over every stone... -What did you mean, by that? (I'm referring to the Burisma and the 2016 DNC server investigations.) -Later that evening, Secretary Perry responds, just to you and Brian McCormick; saying, Just confirmed; the call is being set up for tomorrow, by NSC RP and a little bit later, Mr. Mulvaney replies to all; saying I asked NSC to set it up for tomorrow... -Were these the only responses that you received, to this email? (I don't know... If I had them, I would show them; I don't know.)

Goldman asks, nobody wrote back, and said, "Gordon! what you talking about?" (no) -What did he mean by, turn over every stone?

Schiff interrupts at some point, there was a chain; where Bolton pushed back, and said he did not want the call to President Zelensky made by President Trump, until after the parliamentary elections; so that would be why it was moved from the next day, July 20ᵗʰ, to July 25ᵗʰ; but Ambassador Volker is not on this email, is he?

They (the Republicans) just asked you whether there are any other the key witnesses, that might be able to help this investigation? -and you said Brian McCormick. -You are aware, that the committee subpoenaed him; and that he refused to come to testify... -Are you also aware that Mr. Mulvaney was subpoenaed, and he refused to come to testify... (I did read that in the newspaper, yes.) -Are you also aware, that Robert Blair was, and secretary Perry was; and so, would you include them; as well secretary Pompeo; as key witnesses that would be able to provide some additional information, during this inquiry? (I think they would.)

Now, this was not the first time, as you indicated, that Mr. Mulvaney heard about these investigations into Burisma, and the 2016 election interference; is that right? (I don't know what Mr. Mulvaney heard, or didn't hear; I think there has been a huge amount of exaggeration, over this. My contact with Mr. Mulvaney is actually quite limited.) -He certainly indicated a familiarity with; didn't he indicate a familiarity with what you're talking about, in your email? (Yes, because I think Mr. Mulvaney was in the July 23rd briefing with Mr. Trump; and the May 23rd briefing with President Trump; I don't exactly remember; because there were people sitting behind us, that were coming and going; we were sitting in front of President Trump's desk.)

-You said that you don't have a recollection of referencing Mulvaney, in the July 10th meeting, in Ambassador Bolton's office, is that right? (I don't recall.)

So, when Fiona Hill testified, that in response to a question from Ukrainian officials, at that July 10th meeting, about scheduling a White House visit; that you (i.e.- Sondland) had said, "I spoke with Mr. Mulvaney, and it will be scheduled after we announce these investigations..." -Do you have any reason to dispute that characterization? (I don't have any reason to agree, or dispute it; I just don't remember.) -So, they both remembered it... Remember, they spoke to the NSC legal advisor about it; you would trust that... (Yes; I trust that, if they relayed it to the NSC legal advisor; I don't know if I said it; and I don't know which conversation... again; I've had very limited conversations with Mr. Mulvaney.)

This email indicates that you spoke to President Zelensky, and were relaying what he said, to very senior officials; is that right? (Which email?) -The July 19th email, where you say; well, the subject is, "I talked with Zelensky just now..." -Was there some sort of assurance, that President Zelensky needed to provide, about what he would say to President Trump; just in order to get a phone call from President Trump? (I think that part was verbal; and then there were a lot of communications going on around, back and forth with the Ukrainians; and that's when someone, I don't remember who, came up with the idea of a draft statement; so there would be no misunderstanding about what, in fact, the Ukrainians would be willing to say; that we could rely on; and negotiate something on a piece of paper.)

-So just to place you in time; and we're going to get to (talking about) that draft statement, which was in August; but this is July 19th, or before the July 25th call; do you remember whether there was a need, from any of the White House officials or other National Security officials, for President Zelensky to provide some assurance of what he would say to President Trump; in order for a phone call; not a meeting; but a phone call, was scheduled? (There was initially, apparently a condition; but that condition was obviously dropped, because the phone call took place, and there was no such statement made.) -The phone call took place, as you said, on the 25th of July; when you say, there was no such statement that took place; what do you mean? (Well, the Ukrainians never made a public statement, prior to the phone call on the 25th of July.) I'm not talking about a public statement; what I'm asking, is whether Presidents Zelensky needed to relay, to you, or any other American officials, that he would assure President Trump, that he would do these investigations? (Well, in my email on the 19th, I obviously had just spoken with Zelensky; and he said that he was prepared to receive a call, and he would make those assurances to President Trump, on that call; and then presumably, that would then lead to a White House meeting.)

-And you had been discussing this phone call, for several weeks now; is that right? (Yes; I think with Volker, with Perry, and with Giuliani through Volker and Perry.) -And then, right after you sent this email, that was sharing with the others, that he will discuss the investigations, and he will turn over every stone; indicating that Burisma, and the 2016 election meddling investigations; Mr. Mulvaney responded that he had subsequently asked to set the call up, for the next day.

-Let's go to that press statement, that you were discussing; in August. You testified, I believe; that you understood, that Rudy Giuliani was representing the President's interests, with regard to Ukraine; is that right? (That's what we all understood.) -Who is "we all?" (Secretary Perry, Ambassador Volker, and myself.)

-In August, you and Ambassador Volker were coordinating with Andre Yermak, the Zelensky advisor; about a press statement; and I want to pull up some of the text exchanges that you are referring to; which, as you acknowledged, had helped to refresh your memory. (I think Ambassador Taylor was involved in some of those initial statements, as well.) -But he's not on any of these, so let's go to the first one; on August

9th. This is an exchange between Ambassador Volker and you; where you are discussing trying to set up a White House meeting; and you say to Morrison, "ready to get dates as soon as Yermak confirms." Morrison texts back, "Excellent; how did you dissuade him?" You responded, I'm not sure I did; I think POTUS really wants the deliverable." -What did you mean, there? (The commitment to do the investigations.) -And how did you know, that the President wanted the deliverable? (I don't recall; I may have heard it from somewhere else; I may have heard it from the President; I don't remember.)

-Going to the next Exhibit; on August 10th, this is between you and Andre Yermak; "how was your conversation?" Yermak responds, "hello, good; my proposal, we receive date and then make general statement with discussed things. Once we have a date, will call for a press briefing, announcing the upcoming visit and outlining vision for the reboot of US–Ukraine relationship, including among other things Burisma and election meddling investigations.

You respond, "got it." -That was your understanding of what Zelensky had to say, in order to satisfy Mr. Giuliani; and ultimately, to satisfy the POTUS deliverable. (yes) -Now, the next day, you write an email to Ulricht Brechtbuhl, and Lisa Kenna. The subject of the email is "Ukraine" -Will you read what you wrote there? (Mike; I'm referring to Secretary Pompeo; Kurt and I negotiated a statement from Zelensky, to be delivered for our review, in a day or two. Contents will hopefully make the boss happy enough to authorize an invitation. Zelensky plans to have a big presser (press conference) on the openness subject; including specifics, next week.

-And in your opening statement you referred to "the specifics;" what did "the specifics" represent? (The 2016 election meddling, and the Burisma investigations.) and the "Boss" meant President Trump... (yes) -And the invitation was to the White House meeting... (yes) -Lisa Kenna responds, Gordon, I will pass to "S." Thank you, Lisa

-Two days later, you have a text exchange with Ambassador Volker; and on August 13th, the earlier texts, which we don't have; you may recall, includes this press statement, that includes Burisma, and the 2016 elections... (yes) -So, you will ultimately remember, that after the conversation with Mr. Giuliani, you did pass along the statement to the Ukrainians, that included Burisma, and the 2016 election meddling investigations… (I think there were statements being passed back and forth, between Volker and Ukrainians; and others; to try to work out acceptable English.) -And ultimately, that statement was not issued… (correct) -And the White House meeting, still hasn't occurred… -but you certainly understood, at that time; did you not? -that it was the President's direct instruction; that the White House meeting with President Elect, would not occur, until President Zelensky announced publicly, these investigations that the President wanted; is that right? (that's correct) -And you now know, that the investigations the President wanted, were this investigation into the Bidens, and into the 2016 election meddling… (Yes; I now know that.)

-Let's move ahead, to August 22nd, when you wrote an email to Secretary Pompeo directly; CCing Lisa Kenna. The subject was "Zelensky," -And could you read what you wrote? (Mike; should we block time in Warsaw, for a short "aside," for POTUS to meet Zelensky? I will ask Zelensky to look him in the eye, and tell him that, once Ukraine's new justice folks are in place this September, Zelensky should be able to move forward, publicly, and with confidence, on those issues of importance to POTUS and to the US. Hopefully, that will break the logjam.)

Secretary Pompeo responds, three minutes later; Yes.

-Now, let me unpack this a little bit. He said; in the middle; that "once Ukraine's new justice folks are in place…" what did he mean, by that? (The new prosecutor that was going to be working for President Zelensky… The old prosecutor, I believe; his term was up; or he was being let go; he was the Poroshenko prosecutor; and Zelensky wanted to wait until this new person was in place.) -So, once that new prosecutor was in place, then President Zelensky should be able to move forward publicly, and with confidence on those issues of importance to POTUS… -What did he mean, by "those issues of importance to POTUS?" (Again; the 2016 election, ad Burisma.)

-Were you aware; at this time; that secretary Pompeo had listened in to the July 25th phone call? (I was not.) -If he had, do you believe that he would fully understand what the issues of importance to POTUS, related to Ukraine would be? (I can't characterize what his state of mind was; if he listened in on the phone call, then he concluded what he concluded.) -But after that phone call, it is quite clear that what were those issues of importance to POTUS… (yes) -The Biden investigation and it 2016 election investigation… -And then he says, hopefully that will break the logjam…

By this point, you were aware that security assistance had been on hold for about five weeks; is that right? (I became aware on the 18th of July.) -And you understood that there was a lot of activity within the State Department, and elsewhere; to try to get that a hold lifted; is that right? (That's right; just about everybody in the interagency, and the National Security apparatus, wanted the aid to go to Ukraine… (correct) -So, what did you mean here; when you said logjam? (Like I said to Chairman Schiff; I meant inclusively, anything that was holding up moving forward, on the meeting, and the US Ukraine relationship.)

-What was holding up, at that point? (It was the statements about Burisma, and the 2016 election.) -But what was being held up? (The aid was being held up; obviously.) -Four days later, you said, in your opening statement, that you sent Rudy Giuliani's contact information to John Bolton; is that right? (yes) -Do you know why he asked you for that? (No, I didn't.) Do you know that he was going to Ukraine, the next day? (I knew that he was about to go to Ukraine; I didn't know exactly when his trip was; I thought it was kind of an odd request, given that the White House can get anyone's phone number, that they want to!)

-So, in this email, to Secretary Pompeo, you reference a trip to Warsaw. Ultimately, the Vice President went on the trip; and that was when the conversation that you had testified about earlier; where you said, "we really need to get these investigations, from Ukraine; in order to release the aid…" -And Vice President Pence nodded? (He heard what I said.) -And did he respond, in any way? (I don't recall; no, not a substantive response.) -But you never specifically referenced the Bidens, or Burisma, in that meeting? (I don't remember ever mentioning the Bidens, or Burisma in that meeting.) -You were with a group? You were not alone with Vice President Pence? (That's correct.) -And you know, that at that bilateral meeting with President Zelensky, you testified earlier, that Vice President Pence did not mention these investigations at all; is that right? (I don't recall him mentioning the investigations.)

-So, your testimony is simply, that in a pre-meeting, with a group of Americans, before the bilateral meeting, you had referenced the fact that the Ukrainian need to do these investigations, in order to lift the aid? (I didn't say that. Ukraine had to do the investigations; that we heard from Mr. Giuliani, that this was the case.) -So, that was what informed your presumption? -So, it wasn't really a presumption; you heard it from Mr. Giuliani? (Well; I didn't hear from Mr. Giuliani about the aid; I heard about Burisma, and the 2016 elections.) -But you understood, as we discussed, that a 2+2 = 4; that the aid was conditioned... (well, that was the problem, Mr. Goldman; nobody told me directly, that the aid was tied to anything; I was presuming it was.)

-Well, I want to go ahead to September 7th, okay? When we discussed those text messages where you said there were multiple convos, with President Zelensky and POTUS; and you confirmed; that likely meant, as you said it did; that you spoke with President Trump; is that right? (Again; if my email said I spoke with President Trump personally; I think I did.) -You are relying, pretty heavily; your testimony; on the texts and emails that you were able to review; is that right? (yes) -So, certainly if someone else had taken contemporaneous notes, you would presume that what they are saying is accurate? If both Taylor and Morrison had texts, or emails; if they had notes? (I don't know; some people's notes are great; some peoples' aren't; I don't know, but certainly it would be a helpful refresher to remember; including my own, yes.)

-But you had a conversation on September 7th, according to both Ambassador Taylor and Tim Morrison; where you told Mr. Morrison that President Trump had told you, that he was not asking for a quid pro quo; but that he did insist that President Zelensky go to a microphone, and say that he is opening investigations of the Bidens, and the 2016 election interference; and that Presidents Zelensky should <u>want</u> to do this himself; do you have any reason to dispute, both, Ambassador Taylor's, and Mr. Morrison's testimony about that conversation? (no)

On September 8th, you then had a conversation directly with Ambassador Taylor, about the same phone call, where Ambassador Taylor said that you confirmed, to him, that you spoke to President Trump as he had suggested earlier to you; and that President Trump was adamant that President Zelensky himself; meaning, not the prosecutor general; Zelensky had to quote clear things up, and do it in public; do you recall that? -You don't have any reason to think that Ambassador Taylor's testimony, based on his contemporaneous notes, was incorrect? (I don't know that I got that from President Trump; or if I got it from Giuliani; that's the part I'm not clear on.) -Well, Ambassador Taylor is quite clear on it; that you said President Trump. Mr. Morrison is also quite clear, that you said President Trump...

-You don't have any reason to dispute their specific recollections, do you? (No; if they have notes, and they recall that; I don't have any reason to dispute it.)

-Then, you also told Ambassador Taylor, in that same conversation, that you told President Zelensky, and Andre Yermak, that although this was not a quid pro quo; as the President had very clearly told you; it was, however, required for President Zelensky to clear things up in public, or there would be a "stalemate;" you don't have any reason to dispute Ambassador Taylor's recollection of that conversation, do you? (no) -And you understood that "stalemate" referred to the continuing hold on the aid... (At that point, yes.)

-Ambassador Taylor also described a comment you made, where you are trying to explain what President Trump's view of this was. You had said, that President Trump said, that when a businessman is about to sign a check to somebody, who owes them something; the businessman asks the person to pay up; before signing the check. -Do you recall saying that, to Ambassador Taylor? (I don't recall it, specifically; but I may have.) Ambassador Volker also said that you did.

-So just to summarize here; by the end of the first week of September, before the aid had been released, you had expressed, twice, to the Ukrainians, that you understood that the investigations need to be publicly announced on CNN; in order for the aid to be released; do you recall that? (I didn't say, in order to get the aid; the Ukrainians had said to me, that they had already planned to do an interview anyway, on CNN; and they would use that occasion to mention these items.) -So, at some point, you calculated 2+2 = 4; and therefore, you believed the aid was conditioned on the investigation. (yes)

-And you had a phone call with President Trump, that you relayed to both Tim Morrison, and Ambassador Taylor; whose accounts of that conversation you do not dispute; where President Trump confirmed that President Zelensky needed to publicly announce the investigations; or otherwise, the obvious implication of the "stalemate" would be that the aid would not be released; is that correct? (Again; the implication; I did not hear it directly from President Trump.) -So, you agreed with what Mr. Morrison and Ambassador Taylor testified to, about the conversation you had with President Trump; is that right? (Remind me again; I don't want to misspeak.) -You just said, you have no reason to dispute their accounts, based on their detailed notes... (Were they saying that I said, that President Trump says that the aid would not be released, until the statements were made? -because I said repeatedly, that I don't call President Trump ever saying that to me.)

Schiff interrupts and says, I think what they said; if I can just finish this line of questioning; is that President Trump was adamant, that President Zelensky himself, had to clear things up; and do it in public. -So, what they related was that although President Trump claimed there was no quid pro quo, that he also made clear to you, in that call; that President Zelensky had to clear things up; and do it in public. -Do you have any reason to dispute that? (I don't have any reason to dispute the "clear things up in public;" but President Trump never told me directly, that the aid was tied to that.) -But that same conversation with you, about the aid; he told you that President Zelensky had to "clear things up; and do it in public; correct? (I did not have a conversation with him about the aid; I had a conversation about the quid pro quo.) -But the quid pro quo you are discussing, was over the aid; was it not? (President Trump; I asked him the open-ended question, what do you want from Ukraine? He said, I want nothing; I want no quid pro quo; tell Zelensky to do the right thing; that's all I heard from President Trump.)

-But you also got from President Trump, that is reflected by Ambassador Taylor, that you said he was adamant, that Presidents Zelensky had to quote "clear things up; and do in public." (That part I can agree to, yes.)

Schiff then says, the time is now with minority, for 30 minutes. Nunez clarifies 33 minutes {asshole} So, now Nunez is contending that, only the person in charge of foreign aid, could know anything about what was happening to foreign aid; {but if that was the case, then how did dozens of State Department officials know that the aid was being held; as of July 18th, for 55 days? There are other people, other than the head honcho, that get wind of what's going on; especially when there's $400 million hanging in the balance.}

So, now Nunez is contending that it's a very important part of Ambassador Sondland's responsibilities, for him to impress it upon the EU countries that they need to give more aid. {I don't think so; but if that is his job, it is certainly not anywhere near as important as the dozens of other priorities across this group of 20 European countries.}

Nunez says that in Trump's conversation, {I think he is alluding to the July 25th conversation with Zelensky, he starts off mentioning that he's upset that Germany is not providing enough aid; {and again, this points out that if that was said on that July 25th call, why haven't we heard this before? It is because they won't release the readout of the whole call; they only released some of the things that were said. Again, it's obstruction.}

Nunez is still talking about the Steele dossier! {again, we are in 2020, not in 2015; but he is complaining that we are not going to hear from witnesses he'd like to hear from. Gee, Mr. Nunez, I'm sorry; but there is a hell of a lot more people that we would like to hear from, that are germane to this investigation! -that are being blocked from giving any testimony.

Nunez is now trying to suggest that Sondland should not have been thinking that maybe the aid is being conditioned; but his time expires, and Nunez is finally done.

So now, Castor has some more questions. Castor goes back to this idea that when Sondland had said that "we were told to "Talk to Rudy," Castor is now saying, well really, President Trump just couldn't be bothered with the subject; he just didn't want to talk about it; so he just kind of blithely said, "Oh, just go talk to Rudy about this... Sondland says Rudy was the guy; and Castor says, but President Trump didn't direct you to call to talk to Rudy, did he? It wasn't in order to do it, was it? {Castor is trying to suggest that Trump was simply recommending, that if you want to work on this Ukraine relationship,} -this is the guy you want to talk to; and Ambassador Volker had said, "I didn't take it as an instruction; but just as a comment.

{But Volker was not in the loop; Giuliani knew that Volker was a long-time, top diplomat, and would never participate in this scheme; so he purposely kept him in the dark about it; but Castor is just offering a twisted, farfetched contention here; it becomes clear that this was a well-coordinated scheme, that was all about pressuring the Ukrainians to announce they had opened a criminal investigation related to Joe Biden.}

Sondland says, I do know he testified that, it became very clear to all three of us, that if we wanted to move the relationship forward, President Trump was not really in interested in engaging. He wanted Rudy to handle it; and as I said in my opening statement, Secretary Perry took the lead in making the initial contact with Rudy; and I began working with him. {Volker had also testified, apparently, that he considered that Rudy Giuliani was doing his own communications.}

Castor says, this is because he had his own business he was conducting, in Ukraine, is that right? and Sondland says, I don't know anything about that. Castor alludes to his partners, Lev Parnas, and Igor Fruman; and of course, Lev Parnas has just broadcast in a TV interview, that this scheme was known about, and participated in, by several high-level US Government officials; and he also said, in his interview with Rachel Maddow, that his whole deal was being the point person representing President Trump; and that's even how Rudy Giuliani introduced him to everybody, especially to Dimitri Firtash, who, Parnas claims, would not have given him the time of day, otherwise. Sondland says he never met with Parnas, or Fruman.

Castor says, it is been a lot of important events that we've asked you about; and many times, you've said that you don't recall... (but the idiot is just making the further case, that in a situation like this, documentation is paramount to becoming certain of what these people did, or said, during this time period.

Sondland says that he was miffed about having to dream up theories, as to why things weren't moving along, and the aid wasn't being released; so, he finally called President Trump on September 9th. Sondland says, I asked him what he wants?

At that point, Castor interrupts, to blurt out, -And he said nothing! {Yet, in reality, he first said nothing; and then afterward, he said, except that President Zelensky should <u>want</u> to announce these investigations; that it would be the right thing to do.is what he was inferring; and if the President, of the most powerful country in the world, tells the President of a very vulnerable country, under fierce attack by Russia; that he <u>should want</u> to do something, that would be a clear order I imagine; in most people's viewpoints; would it not?

Castor now is talking about the day after that July 25th call; on July 26th; and how Sondland was at a restaurant in Kyiv, with David Holmes; and this is when that infamous cell phone call was made; where President Trump could be overheard by Holmes. -So, Castor is talking about the conversation that went on, after he hung up from Trump. Holmes says something to the effect, that the President had answered that he was only interested in big things; and Holmes reports that he (Sondland) had said, Oh, there's a lot of big things going on in Ukraine; like the war; Ukraine is under attack by Russia. Castor continues; and he puts words in your mouth, to the effect of "No, the President only cares about investigations, like Rudy is pushing, about the Bidens. -And what's important about this? This is the day after the July 25th call. What's reported by Mr. Holmes; and you confirmed this; it isn't anything different than what happens on the July 25th call. (agreed) -With 2020 hindsight; now that we have the transcript of the call. (The

Bidens were mentioned on the call, but I wasn't making a connection to the Bidens.

-But with regard to the President, you are just mentioning investigations; but you told us, time and again, that you never realized the Bidens were part of any of this Burisma, and the continuum; and you never came to understand that, until it was, maybe as late as September 25th.

Castor is saying that Volker had testified, that the Bidens never came up, when he had that breakfast with Giuliani. {but of course, that's exactly why it didn't come up- Giuliani wanted to make sure of this. He didn't even want Volker to understand that what they were trying to accomplish; that he and the President were using the Ukrainians to ruin Joe Biden's chances of beating Trump, in the upcoming 2020 Presidential election. It's interesting that Holmes testified that Sondland's explanation of what the "big stuff" meant, included investigations of the Bidens; whereas Sondland has been saying, all afternoon, that he didn't know it was the Bidens; that he'd never made any connection between these investigations being asked for, and the Bidens. So, at this point, I kind of tend to think this is bullshit, because, as we just learned from Lev Parnas, in his MSNBC interview, that there were lots of people that understood what was going on, in the undercurrent: Mick Mulvaney, Mike Pompeo, Rudy Giuliani, Lev Parnas, Dimitri Firtash, Bill Barr, as well as key people that were being interviewed now; the three Ambassadors, George Kent; and of course, John Bolton' characterization of a "drug deal" that was being cooked up by Trump and Giuliani. They all knew it was going on; it was a campaign to ruin Joe Biden's chances of beating Trump in the election; so, I don't know why Sondland would say that he "didn't have any idea" that the Bidens were at issue. I think it was because, right after he testified, he got on a plane, and went back to the EU, to continue doing his job. I don't think it would be unreasonable to surmise that Trump would have put him up to this; to saying that he didn't know that this whole thing was about the Bidens. I think that he, and a lot of other people as well, did really know; and this conversation with Holmes; and Holmes is a dedicated public servant; he would have no reason to lie. Holmes was just forthcoming with the details about this phone call, that he overheard; between Gordon Sondland and the President of the United States; yet, on an unsecured cell phone line. President Trump was talking so loudly, that you could probably hear him halfway down the block! -And afterword, Holmes testified that Sondland had told him that "big stuff" meant an investigation of Burisma, and the Bidens; and I believe Holmes.

Alternatively, I can think of lots of reasons, (as I'm listening to Gordon Sondland duck every question, by saying he can't really recall anything clearly), to disbelieve him, and think that he's being disingenuous; and being purposely ambiguous; as some kind of attempt at protecting the President; to try and help Trump beat this rap.

Nunez interrupts, and takes the microphone to say, whistleblower, whistleblower, whistleblower, whistleblower again; then it goes back to Castor; who starts picking at trying to deny that there is any substantiation, that anyone in the administration knew the conditioning of the aid, necessarily had anything to do with the muscling of the Ukrainians, to put forth these consequential announcements. Sondland disagrees, saying that in his August 22nd text exchange with Pompeo, it was obvious to Sondland, that he did understand the aid was also being conditioned.

(This concludes the 30-minute rounds.)

{I am going to move through the 5-minute rounds of questioning by the other committee members; and instead of transcribing everything, I'm going to pick out the interesting and informative highlights; to save a bit of lengthy monotony; there is so much repetition; it seems unnecessary to include it all.}

Where we pick up, Adam Schiff is explaining that, since the original scheduling of these hearings, Mark Sandy, of the Office of Management and Budget (OMB), had come forward to testify, in a closed door session, on the previous Saturday, November 17th; so a summary of his testimony will be released shortly, reporting what he had to offer.

Schiff also remarks that Sandy is not the most senior official at the OMB, and Two other senior officials had been asked to testify, and had refused to comply with their subpoenas.

I want to ask you a few questions with respect to the statement, that you, and Ambassador Volker, and others, were going back and forth with the Ukrainians, to figure out what statement they would need to make, in order to get the aid. You understood that they had to make the announcements, to get the aid; that, you had understood. Similarly, you testified that pretty much everyone could put two and two together; and Mr. Yermak understood that the military assistance was also conditioned on the public announcement of these two investigations... (That was my presumption, yes.) -You put two and two together, and got four... (yes) -Now, you are capable of putting two and two together, and so are the Ukrainians; they can put two and two together, as well. They understood there was a hold on security assistance; there's testimony that they understood that, in July, and August; but it was without a doubt, that it was made public in the newspapers, in September... They understood that the security assistance was being held up? (I don't know if they understood it; but presumably they did; it was public; I assume so.) -And indeed, that was one of the issues that was brought up in that meeting, between Zelensky and Pence, in Warsaw... (I think as I testified previously, I think Zelensky, if I recall, asked the question more openly; like, when do we get our money?)

-So, they understood that they didn't have the money; and it had been approved by Congress; there was a hold on it, and you could give them any explanation... (I could not.) -And if they couldn't put two and two together, you put two and two together for them, because you told them, in Warsaw, that if they were committed to make that public statement, this was likely to get that aid released... (yes) -We've had a lot of argumentation here, about, the Ukrainians didn't know that the aid was held; but the Ukrainians found out; and it was made abundantly clear, that they would have to make the statements in order to get the aid... (correct)

It now goes to Nunez, who yields to Ratcliffe. Ratcliffe summarizes Sondland's testimony; he says nothing new. Ratcliffe says summarizes that on Sondland's call to President Trump, on September 7th, where Trump had told Sondland, "I want nothing…" later in that call, Trump had said, "I want him to do what he ran on…" {and I can guarantee you that Zelensky did not run on the basis of promising that he would strategically investigate anyone's political opponents.}

Ratcliffe contends that in these hearings, nothing but opinion, presumption, and speculation is being put forth, and Ratcliffe says that {Trump's words on the September 7th call} are factual, and not any of what he had just summarized, as far as a recap of Sondland's testimony, was the kind of thing that the Senate is going to find valid. {but Sondland's testimony of what the President said on this phone call is merely a recollection, in itself; and we have heard from several other witnesses, who are exemplary, long-standing foreign service professionals. We have heard from these fine people, telling us lots of recollections that should be considered just as factual, as Sondland's recollection of what the President told him on that September 7th phone call. Much of what is being recounted by the witnesses, is what we could define as evidence; and evidence is not proof, of course; but evidence, in many cases, mere evidence that is substantial enough, will still lead to convictions, in a court of law.}

Of course, Ratcliffe is getting Sondland to repeat his dubious contention, that he didn't really know that this was a subversive scheme; but Sondland is not being truthful, I don't think; he is instead trying to pass off this bullshit, that he didn't know what was going on; and of course, Ratcliffe is trying to personify that; and that's a good example of a key strategy that the Republicans are employing; to personify contentions that are merely deceptions, and interject other things that have no relevance, to the high crimes and misdemeanors that Trump has committed in 2019.

On the other hand, I do believe that Volker did not know about the underhanded scheme; that Giuliani kept him in the dark; but I do believe that Rick Perry knew; although his name never really comes up much in these hearings; and once again, he is government official that is being blocked from testifying.

Ratcliffe's last contention is that reasonable people could look at this, and come to different conclusions; nothing could be farther from the truth! The overwhelming evidence that I've heard come out of these hearings, points unequivocally to dirty, underhanded, unconstitutional thinking, plotting, and actions.

Jim Himes is questioning Sondland now, and he makes a remark that earlier, Devin Nunez had contended that that phrase to describe the scheme, as being likened to a "drug deal." Nunez said that was a characterization of the Democrats. Himes corrects him, and says, no; that was not coming from the Democrats; that was spoken by John Bolton, a US Government official serving in a Republican administration. Himes pointedly asks Sondland, why did the Secretary of State who had commanded you and said keep it up but the good work.

-What confuses me, is that you have said that the Secretary of State was not only aware of, but he applauded your good work. If this had been irregular, or a "drug deal," or a shadow foreign policy; he would've been the one to put an end to it; yet, he did not...

Sondland thinks about that, and replies, "He was apparently taking into account, the totality of what I had been working on; and saying, you're doing a great job." -Right; okay, so he was aware of what you were doing, and said you were doing a great job. He includes this; so, in some sense, he was validating everything you were doing; rather than saying, that what you were doing was irregular.

-Then, why do you think Secretary of State Pompeo said that? -if, in fact, so many other officials were aware, and upset about what was going on? {this subversive plot, to press the Ukrainians to make these underhanded announcements of investigations}; -and when the National Security Advisor thought it was a drug deal, for example? -and Sondland's response was, (I don't know... followed by, (I have no knowledge of his communications with the President.) {Himes is bringing out the fact that these top officials should be informed of what are the top priorities, and each other's views and considerations; and yet, obviously, Pompeo was keeping a secret from Bolton, that he was behind the President's dirty scheme.}

Himes says he thinks that the committee will probably eventually see a transcript of that cell phone call with President Trump; which would potentially be confirming that Sondland had indeed used the word "Bidens" in that call. (which Sondland now denies); so, we still couldn't catch him with perjury, because he saying that he's "unclear," and he doesn't remember. -But if he was found out, as having said "Biden" on that unsecured call, at least it would clearly establish that he knew about the true nature of the scheme.

Himes presses Sondland about what Holmes had testified to; that after this cell phone call from the restaurant in Kyiv to President Trump; that Holmes had overheard Holmes and Sondland had a conversation and Holmes has testified, that Sondland relied, the President does not give an (explicative) about Ukraine… (Sondland says, I think that's too strong… The President was down on Ukraine; and would need a lot of convincing.) {but that does not answer the question. The question is, did you say that to Holmes? and do you believe that the President truly did not give a damn about Ukraine? -but only about his investigations?}

Himes presses Sondland to respond, when Himes asks whether he recalls saying that the "big stuff" was the investigations? and Himes is then asking, "Is that what you believe the President considered big stuff? Do you believe that now? (I really can't opine) I'm not asking for your opinion; I'm asking for your beliefs… (I don't understand your question; I want to answer it; I don't understand it.) -Let's try one more time; do you believe what is alleged, that you said, on this phone call; that President Trump only cares about the "big stuff" that benefits the President? (I don't think the President said that to me on the phone call.) {Here, Sondland is very obviously just playing stupid, in order to avoid admitting anything further that would give him consequences. Himes, of course, is not asking about the phone call; he's just trying to prompt Sondland to say one more time, that he explained to Holmes after the restaurant call to Trump; that big stuff for Trump is not anything about Ukraine; but only about getting his crooked announcements made by Zelensky. So, he ducked that successfully; because Himes' time expired.

It goes to Jordan, and he babbles some obnoxious bullshit. Jordan stupidly asks him, what does President Trump say he wants President Zelensky to do? (to do what he ran on.) -And what did he run on? (Transparency.) {Isn't that a laugh; I think is funny that they keep saying this line. The Republicans keep saying this line about I want nothing I want no quid pro quo; and yet this whole scheme was a tremendous amount of pressure put on Ukraine; many, many different efforts, and many ways of trying to force them to make the announcements; and it was all a quid pro quo; and then the withholding of the aid was basically extortion, so Jordan is just an idiot}.

It now goes to Ms. Sewell: Sewell asks Sondland when it was that he discovered that Burisma meant the Bidens, {and the snake initially says I don't recall; so, Sewell presses a bit}; -Not until the July 25th phone call transcript came out on September 25th? (Sondland says, no; before then); {but I think he knew all along; he's just trying to save face here.} Ms. Sewell gives the legal definition of bribery:

An event of offering, giving, soliciting, or receiving a big item of value; as a means of influence and action. Any item of value that is immediate, as a means of influencing an action of an individual holding a public, or legal duty.

-Do you believe that it was bribery? (I'm not a lawyer, and I'm not going to characterize it.) Sewell asks Sondland what he meant, by saying "We played the hand that we were dealt..." -and also, what did you think would happen, if you did not talk to Rudy, and go that direction, as President Trump asked? (It was very fragile with Ukraine at the time; there was no Ambassador; the Ambassador had left. There was a new President, we thought it was very important to shore up the relationship.)

Ms. Sewell continues, you go on to say, "we all understood that if we refused to work with Mr. Giuliani, we would lose an important opportunity to cement the relationship between the United States and Ukraine; so we followed the President..." -Did you see it as a directive? (I saw it as the only pathway.) -So, you would say the efforts that Mr. Giuliani were undertaking became a part of the formal Ukraine US policy? (I can't opine on that; if what Giuliani was doing was okay and proper, and you said that this was not improper, rogue diplomacy, that would have meant that it would not have involved leadership of the State Department, and the White House; so you're saying that everyone in the chain of command knew about Giuliani's investigations, into Burisma and the Bidens? -I'm just trying to figure out what you thought… (Actually, the President directed us to work with Giuliani; and the State Department and the NSC were knowledgeable of this.)

Ms. Sewell coyly says, it's interesting that Ambassador Taylor knew nothing about it; and clearly, he would be in the chain of information, if he was the Ambassador to Ukraine, right? {She makes a good point; that, no Gordon, you are the Ambassador to the EU; Taylor was Ambassador to Ukraine; so why didn't he know about it? He was there since mid-June. If it was such a regular channel… {Taylor was one that said there was both a regular, and an irregular channel.} Sewell continues, you said you did not want to work with Giuliani, but you did, in fact, work with him… (that's correct) -And do you think the essence of what he was trying to achieve was accomplished? (I don't know what he was trying to achieve.) -You clearly had to have known, Sir, if you think this was actually going down the center lane… (It was clearly important that we work with Mr. Giuliani to get what the President asked for, because it was a directive, an order.) -Surely, you must know whether the mission was accomplished… (I know what Giuliani communicated to us.) -And you thought that was totally fine… -Did you know that was okay? -Did you ask what Mr. Giuliani was trying to achieve? (No)

-I asked whether you thought that it was right for Mr. Giuliani to want to accomplish the efforts that he was involved in, which was to get them to investigate Burisma, and the 2016 election… (All I can testify to, is what Giuliani told me directly, or through Ambassador Volker.) Ms. Sewell yields back.

{Sondland is really showing that he's a snake; he refuses to nail down for us, what he thought of what Giuliani was doing, or trying to accomplish; obviously to most of us, he knew he could not answer that truthfully, without incriminating himself, by exposing that he knew the ins and outs of what was going on; and he remained complicit; even though he must have known it was not above board. People like Trump and Sondland don't care about that; they care about the big stuff; like forwarding their dirty agenda of pressure tactics and bribery, and then doing everything they can, to squirm their way out of being nailed for it, and being brought to justice.}

Next, it goes to Mr. Turner:

Turner says that Ambassador Volker testified yesterday, that the President did not tie, either a meeting for Zelensky, a phone call, or any aid, to investigations of Burisma, 2016, or the Bidens; and you, Ambassador Sondland, said that the President did not tell you that...

{However, Clearly, Ambassador Volker was aware that they would not get the meeting until the investigations were announced.} Turner claims that Volker did not think it was a requirement. Sondland disagrees strongly with that testimony. He says, "He absolutely knew that {Zelensky's announcement} was absolutely a requirement; or we just would have had the meeting, and be done with it. {Turner is alluding to the fact that nobody directly had said that the aid was tied to the investigations. {Next, Turner asks whether Sondland likes President Trump; and Sondland says, yes. Well; birds of a feather...}

Turner now is complaining about that day's headline in the news; "Sondland ties the President to the aid withholding." -and Turner is complaining, because he says what you have presumed; that's not evidence! {So, Turner is saying presumption equals a lack of evidence- not necessarily! I refer you to the scenario I laid out on the bottom of Page 507}.

Turner continues, -No one on this planet told you that President Trump was tying the aid to the investigation. Next, Turner contends that presumption is just "made up" testimony. He contends that Sondland has no evidence that the President was withholding aid, in order to get these investigations. He yields back, and the floor goes to Mr. Carson:

Carson begins:

-In August, is when the emails {between Volker, and Giuliani, and Sondland}, about that statement being devised for the Ukrainians, that included {that the Ukrainians would make} announcements of investigations, Giuliani had insisted that Burisma and the 2016 elections be in the statement. Top Ukrainian officials were participating in this process, so the Ukrainians knew about this quid pro quo by that point, {and of course, much earlier on, as well; we can be pretty certain.}

Carson asks, was pushing the Ukrainians to investigate Burisma, and the 2016 election interference, part of the official State Department policy? -Was it in your mind; your understanding, that Ukraine policy should involve investigations into Burisma in the 2016 election" -into Americans, or debunked conspiracy theories about the 2016 election? (What I testified, is that in order to get President Zelensky a White House visit, Mr. Giuliani conveyed the notion that President Trump wanted these announcements to happen…)

Carson answers his own question; since Sondland was obviously not going to admit this out loud: Of <u>course,</u> it was not was part of official US policy; it was a part of the President's political agenda, and it was done to benefit President Trump, personally and politically!

Carson yields back; and Schiff wants to interject a bit: -My (Republican) colleagues seem to be under the impression that, unless the President spoke the words, "Ambassador Sondland, I am bribing Ukrainian President Zelensky…" that there is no evidence of bribery; or that if President Trump didn't say, "Ambassador Sondland, I'm telling you I'm not going to give them the aid, unless they do this or that…" then there's no evidence of a quid pro quo of military aid. -So, Ambassador, you've given us a lot of evidence of <u>precisely</u> that conditionality, of both the White House meeting, and the military assistance. You've told us, Ambassador, that you emailed the Secretary of State, and said that if these investigations were announced, and the new justice person was put in place, that the Ukrainians would be prepared to give the President what he wants, and that would break the logjam. You have testified, and shown us documents about this; have you not? (yes) Ambassador, we have it, in a written statement; you said the logjam that you're referring to, includes the security assistance; correct? -And we also have seen acting Chief of Staff Mulvaney, himself, (in a televised press conference) acknowledge that the military aid was used to bargain for the announcements of these investigations President Trump wanted… that the military aid was held; in part; for that. (My

Republican colleagues) also seem to say, that while the money may have been conditioned, but they got the money. Yes; they got caught! They got caught out! The deal was, Zelensky had to announce the investigations, in order for Zelensky's government to get a White House meeting. -And indeed, they made no statement; they got no meeting! -But they got caught!

The floor now goes to Mr. Wenstrup. He addresses Democrats' accusation, that Republicans refused to acknowledge that the Russians have interfered in our election; he points out, that they have too acknowledged, that there has been Russian interference, in one form or another, with our elections; going back for many decades! Wenstrup says he's interested in facts- I find that to be a pretty ridiculous statement; Republican committee members are merely interested in sweeping the facts of the matter under the table!

The floor next, goes to Mr. Conaway; and he wants to enter an article into the record about Adam Schiff's claim that the whistleblower has a statutory right to anonymity. The article received three Pinocchio's; (contending there were three lies in the article, I assume); which I guess Conaway accuses or contends that the only reason the whistleblower isn't being allowed to testify, is because the Democrats have something to hide; -but the clear truth is that, the reason whistleblower is not testifying, or revealing his identity, is because Trump has threatened to charge him with treason; and the punishment for that is death! -and that's hellaciously unfair to some CIA agent, who has simply had the integrity to come forward, and reveal that the President is engaging in nefarious, untrustworthy, and unconstitutional behavior!

Mr. Conaway is now referring to Adam Schiff's announcement, that he makes before every hearing; saying that we will not tolerate retribution or reprisal for witnesses who are testifying; and Conaway then points to the fact that Sondland's hotel chain is being boycotted, as an initiative of an Oregon Congressman Earl Blumenauer. Conaway contends that Blumenauer is doing this because it will harm Sondland; and Sondland will then be bullied into doing whatever he wants done. {So, in other words, Blumenauer intended to harm Sondland, so

Conaway is considering that as reprisal; but if this is indeed reprisal, it is not any reprisal for the testimony Sondland has given!

-Because, Sondland's testimony has actually been somewhat damning to President Trump; in exposing the dirty scheme. So, he's not getting reprisal for that; he's getting reprisal for having <u>participated</u> in the dirty scheme. -And even though Sondland keeps trying to avoid saying anything that would expose his knowledge and complicity in the scheme, I think it's pretty evident to many of us watching these hearings and listening to Sondland's testimony, over a longer period of time; that he is as dirty as Trump. He perhaps, is one of Trumps right-hand men; who are also termed henchmen; like we initially refer to Lev Parnas, as being; but this boycotting initiative is not reprisal for testifying; that's my point. Boy, these republicans are just full of these crooked perceptions; aren't they? Spin, spin, spin!

The floor now goes to Ms. Speier, who says, I was somewhat humored by (Conaway's) request, that Mr. Blumenauer not put forth a bullying effort, to get something he wants, done; when all we are talking about here, is the President bullying someone, to get something he wants done! (It gets a laugh)

Next, Speier says she wants to clear up one point; from this article about witness protection, that Conaway was just referring to; when he was talking about that the article got three Pinocchio's. She reads: The law expressly restricts the Inspector General's office from disclosing a whistleblower's identity. It says: The inspector general should not disclose the identity of the employee, without the consent of the employee; unless the inspector general determines that such disclosure is unavoidable, during the course of the investigation; or disclosure is made to an official in the Department of Justice, who is responsible for determining whether prosecution should be undertaken.

She resumes: Nonetheless, the best practice is to avoid disclosure of the Ukraine whistleblower's identity, given the concerns about retaliation. We step into a "bizarrio" when senior policymakers are trying to yank a CIA employee into the public spotlight, in retaliation for making a whistleblower complaint; especially when they are a credible threat to that employee's personal safety.

Speier addresses the room; I don't know why our colleagues on the other side of the aisle... (Conaway interrupts her and says, I believe the article says... -and there are three Pinocchio's...) -to which Speier replies, Mr. Conaway; the President of the United States has five Pinocchio's, on a daily basis; let's not go there! (It gets a big laugh, and applause for almost 10 seconds).

Next, the floor goes to Ms. Demmings, and she says a few words about Sondland's repeated assertions, throughout the hearing, that he hasn't had the ability to access his written records; as part of the President's stonewalling, against any Congressional oversight.

Sondland responds, I've been hampered to provide completely accurate testimony, without the benefit of those documents. Speier coyly asks, would you say the delay in military aid to Ukraine and the reluctance to have a White House meeting, has a benefit to Russia? (I think it could be looked at that way; yes.) -Do you think the President was speaking in code {like a mob boss says, "Take care of him;" instead of, "Go kill him"}, when he was talking about wanting investigations? (I cannot characterize how the President was speaking; but every conversation I've had with the President, has been fairly direct and straightforward.) {and you know that's a lie; as Trump lies multiple times, in the course of any given hour, usually!}

The floor goes to Mr. Stewart; who asks unanimous consent, to enter into the record, Perry's Chief of Staff's response to Ambassador Sondland's comments.

Stewart reads: Ambassador Sondland's testimony today misrepresented Secretary Perry's interaction with Rudy Giuliani, and the direction which the Secretary received from President Trump. As previously stated, (Energy) Secretary Perry spoke with Giuliani only once; at the President's request; and no one else was on the call; and that at no point; before, during, or after the phone call, do the words Biden or Burisma ever come up in the presence of Secretary Perry. {Perry didn't need to speak with Trump, since he knew that Giuliani was coordinating this effort; so, even if it was the truth, that Perry; yet, one of the three amigos, charged with carrying out the scheme; didn't speak much, directly with Trump; which I'd doubt; I think that if Perry and others were compelled to testify, it could be established that Perry was privy to the full picture of what Trump wanted, and how he was plotting to get it.}

Stewart asks that this assertion of Perry's, be entered into the record; and Schiff says, without objection; although I'll also note that they (Perry and his Chief of Staff) had been asked to come and testify; and they refused.

Stewart is now trying to suggest, that the Democrats are being unfair; so, he wants to quote a part of a text that he received, from a friend today, "Crafting a story to hurt another human being, can never be right; it means destroying, and hurting another. It does not justify the anger in politics; it does not give anyone a free pass to destroy other people..." {I might point out, that the Republicans have been trying to craft several stories; bogus contentions, such as, Trump was concerned about corruption in general, in Ukraine; and that's why the aid was held. Ukraine interfered in the 2016 election, and not Russia; there was no quid pro quo; no one knew that the aid was even being held, etc. I have debunked all of these, earlier on in this book, of course.}

Now Stewart is trying to argue, that President Trump's behavior has always been fair! How preposterous! I am not aware of anything that he's done, that was fair to anyone; except his rich pals and other financial interests. I rather agree with what else Stewart is saying Trump hasn't done; but I see things differently; he has indeed betrayed our country; he does appear quite likely to be either a Russian asset, or at least he is complicit with Russia's initiatives; he may well have even committed treason; certainly obstruction of Justice, and Obstruction of Congress; I would say that all of those assertions are true!

Regarding evidence of obstruction; even though the Republicans keep saying that nobody has yet produced any evidence; there's been a ton of evidence, and they just keep saying there's no evidence; so, I think that it was very apropos, that Schiff took a few moments to belittle the Republicans argument, appropriately; by saying, "My colleagues seem to think that, if President Trump didn't say, Ambassador Sondland, I'm going to bribe President Zelensky; then that means there's no evidence of a bribe… Republicans have turned a blind eye to the evidence; which is considerable…

{there have been so many hours of testimony to this effect, so far; and we are only halfway through the total number of hearings that took place, with the Intelligence Committee alone! (There are three other sessions with the Judiciary Committee, immediately after this group of hearings. So far, I have written 198 pages of mostly transcription of the testimony and questioning of the witnesses; there's a lot of evidence of this underhanded scheme, and the subsequent cover-up; and Republicans just want to turn a blind eye to it, and kiss off this whole affront to our democracy.}

Conaway reads one definition of bribery; defined as, obtaining money or property, by threat, for advantage to a victim's property or loved ones… {or something to this backwards effect. and that's interesting; because he says it is obtaining money or property; but a better way to explain bribery, would be: Giving someone money, in exchange for them to do something for you, that they wouldn't otherwise be inclined to provide.

So, obviously, Conaway is purposely try and contort the definition of bribery, in order to deceive listeners, and convince them this is not bribery; but by the second definition I cite, this is classic bribery; because Trump has, in effect, said to Zelensky, make these announcements of bogus investigations, to hurt my rival, and then I will give you $391 million dollars.

Of course, in many instances, offers of giving money in exchange for what the other person wants, involve the person being bribed, being asked to do something that would constitute a very hurtful, destructive, or otherwise disadvantageous action, that would benefit the briber, at the undue peril of others. This is exactly the case, with this scheme of Trump's.

Mr. Stewart is now saying that there was no pressure; which is a ridiculous argument. He is arguing that there's a reason that we withheld the aid. Stewart is arguing that it's a common occurrence for the US to hold aid. They did, in the case of Afghanistan, last year; and in a couple of other countries too, apparently. -But like I said before, those countries are not on the front lines of fighting war against the world's greatest enemy, Russia; literally invading democracy!

Now it goes to Mr. Quigley. He draws an interesting parallel; he says that what Republicans are doing here, might be likened to a situation where somebody set a building on fire; and instead of going after, and prosecuting the arsonist, they want to go after, and prosecute the guy who simply had pulled the fire alarm, to alert the authorities! How true! (and Republicans are ardently defending the arsonist, as well!) Quigley continues, "Whatever the whistleblower did, doesn't change the fact of the President's actions! It doesn't change the President's own words; and it doesn't change Mick Mulvaney's own words; and it doesn't change the body of proof that we have here, also." Well said!

Next, he asks Sondland about the July 10th meeting; and the "prerequisite" mentioned in that meeting, by Sondland. This is the first meeting in John Bolton's office; and Quigley makes reference to his statement, that a condition must be met, before a White House meeting would be granted. Sondland says, I believe someone else testified that I raised that, during the meeting; and I didn't dispute that testimony; that I said it's my understanding, that in order to get this visit, there needs to be an announcement. I don't know if I just said investigations, or if I said Burisma specifically.

{But at the same time this meeting was going on, apparently there was a meeting with Rudy Giuliani.} There was an email Sondland received afterward; I believe from Volker. Quigley recounts: the message you got was underscored; very concerned about Lutsenko... according to RG (Rudy Giuliani), POTUS meeting will not happen...

Sondland says, (this was apparently a meeting that Rudy Giuliani was having, at the same time; in Ukraine; unbeknownst to us.) Quigley points out, -but he is saying something different; Giuliani is saying it's not going to happen; there's no notice about the meeting being conditioned...

The text message was from Volker, to Sondland; and was saying, don't let other people (Giuliani was not part of Government) speak for the US Government! Quigley continues, "Rudy is following directions; and he is saying the meeting is called off; no conditions; and you're also following directions; and you're saying the meeting will happen, under these conditions; and both of you are saying this at the same time!"

Quigley asks, "Who was giving you the instructions to say what you were saying? Was it the Chief of Staff for Secretary Pompeo? Sondland says that he was getting informed through Ambassador Volker; and that he was the one in touch with Giuliani; so Sondland said he didn't talk to Mulvaney or Pompeo about this.

Next, the floor goes to Ms. Stefanik. She starts taking about Burisma, and asking a question about Hunter Biden's son. Sondland acknowledges that Hunter's appointment to the board was "the appearance" of potential conflict of interest, for Joe Biden; Vice President at the time. -But again, Hunter Biden has nothing to do with what this little group of schemers were up.

Next, it goes to Eric Swalwell. He says to Sondland that President Trump has just said, in a tweet about you, that quote, "I don't know him well; I haven't spoken to him much; this is not a man I know well." {-but I don't know; I would say that if you are able to reach the President directly, on your cell phone; and then laugh with him about, that the President of a foreign country, who is under your thumb, will do anything in the world for you; and that "He loves your ass!"

Talking so informally with the President of the United States, in such a familiar tone, would indicate that there is a pretty strong understanding, and friendship between those two, I think it indicates that they were talking all the time; isn't this just more evidence?! Republicans are denying there is any evidence; but I'd say that's evidence. Sondland had just testified, regarding the extent of his relationship with Trump "We (merely) have a cordial business relationship..." {Is it merely cordial, to say to each other, "That fool Zelensky, he loves your ass!"}

When Swalwell asks, Sondland tells us that he paid $1 million for a VIPP ticket to Trump's inauguration; {so that was his donation.} Swalwell says, you testified that "you were <u>playing the hand you were</u>

<u>dealt</u>." When Trump had said they needed to go talk to Rudy, the three amigos decided to do that, even though they would really rather not. Swalwell jokes, "And <u>Trump was the dealer</u>, right? {Sondland laughs heartily.} Swalwell says, although you have said that you didn't think that anything you were doing was wrong; but now, at this point, you <u>do</u> know that what was going on, was wrong, don't you? and Sondland says yes. {more evidence against Trump}

Swalwell continues: So, let's take out any leveraging of security assistance over the Ukrainians and a White House visit, from the picture; would you agree that it was wrong for the President of the United States to ask the leader of a foreign government, to investigate his political opponent? (yes) -Would you agree, that, in addition to making that request for investigations; leveraging a visit at the White House for a foreign government leader who desperately needs a show of US support, in the form of a meeting at the White House; to show their legitimacy, to their people? {Swalwell goes on to lay out a few other similar scenarios involving US domestic politicians}

Sondland offers, every meeting in the White House, has conditions on it…

Swalwell asks, -but if one of those meetings was conditioned on the investigation of a political opponent; that would be wrong… (yes) {However, Sondland next suggests that there's nothing wrong with conditioning a White House meeting on making announcements! That is what he just said! Yet, it's clear that the announcements that the Ukrainian government would be making, would ruin Donald Trump's chief rival in the 2020 election! You see? That's the thing about Sondland he sure appears dirty; but he is just very diplomatic, and half-way convincing, in his cover-up efforts. -But then you catch him saying something like that… It came right off the top of his head! He's basically saying, announcements are fine; we can leverage announcements. Do you see? He's on Trump's team; they are two peas in a pod!

To finish up, Swalwell says, if a guy walks into this room in a raincoat, wet boots, and an umbrella dripping with water, do you have to look outside, to reasonably presume that it's raining?! {Good question!}

Now it goes to the Bill Hurd:
{Sondland ducks basically all of Hurd's questions; I'm not sure, I don't know, etc...

Next, it goes to Mr. Castro. Castro says, others close to President Trump have made it clear that investigations were, in fact part, of the conditions, of US assistance to Ukraine; including Rudy Giuliani, and Mick Mulvaney, acting Chief of Staff.

So, Castro asks, Ambassador Sondland, in his October 17th press conference, Mick Mulvaney said that it is entirely appropriate to politicize US foreign policy; Ambassador, how long did you speak with, or meet with Mr. Mulvaney? (Again; based on my lack of records, I'm going by my memory; I think that I only had one formal meeting with Mulvaney; and it had nothing to do with Ukraine.

Castro says, Mulvaney, in his October 17th press conference; as one of the driving factors (of the quid pro quo), also mentioned the corruption related to the DNC server, he says, no question about that; but as far as the holding up of the money, the demand for an investigation was part of the reason why it was withheld. He asks Sondland, -the look-back to what happened in 2016 "was a part of the things he was worried about; corruption; and that it was absolutely appropriate...) Castro says, Mulvaney said that President Trump has an interest in that investigation; as he is the Chief of Staff, Mulvaney speaks to the President; he has conversations with the President every single day; is it your understanding, that the US Government conditions security assistance on an investigation into a political rival, all the time? (I don't think that would be proper.)

-Let us also say, what Mulvaney said in that press conference, "I have news for you; get over it; there's going to be political influence in foreign policy..."

-Knowing what you know now, Castro asks Sondland, do you agree, that there's going to be political influence in foreign policy? Sondland says, "I think there's a big difference between political influence, and investigating a rival; because politics enters into everything; including foreign-policy."

-But you agree, that the President should not be allowed to ask for the investigation of a political rival, in the context of what is going on in Ukraine…

Sondland agrees, "I believe the President should not investigate a political rival, in return for a quid pro quo." Castro yields back.

It goes to Mr. Ratcliffe, who ask unanimous consent, to enter into the record, the statement issued this morning; from the office of Vice President Pence's Chief of Staff, Mark Short. Schiff says yes, without objection. It amounts to a denial, in anticipation of Mr. Holmes's testimony tomorrow, about this July 26 phone call that he overheard at the café in Kyiv, that Sondland had with President Trump. {It is probably a bit of protective bullshit, perhaps.}

Ratcliffe yields back; and it goes to Mr. Heck; who had questions about Sondland's knowledge of the nature of the investigations, that he was trying to get the Ukrainians to announce the opening of; and Sondland contends that he doesn't believe that what he did was improper. Heck asks, did you realize that those investigations could impact the 2020 election? (Sondland says no)

-Is it ever appropriate, to invite foreign interference in our elections? (no)

Next, Heck reads part of Sondland's statement, then states, you had previously testified, "Had I known of all Mr. Giuliani's dealings, and his associations with individuals now under criminal indictment, I would not have acquiesced to this participation…" {so what Heck is saying, is that, in reading that; it's quite obvious that you, Ambassador Sondland, think what Rudy Giuliani was doing, was either wrong, or that he is not reputable.

Sondland replies, "With 2020 hindsight; yes." Sondland says, "I believe I have a legal obligation, and a moral obligation, to come before the committee, and testify."

So next, Heck talks a little about Sondland's family background; reviewing that his parents had emigrated into the United States, to raise Sondland and his sister here; and remarking that Sondland has obviously become a success story; he's a high-powered, wealthy businessman; and he says, no doubt you're grateful; and it has created a sense of patriotism within you; is that fair to say? (very fair)

Heck asks, "Why then, sir, why does that same standard not apply to Mr. Mulvaney; to come before us? Doesn't that same standard apply to Mr. Duffy, Mr. Pompeo, Mr. Bolton, and Mr. Giuliani? Why shouldn't those same sentiments be within their hearts, to do their patriotic duty? -to do what you have done? Indeed, why doesn't that same standard apply to the President of the United States?

Sondland says, I wish I could answer that.

Heck continues; you can't; because there is no good answer! -But I do appreciate your being here. With that, I yield back.

It now goes back to the obnoxious Mr. Jordan; who reiterates a long-winded tantrum of verbal diarrhea; really saying nothing new.

After that, it goes to Mr. Welch: Welch points out that Sondland has emphasized that his main objective with Ukraine, has been to get this White House meeting; and then Heck says, well; wasn't that also pretty-much the main objective of Ambassador Taylor, and Ambassador Volker; and several other Foreign Service and State Department representatives?

Then, Welch asks Sondland a really pointed question; he says, "As a person who came into public service in order to serve; you had a team of people who shared your desire to help Ukraine; do you feel, in any way, betrayed? -by the double-dealing of the President? This is the real question!

Sondland almost goes on "tilt," because in reality, he was undoubtedly, like he says, "in the loop;" and he was on the betraying end himself; yet he also knows that he should really be answering that he does feel betrayed. Then to top this off, he can't say he feels betrayed, because he has undoubtedly made a deal with the devil (Trump), to try and do everything he can, within his responses, to cast doubt, and make the President look the least bad, that he can muster; in exchange for keeping his job. Sondland has made it pretty evident that he values his job, he likes Trump, and he appears willing to try and muddy the waters; as opposed to answering questions directly and truthfully.

Sondland says, "I don't want to characterize… I would've preferred… I'm not sure… Everyone preferred that the President, simply met with Mr. Zelensky right away; our assessment of Mr. Zelensky, was that he and the President would get on famously; he was smart, he was funny, he was charming; he was the kind of person the President would like. Once the two of them got together, we thought the chemistry would take over; that's why we were pushing for a quick and unconditional meeting."

{So, in other words, Sondland avoids saying anything like, that he was very upset, when he found out that he had been working, all along, for this righteous objective, of getting together the two Presidents; and then, when he suddenly found out, (he really knew all along though), that the President had a subversive motive, he was devasted.) He knew he couldn't say this; although it would be best, under the circumstances perhaps; if it was true; which I'm pretty sure it is not true.

It's an interesting, and intelligently-thought-out question; because he can't answer yes I was upset, without accenting the blame, in the sense of wrongdoing that most of the Democrats on the committee feel toward President Trump; but more probably, he was complicit in the act; so there really <u>was</u> no point, in which he suddenly found out that what he was doing was dirty; I think he knew it all along.

It now goes to Mr. Maloney. Maloney takes an interesting approach; he talks about the cell phone call; from the restaurant; that David Holmes overhears; and so Sondland says that he doesn't remember; but he also doesn't dispute what Holmes had testified, about what Sondland told him that day in Kyiv. (i.e.- the President was only interested in "Big stuff" that benefitted him personally…) -but when Maloney asks him, "Well; then do you dispute that you mentioned "Bidens," in that conversation; as Holmes recounts to us?" Although Sondland first claims he doesn't remember the conversation; yet, he next strongly disputes that he had said "Biden" in his conversation with Holmes; and he has already contended that he didn't have any knowledge that the Bidens were associated with the investigations into Burisma, that he was advocating the Ukrainians publicly indicate they are moving forward with.

I mean, Holmes has no reason to lie. It's pretty obvious that Holmes is the kind of Foreign Service agent who, like Yovanovitch, would certainly never lie about anything of importance, such as this. -And he was entirely clear and succinct, in his memory of this very odd call. So, I really believe it, when Holmes says that he overheard Trump, and then he asked Sondland, what was big stuff? -that Sondland really did tell him Burisma and the Bidens; but I think we can be pretty certain that Trump has put Sondland up, to denying that.

Maloney continues trying to nail Ambassador Sondland on something he might trip up in answering; trying to get him to say anything that would further indicate Sondland was complicit in the scheme. He wasn't successful though, and so he finally says, "Ambassador Sondland, who would benefit from an investigation of the Bidens?" and Sondland wouldn't answer; the wormy idiot; but Maloney persisted, and so finally, Sondland said, "The President." and Maloney says, "There we go! Finally! (And this gets a big round of applause) "That didn't hurt a bit!" Maloney jokes.

Maloney is really fighting hard, to the last, as the hearing is coming to an end shortly. Wounded by the exchange, Sondland says, "You know, I really don't appreciate what you're doing here; I've been forthright; and I really resent what you're trying to do."

Maloney doesn't let up, "You been very forthright; this is your third try! -to do so!" {he gave the first closed-door deposition; and he said "I can't remember, I can't recall, I'm not sure..." for two pages of transcription taken. Then, he came back, for second closed-door deposition; in which he said that his memory had been refreshed; after listening to the revealing testimony of others (a likely story); and now, this is his third time around; so, Maloney is really giving him a stern talking to about this.} He barks, "This is your third time around! -so, you say you've been forthcoming; but we've had; it's taken us three tries, to get it out of you! -We got a doozy of a statement from you this, morning. There was a whole bunch of stuff, that you don't recall (supposedly, but this is not convincing to the Democratic committee members); so, with all due respect, sir, let's be really clear; what it took to get it out of you."

{Maloney then gave Sondland a final jab; saying, "You might say, that the Ukrainians were delivering a personal benefit to Mr. Trump; in exchange for an official act; the White House meeting..."

All of this, kind of aggravated Sondland, you could tell; but then Maloney's time had expired.

It then goes to Val Demmings: She says that talks about a meeting that took place on May 7th, involving President-elect Zelensky, and several other advisers; it took place in Ukraine. Demmings says the subject of the meeting was, to discuss how to handle pressure from President Trump and Mr. Giuliani, about investigating the Bidens. Of course, Sondland denies any knowledge of it; saying he doesn't recall; he doesn't know anything about it; "I don't recall anything about such a meeting a meeting among the Ukrainians." {that's interesting; Zelensky had just gotten elected, on like, April 21st, and he had this meeting already, on May 7th! He already knew he was being pressured! {Actually, it makes sense; because it soon comes out in the newspapers, that Trump and Giuliani had been running the same campaign, with former Ukrainian President Poroshenko.}

Demmings says, "I know you said you don't quite remember when it was, that you came to the realization that Burisma actually meant the Bidens; but back on May 6th, when asked, in a news report, about the role of the former Vice President's son, at Burisma, President Trump told Fox News that "It was a major scandal; a major problem." Then, on May 9th, the New York Times reported that Rudy Giuliani planned to travel to Ukraine; and to meet with President Zelensky; to urge him to pursue the 2016 election, and the involvement of Hunter Biden at Burisma; are you saying that you did not realize, at that time, that Mr. Giuliani wanted to pursue the 2016 election, and the involvement of Hunter Biden, at Burisma?!

Sondland claims that he did not know that; and also, that he didn't pay much attention to any of the (numerous) news reports on the subject.

Demmings presses, you mean, you didn't know; when the person you were directed by the President, to work with; when he was on television, over and over again; talking about Hunter Biden and Burisma in the news; you didn't have any idea of that connection?!

Demmings is nailing him right and left; 'Regarding September 9th, in the text from Ambassador Taylor, "are we now saying that aid is tied to the investigations?" and you had a conversation with President Trump; and President Trump said something to the effect that there is no quid pro quo; do you know what prompted him to say that? -You asked him what he wants, and he goes directly to "no quid pro quo!" -Instead of going directly to a list of things that he wanted! What prompted him to use that term?

Sondland replies, "I have no clue."

She asks him, "Had you discussed your text, from Ambassador Taylor with President Trump; before he made that statement?"

Sondland says, "I did not; I asked him an open question."

Demmings bears down harder, "-And you remember that, directly; although there are several other conversations that you cannot recall; because you don't have your notes, and your documents, and your emails, or other information; but you remember that call specifically; exactly what the President said...

The floor now goes to Kristamoorthi; who also nails Sondland right and left. He picks up on the September 9th conversation with the President; where he had said, "I want nothing, I want no quid pro quo!" I presume that on that September 9th conversation, the President did not mention, that this was the same day that we launched a congressional investigation, into whether there was a quid pro quo. -While you were on that call, did the President mention that? that he said that to you? (no) Sondland says, we didn't have time to talk about it.

Krishnamoorthi continues, "-And I presume that he also did not mention the whistleblower complaint, that also alleged it was a quid pro quo; did President Trump bring that up, in your call, that day? (he did not) -So, then you can't rule out the possibility, that the reason why he started talking about "Quid pro quo," was because of the congressional investigation... (I can't rule that out)

I want to point to a New York Times article, from last week (or in mid-November, 2019). This is about Lev Parnas; some information passed on by his attorney. Lev Parnas is an associate of Rudy Giuliani's; he was recently indicted. (Sondland nods that he is familiar with who Lev Parnas is). Mr. Parnas told a representative of the incoming government; the Zelensky government; that it had to announce an investigation into President Trump's political rival, Joseph Biden and his son; or else Vice President Pence would not attend the swearing-in of the new President; and the Vice President did not attend; possibly because this investigation did not become announced. (The implied question is; since this meeting was in April or May, did you really have no idea, until much later into August or September; that Burisma meant the Bidens? (But Sondland, of course, would not address this.)

Sondland says, "All I know, is that I was part of the delegation; Secretary Perry had invited me, at the last minute."

Krishnamoorthi says, "On October 8th of this year, the President tweets, That you "are really good man; and a Great American; and of course, on November 8th, only a month later he said on camera, "I can just tell you, I hardly know the gentleman..." Sondland says, "Easy come, easy go!" and they laugh. {but this was stated to further show what A wishy-washy liar of a President, that somehow got into office; despite being a totally destructive and incompetent, narcissistic maniac!

Finally, the questioning is over. Nunez makes his final comments first; and Nunez closes with his basic three question spiel; a pathetic ending.

So, now it is time for Adam Schiff's closing statement: Thank you for your testimony today. This is a seminal moment in our investigation; the evidence you have brought forward is deeply significant, and troubling. It has been long hearing, and I know Americans watching around the country, may not have had the opportunity to watch all of it; so let me go through a few of the highlights.

I'm not going to try to paraphrase; I'll just refer your opening statement: "We all understood that if we refused to work with Mr. Giuliani, we would lose an important opportunity to cement relations between the United States and Ukraine; so we followed the President's orders. Mr. Giuliani's requests were a quid pro quo for arranging a White House visit, for President Zelensky. Rudy Giuliani demanded that Ukraine make a public statement, announcing investigations of the 2016 election, the DNC server, and Burisma. Mr. Giuliani was expressing the desires of the President of the United States; and we knew that these investigations were important to the President."

Schiff continues, "Later, you testified, "I tried diligently to ask why the aid was suspended; but I never received a clear answer. In the absence of any credible explanation, for the suspension of the aid, I later came to believe that the resumption of security aid would not occur, until there was a public statement from Ukraine, committing to the investigation of the 2016 election, and Burisma; as Mr. Giuliani had demanded. I shared concerns of the potential quid pro quo regarding the security aid, with Senator Ron Johnson, and I also shared my concern with the Ukrainians."

Schiff then says, "So much for the Republicans' assertion, that "the Ukrainians didn't know; and you can't have a quid pro quo unless the Ukrainians knew;" (Schiff then looks at Sondland) -and you testified today, Ambassador, that the Ukrainians knew.

You further testified Mr. Giuliani emphasized that the President wanted a public statement, from President Zelensky, committing Ukraine to look into corruption issues; Mr. Giuliani specifically mentioned Burisma, and the 2016 elections, including the DNC server, as two topics of importance to the President. In reference to the July 10th meeting at the White House, that you (Sondland) attended with Ambassador Bolton and others, and a Ukraine delegation, you said, "I recall mentioning the prerequisite of investigation announcements, before any White House call or meeting can occur."

You further testified again, "Mr. Giuliani demanded of President Zelensky that he make a public statement about investigations; I knew that the topic of investigations was important to President Trump."

You testified later, "I know that members of this committee frequently frame these complicated issues, in the form of a simple question; was there a quid pro quo? As I testified previously, with regard to the requested White House call and the White House meeting, the answer is yes. We all understood these prerequisites; for the White

House call, and the White House meeting; reflected President Trump's desires and requirements."

Schiff continues, later, on the subject to security aid you testified, "In the absence of any credible explanation for the hold on the aid, I came to the conclusion that the aid, <u>and</u> the White House visit were jeopardized. In preparation for the September 1st meeting in Warsaw, I asked Secretary Pompeo whether a face-to-face conversation, between Trump and Vice President Pence could help break the Logjam?"

Schiff reads, and this is from an email (from Sondland to Secretary Pompeo) which the State Department refused to provide. It reads, "should we block time in Warsaw, for a short pull aside; for POTUS to meet Zelensky? I would ask Zelensky to look him in the eye, and tell him that once Ukraine's new justice folks are in place, in mid-September, that he should be able to move forward publicly, and with confidence, on those issues of importance to the POTUS, and to the United States. {Sondland, by writing this, shows that in August, or before, he knew that there was a difference, between what was important to President Trump; and what was alternatively important for the good of the United States.}

Sondland's last line in the email: "hopefully that will probably break the logjam." -and secretary Pompeo's reply? "yes." -Not, what issues of importance to POTUS? Not, what you talking about Ambassador Sondland?

Because Secretary Pompeo had been on that July 25th phone call, he knew what issues were important to POTUS; and there were two of them; an investigation into 2016 and the DNC server; and the investigation into the Bidens. By the end of August, you (Sondland) testified, "My belief is that, if Ukraine did something to demonstrate a serious intention to fight corruption, specifically addressing Burisma, and the 2016 server; then the hold on the military aid would be lifted. I mentioned to Vice President Pence, before the meeting with the Ukrainians, that I had concerns that the delay in aid, had become tied to the issue of the investigations."

Schiff looks at Sondland: And as you testified; he gave you no response... No, "What you talking about, Ambassador?! Or How could that be?!" He merely took it in due course. -And the record of that July 25th call, with Presidents Trump and Zelensky, was in the Vice President's reading book; just days earlier.

Then, you testified, "My goal, at the time, was to do what was necessary, to get the aid released; to break the logjam; and I believed that the public statement we had been discussing for weeks, was essential for advancing that goal.

Schiff refers now to Republican committee members, "Now, my colleagues seem to believe; and let me add too, about this call you had. with the President. You have confirmed today, that, in addition to claiming there was no quid pro quo; that President Trump was adamant, that President Zelensky had to clear things up; and do it in public. That's what you have confirmed; that is what you also told Ambassador Taylor. So, President Trump would deny there was a quid pro quo; but he was adamant, that Zelensky had to "clear things up; and do it in public."

I've said a lot of things about President Trump, over the years. I have very strong feelings about him; which are neither here nor there; but I will say this, on the President's behalf. I do not believe the President would allow himself to be led by the nose, by Rudy Giuliani, or Ambassador Sondland, or anybody else. I think the President was the one who decided whether the meeting would happen, or whether the hold on the aid would be lifted; not anyone who worked for him; and so the answer to the question, who was refusing meeting with Zelensky, that you (Sondland) believe should take place; that everybody believed should take place; the question is, who was the one, standing in the way of that meeting? Who was the one refusing to take that meeting? There is only one answer to that question; and it is Donald J, Trump; 45th President of the United States.

Who was holding up the military assistance? Was it you (Sondland)? -No; was it Volker? No; Taylor? No; Deputy Secretary Kent? No; Secretary Pompeo? No. Who had the decision to release the aid? There was one person; Donald Trump, the President of the United States.

My colleagues seem to think, that unless the President says the magic words, "I hereby bribe the Ukrainians!" that there's no evidence of bribery, or high crimes and misdemeanors; but let's look to the best evidence of what the President had said; what was his intent? What was the reason behind the postponement of the White House meeting; and the hold on the aid?

-But let's look at what the President's intent; at what's undisputed about what the President was saying. Do you know how we know? -because we have a record of his conversation; with the one who really matters; the other President, Zelensky. He says, "Rudy very much knows what's happening, and he is a very capable guy." This is after he says, he wants a favor. He goes into Crowdstrike, and 2016. "Rudy very much knows what's happening. He is a very capable guy. If you could speak to him, that would be great. The former Ambassador to the United States; the woman was bad news; the people she was dealing with in Ukraine were bad news; so I just want to let you know; and the other thing; there's a lot of talk about Biden's son, that Biden stopped the prosecution; and a lot of people want to find out about that; so whatever you can do with the Attorney General, that would be great. Biden went around bragging, that he stopped the prosecution; so if you could look into it, it sounds horrible to me."

So, it's in the President's mind, when he's placed this otherwise inexplicable hold on the aid; when he refuses to take the meeting, what's on his mind? Biden. He makes it abundantly clear. Understanding, Ambassador Sondland; you say you didn't make the connection, between Burisma, and the Bidens; I'll let the American people judge the credibility of that answer. -But there's no mistaking what Donald Trump's interest was; there is no mistaking at all, what Trump meant, when he had that call with you (Sondland), on an unsecured phone line, on the outdoor terrace (at a restaurant in Ukraine);

He made that abundantly clear to the President of Ukraine, the day before. The question is not, what the President meant; the question is not, whether he was responsible for holding up the aid; he was. The question is not, whether everybody knew it; apparently, they did. The question is this: What are we prepared to do about it? Is there any accountability? -or are we forced to conclude, that this is just, now, the world we live in? -where the President of the United States can withhold vital military aid, from an ally, at war with Russia; an ally fighting our fight, to defend our country against Russia. Are we prepared to say; in the words that Mulvaney used, "get over it; get used to it."

We are not prepared to say that; and I appreciate, Ambassador Sondland, the fact that you have not opined on whether the Present should be impeached, or whether the crime of bribery, or the impeachable offense of bribery, or other high crimes and misdemeanors, have been committed. That is for us (Congress) to decide; in consultation with our constituents, and our conscience.

It is for us to decide; and as much as my colleagues may think otherwise, this is not this not an easy decision, for any of us; and as much as my colleagues may say otherwise; this is not something we relish. For over a year, I resisted this whole idea of going down the road to impeachment; but it was made necessary; not by the whistleblower, but by the actions of the President; and I'm continually struck that my colleagues would suggest, that because the President got caught, we should ignore the facts that he was conditioning official acts, in order to get political favors; in order to get an investigation against his rival.

Getting caught is no defense; not to a violation of the Constitution; or to a violation of his oath of office; and that certainly doesn't give us reason to ignore our own oath of office! We are adjourned. (Adam Schiff gets a big hand, for that brilliant statement, by the way)

Intelligence Committee hearing #6- Cooper and Hale

This is the 6th intelligence committee impeachment hearing. The witnesses are Laura Cooper and David Hale. Adam Schiff gives his opening statement. He says that Laura Cooper and David Hale are National Security professionals one at the Department of State, and the other at the Defense Department.

David Hale is the Undersecretary of State for Political Affairs, and the 3rd most-senior official in the State Department; and the most-senior Foreign Service officer.

Laura Cooper serves as Deputy Assistant Secretary of Defense, for Russia, Ukraine, and Eurasia. She is responsible for a broad range of countries in the Soviet Union and the Balkans. Between them, they have several decades of National Security experience, serving of both Republican and Democrat Presidents.

Undersecretary Fiona Hill was witness to the smear campaign against Ambassador to Ukraine, Marie Yovanovitch; and the efforts, by some in the State Department. to help her. In late March, Yovanovitch reached out to Hill, in an email, that the tempo of social media and other criticisms of her were such that she felt she could no longer function, unless there was a strong statement of defense for her, from the State Department.

Hill pushed to get the State Department to put out a robust full-page statement of defense and praise, for Ambassador Yovanovitch; sadly, to of no avail. That silence continues today.

{Schiff says that Energy Secretary Rick Perry was the chief coordinator of the 3 amigos; being Perry, Curt Volker, and Gordon Sondland.} From her office in the Pentagon, Ms. Cooper oversaw a significant amount of security assistance flowing to Ukraine; and was involved in efforts to understand, and to reverse the suspension of nearly $400 million in US aid. She learned about the freeze, in the last 2 weeks of July. At the first meeting on July 17th, an OMB representative relayed that the White House Chief of Staff had conveyed that the President Trump had concerns about Ukraine, and Ukraine security assistance; and that a hold had been ordered by the President with no explanation provided. Even though the hold on the aid was not made public, word was getting out.

Catherine Croft, Special Advisor for Ukraine Negotiation, worked closely with Ambassador Volker, (who has testified before this committee in a deposition), received separate calls, in July and August, from officials at the Ukrainian Embassy; who had approached him, in confidence; to ask about the OMB hold on Ukraine security assistance. Ms. Croft was very surprised at the effectiveness of her Ukrainian counterparts' diplomatic tradecraft; as if to say they found out much earlier on, than she had expected them to.

The Ukrainians wanted answers; and Croft did not have a good response; but then in late August, Ms. Cooper met with Kurt Volker, with whom she had met many times in the past. During that meeting, they discussed the hold on security assistance.

Volker had revealed that he was engaged in an effort to have the government of Ukraine issue a statement, that would commit to the prosecution of individuals involved in election interference. Ms. Cooper understood that if the focus of the effort were successful, the hold might be lifted. Unbeknownst to her, no such statement was forthcoming; but the aid was abruptly restored on September 11th, just days after three Congressional Committees had launched an investigation into the Trump/Ukraine scheme. With that, Schiff recognizes Devin Nunez, the ranking minority member, for his opening statement.

Nunez starts off claiming that the American people are getting a skewed impression of these events. Then, he goes into the whistleblower once again.

He says some bullshit about the whistleblower complaint; that in order to be considered legitimate, it should have required a first-hand witness to what was being complained about. {But that seems pretty unimportant, in the face of such surprising conduct, taking place in the office of the presidency; and obviously, the White House had the opportunity to dispute what the whistleblower was saying. But instead, Trump had released a summary of what was said on the July 25th phone call with President Zelensky; and that constituted some pretty-solid evidence that there was a scheme going on; especially when combined with the other testimony that has come out, so far.}

Nunez claims that Alexandra Chalupa, whose activities were one of several factors indicating evidence of Ukrainian election meddling in 2016, were aimed at hurting the Trump campaign, supposedly. (I believe Chalupa simply did some research and wrote articles about it; truthful claims, probably; it wouldn't be hard to find upsetting things about is past, that would probably be well-worth mentioning to the public, as they were possibly weighing whether to seriously-consider possibly nominating him, or not.}

Nunez claims that Ukrainian officials were working with Democrats to undermine Trump's candidacy. Next, he mentions Hunter Biden; {and of course, Hunter Biden's activities are not at stake here; and in fact, there has been no evidence that he has committed any wrongdoing.}

Nunez claims that Burisma was the highlight of corruption in Ukraine; {but how could that be? -Because Burisma was a natural gas-producing company, whereas, there is also a lot of oil being drilled for, in the country; and there's also the factor that Russia is a huge producer of oil and gas, and they have corruptly arranged for kickbacks, having built pipelines going through Ukraine, for example; and Russia supplies heating oil to many people in Ukraine; so the corruption of one single gas company in Ukraine could not possibly be the highlight of all corruption in Ukraine, obviously.}

Nunez basically contends, "The presumptions, assumptions, and smoke and mirrors" {assertions of the Democrats, obscure the facts of this case; and he thinks that his (alternate) facts of this case are clear. He goes on to contend that Trump was simply generally "concerned" about giving aid to Ukraine and other countries; {however, he did not mention this, in his phone calls, or otherwise; nor did he otherwise make this known to the American people, to any extent. You would think that, as many Americans know, substantial support being in the US interest; to greatly help Ukraine in fighting the world's fight, against Russia expanding its borders by use of military force; that any good reason for delay or interruption of that aid, would warrant a national address, from his badly abused bully pulpit.

I've stated before, several reasons why, of all countries, Ukraine is the last country that we should ever consider not funding their war with Russia right now. Fighting Russia is not a corrupt effort, of course! -So it is well worth supporting consistently; how could this be reasonably be disputed?!}

Next, Nunez claims that President Zelensky was being extorted; {but it was really the other way around, of course. If Zelensky were being extorted, then he would be having to pay money to Trump, right?}

Nunez says the accusations have changed by the hour; {but really, the accusations simply keep mounting, because we are coming to increasing revelations and realizations that there are indeed several forms of abuse of power, and obstruction of Congress involved; so it is only appropriate for them all to be listed in a hearing such as this.}

He yields back; and Adam Schiff announces the witnesses: David Hale is Undersecretary of Defense for Political Affairs, at the Department of State, since August 30, 2018. Hale joined the Foreign Service in 1984, He holds the rank of Career Ambassador, and was Ambassador to Pakistan, Ambassador to Lebanon, and Special Envoy for Middle East Peace; and Special Envoy Ambassador to Jordan.

Laura Cooper is the Deputy Secretary of Defense, for Russia, Ukraine, and Eurasia, at the Department of Defense. She is a member of the Senior executive Service. Ms. Cooper previously served as Principal Director, in the office of the Assistant Secretary of Defense and Global

Security Affairs. Prior to joining the Department of Defense in 2001, Ms. Cooper was a policy planning officer at the State Department, in the office of Coordination of Counterterrorism.

Schiff says that since the depositions were held at and unclassified level, so will these hearings; any responses that will touch on classified information will be addressed separately.

Schiff swears them in; and first, Ambassador Hale gives his opening statement. He explains that he does not have prepared, a written opening statement; but that he wants to comment on his record. Hale was Ambassador 3 times; serving in both Republican and Democratic administrations; and he says he will be happy to answer the questions of the Committee.

Ms. Cooper then reads her opening statement: I will be answering questions today as a fact witness; to provide facts, and answer questions, based on my experience as Deputy Assistant Secretary of Defense, for Russia and Ukraine. I would first like to describe my background, as well as my role, and vantage point, relevant to your inquiry. I bring to my daily work, and into this proceeding, my sense of duty to US national security; not to any political party. I have proudly served two Democratic, and two Republican Presidents.

I entered into government service through the Presidential Management Internship Competition, joining the State Department in 1999, to work on counterterrorism in Europe, and the former Soviet Union. Inspired by working with the US military, in a Department of Defense rotational assignment, I decided to accept a Civil Service position in a policy organization, for the office of the Secretary of Defense, in January of 2001; where I have remained for the past 18 years.

My strong sense of pride, in serving my country, and dedication to my Pentagon colleagues, were cemented in the moments after I felt the Pentagon shake beneath me, on September 11, 2001. My office was scheduled to move into a section of Pentagon that was under attack; but construction had been delayed, so we were still in an adjacent section of the building, on that day. After we had wiped the black dust from our desks, we tried to get back to work.

I found meaning by volunteering to work on Afghanistan policy, and I gave my 4 years to this mission. I later had the opportunity to move into the leadership ranks in my organization, and have had the privilege to manage issues ranging from defense strategic planning, to homeland defense, and mission assurance.

I accepted the position of Principal Director for Russia, Ukraine, and Eurasia in 2016, and was honored to be appointed formally to the position of Deputy Assistant Secretary of Defense in 2018. In my current role, I work to advance US national security, with a focus on deterring Russian aggression, and building strong partnerships with the front-line states of Ukraine, and Georgia; as well as 10 other allies and partners, from the Balkans, to the Caucuses.

Strengthening Ukraine's capacity to defend itself against Russian aggression is central to my team's mission. The United States and our allies provide Ukraine with security assistance, because it is in our national security interests, to deter Russian aggression around the world. We also supervise security assistance so that Ukraine can negotiate a peace with Russia, from a position of strength. The human toll continues to climb in this ongoing war; with 14,000 Ukrainian lives lost, since Russia's 2014 invasion.

These sacrifices are continually in my mind, as I lead efforts to provide training and equipment, including defensive legal assistance for the Ukrainian Armed Forces. I have also supported a robust Ukrainian Ministry of Defense program, including corruption reform, to show ensure the long-term support of the US, in the transformation of the Ukrainian military, from a Soviet model, to a NATO interoperable force. The National Defense Authorization Act requires the Department of Defense to certify foreign progress, for the USIA to release half of initiative for USAI funds; a provision we find very helpful.

Based on recommendations from me, and other advisors, the Department of Defense, in coordination with the Department of State, had certified, in May of 2019, that Ukraine had taken substantial action to make defense institutional reforms for the purposes of decreasing corruption; increasing accountability and sustaining improvements, and permits a combat capability meriting application of the entire $250 million USAI funds. This brings us to the topic of today's proceedings:

I would like to recap my recollection of the timeline in which these events laid out. I testified about all of this at length, in my deposition. in July, I became aware of a hold being placed on the obligation of the State Department's Foreign Military Financing; or FMF; and the DOD's USAI funds. During the series of interagency meetings, I heard that the President had directed the Office of Management and Budget to hold the funds because of his concerns about corruption in Ukraine.

Let me say, at the outset, that I have never discussed this; or any other matter, with the President; and I never heard directly from him about this matter.

At a Senior-level meeting I attended, on July 26th, chaired by National Security Council leadership; as at all other interagency meetings on this topic; that I was aware the national security community had expressed unanimous support for resuming the funding; as this is in US national security interests.

After the July 26th meeting, there was also a discussion on how Ukrainian anticorruption efforts were making progress. The UG reiterated what we had said in her earlier certification of progress, stating that sufficient progress in defense reform, including anticorruption, had occurred, to justify the USAI spending.

I, and others at the interagency meetings, felt that the matter was particularly urgent, because it takes time to obligate that amount of money; and my understanding was that it was legally required to be obligated by September 30th, the end of the fiscal year. In the ensuing weeks, until the hold was released on September 11th, I pursued redress; first starting on July 31st.

In the interagency meeting, I made clear to the interagency leadership, my understanding at once DOD reaches the point at which it does not have sufficient time obligate all of the funds, by the end of this year, there were only 2 ways to discontinue this obligation of USAI; if the President had directed decision, or a DOD-directed reprogramming action; either of which, would need to be notified to Congress. I never heard that that was being pursued.

Second, I was in communication with the DOD security-assistance-implementing community, to try to understand exactly when we would reach the point at which they would be unable to obligate all of the funds, by the end of the fiscal year.

I received a series of updates, and on the September 5th update, I and other senior Defense Department leaders were informed that over hundred million could not be obligated by September 30th.

Third, I was advocating for a meeting of the cabinet level principles, with the President to explain why the assistance should go forward.

Although I heard of attempts to discuss this the President, I have never heard any details of the conversations, other than a status update, that the hold had not been lifted. After the decision to release the funds on September 11th of this year, my colleagues across the DOD security assistance enterprise worked tirelessly to be able to ultimately obligate about 86% of the funding by the end of the fiscal year; more than they had originally estimated they would be able to.

Due to a provision in September's continuing resolution appropriating an amount equal to the unobligated funds from fiscal year 2019, we ultimately will be able to obligate all of the USAI funds. Given how critical these funds are for bolstering Ukraine security, and deterring Russia, I appreciate this congressional action.

That concludes my opening statement; but before answering your questions, there is one other matter I would like to address. I testified in a deposition before this committee and other committees October 23rd. At that time, I was asked questions about what I knew, about when the Ukrainian government may have learned about the hold on the assistance funds. My answer to those questions, and my knowledge was based on my notes at that time. I have again reviewed my calendar, and the only meeting I can recall the Ukrainians raising the issue with me, was on September 15th, at the Ukrainian Independence Day celebration.

I have however, since learned additional information about this, from my staff. Prior to my deposition testimony, I avoided discussing my testimony with members of my staff, or anyone other than my attorney, to ensure that my deposition testimony was based only on my personal knowledge.

My deposition testimony was publicly released on November 11th. Members of my staff read the testimony, and have come to me since then, and provided additional information.

Specifically, on the issue of Ukraine's knowledge of the hold, and of Ukraine asking questions about possible issues with the flow of the assistance, my staff showed me two unclassified emails they had received from the State Department. One was received on (the morning of) July 25th. The Ukrainian Embassy and House foreign affairs committee were asking about security assistance. The second email was received (in the late afternoon) on July 25th. "The Hill (publication) knows about the FMF situation -so do the Ukrainians."

I did not receive either of these emails, and my staff does not recall informing me about them; and I do not recall being made aware of their content, at the time. I do not have any additional information about precisely what the Ukrainians might have said, or what may have been the source of information about a hold, or any possible issues with the flow of assistance, or what State Department officials may have told them.

My staff have also advised me in the last few days, of the following additional facts, that may be relevant to this inquiry. Again, my staff does not recall reporting them to me, and I do not recall being made aware of them. On July 3rd, there was an email from the State Department saying they heard that the CN is currently being blocked by OMB. This apparently refers to the congressional notification statement for Ukraine sent from the FMF. I have no further information on this.

On July 25th, a member of my staff got a question from a Ukraine Embassy contact, asking what was going on with Ukraine security assistance; because at that time, we did not know what the guidance was, on USAI apportionment.

The OMB notice of apportionment arrived that day, but my staff members did not find out about it until later. I was informed that a staff member told Ukrainian officials that we were moving forward on the

USAI, but they recommended that the Ukraine Embassy check in with (the) State (Department), regarding FMF.

Sometime during the week of August 6-10th, a Ukraine Embassy officer told a member of my staff that a Ukrainian official might raise concerns about the security assistance, at an upcoming meeting. My understanding is that the issue was not, in fact raised. I have no further information about what concerns over security assistance Ukraine may have had, at that time.

My staff also recalled thinking that the Ukrainians were aware of the hold on the security assistance during August, but they cannot pinpoint any specific conversation where it came up.

My staff told me they were aware of additional meetings, where they saw officials in the Ukraine Embassy, in August; and they believe that the question of the hold came up at some point; but they told me they did not find any corresponding email records of those meetings. Consequently, neither they, nor I know precisely when or what additional discussions may have occurred with the Ukrainians in the month of August. if I had more details on these matters, I would offer them to the committee; but this is the extent of additional information I have received since my deposition. (I will answer your questions of the best of my ability). Thank you

Adam Schiff announces that they will forgo the first round of questioning by the Majority and Minority leaders, and their counsel; going directly to the member questioning; being that there have been lengthy questioning sessions over the past few days, by the Minority and Majority leaders and their counsels, so enough has already come out about the scheme, that a staff member round is not necessary, at this point.

Schiff takes the opportunity to address a minority member's claim, that none of their witnesses were called; Schiff says that's inaccurate. He argues that David Hale is a minority witness; he's one of the witnesses the minority requested. Likewise, two other witnesses (Volker and Morrison) were both minority-requested witnesses. (Is none of what Republicans are claiming, accurate?!)

Then, Schiff recognizes himself for 5 minutes; and says, as early as July 25th, the day that President Trump and President Zelensky spoke on the phone; on that date also, according to Ms. Cooper's testimony, there were two emails from the Ukrainian Embassy, asking about what's happening with the aid, and concerned about the status of the military assistance. Schiff asks Cooper, did that connote to you that something was going on with the aid?

Cooper affirms, and clarifies that the email that Schiff was just talking about was an email sent to her staff. The other email, also sent on the 25th reflected outreach to the State Department, by the Ukrainians.

-Your staff also heard in August, inquiries from the Ukrainian Embassy about the hold-up of the aid? (My staff recalled having meetings with Ukrainians at the Embassy, and they believe that the topic came up at some point during those meetings, but they don't recall the specific dates or nature of the discussions.) Schiff says, you are now the 3rd witness who has testified that the Ukrainians found out about the hold, prior to it becoming public; and it may go back to as early as July 25th.

Next, Schiff refers to Ms. Cooper's testimony, that she had met with Kurt Volker in August, and Volker had told her it appeared that the Ukrainians were going to make an announcement of the investigations, that they would commit to the prosecuting of individuals involved in election interference; and if so, this might lift the hold on Ukraine security assistance.

Cooper says that the only things she remembers talking about, in that discussion, were the talks about the lifting of the hold on the aid, and that also after that they had a discussion about what Volker had understood Ukrainians would be committing to, which would supposedly cause the hold to be lifted, she says she's not sure if she talked about the White House meeting or not, but she says that it's likely that this was a part of the conversation.

The floor now goes to Devin Nunez, who yields to Mr. Ratcliffe, who starts out, Undersecretary Hale, Ms. Cooper, I think you both have heard talk about President Trump's general skepticism of providing aid, core aid being provided to foreign countries... Nunez had mentioned this, as he refers to the NSC having launched an investigation specifically into Ukraine, and their corruption; and how effectively they have recently been addressing their corruption issues. The last foreign assistance review process was apparently sometime in late August, or early September. Ratcliffe asks, is it fair to say that the President wanted to ensure that the American taxpayers' money was being effectively and efficiently spent, outside of the United States? (Yes, that is the broader intent of the foreign assistance review, among other goals.

Ratcliffe then brings up Trump's claim that he expects our allies to give their fair share of at foreign aid; as evidenced by a point that he raised during the July 25th phone call, to that effect. (The principle of greater burden sharing is important.) -Is it fair to say that aid is withheld from foreign countries, for a number of factors? (correct) -And it is normal to have delays on aid? (It certainly does occur.) -Last year, Ukraine was not the only country to have aid withheld… (correct) {Aid was withheld from Pakistan because of unhappiness over the policies and behavior of the Pakistani government toward certain proxy groups that were involved, that were involved in conflicts with United States. Aid was also withheld from the 3 states in Central America, and in Lebanon.}

-Were you given a reason why Lebanon's aid was withheld? (no) -Having no explanation for why aid is withheld is not uncommon? (I would say it was is not the normal way we would function; it does happen.)

{Ratcliffe points out that the aid being withheld from Lebanon occurred at the same time that the aid was withheld from Ukraine; however, of course, this could have been strategically implemented as part of the effort to cover up Trump's plot to put pressure on Ukraine, to make these damaging announcements for candidate Joe Biden, in the run-up to the 2020 election.}

Ratcliffe's time expires, and he yields back.

The floor then goes to Jim Himes. (He starts out sarcastically)-The President's acting on some deep historical concern; apparently invisible concern, about corruption; and it is because he so concerned about corruption in Ukraine that he is holding up aid; he was being prudent and judicious… The first part of that is pretty easy to dispose of, because President Trump wasn't worried about corruption in Ukraine. In fact, in the two conversations he had with the President of Ukraine, on April 21st and July 25th, not once does the President of the United States use the word, or mention corruption to the President Zelensky.

The second part of that is more interesting; he is being prudent, holding up the aid. That's not just wrong, it's illegal! Ms. Cooper, I want you to help us. Walk us through this Impoundment Control Act of 1974. The President does not have the authority to, on a whim, or out of prudence, or as my Republican colleagues say, because of a general skepticism of foreign aid.

-Under our Constitution, it's the Congress, and not the President, that has the power of the purse; is that correct? (yes) -Ms. Cooper, wasn't the security assistance to Ukraine authorized and appropriated by the Congress? (correct, yes)

Congress is also concerned about corruption, and must ensure that American foreign assistance is spent wisely, and does not worsen corruption; so, when Congress authorized this money, they must have first determined that these conditions were met.

The floor goes to Mr. Stewart, who thanks the witnesses for doing what they do; and he says that being the President is the most complicated job in the world and, that he couldn't do it without their support. {It's interesting that he would say that; because President Trump has been doing so many things without anybody else's support, or even bringing anyone into the discussion; including most recently, authorizing an attack, to assassinate this Iranian general Sulimani; which caused a huge scare around the world, and it ended up touching off an overreaction on Iran's part. When they retaliated with a strike, they had anticipated the that US may well launch a counterstrike, sending planes into Iran; so they had missiles set up, ready for this. There was no US, attack but an Iranian passenger plane accidentally became shot down by missiles readied to fire, in the case of a US airstrike. There were 300 passengers killed instantly!

On top of that, when Sulimani was killed by the US strike, the reaction in Iran was so severe that while people were demonstrating on the streets, 50 people got trampled! So, my point is that Trump goes off on a whim and doesn't even consult anyone in his administration, and it causes these huge backlashes, and creates severe challenges, for millions of people!

So, how could Chris Stewart be helping his case defending Trump, by suggesting that the President can't do his job without depending on a network of support; while he should, he doesn't; is probably the wrong thing to say; but these Republicans are defending Trump solely because they are just interested in getting their way, against the citizens of this country.

{Here, I am missing a section of the questioning of Hale and Cooper; I think it is about ten minutes of testimony.}

… The floor goes to Ms. Stefanik; she's on the House arms armed services committee. She goes to the importance of Javelins. When asked, both answer that they had not spoken with the President about Ukraine aid. She goes into what other countries where security assistance was on hold.

Stefanik tells us that the aid package to Lebanon was also being held, in the same fashion (correct) -And foreign aid was pulled, from the Northern tribal areas; in countries in Central America. We learn that when Hale had served as Ambassador to Pakistan, security assistance was also withheld, for their failure to conform to our concerns regarding terrorists, and other issues on the Afghan/Pakistan border.

Stefanik says, we talk about the fact that these are hard-earned taxpayer dollars… (and Hale agrees) Stefanik says, the Trump administration has been conducting a foreign assistance review, to reestablish norms that guide the assistance, as we provide aid overseas… (that's correct) Stefanik reads the part of Hale's testimony where he says, the program evaluates the beneficiaries of our assistance, to ensure that our program makes sense, that we further our nation-building strategies, and that we provide assistance to countries that are locked, in terms of their policy, to our allies… (that's correct) Hale's statement had also said that he warmly welcomes this assistance review process. {Still, we never hear of any formal process of this kind ever was underway; at least none of the witnesses testify that they were aware, or working on this specifically; they all just say that they understood that the President had ordered the hold, and that, other than a nebulous explanation that it was pending a review, no one says anything about being a part of a review process regarding Ukraine.}

Next, it goes to Eric Swalwell, who begins: Ms. Cooper, your testimony today destroys two of the pillars of the President's defense; and one justification for his conduct. First, their contention of "No harm, no foul; the Ukrainians didn't know the hold was in place, so it didn't really hurt them. The second pillar is, this President is a real champion of anticorruption; he cares about corruption in Ukraine.

So, I want to go through your testimony today; it's your testimony now, that after an employee came forward to you, you believe you have some evidence that the Ukrainians first inquired about security assistance, to someone in your office, on July 25th of this year; is that right? (Yes) -July 25th is also the day that President Trump initially talked to President Zelensky, where investigations of the Bidens were brought up; is that right? (that was publicly reported, yes)

-Second, regarding the contention that this President is a champion of anticorruption; (Ms. Cooper) on May 23rd, you certified that, as far as it related to your duties, Ukraine had met the corruption concerns for the aid to be released; is that right? (Sir, the Defense Department certified this.) -And after that, inexplicably, the President puts a hold on the aid… (That's what I heard, yes.) -Now, this anticorruption President cares so much about rooting out corruption in Ukraine; did he ever call you to ask you what is going on in Ukraine (in regards to corruption?) (No Sir.)

-Ambassador Hale, did President Trump ever call you, to ask about an update on Ukraine corruption? (no) -Did he ever call your boss, Secretary Pompeo, Ms. Cooper? -Did he ever call the many bosses that you have at the Department of Defense; Secretaries or Acting Secretaries? (I don't know), {Cooper would undoubtedly be made aware, if she had not also been personally asked to provide a report on the matter; as she works directly with the Secretary of Defense}

-But this is the justification; which is that the Obama administration only provided blankets, so the Ukrainians should be grateful, even after being shaken down by the Trump administration! -But the truth, Ms. Cooper, is that, under the Obama administration and the European Reassurance Initiative, $175 million was provided from US taxpayer dollars to Ukraine… (she says she doesn't have that figure specifically, but she knows that the US has provided $1.6 billion in aid, to date) {since 2014}

-Didn't we also train five military battalions in Ukraine; is that correct? (Yes, the training program began in the Obama administration; and we did train many forces.) -And under the Obama administration, which founded the Ukraine Assistance Initiative, we provided the Ukrainians with armored Hum-V's, tactical drones, night vision devices, armored vests, and medical equipment; is that correct? (These all sounds like pieces of equipment that were provided by the Obama administration.) -You do believe that's a lot more than providing blankets, right?! (yes)

-Ambassador Hale, the aid that was held; to Lebanon, and Pakistan; those holds were for legitimate foreign policy objectives; is that right? (I would say that's true of the assistance to Pakistan; I have not heard an explanation for the current hold on Lebanon aid.) {Oh, so maybe Trump is defying Congress, regarding aid appropriated to other countries, as well!}

-And you would agree that withholding aid to investigate a political opponent is not a legitimate foreign policy objective; is that right? (yes) -So, I guess we can agree that even Bernie Madoff made charitable contributions; but that doesn't make him a good guy…

-Ms. Cooper, your testimony today demonstrates the power of moving forward, and defying lawless orders from the President -Because you came forward and testified, we learned this new information which destroys the central defense that the Republicans have put forward. -Because Ambassador Taylor came forward, one of his employees learned that this defense from the Republicans, that all we have is hearsay evidence; Mr. Holmes said, actually I heard the President of the United States tell (ask) Ambassador Sondland (on the phone at the restaurant in Kyiv), where are we with the investigations? -Your courage has aided this investigation, despite the President's continued obstruction. I yield back.

It goes to Mr. Hurd:

Hurd tells us that, in essence, Ambassador Hale is the number 3 guy in the State Department; is that correct? (correct) -You represent roughly 70,000 folks...

-Would you say that you represent them? (I would say that I am part of them.) Hurd tells us that he shared time with them, in Pakistan. Hurd then asks Hale if anybody raised questions about the investigations of Mr. Biden, to him? (no)

Next, Hurd compliments Ms. Cooper's staff; he says he doesn't know if his staff take the time to read a 115-page deposition that he had given, if he had to testify before Congress in the same way. He says to Ms. Cooper, your department; the Department of Defense; had certified that Ukraine had passed the scrutiny, in terms of Ukraine's level of corruption, as of May 23rd. (Sir, I think the wording was along the lines of "sufficient progress has been made; it didn't reference any anticorruption test, per se.) -Was there a reevaluation for the new President? -Did this have an impact? -Hurd asks if there was a renewed investigation, taking into account the new President? (no) Hurd confirms that the review in the spring was based solely on the Poroshenko administration, and not at all on President Zelensky's new regime; and Ms. Cooper says that that is true; and she adds that the review was (specifically relating to) the Ministry of Defense. Ms. Cooper says that now, there's a new Minister of Defense.

-Can you define the difference between FMF and the USAI; and how the Ukrainians actually get the lethal aid provided. Cooper says, there are 3 separate pieces to assessing our overall ability to provide equipment to the Ukrainian Armed Forces; first is foreign military finance system (FMF), a State Department authority. Countries around the world have that central authority; that authority is used for some training and (provision of) equipment. There is also the Ukraine Security Assistance Initiative, which is a DOD authority. Unlike the state authority, the DOD authority is only a one-year authority; and then for the 3rd piece, there's opportunity for defense sales; and that is something that were working with Ukrainians on now, so that they can actually purchase US equipment; but the Javelins were specifically provided under the FMF initially; and now, the Ukrainians are interested in the purchase of Javelins Cooper confirms that there was not all put on that purchase of Javelins.

Hurd asks, what more can we be doing, to help the Ukrainians, against Russian electronic warfare" (What I can say, in this open hearing, is that there is some electronic warfare detection equipment that is included in the USAI package; there is some capability that we are already working to provide them.)

Hurd yields back, and it goes to Mr. Julian Castro:

He says, a few of my Republican colleagues have rattled off countries where there was a hold on US aid; but there is a big distinction between holding up aid for legitimate foreign policy reasons; and holding up aid, as part of a shakedown, because it's in the service a President who has asked for a political favor of that country; to investigate his political rival, I think that's important for us to know. I will ask you Ms. Cooper you said the money was cleared by the DOD on the 23rd May 23 that's correct and it didn't get released until September 11 yes I should just clarify the 2nd half of Ukraine security assistance initiative was notified to Congress I believe it was on May 23; and then there was a waiting period, For congressional approval; and then after that point, at some point in mid-June roughly, it was available.) -So, for 90 days (between when approved, and when it was released on September 11th), the aid had been approved and was available to be sent to Ukraine... (yes, something like that.)

-The hold was not in the national security interest of United States, and a hold might embolden Russia... we heard this from other witnesses that came before us; but this is not the only issue with the hold. We understand that people within the United States Government had significant concerns about the legality of the hold; as it relates to the impoundment control act; this is because the money been authorized by Congress, and signed into law by President Trump. -Ms. Cooper, at your July interagency meetings, were there any discussions about whether the hold could be implemented in a legal fashion? (So, in the July 26th meeting, my leadership raised the question of how the President's guidance could be implemented; and they proffered that perhaps a reprogramming action would be the way to do this, but that more research would need to be done; so, after that discussion, we had a lower-level discussion; at my level, on July 31st.)

-Let me ask you about that July 31st meeting; based the conversation with your colleagues, at the DOD July 31st interagency meeting, did you share your understanding of the legal mechanisms that were available at that time? (yes) -And what were they? (I expressed that it was my understanding, that there were two ways that we would be able to implement the Presidential guidance, to stop obligating the Ukraine Security Assistance Initiative. The first option would be for the President to do a rescission; the 2nd would be a reprogramming action, that the Department of Defense would do.

-Both of those would require congressional notice, and there would be an extra step that the President would have to take... -As far as you know, was there any such notice? (Sir, I did express that I believe it would require a notice to Congress, and that there was no such notice, to my knowledge; nor preparation of such notice.) -And there was never such a rescission, or reprogramming of that money? (No Sir, not to my knowledge. Instead what happened was OMB devised an alternative solution, involving creative footnotes, to implement the hold; but there came a time in August, when the Department of Defense no longer supported these unusual footnotes, because of concerns that there might not be sufficient time for the DOD to implement the funds, before the end of the fiscal year, which would be a violation of the Impoundment Control Act s

-So, despite these concerns in mid-August, about the Impoundment Control Act, about all of these footnotes, the hold nevertheless continued through September 11th, even after the whistleblower had come forward; is that right? (It is correct that the hold was released on September 11th.) -Well, I know that many of my colleagues also shared DOD's concerns about the legality of the hold. {Castro thanks Ms. Cooper for voicing the DOD's concern to the White House, pursuant to the national security interests of the United States. Castro yields back, and it goes to Mr. Ratcliffe:

Ratcliffe takes issue with the headlines that had just came out, because of Ms. Cooper's revealing that there were two emails in late July, in which Ukrainian officials were asking about the aid; but he says that the headlines reported that Ukrainians were asking about the <u>hold</u> on the aid; where in truth, the only thing the Ukrainians may have basically asked, was when might the aid be coming? (Sir, my exact words, were that one email said Ukrainians at the Embassy and the House Foreign Affairs committee were asking about security assistance; and the second email had stated that the Hill (publication) knows about the FMF situation; and to an extent, so does the Ukrainian Embassy those were the exact words.)

Ratcliffe says, the emails don't necessarily mean that they were asking about a hold; correct? (not necessarily) Ratcliffe asks, is it true, that around the same time, OMB put a hold on 15 State Department and USAI accounts, including that account? (I don't know that specific detail...) -But you can't say, one way or the other, whether the inquiries in this email were about the hold... (I cannot say for certain.) -Or whether the Ukrainians knew about the hold, any time before August 28th, when the politico article came out, {revealing that there was a hold on US aid to Ukraine}. (It is the recollection of my staff, that the Ukrainians likely new; but I do not have a certain datapoint to offer you.)

Ratcliffe says, it's not unusual for foreign countries to inquire about foreign aid that they're expecting from the United States... (Sir, in my experience with the Ukrainians, they typically would call about specific things; not just generally checking in on their assistance package.)

Ratcliffe then alludes to Zelensky's press conference on October 10th, where he had contended, right and left, that he did not know about the hold on the security aid, until the release of the Politico article, {but as I've said before, Zelensky would be loath to dispute anything that the Trump administration was publicly contending, undoubtedly due to the reasonable fear of developing any kind of a rift, that might ultimately hamper US support for Ukraine. Sometimes, even as a man of integrity, you just can't afford to be completely honest about everything!}

Ratcliffe yields back, and it goes to Mr. Heck:

-Ambassador Hale, last week the country watched as President Trump attacked and intimidated your colleague, Ambassador Yovanovitch, who was a witness within these proceedings; and subsequently, Secretary Pompeo declined to condemn the attack... I think Secretary Pompeo's silence is nothing less than a betrayal of the men and women whom he swore an oath to lead; and it's a betrayal that has long-term consequences to attracting and retaining a workforce; to their morale, to their effectiveness, and to our overall strength.

-So, Ambassador Hale, I want to give you an opportunity now, to do what Secretary Pompeo did not do; either in March, when the smear campaign on Ambassador Yovanovitch got kicked into high gear, when you, sir, (Hale) pressed for a statement of strong support for her; nor did Pompeo speak up in her behalf last week, when the President attacked her again. I'm offering you the opportunity to reaffirm to this committee, so that Americans who are hopefully watching, will know that that Marie Yovanovitch is a dedicated and courageous patriot; and that she served with grace and dignity; even in the face of that orchestrated and unsubstantiated smear attack against her. Ambassador Hale, I'm giving you the opportunity to demonstrate leadership; an opportunity to send a clear resounding message to the men and women who serve, in dangerous foreign posts surround the globe; that what happened to Marie Yovanovitch was wrong.

Hale says, "I would endorse entirely your description of Ambassador Yovanovitch. I met her when I took this job, and I immediately understood that she was an exceptional officer, doing exceptional work, in a very critical Embassy, in Kyiv. During my visits to Kyiv, I was very impressed by what she was doing there; to the extent that I had asked her if she would be willing to stay on... I support, and believe in the institution, and the people of the State Department. I'm one of them, I have been there 35 years. All of us are committed to America's national security; we are the best group of diplomats anywhere in the world.

If I may, I would like to read a letter that the Undersecretary of Foreign Management wrote, on November 18th, to the ranking member of the Senate Foreign Relations Committee; in response to communication from him.

"A number of department employees have testified before the House intelligence committee's inquiry regarding Ukraine. No employee has faced any adverse action by the Department for their testimony before Congress on this matter. The Department will not discipline any employee appearing before Congress, in response to a subpoena. The Department is also proactively establishing a program of financial assistance, with respect to private counsel legal fees incurred by Department employees.

Hale says, there's additional information, but that's the essence of the message. He says America's security, strength, and prosperity is predicated, in no small part, on the professionalism of the Foreign Service; and Foreign Service officers need to know that, as the highest-ranking professional diplomat in the entire State Department, we have their back...

{We should keep in mind that the State Department has refused to supply any documents relating to the matters being investigated by the House Intelligence Committee; despite the fact that several officials testifying so far, have disclosed that having access to their notes, email and other related documents would have helped them to provide more specifics, as well as clarity. -What if some official's testimony, based on a fuzzy recollection, later is revealed as an incorrect accounting; and they became imprisoned for lying to Congress? How could the State Department begin to have that employee's back?! It is very clear that the State Department speaks with forked tongue!}

Heck says to Hale, thank you for having Ambassador Yovanovitch's back, this evening. With that, he yields back, and it goes to Mr. Jordan:

Jordan asks Ms. Cooper why did the OMB put a hold on the security assistance; and she answers that all she knows is that they were operating at the direction of the President, and they reported that he had concerns about corruption. Jordan contends that this was a very legitimate reason to hold the funds. {regardless of the fact that corruption was not an object in this case. For one thing, the Poroshenko administration was receiving these funds freely without reservation, and it was well known that the Poroshenko administration was corrupt, whereas it was pretty well known that the Zelensky administration was actually going to not be corrupt. As an aside, Zelensky was apparently sworn in couple of days after May 23rd, the date that the DOD eligibility conditions had been signed-off on, in order for Ukraine to receive congressional appropriated funds.

Jordan stupidly reminds us that prosecutor general, Yuriy Lutsenko, was quite corrupt indeed, and yet US aid funds flowed despite this. How could the new Zelensky administration possibly be worse than that?! Jordan remarks that Ukraine's Prosecutor General, Lutsenko was replaced on September 5th, as if this was any part of the rationale for lifting the hold on the aid, on September 11th; but we know it wasn't, because what had been going on in the Poroshenko administration was knowingly quite corrupt; and this did not affect Ukraine's eligibility for US aid, under the circumstances of being under attack by Russia.}

Jordan contends that Trump has a deep-rooted concerned about corruption in Ukraine, {but we hear lots of testimony to the contrary; and least he never brings up this issue with anybody in the Ukrainian government; certainly not with President Zelensky.

Jordan yields back and it goes to Mr. Welch:

Welch goes back to Hale's statement of support of Ambassador Yovanovitch, that he had just made; and he talks about the bond of loyalty that many people in the State Department have. Welch says that Secretary Pompeo had reported that he received a letter from Congressman Sessions, during the fall of 2018, supposedly complaining about Ambassador Yovanovitch. Pompeo had publicly voiced this in early March. Welch asks Hale, was there any basis to the claims? (no)

Undersecretary Hale confirms that it was a personal idea of his to ask Marie Yovanovitch to extend her term, in Kyiv, at the Embassy. Welch adds, obviously an indication that you valued her continued service there. Hale tells us that he had also said to the press in Ukraine, that Ambassador Yovanovitch represents the President of the United States, and America stands behind her statements...

Welch adds, obviously you were trying to give her some public support... (correct.) -And yet weeks later, the President and Mr. Giuliani unleashed what can only be characterized as an ugly smear campaign, to oust her. What was your reaction to the news articles, in which the corrupt Ukrainian prosecutor attacked the Ambassador? (We were concerned; we put out a statement that some of these allegations are an outright fabrication; such as the contended "do not prosecute" list (that Yovanovitch had supposedly given to Lutsenko); and we began to discuss what we could do, to deal with this matter.)

-The problems continued for Ambassador Yovanovitch, as I understand it. She emailed you on March 24th, and indicated that the tempo of social media and other criticisms were such that she felt she could no longer function, unless there was a strong statement of defense for her, from the State Department... (correct) -And Secretary Pompeo was aware of her situation, right? (Yes, I briefed him the next day.)

Pompeo is the ultimate authority that could issue that strong statement of support, correct? (correct) -But he never ever did issue the statement, right? (We did not issue a statement, at that time.) -But in fact, you testified, that around the same time the Secretary did not render assistance, to a long-serving and highly respected Ambassador, he made two phone calls to Rudy Giuliani; is that right?

(That's correct; I've seen the record, that he made those phone calls; one on March 20th, and another on March 29th.) -We don't know what he said to Rudy Giuliani, but we have a pretty good idea what Rudy Giuliani said to him, he would have said, "Get rid of Marie Yovanovitch!"

-When she was recalled, and wanted to find out what happened, Secretary Pompeo would not meet with her... (I can't comment on that period.) And then Mr. Bradfield was next in line; he would not speak with her... Welch continues, it went to the Deputy Secretary (George Kent), he held the meeting... (I was traveling, at the time.) -It would be interesting if we could have Secretary Pompeo be here, to tell us what his conversations were, with Rudy Giuliani; the person who was fomenting the discontent about this Ambassador who was fighting corruption.

He thanks them for their service, and the floor goes to Mr. Maloney:

Maloney brings up that, during Ms. Cooper's deposition, that was the day that the Republicans came down and invaded the skiff; to try and disrupt the deposition process; and they obnoxiously lingered for so long, that at one point, they had planned to order pizza and have it delivered for their sit-in; and so Maloney gets a bit of a chuckle; but he says, in all seriousness, thanks for your forbearance. Ms. Cooper, was DOD able to put all of the security assistance funds into contract, before the end of the fiscal year? (no) -And how much were they not able to obligate? What was left unobligated? (I believe the figure was $35 million; we were able to actually obligate 80%, I think.) -You had mentioned that you were able to provide the rest of the funding, because Congress passed a resolution...

(So, the remainder we are in the process of obligating right now, because of a provision in the continuing resolution.) -So, but for, literally, an act of Congress, you couldn't have spent all the money... (If we had not received the provision, in the continuing resolution, we would have obligated 88%.) -But not the full amount, right? (yes) -Which of course, would be a violation of the law; to not spend money the Congress appropriated... (Sir, I am not a lawyer, but that is my understanding.)

Welch tells us, Ambassador Hale, you served as Ambassador to three countries; Jordan, Lebanon, and Pakistan. -While you were Ambassador to those three countries, did anyone ever ask you to issue support, personally praising the current President of the United States? (Hale doesn't follow, right away.)

Welch explains, let's say you're talking to your superior, and you were having a problem with your job; and you said, how could I do better? -and they said you should publish something personally flattering to the President; would that strike you as unusual? (yes) -So, if you were told to "go big, or go home," would that change your mind? (Hale isn't quite following; so Welch explains), that's what Ambassador Yovanovitch was told, when she went to Ambassador Sondland, seeking advice; and she declined to do so; she said it would strike her as too political... -Is that the approach you might take? -Does that sound sensible? (yes) Welch yields his remaining time back to Chairman Schiff; who gives the floor to Ms. Demmings:

Demmings refers to Hale's testimony, where he had said he was aware that Ambassador Sondland was involving himself in matters that went beyond the normal writ of the Ambassador to the European Union. She asks Hale, as you understood it, who had authorized Ambassador Sondland to work on Ukraine? (I have no firsthand knowledge, but I received a readout on May 23rd, indicating that the President wanted the members of that delegation, including Ambassador Sondland, to carry forth the policies that were discussed in the course of that meeting.)

-So, that occurred within the meeting in the Oval Office, on May 23rd, this is where you heard that information? (In a written readout from that, yes.) Demmings confirms for us, that is clear that the members of the inaugural delegation were indeed empowered by the President; and, as a practical matter, you thought it would be Ambassador Volker and Ambassador Sondland, presumably working with Ambassador Taylor; and these would be the ones really engaging in the continual effort, here. -Did you understand that Ambassador Sondland had direct access to the President? (The few occasions when I had conversations with Ambassador Sondland, he often let me know that he was in direct contact with the with the President. {Hale says that, based on what he knew at the time, he was satisfied that this delegation was who the President wanted to have continue to pursue these policies. Hale knew that Ambassador Volker was a professional, and had been a Foreign Service officer of distinction; and steeped in Ukrainian affairs; and he was part of that group.}

-So, at the time, you were okay with (Sondland's) role; but did your opinion change, about the appropriateness of his role? (As I testified, I was not aware of these various activities related to negotiations over investigations; preconditions related to that; I just wasn't aware of it, so I had no reason to be making any judgments...) When asked, Hale discloses that he was surprised by what he saw, in the media, about the text messages between Sondland and Taylor.

Deming says, you are the undersecretary for political affairs; and in that capacity, you are responsible for the management of the United States' bilateral relationships, with every country in the world that we recognize the management of our policies towards those countries; as well as our policies as they relate to multilateral organizations; does that include US policy and relations with Ukraine? (It does; and when we have a Special Envoy who works directly with the Secretary, that Special Envoy will take the day-to-day responsibilities.) -How about US policy and relations with the European Union? (Yes, I am.) -But you were not aware of Ambassador Sondland's activities on behalf of President Trump? (That's correct.)

{That is interesting; he was supposed to be in the loop with respect to management of US policies pertaining to Ukraine, and to the EU; yet he had no knowledge of the basic goals Sondland was working toward... Well, of course not! If he had been informed that Sondland was involved in a pressure campaign, to get Zelensky to participate in Trump's corrupt plan, Congress would not have had to wait, to hear from him about this odious plot!}

Ms. Demmings yields back, and the floor goes to Mr. Krishnamoorthi; who says to Hale, you and your colleagues were told to gather records at the State Department; supposedly to be provided to Congress, right? {Apparently, they were gathered in order to keep Congress from ever seeing them.} (I was not involved in the decision-making on that; I have no responsibility to gather documents. I understood that it was underway; I certainly received the documents that I described earlier.) {the ones that he had requested to see}.

-Did they include electronic files and emails, for instance? (I can only speak to the documents that were made available to me; but yes, they did include emails and paper documents.) -How about tape recordings; would they be among the files that were gathered? (he doesn't know) -Then you can't rule out that possibility... (I don't know; I can't really comment on that.)

Hale doesn't know who were the individual custodians that collected the documents. Krishnamoorthi clues us in, you <u>are</u> aware that despite the fact that a duly authorized congressional subpoena has been served on the State Department, we have yet to receive a single document... (I understand that.)

Krishnamoorthi then asks Ms. Cooper if, during any of her interagency meetings last summer, anybody had brought up the subject

of the lack of Allied funding, as a reason for why there should be a
hold on military assistance to Ukraine? (I can only speak to the three
(related) meetings that I attended; and I have no recollection of the issue
of Ally burden-sharing coming up... I did provide information, in my
deposition, about what I thought was a completely separate query, that
I had received in mid-June; from the Secretary of Defense's front office.
One of the questions, was a question about the degree to which allies
were contributing to Ukraine's security assistance.)

-But after the hold was put into place, you hadn't heard any concerns
about a lack of Allied funding, as a reason for why the hold should be
in place... (In those meetings that I attended, I did not hear that; I do
not recall hearing that. The only reason I heard was that it was due to
the President's views on corruption; I had no other information.) (same
question to Hale) -You didn't hear about the lack of Allied funding, as
a reason for the hold being put in place; after July 18th? (No, I never
heard a reason for the hold.)

Krishnamoorthi says, one of my colleagues suggested the hold was
put in place to assess whether or not President Zelensky was legit; I
assume that was not a reason that was offered, either... (Both of them
said no.) -What is the importance of a world leader having a meeting
at the White House? (he asks Hale); in particular for a new leader?
(It's an extremely important opportunity to demonstrate the strength
of our relationship, for the building of that relationship, at a personal
level, and a professional level...) 'How about for President Zelensky;
how important was it for him, to have this White House meeting with
President Trump? (I never talked to President Zelensky about that,
myself, before he became President. I met with President Poroshenko.)
-But as an expert on these matters, is it fair to say that, for a new leader
such as President Zelensky, having a meeting at the White House, with
President Trump, is extremely important for his image that he projects;
especially towards folks like Russia? (Well, an Oval Office meeting is
incredibly valuable for any foreign leader, on general principle; and for
Ukrainian President Zelensky, as you just said, to demonstrate that the
bond between Ukraine and the United States is strong, and that there
is continuity in our policies; and that we will continue to work together,

toward our policy goals, including countering Russian aggression and intimidation of Ukraine).

Krishnamoorthi yields back; and Adam Schiff says, that concludes the member questioning; Mr. Nunez, do you have any concluding remarks?

Nunez winds up, (Here comes the barrage of bulllshit):

What did we learn from the Democrats' impeachment inquiry? They promised the country a fair hearing; what did they deliver? The impeachment version of three-card monte; a notorious con card trick; with the mark, in this case, President Trump and the American public. We stand no chance of winning. {-and when it comes to any possible defense of what has gone down, that's as right as rain!}

Democrats promised the whistleblower's testimony; in fact, they told us that we need to speak with the whistleblower. -And then we learned that the whistleblower coordinated with the Democratic staff, before alerting the intelligence community's Inspector General, to hide their con. Democrats pound the table, and gaslight the country; telling us that the whistleblower is entitled to an imaginary statutory right of anonymity. -And they have accused us of trying to "out" the whistleblower, knowing that they're the only ones that know who he is.

They say that, when the facts are against you, argue the law; and when the laws against you, argue the facts. If both are against you, pound the table, and yell like hell! It seems that law school these days is teaching students a fourth tactic; when the facts and the law is against you, you simply break the game, and hope your audience is too stupid to catch your duplicity.

This is not an impeachment inquiry; it's an impeachment inquisition. In the Middle Ages, the accused was allowed to bring his own suit against a person who is even vaguely a subject of the lowest regard; and now, the accused are denied any right to confront their accusers... Incredible! -Maybe not so much, given the Democrats' track record. In ages past, the accused victim had more rights than the Democrats are giving the President. After all, inquisition victims had the right to know their accusers name. {Idiot, the name is Congress!}-For those of you at home, you can change the channel, turn down the volume, or hide the kids... I yield to Mr. Schiff, for story-time.

{Without missing a beat, Adam Schiff cordially says,} "I thank the gentleman, as always, for his remarks..." (Schiff is smiling a bit sarcastically, as he says this, and he gets a big laugh from the gallery!) Schiff continues, "This has been a long day, and I have said most of what I wanted to say, earlier in the day; but I wanted to share a few reflections, on two words that come up a lot, in the course of these hearings. Those words are "corruption," and "anticorruption." We are supposed to believe or imagine; listening to my colleagues; that Donald Trump is a great anticorruption fighter; that his only concern about Ukraine was that it would fight corruption; but let's look at that argument... Let us look at the President's words, and look at his deeds:

Ambassador Yovanovitch was an anticorruption champion; no one has contradicted that. Everyone who has come forward to testify here, has said she was an anticorruption champion; and on the day she was recalled (by Trump), she was at a reception acknowledging another anticorruption champion; a woman who had acid thrown in her face, and died a painful death, after months.

Yovanovitch was recalled back to Washington because of the vicious smear campaign by the President's lawyer, Rudy Giuliani, among others. She was recalled; that is not anticorruption; that is corruption! -And one of the people responsible for the smear campaign, in addition to Mr. Giuliani; and there is a long and sordid list of those who were involved; is a man named Lutsenko; someone who the minority's own witness acknowledges has a poor reputation; as self-serving and corrupt.

-And what do we see, about Mr. Lutsenko and his predecessor, Mr. Shokin? What does the President have to say against these corrupt former-prosecutors? He praises them! He says they were treated very unfairly! That's not anticorruption; that's corruption! -And when Ambassador Sondland testified today that there was unquestionably a quid pro quo, and everybody knew it; conditioning a White House meeting that Ukraine desperately needed, to show its friends and foes alike, that it had the support of the President of the United States; when that official act was conditioned on the receipt of things of value to the President; a political investigation; that was not anticorruption; that was corruption!

-And when Ambassador Sondland testified today, that he could put 2 and 2 together, and so can we! -that there was also a quid pro quo on the military aid; that that aid was not going to be released unless he released a public statement of these political investigations; that's not anticorruption; that is corruption!

(Schiff's closing statement continues on the next page)

-And let's look at the President's words, on that phone call; that infamous phone call on July 25th; does he ask President Zelensky, "How is that reform coming? -or, what are you doing to root out corruption? -or, What about that new anticorruption court?"

Of course not! Of course not! Are we really to believe that this was his priority? No! What does he ask? I want you to do this favor, and investigate this crazy 2016 server conspiracy theory; that the server is somewhere in Ukraine… and more ominously, investigate the Bidens… That's not anticorruption; that is corruption!

-And the next day, when he's on the phone to Ambassador Sondland; that afternoon at a restaurant in Kyiv; what does he want to know about? -Does he want to know how Zelensky is going to fight corruption? Of course not! The only thing he brings up, in that call, is the investigation he wants into the Bidens; that's not anticorruption; that is corruption!

Every now and then, there's a conversation that really says all you need to know; sometimes it doesn't seem all that significant at first, but I'll tell you, this one really struck me. It was a conversation that Ambassador Volker related, in his testimony; a conversation just this past September, when he is talking to Andre Yermak; the top advisor to President Zelensky. Volker is advising him, as indeed he should, "You know, you may not want to go through with the investigation or prosecution of former President Poroshenko;" that engaging in political investigations is really not a good idea… -and you know what Yermak says? "Oh, you mean, like you want us to do with the Bidens, and the Clintons?"

There is a word for that too; and it's not corruption, or anticorruption; it's called hypocrisy!

This is the problem, here. We do have an anticorruption policy, around the world; and the great men and women in your department Undersecretary Hale, and in your department Ms. Cooper; they carry that message around the world; that the United States is devoted to the rule of law.

But when they see a President Of the United States who is not devoted to the rule of law; who is not devoted to anticorruption; but instead he demonstrates, in word and deed, corruption! -they are forced to ask themselves, what does America stand for anymore???!!! that concludes this evening's hearing. (Powerful stuff!)

Once again, I'm going to pause to briefly interject some comments on the most recent developments during the Senate impeachment trial. I haven't been watching this trial, because every time I tuned into it briefly, it sickens me to hear the ridiculous rationalizations being cast about by President Trump's legal team, and other Republican Senators.

The other reason why I have not bothered to tune into the many hours of bogus defense tactics from the Republican side, is that I find the New York Times captures probably most of the important points being made, and the essence of the arguments being made against Trump becoming impeached.

I was particularly taken aback when I read in one article in yesterday's paper, which was January 29th, where I understand that the argument being put forth by the Republicans is that abuse of power and obstruction of Congress are not impeachable offenses. I ask, if they are not impeachable offenses, then what is?

Another article I read in today's paper January 30th, was saying that, provided a President believes that becoming reelected is in the best interest of the country, that a quid pro quo to quench that objective is okay. Even if I were to believe that; which I don't; in this case, it was not only a quid pro quo; which maybe could be arguable to be not too bad, as long as it merely involved withholding of funds to a foreign country where such withholding is not of any significant consequence to US national security.

However, in this case, the withholding of the military aid funding for Ukraine, gave Russia a significant edge, over their previous military and negotiating position.

My observation is that the Trump Administration seems to be summarily opposed to the laws of natural development. An article I was reading in the New York Times today (February 17, 2020) was about the Trump administration's current initiative to grant unilateral authorization for one official, to be able to bar transactions between the US and any other country. We have seen Trump make audacious and ridiculously nasty attempts to stem the tide of natural development; whether it is related to immigration, climate control, interrupting naturally-developing international trading relationships, etc... Although he somehow thinks he can, I know from experience, that you can't fight, disregard, or disrespect nature, or the natural order; and have any continuing success; I would say that you just tend to cause a lot of difficulty and hard feelings, as you make these drastic attempts.

I will take this opportunity to talk briefly about a couple of other recent New York Times articles:

An article in the NY Times last Saturday (2/1/2020) said that Democrats had failed to defeat Trump, in terms of our general knowledge of his certain imminent acquittal, at this point; but I don't think that's really quite accurate. I think that all of this damning testimony has definitely defeated Trump, and any of his arguments against what has come to light regarding Trump's obvious corruption, and corrupt dealings; at least for any reasonably-intelligent soul, even modestly following along.

All that the Democrats really failed to defeat, is merely the solidarity of the Republican-majority Senate; which they were never going to defeat; and that is why it took so many months, for many Democratic Congressmen and other leaders; most notably, Nancy Pelosi, of course; to get on board with impeaching Trump.

I think the main reason they went through with this exercise, is for a potential benefit that can now come about, as a result of all that was revealed about this fairly-wide-handed Republican conspiracy, over the course of the last couple of months; but really, in some senses, this especially-mean-and-nasty solidarity effort has been going on pretty much since Trump first took office.

As it turns out, what the Republicans had to pretend to ignore, as being insignificant; (when much of what was being testified-to was, in reality, very significant); paves the way for Democrats to trumpet many reports of the ridiculous contentions and rationalizations made by the Republicans involved; especially those of Republican Senators; all over the country; in an effort to help the general public become aware of what is really going on politically here; which is that a couple of leaders at the top; being McConnell, Pompeo, Mulvaney, and Trump; and apparently, even including the State Department top officials and Defense Department top officials, as well; have realized that, as long as Republicans are in the majority, in the Senate; every Republican lawmaker's conservative agenda gets hammered all the way home, on every issue, from Supreme Court confirmation of people of poor integrity like Cavanaugh, to backing of nasty, inhuman immigration initiatives, to reversal of many dozens of very important and necessary regulations, that were in place prior to this crooked, immoral and unfit group of Republican Senators, led by the anti-Christ Mitch McConnell; or the grim reaper, if you would rather call him that.

This has been the most horrible nightmare administration, that has so badly hobbled and crippled the American people, in ways many will only find out, after the fact; when they are destitute in a crashed economy once more; children dying or rendered mentally incompetent as a result of Government allowance of toxic chemical use all around them; or burning their homes to ashes because instead of addressing global warming, Republican lawmakers are stepping up production of petroleum products and natural gas, which only exacerbate the effects of fossil fuel ecological planetary destruction.

And the propaganda machine that is the internet and social media, keeps churning out lies and false contentions, on a level so prominent, that poor unenlightened souls by the tens of millions are buying the rhetoric, that we are even doing the slightest bit well; but we are instead suffering, under a mercilessly-oppressive Republican leadership that could care less about anything besides continuing to stay in power.

It's a damned shame. But because of the confrontation over the past several months; really for the better part of a year, if you include the end of the Mueller report saga; I am thinking that, people who do know better, are probably going to come out of the woodwork, like I am doing so, in writing this book; and we are together going to make a big push to reveal the awfulness that is the Republican takeover of the country; viciously against the interests of the common man. We can prevail, as of November, because the Republicans have most recently showed their true colors, loud and clear; and now we have an opportunity to air their dirty laundry to the rest of the country; and the whole world.

America is a principled country, and we need to throw these Republican thugs out on their ear, so that the country can act with good integrity, to once again spread Democracy around the world again; and not corruption, like is now the practice of the Trump administration.

Intelligence Committee hearing #7-
Dr. Hill and David Holmes

This is Day 5, and it is the 7th Intelligence Committee impeachment hearing. The witnesses are Dr. Fiona Hill, and David Holmes. Fiona Hill was the former National Security Council Senior Director for Europe and Russia, before Tim Morrison took over her post in July. She was the top Russia official on the National Security Council. She was also a veteran National Security official in Washington, for multiple Presidents.

David Holmes is a career Foreign Service officer who was based at the Embassy and Kyiv. His testimony revolves around his notetaking responsibilities at a meeting and Kyiv where he was asked to stay outside of the room during a discussion between Gordon Sondland and Zelensky's top advisor Andre Yermak, following the meeting that he had taken notes on.

Adam Schiff gives his opening statement:

Yesterday morning, we heard from Ambassador Gordon Sondland, American Ambassador to the European Union. As the de facto leader of the "Three Amigos," he had regular access to President Trump, and the new Ukrainian President, Volodymyr Zelensky; pressing for two investigations Trump believed would help his reelection campaign. The first investigation was of a discredited conspiracy theory that Ukraine, and not Russia, was responsible for interference in our 2016 election. The second investigation was into the political rival Trump apparently feared most; Joe Biden. Trump sought to weaken Biden, and to refute the fact that his own election had been helped by a Russian hacking and dumping operation, and a Russian social media campaign, directed by Volodymyr Putin.

Trump's scheme stood in contrast to the long-standing foreign policy of the United States, by undermining US military and diplomatic support, of a key ally; and it set back US anticorruption efforts in Ukraine. In conditioning a meeting with Zelensky, along with military and security aid, on an investigation of his rival.

Trump put his personal and political interests above that of the United States. As Ambassador Sondland would later tell Foreign Service officer David Holmes, immediately after speaking with President Trump; that the President did not give an (expletive) about Ukraine; he only cares about "big stuff" that benefits him; like the Biden investigation that Giuliani was pushing.

David Holmes is here with us today; he is a Foreign Service officer currently serving as a political counselor to the US Embassy and Kyiv. Also with us today, is Dr. Fiona Hill, the former National Security Council Senior Director for European and Russian affairs; whose job as a National Security Council Senior Director, was the coordination of US policy toward Ukraine. Dr. Hill left the NSC in July, after more than two years in her position.

Dr. Hill, and Mr. Holmes each provide unique perspective on issues relating to Ukraine; Dr. Hill, from Washington DC; and Mr. Holmes, from on the ground in Kyiv, In early 2019, Dr. Hill became concerned by the increasing prominence of Rudy Giuliani, the President's personal lawyer, who, as she has testified, was quite frequently on television, and in public appearances, stating that he had been given some authority over matters related to Ukraine. Dr. Hill was not alone, in her concerns. The National Security Advisor, John Bolton, was also paying attention; as were other NSC and State Department officials, including Holmes, at the US Embassy, in Kyiv.

Bolton viewed Giuliani as a "hand-grenade," that was going "blow everybody up," and that he was yet, powerless, to prevent the former Mayor from engineering former Ambassador to Ukraine, Marie

Yovanovitch's firing, in late April, or her recall. Holmes was stunned by the intensity, and the consistency of the media attacks on Yovanovitch, by name, as a US Ambassador; and the scope of the allegations against her. Yovanovitch's dismissal, as a result of Giuliani's smear campaign, was one of several things that unsettled Dr. Hill. Another was the role of Gordon Sondland, who emerged as a key player in Ukraine policy, in May; where he was named as part of the US delegation, led by Energy Secretary Rick Perry, at President Zelensky's inauguration. Lieutenant Colonel Alexandra Vindeman also attended the inauguration, and as Holmes recalls, during a meeting with President Zelensky, Vindeman took the opportunity to advise the Ukrainian leader to stay out of US domestic politics.

Another concern that arose for Dr. Hill, at around this time, was her discovery of the NSC back-channel on Ukraine. Dr. Hill learned that, as an Embassy staff member who did not work on Ukraine, Sondland may have been providing Ukraine information to President Trump, that Dr. Hill was not made aware of.

According to Holmes, following the Zelensky inauguration, Ambassador Sondland and Secretary Perry took a very unconventional role, in formulating our priorities for the new Zelensky administration; personally reaching out to the new President Zelensky and his Senior team. Sondland's newfound assertiveness also concerned Dr. Hill, who previously had enjoyed a cordial relationship with the Ambassador.

On June 18th, Dr. Hill had a blowup with Sondland, when he told her that he was in charge of Ukraine policy. Dr. Hill testified that Sondland "got testy with me, and I said, who has put you in charge? -and he said, "The President."

On July 10th, Dr. Hill was part of the meeting, at the White House, with a group of US and Ukrainian officials, including Bolton, Sondland, and Energy Secretary Perry; a member of the three amigos. The meeting was intended, among other things, to give Ukrainians a possible opportunity to convey, that they were anxious to set up a first meeting, between their new President Zelensky, and President Trump.

Ambassador Sondland interjected, to inform the group, that according to White House Chief of Staff, Mick Mulvaney, the White

House meeting with President Trump, sought by the Ukrainian President, would happen if Ukraine undertook certain investigations.

Hearing this, Bolton abruptly ended the meeting. Undeterred, Sondland brought the Ukrainian delegation, and the and the NSC Director, Lieutenant Colonel Vindeman, downstairs to another part of the White House; where they were later joined by Dr. Hill.

At this second meeting, Sondland was more explicit; Ukraine needed to conduct these investigations, if they were to get a meeting, at all. Bolton had directed Dr. Hill to report this to the NSC lead counsel, John Eisenberg. Bolton said, "You go and tell Eisenberg that I am not part of whatever "drug deal" Sondland and Mulvaney are cooking up, on this; and you go ahead and tell him what you heard, and what I said."

Dr. Hill did so; as did Lieutenant Colonel Vindeman, who separately approached the same lawyer. On July 18th, the day before Dr. Hill left her post at the NSC, Holmes participated in a secure interagency video conference on Ukraine; and towards the end of the meeting, a representative of the Office of Management and Budget announced that the nearly $400 million in security assistance to Ukraine was being held up; and that the order had come from the President; also that it had been conveyed to OMB by acting Chief of Staff; without further explanation.

Holmes, unaware of the hold, prior to the call, was shocked! He thought the suspension of aid was extremely significant; undermining what he understood to be long-standing US National security goals in Ukraine. One week later, on July 25th, President Trump spoke with President Zelensky by phone. When President Zelensky brought up US military support, and noted that Ukraine would like to buy more Javelin antitank missiles, from the United States, Trump responded by saying, "I would like to you to do us a favor, though…" Trump then requested that Zelensky investigate the discredited conspiracy theory, of Ukraine interference in the 2016 election. Even more ominously, Trump asked him to take a look into the Bidens.

Neither request had been included in the official talking points, that were prepared by NSC staff; but both were in Donald Trump's personal interests, and in the interest of his 2020 reelection campaign; and it became obvious that the Ukrainian President knew about both topics in advance; in part, because of efforts, by Ambassadors Sondland and Volker, to make President Zelensky acutely aware of President Trump's demands.

The next day, on July 26th, in Kyiv, Holmes served as a notetaker, at a meeting between Ambassadors Taylor, Volker, and Sondland, meeting together with President Zelensky and other Senior Ukrainian officials. Zelensky said that, on the previous day's call, President Trump had three times raised some very sensitive issues, that he would have to follow up on those issues, when the two Presidents met in person.

Although he did not realize it at the time, Holmes came to understand that the "sensitive issues" were the investigations that President Trump demanded, on the July 25th call. Following the meeting with Zelensky, Holmes accompanied Ambassador Sondland to his separate meeting, with the Ukrainian President's top advisor, Andre Yermak; but Holmes was not allowed into the meeting. He waited for 30 minutes, while Sondland and the Ukrainian met alone, without any notetakers to report what they said.

After the meeting, Sondland, Holmes, and two others of the department staff, went to lunch at a nearby restaurant; and they sat on the terrace of a local restaurant. At some point, Sondland pulled out his cell phone, and called the White House; asking to be connected with the President. When Trump came on the line, Holmes could hear the President's voice clearly. Holmes recalled that the President's voice was very loud and recognizable.

Ambassador Sondland held the phone away from his ear, presumably because of the loud volume President Trump was speaking in. Sondland said he was calling from Kyiv, and he told the President that "President Zelensky loves your ass…" Holmes then heard President Trump ask, "So he's going to do the investigation?"

Ambassador Sondland replied, "He's going to do it…" adding that President Zelensky "Will do anything you ask him…" After the call ended, Holmes took the opportunity to ask on Sondland for his candid impression of the President's views on Ukraine. At this point, Sondland revealed that "President Trump doesn't give a (expletive) about Ukraine;

the President only cares about "big stuff," that benefits the President; like the Biden investigation that Mr. Giuliani was pushing.

A month later, National Security Advisor Bolton traveled to Kyiv. Between meetings with Ukrainian Government officials, Ambassador Bolton expressed to Ambassador Taylor, his frustration about Mr. Giuliani's influence with the President. Bolton made it clear, however, that there was nothing he could do about it. Bolton further stated that the hold on security assistance would not be lifted, prior to the upcoming meeting between Presidents Trump and Zelensky, in Warsaw. It would hang, on whether President Zelensky was able to favorably impress President Trump.

Trump subsequently canceled his trip to Warsaw; and Sondland, Volker, and others continued to press for a public announcement of the opening of investigations by Zelensky. On September 8th, Taylor told Holmes that, now, they were insisting that Zelensky commit to the investigation, in an interview with CNN.

Holmes was surprised that the requirement was so specific, and concrete; since it amounted to nothing less than a demand, that President Zelensky personally commit to the specific investigation into President Trump's political rival; on a cable news channel.

On September 9th, this committee, along with the Foreign Affairs, and Oversight Committees, launched an investigation of this corrupt scheme. President Trump released the hold on the aid, two days later; and once this had been revealed, the Ukrainians canceled the CNN interview, shortly thereafter.

Two weeks later, on September 25th, the transcript of the July 25th call was released by the White House, and the details of the President's scheme started coming into view.

In the coming days, Congress will determine what response is appropriate. If the President abuse his power, and invited foreign interference into our elections; if he sought to condition, coerce, extort, or bribe a vulnerable ally, into conducting investigations to aid his reelection campaign; and did so by withholding official acts; the White House meeting, and hundreds of $millions of dollars in military aid, it will for us to decide, whether those acts are compatible with the office of the presidency.

Schiff then recognizes Devin Nunez to make his opening statement Nunez starts off:

Throughout these hearings, Democrats struggled to establish that President Trump has committed an impeachable offense, on his phone call with Ukrainian President Zelensky. The offense itself changes, depending on the day. It ranges from quid pro quo, to extortion, to bribery, to obstruction of justice; and back to quid pro quo. {Here we go again, the repetition of ridiculousness, because of course we know that it is "all of the above;" not just one of those.}

It's clear why the Democrats have been forced into this carousel of accusations... Nunez claims that Trump had good reason to be wary of Ukrainian election meddling against his campaign. {Yeah sure,} the widespread corruption in that country... {Then he claims that Zelensky didn't know that the aid had been paused, but we know, from testimony at these hearings, that this is not true. Zelensky knew as early as mid-July; nothing new.}

Nunez has this right, that President Trump got caught. {The only reason why he backed down and released the aid, was because he got caught; this we know is quite critical. Nunez urges Americans to consider the credibility of Democrats on this committee, but I would urge Americans to consider the lack of credibility on the part of the Republican committee members instead. What the Democrats are doing is proper and just.}

Nunez says it's not President Trump that got caught, it's the Democrats that got caught. {Here we have it again, that one key Republican strategy is to launch the same accusation back at Democrats, as the Democrats are launching against President Trump. It is probably somewhat effective to the Republican base, and this is unfortunate, because as these hearings point out and emphasize, Trump is the only one worthy of being accused.}

Nunez goes into the same things again; false allegations regarding the Steele Dossier, {which was paid for by a group of Republican candidates running against Trump in 2016; Republicans who were seeking to expose the Russians' potential leverage over Trump, that should have clinched the public revealing Trump's apparent unfitness for office.}

Nunez goes on about secret depositions and transcripts; {but we've already discussed, that only because Bill Barr's Justice Department would not open an investigation, indicated necessary and warranted by the whistleblower complaint, this had forced Congress to do the investigation itself; and these investigations always start out with closed hearings; so that's what the intelligence committee conducted.

-And now, we are in the 2nd phase, where the Intelligence Committee is holding public hearings to broadcast the odiousness that's been discovered, about Trump's dealings with Ukraine}.

Nunez goes back to the nude photos, {I discussed this earlier}; he goes back to Alexandra Chalupa; and claims that they smeared the Trump campaign. {This is bullshit.} Apparently, the Republicans wanted to call Alexandra Chalupa, to question her at these hearings; but we can be sure that those questions would be relating to her written articles in 2016; and they would be defending the false legitimacy of Trump's campaign-smear allegations. Of course, this has nothing to do with what Trump has maliciously forced upon the new President Zelensky.

Nunez goes back to, how one of the witnesses had admitted that he had merely inferred, {and had not been informed directly somehow, for example}, that the aid was being held, on condition of the announcement of these investigations; but to that point; Adam Schiff had once before sarcastically suggested, that the Republicans seem to think that, unless President Trump told the witnesses appearing before the committee, "I am bribing President Zelensky; and I am withholding aid because I want President Zelensky to make announcements; otherwise, I won't release the aid..." that Republican Committee members are suggesting that if Trump didn't actually say these words, then there's no evidence of his conditional withholding of the aid! I suppose this illustrates one very important reason why circumstantial evidence is quite valid in court, in many instances.

Nunez says, whether the Democrats will reap the political benefit they want from this impeachment remains to be seen. {On that point I would wholeheartedly agree. I think that the benefits to be reaped is for Democrats to broadcast widely to the American public how the Republicans have conducted themselves during these hearings, and trumpeting the ridiculous contentions and twisted statements misrepresenting the facts and the significance of what Trump has orchestrated, against the interests of the common man in the US. Only if trumpeting this out is successful enough, will the Republican majority in the Senate come to an end, as well it should; as of our 2020 election votes.

Nunez says the damage that Democrats have done to this country will be long-lasting. {This is yet another example of how Republicans are just saying, you know; I'm rubber your glue; what you say bounces off me, and sticks to you! That's a ridiculous, immature game; because the facts are that the damage that the Republicans have done to the to US, the citizens of this country, is definitely going to be long-standing, in terms of the impact of all of the bad decisions: Starting a horrendous trade war with China and other countries around the world, initiatives such as the committing of humanitarian atrocities at the border, the rounding up, and deporting of struggling immigrants trying to establish themselves and become productive workers and useful consumers in the US, really beefing up production of oil and gas which will quicken the pace of global warming which is pretty-quickly making this planet uninhabitable, rolling back financial regulations which make US financial markets vulnerable once again to a market crash, resulting in even further economic hardship, to the remaining middle-class; which had already shrunk considerably, due to the 2008 crash, which was orchestrated under deregulated Republican rule; this administration has given tax cuts to the wealthy which has resulted in several trillion dollars in added National debt which we didn't need; Trump has rolled back environmental regulations on pollution, on dumping of coal ash, and Scott Pruitt as head of the EPA at one point approved 300 new chemicals instantly, that were previously waiting to become evaluated one by one; we can be certain that some of those chemicals are toxic and should not have been approved, but now they are on the market, and we are being exposed to these additional toxic substances in our everyday lives; I could go on, but I think you get the point. All of these things that I have just listed, constitute decisions and actions and initiatives that will have caused lasting damage, even if we are able to throw Trump out of office and get a new decent President as of November.

How will we ever repair the breakdown of trade between China and the US?! There are aspects of the stupidity of Trump's moves, and his trade war tactics with China, that are less apparent to the average onlooker; things like, sure, we only import 18% of all we import, from the world as a whole, from China; but what isn't quite so apparent, is that when US companies buy Chinese parts, and other Chinese products that will be used in the further production of US products, the fact that, what we can buy from China in these respects is so inexpensive, compared to what US companies' prices are for these same parts, or products, or supplies perhaps; causes US product prices to increase significantly. -And then there is the fact that the US no longer produces some products, in cases where US companies are no longer able to purchase Chinese components, at their previously great prices.

These kinds of unfortunate side effects, of Trump's narcissistic bluster towards China, and several other important trading partner countries around the world, will take years to repair; and some of these, what were particularly advantageous importing and exporting arrangements between the US and other foreign countries, will likely never become reestablished; because for example, in the case where a US company that had relied on a Chinese supply of parts, that are only inexpensively produced in China; that US company may well find that it simply has to get out of that business, and begin making a new product line. This being the case, even if previous normal trade relations were to become instantly restored, US demand for what was being exported from China may fall off sharply, related to some parts or other components that used to be coveted by US companies, but are no longer needed.

Anyway, back to the Dr. Fiona Hill and David Holmes impeachment hearing:

{We resume midway through Devin Nunez's opening statement}

Nunez next says, that Democrats have pitted people, across the country, one against the other. {But that, of course, is the Trump administration's trick. That is exactly what the 2016 Internet and social media campaigns were designed to do; to more deeply polarize us, by contending a bunch of lies and distortions which would make people who were on the conservative side, indignant at what they been told that Democrats are thinking, saying, and doing; and on the other hand, Democrats are tuning in briefly to Fox News, and also seeing other conservative news reports which are pretty shocking, in terms of their grossly misleading character; taking everything way out of context.

Then again, there are reporters and activists on the left who probably also tend to distort their representation of how the average conservative views the many controversial issues of today's world; (I'll have to get a hold of more info summarizing the major issues of the moment.)

Next, Nunez is saying that Democrats have poisoned the minds of fanatics. {These guys don't need any poisoning, from anyone. Both Democratic and Republican extremists alike, they were already poisoned, long before any impeachment hearings began!

Nunez contends that these proceedings have inflicted many wounds that will need to heal; but of course, in truth it is the Republicans who have wounded the common man in this country, and then lied about it, and contended that everything is going great in the country.

But to the astute observer, that is far from the case.

Nunez says he hopes the Democrats will turn their focus to governing, for a change; but the truth is that this Congress has drawn up and passed over 100 bills, which remain sitting on Mitch McConnell's desk; Democrats, now holding the majority in the House of Representatives, have been working all along, to improve everything from the prescription drug prices to lowering medical costs, to... (I suppose I will have to find out the nature of those 100 bills and maybe list the several most important ones perhaps.)

Nunez says that, under House rule 11, the minority is entitled to have a day of hearings themselves; he asserts that under clause 2J1, Republican members hereby transmit their request, to convene a day of minority hearings. {We will see what Adam Schiff has to say about that.}

Next, Nunez brings up an assertion that Fiona Hill made, within her earlier statement; she had claimed some committee members denied that Russia meddled in the 2016 election. as I noted my opening statement on Wednesday that in March 2018 intelligence committee Republicans published the results of a year-long investigation into Russian meddling; a 240-page report. (he holds it up) We analyzed the 2016 Russian meddling campaign, the US Government reaction to it; and Russian campaigns in other countries; and provided specific recommendations to improve American election security. I asked my staff to hand these reports to our two witnesses today; just so we can have a recollection of their memory.

{I don't know what that silly statement is supposed to mean! -But addressing his Bruhaha about this report, stemming from an investigation Republicans would contend is much more accurately researched, than the Mueller investigation. This obviously is so that they can assert some alternate narrative. They cannot abide by all the damning revelations within the Mueller report, of course. They have to spin things differently. There is the official report, based on an exhaustive 3 year thorough investigation, and the consolidated, summarized results of an expansive team of CIA and FBI personnel; who's full-time job is Governmental investigation; and this wasn't even completed and drawn up into the Mueller report until mid-2019 -But the Republicans still need to reject this, because it is too revealing, about what the report indicates has been happening, in terms of apparent, contact, coordination, and cooperation, between Russian operatives, and a whole group of Trump campaign representatives and assistants; from campaign manager Paul Manafort, to Roger Stone's WikiLeaks connections to release Russian-hacked Clinton emails, to Trump's relatives meeting with Russians in the Trump Tower, etc...

Anyway, that aside, let's look at what Nunez is trying to infer, here. He is basically contending that it wasn't correct, for Dr. Hill to have assumed that Republican Committee members are denying that it was the Russians, who hacked us in 2016; as evidenced by this suddenly-appearing Republican version of an investigative report; they don't trust or believe America's intelligence agencies; they feel the need to look to other sources, to get a more accurate appraisal! Of course, the real reason they make such contentions is because they need a mechanism to spin out lies and distortions, and utter fabrications of facts that are not even real; but they will get some percentage of us to believe their falseness.

Anyway, these Republican Committee members speak out of both sides of their mouth; in Nunez's earlier opening statements, he asserted that it was Ukraine instead, that did the meddling, and also that the meddling was against the Trump campaign, and for Hillary. Nunez even started off, right from the beginning, calling this very serious Mueller investigation "The Russia Hoax;" in order to stay in lock-step with his pal Donald Trump. It's a hoax, in one sentence; and it's a very serious Russian meddling effort that had transpired, warranting a full independent Republican investigation, producing a 240-page report; in the next sentence. This stuffed-shirt, rabble-rousing phony doesn't know his ass from his elbow, of course.

Nunez continues on with his carrying-on:

As America may or may not know, Democrats refused to sign on to the Republican report. Instead they decided to adopt minority views filled with collusion conspiracy theories. Needless to say, it is entirely possible for 2 separate nations to engage in an election meddling at the same time.

{The spin here, is that if a few extremists from other countries try to cast aspersions on one candidate, it's just as significant to investigate this too. Bolder-dash! They just don't want to have to face what we all know, because a host of intelligence sources all confirm, it was Russian efforts and initiatives that were very effectively-deceptive, and convincing of a number of lies and false contentions that could have only swayed people to vote for Trump.

Nunez says, "Republicans believe we should take meddling seriously by all foreign countries, regardless of which campaign is the target..."

He is trying to muddy up the waters, by suggesting that meddling comes from different countries, for and against both sides. No! The meddling, the very seriously-impressive, massive disinformation campaign, the likes of which no one has ever seen before, was uniquely undertaken by Russia, because there is nowhere else in the world, where a cauldron of corrupt filth that is the Russian Mob/Government, could exist.

We need to be mindful of the treachery that can be put into effect, when you combine the sickest minds, with a lot of Mob money buying the most sophisticated deviant hackers; individuals who would think it would be cool to deceive an entire nation into believing everything is running smoothly; while every previous democratic process was slowly becoming undermined, and taken away from the citizens of that country; unbeknownst to many.

Nunez wants to give a copy of the report to the witnesses.

He says, "I would like to submit, for the record, a copy of our report, entitled, "Report on Russian active measures." I yield back...

{I have not heard about this Russian meddling report that the Republicans put out; that's the first I've heard of it; but right away, I can make an educated guess that it was spawned out of a refusal to publicly-reveal that it calls them out on their crookedness. This is the 2 ½ year-long Mueller investigation that we paid millions of dollars to have quite an extensive network of investigators look at this from all sides, and they came up with a very conclusive 440-page report. If the Republicans are basically saying, "That's worthless, and instead you have to listen to us, in order to understand what really happened with the Russian meddling;" well, right there, you can see that; as Republican Committee members are no experts at an investigation; they are just sitting in their offices all day long, figuring out how to make all of the Governmental decisions, and all of the laws go the way of their cronies and special interests. They don't have time to investigate; they are just pretty undoubtedly throwing a bunch of contrary contentions, to what was reported in the Mueller report, to spin out an alternative narrative; the Republicans are very good at that; Trump especially!

Adam Schiff now introduces the witnesses to us:

Before returning to government, Dr. Hill was a Senior official fellow at the Brookings Institution, where she directed the center on the United States and Europe. she previously worked at the National Intelligence Council Eurasia Foundation, and the John F Kennedy school of Government.

David Holmes is a political counselor at the US Embassy, in Kyiv, where he serves as the Senior policy and political advisor to Ambassador Taylor. Holmes is a career Foreign Service officer, who has previously served in Moscow, New Delhi, Kabul, Bogotá, and Grenada. He has also served on the staff of the National Security Council, as special assistant to the United States Secretary of State.

Schiff then swears in the witnesses; and then Adam Schiff recognizes David Holmes for his opening statement:

Holmes tells us that he is a career Foreign Service officer with the Department of State since August of 2017; he's been a political counselor at the US Embassy, in Kyiv. While it is an honor to appear before you today, I want to make clear that I did not seek this opportunity. I testify today, as you determined that I may have something of value to these proceedings, and issued a subpoena. It is my obligation to appear and tell you what I know. Indeed, as Secretary Pompeo has stated, I hope that everyone who testifies will do so truthfully, and accurately. When they do that, the oversight role will have been performed; and I think America will come to see what took place. That is my only goal; to testify truthfully and accurately, to enable you to perform that role. To that end, I put together statement that lays out the specifics of my recollection of events that may be relevant to this matter.

By way of background, I have spent my entire professional career, as a career Foreign Service officer, like many of the public servants who have testified, in these proceedings. My entire career has been in the service of my country. I am a graduate of Pomona College in Pomona, California; and I have a second degree, in international affairs, from the University of St. Andrews, in Scotland; and the Woodrow Wilson School of Public and international Affairs.

I joined the Foreign Service in 2002 during a political merit-based process under the George W Bush administration. I have proudly served the administrations of both parties; and worked with their appointees; both political and career. Prior to my current posting, in Kyiv, Ukraine, I served in the political and economic sections of the US Embassy, in Moscow, Russia.

In Washington, I served on the National Security Council staff, as Director of Afghanistan; and as Special Assistant to the Undersecretary of State. My prior overseas assignments include New Delhi, India, Kabul, Afghanistan, Bogotá, Columbia, and Christiana Kosovo.

As the political counselor at the US Embassy in Kyiv, I lead the political section, covering Ukraine's internal politics, foreign relationships, and security policies. I serve as a Senior policy and political advisor to the Ambassador. The job of an Ambassador's political counselor is to gather information about the host countries, on the political landscape, and to report back to Washington; to represent foreign policy to foreign contacts, and to advise the Ambassador of policy developments and implementation. In this role I'm a Senior member of the embassy's country team, and I am continually involved in addressing issues as they arise.

I'm also often called upon to take notes, in meetings involving the Ambassador, or visiting Senior officials with Ukrainian counterparts. For this reason, I've been present in many of the meetings with President Zelensky and his administration; some of which may be germane to this inquiry. While I am a political counselor at the Embassy, it is important to note that I am not a political appointee, not do I engage in US politics in any way. It is not my job to cover, or advise US politics; on the contrary, I am a political foreign policy professional, and my job is to focus on the politics of the country in which I serve; so that we can better-understand the local landscape, and better-serve the US National interests there.

In fact, during the time period we are covering today, my colleagues and I followed direct guidance from Ambassador Yovanovitch and

Ambassador Taylor to focus on doing our jobs, as foreign policy professionals; and to stay clear of Washington politics.

I arrived in Kyiv, to take up my assignment, as political counselor, in August of 2017; a year after Ambassador Yovanovitch had received her appointment. From August 2017, until her removal from post, on May 20th of this year, I was Ambassador Yovanovitch's chief policy advisor, and I developed a deep respect for her dedication, and her determination, decency, and professionalism. During this time, we worked together closely, speaking multiple times per day; and I accompanied Ambassador Yovanovitch to many of her meetings with Senior Ukrainian counterparts.

Our work in Ukraine focuses on 3 policy priorities; peace and security, economic growth and reform, and anti-corruption and the rule of law. These policies match the 3 consistent policies of the Ukrainian people since 2014; as measured in public opinion polls: Namely, to end the conflict with Russia and restore National unity and territorial integrity, responsible economic policies that deliver European standards of growth and opportunity, and effective impartial rule of law institutions that deliver justice, in cases of bilevel official corruption.

Our efforts on this foreign-policy priority merit special mention, because it was during Ambassador Yovanovitch's tenure that we achieved the hard-fought passage of a law establishing an independent court to try corruption cases. These efforts strained Ambassador Yovanovitch's relationships with President Poroshenko and some of his allies, including Prosecutor General Yuriy Lutsenko, who resisted fully-empowering truly independent anticorruption institutions, that would help ensure that no Ukrainians, no matter how powerful, were above the law.

Despite this resistance, the Ambassador and the Embassy kept pushing anticorruption and other priorities and policies towards Ukraine. In May, the situation at the Embassy in Ukraine changed dramatically, beginning in March. Specifically, the 3 priorities of security, economy, and justice, and our support for the Ukrainian Democratic resistance to Russian aggression, became overshadowed by a political agenda promoted by former New York City Mayor Rudy Giuliani, and a cadre of officials operating with a direct challenge from the White House, that began with the emergence of press reports, critical of Ambassador Yovanovitch, with a direct channel to the White House and matching nations; by then-prosecutor Lutsenko and others, to discredit her.

In mid-March, Embassy colleagues learned, from their Ukrainian contacts, that Mr. Lutsenko complained that Ambassador Yovanovitch had destroyed him, with her refusal to support him until he followed through, and ceased to use his position for personal gain. In retaliation, Lutsenko made a series of unsupported allegations of against Ambassador Yovanovitch, mostly suggesting that Ambassador Yovanovitch improperly used the Embassy, to advance political interests of the Democratic Party.

Among Mr. Lutsenko's allegations, were that the Embassy had ordered an investigation of a former Ukrainian official solely because that official was the main Ukrainian contact of the Republican Party and President Trump, personally; and that the Embassy had allegedly pressured Lutsenko's predecessor to close a case against a different foreign official, solely because of the connection between that official's company, Burisma, and former Vice President Biden's son.

Mr. Lutsenko also claimed that he never received $4.4 million in US funds intended for his office; and that there was a tape of Ukrainian officials saying that he was trying to help Hillary Clinton in the 2016 election. Finally, Mr. Lutsenko publicly claimed that Ambassador Yovanovitch had given him a "do not prosecute" list, containing the names of her suppose-ed allies.

The State Department called this an outright fabrication; one that Mr. Lutsenko later retracted. Mr. Lutsenko had said, that as a result of these allegations, Ambassador Yovanovitch faced serious problems in the United States. Public opinion polls had indicated that Ukrainians generally didn't believe Lutsenko's allegations; and on March 22nd, President Poroshenko issued a statement of support for Ambassador Yovanovitch.

Following Mr. Lutsenko's allegations, Mr. Giuliani and others, made a number of public statements, critical of Ambassador Yovanovitch, questioning her integrity, and calling for her removal from office. Mr. Giuliani was also making frequent public statements pushing for

Ukraine to investigate interference in the 2016 election, and issues related to Burisma and the Bidens. For example, on April 19th, the New York Times reported that Mr. Giuliani had "Discussed the Burisma investigation, and its intersection with the Bidens, with the ousted Ukrainian Prosecutor General, and the current prosecutor.

On May 9th, the New York Times reported that Mr. Giuliani said he planned to travel to Ukraine, to pursue investigations into the 2016 election interference and into the involvement of the former Vice President Biden, his son Hunter, and the Ukrainian gas company. Over the next few months, Mr. Giuliani also issued a series of tweets, asking why Biden shouldn't be investigated; and attacking the new President of Ukraine, Volodymyr Zelensky, for being silent on the 2016 election, and the Biden investigations; and Giuliani complained about the New York Times attacking him, for exposing the Biden family history, of making millions from Ukrainian criminals.

Around this time, the Ukrainian Presidential election was approaching, and the political newcomer, entertainer Volodymyr Zelensky, who had played the Ukrainian President on television, was surging in the polls, ahead of Mr. Lutsenko's personal ally, Mr. Poroshenko.

On April 20th, I was present for Ambassador Yovanovitch's third, and final meeting with then-candidate Zelensky, ahead of his landslide victory, in a runoff election the next day. As in her two prior meetings, that I also had attended, they had an entirely cordial and pleasant conversation, and signaled their mutual desire to work together.

However, the negative narratives about Ambassador Yovanovitch had gained currency, in certain segments of the United States press. On April 26th, Ambassador Yovanovitch departed for Washington DC, where she learned she would be recalled early. The barrage of allegations directed at Ambassador Yovanovitch; a career Ambassador, was unlike anything I've ever seen, in my professional career.

Following President-elect Zelensky's victory, our attention, at the Embassy, focused on getting to know the incoming Zelensky administration, and on our preparations for the inauguration, scheduled for May 20th, the same day that Ambassador Yovanovitch departed from Kyiv.

It quickly became clear that the White House was not prepared to show the level of support, as that of the Zelensky administration, that we had initially anticipated. In early May, Mr. Giuliani publicly alleged that President Zelensky was "Surrounded by enemies of the US President;" and Giuliani canceled his visit to Ukraine. Shortly thereafter we learn that Vice President Pence no longer planned to lead the Presidential delegation, at the inauguration.

The White House then whittled down the initial proposed list, for the official delegation to the Presidential inauguration, from over a dozen individuals, to just Energy Secretary Rick Perry, Kurt Volker (representing the State Department), National Security Council Director Alex Vindeman (representing the White House), Temporary Acting Charge of Affairs Joseph Pennington (representing the Ukrainian Embassy), and Ambassador to the European Union, Gordon Sondland.

While Ambassador Sondland's mandate, as the accredited Ambassador to the European Union, did not cover individual member states; let alone nonmember countries like Ukraine; he made clear that he had direct, and frequent access, to President Trump, and Chief of Staff Mick Mulvaney; and he portrayed himself as the conduit to the President, and Mr. Mulvaney, for this group.

Secretary Perry, Ambassador Sondland, and Ambassador Volker later styled themselves the "Three Amigos," and they made clear that they would take the lead, on coordinating the policy with the Zelensky Administration.

At around the same time, I became aware that Mr. Giuliani, President Trump's personal lawyer, was taking a direct role in Ukraine policy. On April 25th, President Zelensky's childhood friend and campaign chair, who was ultimately appointed as the head of security services of Ukraine, indicated to me privately that he been contacted by someone named Giuliani, who said he was an advisor to the President. I reported this message to Deputy Assistant Secretary of State, George Kent.

Over the following months, it became apparent that Mr. Giuliani was having direct influence on the foreign policy agenda; and the

"Three Amigos" were executing it, on the ground, in Ukraine. In fact, at one point, during a preliminary meeting of the inaugural delegation, someone wondered aloud, why Mr. Giuliani was so active in the media, with respect to Ukraine?

My recollection is that Ambassador Sondland then stated, "Damn! Every time Rudy gets involved, he goes and F's everything up!"

The inauguration took place on May 20th, and I took notes at the delegation's meeting with President Zelensky. During the meeting, Secretary Perry passed President Zelensky a list, that Perry described as "people he trusts." President Zelensky told Secretary Perry that he would seek advice with the people on this list, on issues of energy sector reform; which was the topic of the subsequent week's meetings between Secretary Perry, and key Ukrainian sector energy contacts.

Embassy personnel were excluded from some of these meetings, by Secretary Perry's staff. On May 23rd, Ambassador Volker, Ambassador Sondland, Secretary Perry, and Senator Ron Johnson; who had also attended the inauguration, although he was not part of the official delegation; they returned to United States, and briefed President Trump.

On May 29th, President Trump signed a congratulatory letter to President Zelensky, which included an invitation to visit the White House, at an unspecified date. It is important understand that the White House visit was critical to President Zelensky. President Zelensky needed to show US support at the highest levels, in order to demonstrate to Russia, and President Putin, that he had US backing; as well as to advance his ambitious anticorruption reform agenda at home.

President Zelensky's team immediately began pressing to set a date for that visit. President Zelensky and Senior members of his team, made clear that they wanted President Zelensky's first overseas trip to be, to Washington, to send a strong signal of American support; and made plans for a call from President Trump as soon as possible.

We at the Embassy also believe that meeting was critical to the success of the Zelensky administration, and its reform agenda; and we worked hard to get it arranged.

When President Zelensky's team did not receive a confirmed date for the White House visit, they made alternative plans for President

Zelensky's first overseas trip to be, to Brussels instead; in part, to attend an American Independence Day event that Ambassador Sondland hosted on June 4th. Ambassador Sondland hosted a dinner in President Zelensky's honor, following the reception, which included President Zelensky, Jared Kushner, Secretary Pompeo's counselor Ulricht Brechtbuhl, Senior European officials, and comedian Jay Leno, among others.

Ambassador Bill Taylor arrived in Kyiv, in charge of affairs on June 17th. For the next month, the focus of our activities, along with those of the three amigos, was to coordinate a White House visit. To that end, we were working with Ukrainians, to deliver things that we thought President Trump my care about; such as commercial deals that benefit the United States; which might convince President Trump to agree to a meeting with President Zelensky.

The Ukrainian policy community was unanimous, in its recommendations, and in recognizing the importance of securing the meeting, and President Trump's support. Ambassador Taylor reported that Secretary Pompeo had told him, prior to his arrival in Kyiv, "You need to work on turning the President around, on Ukraine."

Ambassador Volker had told us that the next five years, would hang on what could be accomplished in the next three months; I took that to mean that, if we did not earn President Trump's support in the next three months, we could lose the opportunity to make progress during the whole of President Zelensky's five-year term.

Within a week or two, it became apparent that the energy sector reforms and commercial deals, and the anticorruption efforts on which we were making progress, were not making a dent, in terms of persuading the White House to schedule a meeting between the two Presidents.

On June 27th, Ambassador Sondland and Ambassador Taylor had a phone conversation; the gist of which Ambassador Taylor shared with me at the time; that President Zelensky needed to make clear to President Trump that President Zelensky was not standing in the way of "investigations." I understood this meant the Biden and Burisma investigations, that Mr. Giuliani and his associates had been speaking about, in meetings, since March.

While Ambassador Taylor did not brief me on every detail of his communications with the three amigos, he did tell me that on a June 28th call with President Zelensky, Ambassador Taylor and the three amigos, it was made clear that some action on Burisma, and the Biden investigation, was a precondition for an Oval Office visit.

Also, on June 28th, while President Trump was still not moving forward on a meeting with President Zelensky, he met with Russian President Putin, at the G 20 Summit, in Osaka, Japan; a further signal of lack of support to Ukraine. We became concerned that, even if a meeting between Presidents Trump and Zelensky could occur, it would not go well; and I discussed, with Embassy colleagues, whether we should stop seeking the meeting altogether.

While the White House visit was critical to the Zelensky administration, a visit that failed to send a clear and strong signal of support, likely would be worse, for President Zelensky, than no meeting at all.

Congress has appropriated $1.5 billion in security assistance for Ukraine since 2014. This assistance has provided crucial material and moral support, to Ukraine, in their defensive war with Russia. It has helped Ukraine build its Armed Forces, virtually from scratch, into arguably the most capable and battle-hardened land force in the world.

I've had the honor of visiting the main training facility, in Western Ukraine, with members of Congress, and members of this very Committee; where we witnessed, firsthand, US National Guard troops, along with allies, conducting training for Ukrainian soldiers. Since 2014, National Guard units from California, Oklahoma, New York, Tennessee, and Wisconsin have trained, shoulder to shoulder, with Ukrainian counterparts.

Given the history of US security assistance to Ukraine, in a bipartisan recognition of its importance, I was shocked, when on July 18th, an Office of Management and Budget staff member surprisingly announced there was a hold on Ukraine the security assistance. The announcement came toward the end of the nearly two-hour National

Security Council secure videoconference call, which I participated in; from the Embassy in Ukraine. The official said that the order had come from the President, and had been conveyed to OMB by Mr. Mulvaney, with no further explanation.

This began a week, or so, of efforts by various Agencies, to identify the rationality for the freeze, to conduct a review of the assistance, and to reaffirm the unanimous view of the Ukrainian policy community, of its importance.

Our Agency counterparts confirmed to us, that there had been no change in Ukraine policy; but they could not determine the cause of the hold, or how to lift it.

On July 25th, President Trump made a congratulatory phone call to President Zelensky, after his party won a commanding majority in the parliamentary election. Contrary to standard procedure, the Embassy received no readout of that call; and I was unaware of what was discussed on the call, until the transcript was released on September 25th.

Upon reading the transcript, I was deeply disappointed to see that the President had raised none of what I understood to be our interagency agreed-upon foreign-policy priorities in Ukraine, and instead had raised the Biden/Burisma investigation; and referred to theory about Crowdstrike, that supposedly connected Ukraine, to the 2016 election.

The next day, on July 26th, I attended meetings at the Presidential administration building in Kyiv with Ambassador Taylor, Ambassador Volker, and Ambassador Sondland; and I took notes during those meetings. Our first meeting, with President Zelensky's Chief of Staff, was brief; as he had already been summoned by President Zelensky, to prepare for a subsequent, broader meeting; but he did say that President Trump had expressed interest, during the previous day's phone call, in President Zelensky's personnel decisions, related to the Prosecutor General's office.

The delegation then met with President Zelensky and several other Senior officials. In the meeting, President Zelensky stated that, during their July 25th call, President Trump had "Three times, raised some very sensitive issues," and that he would have to follow up on those issues, when he and President Trump met, in person.

Not having received a readout of the July 25th call, I did not know, at the time, what those sensitive issues were. After the meeting with President Zelensky and Ambassadors Volker, and Taylor, we quickly left the Presidential administration building, for a trip to the front lines.

Ambassador Sondland, who was to fly out that afternoon, stayed behind; to have a meeting with Andre Yermak, President Zelensky's top aid. As I was leaving the meeting with President Zelensky, I was told to join the meeting with Ambassador Sondland and Mr. Yermak, to take notes.

I had not expected to join that meeting, and I was a flight of stairs behind Ambassador Sondland, as he went to meet with Mr. Yermak. when I reached Mr. Yermak's office, Ambassador Sondland had already gone into the meeting; and I explained to Mr. Yermak's assistant, that I was supposed to join the meeting; and I strongly urged her to let me in; but she told me that Ambassador Sondland and Mr. Yermak had insisted that the meeting be one-on-one, with no notetaking.

I then waited in the anteroom until the meeting ended, along with a member of Ambassador Sondland's staff, and a member of the US Embassy staff. When the meeting ended, the two staffers and I accompanied Ambassador Sondland out of the Presidential administration building.

Ambassador Sondland said that he wanted to go to lunch. I told Ambassador Sondland that I would be happy to join him and the two staffers, for lunch; if he wanted brief me out, on his meeting with Mr. your Mac; or discuss other issues. Ambassador Sondland said that I should join him.

The four of us went to a nearby restaurant and sat at the outside terrace. I sat directly across from Ambassador Sondland; and the two staffers sat off to the side. At first, lunch was largely social. Ambassador Sondland selected a bottle of wine that we shared, among the four of us; and we discussed topics such as marketing strategy, for Sondland's hotel chain.

After this, during lunch, Ambassador Sondland said that he was going to call President Trump, to give him an update. Ambassador Sondland placed a call on his mobile phone, and I heard him announce himself several times; along the lines of "Gordon Sondland, holding for the President. It appeared that he was being transferred through several layers of switchboards, and assistants; and then I noticed that Ambassador Sondland's demeanor changed; and I understood that he had obviously been connected with President Trump.

While Ambassador Sondland's phone was not on speakerphone, I could hear the President's voice, through the ear-piece of the phone. The President's voice was loud, and recognizable. Ambassador Sondland held the phone away from his ear for a period of time, presumably because of the loud volume.

I heard Ambassador Sondland greet President Trump, and explain that he was calling from Kyiv. I heard President Trump then clarify that Ambassador Sondland was in Ukraine. Ambassador Sondland replied that, yes, he was in Ukraine; and he went on to state that President Zelensky loves your ass.

I then heard President Trump ask, "So is he going to do the investigation?" Ambassador Sondland replied that he's going to do it; adding that President Zelensky will do anything that you ask him to do.

Even though I did not take notes of these statements, I have a clear recollection that these statements were made. I believe that my colleagues who were sitting at the table also knew that Ambassador Sondland was speaking to the President.

The conversation then Shifted to Ambassador Sondland's efforts on behalf of the President, to assist a "rapper" who was jailed in Sweden. I could only hear Ambassador Sondland's side of the conversation. Ambassador Sondland told the President that the rapper was quite kind of "F"-ed there, and should have pled guilty. Sondland recommended that the President wait until after the sentencing; or it will only make it worse; and added that the President should let him get sentenced, and then play the racism card; and give the rapper a tickertape parade when he comes home. {This is the official business of the President?!}

Ambassador Sondland told the President that Sweden quote, "Should have released him on your word, but you can tell the Cardicians that you tried!"

After the call ended, Ambassador Sondland remarked that the President was in a bad mood, as was often the case early in the morning. I then took the opportunity to ask Ambassador Sondland for his candid impression of the President's views on Ukraine; and particularly I asked him if it was true, that the President did not give an (expletive) about Ukraine? Ambassador Sondland agreed the President didn't give an (explicative) about Ukraine. I asked why not? Ambassador Sondland stated that the President only cares about "big stuff." I noted that there certainly was "big stuff" going on in Ukraine, like a war with Russia. Ambassador Sondland replied that he meant the "big stuff" that benefits the President; like the Biden investigation, that Mr. Giuliani was pushing.

The conversation then moved on, to other topics. Upon returning to the Embassy, I immediately briefed my direct supervisor; the Chief of Mission, about Ambassador Sondland's call with President Trump, and my subsequent conversation with Ambassador Sondland; and I told others at the Embassy about the call. I also emailed an Embassy official in Sweden, regarding the issue with US rapper that was discussed on the call. July 26th was my last day in the office; as I had a long- planned vacation, that ended on August 6th.

After returning to the Embassy, I told Ambassador Taylor about Sondland's July 26th call; and I also repeatedly referred to the call, in conversation with Ambassador Sondland, and in meetings and conversations; when the issue of the President's interest in Ukraine was potentially relevant.

At that time, Ambassador Sondland's statement of the President's lack of interest in Ukraine was a particular focus. We understood that if we were to secure a meeting between President Trump and President Zelensky, we would have to work hard, to find a way to explain Ukraine's importance to President Trump, in terms that he found compelling.

Over the ensuing weeks, we continue to try and identify ways to frame the importance of Ukraine, in ways that would appeal to

President Trump, to determine how to lift the hold on the security assistance, and to move forward on scheduling a White House visit for President Zelensky. Ukrainian Independence Day, August 24th, presented another opportunity to show support for Ukraine. Secretary Pompeo had considered attending; as National Security Advisor Bolton had attended in 2018, and Defense Secretary Mattis had attended in 2017; but in the end, nobody senior to Ambassador Volker attended.

Shortly thereafter, on August 27th, Ambassadors Bolton and Volker visited Ukraine, with welcome news that President Trump had agreed to meet President Zelensky, on September 1st, in Warsaw. Ambassador Bolton further indicated that the hold on security assistance would not be lifted, prior to the Warsaw meeting, where it would hang on whether President Zelensky was able to favorably impress President Trump.

I took notes at Ambassador Bolton's meeting that day, with President Zelensky and his Chief of Staff. The Ambassador told Zelensky's Chief of Staff that the meeting between the Presidents, in Warsaw, would be crucial to cementing the relationship. However, President Trump ultimately pulled out of the Warsaw trip; and the hold remained in place, with no clear means to get rid of it.

Between meetings on August 27th, I heard Ambassador Bolton express to Ambassador Taylor, and National Security Council Director Tim Morrison, his frustration about Mr. Giuliani's influence with the President, also making clear that there was nothing he could do about it. He recommended that Mr. Lutsenko's replacement Prosecutor General open a channel with his counterpart, Attorney General Bill Barr, in place of the informal channel between Mr. Yermak and Mr. Giuliani.

Ambassador Bolton also expressed frustration about Ambassador Sondland's expansive interpretation of his mandate. After President Trump canceled his visit to Warsaw, we continued to try and appeal to the President's foreign policy, in National Security terms. To that end, Ambassador Taylor told me that Ambassador Bolton had recommended that he, Ambassador Taylor, send a first-person cable to secretary Pompeo, articulating the importance of the security assistance.

At Ambassador Taylor's direction, I drafted and submitted the cable on Ambassador Taylor's behalf on August 29th, which further attempted to explain the importance of Ukraine security assistance, to our own national security. By this point, however, my clear impression was that the security assistance hold was likely intended by the President; either as an expression of dissatisfaction with Ukrainians, or because the Ukrainians would not agree to the Biden investigation; or as an effort to increase the pressure on them to do so.

On September 5th, I took notes at Senator Johnson and Senator Chris Murphy's meetings with President Zelensky. I think this is when President Zelensky ask about the security assistance. Although both Senators stressed strong bipartisan support for Ukraine, Senator Johnson cautioned President Zelensky, that President Trump had a negative view of Ukraine, and President Zelensky would have a difficult time overcoming this. Senator Johnson further explained that he had been shocked by President Trump's negative reaction, during an Oval Office meeting on May 23rd, when he and the three amigos had proposed to President Trump, that President Trump meet with President Zelensky, and show support for Ukraine.

On September 8th, Ambassador Taylor told me that now, they are insisting Zelensky commit to investigations, in an interview with CNN; which I took to refer to the three amigos. I was shocked, that the requirement was so specific, and concrete. What we had advised our Ukrainian counterparts, was to voice a commitment to following the rule of law, and generally investigating credible corruption allegations. Yet, this was a demand, that President Zelensky personally commit, on a cable news channel, to a specific investigation of President Trump's political rival.

On September 11th, the hold was finally lifted, after significant press coverage, and bipartisan congressional expressions of concern about the withholding of the security assistance. Although we knew the hold was lifted, we were still concerned that President Zelensky had committed, in exchange for the lifting, to give the requested CNN interview.

We had several indications that the interview would occur. First, the news conference in Kyiv was holding firm, for September 14th, and CNN's Fareed Zacharia was one of the moderators. Second, on September 13th, an Embassy colleague had received a phone call, from another colleague who work for Ambassador Sondland. My colleague had texted me regarding that call. "Re: the Sondland and Zelensky interview, someone said the Zelensky interview is supposed to be today, or Monday; and they plan to announce that a certain investigation, that was put on hold, will progress. He said he did not know this was decided, or whether Sondland was still advocating for it; apparently, he's been discussing this with Yermak.

Finally, also on September 13th, Ambassador Taylor happened to run into Mr. Yermak, on our way out of a meeting with President Zelensky, in his private office. Ambassador Taylor again stressed the importance of staying out of US politics; and said that he hoped no interview was planned. Mr. Yermak did not answer, but shrugged in resignation, as if to indicate that he had no choice. In short, everybody thought it was going to be an interview that the Ukrainians believed that they had to do.

The interview ultimately did not occur. On September 21st, Ambassador Taylor and I collaborated on input that he sent to Mr. Morrison, to brief President Trump ahead of a September 25th meeting, that had been scheduled with President Zelensky, in New York, on the margins of UN General Assembly. The transcript of the July 25th call was released that same day. As of today, I still have not seen a readout of that September 25th meeting.

As the impeachment inquiry has progressed, I have followed press reports, and reviewed the statements of Ambassadors Taylor and Yovanovitch. Based on my experience in Ukraine, my recollection is generally consistent with their testimony. I believe that the relevant facts were therefore being laid out, for the American people.

However, in the last couple of weeks, I read press reports expressing, for the first time, that certain senior officials may have been acting without the President's knowledge; or freelancing, in their dealings with Ukraine.

At the same time, I also read reports noting the lack of first-hand evidence, in the investigation; suggesting that the only evidence being elicited at the hearings was hearsay. I came to realize that I have firsthand knowledge regarding certain events on July 26th, that had not otherwise been reported; and that those events would bear on the question of whether President Trump did, in fact, have knowledge that senior officials were using the levers of diplomatic power, to influence the new Ukrainian President to announce the opening of a criminal investigation, against President Trump's political opponent.

It was at that point, that I gave communicated to Ambassador Taylor, my realization that the incident I had witnessed on July 26th had acquired greater significance; which is what he reported in his testimony last week; and this is what led to the subpoena for me to appear here today.

In conclusion, I'd like to take a moment to turn back to Ukraine. Today marks exactly 6 years, since throngs of pro-Western Ukrainians spontaneously gathered on Kyiv's Independence Square, the beginning of what has become known as the Revolutionary of Dignity.

When the protests began, in opposition to a turn towards Russia and away from the West, it took the better part of three months to reject the entire corrupt repressive system that had been sustained by Russian influence in the country.

Those events were followed by Russia's occupation of Ukraine's Crimean Peninsula, and an invasion of Ukraine's Eastern Donbas areas; an ensuing war that has caused almost 14,000 (Ukrainian) lives.

Despite the Russian aggression over the past five years, Ukrainians have rebuilt a shattered economy, have adhered to a peace process, and have moved economically and socially closer to the West; toward our way of life.

Earlier this year, large majorities of Ukrainians again chose a fresh start by voting for a political newcomer as President, replacing 80 percent of their Parliament, and endorsing a platform consistent with our democratic values, our foreign priorities, and our strategic interests.

This year's revelation at the ballot box underscores that, despite its imperfections, Ukraine is a genuine and vibrant democracy, an example to other post-Soviet countries and beyond; from Moscow to Hong Kong.

How we respond to this historic opportunity will set the trajectory of our relationship with Ukraine, and will define her willingness to defend our bedrock international principles, and our leadership role in the world.

As we sit here today, Ukrainians are fighting a hot war, on Ukrainian territory, against Russian aggression. This week alone, since I have been here in Washington, two Ukrainian soldiers were killed, and two were injured by Russian-led forces in Eastern Ukraine; despite the declared cease-fire. I learned overnight, that seven more were injured yesterday.

As Vice President Pence said, after his meeting with President Zelensky in Warsaw, the US-Ukraine relationship has never been stronger. Ukrainians and their new government earnestly want to believe that. Ukrainians cherish the bipartisan American support, and the sustained Euro-Atlantic aspirations; and they recoil at the thought of playing a role in domestic US politics, or elections.

At a time of shifting allegiances, and rising competitors in the world, we have no better friend than Ukraine; a scrappy vowed and determined, and above all, a dignified people, who are standing up against Russian authoritarianism and aggression. They deserve better. We are now at an inflection point in Ukraine. It is critical to our national security, that we stand in strong support for our Ukrainian partners.

Ukrainians are freedom-loving people; people everywhere are watching the example we set here, of democracy, and the rule of law. Thank you.

Next, Dr. Fiona Hill gives her opening statement:

I have a (relatively) short opening statement. I appreciate the importance of Congress's impeachment inquiry, and I'm appearing today as a fact witness; as I did during my deposition on October 14th; in order to answer your questions about what I saw, what I did, and what I knew; and what I know with regard to the subject of your inquiry. I believe that those who have information that the Congress deems relevant, have a legal and a moral obligation to provide it.

I take great pride in the fact that I am a non-partisan policy expert, who has served under three Republican and Democrat Presidents. I have no interest in advancing the outcome of your inquiry in any particular direction, except toward the truth.

I will not provide a long statement, because I believe that the interest of Congress and the American people is best served, by allowing you to ask me your questions. I'm happy to expand upon my October 14th deposition testimony, in response to your questions today; but before I do so, I'd like to communicate two things: First, I'd like to share a little about who I am.

I'm American by choice; I became a citizen in 2002. I was born in the Northeast of England, in the same region that George Washington's ancestors came from; me and my family have deep ties to the United States. My paternal grandfather fought in World War I, in field artillery, and survived being shot, shelled, and gassed, before American troops intervened to end the war, in 1918.

During the second World War, other members of my family fought to defend the free world from fascism, alongside American soldier, sailors, and airman. The men in my father's family were coal miners. My family has always struggled with poverty; but my father Alfred was 14, he joined his father, brother, and cousins, working in the coal mines, to help put food on the table.

When most of the local mines closed, in the 1960s, my father wanted to emigrate to the United States, and work in the coal mines in West Virginia and Pennsylvania; but his mother, my grandmother, had become crippled from hard labor, and my father couldn't leave her; so he stayed in North England until he died, in 2012.

My mother still lives in my hometown today. While my father's idea that we should emigrate to the US was thwarted, he loved America; its culture, its history, and that it was a beacon to the world. He always wanted someone in our family to make it to the United States.

I began my University studies in 1984; and I just learned I went to the same university as my colleague, Mr. Holmes; St. Andrews, in Scotland.

In 1987, I won a place as an academic exchange student, to the Soviet Union. I was there for the signing of the Intermediate Nuclear Forces INF treaty. I was there when President Ronald Reagan met

Soviet leader Mikhail Gorbachev, in Moscow; and this was a turning point for me. A professor that I met there, told me about graduate scholarships in the United States; and the very next; year thanks to his advice, I went to America, to start my advanced studies at Harvard.

Years later, I can say with confidence, that this country has offered me opportunities I never would've had in England.

I grew up poor, with a very distinctive working-class accent. In England, in the 1980s and 1990s, this would have impeded my professional advancement; this background has never set me back, in America.

For the best part of three decades, I built a career as a nonpolitical national security professional, focused on Europe and Eurasia and especially the former Soviet Union have served our country under three Presidents. In my most recent capacity, serving on the National Security Council under President Trump, and in my former capacity, as Director of National Intelligence for Russia and Eurasia, under Presidents George Bush and Barrack Obama. In that role, I was the intelligence community senior expert on Russia, and the former Soviet republics, including Ukraine.

It was because of my background and experience, that I was asked to join the National Security Council, in 2017. At the NSC, Russia was part of my portfolio, but I was also in charge of US policy for all of Western Europe. Part my portfolio was coordinating US policy for all of Western Europe, and all of Eastern Europe, including Ukraine and Turkey, along with NATO and the European Union.

I was hired initially by General Kellogg... I started working in April 2017, when General McMaster was national security advisor; when they thought it could help them with President Trump's stated goal of improving relations with Russia, while still implementing policy signed to deter Russian obstruction to the United States; including the unprecedented and successful Russian operation to interfere in the 2016 Presidential election.

This relates to the second thing I wanted to communicate: Based on questions and statements that I've heard; some of you on this committee appear to believe that Russia and its security services did <u>not</u> conduct a campaign against our country; and that perhaps, somehow, for some reason, that Ukraine did.

This is a fictional narrative; and it is being perpetrated and propagated by the Russian security services themselves. The unfortunate truth, is that Russia was the foreign power that systematically attacked our Democratic elections in 2016.

This is the public conclusion of our intelligence agencies, confirmed in bipartisan public reports; there is no dispute. Even if some of the underlying details must remain classified. The impact of the successful 2016 Russian campaign remains evident today. Our nation is being torn apart; our highly professional expert Foreign Service is being undermined; US support for Ukraine, which continues to face armed Russian aggression, is being politicized.

The Russian government's goal is to weaken our country, to diminish America's global role, and to neutralize a perceived US threat to Russian interests. President Putin, and the Russian Security Services aim to counter US foreign policy objectives in Europe, including Ukraine.

Russia, or Moscow, wishes to reassert political and economic dominance. I say this, not as an alarmist, but as a realist. I do not think long-term conflict with Russia is other desirable or inevitable. I continue to believe that we need to seek ways of stabilizing our relationship with Moscow, even as we counter their efforts to harm us right now. Russian security services and their proxies have geared up, to repeat their interference, in the 2020 election. We are running out of time to stop them. In the course of this investigation, I would ask you please, not to promote politically-driven falsehoods, that so clearly advance Russian interests.

As Republicans and Democrats have agreed for decades, Ukraine is a valued partner of the United States, and plays an important role in our national security. As I told the committee last month, I refuse to be part of an effort to legitimize the alternative narrative, that the Ukrainian government is a US adversary; and that Ukraine attacked us in 2016. These fictions are harmful, even if even if they are deployed for purely domestic political purposes.

President Putin, and the Russian security services operate like a super PAC; they deploy millions of dollars to weaponize our own political opposition research, and false narratives.

When we are consumed by partisan rancor, we cannot combat these external forces, as they seek to divide us against each other, to degrade our institutions, and destroy the faith of the American people, in our democracy.

I respect the work that this Congress is doing, in carrying out its constitutional responsibility; including this inquiry; and I'm here to help you, to the best of my ability.

If the President, or anyone else, impedes or subverts the national security of the United States in order to further domestic policy, political, or personal interests, that is more-than-worthy of your attention. We must not let domestic politics stop us from defending ourselves against the foreign powers who truly wish us harm us. I am ready to answer your questions. Thank you.

Adam Schiff announces that he and the lead counsel, Daniel Goldman, now have their 45 minutes to question the witnesses. Schiff says that Fiona Hill's story is a lot like Alexandra Vindeman's; in terms of their emigrating here coming from a poor number underprivileged background; and Schiff remarks that these kinds of stories are powerful; and here they are being told by two of our government's highest-ranking officials. Schiff says, the report that my colleagues gave you, (Schiff is referring to the report that Devin Nunez was talking about in his opening statement that he insisted on giving to the witnesses) {So now we find out that, first of all, the Republicans produced that report during these investigations; I guess they knew they needed to back off of their assertion that Russia had nothing to do with the election interference; it was all Ukraine. Schiff then says that their report calls into question the intelligence community's findings, that Russia intervened to help one side; to help Donald Trump, at the expense of Hillary Clinton; nobody questions that finding; not the FBI, nor does the Senate Bipartisan Intelligence Committee report, nor does the minority Committee report, nor this Committee. The Republican House Intelligence Committee report is an outlier.

Schiff asks Dr. Hill why the Russians would want to push this narrative, obviously so that the public can hear, that it's because Russia was severely sanctioned, as a consequence for interfering in our election in such a dastardly way, on such a large scale; and Russia has been suffering under the weight of those sanctions, which are very crippling economically to Russia; so if they can promote a new narrative, that it wasn't them that did the hacking; instead it was Ukraine; they might then have a much better chance at arranging for the sanctions to be lifted. I believe this is the paramount motivation.

I was wrong about guessing that was what she was going to explain to us, though; Dr. Hill says that Russia's interest is to delegitimize our entire presidency. She says, Russia really likes that they have seeded disinformation, and seeded doubt; they have everybody questioning the legitimacy of the Presidential contest; they would like to pit one party against the other. She says, Russia wants to arrange it so that the one who got elected would be beholden to Russia; and we can see that this would be another reason why Russia would support Donald Trump's election; because apparently Russia has a lot of dirt on him; which is why the Christopher Steele investigation was sought by Trump's competitors; because it was obvious enough that Russians do have things to hold over his head; and Trump also has borrowed almost all of the money he has borrowed, from Russia; these are corrupt lending sources that want more than interest to be paid on the loan! So, Russia really appears to have him over a barrel; although we haven't yet proved that, because he's managed to hide his tax returns, and keep everybody from finding out about what is behind his financial endeavors they certainly couldn't be very legitimate otherwise he wouldn't have to hide his tax returns and all of these other business transactions through Deutchebank; and on record with his accounting firm Mazars, etc…

Schiff points out that the Russians seek to sow discord in the United States, along ethnic lines, religious lines, geographic lines, racial lines; along all those lines. Schiff then brings up another reason that Russia would like to try and change the narrative; in order to try and drive a wedge, in the goodwill relations between the US and Ukraine.

Schiff quotes a section of Holmes's opening statement, saying that, while we had advised our Ukrainian counterparts on following the rule of law, and generally investigating credible corruption allegations; this was a demand that President Zelensky personally commit, on a cable news channel, to a specific investigation of President Trump's political rival.

{Schiff wants to make a point about hypocrisy; here we are urging Ukrainians the following the rule of law, and to only investigate genuine, credible allegations; and what are we doing? We are asking them to investigate the President's political rival! He says, Ukrainians are pretty sophisticated actors; they can recognize hypocrisy when they see it. -But what does that do to our anticorruption counselling efforts, when the Ukrainians see that we are engaging in corruption ourselves? Doesn't Trump see how his behavior, as a US President, undermines the very thing we stand for, that gives the concept of Democracy its life breath?! -for all others around the world to see, and emulate? Wouldn't the world work so much better, if many other nations took lessons from our example; well now how can we tout democracy, if it can be so easily undermined? The answer is, it can't be undermined; we cannot allow it. If we act in the same spirit as our forefathers in this country, we owe it to the humanity of the future to do what we have to, to prevail over this kind of tyranny!}

Schiff next comments that the Ukrainians are sophisticated enough actors that they can see when we are saying, do as we say, and not as we do. Schiff also brings up the part of Holmes's statement where he explains that, even after the hold had been lifted, the Ukrainians still apparently felt obligated to make these corrupt announcements, in a CNN interview. Schiff points out that in explaining this during his statement, Holmes is driving it home, that the Ukrainians may have felt like they couldn't avoid it; but they definitely did not want to engage in the corruption that Trump was trying to force them into. Holmes points out that, well even though the hold on the security aid had been lifted, we also know that at this point, when Taylor runs into Yermak, between meetings in mid-September; Holmes reminds us that the Ukrainians had not yet gotten their White House meeting, and there were other forms of support and assurance they needed from the US.

This brings up an interesting point: the Ukrainians did ultimately cancel the CNN announcement; but they did so because other US diplomats had obviously convinced them that whatever they do, support from America will not have to be predicated on engaging in corruption. The world is at least beginning to see, that there is a marked distinction between American values and ideals, versus Donald Trump the narcissistic maniac; Good! -then we are making progress already!

One of the stronger motivations for Ukrainians to have still remained willing to make these corrupt announcements, Holmes says, is that at this point in time, Zelensky had been trying to arrange a summit with President Putin, to try and work out a peace agreement; and this is another huge reason why Ukraine needs a show of strong US support, in order to be in a better bargaining position. Schiff now yields to Mr. Goldman:

Goldman asks Hill just who it was, that Sondland had told her had put him in charge of Ukraine policy? -and she answered that Sondland said it was the President. Goldman asks Holmes if he also understood that Sondland had the authority of the President? Holmes says he understood that the President had told Sondland to work with Rudy Giuliani; a slightly different message; still, then Holmes says that yes, Sondland had held himself out as somebody with direct contact with, and being directed by the President.

Even though Holmes had said in his opening statement that he didn't know what the sensitive issues that Zelensky was referring to about (mentioned within the July 25th phone call) on the next day on the 26th, when Holmes was taking notes in the meeting between Sondland, Volker and Zelensky; but he said that even then, at that point, he did suspect that the sensitive issues had something to do with the investigations of Biden.

Goldman refers to the fact that when Sondland made this call to President Trump, from the restaurant in Kyiv, it was not only out in public, on the terrace of a restaurant; but it was an unsecured cell phone call with the President; that others could pretty easily be listening in on; that's not too bright either.

Holmes says that when Trump first came on the line, he was so loud that Sondland winced and then held the phone away from his ear; and that's why the volume was at such a high a level, that Holmes could definitely identify that it was Trump.

{You know? -Just thinking about the fact that, as is revealed within his closer personal circles, President Trump doesn't give a flying you know what about Ukraine, is this really the man we elected for President in this country?! -a guy who doesn't even give a hoot about an ally that is fighting the world's fight against Russian expansion? What kind of a joker is he? Why the hell should he even be anywhere close to the White House? This is a total cluster flock! skews my French.}

Goldman asks Dr. Hill, saying that during your 2 ½ years in the White House you listened to a number of Presidential phone calls is that right that's right she says sometimes multiple calls per week so over 2 ½ years were talking probably well over hundred phone calls Presidential phone calls Goldman was can ask her if she'd ever heard another phone call of a similar nature; but she speaks up first and says that she doesn't want to comment on the call and that she considers a Presidential call to have executive privilege.

Goldman points out that the transcript of this call was released publicly, and so he just wants to ask her if she's heard other phone calls that were anything like along these lines? she doesn't want to compare this with other phone calls she wants to stick to talking about this phone call; and she says that she found, both the subject matter, and the way it was conducted, surprising!

Goldman asks her why she was very shocked, and very saddened to read that the transcript; as she has earlier testified. Hill says, because of the nature of the discussion, and the juxtaposition of the issues in which they were raised, and also given the fact she herself, along with Ambassador Bolton, feared having a call unless it was very well prepared, and they were confident that the issues that Ukraine and the US were most-generally together-interested-in, were going to be raised. She saw that, with this call, this was not the case.

Holmes says that when Yermak brought it up to him, that Zelensky had said that there were "personnel" issues that Trump had brought up with him, on that July 25th call, and Holmes's statement today made it seem like that was just a nebulous thought in Holmes his mind, at the time; but after reading the transcript of the call released on September 25th, he now knew that it was a reference to the former Prosecutor General Lutsenko; and this was obviously troubling Zelensky, because Zelensky knew Lutsenko was corrupt, and he was in the process of replacing him; and yet, Trump was praising Lutsenko, and saying that he had been treated unfairly; so yes, that <u>would</u> cause a personnel issue!

Holmes reports that Lutsenko was not a good partner to the Embassy, in Kyiv; he had failed to deliver on the promise that he had committed to, when he took office; and he was using his office to insulate and protect political allies, presumably while enriching himself with their payoffs for doing so.

Goldman says, is another way to describe that, corrupt?! (yes)

Next, Goldman points out that some of President Trump's most senior advisers had informed Trump that this idea that Ukraine had been responsible for the 2016 election interference was false; so, in other words, Trump is just impervious to reason, and only believes dictators and conspiracy theorists!

Goldman reads an excerpt from a February 2, 2017 news interview, with President Putin and Prime Minister Orban, of Hungary. Putin says, "As we all know, during the Presidential campaign in the United States, the Ukrainian government adopted a unilateral position in favor of one candidate; that certain oligarchs; with the approval of Ukraine's political leadership; funded this candidate, or female candidate, to be more precise…" {alluding to Hillary Clinton, of course)

Goldman says, Dr. Hill, you spent 3 years working in Russia; why would it be to Vladimir Putin's advantage to promote this theory of Ukraine interference? (first of all, to deflect from the allegations of Russian interference; 2nd of all to drive a wedge between the United States and Ukraine, which Russia essentially wants to get Ukraine back into its sphere of influence. Thirdly, to besmirch Ukraine, and its political leadership, and to degrade and erode support for a new regime in Ukraine, in the eyes of other key partners, in Europe and elsewhere.

Goldman says, President Zelensky was elected in April, and his inauguration was on May 20th, is that right, Dr. Hill? (yes) -And back in May this year, do you recall that President Trump had a phone conversation, in early May, with President Putin... (I do) -And that he also then met in mid-May with Prime Minister Orban, who had joined President Putin at this conference... (That's correct.)

-Now, that happened in-between the time when President Zelensky was elected on April 21st, and the date of his inauguration, on May 20th, is that correct?

(yes) -And in fact, isn't it true that President Trump had asked Vice President Pence to attend the inauguration? (Yes; and after his congratulatory phone call with President Zelensky, on April 21st, I myself, and many others at the State Department, were very eager to have Vice President Pence go to Ukraine, to represent the US President.)

{Holmes also says that he understood that this was the plan. Goldman points out that it's interesting, that on the same day that President Trump called off sending Pence to Zelensky's inauguration, Trump had also had a phone call with Victor Orban, who is a chum of Putin's; and we also know from Lev Parnas's interview with Rachel Maddow, that on that same day, President Zelensky had told Lev that he refused to make the announcement of the investigation Trump was demanding; knowing full well that Trump had threatened that Vice President Pence would not be coming the inauguration, if Zelensky would not agree to make that announcement.

{You know, what kind of President would behave in such a thug-like manner? When he is called out for doing something dirty, or crooked, with some other shady character, first he says that he doesn't know that person, then, when a slew of pictures with that guy appear all over the news, he shrugs that off, and then next denies, that he said or did what he is being called out for having done or said; then once it has subsequently become firmly established, through corroborating sources, that in fact he is indeed guilty of what he had been accused of, he either still denies this; and somehow this is believable to his base! -Or he finally says, yeah, I did it, but so what? -No big deal; even though the whole reason why it made the news and was being talked about in the first place, because it is a big deal! -Things like, inviting foreign interference into our election; that by itself is a big deal; but then the fact that he held a particularly vulnerable ally over a barrel, pressuring him for months to become complicit in Trump's crooked scheme, while also withholding important American support, that would keep Russia at bay, during the middle of a hot war, where Russia was continually invading our ally, Ukraine.

Somehow, the President's defense team at the Senate impeachment trial said that they don't consider this to have be an impeachable offense; that it doesn't rise to the level of an impeachable offense. We know that this is not at all true; those Republican Senators know Trump's behavior is impeachable, and it should be impeachable. However, the only thing that's important to the Republicans in government, is to stay in power; and as long as they have a majority in the Senate, where the muscle is, to either make decisions of integrity, in the interest of the American people; or conversely to make crooked decisions and take crooked actions to protect a crook in a crooked administration; that power lies with the Senate majority completely, of course; that's what we have just learned!

Therefore, it is our only path to justice, and the continuance of American Democracy, to make sure that, as of election day this November, the Republicans will no longer hold a majority in the Senate. In fact, because of the way that Mitch McConnell and the other Republican Senators have behaved, throughout President Trump's term, and especially throughout the impeachment proceedings and the trial, once the Democratic Senators do become the majority in the Senate, they should immediately adopt a resolution to bar Republican Senators from ever achieving majority status that would allow them to visit these severe injustices upon the American people again.

They should adopt a resolution that states that, should the Republican Senators ever become a majority in the Senate again, that they will never have a majority vote on any issue; that the most they can sway any decision is up to 50% of the Senators. They honestly don't deserve any more than that; that should be the absolute limit.

During these hearings, we heard more odious aspects about the mentality of Trump, like that he goes from confirming, with Sondland on a cell phone call, that his foreign President patsy is going to do something corrupt, that Trump has put great pressure on him to do; to discussing his great concern about a rapper. A rapper! How could the President of the United States be talking about a rapper in the middle of the business day?!

Of all the important officials, heads of large companies, and highly-influential others, to be discussing important matters with, and with a whole host of critical issues plaguing our nation, Trump's present concern is about one, of a thousand entertaining nonsense-spewers; not that I don't find some rappers impressively-skilled and entertaining; but let's face it; they are not exactly well-versed in the panacea of world issues within a normal President's circle of influence!

Goldman asks Hill about the time period last spring, when Rudy Giuliani was on the news particularly a lot of the time; and Ms. Hill had testified earlier, that it was really bothering her, and also John Bolton. At one point, Hill had brought to Bolton's attention the smear campaign tactics of Giuliani, toward Yovanovitch, and she expressed great regret about how this was unfolding.

Hill then asked Bolton if there was anything that they could do about this smear campaign; and she says he had a pained look on his face, and had indicated with body language, that there wasn't much they could do about it

In the course of that discussion, this is when Bolton famously said, "Rudy Giuliani is a hand grenade, and he's going to blow everybody up!"

Hill says that, at this time, Giuliani was frequently on television, making incendiary remarks about everyone involved; and that, "This was clearly causing issues that would probably come back to haunt us; in fact, that's where we are today…" she

Holmes says Yovanovitch was removed following this media campaign, cooked up by Rudy Giuliani and Lutsenko, over in Ukraine; within the smear campaign, they had criticized Yovanovitch for not looking into some of the issues that Lutsenko was trying to impress upon her were important; or so they said. -But once they had succeeded in getting her removed, news commentators in Ukraine were impressed; it seemed to demonstrate that Giuliani and Lutsenko had power in Ukraine. {look up who Joseph Penniman, he was part of the 5-person US delegation at Zelensky's inauguration. (Perry, Volker, Sondland, Vindeman, and Joseph Penniman.)

Goldman is now asking Holmes about this list of people, that Rick Perry had given Zelensky at the inauguration; and I think it was on the Rachel Maddow show that I learned this list contained the names of several American oil and gas entrepreneurs that Rick Perry was familiar with; and although Zelensky was told, by Perry, that these are people that he trusted, and that Zelensky could get advice from; I think what actually ended up happening is that these people then exploited their direct connection with Zelensky, and they ended up becoming awarded some sweetheart natural gas leases; or perhaps other energy-deal-related contracts with Ukraine; so I think that Rick Perry is looks a bit dirty as well because I am pretty sure you're not supposed to financially benefit, nor arrange for your cronies in the energy business to benefit, from your official relations with a foreign President.

Holmes tells Goldman that he was aware that, at the inauguration, Zelensky was, by then, already feeling some pressure about the investigations; and that was, as of May 20th! The funds got released on September 11th, and the pressure was on for that whole period of time. -And here it is February 6th, and they still haven't gotten their White House meeting! I'm sure Putin must be enamored with the way Trump is not offering full support to Ukraine, in the face of Russian border expansion efforts.

Fiona Hill's response to Goldman's questioning, about how obvious it was that the investigations into Burisma (that several officials knew about, from internal complaints about what Giuliani and Sondland were doing) meant investigations of the Bidens?

Goldman asks her, when you heard Burisma, did you realize the connection between Burisma and the Bidens? {as you might remember, Sondland had contended that he didn't know that the investigation into Burisma was in connection with the Bidens, until the September 25th release of the July 25th call transcript; and as I mentioned before, he certainly would want to say this, in order to distance himself from his apparent complicity with the underhanded scheme; but what Fiona Hill says here is that during this whole period of time, from the spring, through the summer, she had witnessed Rudy Giuliani saying on TV news and interviews, multiple times, that they were interested in investigating Burisma because Hunter Biden, Joe Biden's son had secured a position on the board, making $50,000 a month; and that seemed very inappropriate since Hunter Biden didn't have the background for this.

-But Fiona Hill says that Giuliani was talking about Burisma and the Bidens in the same breath multiple times on TV different news stations; I find it very hard to believe that Sondland really didn't know he had been {pushing for something dirty.}

When Goldman asks him next, Holmes also agrees that anyone involved in Ukraine matters in that spring and summer would also be aware that the investigations being pushed for were connected to the Bidens.

Sondland had testified that his recollection of that July 10 meeting where he had suddenly interjected, when Mr. Doniluk asked about getting a White House meeting; at that point Sondland said that we have an agreement that the meeting will only be granted if the investigations are pursued; but Sondland had said in his hearing yesterday, that to his recollection, the meeting did not end abruptly; as others had testified; and so we are now listening to Fiona Hill, who was at that meeting, and she said that when Sondland talked about the quid pro quo, that she saw Bolton "stiffen" (was her words), so he had a visceral reaction to it; and as I said before, he might've been graceful about how he did it, but it's pretty clear that this ended everything; he then wanted no more to do with this, after that; and this is where he told Hill that he didn't want to be part of any "drug deal being cooked up by Sondland and Perry." {Isn't that funny?! -as I had guessed, and said I would have done this myself; Fiona Hill says that Bolton looked up at the clock and then down at his watch; and he said, well, it was nice to see you; but I've got another meeting..."

Goldman refers to Holmes's deposition testimony that by late August Holmes said he had a clear impression that the security assistance hold was somehow connected to the investigations that President Trump wanted; how had you reached that clear conclusion? (We had been hearing about the investigations since March; months before; and President Zelensky had received a congratulatory letter from the President saying he would be pleased to invite Zelensky for a meeting, following his inauguration, in May; and we had not been able to get that meeting; and then the security hold came up, with no explanation.

Holmes says that the Ukrainians are sophisticated enough that when the hold was put in place, and there was no explanation; that they would've drawn that conclusion. Holmes further says that this was the only logical conclusion that he could reach. (Goldman uses the 2+2 = 4 analogy again.)

At this point, that ends Majority leader and his lead counsel's 45-minute questioning segment. They are taking a break, and when they come back, it's Devin Nunez and his counsel, Mr. Castor's turn, for their 45 minutes.

Nunez begins by asking Fiona Hill whether she knows who a number of people are; and has she met with any of them: Alexandra Chalupa, Nellie Orr, Bruce Orr, and Glenn Simpson? Hill says that Bruce Orr had attended some of the meetings that she was at, when she was the national intelligence officer for Russia.

Castor then asks Hill, how about Glenn Simpson? (no) Next, he asks Hill about Christopher Steele. Hill says that, at one time, Christopher Steele was a partner with her in some shared position; that Christopher Steele had retired from the British intelligence services in 2009.

Hill had stated in her deposition that she had seen the Steele Dossiers before they became publicly released; that she was shown them by a colleague, at the Brookings Institution. She tells us that it was the President of the Brookings institution, a Mr. Talbert; he had been sent a copy of it, and he showed it to Hill; this was the day before it was published.

Castor quotes that Fiona Hill had said that the dossier was a "rabbit hole." Nunez asks if she knows who hired Steele to do the investigation, and write the dossiers? -and Hill accurately says GPS fusion. {it's interesting that Fiona Hill seems to take for granted what the Republicans in the committee had told her; that the money to fund the Steele Dossier research was paid by the Democratic National Committee; and Nunez tries to get her to agree that it was the Clinton campaign who had actually funded it.}

Hill says, I don't know for sure... {but I suppose she hasn't read the same articles that I have, explaining that it was actually a group of Republicans who funded it, and who had the idea in the first place, to have these investigations performed on Trump.}

Nunez now yields to Castor. We find out that Hills last day was July 19th; so, she wasn't involved at the time of the July 25th call, or afterward. Castor is asking Hill about why it is, that she wasn't in favor of that July 25th call between the Presidents being made; and why Bolton also was not in favor of that call being made, as Hill contends; and she explains that, a call such as this, should be a well-prepared call, that discusses a range of issues that are of a bilateral nature and of mutual interest; and this preparation had not been done; and I suppose they also knew that Trump was very unsophisticated; so this probably could not go well.

Hill says that she learned about the security assistance hold on July 18th, (the day before she resigned); {and I guess that tells us a little bit about why she left. Perhaps this was the last straw; that she already knew that the White House meeting was being withheld, and that Giuliani and Sondland were running around pressuring the new Zelensky administration to do something corrupt, as ordered by Trump.}

Interestingly, Hill tells us, that for many months before she left, they were engaged in a full-scale review of foreign aid being given to multiple countries; but let's not forget that Trump has been in office since 2017, and it's quite possible that, in anticipation of pulling off this scheme to coerce the Ukrainian President into publicly pursuing investigations on his political rival, that it would work well to leave open the possibility that security assistance could be part of a quid pro quo, to force this corrupt announcement of investigations. Trump would be covering his tracks, in this respect, if it appeared that he was reviewing multiple countries' foreign aid.

However, as I said before; although a hold, pending a review of this kind might be a good excuse perhaps, to pose as a legitimate reason to withhold aid from a foreign country; the one country that this would not ever apply to; because of the situation with Russia attacking Ukraine; is holding up military aid to Ukraine in fighting this war; so once again, Castor and the Republicans are contending a bullshit reason, for why it might be at all reasonable to have withheld Ukraine military aid; under any circumstances really; because, for the sake of peace and Democracy, we want to be strongly fighting this war against Russia's expansion.

Castor asks Hill about Volker, and apparently, Ambassador Volker became appointed as a Special Envoy for negotiations towards the war in Russia, when Russia attacked the Donbas area, on the Northern border. Hill says that Volker is an extraordinarily accomplished diplomat, and that she's worked with him in many capacities. Previously, he's been the Ambassador to NATO, he's held a number of positions at the State Department; and Hill says she knows him personally.

Castor tries to suggest that Sondland had just kind of been "spinning" a bit, when he told Fiona Hill that the President had put him in charge of Ukraine. He had testified to this originally; but he backtracked in his yesterday's public testimony; again, trying to protect Trump, if not distance himself from complicity with the scheme. Sondland had said yesterday, that maybe I misspoke when I told Fiona Hill that the President had appointed me; suggesting that who was <u>really</u> giving him that responsibility was the Secretary of State, or Mike Pompeo.

Hill says that she remembers Sondland talking about Chief of Staff Mulvaney being someone that he was, at times, getting instructions from. Hill also tells us that there were other people in the room, during the meeting where Sondland said that the President had put him in charge of Ukraine policy.

Castor asks Hill if she considers Volker to be a man of integrity; and that he had always worked in the best interest of the United States (yes).

-When did you first learn of Ambassador Sondland's involvement, and how did you feel about it" (Ambassador Sondland had some perfectly logical involvement in the Ukraine portfolio; we work very closely with the European Union, on matters related to Ukraine. The Ukrainian dialogue with Russia was in a format known as the Minsk process, which was led by the French and the Germans; and Ambassador Volker was trying to find out ways that he could work closely with the French and Germans, to move along resolution of the conflict between Ukraine and Russia; and the European Union, which was the umbrella organization, in terms of funding assistance, was heavily active in offering assistance to the Ukrainian government, as well as military assistance in the conflict. It is perfectly logical that Ambassador Sondland would play some kind of role, as Ambassador to the European Union.)

Castor asks if Hill had any concerns when Sondland had contended that he was playing a major role in Ukraine policy. Hill explains that after Ambassador Yovanovitch was pushed out of her position, this is when Sondland had first approached her; and at that point, Sondland's role seemed to grow larger.

-And at that point, did you express any concerns to him directly? (I did; I asked him quite bluntly, in a meeting we had in June, after the Presidential inauguration when I had seen that he had started to step up to a much more proactive role in Ukraine.) When Hill asked, Sondland had told her that he was now in charge of Ukraine. When she had asked Sondland, "Who put you in charge?" He had said, "The President." (It was surprising when he told me; we had never been told this. Ambassador Bolton then indicated that he thought Ambassador Sondland was now playing a leading role in Ukraine.

Castor's expresses his understanding that Sondland was given a large portfolio... (He had told us that he had been given a very broad portfolio by the President, and his job was to go out and make deals in Europe; I listened to his testimony very carefully yesterday; he said that anything that had to do with the EU itself, and the European Union member states, was within his portfolio.)

Castor stupidly asks Dr. Hill whether, at the time that she left, was she encouraged about the way that things were going between the US and Ukraine?

{Of course she wasn't! -which is probably why she resigned!}

Hill says, one thing that she was upset about was the removal of Ambassador Yovanovitch; and it wasn't just that she was removed; because a President has a right to do that; but it was the circumstances; that she was unjustly maligned repeatedly on television, and in all kinds of exchanges; that was completely unnecessary! -and then Hill was also very upset that there was what she called a "different channel" in operation in Ukraine; and of course, she's referring to Giuliani, Sondland, and Perry; maybe mostly Giuliani and Sondland.

She said that the Giuliani/Sondland channel was domestic and political in nature; as opposed to the regular channel promoting bilateral relations and US foreign-policy to Ukraine, which was the long-standing effort that Fiona Hill was engaged; in and this went severely against the grain, for her, I'm sure; that's undoubtedly why she left!

Castor says did you think, on your last day, that Ukraine policy was moving in the right direction? (I did not.) -Why was that? (Well, I was concerned about two things in particular; one was the removal of Ambassador Yovanovitch. For the record, the President has a perfect right to remove an Ambassador at any time, for any reason; but I was very concerned about the circumstances in which her reputation had been maligned, repeatedly, on television, and in all kinds of ways; and I thought this was completely unnecessary; if the President wanted to remove an Ambassador, which he had done quite frequently, and there were a number of Ambassadors removed who were not political, but career professionals; that was done; but without these kinds of interventions. I wondered what kind of message it was, that was being sent... And secondly, it was very clear, at this point, that there was a different channel now also in operation, in relation to Ukraine; it was one that was domestic and political in nature, that was very different from the channel that I, and my colleagues were focused on; which was on Russian relations, and US foreign policy toward Ukraine... And these traversed at this point.)

-Getting around to Ambassador Yovanovitch's separation from post; did you have any conversations with officials at the State Department about your concerns? (I did) -Who did you relate these concerns to? (Directly to my counterpart, Assistant Secretary Phil Rieger. I also spoke to David Hale, in the context of larger meetings about many other issues. I covered broad portfolio myself, and we would often talk about individual items; and I had private discussions with Deputy Secretary Sullivan; and he, of course, has appeared before Committees here, in the course of his nomination to be Ambassador to Russia; and he has spoken about that himself.)

{Castor goes back to the Javelins, yet again; this is getting quite monotonous, especially since this has nothing to do with these proceedings.}

The Trump administration changed course, from its predecessor, providing lethal defensive assistance to Ukraine; are you in favor of arming Ukraine with javelins? I was not initially in 2015, before I joined the government; and I'm sure many people in the committee have seen that I wrote an opinion piece, with a colleague at the Brookings Institution. I was very worried, at that point in time, that the Ukrainian military was not in a state that it could take on to take on more sophisticated weapons... I thought it was not a sustainable plan, given the overwhelming force that the Russians could exert on the Ukrainians. However, when I came into the government in 2017, and started to interact with my colleagues from the Pentagon, who we had here yesterday, I realized that in fact there had been an awful lot of work done by them on the idea; and I saw that there was a clear and consistent long-term sustainability of the Ukraine military.

{Castor, once again, goes on about the Obama administration didn't provide them; blah, blah, blah...}

{I was thinking a bit more, on this Javelin thing. When the Ukraine/Russia conflict first started up, in 2014, it really wasn't a war; it was a sudden occupation of Crimea, but it was a peaceful occupation of Crimea; and so, if you remember, we learned that in 2011, Obama had voiced objection to providing the Ukrainians with lethal weapons, such as Javelin missiles; because he was reasonably concerned that it would inflame the Russians, and make things spin out of control even more.

That stance became a policy, that stretched through several years of his Presidency; so, when the heat got turned up militarily, it didn't suddenly get turned up, it gradually ramped up, and became more and more of a hot war.

So, it wasn't a situation where Obama should have suddenly realized that lethal weapons needed to be sent right away, to Ukraine; and then again, Obama's whole thing was, let's negotiate instead of having wars; so, I'm sure he was holding off on the military side for that reason too. -But what Hill says, is that there was an initiative within the department, because these Defense Department, and State Department folks are on the front lines more; and they realized that the Javelin antitank missiles had become pretty necessary, in order to keep Russia from advancing further into Ukraine territory; that's what Javelins do best, is keep the tanks from rolling further into the country; and there was a slow turning of the tide, from the position of, let's not provide lethal weapons; to, "We need to stop the Russians from gaining ground; let's provide these Javelins!" -and again, I don't think Trump personally had much to do with this; it was undoubtedly all initiated by the State Department and the Defense Department; and then Trump probably just signed off on it, when asked.}

{While I have been thinking that all this talk about Javelins is quite irrelevant to the matter at hand; actually, now that I think about it, Javelins are relevant in one respect. At some point within these hearings, a Republican Committee member asks whether Ukraine was destitute, and totally out of supplies because of the hold on the security funds; and the official being asked, truthfully said no, that was not the case; and of course, this was to indicate to the public watching, that the hold on the appropriated funds wasn't really hurting anything. -But one point the Republicans have brought up repeatedly, is how essential the Javelin missiles are; and several witnesses have said that Javelins are the only effective defense against Russia rolling tanks further into Ukraine. Yet, when Zelensky asked Trump to sell more Javelins; on that July 25th call; Trump had not said okay to that request; he instead strongly indicated that Zelensky would first have to satisfy Trump's demands regarding the investigations. In other words, even though the Ukrainians were not completely out of money and supplies then, they were purposely being cut off from buying-in any of the most crucial weapons needed to stave off the Russians' further advances into Ukraine territory.}

Nunez asks about whether either Hill or Holmes are familiar with Sergei Lutsenko. Holmes say yes, and that he has met with him. Nunez tells us that Lushenko was a journalist; and then he was in the Ukrainian Parliament; and he asks Holmes if Lushenko is currently in the Parliament.

Holmes replies that, no, he is once again a journalist, at this point. Nunez asks Homes if he is aware that, when Lushenko was a member of Parliament, that he had provided information from Fusion GPS?

Holmes is not aware; but offers he does know that, as a journalist, he has provided information, in the course of his work. Nunez asks if Homes considers the information in the infamous "Black Ledger" to be credible; and Holmes says that it is seen as credible information. Nunez says, Bob Mueller didn't find it credible; at least he didn't necessarily indicate that it was, in his report…

Holmes says he is aware that the Black Ledger was used in other prosecution proceedings, and it was considered credible; proceedings where people like Mike Flynn and the Paul Manafort were sent to prison based on entries in that Black Ledger. {Republicans spin out the stupidest arguments; and they are trying to put them over on top officials with decades of experience, besides their being very enlightened individuals.}

Holmes refutes Nunez's idea that the reason why Lushenko released the Black Ledger, was to hurt the Trump campaign; and Holmes says, no; the reason why he released the Black Ledger; which is the same motivation that he's always expressed; it is to expose corruption in Ukraine.

{Nunez is trying to say that, a part of the reason Lutsenko released the Black Ledger, was to hurt the Trump campaign.} Holmes knows the journalist; and says, "He's not said that to <u>me</u>."

Nunez stupidly asked Holmes whether he thinks it's appropriate to have foreign operatives dig up dirt, on political rivals, in foreign countries… {Why, that's exactly what Trump has been doing! -And these stupid Republicans are trying to pass their effort off as a reasonable argument for why Trump shouldn't be removed from office for this very behavior! Why are they asking the witnesses to tell us how wrong they think that would be?!!!}

{Can these Republicans really even begin to think, that their efforts might be successful, in fooling the public into believing they have any kind of reasonable argument, for why Trump should not be removed from office? -Of course, then again, this Republican Committee probably doesn't really need to offer up much of a defense; they are all banking on the Senate voting to keep Trump in office, no matter what becomes revealed at these hearings. -And the way I figure it, it stands to reason that the only objective of the Democrats who are spearheading this confrontation process, is to begin to get the word out to the public, of how crooked and dirty Trump is; ahead of the November elections. We also can all broadcast all of the immoral, stupid and corrupt things that came out of the mouths of the Republican defenders, over the course of these several months. Hopefully, Democrats can artfully drag this out long enough for the public to see how bad Trump is, for themselves.}

Holmes, of course, answers in the affirmative. Dr. Hill also answers yes, to the same question. At this point, Nunez passes the questioning back to Castor:

-Ambassador Volker had testified that he was very pleased with the size of the delegation, at the inauguration; although the Vice

President was unable to make the trip; and instead it was Secretary Perry, Ambassador Volker, and Ambassador Sondland, in his place. I understand, Dr. Hill, that you were involved with some of the logistics, including the delegation that was put together. (that's correct.) -What can you tell us about the Vice President's role, in attending or not attending? (Well, I know that you have the testimony of Jennifer Williams, who worked in the Vice President's office; I would defer to her, as being much closer to decisions that were made about the Vice President's attendance. I will say, that I and many others, had hoped that the Vice President would be able to attend. What I know, from my perspective, because I was not involved intimately, in discussions with the Vice President and his immediate staff, was that there were some questions about his schedule. The President and the Vice President cannot be out of the country at the same time, and there was some question about Presidential travel in the same timeframe; and there was quite a bit of back-and-forth as to whether it would really be feasible for the Vice President, in that timeframe, to go. I wasn't aware of the extent that Ms. Williams was involved in the discussions.)

-Right; the President was traveling in Japan, and then he was headed to Europe for the D-Day anniversary. The Vice President's office, according to Ms. Williams, provided 4 days, at the end of May, for this trip- May 29th through June 1st; and as it turned out, the Ukrainians decided on May 16th, to schedule the inauguration for 4 days later. By this point in time, the Vice President had been rerouted for a trip to Canada, for the US MCA.

-But you don't have any evidence that the Vice President was asked not to attend, for any other reason... (I personally do not, but I defer to miss Williams.)

-Ms. Williams had testified that she heard it from the Chief of Staff's assistant. Apparently, there was a question whether Prime Minister Ormand had influenced this decision; having been talking to Trump on May 13th, as well.

(The meeting with Ormand was very likely in the middle of the day, around lunchtime...) {This is being asked because they are trying to conjecture whether possibly Ormand's influence was a factor in Trumps decision to call off Pence's visit; but of course, this is just a smoke screen, as we already know now, from interviews with Lev Parnas, that the Ukrainians had been pressured that the Vice President would not come to the inauguration unless they agreed to do the investigations; and they told Lev no, they wouldn't; on May 13th.}

Castor asks Hill whether she thought the size of the delegation was adequate; {he was really just trying to cover up trying to make an excuse for why it might've been okay for the VP to have not showed up} but Hill says back to him, that actually it would have been better if the delegation was smaller; because the US taxpayers would be paying for the travel and accommodations, for whoever was going to be at the inauguration; so it is best if just the President or the Vice President, and maybe a few other key people were to attend.}

Hill continues, (Secretary Perry was a key person to be there, in this case; he has deep knowledge of the energy industry; between that, and his former governorship; and Perry himself is an extraordinarily good advocate of US interests, particularly in energy sphere. One of Ukraine's Achilles' heels, in addition to its military disadvantage with Russia, is in fact, energy. Ukraine remains for now the main transit point for Russian oil and gas to make its way to Europe; and this has been manipulated repeatedly, especially since 2006, by the Russian government. In fact, as you may remember, there was a huge dispute in the Reagan era, between the US and Europe, about whether it made sense for Europe to build pipelines from the Soviet Union to bring oil and gas to the European markets.)

Castor now asks Holmes, what he thinks about the size of the delegation also... Holmes says he thinks it was fine.

Nunez segues into Burisma; he goes back to September 2015 Jeffrey Piatt was the Ambassador to Ukraine; {Holmes knows him} -Is he credible? (yes) -He had called for an investigation into Zlochevsky, the owner of Burisma. Nunez says that Deputy Secretary Kent had concerns, at the time, about Hunter Biden's position appearing as a conflict of interest for the Vice President Joe Biden.

Nunez says that Burisma rooted $3 million into Hunter Biden's accounts, in pay, over the years. {$50,000 a month is what I heard.}

Nunez goes through about 6 contentions asking them both did you know such and such happened? -and they both said no they don't, and I think probably at least half of what he was contending was bullshit, that he was hoping the public was buying, perhaps; but I don't know either.

He goes back into Trump having concern about meddling in the 2016 election by the Ukrainians, {false!} Nunez asks if Hill had ever briefed the President about any of these issues; and she says that she only would have become involved if the President had asked for information; which he didn't; {and we're actually talking about a 2015 timeframe} Hill tells us that Ukraine was not a top foreign policy issue priority, at this time. There were many other issues, from Syria, to Turkey, and others; so, there weren't that frequent briefings on Ukraine; they would mainly take place when there was a scheduled meeting; and there hadn't been too many of those.

Castor stupidly says, there are complications when the child of a US official is involved in Government employment, in terms of "conflict of interest" troubles. Hill says, any family member related to the US President or Vice President, Congress, or the Senate, is open to all sorts of questions about the optics; and perhaps could have undo outside influence, if they take part in any kind of activity that could be misconstrued as being related to the parent, or the family member's work.

{But I'm glad Castor brought this up, because all throughout the rest of this year, hopefully that issue is going to be trumpeted by the Democrats seeking to gain election of Senators, in order to gain a Democratic majority; and also to convince people to vote Trump out of office, because Trump has violated in spades, the idea of nepotism, and conflicts of interest. All of his family members are involved in government, and they have no background, and absolutely no business being in those positions. This is very disadvantageous for the country; and Trump hasn't even a clue of how dangerous, ineffective, and trouble-causing it is, to have totally inexperienced people in these high positions!}

Apparently, at one point, Sondland had contended that he had had coffee with Dr. Hill, on her last day at work; and Hill says that that was fabricated. Hill's lawyer said that that was a fabrication. Hill says, "In my office, we don't have coffee machines; all I could've offered him was a glass of water! -But at one point in 2018, Sondland found out where she was going to be traveling to, in Jackson Hole, Wyoming, and he asked her to meet for coffee. However, this was a full year before Hill had resigned. She remembers that it was a nice coffee; and suggested that he might've conflated those 2 meetings together. -But the meeting that he was referring to, was that he was to come in to meet with our director for the European Union; this was during my last week in the office; and as I was in my office, at the same time, for a brief period before going into another meeting, we agreed to sit down with the director of the European Union. Colonel Vindeman was at this meeting, as well as the assistant that Sondland had brought with him from the State Department; and that meeting wasn't over coffee.

Sondland had indicated in his testimony that, at this point, Hill was upset with him, with Ambassador Bolton, and with the way things are going. Hill had said that that was an outright fabrication; she recalls that she said this at her deposition, and October 14th. Hill says, "Unfortunately, I had a bit of a blowup with Ambassador Sondland, and I had a couple of testy encounters with him. One of those was on June 18th; this is when I actually had said to him, who put you in charge of Ukraine? -and I admit, I was a bit rude; that's when told me it was the President. At this other meeting, as he depicted, I was actually, to be honest, angry with him; but when women show anger, it's not fully appreciated; it is pushed onto emotional issues, or deflected onto other people; but what I was angry about, was that he wasn't coordinating with us. I actually realized, having listened to his deposition, that he was absolutely right; that he wasn't coordinating with us because we weren't doing the same thing he was doing. So, I was upset with him, that he wasn't fully telling us about all the things he was doing; and he had said to me, "-But I'm briefing the President, I'm briefing Chief of Staff Mulvaney, I'm briefing Secretary Pompeo; and I talk to Ambassador Bolton; who else do I have to also deal with?!" We have a robust interagency process that deals with Ukraine; Mr. Holmes, Ambassador Taylor, and several other people; but it struck me, when you put Ambassador of Sondland's emails up on the screen, in these emails, <u>he</u> was being involved in a domestic political errand, and <u>we</u> were being involved national security, and foreign-policy; and those things had just diverged; so he was correct! I had not put my finger on it, at that moment. I was irritated with him because he wasn't fully coordinating; I did say to him, "Ambassador Sondland, I think this is all going to blow up-(and here we are); and after I left my next meeting, our director from the European Union talked to Ambassador Sondland much further, for a full half-hour, to figure out how could we coordinate better after I had left the office?

{This was just a few days before she resigned his feeling was that the national security Council} Hill continues, "Ambassador Sondland had said we were always trying to block him; yet what we were trying to do, was to block (our normal operations) from straying into domestic or personal politics; that was precisely what I was trying to do! So, Ambassador Sondland was not wrong, that he had been given a different remit... At that moment, during yesterday's hearing, I started to realize how those (two objectives) had diverged, and I realized in fact, that I wasn't being fair to Ambassador Sondland; because he was carrying out what he thought he had been instructed to carry out..."}

{Sondland has definitely been talking a good game, throughout these proceedings; you could see how he became a successful businessman; but all of his feigning innocence, yet being a prominent negotiator, right at the center of the mental machinery of this crooked scheme, has led me to come to the pretty-certain conclusion that he was knowingly involved; and purposely pulling some punches, to give the impression that he was not to be bothered or discouraged, by State Department officials or Foreign Service officers, from whatever he had set his sights on arranging and negotiating, throughout the spring and summer months.}

(Back to my Impeachment hearing summary.)

At this point, Nunez takes over and, once again, lays out the Ukrainian 2016 election meddling scenario, and he asserts that

President Trump at that point was convinced that Ukraine had done the meddling, even though Hill repeatedly has stressed that this is a false narrative, and didn't happen. So Nunez finishes laying out his scenario, and he asks, isn't it the President at the end of the day that makes these decisions? -and Hill responds, my point, Mr. Nunez, is that we, at the national Security Council were not told, either by the President directly, or by Ambassador Bolton, that we were to be focused on these issues, as a matter of US foreign policy toward Ukraine; so when you're talking about Ukraine, in 2016, I never personally heard the President say anything specific about 2016 and Ukraine; I understand that he said plenty of things publicly, but I was given a directive on July 10th, by Ambassador Bolton, very clearly to stay out of domestic politics.

At this point, Mr. Castor takes over, and asks if she believes that they had already had discussions about investigations into Ukraine meddling by July 19th? Hill says, we had already had a discussion with Kurt Volker by that point, and it was his assistant Chris Anderson, who had indicated that he had met with Rudy Giuliani. At this point, Ambassador Sondland make comments about meeting with on May 23rd, where they had been instructed to work with Rudy Giuliani. They gave us every impression that they were working with Rudy Giuliani at this point; and Rudy Giuliani was also saying this on the television; and he said subsequently, that he was coordinating with the State Department. So, it is my belief that it was known by then.

Castor then floated this idea that when Trump said, in that meeting on July 10th, for Sondland and Volker to "speak with Rudy," Castor is contending that perhaps Trump had just not wanted to be bothered with this issue, and made an off-the-cuff dismissal, for Sondland and Volker to just talk to Rudy, and leave him out of it.

Hill says she only learned that from that Ambassador Volker's deposition, so, in that particular timeframe, I was not aware. In fact, Gordon Sondland did refer to Rudy Giuliani again; and Mr. Bolton had warned Ambassador Volker not to meet with Rudy Giuliani.

Castor says that Morrison had testified that Dr. Hill had expressed concerns about Alex Vindeman, but Hill says that she never made any remarks about Vindeman's general trustworthiness, and she was surprised when Mr. Morrison had made that assertion, during his deposition. She says, it was a very specific point that was made (about Vindeman), and again, these are personnel issues. I'm not sure that we would want to have our private personnel issues come before the committee; but you've asked me about this, so, I had a couple of very short transition meetings with Mr. Morrison; and again, Mr. Morrison had not been working in our department; he was just taking over the position, which he had only held for 3 months. I had worked as the Senior Director for Europe and Eurasia for more than 2 years, at this point, and I had been working with Colonel Vindeman. In the course of one of the meetings, sometime in the June timeframe, I sat down with Mr. Morrison and John Earth, and we went over the organizational charts, discussing who was staying, and who was leaving after the summer; and we talked about everybody's strengths and weaknesses; (not just Vindeman's). I also asked my staff to give me feedback on anything that I wasn't doing well, as far as they thought; I liked to learn too. I said that I was concerned about the way things were trending, in Ukraine policy; so, Colonel Vindeman is a highly distinguished, decorated military officer. He came over to us from the Chairman's office of the Joint Chiefs of Staff; and we were evaluating him, in terms of his future; and we were evaluating and looking at him in the context of the U.S. Army. I was concerned that if, for example, Colonel Vindeman might decide to leave the military, that perhaps he wasn't well-suited as someone to be much more political. I did not feel that he had the political acumen to deal with something that was straying into domestic politics; not everyone is suited for that; but that did not mean, in any way, that I was questioning his overall judgment, nor was I questioning in any way, his substantive expertise. He is excellent on the issues related to Ukraine, Belarus, Moldova, and Russian defense issues; taking charge of the Russian campaign, thinking through what the Chairman's office in the Pentagon; this was a very specific issue, because by June, we saw that things were diverging, and needed a completely different sensitivity. Some people in my office had worked at the highest levels of advisory positions, and Colonel Vindeman had come from Capitol Hill; and Mr. Morrison had come from Capitol Hill, and he knew politics inside out; and we said that Colonel Vindeman did not; and we were concerned about how he would manage, what was becoming a highly-charged and potentially partisan issue, which there had not been before. (meaning, before a guy like Trump got into office.)

Hill says that in the July 10th meeting, Vindeman was justifiably alarmed when he realized there was this highly-political aspect of the meeting, discussing what we were looking for eventually, with President Zelensky.

Castor then addresses Holmes; he says Ambassador Taylor was engaged in obtaining information for the President, about the European allies' burden sharing in the region, as the decision about aid was (supposedly) being debated. Holmes says after the hold was placed on the security assistance, many people were scrambling to try and understand why; I believe it was Sen. Johnson who had said the President was concerned about burden-sharing, as well; and so we were trying to interpret what was happening; we were looking at the facts, as far as what the European Union had provided, and what we had provided. It was very illuminating; we learned that the United States had provided, in combined civilian and military assistance since 2014, about $3 billion, plus the US had made $3 billion in loan guarantees. The European Union, and Europe had provided $12 billion over the same time period.

Holmes says he thinks that he provided that information to the White House in August, (yet, the hold was not release until a month and a half later). If the concern was that we weren't spending as much as others on supporting Ukraine, then that information showed a different story.

This concludes the 45-minute rounds of questioning, for the Chairman and the Minority leader; so now it goes to five-minute questioning, by the committee members.

Adam Schiff recognizes himself for the first 5 minutes:

Schiff cautions the witnesses, that when the minority is saying, "Are you aware of (one fact or another), that these contentions are not necessarily facts. Schiff says, if you have personal knowledge of what is being alluding to, such as so-and-so has testified such-and-such, this is one thing; but if they are contending that somebody has testified to something that you don't have personal knowledge of that testimony, you shouldn't take it for granted that the contentions are true.

Schiff immediately says that one of these points was that it was contended by the Republicans that VP pence had canceled his trip to Ukraine because of a conflict with a trip in Canada, and Schiff says, that was not the case; that was not Ms. Williams' testimony. Ms. Williams had said, "I asked why VP pence would not be attending, and I was informed that the President had ordered it…"

Schiff then refers to the Republican attacks on Colonel Vindeman, suggesting that he has dual loyalties; that he's not really loyal to America, his loyalty is to Ukraine. He addresses Dr. Hill, I want to ask you, as a fellow immigrant, what you think of those kinds of allegations?

Hill says, I think that's unfortunate, because this is a <u>country</u> of immigrants; everyone here had emigrated to the United States, at some point in their family history, of course; and this is what, for me, really does make America great. This is why I chose to come to America; and I think that it's unfair to castigate anyone here; everyone is either Anglo-American or British-American, or a naturalized citizen; I certainly do not believe that my loyalty is to England! It is to the United States! This is my country, and the country that I serve…

And she indicates her belief that everyone in her office, she feels certain, thinks the same way; and that is deeply unfair for the allegations that Colonel Vindeman suffered.

Schiff asks Hill, you gave testimony that Ambassador Sondland's role was to make deals; I want to ask you about one particular deal, the deal that John Bolton called a "drug deal." Schiff says, when Mr. Goldman was asking you about the July 10th meeting (in fact there are 2 meetings; one in Ambassador Bolton's presence and other one in the wardroom), I got the impression there was more that you wanted to say about that. Would you like to walk us through a little more detail?

The reference that Ambassador Bolton made, was after Hill had returned from the wardroom meeting. Hill says, I know that there have been some discrepancies about the sequence, in the meetings. What happened a little after the first meeting, that Ambassador Bolton had called short; he told me to hold back in the room, as he was escorting out the Ukrainian visitors, along with secretary Perry, and Ambassadors Volker and Sondland; and I guess they wanted to take a quick photograph outside of his office; and I noticed that secretary Perry and others have tweeted out that photo, it was a beautiful sunny day; the picture was of all them standing just outside of Ambassador Bolton's office. So, after the picture, Ambassador Sondland says let's reconvene in the wardroom to discuss a couple of next steps; which, to be honest was a little unusual; we don't normally head into a room in the White House to discuss next steps with foreign delegations; particularly on next steps for setting up a meeting! -And Ambassador Bolton wasn't prepared to do that; which is why he ended it abruptly...

Hill hung back from the wardroom meeting briefly, and Bolton told her to go down there, and find out what was going on, and come right back and report to him. Hill says, as she entered the wardroom, Sondland was in an exchange with Vindeman; and that's the point at which Hill realize that Colonel Vindeman was quite alarmed. Hill then alluded to Sondland's testimony yesterday, that he refutes the idea that there was any yelling or shouting going on in those meetings, and Hill asserts, I never said that; there was no yelling or shouting in the meeting. That's an embellishment that has come up as people have retold the story, probably. The exchange between Vindeman and Sondland, was Sondland saying, well, we have an agreement with the Ukrainians, that they're going to do something for us in order to get this meeting that they wanted.

Hill recounts for us, that in the meeting, were the Ukrainian delegation, Sondland, Volker, Vindeman, and herself. When she first came in, Sondland was saying to Vindeman, I have a deal with Chief of Staff Mulvaney, that there will be a meeting, if the Ukrainians announce these investigations into the 2016 and Burisma.

Hill says that she and Vindeman knew that, since Giuliani was on the TV mentioning Burisma in connection with the Bidens, that when Sondland mentioned the 2016 election and Burisma, they all knew that this meant, opening a political investigation, to cast aspersions on the Bidens.

Vindeman had said back, that this is inappropriate; we are the National Security Council; we can't be involved in this! Hill says she learned from Holmes's testimony today, that Vindeman had in fact, even warned the Ukrainians against getting involved in US domestic politics. so at this point in the meeting, Hill had said, this is an issue that we need to sort out by ourselves, and we should not be talking about this in front of the Ukrainian delegation; and Sondland agreed; and we asked the Ukrainians to move out into the corridor; but that was also pretty awkward; because they shouldn't have been standing around by themselves in the corridor, either!

At this point, Hill says she pushed back at Sondland, saying, I know we have our differences, about whether or not we should have this meeting, and we are also trying to figure out if we shouldn't have it, after the Ukrainian parliamentary elections; which by that point, I think had been set for July 21st; and Hill had said, Ambassador Bolton would like to wait till after that, in order to see whether President Zelensky gets the majority in the parliament; which would enable him to form a cabinet; and then we can move forward…

Ambassador Sondland, at that point, said okay, fair enough; he knew he wasn't going to be able to push this further.

After this meeting, Hill says she went back up to speak with Ambassador Bolton; which is when she got the instruction to go see John Eisenberg, at the NSC counsel's office.

Now it's Nunez's turn first, for his 5 minutes; he yields to Jordan. Jordan goes through this ridiculous long litany of events that have been testified to, trying to ridicule Holmes about why it was that if this phone call, that he had overheard, between Sondland and the President, at the restaurant, was such an extraordinary event; which Holmes has recounted that he told lots of people about; why did Taylor fail to mention this phone call, in his testimony, at the first hearing?

Holmes says, immediately after I got back to the Embassy after this lunch on July 26th, I told my direct supervisor, the Deputy Chief of Mission. I would have told Ambassador Taylor immediately, except that he was on the front lines of the war, that afternoon.

Holmes then went on vacation over the weekend; and the following Tuesday, he was in Ambassador Taylor's office, and he says that he had brought up the phone call with Ambassador Taylor, at that point. Holmes said that the context they discussed the call in, was the main point, being the President doesn't care about Ukraine; and so therefore, they were going to have a tough time convincing President Trump to get on board with anything positive for the new Ukrainian regime; even though they knew that this was an important objective; that it was important for Ukraine to have solid US support, because of the Russian invasion, particularly.

From there, Jordan just goes on this ridiculous rant, trying to browbeat Holmes. I'm not even sure what Jordan's point is, except to try and make a mockery out of the proceedings; but still, it remains most relevant that what Holmes was so surprised about is that he learned that the President doesn't care about Ukraine; and this is a country that he should very much care about, especially in light of them being on the front lines of the whole world's war with Russia, to keep them from exerting military force, in order to try and capture new territory.

Holmes, making ketchup out of a rotten tomato, acknowledges that everybody in the office knew about this phone call, by the time he got back from his vacation; because he had gone back and talked to the chief of Mission about it right away, after the lunch; so when he brought it up again on Tuesday, everybody in the meeting was nodding, because they all knew, as a result of hearing about this phone call, they knew that President Trump wanted the Biden investigation before he would consider allowing the Ukrainians a White House meeting, or lifting the hold on the aid. Jordan's time expires.

Jim Himes is up next. He quotes Dr. Hills earlier testimony, that some of the Republicans keep touting this idea that it was the

Ukrainians, not the Russians, who meddled in the 2016 election. Himes says that regardless of what's true or not true, in terms of who meddled; just the Republicans creating some ambiguity about what happened; is damaging. Himes says that the report that the Republicans have just released during these committee meetings, differs, in material ways, from the (Mueller) report that was based on 17 intelligence agencies in the US, regarding the Russian meddling in our elections.

Himes says, "A day does not go by, in which Devin Nunez does not speak of a Russian hoax; and this is an area in which context is pretty important. Next, Himes quotes one official's recent public statements, "Why did the Democratic National Committee turn down the DHS offer to protect against hacks; it's all a big damn hoax! Why did the DNC refused to turn over the server to the FBI; it's all a big damn scam!

Dr. Hill, do you know who said those things? (I don't) -It was the President of the United States, Donald J Trump! Himes says, tell me if you agree, Dr. Hill, that ambiguity, and attempting to name and shame Democrats, for the Russians' attacks of 2016; that is not in the service of our national security…

Himes says, Dr. Hill, you characterized the idea of Ukraine meddling in the US election in 2016 as a "fictional narrative." Himes asks her if she is aware of any Ukrainian meddling efforts? and Hill says, I brought with me 2 exhibits.

Hill says that during her deposition, she was presented with 2 pieces of information, by the Republicans actually; one was an op-ed that Ukrainian Ambassador Charney wrote in 2016, in the Hill. This was during the Presidential campaign, when President Trump was then the nominee for the Republican Party; and he says Ambassador Charney was then still the Ukrainian Ambassador to the United States; and the op-ed was being critical of President Trump; who was then the nominee for the Republican Party; for making comments about Ukraine, Crimea, and Russia…

Himes interrupts her there, to tell us, the President, at that time, said, "The people of Crimea, from what I've heard, would rather be with Russia, than where they were." so Ambassador Charney is responding to that, in the article…

Hill says, that's correct, he just uses this as a peg, because to be honest, the whole article is actually about Ukraine; and this is classic material for anyone who wants to write an op-ed. It's classic, when writing an op-ed, to pick something somebody else had said, to center the article around; and then proceed to say what you want to say; so, Ambassador Charney talks about Ukraine's position vis-à-vis Russia, and the Russian aggression against Ukraine.

At this point, Himes wants to make sure that the public understands what was being objected to, by the Ambassador writing this article in the Hill. The op-ed had said, even if Trump's comments are purely speculative, and do not reflect a future foreign-policy, they offer appeasement of an aggressor, and support the violation of the sovereign country's territorial integrity; and breach of international law.

Himes says, that's the attack on candidate Trump; does that sound like election interference to you? Hill answers, I would say it's probably not the most advisable thing to do, as an Ambassador; because you never know who is going to win the election. -But I think the 2nd piece that was presented to me; and I want to thank Mr. Castor for making me go back and read it again; because when you asked me the questions about it, I did remember the piece, because Vogel was a very well-known and extremely good journalist, and I remembered reading this back in January 2017, but it had been a long time between that, and October at my deposition; and you gave me a copy, and I went back and read it again; because I think it is actually extraordinarily important; it gets to this issue. Mr. Vogel points out that the Ukrainian government had bet on the wrong horse; they bet on Hillary Clinton winning the election; and so they were trying to curry favor with her campaign; it is quite evident here; and he relates to some Ukrainian officials, like the interior minister, and he names other people, and talks about how they were trying to collect information on Mr. Manafort, and other people as well... However, the crux of the article was that Vogel had said there was little evidence of a top-down effort, by Ukraine. He makes a distinction between the Russian effort, that was directed by Russian President Putin, and all of the country's military and foreign intelligence services; and (comparing this to a bit of bad press in Ukraine), I don't think that those two things are exactly the same.

Hill continues, I also mentioned my deposition of October 14th, that in fact, many officials from many allied countries, including Ukraine, also had bet on the wrong horse; they believed that secretary Clinton was going to win. Then, Mr. Vogel said some pretty disparaging things about President Trump; but I can't blame him for feeling aggrieved (about what he was writing about Trump's perspective).

Then, (after Trump had won the election), when we were setting up our first visits, to 50 countries, including the European Union, we thought it prudent to collect as much as possible about comments that people had said about the President's campaign, when he was a either one of the candidates, or later the nominee for the Republican party; when he was actually running against Hillary Clinton; and I'm sorry to say; and maybe I shouldn't here because it will have consequences; but an awful lot of senior officials, and their governments; including in our government, had said some pretty hurtful things about the President; and I would take offense, if I were the President... The difference here, is that this hasn't had any major impact on his feelings toward those countries; not that I have seen!

But, for the President to say that Ukraine tried to "take me down;" while I I've seen some ill-advised Ukrainian officials; and Ambassador Charney has been removed; the fact is, I could name a host of Ambassadors from Allied countries who Tweeted out, and made public comments about the President, as well; and it did not affect security assistance, or having meetings with them. -If it had, there would be lots of people that he wouldn't have met with!

Himes asks for unanimous consent to enter in a Politico article from December 2016, entitled "Russia accuses Ukraine of sabotaging Trump." It outlines Russian senior officials making allegations that there was Ukrainian interference in the 2016 election. {Himes wants to emphasize how Russia has been at the center of what really is a Ukrainian narrative "hoax!"} Schiff says yes, without objection; and the floor now goes to Mr. Conaway

Conaway yields to Ratcliffe:

Ratcliffe first surprisingly tells us that it was the Republicans, that first identified that Russian hacking was occurring in the 2016 election timeframe, but he also clarified that what the Republicans objected to was the Democrats launching allegations that the Trump campaign was participating in, or complicit with the Russian scheme; and that was something that Bob Mueller could not prove beyond a reasonable doubt; however, the investigation into the Russian meddling did open up of Pandora's box revealing many bad actors; several of which are in prison now because of the investigation that Bob Mueller started, and had to conduct for 2 ½ years; that's how much odious happenings were going on.

But in terms of the allegations that the Trump administration was conspiring with the Russians, the sure seemed to be several pieces of evidence that would give rise to suspicion that this was happening; and we also have to take into account that there were quite a few people who were interviewed by Mueller and his team who lied to them who misled them who denied what later proved to be accurate allegations of what they had done; people were trying to throw Mueller's team off the scent left and right; and just because Mueller couldn't unquestionably established a conspiracy between the Trump campaign and the Russians, it doesn't mean that one did not indeed exist.

Ratcliffe, along with Jordan, and Conaway, Turner, and maybe one or two other Republican Committee members, are just a bunch of heckling idiots, that are just trying to throw a monkey wrench into the machinery here; but at this point, Ratcliffe is heckling Holmes about the fact he can't tell us everything that was said in that phone conversation between Sondland and Trump, on the terrace at the Restaurant; or maybe it's upsetting to Ratcliffe what he doesn't know about the conversation that transpired between Sondland and Trump that he had overheard; I really don't know what these guys are going after. They certainly aren't trying to find out facts, they are just trying to upset the applecart, in any way they can.

Anyway, so Ratcliffe goes on with his mad rant, for couple minutes, and he's asking Holmes what did President Trump say on that call, after Trump had asked about whether Zelensky was going to agree to announce the investigations, and Sondland had said yes, he'll do anything you ask. -But just why Ratcliffe is asking what he said after that, as the conversation turned to Sweden, certainly wouldn't have any bearing on what is being discussed here, would it?

The important point is that Trump asked about the investigations and he got his answer, and he was satisfied; so, he could move on to other topics. Ratcliffe's time finally expires.

{-Boy, is he going to go down in history as a heckling menace! It pains me to realize the fiber of some of (what are yet) our highest Congressional representatives, that they are so ill-willed as to try to heckle and belittle government officials of great integrity; with integrity enough to come before Congress, when they have been ordered not to, by a corrupt President.

I sure as hell hope that the Republicans never become in the majority again in my lifetime. I don't know about you all, but I want them out, as of November; and never to be able to come back in and have majority say in this country again.

Republicanism, as represented by these nasty thugs, is just reprehensible; I hope the memory of this outrageous display will become burned into the minds of our young people, so we will be prevented from allowing the stench of these assholes to permeate Federal chambers, for at least another couple of generations; unless and until they can learn some decency and respect for humanity; not just for themselves as oppressive leaders.}

The floor goes to Ms. Sewell: Sewell says, both of you Holmes and Hill, have witnessed this smear campaign on Marie Yovanovitch; Sewell asks Hill what her experience is, and her knowledge about Yovanovitch's work; and does she consider that it was a smear campaign, the way Marie Yovanovitch was characterized?

Hill says, I have the highest regard for Marie Yovanovitch, in terms of her integrity, and the high standards of the work that she's done, as Ambassador of Ukraine, and during her whole career. I do believe it was a smear campaign against her; and I wanted to say that this is unnecessary; it was (Trump's) decision to have a political Ambassador replaced in Ukraine; that would be perfectly acceptable; it's the right of the President to do that; but why was it necessary to smear her?!

Sewell asks Holmes if he agrees with that? Holmes replies, she's extremely professional, and is respected by Ukrainians; and also by American senior officials, members of this Committee, and Congress. She is extremely dedicated, and hard-working; I did see it as a smear campaign...

Sewell asks, what effect did this have, on the morale of other professionals that you work with in Ukraine? (It was a very confusing time; as I said before, the President has the right to remove an Ambassador for any reason, or no reason at all. But it was not clear to us, why this was happening; or why people weren't standing up for her.

Sewell turns the subject to Dr. Hill's boss, Ambassador Bolton. Did your boss tell you that Giuliani was quote, a hand grenade? (he did, yes) What do you think he meant by his characterization? (What he meant by this, was pretty clear to me; the context of all of the statements that Mr. Giuliani was making publicly, about investigations that he was promoting; the storyline that he was promoting; the narrative, it was going to backfire; and I think it has backfired.)

-Was that narrative also inclusive of falsehoods about Ambassador Yovanovitch? (At that particular juncture, Ambassador Bolton made that comment absolutely because it was in the context of my discussions with him, about what was happening to Marie Yovanovitch.)

-I was struck by your testimony, that receiving hateful calls and being accused of being a source mole, at the White House... Are you a "never-Trumper?" or have you been true to your profession, and remained nonpartisan? (I honestly don't know what the definition of a never-Trumper is, but it's a puzzling term, to apply to a career where a nonpartisan official says, I choose to come into the administration; I could've easily said no, when I was approached...)

-But you didn't sign up, to have hateful calls, and Tweets and threats... Hill says, unfortunately, where we are today, that comes with the territory; you're constantly having to deal with these... As I said in my deposition, this could happen to any single person in this room; you get labeled and slandered, {by Trump, and people in his administration, and the press, and Fox News- they can just take it and run with it}, and it creates a nightmare, just like it did for Ambassador Yovanovitch.

They agree that this should <u>not</u> become the new normal. Hill says that she is more determined to do her work now; because she says, we can't let this stand! I don't think anyone here wants to let this stand! {Well, the Republicans obviously do; they don't care how dirty government gets; we can see that very clearly now!}

Sewell says, I think this is actually what <u>has</u> become the new norm, and its leader, at the top layer is the President; and unfortunately, I'm especially disheartened by his treatment of women, and I think that the fact of the matter is there's a long line of strong talented women, who have been smeared and victimized by this President; and you can either choose to ignore it, or do something about it; and that whether you voted for him, or support him, or not, that doing so is wrong... You could simply just remove someone; you don't have to smear them... she yields back her time, and it goes to Mr. Turner

Turner says he laments the attacks that were made on Ms. Stefanik.

{I haven't heard about this; only about nasty things the President has said, or Fox newscasters, perhaps.} Turner says they are violent, and hateful. Turner contends that Volker did communicate with the President and he said that President did not did not condition either phone call a meeting or for a on Ukrainian investigations. {You see, we keep debunking these ridiculous claims of Presidential innocence, but they keep coming right back and restating them! They should personally have to pay a $1,000 fine every time they repeat an earlier-debunked falsehood; maybe that would clear up this injustice! Just a joke}

Blah, blah, blah, we have a direct statement from the President of Ukraine that he did not feel pressure... {but we've already long-since explained how Zelensky would've been a fool to deny anything that the Trump administration wanted him to say publicly, he knew he was at the mercy of the tyrant Trump. Turner is just, once again, trying to throw everybody off the scent; but of course, we haven't had a dozen or more officials come and each spend a day testifying about their upset over President Trump, and the rogue force of people he was ordering around, in this crooked scheme that they were doing; we wouldn't have

3 separate Congressional Committees, all up in arms about all this, if there was no issue at hand, would we?}

Turner then reads the first statement of the independent investigation report that the Republicans suddenly drummed up in the middle of these hearings, which inescapably must acknowledge that there was Russian meddling with the 2016 elections, right in the opening of the report... However, we know that the Republicans are just trying to play 3 card monte, and say one thing at one moment, and the opposite thing in the next; anything to confuse the public, and throw the scent off of the odious crap that's been going on; but the fact of the matter is when Hill said that the Republicans are trying to go promote this false narrative that it was the Ukrainians and not the Russians that did the meddling, the reason she said this is because within these hearings, several Republicans have said just that. They said President Trump was wanting to look into the Ukrainian meddling, and he was convinced that there was a server in Ukraine that had some evidence of this, and such.

If Trump could even begin to truly acknowledge the reality of the incredibly multifaceted, devastating disinformation campaign the Russians perpetrated on US citizens, in favor of putting him in office; yet he still lost by 3 million votes, I think. Anyway, if he could even begin to fathom that, the crooked dumbbell that he is, he would have easily dismissed any few incidents of malignment made by forces on the other side.

If these Republicans had not contended legitimate concern for Ukrainian meddling, left and right, throughout these hearings, then Dr. Hill wouldn't have to say such things. Even if the Republicans at one moment were trying to say that it was the Ukrainians and not the Russians who meddled in the 2016 election and then they want to turn around and procure this Republican version of the investigation into the 2016 meddling, it's all smoke and mirrors. There is no defense against what Trump did, so they want to try and criticize the process, and try to undercut the credibility of these fine officials, testifying out of their sense of duty, and outrage at this wrongdoing.

So, now Turner nitpicks that Hill had said that Sondland had met with Giuliani, and Turner points out that Sondland said that he had never met with Giuliani and so he's trying to ridicule Hill; but the thing is, that we can't believe Sondland, I think that's pretty well-established; he has flip-flopped on what he is attested to, and he has obviously been protecting himself and trying to keep his job which, he lost anyway after- but even if Sondland had never met, in person, with Giuliani, what difference would there be, whether they met in person, or they had only emailed with each other, or written letters to each other, or merely talked on the phone; it's still a communication process; and Trump had told Sondland to "talk to Rudy," so we know that he needed to get his orders from Rudy; and it doesn't matter if those came in a face-to-face meeting, or through some other communication, right?

Turner tries to make a mockery out of the proceedings again, this time saying, "Do you want to impeach a President because he didn't take a meeting?"

{No Mr. Turner, that is not what this is about; this is about the President of the United States bearing down on the new President of the country that is fighting everyone's fight with Russia; and threatening him that if he doesn't do dirty favors that will help Trump clinch reelection, that he will thwart all their efforts in reasonably fighting the Russian invasion, and Trump would let their country get overrun by Russia; that's what's at stake here! -and yes, that definitely is impeachable; and it should have been removal-able, as well!}

Turner now tries to claim that overhearing Sondland say he'll do anything you ask and he loves your ass, that Holmes had reported to this Committee, Turner says, Mr. Holmes that information had nothing whatsoever to do with the subject matter of any of these hearings... {Are you kidding me?! That was getting it right from the horse's mouth- sorry to cast aspersions on the poor horses- Trump doesn't give a damn about the world; only about getting his!}

Turner contends Sondland's words were merely anecdotal, and extraneous; and he's trying to browbeat Holmes for having made those statements. Incredulously, he thinks that what Holmes has revealed embarrasses Zelensky; but the truth of the matter is that, it is because of Trumps nasty scheme, that it became necessary to expose this fateful conversation; even if in the process it <u>had</u> made Zelensky look weak. (It didn't) -But for those of us who are not Republican lawmakers, we actually see that President Zelensky was being very strong, in resisting Trump and his intricate network of operatives trying to press him into doing these dirty things for Trump.}

Schiff interrupts, "The time of the gentleman has expired."

It now goes to Mr. Carson. Carson refers to the letter that Trump wrote to Zelensky, on May 29th, congratulating him for winning the election. The final sentence said, "I would like to invite you to meet with me at the White House, in Washington DC, as soon as we can find a mutually convenient time." Carson asks, Dr. Hill, was this congratulatory letter drafted consistent with the normal procedures that the NSC uses to send letters to foreign heads of state?

Dr. Hill says, the first part of it was; except for the last paragraph. {She explains later}

Dr. Hill, you also testified that Ambassador Sondland told you that he had dictated that line to the President, and that Mr. Mulvaney had told him to add that to the letter, is that correct? (that's correct) -You had said that you were "nervous about that;" why? (Because at this juncture, it had become quite apparent that the President wasn't very keen on meeting with Mr. Zelensky; for all the reasons that we have been trying to lay out, here today; and once something like that is put in a letter, it raises the expectation of an invitation, coming shortly. {It was disingenuous, they all knew.}

Carson says Giuliani's campaign of lies ultimately led to Yovanovitch's recall, in May... You had also testified that her removal was pretty dispiriting; and a turning point for you...

Hill explains, Ambassador Yovanovitch is a person of great integrity; she is one of our finest Foreign Service officers, and had it been a decision to replace her with a political appointee, that was perfectly within the rights of the President. Sometimes it's even highly-advisable. What was dispiriting was all of the accusations that were being fired at Ambassador Yovanovitch; she was Tweeted about, even by members of the Presidents family! We all firmly believe that Mr. Giuliani and others had decided, for some reason, that Ambassador Yovanovitch was some sort of personal problem for them; and that they had decided to engage in just the kind of things that we've been discussing here; and frankly, she was an easy target, as a woman.

Schiff cautions the witnesses again about (supposed) "fact representations" about what prior witnesses said, or even what you have said; they may not be consistent with the facts. (Schiff gives this example:) This is from Ambassador Sondland's opening statement: After the Zelensky meeting, I also met with Zelensky's senior aide, Andre Yermak. I don't recall the specifics of our conversation, but I believe the issue of investigations was probably a part of the agenda, at that meeting…

Schiff now recognizes Dr. Wenstrup; who goes into another whirlwind of verbiage. In the middle of his diatribe, he suggests that, oh yes, us Republicans "Knew that the Russians did make an effort to meddle in our elections; but that they had been doing this ever since the Soviet Union."

He's trying to make it seem as though Russia was just engaging in their normal manner that they always try to interfere with the US; but no; what Russia did in 2016 was prolific! it was a far-more-rampant, and highly concentrated effort than we've ever seen; and it was successful in electing a President who has since, coincidentally, thrown every advantage to Russia; and whom the President himself said at a Worldwide press conference, that he trusted Putin's word, over the word of his country's intelligence agencies. Whatever else Trump is, he's an idiot; or even worse, he's a puppet of Putin.

Wenstrup, once again, takes us to this to this Alexandra Chalupa topic; who is a Democratic National Committee operative; Republicans really want her to come and testify at these hearings. -But whether there was some Trump-bashing going on, on the Democratic side, or not, this has nothing to do with what the President has done here, which is a full-scale corrupt effort.

Wenstrup rhetorically asks, was it good for America to claim that Trump had conspired with Russia, or colluded with Russia, when he had not? But you see, the Republicans claiming that he has not conspired with Russia, this is just engaging in the same strategy, as the Democrats, having claimed that Trump had conspired with Russia. We start with a claim, without anything else to back it up.

On the Republican side, there's very little to back up the claim that he did not conspire at all with Russia, simply because we know that there were several meetings and phone calls, and other communications between people in the Trump campaign and Russia. Why, just the fact that Paul Manafort was the campaign Chairman, who we know was very dialed into Russian organized crime, and a major operative conducting political smears directed by Russia; this is what Paul Manafort was best at; at least, I think that's what I heard, in a recent documentary.

On the other hand, the claim that Trump <u>was</u> colluding with Russia, that did receive some news sensationalism, there at least was <u>some</u> evidence, and there might even be a strong possibility that collusion and conspiracy actually had occurred; and in the light that US Government officials had become well-aware of this suggestive evidence, it certainly constituted good reason to investigate, because this is a grave violation of US Democracy, and the fundamental principles that our country is supposed to operate based upon!

Wenstrup boringly goes to the whistleblower again… Well, there actually is one thing that he says, that probably has some truth to it; which is that "coups create division."

Trump's regime is definitely a coup! And we definitely have us a heap of division in this country right now! –And Trump has probably sowed most of it! He is going to be the sorriest political figure that ever walked the earth; well, maybe except for Hitler.

Dr. Hill wants to respond to this diatribe. She basically says that we are here as fact witnesses, merely to tell what we know and what we have heard; and she takes a rather charitable posture after this, accenting that we do need to come together as a country, so that we can move forward with our Democracy; I think she is a bit naïve, to think that we are still operating in what could be corrected, as a political system gone mildly awry. It is very evident to me that this country has been taken over by thugs; a thug in the white house, and a whole group of Republican thugs; some speaking out at these hearings.

The floor goes to Ms. Speier:

Speier recounts a story about Dr. Hill when she was a little girl, that at school, somebody lit her hair on fire! -And she simply put it out and kept going, on her merry way; which was pretty indicative of her tenacity, and her ability to keep plodding ahead, even when the going gets tough. Speier calls Hill "Steely."

Speier talks about the systematic character assassination that Marie Yovanovitch suffered. This smear campaign had actually started in 2018. Speier brings up that Hill said in her deposition, that besides being disappointed in the publications that were printing smears on Marie Yovanovitch's character, the constant drumbeat of these accusations that Giuliani was making on the television were also very disturbing to Hill. Speier points out that Giuliani had no standing, as a government representative; yet, he frequently met with top Ukrainian officials throughout the year. Hill characterized Giuliani's efforts as "a massive complication, in terms of our engagement with Ukraine."

Speier asked her to explain. "We were actually conducting, what the American people might find, a boring standard bilateral policy toward Ukraine, pushing them on issues of performing in the energy sector, more broadly. We were concerned about corruption in Ukraine; and we tried to help Ukraine protect its sovereignty against Russian aggression.

-How did Mr. Giuliani's affect this activity? "We had worked out, over the course of two years, in close connection with the Embassy in Kyiv, and the interagency agreed-upon "action plan;" and these were things that Colonel Vindeman and others were working on. We were basically moving forward on various issues; {we had a drawn up} list of items. Rudy Giuliani and the {other rogue actors} didn't care at all about this. Ambassador Sondland wasn't interested in {the department's work) either; it was quite boring; it wouldn't make for good copy in the press; it was the kind of thing that everybody, in a routine, found useful.

Speier says to Holmes, <u>you</u> know the incredible power that Russia wields against Ukraine; and we know that the White House meeting for President Zelensky has still not yet happened; doesn't that make Ukraine look weaker, in this conflict with Russia? (absolutely). -Putin's false claim of Ukraine intervention into the election also benefits Russia, doesn't it? (yes) -So, when President Trump meets privately with Vladimir Putin, at the G 20 summit, who does that benefit?

Holmes says, "It doesn't help Ukraine…" -And by President Trump calling Ukraine corrupt, and not North Korea, for instance, does that accrue to Russia's benefit? {She means that Trump makes friends with Kim Jong-Un, and brushes off overtures from Ukraine leadership.} -Again, it doesn't help Ukraine…

Speier yields back, and the floor goes to Mr. Stewart. He goes into a rant about 2 ½ years of the Democrats trying to go after Trump, {but we know that there has been good reason for them to have been confronting Trump, as he had been doing dirty things, since the early days of his campaign, and throughout his Presidency.} Stewart says that we've gone through 7 weeks of hearings; that's interesting, it doesn't seem like it's been that long; but I guess they started with closed-door depositions, and that was probably about half of this overall time, of seven weeks; whereas, all that the public generally heard, were news reports about what was publicly released, of their depositions.

Stewart thinks it's ridiculous to impeach and remove a President for this, {but if the President can't be impeached, or supposedly shouldn't be impeached, for doing all of the subversive, crooked things that threatened our own security and weakened our worldwide fight against Russia; I should point out that, had Congress not found out about this scheme, in the nick of time, Trump would have undoubtedly been successful in forcing the first non-corrupt President of Ukraine, to begin engaging in corruption, as one of his first acts as President; countering the United States' long-standing practice of discouraging other countries from engaging in corruption. If you think about it, corruption is the worst part, of the worst governments. It allows oppression and other atrocities to be carried out by government; and this is what we have spent the last 100 years fighting against; so if we now have a President who casts all of that aside, and instead promotes corruption; and he routinely engages in corruption, and forces other countries' leaders to engage in corruption, isn't that the very definition of why impeachment was created, as part of our constitutional mandate?!

Stewart says that there is zero evidence against President Trump, {but if that were true, then how could we possibly have, as he recounts, hundreds of hours of related testimony by government officials? Is he saying that government officials are just full of it; the whole pack of them? Who else is going to protect the interests of the US, and our long-standing ideals, goals, and objectives; and the United States' working relationships with and it's working with other foreign countries?

Stewart contends that all of the Democratic committee members who have said that they are saddened to have to impeach a President, that they are really, instead giddy about this idea; and that all of the American people know this to be true. {Once again, we can see that the Democrats in this situation are going forward with what the Constitution charges them to confront, in a crooked President; and although many of us would be ecstatic if Trump could actually become removed in the coming weeks, one big problem is that the whole country doesn't feel this way, and instead there is something like 40% of voters who are buying the right-wing media contentions, and taking seriously the false and misleading tweets that the President has put forth; knowing full well that he has a uniquely-effective bully pulpit, to be able to perpetrate such lies and twisted truths; and yet, a reasonable percentage of Americans will falsely believe what he saying.

Stewart calls the intelligence committee hearings "the warm-up band;" {that they are somehow insignificant, in what they do, and in what they what their performance has been; compared to the Senate, that we are just about to have this matter go into their hands, at this point; but {by a few later} we sure know what happened, once the ball got into the Senate's court, their performance was anything but honest, or marked by any significant degree of integrity; well, except for the true story that the impeachment managers, Adam Schiff, and Zoe Lofgren particularly, among a few others; the true stories that they told about what had come out of all this testimony; and it was a very damning picture; yet the Republicans Senators stood in solidarity against all reasonable ideology, and acquitted a crooked, corrupt President; merely so that these Republican lawmakers could keep raping the country with their unilateral decisions and actions, as they have been, at very least, financially speaking.}

Stewart goes through the usual litany about the whistleblower, and Hunter Biden, and etc. etc. Alexandria Chalupa, the Steele dossier; and course none of these things have anything to do with the crooked scheme.

Anyway, so Stewart yields back, and the floor goes to Mr. Quigley:

He recounts Hill's testimony, that Bolton had directed her to "Go and tell Eisenberg that I am not part of any drug deal that Sondland and Mulvaney are cooking up on this... You go and tell him what you've heard, and what I said..."

Quigley reads a quote from Hill's testimony of what John Bolton had told her at this July 10th meeting, after he had abruptly ended it. {I thought it would be good to mention again, that John Eisenberg is chief lawyer for the National Security Council when she first went to Eisenberg on July 10 after that wardroom meeting Eisenberg.}

Quigley asks Dr. Hill to tell us about that interchange with Eisenberg. Hill replies that she didn't have a lot of time {at that moment}, so she gave him the quick-and-dirty version of what had transpired in the meeting, and made an appointment for her to come back the next day, and illuminate more about the situation. Hill says, "I also wanted to bring with me my colleague Senior Director for Energy, Will Schofield, who had been sitting with me on the sofa, during the first portion of the July 10th meeting. I also suggested that he speak to Colonel Vindeman separately, because Colonel Vindeman was in the room when I arrived {at the Wardroom follow-up meeting}, and had obviously been engaged in a discussion beforehand.

Dr. Hill says that when she talked with Eisenberg, that he had taken this all very seriously; {as well he should; this is very irregular meeting activity for a White House meeting.} -Who was at this second meeting? Hill answers, "Mr. Doniluk, Mr. Yermak and his aide, Ambassador Volker, Ambassador Sondland, and a couple of people from the State Department. I wondered for a while, if one of Secretary Perry's group had been there too; but I honestly can't remember. Ambassador Volker didn't speak much during the meeting but he was there Ambassador

Sondland was doing most of the speaking. Ambassador Sondland had said that he had an agreement with Mr. Mulvaney, that the White House meeting would go forward if the Ukrainians were going forward with the investigations."

Quigley asks Hill how the Ukrainians in the meeting reacted to Sondland's bringing up the necessity of their announcement of investigations, in order for a White House meeting to occur; and Hill says that they were pretty and passive at that meeting. She said that in the meeting with Ambassador Bolton, the first meeting on July 10th, Andre Yermak's aide was, at points, whispering to Mr. Yermack, a number of times during that meeting. Hill says, of course I'm not sure if he wasn't just translating, because I'm not sure how good Yermak's English is...

Hill further says, that Mr. Doniluk, whom she knows speaks English quite well, had looked very alarmed, at hearing Sondland say they needed to perform some troubling deed, in order to get a White House meeting; and Mr. Doniluk had seemed most alarmed by the back-and-forth, between Sondland and Vindeman, over the inappropriateness of the arrangement that he and Mulvaney had cooked up. {Actually, Trump was the one that cooked this up, of course.}

Hill says that arguing about the meeting, in front of the Ukrainian delegation, was obviously very uncomfortable for Doniluk.

Quigley yields back, and the floor goes to Ms. Stefanik:

{It's interesting; Ms. Stefanik makes a point that the Republican committee members, who had just suddenly procured this report about the Russian meddling; but she said, that within this Republican Lawmakers' report, they suggest ways of combating against this type of activity in the future. Yet, now that it is three months later, as I write this; a couple weeks into February, we hear on the news that the Trump administration had recently been informed, by US intelligence agencies, that the Russians are, in fact, currently engaging in another disinformation campaign aimed at affecting the 2020 election, in favor of President Trump being reelected; and yet the Trump administration was sitting on this information; and they did not bring any of this to the attention of the public; they kept it under wraps; and somehow some Democrats were able to discover news of what is now happening, once again. I think it's also interesting that the Russian campaign is reportedly aimed at helping Bernie Sanders get the Democratic nomination; perhaps the Russians think that it would be easier for them to run a disinformation campaign and smear Sanders that it would be to attack Biden. I don't know about that; I still would much prefer Bernie Sanders get the nomination. Whoops! A month later, as I make my final edits here, I suppose now that he won't; and I can also understand that it could be risky to bet on Sanders at this moment in history. I think we just have to transition, from way whacky, to Sane and reasonable; and then maybe next election we can elect a President who will actually do what Sanders would have done; like eliminate health insurance profiteering off of American citizens, run a crash campaign to develop clean energy, and eliminate coal mining, drilling for oil and gas, also refining, and also all distribution to gas stations. We need to close them all. We also need to develop a US Government that acts on behalf of the common man; giving everyone protection from being screwed over by the shrewd, uncaring plunderers; these are all things that we have to accomplish, as we near a greater ideal of justice for all. (Don't say it can't be done.)}

Next, Stefanik has the nerve to say that, to have our Democratic colleagues making untruthful statements, just reeks of political desperation, and their continued obsession to manipulate mainstream media coverage..." {Well, if you substitute Republican for Democrat in that last statement, and you substitute mainstream media for Fox News and right-wing media, there you have it again; evidence of the Republicans employing a strategy of accusing the other side, of what only your site is doing!}

Stefanik recounts that Hill had testified that she handed off her duties at the NSC to Tim Morrison on July 15th, physically; but she had actually left the White House on July 19th. So, Stefanik says, well then you were no longer an employee of the White House, as of the July 25th phone call, is that right? -and Hill says, "Well technically, I was on the payroll until the end of August..."

Stefanik brings up the Javelins once again. Next, she is trying to suggest that the Trump administration was merely waiting to see if Zelensky could implement reforms in the country; in light of their government's long-standing problem with corruption; before a White House meeting of support might occur. {But the truth is, that we have been providing full support for Ukraine, even when they were very much a corrupt government, under President Poroshenko Zelensky's predecessor; and this had never stopped the Trump administration from giving full support to Ukraine.}

Stefanik tells us that Trump actually did meet with Zelensky at the UN building recently; {I did not know that; but Holmes points out that Trump had invited Zelensky for an Oval Office meeting, and that meeting has still not yet occurred; not even by now, toward the end of February 2020. We've heard throughout these hearings that an Oval Office meeting with the President of the United States is a very strong show of support for any new foreign leader; and the lack of a show of support, so far, for the new Ukrainian foreign leader, certainly inures to the benefit of Russia.}

She yields back, and it goes to Eric Swalwell:

Swalwell brings up the phone call that Sondland makes, to President Trump, on September 9th, where Sondland had testified that he just asked this very nonspecific question, of what do you want with Ukraine? -And Trump responds, I want no quid pro quo! So, Swalwell jokingly likens this to a guy who has just gotten pulled over for speeding, and the officer asks him, do you know how fast you were going? -And he replies, I did not just come from robbing that bank!

Swalwell just gets it from Hill one more time, her testimony that the reason she went to Eisenberg, was because she saw a link between the White House meeting that the Ukrainians desperately needed, and the quid pro quo, that the Ukrainians must first announce investigations; and establishes that it was as early as July 10th, that the President's lawyers had received word that there was concern about this linkage.

Swalwell says, Dr. Hill, you testified you had evidence that, as recently as this year, President Trump believed he had heard about someone named "Cash…"

Hill says, it's not really evidence; I want to be clear about this; I was asked questions about this in my deposition; to be honest, I was surprised that I was asked the question…

-But you heard that name cash? Hill says, yes, I heard it in passing, and I explained the circumstances under which this had come up; but I was asked the question in my deposition about this… the only person by the name of Cash, had worked (as Ukraine Director) at the National Security Council; this was Cash Patel;

-And prior to working at the National Security Council, from 2017 to 2018, he had worked for ranking member Nunez… Hill says, I didn't know that until after my deposition, when I looked him up; I didn't know about his past, before the NSC; that he was connected with Devin Nunez… {but now we all do, of course.}

Swalwell also tells us that, the day before this hearing, there was an article in the Daily Beast, reporting the indicted Ukrainian, Lev Parnas, has been working with ranking member Devin Nunez, on Mr. Nunez's overseas investigations. "Lev Parnas Helped Devin Nunez With His Investigations," was the headline of the article; and Swalwell asks that it be entered into the record.

Swalwell cites a second article, entitled, "Lev Parnas, an Indicted Associate of Rudy Giuliani, Helped Arrange Meetings and Calls in Europe, That Helped Rep Devin Nunez in 2018." Parnas's lawyer, Ed McMahon, also told the Daily Beast that Nunez's aide, Derek Harvey, had participated in the meetings, which were arranged to help Nunez's investigative work.

Swalwell points out that Devin Nunez has been accusing Adam Schiff of being a "fact witness," as Republican Committee members had made repeated accusations that Schiff had met with the whistleblower, or knows the whistleblower; but Swalwell suggests that Nunez was perhaps just projecting; and it was Nunez himself, who was subversively working, even with indicted individuals, surrounding this Committee's investigation! {There sure are some dirty dealings in this Republican party, at present.}

{As and aside, I wondered why people kept using this term "hot war," and I just realized that the reason is because, I just heard Holmes use a term that is the alternate to a hot war; that is a "frozen conflict," interesting.

Holmes closes by bringing up how Mr. Turner had suggested earlier that it had somehow cast embarrassment on President Zelensky, for Holmes to talk about this phone call, between Sondland and the President, at the restaurant.

Holmes says, "I have the deepest respect for President Zelensky; this is a guy, of Jewish background, from a post-Soviet industrial suburb, in Southern Ukraine, who made himself one of the most popular entertainers in the country; and somehow got elected President; and he is not to miss that opportunity. This is a Ukrainian patriot; this is a tough guy, and frankly, he went withstood of a lot of pressure, for a long time; and he did not give that interview, with CNN. I have the deepest respect for him; and the Ukrainian people have the deepest respect for him, and have chosen him, to help deliver the full measure of promise, of their Revolution of Dignity; and I think that merits all of our respect."

Swalwell yields back, and the floor goes to Mr. Hurd:

Hurd says, we are here because of 2 statements made during the July 25 phone call to the Ukrainian President Zelensky; do us a favor though, in reference to the 2016 presidential election; and he mentioned the word "Biden." Those statements were inappropriate, and misguided foreign-policy; and it is certainly not how the executive, current or future, should handle such a call. Over the course of these hearings, the American people have learned about the series of events that, in my view, undermine our National security, and undercut Ukraine; a key partner on the front lines against Russian aggression.

We've heard US officials giving uncoordinated, confusing messages, that created doubt of certainty, at the time when a new, reformist administration had just taken office, and was ready to fight corruption, and work with us to advance the US agendas.

I disagree with this sort of bumbling foreign-policy; but through these hearings, many of my colleagues have unwittingly undermined Ukraine government, by suggesting that it is subservient to the United States; and without the United States, they would not be able to function. Ukraine is in a hot war with Russia, and they are holding their own. {Hurd is absurdly suggesting that Democrats have hurt Ukraine's feelings, in asserting, during public hearings, that they need someone besides themselves, to fend off the vicious Russian attacks.}

We could benefit from the experience of the Ukrainians; not the other way around. {I think Hurd is turned around!}

We are here, talking about one of the most serious constitutional duties we have, as members of Congress; impeachment and removal of the President of the United States. After weeks, we've learned a few things; committee members have many different opinions on whether the call was concerning, or not; and just because Vice President Biden is running for President, does not mean that Burisma, and his ties to it, are not concerning.

We haven't heard from Rudy Giuliani, and we haven't heard from Hunter Biden {but again, this has nothing to do with what Trump did; which is what these hearings are supposed to be about, right?}

Hurd brings up wanting to question the whistleblower, for the umpteenth time; {I wonder, has there ever been a case where an informing whistleblower, being a CIA agent, or some other member of a US intelligence agency, coming forward in the proper channels and making a whistleblower report, that then goes to the Inspector General; has there ever been an instance where having that whistleblower further interrogated, by those whom he has reported their evident wrongdoing; Has whistleblower interrogation ever been necessary, as a basis for legitimizing the complaint? I heard that the Inspector General spends a few days determining if the complaint appears credible; and I understand that this complaint had passed muster, in this respect; so, I don't know what possible basis the Republican committee members could have, for insisting that the whistleblower be further interrogated. My understanding is that a whistleblower is simply pointing something out which needs to be investigated, and it is the investigation subsequently moved-forward-with, is what bears scrutinizing; not the whistleblower himself.}

Hurd calls this a very partisan process; {but if it if he thinks this is partisan, wait till we get to the Senate, where all of these strong arguments are put forth, as to what was terribly wrong with the plans and strategies that President Trump and these bad actors he surrounded himself with, had cooked up, and went forward with executing; and yet the Republican Senators, in solidarity, all voted to acquit President Trump; now that's partisanship of the dirtiest, rottenest kind!

That is a partisan power-play stronger than anything I can ever remember; a very unjust partisan power-play, at that!

Hurd yields back, and the floor now goes to Mr. Castro: {This is Julian Castro, who was a presidential candidate, until a couple of months ago.} Castro says that he had been running for President because what had happened was vile, irresponsible, and dangerous; {I would wholeheartedly agree!}

Castro continues, we have now heard and seen substantial evidence that, in fact, the President tried to trade a political favor, for official government resources. The most damning words come from no one else, but the President himself; on that phone call with the Ukrainian President; where he asked for a favor, and mentioned investigations; and then he mentions the Bidens and Burisma. However, as Mr. Holmes has testified, Mr. Holmes also overheard the President speaking to his hand-picked ambassador, Ambassador Sondland, about investigations. Mr. Holmes has also said that, in the office, everybody knew; at least, that it was in the President, who wanted the investigation of the Bidens. In addition, although Mick Mulvaney and Rudy Giuliani have not come before this committee, they have spoken publicly, on the issue of investigations. Mick Mulvaney, the President's Chief of Staff; the person who usually works with the President most; day in, and day out; went in front of the news cameras, and basically admitted that an investigation had something to do with holding up of the financial aid; and that this process was politicized. Rudy Giuliani, the President's personal lawyer, also essentially admitted that these investigations were at issue; he also said that he thinks he's done nothing wrong, because he was working at the direction of the President. So, we have seen and heard, substantial evidence of wrongdoing, by the President of the United States. This Congress will have to continue to take note of these very important issues, to the people. My concern today, is that I also feel as though the cancer of wrongdoing may have spread beyond the President; and into others of the executive branch; and I want to ask you (Dr. Hill, and Mr. Holmes) a few questions about that; but before I do, I would like to enter two articles into the record; one entitled, "After boost by Perry, Backers Got Huge Gas Deal in Ukraine." The other headline was from a Wall Street Journal article, "Federal prosecutors Probe Giuliani's Links to Ukrainian Energy Products."

Castro continues, Mr. Holmes, you indicated that, when Secretary Perry went to Ukraine, he had private meetings with Ukrainians; and before he had those private meetings, he had a meeting with {he had a talk with Zelensky) and others, including yourself; where he presented a list of American {Energy companies who were to be used by Zelensky as} advisers, for the Ukraine energy sector... Do you know who was on that list?

Holmes answers, sir, I didn't see the names on the list myself..."

-Do you know if Alex Greenberg and Michael Glaser were on that list? Holmes says, I have since heard that Michael Glaser's on the list.

-Before Secretary Perry did this, we also heard testimony before, that Ambassador Sondland had also had a private meeting {with Andre Yermak; Holmes told us that Sondland told Yermak's assistant not to let anyone else in.} -How unusual is it, for US Government officials, to have private meetings where they insist that nobody else be included?

Holmes says, it's very rare; almost never.

-You have said you are here, as a fact witness; but you're also here, in the service of this country; and it is a precedent that this Congress will set. Putting aside President Trump personally; if the Congress allows a President of the United States, now or later, to ask a foreign government to investigate his political rival, what precedent does that set, for American diplomacy? -and for the safety of Americans overseas? -and for the future of our country?

Holmes says, <u>that</u> would be a very bad precedent, if that was ever the case, going forward; I would raise objections... Dr. Hill says, that is a very bad precedent.

Thank you both. Castro yields back, and the floor goes to Mr. Ratcliffe:

Mr. Ratcliffe yields to Mr. Conaway:

Conaway says, the Russians' objectives are to foment unrest within the nation; to cause us to have a loss in the confidence of our elections... This issue is very divisive... {but of course, it is not intended to be divisive; it is merely intended to be informative. It is only divisive, to the extent that there are many of us in this country who unfortunately are buying a lot of the lies and doubletalk, from Republican politicians who are trying to say that this was no big deal; and yes, that causes some division, to have some people hanging onto that false notion, and to have many others who are watching these hearings, or following major news coverage of what is truly going on; who are realizing that there is a very significant violation that happened here; and it is going to be hard to reconcile one with the other; especially when Republican Senators, in solidarity, intend to let nothing stop them, in their path to acquit this crooked President. This does not help the country in terms of divisiveness. However, there would be a great relief of divisiveness, if the Republican Senators were to simply admit the truth; that went Trump and his pals did is very wrong, and was very damaging; and it sets a very bad precedent for the future, if Presidents can get away with this kind of autocratic behavior in the United States, like unfortunately happens in many other countries around the world.}

Conaway expresses great concern, that if we did away with fracking, we would not be the premier resource for oil and gas in the world; {but, of course, this would only be bad for those making money off gas and oil extraction, and sales. If, for example, we all were to drive cars that run on electricity, the American public would be getting their transportation needs met, and we wouldn't miss oil at all, right?}

Now Conaway is referring to the US media station, "RT" that shows Russian propaganda; and I suppose this is why he was talking about fracking. Dr. Hill, at this point, tells us that in 2011, she was at some kind of a summit meeting sitting next to Putin, and this was the first time she heard, that if the United States stepped up their fracking operations, this would be a harmful competition to Russia, whose only major resource is oil and gas; they wouldn't want to have their sales significantly diminished by the US is fracking operations, especially given the US has a great deal of natural gas and oil to be tapped into. {Of course, we should not be tapping into oil and gas. Ideally, we should just leave it there!}

In another browbeating tactic, Conaway suggests that it was inappropriate for Holmes to have told a number of people about this conversation between Sondland and the President, at the restaurant. {Conaway's alluding to this, totally dismisses how outlandish it is, that we have a President who doesn't care about, as important of a country as Ukraine is, to every other country in the world right now; that might have to worry about Russia expanding to capture their territory as well; Trump wants to make non-corrupt leaders corrupt, and his biggest concern of the moment is some "rapper" that got arrested and in another country. That is truly so embarrassing, as Conaway says; but it is not Mr. Holmes' fault, the way I see it, if such an outlandish scenario exists that probably anybody privy to that phone call between Sondland and the President at that restaurant, would be blabbing that to everybody they knew!

Holmes responds, "Sir, I think it was Gordon Sondland, who showed indiscretion, by having that conversation... so, Holmes only gets to say half of his answer, before being obnoxiously bullied through and cut off by the crass, nasty Conaway. Of <u>course</u>, Sondland was the one showing indiscretion by having that conversation in public in a restaurant; I mean, Sondland did choose to place that call, he could've done it later; but actually, it's a very good thing that he did it in front of a foreign service officer who, unlike Sondland, had some integrity; because otherwise we might still have been missing a key first-hand eyewitness of the President's corrupt motives, and solid verification that it was the President, who was running this scheme. {Even though the crooked Republican Senators will acquit Trump, the American people will have a much clearer picture of what not to vote for, in the 2020 election!}

Even though Conaway tries his best to disallow him to answer his obnoxiousness, Holmes does manage to get in edgewise, that he only informed the people who did need to know; and he had also explained earlier, that the people that he worked directly with in his department did really need to know, because this would help them to face the real problem; which was what could they do to bring Trump on board with support for Ukraine; to get Trump to meet with Zelensky in the Oval Office? Due to Holmes's new information, it had become suddenly very clear to all of them; to Taylor, to Holmes, to all of the people in their office, working on this problem of getting the two Presidents together; but now they unmistakably knew, that the President was holding Zelensky over a barrel, to make these announcements of investigations, before he would do anything further, as far as supporting Zelensky and Ukraine's objectives; at least, now they knew what they were dealing with; where there might have been some doubt, before.}

Holmes adds that he would hate to think that what he brought before the committee, having become subpoenaed to appear, that anyone would consider that he shouldn't have disclosed about such a call. He says, I was subpoenaed to share what I know, and what I've done. {Conaway is so freaking obnoxious; he interrupts Holmes before he can answer Conaway's ridiculous rant; and then he refuses to obey the chair who is only trying to enforce the standards that are written about this resolution 660; the way that impeachment hearings are supposed to go. The committee members are not supposed to interrupt or prevent the witnesses from answering; and here Conaway is stupidly thinking that Adam Schiff was out of line, in trying to discourage the inappropriate behavior of a rogue committee member; he doesn't even have a clue of what a jerk he is! Maybe I <u>would</u> say, that this committee member should be ashamed of himself, but I know these Republican hecklers, as such poor excuses for United States lawmakers, they <u>have</u> no shame.

Schiff says, we allow those asked the question to answer; even if those who asked the question, don't want to hear the answer...

Conaway's time has expired, it now goes to Mr. Heck:

Heck wants to talk about regular, and irregular foreign service channels; and he says, in my experience, (other) Presidents have used regular and irregular channels... (Holmes agrees) -And generally speaking, provided those channels were closely coordinated; and as long as both, the regular and the irregular channel, would be furthering the

US foreign policy, toward that country, and also our National security interests, {this would be above board.} (Holmes agrees)

Heck asks him, do you believe that Mr. Giuliani's efforts were closely coordinated with the regular channel? (no, they were not) -Were they in furtherance of American foreign policy, as you understood it? (No, Sir) he asks Holmes, "If Russia were unchecked, do you think that they would subjugate Ukraine, and attempt to render it a client state, if not occupy it?"

Holmes says, absolutely Sir; it has been said, that without Ukraine, Russia is just a country but with Ukraine, it's an empire.

Heck reminds us, that if someone tells a lie, over, and over again, enough times, people begin to believe it. He reads an example: "The President didn't solicit assistance from Ukraine, in a clear violation of federal law…" Heck says, yes he did! "The President didn't withhold vital military assistance, in furtherance of its objective to obtain campaign assistance…" Heck again says, yes he did! "Rudy Giuliani was just working independently, on his own…" -No he wasn't!

"All this is business as usual; it happens all the time…" No it doesn't!

"It's okay to attack patriotic diplomats in public service, if they stand in your way, and have the courage to speak out…" no it isn't! -And those are just some of the big lies; but here's the big truth: the President <u>did</u> it; he <u>did</u> it! heck says, it was an auspicious idea, the idea of our democracy; this notion of democracy, self-governance, of freedoms, of speech, and of press, and of religion, of expression, and of assembly. Most of all, that we rooted this in the premise of the "rule of law."

-Not monarchs, not military strongmen, but the rule of law. Others helped <u>us</u> to get here; and we wouldn't be here without them. {Heck explains that, without the allied assistance of the French, we may not have won the Revolutionary war, and gained our independence; Ukraine needs <u>us</u> at this moment}

Heck continues, frankly, I feel like we are almost in a little bit of a "pay it forward" moment; so, when the President <u>did</u> it, it could have risked the security of Ukraine; a strategic ally, and a nascent Democracy; with their masses yearning to breathe free. Six years ago, this day, were working to sign that memorandum of agreement with the European Union; they rose up and took to the streets, because they frankly wanted what we have… -And when the President <u>did</u> it, he put our own national security at risk; but what he did, most importantly, was put at risk that idea that makes us exceptional; as I do believe that America is truly exceptional; a country rooted in something that nobody has ever tried before; the rule of law. He put <u>that</u> at risk, when he did what he did. The President <u>did</u> it; and the only question that remains, is what will we do?

Heck yields back, and the floor goes to Mr. Jordan once again, unfortunately.

Putin in Russia weaponized our own political opposition research in 2016; that's exactly what happened, Jordan tells us, but his version is that the DNC hired fusion GPS, who hired Christopher Steele, who gave the Russians a bunch of dirt that he had compiled in a dossier, and {Democrats} used it as part of their investigation that they opened in July of 2016… {but Jordan has it backwards; Christopher Steele did not go over to Russia to provide them with information; Christopher Steele went over to Russia to confirm allegations, that the people who paid him {Republican competitors for the Presidential nomination in 2016} were making about Trump's connections to Russia. These Republicans just twist everything don't they?}

Jordan tells us that the Mueller investigation cost $32 million, and that it involved 19 lawyers, 500 search warrants, and 28 subpoenas. He claims that they came back in the spring and told us that there was no conspiracy, no collusion, no coordination between the Russians and the Trump campaign; {No Mr. Jordan, that's not what the Mueller report told us; it said that they couldn't prove it; they couldn't put their finger on the specific communications, but anybody following what had apparently transpired, over the course of 2016, between the Trump campaign and Russian operatives, would be able to put 2 and 2 together, and realize that there were some crooked arrangements, and coordinated subversive strategies being carried out ; such as the carefully timed release of Hillary's hacked emails; and it was also conveniently to Trump's benefit, everything that Russia was doing; so when they say that Trump was duly elected, that really is a repeated falsehood. Trump was not duly elected; he was elected because people bought Russian disinformation; and even then, he still lost, in terms of the number of votes for him versus Hillary.}

Jordan thinks that the nation is being torn apart by what the Democrats have done. The Russians are doing exactly what they did before; due to those naysayers who have been talking about the impact of a successful 2016 election campaign, it remains evident today, that our nation is being torn apart. {Yes, but our nation is being torn apart not because of Russia; our nation is being torn apart because of Republican lawmakers' crooked initiatives, and their broadcast of lies, plain and simple. They have no integrity; they don't care about the Constitution, and the principles of democracy. They only care about getting theirs; and they don't care about the masses of people who have to suffer, in order for them to get it.}

Jordan goes on, and on; this same nonsense that he has spewed, for weeks now; whistleblower, whistleblower, etc… Jordan thinks is preposterous that, on a Sunday morning TV interview, Nancy Pelosi said that the President is an imposter. {and it is preposterous to have to say; but she said it only because it's true! Trump had represented that he was a self-made man; then we find out, in a 7-page New York Times article about him and his father and his brother, that he was first given a little money, by his father; and he later stole a lot more of his father's money and assets, when his father was very old, and not able to protect himself better. Trump had represented himself as a dealmaker, but we found out that he had, many times, stiffed contractors he had hired for his building projects, and that is one of the ways he has benefitted from the deals he's made. Trump hasn't made a deal with China; just a very troubling and hurtful mess, with his unilateral trade war; he withdrew the US from the Iran deal, that was a worldwide joint effort, which took President Obama many months to put together with a larger group of our allies; he befriended Kim Jong-Un, but was ultimately unable to make any new headway in negotiations on the United States' behalf; he has many times said, that the economy is markedly improved, but if you take away the relaxed banking regulations, that allowed more money to get pumped into the economy, if you take away the oil and gas production, that has indeed added to the economy; but at the expense of global warming being accelerated; if you take away the pollution-related EPA regulations that were rolled back; so that now, companies can dump pollutants into the rivers again; if you take all that away, you've got, not only a lack of any real economic progress; but there is a whole list of hidden and lied-about ills that this country has actually suffered, as a result of President Trump's hoax as a leader. Trump has done nothing positive; at least, I cannot think of a single thing positive that Trump is done; and I can think of a lot of negative things that Trump has done to this country.}

Jordan yields back and the floor now goes to Mr. Welch:

Welch says that he wants to use his time to make a statement, to his Republican colleagues, and to the American people:

Today's witnesses, and the ones we've been privileged to have, over the last 2 weeks, have provided an invaluable service to our country; not just in all of your professional careers, but in your having the courage, and the patriotism, to share your {disclosures of apparent wrongdoing} with the American people; and you do so at considerable risk to yourselves, when you clearly step forward, for the simple fact that believe it's your duty. -And all of your testimony reaffirms the very central fact, that President Trump conditioned our foreign policy and national security, on getting a valuable political benefit from Ukraine; he wanted Ukraine's new President to create ethical questions about Joe Biden, by publicly announcing investigations; and to pressure President Zelensky into taking actions that would benefit his personal political interests.

He withheld vital military aid to Ukraine, and he refused to meet with President Zelensky in the Oval Office; and as we heard from Mr. Holmes and Dr. Hill today, that meeting was extraordinarily important to Ukraine, and extraordinarily important at sending a message to Russia, of unyielding support {for Ukraine.} The witnesses have made it absolutely clear what the President did; and it's equally clear, that President Trump has launched a cover-up, and a disinformation campaign, to hide this abuse of power from the American people.

479

That is why the administration refuses to provide documents to this committee; and it is why the White House is taking the unprecedented position that Senior officials could ignore congressional subpoenas, and refuse to testify. That's why acting Chief of Staff Mulvaney, Secretary Pompeo, and others have not testified. Now, the President, and even some {Republican lawmakers} in this committee are protecting this {otherwise ongoing ability}.

-Is this normal? It is not; it must never be. No other President has betrayed his office like this, by putting his own small political interests above those of our national security. If it happened with a military commander, a court-martial would follow; if it happened with a Corporation, the CEO would be fired. We all know this {type of behavior} is wrong; but the President continues to say it isn't. He says it is perfect; and he would do it again tomorrow. The same rules apply to Mayor's, Governors, members of Congress, CEOs, and everyone else. They apply to the President, whether you're a Republican or a Democrat; whether you like MSNBC or Fox. {I should hope that} Every American believes in our founding principle, that no American is above the law; not even the President!

Welch then points out, that on July 24ᵗʰ, that was the day that Bob Mueller gave a press conference, warning us that the Russian disinformation campaign that we suffered the attack of in 2016, is alive and well, and on course to happen again in this upcoming election; and so, one day later, on July 25ᵗʰ, President Trump calls the President of Ukraine and asks him to interfere in our elections; so, instead of fighting interference in our election, Trump is inviting interference in our election; and that is completely un-American misconduct. It corrupts our democracy; it corrupts how we implement foreign-policy; it threatens our National security, and the security of all Americans. In my view, it is a clear betrayal of the President's oath of office.

Welch yields back, and it goes to Mr. Maloney:

Maloney asks unanimous consent to enter an ABC news story into the record, with a headline of, "70 Percent of Americans Say That Trump's Actions, Tied to Ukraine, Were Wrong." Published on November 18ᵗʰ; and a New Yorker story entitled, "The Invention of the

Conspiracy Theory on Biden and Ukraine; How a Conservative Dark Money Group Targeted Hillary Clinton in 2016, spread the discredited story that led to President Trump's impeachment."

Maloney probes Dr. Hill about Sondland, {because Sondland had most recently testified that he did not know that Burisma meant "the Bidens," until much later on- the end of August, supposedly.} So, he asks, once again, about the July 10th wardroom meeting, where they were having a dispute over the inappropriateness of this quid pro quo, that was being forced upon the Ukrainians; and he asks Hill whether, in her judgment, Sondland really had no idea, at that time, that Burisma meant the Bidens.

Hill answers, it is not credible to me, that Sondland was oblivious; he had used the term "Burisma" in that July 10th wardroom meeting, and it is {just} not credible to me..." and I should think it seems really incredible to any reasonable soul; knowing that he was at the very center of carrying out this scheme to pressure the Ukrainians; without even knowing what he was pressuring them about; that is very incredible, of course, and Maloney just wanted to point that out.}

He yields back, and the floor goes to Val Demmings:

Demmings says, we all know now, that in July, the President sent an order to the Office of Management and Budget (OMB), that congressionally-approved military aid to Ukraine was to be put on hold. Both of you have expressed that Ukraine is on the front lines; the first line of defense against Russian aggression and expansion into Europe; and that Russia's priority is to undermine the United States; is that right? (they both agree) -In your professional opinion, Dr. Hill, is it in the interest of the United States to support Ukraine, with the much talked about military aid? (Dr. Hill and Mr. Holmes both say yes.)

Demmings then asks Holmes, isn't it true, that even though the security assistance was eventually delivered to Ukraine, {just} the fact that it was delayed, to a country that is actively in a hot war, doesn't that signal to Russia, that perhaps the bond between Ukraine and the United States was weakening? (absolutely!) And even the appearance, that the US-Ukraine bond is shaky, could embolden Russia to act with even more aggression? (that's correct) -And you also testified that it was the unanimous view of the Ukraine policy community, that the aid should be released, because supporting Ukraine is in our national security interests? (yes)

-Dr. Hill, why was the entire Ukraine policy community unanimously in agreement on this? Hill answers, I have actually had this experience before; I just wondered if you would indulge me for a moment; in 2008, Russia also attacked the country of Georgia. I was the National intelligence officer at that time, and we had warned, in multiple documents, to the highest levels of government, that we believed there was a real risk of a conflict, between Georgia and Russia; in fact, we also believed at that point, that Russia might attack Ukraine. This was in 2008, when both Georgia and Ukraine sought membership in NATO; and Russia threatened them both, that if they proceeded with their request for NATO membership, that there would be consequences; and in the wake of that attack on Georgia, President Putin made it clear to the President of Georgia, that this was related to the highest levels of the Georgian government. Putin had said that your Western allies, your Western partners, they didn't deliver; I threatened, and I delivered! We {in the US} had made all kinds of promises to Georgia and Ukraine, and we didn't come through; so Putin is always looking out to see if there's any hints, that we will not follow through on promises that we've made; because he will always follow through on his threats. He threatened Ukraine in 2008, and it wasn't until 2014, when Ukraine tried to conclude association with Russia, that he struck; but he had been threatening this since 2008.

Demmings asks Holmes, what kind of message does it send, other allies, about the United States, when military assistance gets held, with absolutely no explanation? Holmes says, it calls into question the extent that they can count on us.

Demmings says, policies change, but US interests don't; at least, not for those true public servants who are committed, and dedicated to protecting our nation. Thank you both, for being two of them.

She yields back, and the floor goes to Mr. Krishnamoorthi:

Krishnamoorthi addresses Dr. Hill: You've been accused of being a mole for George Soros, in the White House; is that correct? (yes, that's correct) {Hill had disclosed this in her deposition.} -And a conspiracy was launched against you, by convicted felon, Roger Stone, on the show, "Info Wars," run by Alex Jones. Stone wasn't a convicted felon, at the time; this was in 2017... In fact, more recently, before Mr. Stone was due at his trial, they were at it again; repeating the same smear against you; touting, "We here at "Info Wars" first identified Hill as a globalist leftist, working with George Soros, accused of insider trading; who had infiltrated an ambassador's staff..." He said that on May 31st, in 2017. {Having been smeared this way, Dr. Hill was especially upset when they started the smear campaign on Marie Yovanovitch.}

Hill says, I was furious, because this is, again, just this whipping up, of what are, frankly, anti-Semitic conspiracies, {drummed up} to basically target nonpartisan career officials... {We then learn that Alex Vindeman is also of Ukrainian Jewish descent; I don't know if the Jewish part has much to do with the reason for the smear; I suspect probably not; but I don't think it's any coincidence that all three of them, Marie Yovanovitch, Dr. Hill, and Colonel Vindeman, were easy targets for a smear, because they were first generation immigrants.}

{They then talk a little about anti-Semitism; and I suppose it is possible there is some ties to Hill's smears; as she was falsely tied together with George Soros; who is also Jewish; but I won't go into this any further.}

Krishnamoorthi brings up how Hill had testified that she had concerns, about "Rudy Giuliani's increasing role in Ukraine, between January and March of 2019." We then learn that Dr. Hill had served in both, the Bush administration, and the Obama administration. {He jokes that neither President Bush's lawyer, nor Obama's lawyer, were ever directing, or heavily influencing Ukraine policy.}

Hill explains that her concern was for someone like Rudy Giuliani, to have such a strong influence in foreign policy, as that policy may be operating not in the best interest of America; but perhaps in the best interest of Rudy Giuliani, or his clients, or business associates. Hill explains, as I said in my deposition, that's what I thought, at first...

Hill first attributed the reason that Rudy Giuliani was over in Ukraine, was for purposes of making business deals for some of his clients; using the strength of his relationship with the President, to muscle into meeting with influential people, who otherwise would not even receive him.

Next, Krishnamoorthi talks about Igor Fruman and Lev Parnas; but he also says that Dimitri Firtash is here in Chicago, and has been indicted. {That, I didn't know. I had last heard that he had eluded extradition, and that last year, Bill Barr dismissed his case, in exchange basically for Firtash's funding a part of Trump's Ukraine scheme, through having passed money on to Lev Parnas, after which he made donations to Trump's Super-PAC, and another official who orchestrated the removal of Marie Yovanovitch.}

Krishnamoorthi asks, is it possible, that the foreign policy in Ukraine is being run to promote their interests personally, and not the interests of the US? -or Ukraine and not our own? There was a subversion of American foreign policy to push these people's personal interests…

Adam Schiff then announces, "That concludes the member questioning; now we go to closing statements…"

Nunez gives his closing remarks; he goes right away into the whistleblower- {big surprise!} then the Steele Dossiers, then Buzzfeed publishes the dossiers, and then he squawks about what were probably just a few stray media reports, claiming that impeachment began as early as December of 2016; but I'm sure that was just a rogue newspaper or two; or a few isolated TV news reports; none of the major sources talked about impeachment, that I am aware of, until the Mueller report came out, and we saw that there was impeachable behavior, on the President's part; even though it was being covered up and well-hidden. but Nunez goes on this litany; there were two other news stories, saying that there was an article of impeachment filed against President Trump in 2017; and then several months later, supposedly there was another article, saying that there were two more articles of impeachment filed in mid-2-17; but of course, there really were no articles filed until after the Intelligence Committee hearings, in November of 2019; so this was just a few rogue news stories; maybe even in the National Enquirer! -But again, it wasn't as though this was a prevalent message going through the US news networks. I never heard anything like this in the news that I watch, at least; so, I wouldn't give any credence to what Nunez is trying to "Trump-up" here. (excuse the pun)

Nunez next claims that the FBI used fabrications of the steel dossier to get a warrant to spy on a campaign associate of Trump's. Surprisingly, Nunez brings up that op-ed article, that was in the times last year, written by an anonymous official in the White House, assuring US citizens reading the paper, that there were still people in the White House, that were working against what the President was blithely, foolishly, stupidly, dangerously, summarily deciding and moving forward with; there were people who would take papers off of Trump's desk, and hide them; or try to postpone some of these harebrained ideas, that Trump had. In a way, I at least was somewhat heartened to hear, at that point, that there, at least, were a few people in Trump's orbit, that were pushing back against his crazy narcissistic plans and ideas.

Then Nunez says "Russia hoax" once again, {but if it was a hoax, then what false premise is it based upon? certainly not any of the premises brought forward by all of these fine US officials and foreign service officers!}

Nunez says that Mueller's report debunked the conspiracy theory that the Trump campaign worked with the Russians; {but that report did not debunk this; in fact, it indicated that apparently, there was some communication between the Trump campaign and Russians, and some receptiveness to hearing out Russian operatives at a Trump Tower meeting in June of 2016, the revelation that Paul Manafort, who worked on Russian initiatives to smear opposition candidates, running for President in countries whose Governments are under Russian influence; as well as the revelation that Trump continued to work on a Moscow Trump Tower project, for several months after announcing that he had abandoned that project; there was, in fact, some evidence of apparent collusion; it just could not be established beyond any reasonable doubt;

it happened, but Mueller couldn't necessarily prove it. -This is not a debunked conspiracy theory, by any measure!}

Nunez says that, on September 13th, Democrats took the extraordinary step of holding a press conference, and issuing a press release related to the whistleblower's complaint. {Why is that extraordinary? It was a pretty outrageous thing to discover, that the President was engaging in this foul activity; why shouldn't the citizens of this country become aware of this?}

Nunez then contends that the whistleblower had spoken with people within the intelligence committee, before the complaint was issued. {That certainly has never been established; and in fact, it has been denied categorically, that Adam Schiff or anybody else on the Democratic side of the intelligence committee, even knows the identity of the whistleblower; no discussion had taken place; I'm pretty certain of that; it was just the complaint that was the full extent of the information obtained from the whistleblower, who is rightfully to be protected from retaliation; and the Republicans are just trying to desperately do anything they can, to try and make the Democrats' sound case look illegitimate; but it was a legitimate complaint, and it was legitimately followed up, by the Inspector General. He had determined that the complaint was credible; and yet, the White House still wouldn't let him send it on to Congress; and then he finally did intimate to Congress, that a whistleblower complaint had been filed, and was deemed credible; but for some reason, it wasn't being acted upon, by Bill Barr's Justice Department; which is yet another cover-up of injustice.}

Nunez accuses the Democrats in this committee of playing dirty tricks; {but we know that Republicans are the real tricksters; we have witnessed them twisting and distorting everything, for weeks. Many Republican Committee members have made false contentions, over and over again; so that less-sophisticated souls might well be inclined to buy the propaganda, and the twisted reasoning being offered by the Republican side of this Intelligence Committee.}

Nunez says, the verdict was decided before the trial ever began; {boy, was he ever right about that! The Senate probably knew they would acquit him, the day the intelligence Committee investigation began; even long before any impeachment hearings were to begin! I certainly didn't have any doubt about that, which is why I began writing this book during the first week of the hearings; because knowing that the Republican Senate, or actually just the Republican Congress, in general, was going to be corrupt and complicit in condoning Trump's abominable behavior; since I knew that that was almost invariably what was going to happen, I started writing this book, which will cover the impeachment hearings; but subsequently, I will create a much more abbreviated summary of these Intelligence Committee hearings; capturing the highlights and the most important points, as I see them.

I'm going to try and limit the length to around 25 pages, but the length will really be determined by what seems of utmost importance to reveal; but it certainly won't be 300 pages like the transcription and commentary has been so far!

Nunez delivers another of those reverse-psychology examples; he claims that the Democrats, going forward with these hearings, was not meant to discover the facts; it was designed to produce a specific storyline... {boy, is that ever true; of the Republicans only! -Not at all true of the Democrats, who have been asking probing questions, to get at the truth; and there's 300 pages of the truth, that I've written here.}

Nunez says he thinks this is a wasted effort, and that it's sacrificing time that could be spent on other congressional initiatives. {However, it seems there's really no point in spinning their wheels anyway; because the Congressional House of Representatives has already passed a hundred or more bills, that sit on Mitch McConnell's desk, because won't even discuss a single one of them, on the floor of the Senate; so what's the point of continuing to go through all of that legwork, if the end product is just going to sit on somebody's desk?!

So, it just goes to show what the priorities of the Republicans are; they think it is very important to confront a President who has been doing almost nothing but crooked, nasty, mentally sick things. As Devin Nunez aptly describes, Republican lawmakers think that confronting this abomination of a President is a waste of time. It just goes to show what a worm Devin Nunez is; he was also engaged in doing these Trumped-up investigations in Ukraine, as a component of the long-planned scheme. In fact, Lev Parnas who was Trump's right-hand man, tying together Dimitri Firtash's money with the US donations that Parnas made, to grease the palms of those who would later remove Yovanovitch.

Parnas was negotiating with Zelensky on behalf of Trump; and the very day that Parnas had reported back to Trump (on May 13th) that the Ukrainians were not on board with making these bogus announcements of investigations, then later that same day, President Trump gave the order that Vice President Pence will not be attending Zelensky's inauguration; because that was what Trump had warned, in order to exert yet more muscle over Zelensky, to get him to do his dirty bidding.

Nunez says he thinks of the Democrats, as possessive of the "tyranny of the majority," in this situation; yet the majority in the House, bringing the initial charges of impeachment, to a corrupt President; this is not the majority that we are really dealing with here; the majority we are really dealing with here, is the one that has the power to either acquit, or remove him from office. That majority is the Republican majority, and yes, Mr. Nunez, there is very much a tyranny of the majority in store for us, in another couple of weeks.

Nunez is very succinctly describing the Senate trial; it's sort of a vision of things to come, as he is saying this, at the final hearing of the intelligence committee proceedings, against Trump's Web of deceit, and cover-up; and his encouragement of corruption within our allied countries.

Nunez continues, they will impose their absolute will on this body, through their sheer force of numbers. {yes, Devin Nunez, I cannot have said it better; that's exactly what the Senate proceeded to do, once the articles of impeachment migrated over to them.}

Nunez says he thinks that when this matter goes over to the Judiciary Committee, that they're going to view things differently; but if he had half a brain, he would realize that that's never going to happen, because in the House of Representatives the Democrats are in the majority; and the Democrats are the only ones that are looking at this pragmatically, sensibly, and open mindedly; so it's pretty much a foregone conclusion, that once Congress decided to impeach him or I should say that once the intelligence committee finish with these hearings and wrote up there report to the Judiciary Committee it was a no-brainer for me that the Judiciary Committee was going to come to a similar conclusion; and that the impeachment would go through; so, at least, we have that on record, as a successful confrontation to this lawless, crazy President!

Nunez finally yields back; now it's time for Adam Schiff's closing statement:

Schiff first talks about the attacks on Dr. Hill, because of her opening statement, accusing the Republican Committee members of asserting that the interference in our election was not a Russian interference; but it was a Ukrainian interference. So, Schiff wants to make sure that the American public understand that Trump has created this false narrative himself, in tweets, daily, weekly; you know, not only has he called it the Russia hoax; as he has also called the Ukrainian ordeal a hoax; but the fact that he has the bully pulpit, and as the President, whatever he says repeatedly, in his tweets, on TV, and otherwise; like when he is standing in front of the helicopter that he does every week, to try and pretend he is busy doing anything but making trouble; but he and other Republicans have pushed this narrative, and several of these Republican Committee members were repeatedly saying, throughout these hearings, defending Trump, by saying that he only had legitimate concerns, about Ukrainian meddling in our election in 2016; and about a few Ukrainians' comments against Trump, at that point in 2016; and these Republican lawmakers certainly have not acknowledged that the Russian disinformation campaign was very ingeniously designed to fool people into voting for Trump, even though it was dead against their interests; and boy, have we paid for that; even though, like every other bad thing Trump has done, he seems to have covered it up, well enough to keep going.

But once we eventually uncover all the bad stuff that Trump has done, there's going to be a huge realization, of the terrible, and awful, and mentally ill direction that this defective leadership has taken this country <u>way</u> downhill; and changed for the worse, the level of confidence that most other countries in the world, will ever have for America again; unless this terrible wrong can be righted, where we remove Trump, and remove Republicans from the majority.

Schiff says, I wish I had heard some of that righteous indignation that the Republicans were piping out today, at the time that President Trump stood with President Putin in Helsinki and denounced the US intelligence agency reporting; that when the President questioned the fundamental conclusion of our intelligence agencies; but of course, they were silent, when the President said that.

They showed indignation today, but they will cower when they hear the President questioning the very conclusions that our intelligence community has reached; but we saw something interesting also today; my colleagues sought to use you, Dr. Hill, to besmirch the character of Colonel Vindeman; and I thought this was very interesting. It wasn't unexpected, but it was very interesting for this reason; they didn't really question anything Colonel Vindeman said; after all, what Colonel Vindeman said, was what you said; he was in that July 10th meeting; he heard the same quid pro quo; the same comments by Sondland; if you Ukrainians want this meeting, we have an agreement about this; you've gotta announce that you're doing these investigations. He heard the same quid pro quo that you did; so why are they <u>smearing</u> him?

Mr. Holmes, you testified that Colonel Vindeman had said he warned President Zelensky against getting involved in US politics; they didn't take issue with <u>that</u>; so why smear this purple heart recipient, just like the smear of Ambassador Yovanovitch? It's just gratuitous; you don't question the facts; it's just this gratuitous the attack on you, Mr. Holmes; that you are indiscreet when you mention this {outrageous} conversation to others. I think you're quite right; that the act of indiscretion was when the Ambassador to the EU calls the President, on an insecure line, in a country known for Russian telecommunications eavesdropping. -That's <u>more</u> than indiscretion; that's a <u>national security</u> risk; but why attack you, Mr. Holmes? They didn't question anything that you said; they didn't question what conversation you overheard, of Ambassador Sondland's; they didn't question what the President had said; they acknowledge that the one thing that the President wanted to hear that day, {the day} after his phone call with Zelensky; it was, is he going to do the investigations? and Sondland said yes, he'll do anything you ask… They don't question that! -So, why do they attack you? They didn't question your testimony when you asked Sondland what the President thinks of Ukraine… well I guess we are not going to get to hear the last of Adam Schiff's final summation, as my DVR recording cuts off when he says President Trump doesn't give a (Schiff says, I want to say the word) about Ukraine.

{This concludes my transcription and commentary on the House Intelligence Committee Impeachment hearings.}

The House Judiciary Committee Hearings:
(Four Professors Weigh in on the Trump Impeachment)

Mr. Nadler, as the Majority leader of this Committee, will preside over this set of hearings and debates. Four experts, (three hired by the Majority Democrats, and one hired by the Minority Republicans) will give their opinions on the matter.

I will limit my transcriptions strictly to the opening statements of the four expert witnesses. I will not continue on, with transcribing the Committee-member questioning; as I find it is almost entirely a duplication of earlier testimony and arguments that we will have already heard, here. Instead, I will just transcribe each of their initial presentations to the committee, inserting my commentary, as usual.

Following this segment, I will transcribe the opening statements that were made within the next Judiciary Committee hearing taking place after this hearing.

In the case of both of these final transcripts within my book, I merely wanted to capture the opening statements, and insert my comments, at various points. I believe this will be very illuminating, in itself; and, as I said at the beginning of the book, I am seeking to minimize length and repetition, without sacrificing any important content.

Before moving on to the Judiciary Committee hearings, I will summarize Mark Sandy's testimony, as it was later discussed in a news interview. I include this in order to show the corrupt manner of workings that Trump orchestrated within the Office of Management and Budget, pertaining to the hold put on the Ukraine financial aid.

Following these three segments, the final segment of Judiciary Committee hearing transcription for this book, will be transcription of the last debate of the Judiciary Committee, the night before the vote to impeach President Trump was cast.

It is a transcription of only the Democratic Committee members' commentary; as I assume they had probably covered pretty thoroughly, the arguments made by the Republicans as well, over the course of the Judiciary Committee hearing process; and they offer their final rebuttals, and closing thoughts regarding what seems most significant about this situation involving the President.

The very last section of my transcription is in all caps, because that was how the file was given to me. It is also not a perfect transcription; it was derived from voice transcription software, recording as the hearing proceeded. I have done my best to make it substantively correct.

Here, in this initial Judiciary Committee hearing segment, Mr. Nadler starts by giving an introductory statement regarding the credentials of each Professor testifying here:

Noah Feldman is the Felix Frankfurter Professor at Harvard Law School. Professor Feldman has authored 7 books, including a biography of James Madison, and a Constitutional law casebook, as well as many essays and articles on Constitutional subjects. Professor Feldman received his undergraduate degree from Harvard College, he has a Doctorate of Philosophy from Oxford University, where he was also a Rhodes scholar, and he earned his JD from Yale Law School. He also served as a law clerk for David Souter of the United States Supreme Court.

Pamela Carlin serves as a Kenneth & Harlem Montgomery Professor of Public Interest Law, and a co-Director of the Supreme Court Litigation Clinic at Stanford Law School. She is the co-author of several leading casebooks, including a monograph entitled, "Keeping Faith for the Constitution," and dozens of scholarly articles. She served as a law clerk, for justice Perry Blackburn, of the United States Supreme Court, and is a Deputy Assistant Attorney General, in the Civil Rights division of the United States Department of Justice; where she was responsible, among other things, for reviewing the work of the Department's voting sector. Professor Carlin has earned 3 degrees from Yale University; an MBA in history, an MA in history, and a JD from Yale Law School.

Michael Gerhart is the Burden Craig Distinguished Professor of Jurisprudence, at the University of North Carolina's School of Law; and the Director of USC's Center of Law in Government. Professor Gerhart is the author of many books, including, "The Federal Impeachment Process," "The Constitutional and Historical Analysis," as well as more than 50 other publications, on a diverse range of topics in Constitutional law, federal jurisdiction, and the legislative process. He received his JD from the University of Chicago Law School, his MS from the London School of economics, and his BA from Yale University.

Jonathan Turley is the Jay T. & Maury C. Shapiro Chair of Public Interest Law, at George Washington University Law School, where he teaches torts, criminal procedure, and Constitutional law. After a stint at Tulane Law School, Professor Turley joined the George Washington Law faculty in 1990; and in 1998, he became the youngest Chair-Professor in the School's history. He has written over 3 dozen academic articles, for a variety of leading law journals, and his articles on legal and law policies appear frequently in national publications. A Chicago native, Professor Turley earned degrees from the University of Chicago, and Northwestern University School of Law.

I now welcome all our distinguished witnesses, and we are thankful for their participation in today's hearing.

{Nadler swears in the witnesses. He then asks the witnesses to give their summaries within a 10-minute timeframe each; and there is a time clock to keep them on that schedule.}

Professor Feldman begins:

I serve as the Felix frankfurter Professor at the Harvard Law School. My job is to study and teach the Constitution, from its origins until the present. I'm here today to describe 3 things: Why the Framers of our Constitution included a provision for the impeachment of a President;

what that provision providing for impeachment, of "High Crimes, and Misdemeanors" means; and lastly, how it applies to the question before you, and before the American people; whether President Trump has committed impeachable offenses, under the Constitution.

Let me begin by stating my conclusions: The Framers provided for the impeachment of a President because they feared that the President might abuse the power of the Office, for personal benefits, or to corrupt the electoral process, to ensure his reelection; or to subvert the national security of the United States.

High Crimes and Misdemeanors are abuses of power, and of public trust, connected to the Office of the president. On the basis of the testimony, and the evidence before the House, President Trump has committed impeachable high crimes and misdemeanors; by corruptly abusing the Office of the presidency. Specifically, President Trump has abused his Office, by corruptly soliciting President Volodymyr Zelensky of Ukraine, to announce the investigations of his political rivals; in order to gain personal advantage, including in the 2020 presidential election.

Let me begin now with the question of why the Framers provided for impeachment, in the first place. The Framers borrowed the concept of impeachment from England; but with one enormous difference: The House of Commons, and the House of Lords were using impeachment in order to limit the <u>Ministers</u> of the King; but they could not impeach the King; and in that sense, the King was above the law.

In stark contrast, the Framers, from the very outset very outset, at the Constitutional convention, in 1787, made very crystal clear that the President would be subject to impeachment; in order to demonstrate that the President was subordinate to the law.

I would like you to think, now, about a specific date; at the Constitutional convention; July 20th, 1787. It was the middle of a long, hot summer; and on that day, two members of the Constitutional convention actually moved to take out the impeachment provision, from the draft Constitution; and they had a reason for that. The reason was that they said the President will have to stand for reelection; and if the president has to stand for reelection, that is enough. We don't need a separate provision for impeachment.

When that proposal was made, significant disagreement ensued. The governor… immediately said, "If the President cannot be impeached, he will spare no efforts or means, whatsoever, to get himself reelected."

Following that, George Mason of Virginia, a fierce Republican critic of executive power, said, "No point is more important than impeachment being included in the Constitution; shall any man be above justice?" he asked; thus, expressing the core concern:

The president must be subordinate to the law; and not above the law. James Madison, the principal draftsman of the U.S. Constitution, then spoke up; he said it was "Indispensable, that some provision be made for impeachment…" -Why? -because he explained that standing for election was "Not a sufficient security against presidential misconduct, or corruption. "A President," he said, "might betray his trust, to foreign powers; a President in a corrupt fashion, could abuse the Office of the presidency," said James Madison, "which might be fatal to the Republic."

-And then, a remarkable thing happened in the convention; Gouverneur Morris of Pennsylvania; one of the two people who had introduced the motion, to eliminate impeachment in the Constitution; got up and actually said the words, "I was wrong…" -He told the other Framers present, that he had changed his mind, on the basis of the debate on July 20th, and that it was now his opinion, that in order to avoid corruption of the electoral process, the President would have to be subject to impeachment; regardless of the availability of a further election.

The up-shod of this, was that the Framers put impeachment in the Constitution, specifically in order to protect against abuse of Office, with the capacity to corrupt the electoral process, or lead to personal gain.

Now, turning to the current language of the Constitution, the Framers used the words "High Crimes and Misdemeanors" to describe those forms of action that were clearly impeachable. These were not abstract terms; to the Framers, "High Crimes and Misdemeanors" represented very specific language, that was well understood by an entire generation. The Framers had borrowed from the impeachment trial in England, that was taking place, as the Framers were speaking; which was referred-to, in fact, by George Mason. The words "High Crimes and Misdemeanors" referred to abuse of the Office of the presidency, for personal advantage, or to corrupt the electoral process, or to subvert the national security of the United States.

There's no mystery about the words, High Crimes and Misdemeanors; the word "High" modifies both crimes and misdemeanors; they are both high; and high means connected to the Office of the President. The classic form that was committed to the Framers was the abuse of Office for personal gain, or advantage. When the Framers specifically named bribery as a high crime and misdemeanor, they were naming one particular version of this abuse of Office; the abuse of Office for personal or individual gain.

The other forms of abuse of Office, are abuse of Office to affect the elections, and abuse of Office to compromise national security, were further forms that were familiar to the Framers.

Now, how does this language of high crimes and misdemeanors apply to President Trump? Let me be clear; the Constitution gives the House of Representatives; that is, the members of this Committee, and the other members of the House, sole power of impeachment. It is not my responsibility, or my job, to determine the credibility of the witnesses who have appeared before the House thus far. That is your Constitutional responsibility.

My comments therefore will follow my role; which is to describe, and apply the meaning of impeachable offenses, to the facts described by the testimony and evidence before the House.

President Trump's conduct, as described in the testimony, and evidence, clearly constitutes impeachable high crimes and misdemeanors, under the Constitution. In particular, the other memorandum, and other testimony, relating to the July 25th phone call between the two presidents; President Trump and President Zelensky; more than sufficiently indicates that President Trump abused his Office, by soliciting the President of Ukraine to investigate his rivals, in order to gain personal political advantage, including in relation to the 2020 election.

Again, the words "abuse of Office" are not mystical or magical; they are very clear the about this. Abuse of Office occurs when the President uses a feature of his power; the awesome power of his Office; <u>not</u> to serve the interests of the American public, but to serve his personal individual partisan electoral interests. That is what the evidence before the House indicates. Finally, let me be clear that, on its own, soliciting the Leader of a foreign government in order to announce investigations of political rivals; and to perform those investigations, would constitute a high crime and misdemeanor; but the House also has evidence before it, that the President committed two further acts, that also qualify as high crimes and misdemeanors.

In particular, the House has evidence that the President placed a hold on critical US aid to Ukraine; and conditioned it its release, on announcements of the investigations of the Bidens, and of the discredited Crowdstrike conspiracy theory. Furthermore, the House also heard evidence that the President conditioned a White House visit, desperately sought by the Ukrainian President, on announcement of the investigations. Both of these acts constitute impeachable high crimes and misdemeanors, under the Constitution. They each encapsulate the Framers worry, that the President of the United States would take any means whatsoever, to ensure his reelection; and that is the reason why the Framers provided for impeachment, in a case like this one.

Nadler says, the gentleman's time has expired.

Then, the Republican Committee members started heckling again; as we could anticipate. Through the din, Mr. Armstrong introduces a motion to suspend any further hearings until December 11th, in order to give Republican Judiciary Committee members time to respond to letters that they have received. Immediately, a democratic Judiciary Committee member moves to table the motion, and Nadler recognizes that. He indicates the matter is settled, and not debatable; all in favor... {It is kind of ridiculous; every time a ridiculous Republican motion is asked for, and there is a motion to table it, from the Democratic side, the Chairman calls for a vote. Before this, he already asked for All

Committee members to either say aye, or nay, all at once; and he judged that the ayes have it; but the Republicans can ask for a roll-call, where each member will be asked to say aye or nay. The Judiciary Committee, I believe, is made up of 25 Democrats and 17 Republicans, and of course, these days, every one of them stands in solidarity for their side; so it is just a purposeful waste of time when the Republicans ask for a roll call; because it takes a couple of minutes to read each of their names. It is still going to be the same outcome, that the Democrat Majority is going to prevail; but these Republicans are just hecklers; they just want to stop the process; they want to stop justice in motion; they only want their own crooked way. (This is called a procedural vote, by the way.) The news commentators tell us that the purpose of this is just to "gum-up the works."}

Pamela Carlin gives her opening statement:

Twice I've had the privilege of representing this Committee and its Leadership, in voting rights cases before the Supreme Court; once when it was under the Leadership of Jim Sensenbrenner, and with Mr. Chavez; and the other is when it was under the Leadership of Chairman O'Connor. It was a great honor for me, to represent this Committee, because this Committee has had a key role, over the past 50 years, in ensuring that American citizens have the right to vote, in free and fair elections.

Today, you are being asked to consider whether protecting those elections requires impeaching a President. That is an awesome responsibility; but everything I know about our Constitutional values, and my review of the evidentiary record here; Mr. Collins, I would like to say to you sir, I read the transcripts of every one of the witnesses who appeared at the live hearing; because I would not speak about these things without reviewing the facts; so, I'm insulted by your suggestion that, as a law Professor, I don't care about them; but everything I read on those occasions {substantiated} that when President Trump invited, indeed <u>demanded</u> foreign involvement in our upcoming election, he struck at the very heart of what makes us a Republic to which we pledge allegiance. That demand, as Professor Feldman just explained, constituted an abuse of power indeed!

As I want to explain in my testimony, drawing a foreign government into our elections is an especially serious abuse of power, because it undermines democracy itself. Our Constitution begins with the words. "We, the people..." for a reason. The Government, in James Madison's words, derives all its powers directly, or indirectly, from the great body of the people; and the way you derive these powers, is through elections.

Elections matter; to both the legitimacy of our government, and to all of our individual freedoms; because, as the Supreme Court declared more than a century ago, voting is preservative of all rights.

So, it is hardly surprising that the Constitution is marbled with provisions governing elections, and guaranteeing governmental accountability. Indeed, the Majority of amendments to the Constitution, since the Civil War, dealt with voting, with terms of Office, and among the most important provisions of our original Constitution, is the guarantee of periodic elections for the presidency; one every 4 years.

America has kept that promise for more than two centuries, and has done so, even during wartime. For example, we invented the idea of absentee voting so that union troops could support president Lincoln, and could stay in the field, during the election of 1864.

And since then, countless other Americans have fought and died, to protect our right to vote. The Framers of the Constitution recognized that elections could not guarantee that the United States would remain a Republic. One of the key reasons for including the impeachment were the risks that unscrupulous officials might try to win the election, or rig election process. {She refers to Alexandra Hamilton, and William Devi, who both warned of what has now happened in the Trump era:} Devi warned that unless the Constitution contained impeachment provisions, a president would spare no means whatsoever, to get himself reelected; and George Mason insisted that, a president who procured his appointment in the first instance; through improper, corrupt action; should not escape action by repeating his guilt.

Mason was the person responsible for adding high crimes and misdemeanors to the list of impeachable offense; so we know, from that,

that the list was designed to impeach a president who acts to subvert our election, whether that election is one that brought him into Office, or is an upcoming election, where he seeks additional term.

Moreover, the founding generation, like every generation of Americans since, was especially concerned to protect our government, and our democratic process, from outside interference.

For example, John Adams during the ratification, {basically when states had to approve of, and submit they would abide by, the final draft of the Constitution} -but Adams had expressed concern with the very idea of having an elected president; writing to Thomas Jefferson that, You are apprehensive of a foreign interference, intrigue, influence; so am I; but as often as elections happen, the danger of foreign influence recurs...

-And in his farewell address, President Washington warned that history and experience prove that foreign influence is one of the most baneful foes of Republican government; and he explained that this wasn't perfect, because foreign governments would try and foment disagreement among the American people, and influence what we thought. The very idea that a president might seek the aid of a foreign government in his reelection campaign, would have horrified them!

-But based on the evidentiary record, that is what President Trump has done. The list of impeachable offenses that the Framers included in the Constitution, shows that the essence of an impeachable offense is a president's decision to sacrifice the national interest, for his own private ends.

Treason is the first thing listed, lay in an individual giving aid to a foreign enemy; that is, putting a foreign enemy adversary's interest above the interests of the United States. Bribery occurred when an official solicited, received, or offers a personal favor or benefit, to influence official action; risking that he would put his private welfare above the national interest.

And high crimes and misdemeanors captured the other ways in which a high official might, as Justice Joseph Story explained, disregard public interest in the discharge the duties of political Office.

Based on the evidentiary record before you, what has happened in the case today is simply one that that I do not think we have ever seen before; a president who has doubled down, on violating his oath, to faithfully execute the law, and to protect and defend the Constitution.

The evidence reveals a President who used the powers of his Office, to demand that a foreign government participate in undermining a competing candidate for the presidency.

As President John Kennedy declared, the right to vote, in a free American election, is the most powerful and precious right in the world. -But our elections become less free, when they are distorted by foreign interference. What happened in 2016 was bad enough; there is widespread agreement, that Russian operatives intervened to manipulate our political process; but that distortion is magnified, if a sitting president abuses the powers of his Office, actually to invite foreign intervention.

To see why; imagine living in a part of Louisiana, or Texas, that's prone to devastating hurricanes and flooding. What would you think if you lived there, and your governor asked for a meeting with the President, to discuss getting disaster aid, the Congress has provided for {your state}, what would you think, if that President said, I would like you to do us a favor, though; I'll meet with you, and I'll send the disaster relief, once you brand my opponent {in the upcoming election} a criminal!

Wouldn't you know, in your gut, that such a President had abused his Office? -that he had betrayed the national interest, and that he was trying to corrupt the electoral process?

I believe that the evidentiary record shows wrongful acts on that scale. Here it shows a president who delayed meeting with a foreign Leader, and the providing of assistance that his own advisors agreed, serves our national interests, in promoting democracy, and eliminating Russian aggression.

Saying, "Russia, if you're listening…" You know, a president who cared about the Constitution would say, "Russia, if you are listening, butte out of our elections!" -and it shows a president who did this, to strong arm a foreign Leader into smearing one of the President's opponents, in our ongoing election season.

That's not politics as usual; at least, not in the United States, or in <u>any</u> mature democracy. It is instead, a primary reason why the Constitution contains an impeachment power. Put simply, a president should resist foreign interference in our elections; not demand it; and not welcome it. If we are to keep faith with our Constitution, and with our Republic, President Trump must be held to account. Thank you.

Michael Gerhart now gives his opening statement:

It is an honor and privilege, to join the other distinguish witnesses, to discuss the matter of grave seriousness to our country, and to our Constitution; because this House, the people's House, has the sole power of impeachment. There is no better forum to discuss the Constitutional standard for impeachment, and whether that standard has been met, in the case of the current President of the United States.

As I have explained in the remainder of the balance of my opening statement, the record compiled so far, shows the President has committed several impeachable offenses; including bribery, abuse of power, and soliciting a personal favor from a foreign Leader, to benefit himself personally; also of obstructing justice, and of obstructing Congress.

Our hearing today should serve as a reminder, that one of the fundamental principles that drove the founders of our Constitution to break from England, and to draft their own Constitution, is the principle that, in this country, no one is above the law. We have followed that principle since before the founding of the Constitution. It is recognized around the world, as a fixed, inspiring American ideal.

In his 3rd message to Congress, in 1903, President Theodore Roosevelt delivered one of the finest articulations of this principle. He said, "No one is above the law, and no man is below; nor do we ask any man's permission when we require it of him. Obedience to the law is demanded as a right; not as or a favor.

Three features of our Constitution protect the fundamental principle, that no one, not even the president, is above the law. First, in the British system, the public had no choice over the monarch who ruled. In our Constitution, the Framers allowed elections to serve as the crucial means of ensuring presidential accountability.

Second, in the British system, a King could do no wrong; and no other parts of government could check his misconduct. In our Constitution, the Framers developed the concept of "separation of powers," which consists of checks and balance designed to prevent any branch, including the presidency, from becoming tyrannical.

Thirdly, in the British system, everyone but the King was impeachable; our Framers' generation pledged their lives, and their fortunes, to rebel against a monarch, when they saw he was corrupt, or tyrannical, and entitled to do no wrong.

In our Declaration of Independence, the Framers set forth a series of impeachable offenses that {defends this Committee against tyranny and corruption.}

When the Framers later convened to fill out the first draft of our Constitution, they were united around the simple, indisputable principle, that was a major safeguard for the public. We, the people, against tyranny of any kind, the people who would overthrow the king were not going to turn around, just having secured their independence from the corrupt monarchial tyranny; and create an Office that, like the King, was above the law, and could do no wrong.

The Framers created chief executives to bring energy to the administration of federal laws; but to be accountable to Congress, for treason, bribery, or other high crimes and misdemeanors.

The Framers' concern, about the need to protect against a corrupt president, was evident throughout the convention; and here, I must thank my prior to friends who have spoken, and referred to a North Carolinian, William Beatty; I will refer to another North Carolinian at the time of the Constitutional convention; James Iredell; whom President Washington later appoints to the Supreme Court; he assured his fellow delegates, that the Presidency is of a very different nature than a monarch. He is to be personally responsible for any abuse of the great trust placed upon him; and this brings us, of course, to the crucial question we are here to talk about today; the standard for impeachment.

The Constitution defines treason; and the term bribery basically means using Office for personal gain; or I should say, misusing the Office for personal gain. As Professor Feldman pointed out, these terms derive from the British, who understood the classifications that would be impeachable, which they referred to as "political crimes."

To refer to political crimes, in which is included great offenses against the United States, and attempts to subvert the Constitution, when the President deviates from his duty, or dares to use his power, vested in him by the people; he breaches the public trust, and causes serious injuries to the public.

In his influential essay on the Federalist papers, Alexandra Hamilton declared that impeachable offenses were those offenses where perceived misconduct, or otherwise the violation of some public trust, related to injuries done immediately to society itself.

Several themes emerged from the Framers' discussion of the scope of impeachable offenses; impeachment in practice.

We know that not all impeachable offense are criminal; and we know that all felonies are not impeachable offenses. We know further, that what matters, in determining whether a particular misconduct constitutes a high crime, or misdemeanor, is ultimately the context in which in the gravity of this conduct in question.

After reviewing the evidence that has been made public, I cannot help but conclude that this President has attacked each of the Constitution's safeguards, against establishing a monarchy in this country; but the context of gravity of the President's misconduct are clear. The favor he requested, was to receive, in exchange for use of his presidential power, Ukraine's announcement of a criminal investigation into a political rival. This foreign action could then be used in this country, to manipulate the public into casting aside the President's political rival, because of concerns about his current corruption.

The gravity of the President's misconduct is apparent will compare it to the conduct of the one president who resigned from Office, in order to avoid impeachment, conviction, and removal from Office.

The House Judiciary Committee, in 1974, approved 3 Articles of Impeachment against President Richard Nixon; who resigned a few days later. The first Article charged him with obstruction of justice.

I won't read them all, but my report identifies a number of factors that I will lay out here, right now, that suggest the President himself has obstructed justice.

If we look at the 2nd article of impeachment against Richard Nixon, it charged him with abuse of power, for ordering the heads of the FBI, the IRS, and the CIA, to harass his political enemies. In the present circumstance, the President has engaged in a pattern of abusing the trust placing placed in him by the American people, by soliciting foreign countries, including China, Russia, and Ukraine, to investigate his political opponents, and interfere on his behalf, in elections where he is a candidate.

The 3rd article approved against President Nixon, charged that he had failed to comply with four legislative subpoenas; in the present circumstance, the President has refused to comply with, and directed at least 10 others in the administration not to comply with lawful Congressional subpoenas; including Secretary of State Mike Pompeo, Energy Secretary Rick Perry, Acting Chief of Staff and Head of the Office of Management and Budget, Mick Mulvaney.

Senator Lindsey Graham, now chair of the Senate Judiciary Committee, said when he was a member of the House, on the verge of impeaching President Richard Nixon; the day that President Nixon refused to answer that subpoena, is the day he was subject to impeachment.

-But as he took that power of the impeachment process away from Congress, and he became the judge and jury, that is a perfectly good articulation of why "Obstruction of Congress" is impeachable.

The President's defiance of Congress was all the more troubling, due to the rationale he claims are his obstructionist arguments; and those of his subordinates. His White House counsel's October 8th letter to the Speaker, and the three Committee Chairs, boils down to the assertion that he is above the law. I will not reread that letter here, but I do want to disagree with the characterization, in the letter, of these proceedings; since the Constitution expressly says; and the Supreme Court has unanimously affirmed; that the House has the sole power of impeachment; and that, like the Senate, the House has the power to determine the rules for its proceedings.

The President and his subordinates have argued, further, that the President is entitled to absolute immunity from criminal procedure; even from <u>investigation</u> of any criminal wrongdoing; including shooting someone on Fifth Avenue!

The President has claimed, further, that he is entitled to absolute executive privilege, not to share any information he doesn't want to share with another branch; he has also claimed the entitlement of being able to order the executive branch, as he has done, not to cooperate with this body, when it conducts an investigation of the President.

If left unchecked, the President would likely continue his pattern of soliciting foreign interference, on behalf of the next election; and of course, concerning obstruction of Congress, the fact that we can easily transpose the articles of impeachment against President Nixon on the action of this President, speaks volumes; but that does not even include the most serious national security concerns, and election interference concerns, that are at the heart of this Presidential misconduct.

No Presidential misconduct is more antithetical to our democracy; nothing injures the American people more than a President who uses his power to weaken their authority, under the Constitution; as well as the authority of the Constitution itself!

{Gerhart sees that his time has just expired.} May I read one more sentence? {Nadler answers, "The witness may have another sentence, or two."} if Congress fails to impeach here, then the impeachment process has lost all meaning {well, for now; but if history repeats itself, in the long run, this foul president will be brought to justice, and the country's leadership will return to its ideal standards before too long.} -and along with that, our Constitution's carefully crafted safeguards, against the establishment of a King on American soil. Therefore, I stand with the Constitution, and I stand with the Framers, who were committed to ensure that no one is above the law. Thank you.

Professor Turley now gives his opening statement:

It is an honor to appear before you today, to discuss what are the most consequential functions you are given by the Framers; and that is the impeachment of the President of the United States. 21 years ago, I sat before you, Chairman Nadler, and this Committee, to testify in the impeachment of President William Jefferson Clinton.

I never thought that I would have to appear a 2nd time, to address the same question with regard to another sitting president. Yet, here we are.

The elements are strikingly similar; the intense rancor and rage of the public debate is the same; the atmosphere that the Framers anticipated; the stifling intolerance of opposing views, is the same... {Is this anywhere near the same scenario as what it was like, when Clinton weas getting impeached? At that point, there was bipartisanism. Both sides cooperated with each other. True, there was outrage among quite a number of us, because this was sexual misconduct, involving a President who took full advantage of his power differential between him and Monica Lewinsky; but in light of the fact that Clinton was a very bright and sensible President, and he was doing well by many measures. A little inappropriate, yet consensual sexual behavior on the part of the President was probably not why the Republicans were really crying foul, I don't think. It was dissatisfaction over the fact that Clinton was not forwarding the conservative agenda. Now, that was a partisan, politically-motivated initiative. There was nobody suffering great tyranny, the President was not wielding his power to cater to special interest groups, at the expense of the nation's suffering; he was not defying every norm, as far as how we treated immigrants, or banning certain races or religious affiliations from coming to America, as had been an available option, since the beginning of American democracy; Clinton was not smearing any stellar foreign service agents, or unjustly spreading undercutting innuendo about his competing candidates; he was not defying the long-standing structure of government which gives Congress the power of the purse; he was not engaging in a crippling trade war, that made it necessary for a sizable portion of US businesses to have to develop new supply chains in order to continue making their products; you get the point.

There is real reason for the opposite party to be furious with the way the President was conducting himself, way against the interests of the common man in this country. Back then, it was just things like, upset over a few billion dollars of welfare being funded by the government, and such.

Then again, Clinton was ultimately impeached; and in the trial that ensued, the witnesses that both the Minority and Majority parties in the Senate wished to have appear, were indeed called; a full and fair debate was carried out in that trial; and the Senate acquitted Clinton because it was reasonable to do so.

In this impeachment ordeal, the President was a dirty dealing so and so; and he then prohibited witnesses called, from coming to testify; he wouldn't turn over a single document to Congress, in their investigation; he even contended he was immune from any investigation into his wrongdoing!

-And despite all of this, There wasn't a single vote, from the House or the Senate, admitting Trump was guilty; to the contrary, the other side just made clever quips, denied the evident truth of the matter, and tried to put forth every manner of distraction; eating up an immense portion of time, arguing points that had absolutely no bearing on the issue at hand, of the President's impeachable offenses.

And ultimately, a dirty dog of a President was acquitted. But based on the recent history in how, in solidarity, the Republicans have subverted every pure and righteous principal of democracy, by using their Majority votes, and even their unanimous Minority votes, to block all reasonability in their legislative missteps; we could have easily predicted the final outcome that occurred; I did by the end of the first impeachment hearing, which is when I began writing this book. No, Mr. Turley, this atmosphere is nothing like the Clinton era; so, you are full of it, right from the start!

{Back to Turley's opening statement:}

I'd like to start therefore perhaps incongruously by stating the irrelevant fact that I'm not a supporter of President Trump; I voted against him. {That is irrelevant; none of us would have thought that a law Professor would have been enough of an idiot to do that!}

My personal views of President Trump are as irrelevant to my impeachment testimony, as they should be to your impeachment vote. {Not if you think the guy is a mentally ill maniac!}

President Trump will not be our last president, and what we believe in the wake of this scandal, will shape our democracy for generations to come. {If the Trump era really does shape our democracy, then democracy is doomed!}

I'm concerned about lowering impeachment standards to fit A paucity of evidence, {paucity means a smallness, or insufficiency- I suppose he wouldn't dare attach that word to the mountain of evidence we have heard against Trump, here. It's a good thing for him, that most people don't know what the word "paucity" means!}, and an abundance of anger. I believe this impeachment not only fails to satisfy the standard of past impeachments, but would create a dangerous precedent for future Presidents. {Oh; and letting this lawless, autocratic narcissist continue on screwing the country over in an undemocratic fashion, by acquitting him, this won't create a far more dangerous precedent?!}

We resume with Professor Turley's statement:

My testimony lays out the history of impeachment, from early English cases, to colonial cases, to the present day. The early impeachments were raw political exercises, using fluid definitions of criminal and noncriminal acts. When the Framers met in Philadelphia, they were quite familiar with impeachment, and its abuses; including the Hastings case, which was discussed in the convention; a case that was still pending for trial in England. Unlike the English impeachments, the American model was more limited; not only in its application to judicial and executive officials, but it's grounds.

The Framers rejected a proposal to add "maladministration," because Madison objected, as so vague a term, would be the equivalent to a tenure during the pleasure of the sentence.

In the end, the very standards that had been used in the past, newly rejected corruption, obtaining Office by improper means, betraying the trust to a foreign power, negligence, perfidy, speculation, and oppression. perfidy is lying, and speculation and self-dealing are particularly relevant to our current controversy.

My testimony explores the impeachment cases of Nixon, Johnson, and Clinton. The closest of these 3 cases, is the 1868 impeachment of Andrew Johnson. It is not a model, or an association that this Committee should relish. In that case, a group of opponents of the President, called the radical Republicans, created a trapdoor crime, in order to impeach the President. They even defined it as a high misdemeanor.

There was another shared aspect, besides the atmosphere of that impeachment, and also the unconventional style of the two presidents; and that shared element is speed. This impeachment would rival the Johnson impeachment, as the shortest in history; depending on how one counts the relevant days.

Now, there are 3 commonalities, when you look at these past cases; all involved established crimes. This would be the first impeachment in history, where there would be considerable debate, and in my view, not compelling evidence of the commission of a crime.

Second, is the abbreviated period of this investigation; which is problematic and puzzling. This is a facially incomplete, and inadequate record, in order to impeach a president.

Allow me to be candid, in my closing remarks; as we have limited time. We are living in the very period described by Alexandra Hamilton; a period of agitated passions. I get it; you're mad; the President is mad; {You know, just the fact that Trump is angry, is strong evidence that he is not well in the head. He has done something so odious, that millions of Americans were very alarmed to hear about it in the news. His scandalous scheme had so many steps to it, and Trump and his rogue operatives made so many rancorous attempts to illicitly pressure a new foreign government, to engage in corruption for the first time; that it was covered in the news for months! Any halfway-sane individual would feel quite small and embarrassed to be found out, having done these unscrupulous acts; yet instead, Trump is angry?! -I think he is angry that anyone would judge him objectively. If the Emperor doesn't want to wear any clothes, for Heaven's sake, don't anybody say anything when you see him nude! -Just act as if everything is fine, and he is grand!}

{Back to Turley's odd explanation:}

My Republican friends are mad; my Democratic friends are mad, my wife is mad, my kids are mad, even my dog seems mad. {Yeah, right; everybody is equally entitled to be angry. The Republican lawmakers are getting every crooked thing they want to happen, under this crazy administration, even if we all are suffering for it; but they are angry because we want to end their reign of terror on the country; gee, poor Mitch…}

{We have so little time, but he wants to tell us all about his dog!} He is a golden doodle, and they don't get mad; so, we are all mad; where has that taken us? Well, will the slipshod impeachment make us less mad? Will it only invite more madness to follow every future administration?

That is why this is wrong. It's not wrong because President Trump is right; {No, of course President Trump isn't right; not right in the head; not right about anything, I don't think.}

His call was anything but perfect. It's not wrong because the House has no legitimate reason to investigate the Ukrainian controversy; {there is no controversy; Trump coordinated a dirty scheme.} it's not wrong because we're an election year; there is no good time for impeachment.

No, it's wrong because this is not how you impeach an American president. This case is not a case of the unknowable; is it case of the peripheral. {We know everything we need to know, in order to judge what has occurred; and it is not peripheral when we have such accounts, as when Sondland called Trump, from the restaurant in Kyiv; they were both so stupid that Sondland didn't think to make such a call privately; and Trump was equally stupid, for not even asking if anyone else was in earshot! They both were stupid not to suspect that the Russians might well be listening in, on their unsecured cell phone call; and could later hold them over a barrel, to solicit their own favors!}

{Back to Turley's ridiculousness:}

We have a record of conflicts; defenses have not been fully considered; un-subpoenaed witness with material evidence. To impeach a president on this record, would expose every future president to the same type of inchoate {This means in the first stage of development, just begun; yeah, sure; we've been screaming about this since September; and we've had 9 all-day hearings to bring it all out; how long must a guilty party have, before punishment is okay to levy, in your opinion?}

{Turley Continuing; okay, the just begun 2 months ago} impeachment; the principal often takes us to a place we would prefer not to be. That was the place 7 Republicans found themselves in, in the Johnson trial. {He is talking 100 years ago, now!} when they saved the president from acquittal, that they despised. {They despised him, and didn't acquit him, or didn't remove him?}

For generations, they even celebrated it as profiles of courage. Senator Edmund Ross said that it was like looking down at his own grave, and then he jumped, because he didn't have any alternative.

It's easy to celebrate those people from the distance of time and circumstance, in an age of rage. It's appealing to listen to those saying, forget the definitions of crimes. Just do it; like this is some impulse, like buying Nike sneakers.

You can certainly do that; you can declare the definitions of crimes alleged are immaterial; and just an exercise of politics; not the law. However, those legal definitions and standards which I've addressed in my testimony are the very thing to divide rage from reason.

This all brings up to me, and I will conclude with this; it's a scene from, "A Man for All Seasons," with Sir Thomas Moore. When his son-in-law, William Roper, suggested that Moore was putting the law ahead of morality, he said Moore would give the devil the benefit of the law. When Moore asked Roper, would he instead cut a great road through the law, to get after the devil? -Roper proudly declared Yes, I'd cut down every law of England, to do that.

Moore responds, -And when the last law is cut down, and the devil turned around on you, where would you hide, Roper? -all the laws being flat? He said, this country is planted thick with laws, from coast-to-coast; man's laws, not God's; and if you cut them down; and you're just the man to do it; do you really think you could stand upright in the winds that would blow, then? And he finished by saying, yes, I'd give the devil the benefit of the law, for my own sake.

So, I will conclude with this: Both sides of this controversy have demonized the other, to justify any measure in their defense, much like Roper perhaps. {Here he goes again, trying to claim that there is just as much equity to the arguments of either side; yet we've just heard from three distinguished, leading Ivy League Law School Professors, just how despicable, and tailor-made for impeachment, that Trump's words and actions should be judged, by this body of Congress; but like Turley himself said, a few paragraphs earlier, you can't argue that the Democratic Congressmen heading up this initiative don't have a very adequate reason to investigate the Trump/Ukraine scandal.}

{He is finally winding down:}

-that's the saddest part of all of this; we have forgotten the common article of faith that binds each of us to each other in our Constitution. {What's that? Protect scum, in the hopes that scum will protect you, next time around, or something?!}

However, before we cut down the tree, so carefully planted by the Framers, I hope you will consider what you will do when the wind blows again, perhaps for a Democratic president. Where will you stand then; {I would hope that the sensible, well-meaning Democrats will stand in the Majority!} when all the laws being flat... (Trump has certainly flattened the entire rule of law, for now.} Thank you again for the honor of testifying today.

{Okay; I hear you; you're saying it isn't against the law to act like a dirty rotten bastard; okay, maybe not; but this presidential behavior sure fits the ideal mold of impeachable behavior, at very least, I would say; along with those three legal scholars who just spoke before you.}

This is the Second Judiciary Committee Hearing
(The Hearing After the one with the 4 expert witnesses)

Mr. Nadler recognizes himself first, for a brief opening statement; and then Mr. Collins' opening statement will follow.

Then, Mr. Burke makes his opening statement; and then Mr. Castor will give his opening statement; which, as you'll see, I have interjected quite a bit of commentary within this text!

Nadler begins:

No matter his party or his politics, if the President places his own interests above those of the country, he betrays his oath of Office. If the president the United States, the Speaker the House, the Majority Leader of the Senate, the Chief Justice of the Supreme Court, and the Chairman and ranking members of the House Judiciary Committee, all have one important thing in common; we've each taken an oath, to preserve, protect, and defend the Constitution of the United States.

If the President puts himself before the country, he violates the President's most basic responsibility; he breaks his oath to the American people. If he puts himself before the country, a matter that threatens our democracy, then our promise to the American people requires us to come to the defense of the nation. That oath stands, even when there is politically disagreement; even when it might bring us under criticism; even when it might cause a surge of the members of Congress; and even if the President is unwilling to honor his oath, I am compelled under my own.

As you heard in the last set of Hearings, the Framers of the Constitution were clear in their vision for our new nation. They knew that threats to democracy could take many forms that we must protect that we must protect against. They warned us against the dangers of would-be monarchs, fake populists, and charismatic demagogues. They knew that the most dangerous threat to our country might come from within, in the form of a corrupt executive, who puts his private interests above the interests of the nation.

They also knew that they could not anticipate every threat that a President may someday pose; so, they adopted the phrase, "Treason, Bribery, and Other High Crimes and Misdemeanors," to capture the full spectrum of possible presidential misconduct.

George Mason, who proposed the standard, said that it was meant to capture all manner of great and dangerous offenses against the Constitution. The debates around the framing made clear that the most serious of such offenses include abuse of power, betrayal of the nation, and foreign entanglements, and corruption of public Office. Any one of these violations of the public trust, compel members of this Committee to take action. When combined, a single course of action, they state the strongest possible case for impeachment, which is removal from Office.

President Trump put himself before country. Despite the political partisanship that seems to punctuate our hearings these days, I believe that there is common ground around some of these ideas, common ground in this hearing room, and common ground across the country, at large. We agree, for example, that impeachment is a solemn and serious undertaking; we agree that it was meant to address serious threats to democratic institutions, like our free and fair elections; we agree that, when the elections themselves are threatened by enemies, either foreign or domestic, we cannot wait until the next election to address them the threat.

We surely agree that no public official, including, and especially the President of the United States, can use his public Office for private gain; and we agree that the President Can't put himself before the country, and the Constitution. His oath of Office's promise to American citizens, require the President to put the country first. If we could drop our partisanship for just one moment, I think we would agree on a common set of facts, as well.

On July 25th, President Trump called President Zelensky, of Ukraine, and asked him for a favor. That call was part of a concerted effort by President Trump, to compel the government of Ukraine to announce investigations; not an investigation of corruption at large, but an investigation of President Trump's political rivals; and only his political rivals. President Trump put himself before country.

The record shows that President Trump withheld Military aid allocated by the United States Congress, for Ukraine. It also shows that he withheld a White House meeting from President Zelensky. Multiple witnesses, including respected diplomats, national security professionals, and decorated war veterans, all testified to the same basic facts: President Trump withheld the aid, and the meeting, in order to pressure a foreign government to do him that favor. President Trump put himself before country; and when the President got caught, when Congress discovered the aid was being withheld from Ukraine, the President took extraordinary and unprecedented steps to conceal evidence from Congress, and from the American people.

These facts are not in dispute. In fact, most of the arguments about these facts appear to be beside the point. As we review the evidence today, I expect we will hear much about the whistleblower.

{Just as an aside, during the impeachment trial, the argument was offered that Trump did not have a subversive motive, because he considers that the country would be best off if he were to continue as President. However, isn't it the reason why we vote, because the <u>American people</u> are supposed to decide whether it is best for the country, for an incumbent Leader, such as Trump, to continue to be president. If we allow a sitting president to engage in this type of behavior, then it figures that what we will potentially end up with, is a struggle, between the incumbent president, deceiving the people in order to stay elected; versus a nominee from the other party also perpetrating their most potent hoax, or propaganda; doing their best to trick the American people into thinking that they are a far better option than the incumbent. This idea flies in the face of the way our democracy has always worked in this country, where the true nature and background of the candidates is broadcast, in various news and documentary formats, and the people cast their votes, to decide who should be at the helm as the country's president.

A whistleblower brought his concerns about the July 25th call, to the Inspector General of the intelligence community. Let me be clear; every fact alleged by the whistleblower, has been substantiated by multiple witnesses; again, and again; each of whom has been questioned extensively, by Democrats and Republicans alike; and their claims also match up with the president's own words, as released from the White House.

-Words that he still says were perfect! I also expect to hear complaints about the term "quid pro quo;" and the contention that a person needs to verbally acknowledge the name of a crime while he is committing it, for it to be a crime at all! {How absurd!} The record on this point is also clear. Multiple officials testified that the president's demand for an investigation into his rival, was a part of his personal political agenda, and not related to the foreign policy objectives of the United States.

Multiple officials testified that the president intended to withhold the aid until Ukraine announced investigations; and yes, multiple officials testified that they understood this arrangement to be a quid pro quo, for the President's political personal political advantage.

President Trump put himself before country. The President's supporters are going to argue that this whole process is unfair. The record before us is clear on this point, as well. We invited the President to participate in this hearing, to question witnesses, and to present evidence that might explain the charges against him. President Trump chose not to show. He may not have much to say in his own defense, but he cannot claim that he did not have an opportunity to be heard.

Finally, as we proceed today, we will hear a great deal today, about the speed with which the House is addressing the President's actions, to the members of this Committee, to the members of the House, and to my fellow citizens.

I want to be absolutely clear: The integrity of our next election is at stake; nothing could be more urgent! The President welcomed foreign interference into our election, in 2016. He demanded it, for 2020; then he got caught. If you do not believe that he will that he will do it again, let me remind you that the President's personal lawyer spent last week back in Ukraine, speaking with government officials, in an apparent attempt to generate the same so-called "favors," that brought us here today; and forced Congress to consider the impeachment of a sitting president. This manner of conduct represents a continuing risk for the country. The evidence shows that Donald J. Trump, the President of the United States, has put himself before his country. He has violated his oath; his most basic responsibilities to the people. He has broken his oath; I will honor mine. If you would honor yours, then I would urge you to do your duty.

Let us review the record here; in full view of the American people. Then, let us move swiftly, to defend our country, as we promised that we would!

I now recognize the gentleman from Georgia is recognized Doug Collins is the Minority leader. {So, before Collins speaks, one of the Republican Committee members demands a point of order; so, when Nadler can't contain this, due to multiple Republicans clamoring for the point of order to be heard, Nadler finally says, state your point of order.

Last week, Mr. Chairman, you were furnished with a proper demand for a Minority hearing, pursuant to clause 2J1 of rule 11. {He claims that Nadler is guilty of an egregious violation; I don't see it; they just want to bulldoze and heckle; since there is no other defense.} The heckler continues, you are refusing to schedule that hearing, therefore I insist on my point of order, that you immediately schedule a Minority hearing day.

Nadler counters, that is not a proper point of order, for today's hearing. As I told the ranking member, several times now, <u>that</u> is not a proper point of order. As I told the ranking member several times now, I am considering the request. The ranking member thinks we would be violating the rules of the House, if we considered articles of impeachment before holding a Minority-day hearing. This point of order would be timely, at a moment where we might consider articles of impeachment. That is not the purpose of today's hearing; the point of order is not timely.

The gentleman from Georgia (Doug Collins), is recognized... Collins continues to grumble about not immediately getting their hearing scheduled. Collins says, there are famous moments in impeachment. There are famous lines from the impeachment; such as, from the impeachment of President Nixon, "What did he know, and when did he know it?" In the Clinton impeachment, there was, "I did not have sex with that woman!" What will be known about this one is probably "Where is the impeachable offense?" {Oh, no; it will be, Wow! A whole body of Republican lawmakers can be that complicit in blatant corruption, and obstruction of a Congressional investigation?!}

Collins continues, why are we here? I'll tell you, this may become known as the "focus group" impeachment, because we don't have anything; nobody understands what the Majority is really trying to do. {Lots of us do; you guys just hope there's enough voters that might be stupid enough to buy your twisted contentions and explanations, that along with a massive Russian disinformation campaign, your crooked buddy Trump might be able to get re-elected.}

Collins thinks the Democrats on this Committee merely intend to interfere, and basically make sure that they believe the president can't win next year, if he's impeached. {No; that's not it, at all; they are here to stand up and scream out to the American people, just what a sleazeball is yet allowed into the White House.}

Collins continues, the "focus group" impeachment takes words, and then takes people, and says, how can we explain this better? -because we don't have the facts to match it. {That's right Doug; you don't pay attention to all those messy words; you all just ignore all of those; and the gravity of who is testifying; and vote to acquit, right? -to keep your crooked crony in power, right?}

Collins keeps spewing, the "focus group" impeachment says, you know, we really aren't working with good facts; but we need a good PR move, that's why we're here today. {You're right, Doug; it is good PR for the only reasonable force in government, the Democrats, to confront all of the crooked, incompetent acts of the President, and his Republican thug protectors.}

Collins says, this is all about a clock and calendar; it really became evident to me that this was true; because last Wednesday after we had a long day and hearings, the next morning, before anything else could get started, the Speaker of the House walked up to the podium, and said go write articles of impeachment! I appreciate that the Majority practiced for two days, this week, on this hearing. {As if you Republican jokers didn't conspire into the wee hours of the morning, on how you each could offer dismissive, insulting comments, to try and deter a righteous, proper process of explaining how nasty and disadvantageous Trump and his crooked clan have been continually trying to do bad things and then cover it up.}

Collins says, I appreciate the fact that that you've got to try and get it right; try and convince the American people of your problem, {What?! The Democratic Committee members are trying to tell the American people that Democratic Committee members have a problem?! No, The Democrats are trying to tell the American people that we all have big problems; as long as Trump is in Office! Gee, as if many of them aren't quite well-aware of that already!}

Collins rants away, but your Speaker has already undercut you; she took the thrill out of the room; you're writing articles of impeachment; why couldn't we just save that time today; if you're going to go and write the articles of impeachment, go ahead and write them. Well this is probably the reason for that; because the Chairman has laid out some amazing claims none of which I think, after this hearing today, the American people can honestly look at it, and see that there was overwhelming evidence that he abused his power; because the Speaker; another claim that she said; to do impeachment, you have to be so compelling, and overwhelming, and bipartisan; all of which we are not.

{I do think that Nancy Pelosi made a mistake in contending that impeachment must be bipartisan, because although because I'm sure that did hold true throughout history up until more recently, but during the last several years, if not a few decades, that the 2 parties have been dead set against each other and vote in solidarity on everything; so what she should have said, was that regardless of how the Republicans react to this initiative, the Democrats do hold the Majority here and believe very strongly that the President has committed impeachable offenses, and we intend to broadcast what we have discovered to the American people; regardless of the fact that Republicans hold the Majority in the Senate, and they will push their partisan agenda. But partisan rancor is beside the point here; the point is that a lot of government officials and foreign service workers were quite alarmed and upset by what President Trump has been scheming, to stack the deck against his most likely rival in the upcoming election; and in this country, we don't just sit back, and allow elected officials to conjure up their hoaxes, like this scheme, intended to fool the American people into thinking that a good, solid candidate's motives, and their record, have been called into question, which Trump knows would call the American people's confidence into question related to that candidate.}

Collins continues, so why are we here? Let's look at the three things that typically are associated with making your case against… motives, means, and opportunity. {The Democratic Committee members' motive is to do this before November 2020; (he tries to mock the Democrats, as usual) "We have to do this, because if we don't impeach him, he'll win again, next year! {He'll win if he can cheat crookedly enough, like he has been trying, so desperately, to do all year.}

Collins contends, the reason he'd win is because, as recently as last week, with the jobs report, on the economy. {Here's another example of how Trump has cheated the American people; do you all realize how many valuable things were sacrificed, in order for the economy to perform just a touch better?! -Wait 'til I show you later.}

Collins' great evidence of how well the economy is doing, was to say, I had a man come up to me at the grocery store this week; and he said keep doing what you're doing; I've never seen an economy this good! People are working, people are being taken care of; and this {impeachment ordeal} is just a little distraction! {Yes, this is sort of indicative of how this administration gauges how well it is doing; can an excited group of folks at a rally testify to it? Well then, it must mean everything is great! -If you remember, throngs of people cheered Hitler once, too. If we don't get rid of Trump, he might even be worse! Don't kid yourself; Trump is a dangerous maniac, who can make himself appear cool and effective, to less-sophisticated souls; of which there tend to be a lot of in the US, perhaps.}

(Picking back up) -they lost; and in January 2017 just a few minutes, and the Washington Post confirmed what every Democrat had been talking about; now is the time for impeachment. {Even if an article of this nature appeared in a major paper, maybe it was even planted by Republicans, so they could make such twisted contentions, as that, in January 2017, all of the Democrats called for impeachment; I sure don't remember hearing anything about this; I remember hearing that there was a lot of upset about the Russian disinformation campaign, but all that the Democrats were calling for at that point, to my knowledge, was an investigation into that, which Bob Mueller was subsequently hired for.

Collins says that the Democrats started with {calling for} impeachment; and then spent two years trying to figure out what to impeach him for. {I would say that's a pretty twisted way to look at the facts. The facts are that we kept discovering every month, or in some cases, every day or every week, some alarming and outrageous cruel, unjust, corrupt activity became apparent to lawmakers; and through the news, to the American people as well; and there were plenty of Democrats upset about the way the Trump goes about things, in such a dirty, upsetting manner. So, I dispute the idea that Democrats first called for impeachment, and then later conjured up some false premise to bring a case against the President, based upon. I submit that it was the president's own behavior, and the actions of those officials, and appointees, who have been acting under his influence, that has become the basis for much upset, and concern over Trump's apparent unfitness for Office.

Collins contends that the Democrats are constantly tearing down President who was working for the American people. Boy, that's a good joke! This President has been working solidly against the American people, and only for big money, special interests, and launching a whole host of conservative extremist policies decisions and actions, to please himself.

Collins takes issue with Nadler's statement that a president is to be held accountable to his oath of Office, and Collins thinks that the Congress should have to be held count accountable to their oath of Office too. {It seems very clear to me that the Democrats, in this ordeal, are indeed talking about what that oath means, and acting in a way that stands on that oath; whereas, Collins is just talking about the fact that there is an oath. He thinks that this process isn't fair, and it is not of a proper decorum; and a fact pattern, {yes, the facts do add up to a pattern, of lies and deceit!} that you're having to force against a President you don't like. {Well, Collins is right about that; we certainly do not like President Trump!}

Collins rants on; what was the opportunity? The opportunity came last November; they got the Majority, and the opportunity began; and they began their impeachment run. {but actually, in November, there wasn't any broad support for impeachment; there were only a few stray Congressman who were pretty outraged by what Trump had been up to, and I think it was perfectly reasonable to feel that way. However, what we heard from the overwhelming Majority of Democratic House members, was a pretty solid argument against impeachment, due to the fact that the Senate was pretty much undoubtedly going to acquit, even if Trump were impeached; and there were other political risks that would weigh on the popularity and electability, of whoever would become the Democratic nominee for president, this year.}

Collins contends that this was a "baked deal," from the start; (that's all Collins has, though; a bunch of cool "bully-words," mainly effective only for those who would buckle easily under them.} that as soon as the House became a Democratic Majority, that plans to impeach President Trump were a foregone conclusion. {that's not what I heard, and I watched the news every day. There was quite a bit of ambivalence, for months; but what eventually broke it down, was the fact that Trump kept doing outrageously nasty and foolish, and completely off-the-rails crap all the time; constantly! -and eventually, he pissed off dozens and dozens more House members. Trump is like that wise guy, that just keeps asking for it; but his Republican lawmaker protectors yet managed to keep him from getting what he deserves. -Well, they can't stop voters from coming to understand what a phony and a flim-flam man he is, and vote him out, in November of 2020.}

Collins criticizes that, rather than proof, the Democrats are relying on presumption; but in a case where no proof can be unquestionably established, presumption has always been a valid standard. Consider the scenario where a policeman walks into a room, he sees a guy shot and dying on the floor, and a man with a smoking gun in his hand. The Officer cannot prove that the man with the gun shot the other man; but that man with the gun may well end up in prison, merely due to a presumption that becomes increasingly obviously evident, as more facts around the situation are discovered.

Collins criticizes, that some of the witnesses had inferred things, and that was being considered as evidence, and he thinks that is invalid. {But once again, "inference" is also valid in legal proceedings, in court. Using our example of the man with the smoking gun in his hand, suppose upon further investigation, we find out that several other people, who were in that same room before the violence began, witnessed the man with the smoking gun say to the other say to the dying man, "You slept with my wife, I'm going to kill you! If then we find the man dead on the floor and the guy who said I'm going to kill you has a smoking gun in his hand, that's an inference that's valid, right?

Collins contends that the Democrats made their whole case based on Gordon Sondland; {but there were something like 14 witnesses who gave testimony and depositions, and all of this testimony had corroborated what Sondland had contended. In fact, at Sondland's first deposition, he didn't admit anything! He said he can't recall, about a hundred times! It was only after other witnesses came forward, that he realized he had better come back and tell the truth, or he may well suffer punishment for perjury, and or lying to Congress.}

Collins refers to the phone call in early September, when Sondland asks the president what does he want with Ukraine? -And the president answers, I want nothing; I want President Zelensky to do what he ran on. {Well, what Zelensky ran on, was a platform of rooting out corruption; so how might, going through with the corrupt act of Trumping up false accusations about Trump's political opponent, how does that fit in with Zelensky doing what he ran on? But in fact, we know, regardless of the lies constantly on his lips, that President Trump did <u>not</u> really want Zelensky to do what he ran on; that was just another of Trump's lies; he wanted Zelensky to do the opposite of what he ran on, and instead, become complicit in Trump's corrupt scheme.}

{Collins criticizes, that Adam Schiff, the Chairman of the Intelligence Committee, is not here at this hearing; {but somebody should explain to Mr. Collins that this is a <u>Judiciary Committee</u> hearing; why would the attendance of an Intelligence Committee member be expected at this hearing?}

Collins then contends that Adam Schiff "made up the call;" I don't have any idea what he means! Schiff merely read, to the American people, the call summary that the White House had released on September 25th!

He says that Adam Schiff started the fairytale that we are having today; you can't even put the transcript in the right... just read it! {Well, Mr. Collins, we don't even have the transcript of the July 25 phone call. The president won't release that. All we have is the call summary that was publicly released; but that readout is certainly damning enough, in itself; and Adam Schiff has not misrepresented that; he has merely talked about what that summary indicates, and a verbatim account of what President Trump said to President Zelensky. Collins then accuses Democratic Committee members of misleading the American people. {This is another often-employed strategy of the Republican Committee members: to suggest that the Democratic Committee members don't possess the mental resources to properly understand how to interpret the true nature of what has transpired. However, that strategy won't work on people with any reasonable amount of overall intelligence perhaps. I do have some faith that the Majority of voters possess reasonable levels of intelligence, even though it has become evident that they are pretty easily tricked, at times; or if there is some question in their mind, as to what the true facts of the matter are, politically-speaking, they would seek further explanation from those who obviously do possess greater levels of intelligence, in this respect. Bullies like Collins believe that the ability to publicly make your opponent look bad, shows the highest level of intelligence; but if this involves embracing and selling false premises, it is really the epitome of self-deception.}

Collins thinks that Adam Schiff has violated his oath, what he swore to the American people, to uphold the Constitution. He says that's the most massive malpractice he's ever seen. {This is just another one of those times when the Republicans accuse the Democrats of doing something that only they are doing; because what the Republicans have been doing is certainly a violation of their oath, and malpractice big time.}

Collins says that the Democrats don't care about what was actually in the transcript; {but once again it's just the other way around. The Democrats are holding these proceedings because they do care what that transcript shows, about the president's scheme, and his overall character. The Republicans don't care how corrupt President Trump's scheme was; they just want to defend him, in order to keep him in power; because this inures to their benefit; their crooked benefit at that.}

Collins says the witnesses that testified last week don't even care that the aid got released. {That is absolutely correct; as well they should disregard such an irrelevant contention; because the aid only got released after Trump got caught, and he realized that he would no longer be able to put pressure on Zelensky to make these corrupt announcements of investigations; and he also realized that now it was all out in the open, and if he didn't, at that point, release the aid, then Trump's crooked Republican defenders couldn't say what Collins is saying now, as at least a weal defense; that the aid was ultimately released. But we should keep in mind, had Bill Barr's Justice Department continued to sit on the whistleblower complaint, as it had, for weeks; not ever informing Congress of it, we can be pretty certain that President Trump would not have released the aid until President Zelensky made the announcements of the investigations that Trump was forcing him into. -And we also know, that as a result of a very long-standing pressure campaign on President Zelensky, that he indeed had finally given in, even though he held out for several months; but he had gone as far as scheduling a CNN interview where he had told others that he planned to make an announcement that those investigations had been opened. I suppose, that from Trump's point of view, it's just a shame that the Inspector General had enough integrity to contact Congress, and tell them that a whistleblower complaint existed. If he hadn't done that, then there was a pretty strong chance that Zelensky would have indeed made those announcements which would have been very damaging for Biden.}

Collins contends that Adam Schiff was claiming that there was clear collusion, in plain sight; before the Mueller report even came out. {I'll bet dollars to doughnuts that this is a twisted statement, and that Adam Schiff merely alluded to the fact that it sure looked like collusion; which is why an investigation was deemed necessary.}

Collins says, we've taken a dangerous turn in this Congress. {I would say that we certainly have! Republican lawmakers, across the board, have taken a very immoral turn!} Collins calls what the Democrats initiatives are a "political vendetta;" {but I should think that the real political vendetta was when the Senate, having the only real power to do something about stopping Trump's corruption, pooh-poohed the Democrats very strong case against Trump, and thumbed their noses at the integrity of the impeachment managers.}

Collins says that the Democrats had believed, that having Bob Mueller come and speak, at a press conference, would strongly implicate Trump; {And unfortunately it seems true that many were falsely convinced of this, but they should have realized up front, that Bob Mueller was hired by the Justice Department, and therefore somewhat beholden to Trump's great protector, Bill Barr. -And had we known how impotent his reporting of Trump's wrongdoing would be; simply because of a current opinion that a sitting president cannot be indicted; the smartest of us should have realized that it would only help Trump's and the Republicans' case, to have Mueller speak publicly. On the other hand, if this had been a true press conference, and a sea of reporters could've asked a bunch of questions of Mueller, then it might've been worth it; but you see, the Justice Department had a handle on all of this, as Trump had already established that this would be the first administration to give press conferences without allowing any questions from the audience. To clinch things even further, we also learned that Bill Barr and Bob Mueller had been buddies for many years. The upshot, was that the deck was stacked against any real justice; and Bill Barr unfortunately had the power to keep a lid on the revelation of any serious wrongdoing on the President's part, or on the part of his campaign; this would all be squelched.}

Collins considers that this hearing is the movie version of the Schiff report; {but Adam Schiff had actually written this report, given to the Judiciary Committee, with the help of a number of other Committee members.}

Collins points out that Devin Nunez is here, {this was his prerogative, assuming he was legitimately invited; but this particular hearing is for the purposes of listening to four legal experts, about any relevant considerations about the pros and cons of impeachment, in these circumstances; so again, I don't see that there's any call for Adam Schiff to be at this particular hearing.}

Collins thinks that the Intelligence Committee is issuing subpoenas for vendettas; {this is just so twisted. Collins is right about one thing; the institution of Congress is in danger! Collins criticizes, that after only the first day of hearings, Nancy Pelosi had said, go write articles of impeachment; and Collins contends that she did this in the spirit of, "facts be damned;" {but if she said it, I'm sure she said it because, although proof could never be established in a situation like this, especially when the President and his complicit officials are powerfully covering up everything they can, Pelosi knew that all we were going to get was presumption and inference; however, I remember sitting through that first hearing and thinking, as I'm sure Nancy Pelosi was, that it is seems clearly evident that the President engaged in, and was the instigator of this crooked scheme; so I don't think Nancy Pelosi was out of line, in suggesting that people start working on developing articles of impeachment, because it looked inevitable, that this is what these proceedings were going to lead to, even at that early point.}

Collins says that Democrats are desperate to have an impeachment vote on this President. {Of course they are! I could hardly think of a behavior that would be more worthy of impeachment. We've never had another President in my lifetime, who has commanded a force of rogue operatives anything like this! Collins and other Republicans think that none of this matters, because the economy is doing well; or so they keep contending. Republicans do hide behind the economy, but later in this book I will establish that the economy isn't really any better, in fact it's much worse, if you look at the United States' comprehensive situation, as compared to just before Trump took Office in January of 2017.}

Collins says this is about a clock and calendar, because they can't get over the fact that Donald Trump is president of the United States; and Collins contends that the Democrats don't think they have a candidate that can beat Trump. {But the Democrats certainly do accept the fact that Donald Trump is president of the United States, and that's why they feel the need to get them the hell out of there! And when the Republican Committee members say the Democrats think that they don't have a candidate who could beat Donald Trump, they are just trying to hide the fact that there are a stage full of candidates who are getting votes in the primaries, specifically because there are lots of Democrats that think the candidates that are running, could be Trump in an election. Why else would they waste time casting a vote? For Republican lawmakers, it's all just smoke and mirrors.}

Collins suggests that Adam Schiff was supposed to be the star witness here today; {but that doesn't really make any sense; today the star witnesses are the 4 legal experts, you idiot!}.

So, Collins yields back, but then right away, a couple of the heckling Republicans are again pushing on this issue of scheduling a Minority hearing day. Nadler is not willing to do this at this point, and his explanation seems reasonable to me; the rules by which an impeachment is governed require a Minority hearing day if articles of impeachment are going to become considered by the Committee. Nadler points out that we are not at that point yet, (We haven't planned any vote on whether to even draft any articles of impeachment yet); so, in his view, as Chairman, he thinks the scheduling of Minority hearings is premature.

Nadler explains, the point of order, would be in order, at the meeting where we are considering articles of impeachment. We will now hear presentations…

The Republicans ask to appeal this decision; and Nadler says, there is no decision to appeal; it was not a ruling, or a motion… {the Republicans are really heckling now; several of them are saying, you made a ruling on the point of order. Nadler says, the gentleman will suspend; it was not a recognizable point of order; it was not an order; it is not time to make that order; there is no ruling to appeal.

At one point, Collins asserts that the rules pertaining to impeachment, don't state that the Minority day of hearings isn't to be scheduled until it is decided that the writing up of articles of impeachment are being considered

{But then again, the rules also don't say, that the Chairman does not have the prerogative to delay the scheduling of the Minority hearing, until such time as it seems, at all, necessary.

Collins is clever; but on another level, he also seems kind of stupid. Thinking about him, and the similar mentality of several other Republican lawmakers I have been hearing from here, gives rise to a new theory I am considering; that if you are always devoting your metal energy to figuring out how to be increasingly clever, it keeps you from using your mental resources, more exclusively for objective assessment; which would seem much more intelligence-building.

Personally, I find that my objective assessments of my own behavior and thinking, for instance, can sometimes lead to my calling myself stupid, for having thought and believed as I had, surrounding certain situations I had found myself in. Others have advised me that I shouldn't be so down on myself; but to the contrary, I also realize that we are all humanly imperfect; and I am not unduly disturbed to discover that I have done something stupid; I spend my energies rather in considering how I might amend my inclinations to fall for illusions that cause trouble or harm.

I say that Collins is stupid, in this instance, because he doesn't see how it is of much greater importance to keep American democracy from going off the edge of a cliff, by allowing, or at least condoning presidential behavior that goes against everything we stand for; and have for generations. Tyranny reigns for shorter periods of time in the US, such as the gangster era; but the integral Leadership which resounds throughout the land, produces a few exceptional individuals, who draw on the backing of sound, reasonable, mature institutions, such as the FBI, the Police, and the Courts; and thereby ultimately ends the injustice.

The Trump administration has now packed the courts full of ultra-conservative nuts, and incompetent conspiracy theorists; and even then; having a sweeping Majority in the Supreme court that will consistently rule in his favor, Trump wants even to disqualify the losing judges in the matter, from writing deservedly-scathing dissents about these ridiculously-inappropriate rulings in Trump's favor; what a tyrant! He not only wants to win all the time, no matter how dirty he has to act in order to do so; but then he wants to prevent anyone from pointing out his foul ways of thinking and acting, employed to get him the results he wanted, at everyone else's expense!

That is the trouble with developing a mindset, to always win what you want, no matter what. Sometimes, we should instead do ourselves, and everyone else, the favor of coming to realize that the advantages we personally might appreciate, by forcing a given outcome to come about, are outweighed in importance, by the disadvantages that would also necessarily occur, as a side-effect; such as promoting massive oil and gas exploration, at the expense of ramping up global warming even much faster, and moving in the exact opposite direction than we should be, in terms of mobilizing a sizable work force to develop and implement renewable energy sources, and get away from burning fossil fuel, for instance.

And we can readily this kind of immature thinking, at the heart of Trump's mental processes, as well as within the minds of many other conservative nut-jobs in power currently, in the vastly-conservatives-dominant US Government, at the moment. They would rather denounce whoever they are hurting, than consider letting-up any. The rest of us are charged with properly removing their ability to call the shots, since this is the immature, inconsiderate, disrespectful way that they would try and guide this great nation.}

Anyway, back to the hearing:

This heckling goes on for probably close to a minute, and it gets pretty hairy; but Nadler finally bangs his gavel repeatedly, and becomes more powerful, and he asserts that this hearing will be conducted in an orderly fashion; the gentleman will not yell out, he will not attempt to disrupt the proceedings. We will now hear presentations of evidence by counsels to the Judiciary Committee, for up to 60 minutes; equally divided.

Mr. Burke, you may begin.

Burke starts off, before I came here today, my son asked me, "Dad, does the president have to be a good person?" Like many questions by young children, it had a certain clarity, and it was hard to answer. I said, son, it is not a requirement that the President be a good person; but that is the hope!

So, it is not a requirement that the President be a good person, and that is not why we are here today; that is not the issue; but in the very document that created the awesome presidency and its power, we <u>have</u> made it clear, there is a requirement that the President be a person who does not <u>abuse</u> his power. It is a requirement that the President be a person, instead, who does not risk the national security of this nation, and the integrity of our elections; in order to further his own reelection prospects.

It is a requirement, that the President not be a person who acts as though he's above the law, and putting his personal and political interests above the nation's interests. That is the lesson of the founders; they were concerned that someone would be elected president, who would use all the power of that Office to serve his own personal interests, at the expense of the people who elected him.

They decided that there needed to be a remedy, because they had suffered the abuses of King George; when they <u>had</u> no remedy. {The founders} imposed, that if a president commits a grave offense; a high crime, or misdemeanor; this body has the power to impeach that President. They wanted to ensure that a president could not serve his own interests, over that of the nation.

It flows from the very oath that all members of this body must take; to support and defend the Constitution, and bear true faith and allegiance to the same. That is why we are here today; and it is an unfortunate occasion, that these proceedings are necessary; but the President's actions have left us no choice.

The founders were very clear, in spelling out what they thought to be the greatest abuses, that would raise the most concern for our nation.

The Constitution spells out the warning signals, such that if a president violated or committed one of these, that would be a reason to potentially impeach that President, if there were an abuse of power, a betrayal of the national interest, or corruption of elections.

And what is so extraordinary about the conduct that we will be talking about today, is that President Trump didn't violate <u>one</u> of these; but all three!

First, the evidence is overwhelming that the President abused his power by pressuring Ukraine, and its new President to investigate a political opponent. The evidence is overwhelming, that the President Abused his power, by ramping up that pressure; by conditioning a wanted White House meeting, and a needed Military aid that had been approved, in order to get that president to investigate a political rival.

It is clear and overwhelming that, in abusing that power, the President betrayed the national interest, by putting his own political prospects over the national security of our country. It is clear that the President was corrupting our elections, by inviting foreign interference, to knock out an adversary; to help his prospects in the reelection.

It is why, in the beginning of the Constitution, James Madison had said that, because the presidency was to be administered by a single man, his corruption might be fatal to the Republic; and this scheme, by President Trump, was so brazen, so clearly supported by documents, actions, sworn testimony, and uncontradicted contemporaneous records, that is hard to imagine, that anybody could dispute those facts; let alone argue that that conduct does not constitute impeachable offense.

This is a big deal! President Trump did what a president of our nation is not allowed to do; it is why last week, the Constitutional scholar Professor Gerhart, said if what we are talking about is <u>not</u> impeachable, then <u>nothing</u> is impeachable.

President Trump's actions are impeachable offenses. They threaten our rule of law, they threaten our institutions, and as James Madison warned us, they threaten our Republic.

Let me begin where we must, with the facts, and evidence. First, it's important to understand why Ukraine was so important to our national security. Ukraine was under attack by an aggressive, hostile neighbor. Russia had already encroached on its territories; Ukraine was at great risk, that Russia would again take further territory.

Europe had stake in this; and so did we. I'm going to turn to an expert on this. Ambassador Taylor, who is one of the most highly decorated and recognized diplomats. For over 40 years, he served our country honorably; and he was appointed by President Trump himself, to be in charge of the US Embassy in Ukraine.

{Video footage rolls, of Taylor, saying:} The Russians are violating all of the rules, treaties, and understandings that they committed to, that actually kept the peace in Europe for nearly 70 years. That order, that kept the peace in Europe, and allowed for prosperity, as well as peace, in Europe, was violated by the Russians. It affects the world that we live in; that our children will grow up in; this affects the kind of world that we want to see evolve...

Burke resumes, that is Ambassador Taylor explaining why Ukraine was so important; and explaining why the president's action so significantly threatened our national security, our national defense policy, and our national interests. You've already heard the significant proof, that President Trump himself told the new President of Ukraine; President Zelensky; that he wanted him to investigate a political rival;

former Vice President Joe Biden. You will hear a lot about that today; but that proof is only the tip of the iceberg. There were so many important events, and meetings, and contemporaneous texts messages, emails, and other documents, that show this happened; and it happened exactly as it as is alleged.

It is clear that, in the scheme to pressure Ukraine to investigate a political rival, the person at the center that scheme was president Donald Trump. The facts cannot be disputed. President Trump used the powers of government for a domestic political errand; to put his political interests above that of the nation.

I'm going to turn to another expert; Fiona Hill, the National Security Council Senior Director in the Trump administration. She's going to explain what happened...

{Video footage rolls, of Dr. Hill, saying:} but it struck me when yesterday, you put up on the screen, Ambassador Sondland's emails, and who was on these emails; and he said these are the people you need to know. He was absolutely right; because he was involved in a domestic political errand; and we were involved in national security foreign-policy; and those two things had just diverged...

{Burke resumes} -and that tells you what the evidence shows; the President put his own domestic political interests above the nation's national security and foreign policy. A president cannot abuse his power, to secure an election. He cannot do that, at the expense of the American people. That is impeachable.

The President has tried to make excuses for his conduct; for why it's not wrongful, or corrupt, or an abuse of power; but the truth holds together. It makes sense, it is consistent with the evidence; when someone is offering an excuse that is not true, that is not consistent with the evidence, it does not make sense; it cannot be squared with what the facts show; and you will see that his excuses do not make sense.

The facts are clear, that President Trump put his own political and personal interests over the nation's interests. I'd like to go through what you're going to hear today, about the President's scheme.

From the facts that we have, first you will hear that President Trump's personal lawyer, Rudy Giuliani, pushed Ukraine to open an investigation of President Trump's political rival. Mr. Giuliani wanted the July 25th call; he wanted public statements, that Ukraine should investigate former Vice President Joe Biden. He tweeted about it; he put pressure on the new Ukrainian President; he went to Ukraine, and later he went again, with the assistance, and the direction of US officials who were told to aid the President's personal lawyer, on the President's behalf.

You'll hear that President Trump told his aides that he was relying on for Ukraine, that he wanted them to "talk to Rudy." What you're going to hear is that his close advisors had just gotten back, on May 23rd, from the inauguration of President Zelensky; they told President Trump, "We were impressed that he was elected on an anti-corruption platform; you should schedule a White House meeting; it's very important! it's very good for the United States." -and the President's response was, "talk to Rudy," who'd been out there saying that what the Ukrainian President had to do, was investigate Trump's political rival.

You'll hear that President Trump's advisors told President Zelensky, that President Trump would not schedule the White House meeting, unless he announced a Ukrainian investigation of former president Vice President Biden. There is documentation and sworn testimony that this happened; and there is no question, from the evidence, that the President did this.

President Zelensky desperately needed a White House meeting; both to show Russia that the US was still supporting Ukraine against Russia, and for Zelensky's own credibility, as a new President. You will hear that, to ramp up the pressure, what President Trump did, was he told his agencies to withhold Military security aid, that had been approved, and was supposed to be released to Ukraine; hundreds of millions of dollars; in order to put more pressure on Ukraine.

All of the agencies involved, the State Department, the Defense Department, and the National Security Council, said the aid should be released; and it is prudent to release it; and so, President Trump personally stopped it. And again, the contemporaneous evidence shows, and proves this.

People said that they were shocked! Ambassador Taylor said he was in astonishment! A witness said that it was illogical to do this; and the president never offered an explanation. Ultimately, it was discovered why he didn't; then on the July 25th call, President Trump explicitly told them he wanted them to conduct Ukrainian investigations; one into a US citizen; his political rival; and the other about the origins of interference into the 2016 election; some conspiracy theory; when all of our intelligence agencies agreed that Russia interfered with the 2016 election; once again, another investigation intended to help the President, politically.

And we know, the President cared about the investigations that would help him politically; and not Ukraine; and not the national security interests.

You don't have to take my word for it; let me play you something from David Holmes, who had worked in the US Embassy in Ukraine, and was speaking to Ambassador Sondland; whom President Trump had appointed. Ambassador Sondland had just come to Ukraine on July 26th, and met with President Zelensky. Afterward, Ambassador Sondland went to a restaurant with David Holmes, the US political affairs Counselor in Ukraine; where Sondland called President Trump on his cell phone. Mr. Holmes could hear that call...

{Video footage rolls of Holmes, saying:} ...and I heard Ambassador Sondland talking with the President. He explained that he was calling from Kyiv. I heard President Trump clarifying that he was in Ukraine. Ambassador Sondland replied, yes; I am in Ukraine; and he went on to state that President Zelensky "loves your ass." I then heard President Trump ask, so is he going to do the investigation? Ambassador Sondland replied that he's going to do it; adding that President Zelensky will do anything that you ask him to do...

Burke resumes, that is sworn testimony by David Holmes; who heard it from the President Himself; and it was clear to everyone; the most experienced people in government; that Donald Trump had appointed himself, into their positions; they knew what was going on. Let's look at a text message from Ambassador Taylor, around this time in {early} September. He wrote, "as I said on the phone, I think it's crazy to withhold security assistance for help with a political campaign!

Burke continues: Again, that is President Trump putting his own political and personal interests over the nation's interests; to hold aid desperately needed by Ukraine in order to combat Russia, and to show US support; purely in order to help his own campaign.

There have been other excuses offered by the president. The first excuse offered by President Trump, is that the aid was ultimately released... but the aid was only released after President Trump got caught doing this scheme.

On September 9th, the Committees of this House started an investigation; announce that they are investigating his conduct, with regard to Ukraine. Two days later was when he released the aid; and there was a news article in the Washington Post, on September 5th, exposing this scheme; and it was only after that, that he met with President Zelensky; and not in the White House, but in New York.

Another excuse offered by the President, was that it was motivated by "general corruption concerns;" and again, the evidence does not prove that it was plausible to hold aid. President Zelensky, in fact, was elected on anticorruption platform; he was reform candidate. President Trump's own people told him again and again, that President Zelensky is doing it the right way; just be supportive...

On his call with President Zelensky on July 25th, President Trump ignored the talking points that were prepared, for him to talk about corruption. He only wanted to talk about two things; the two investigations that helped him politically.

Every intelligence agency unanimous supported releasing the aid to Ukraine, that was appropriated. They did a study; a corruption study, and said release it. The White House never provided an explanation. The aid had already been approved; it was not for any corruption issues, that President Trump withheld it.

The next, is that Ukraine was not pressured, and the argument about that is that they haven't said that they were pressured... Well, Ukraine <u>was</u> pressured <u>then</u>, and still is pressured. They are desperately in need of the United States' support, in the battle against the threat of Russia. They've had to be careful what they said; but contemporaneous documents from Ukrainian officials themselves; emails and texts from

Ukrainian officials themselves, show the pressure that they felt It showed that they knew what President Trump was doing; showed what they had to do...

This is one from Bill Taylor to Ambassador Gordon Sondland, and Kurt Volker.

"Gordon, one thing Kurt and I talked about yesterday was Sasha Doniluk's point {Doniluk was Zelensky's Senior aide} that president Zelensky is sensitive about Ukraine being taken seriously; not merely used as an instrument in Washington domestic reelection politics."

They not only felt pressured, they got the message; they were not going to get a White House meeting; they were not going to get Military aid, unless they furthered Trump's reelection efforts.

Another one of their arguments made, is President Trump never said "quid pro quo," and what you will hear is that, on the call with Ambassador Sondland; after a Washington Post article came out September 5th, exposing the Ukrainian scheme... Days after that, President Trump was on a phone call with Ambassador Sondland; and without prompting, said there was "no quid pro quo," because he got caught!

And these are offerings defense; but even in Ambassador Sondland's sworn testimony, he said that he didn't buy it; because by then, President Trump not only was not dissuaded; he again described what he wanted; he didn't want Ukraine to actually conduct these investigations; he wanted them to announce the investigations of his political rival, to help him politically.

You will hear more about that; again, none of these excuses hold water; and they are refuted by testimony, contemporaneous records. You will hear it suggested that we should wait to proceed with these impeachment proceedings, because we have not heard from all of the witnesses, or obtained all the documents; but the reason we have not heard from other witnesses and documents, is because President Trump himself has obstructed the investigation!

He's directed his most Senior aides, who are involved in some of these events, not to come and testify; to defy subpoenas. He has told every one of his agencies with records that would be relevant, not to produce those records to us; to try to obstruct our investigation!

Now, this is evidence that President Trump is replaying the playbook used in the prior Department of Justice investigation; in an investigation he directed his White House counsel to create a false, phony record, and document lying, and denying that President Trump told him to fire the special counsel. He did many other things to interfere with that investigation; he attacked the investigators, and the witnesses; he called them horrible names; just as he has done here.

President Trump thought he got away with it on July 24th; that was the day that the special counsel (Bob Mueller) testified before this Committee, and the House Intelligence Committee. It was exactly the following day, that President Trump spoke to President Zelensky, in furtherance of his Ukraine scheme. He thought he had gotten away with it; he thought he could use his powers to interfere with an investigation, so he could do what he wanted, and act like he was above the law; and if he got caught, he would again use his powers to try and obstruct this investigation.

He would again use his powers to obstruct the investigation, and prevent the facts from coming out; and that's exactly what he did.

But fortunately, because of the true American Patriots who came forward and testified, despite these threats by the President, against the people who worked in his own administration, they told the story; they, on their own, produced documents that provide uncontroverted, clear, and overwhelming evidence, that President Trump did this scheme.

He put his political reelection interests over the nation's national security, and the integrity of the elections. He did it intentionally, he did it corruptly; he abused his powers, in ways that the founders feared most; no person in this country has the ability to prevent investigations, and neither does the President. Our Constitution does not allow it. No one is above the law; not even the president.

One of the concerns and requirements of finding an impeachable offense, is as an urgency; a sense that this {violation} could be repeated. Well, again, first all of the Constitutional experts who have testified in the press, have recognized that obstructing an investigation is impeachable; but here, the re-offense we are talking about that's being interfered, and obstructed with, is that he is going to interfere with the very election that's coming up; and I submit to you, given what happened with the Department of Justice investigation; given what's happening here; if, in fact, President Trump can get away with what he did, again, our imagination is the only limit to what President Trump may do next; or what a future president may do next, to try and abuse his or her power, to serve their own interests, over that of the nation's.

I would like to turn back to what the founders are most concerned about, in terms of the ABCs of potential presidential abuses. It is extraordinary, that the President's conduct was a trifecta; it checked all 3 boxes. Let's begin with abuse of power; what that means, is to use the power of the Office, to obtain improper personal benefit, while ignoring the national interests; or when he acts in ways that are grossly inconsistent with, and undermine, the separation of powers, that is the foundation of our democratic system.

Now, this question of whether the president engaged in abuse of power, came up before, when this Congress considered the impeachment of President Nixon; and after an action was taken, the President famously said, that if the President does it, is not illegal.

This body rejected that, because that's not so; that goes directly contrary to what the Constitution says; but President Trump has said the same thing, in responding to the prior investigation by the Department of Justice, and defending his conduct. Trump had said, "Here, I have, in article 2, I have the right to do whatever I want, as President." -That he has to the right to do whatever he wants, as President; that is wrong! President Nixon had said a similar thing; that is not what the Constitution provides, that is not what the country demands. He does not have the right to do whatever he wants!

Turning to the 2nd abuse of power concern, betrayal of the nation; of most concern, it is betrayal of the nation about informed powers. The American people have suffered foreign influence, when President Trump treated Military aid that had been approved; taxpayer dollars; and decided to treat it as his own checkbook, to try and further his own reelection chances. That reflects what the founders were concerned about; and finally, corruption over our elections; the Framers knew that corrupt Leaders are Leaders who act corruptly, and concentrate their powers, to manipulate elections, and undercut adversaries.

They talked about it frequently; one of the Framers thought that electoral treachery, particularly involving foreign powers, was a critical abuse that could support, and lead to impeachment.

Now, the American people learned, last election, how dangerous foreign intervention in our elections can be. Let me show another clip, of presidential candidate Trump, on the campaign trail. {Trump says:} Russia, if you're listening, I hope you're able to find the 30,000 emails that are missing; I think you'll probably be rewarded mightily by our press..." -and Russia <u>was</u> listening; within approximately 5 hours of President Trump's invitation to Russia, to interfere in our election, by trying to hack in obtain the emails of his political opponent; Russia, in fact, tried to do that; for the first time!

The very Officers who were then indicted by the Justice Department, for that conduct; they took candidate Trump's invitation.

Now, the American people learned a lesson; but President Trump, unfortunately, apparently learned a <u>different</u> lesson. Let's look:

{Another clip of Trump plays:} "Well, I think that if they are honest about it, they would start a major investigation into the Bidens..." {that's Trump talking about Ukraine, while his helicopter copter is idling in the background.} -A simple answer; what did he want President Zelensky to do? -So, even after he got caught, he is saying again; {Zelensky's} foreign nation, depended upon US support militarily, and otherwise; and again, {President Trump is telling them what to do; and unlike in 2016, when he only had a campaign platform; he was again extending an invitation platform to of foreign power; but now, he has the leverage of government under his control; to not only invite interference, but to put pressure on that country to do it; and that's exactly what he did!

You will hear more about that, in the presentation by the House Intelligence Committee; and what's most striking, as we come back to this issue that the Framers were most concerned about, it was the continuing risk of wrongdoing.

The fact that President Trump did this after he was caught, shows the risk of what will happen, if this body really does believe he can act as though he were above the law. He really does believe this; it is evident by this conduct, that he can put his personal and political interests over the nation's interests; over the national security interests; over the nation's integrity of its elections.

So, of course, we do have an election coming up; and that's not a reason to postpone this discussion, it's a reason that we <u>must</u> have this discussion, to make sure this President doesn't do it; to make sure future presidents do not do it.

It is the hope, that in these discussions, we put aside political rancor, and disagreements, and have a fair discussion about the facts, and this conduct; not just as it relates to President Trump, but as to the presidency itself, for future presidents.

My son, and our children, and our grandchildren; they will study this moment in history; they will read all of your remarks; they will learn about all of your actions; and that is not a reason to vote for or against impeachment; for that, you must vote your conscience.

But it is a reason to have a fair debate, about what the undisputed facts show; to recognize that it is wrong, it is very wrong, and it cannot happen again; with this President, or any President. It is a reason to talk about whether we want our children, and grandchildren, to live in a country where the president elected by the people can put his own personal and political interests, over the interests of the people who elected him.

It is a reason for these debates to begin fairly, and focus on the facts; to make sure the presentations we are going to hear, will not distort the record. A focus on process, or to raise extraneous matters that are really intended to distract, rather than focus on what the conduct was, at issue here; it is a reason to focus on the facts, and what is in the country's best interest.

History, and future generations, will be the judge.

Adam Schiff says, thank you Mr. Burke.

Mr. Castor you are recognized for 30 minutes… {The Republicans interrupt Nadler again, and insist on making a point of order, before the hearing continues. The point of order, is that the witness has used language which impugns the motives of the President; they are upset because it casts the President in a bad light, of course. "Those words should be stricken from the record!"

Nadler responds, "The rules {we determined for this set of hearings} are sustained; the witnesses are not constrained; the point of order is not sustained. The witnesses are not subject to the rules of the Committee… The topic of the hearing is the President's misconduct, so none of us should be surprised that we are hearing testimony that is critical of the President I do not find that the witness's comments are disorderly; I find that they are pertinent to the subject matter of this hearing.

{Nadler continues} The witness <u>would</u> be able to continue; except that his time has expired. the general suspended the general suspended he's talking about {A Republican Committee member voices objection:} He is not talking about the conduct of the president; he's talking about the motives, and the character of the President of the United States!

Nadler reasserts, the rules of the forum apply to members of the House; not to witnesses. {A Republican Committee member asks to appeal the ruling.}

Nadler explains, that is not a ruling; the point of order is not sustained! {One of the Democrats says, I move to table the point of order} and Nadler says, the motion is sustained; and it is not in debate. All in favor of the motion to table, say Aye-

Nadler announces that the "Aye's" have it; the motion to table is sustained. As could be predicted, the Republicans asked for a rollcall, to delay the proceedings. All of the Democratic Committee members vote to table the point of order. The political reporter announces 24 Aye's, and 15 Ney's.

Nadler continues, Mr. Castor is recognized. Next, the Republicans ask for a parliamentary inquiry. Nadler maintains; I will not recognize the parliamentary inquiry, at this time.

Good morning; my name Steve Castor, I am a Congressional Staff member; I serve in the Oversight Committee, with Mr. Jordan; and also, for the purposes of this investigation, I will share, as a Staffer with the Judiciary Committee, and Mr. Collins in the House permanent Committee on intelligence; and with Mr. Nunez. I'm sure is atypical for a staffer to be presenting, but again, thanks for having me.

The purpose of this hearing, as we understand it, is to discuss whether President Donald J. Trump's conduct constitutes a high crime; it does not. Such a Committee could consider impeachment to remove the President, and should not.

This case, in many respects, comes down to 8 lines in a call transcript. Let me say clearly and unequivocally, that the answer to that question is no. The record of the Democrats inquiry does not show that president Trump abused the power of his Office, or obstructed Congress. {How else could you possibly consider his blockade of all documentation and cooperation otherwise?!}

To impeach a president that 63 million people voted for, over 8 lines in a call transcript, is bologna. {This is about a year-long carefully-orchestrated scheme; not merely a phone call.}

Democrats seek to impeach President Trump, not because they have evidence of High Crimes and Misdemeanors, but because they disagree with his policies. {Yes, but that's beside the point.}

This impeachment inquiry is not the organic outgrowth of serious misconduct {Yes it is!!} -and Democrats have been searching for a set of facts in which to impeach President Trump since his inauguration, on January 20th, 2017. Just 27 minutes after the president's inauguration that day, the Washington Post ran a story that the campaign to impeach the president has already begun. {There is nothing wrong with this, if several intelligent politicians and legal experts have assessed that this might be a proper response to Trump's damaging behavior.}

The article reported that Democrats, and liberal activists mounted broad opposition, to stymie Trump's agenda.

Their first impeachment strategy was based on the belief that the Constitution's emoluments clause would be the vehicle. {Trump was visibly enriching himself, by inviting foreign diplomats to Washington, and having them stay at his hotel, near the White House; and there were other ways in which Trump was obviously using his Office to augment his business income; he also had pledged to disavow himself of all other business interests, but the legal paperwork he drew up still indicated he would be earning a future benefit, based on revenue taken in by his businesses, after he leaves Office.}

In the first 2 years of the administration, Democrats of the House introduce articles impeachment to remove President Trump from Office, on several very different factual bases. {There were several different ways Trump was very apparently engaging in impeachable conduct.}

On January 3rd, the very first day, Congressman Sherman introduced articles of impeachment against the President; and on the same day, representative Kelly said, we are going to go in there, and we are going to impeach the President. In May of 2019, representative Green said on MSNBC, that if we don't impeach this President, he will be reelected. {That's just one man's speculation; it doesn't mean anything!}

Even Speaker Pelosi, who is said that impeachment is a somber, and prayerful exercise, has called President Trump an imposter {A rose by any other name…} -and said it is dangerous to allow voters to judge his performance in 2020. {With all of the disinformation; between what the Russians are up to, combined with the lies, false reports, and false promises he can broadcast with unique effectiveness due to his bully pulpit of "con"}

This session has reflected that the Democrats have used the power of their Majority. {As well they should, under the circumstances; too bad it won't be enough to stamp him out of the political sphere right away.}

In the last 11 months, in the Oversight Committee, the Democrats first announced witness was Michael Cohen, a disgraced felon who pleaded guilty to lying to Congress, when he came before us the Oversight Committee; and he even lied again, as many as 8 times, to the Oversight Committee. {Yes, it is disgraceful that Cohen did the dirty work, to cover up Trump's routinely-immoral and criminal actions; but he then came clean, after all; and gave us some astoundingly awful reports about the true nature of Trump's business and political conduct.}

Democrats demanded information about the President's personal finances; and even subpoenaed the president's accounting firm, for large swaths of sensitive and personal financial information. {No other

President has hidden their personal financial particulars; why should Trump be able to?

Castor talks about how Michael Cohen lied to Congress, numerous times in his initial testimony; but that's because, at that point, he was simply continuing his allegiance to President Trump; in which he had pledged, and upheld, for many years; but then at some point, within a few weeks after that first round of testimony to Congress, Michael Cohen had a change of heart, and decided to come forward with the awful truth about Trump. So, when Castor tries to make it seem as though Michael Cohen is just a liar, and of questionable credibility, this is just one more of Castor's twisted statements, also reflective of the Republicans' defense strategy, which is to, as Mr. Burke put it, create distractions and not talk about the issue at hand; which is the misconduct of the president.}

Back to Castor's diatribe: The subpoena was issued with the objection of many Republicans; {in other words, once the Republicans knew that Cohen was going to tell the truth, and no longer protect the president's corruption, the Republican Committee members tried to prevent Cohen from coming to testify truthfully, about all that he knows regarding President Trump, and his own history of being a fixer, and covering up Trump's illegal and immoral conduct.}

In the Ways and Means Committee, the Democrats demanded the president's personal tax return information; the reason they cited for wanting the president's tax returns was to oversee the IRS's audit process for presidential tax returns. you can judge that for yourself. {Officials are blowing the whistle, all over the place, regarding Trump's conduct; in this case, an IRS staffer wrote to Congress, of irregularities in the auditing process related to Trump's tax returns. Trump's dirty dealings resound throughout government; but he keeps effectively blocking the path to being brought to justice.}

In the Financial Services Committee, Democrats demanded and subpoenaed the presidents bank records, going back 10 years. {This was after Michael Cohen testified that Trump had routinely inflated the value of his assets on paper, when applying for financing; and he falsely undervalued those same assets, when applying for insurance coverage.

Our President is an outlaw who covers his tracks well; but he will still go down in history as an outlaw!}

The Financial Services Committee staff, and Republicans tell me that the information demanded would cover every credit card swipe, debit card purchase, in every member of the Trump family, including his minor child. The reason the Democrats gave, for why they wanted such voluminous personal information about the Trump family, was financial industry compliance with banking statutes, and regulations. {Yes; credible witnesses have testified that Trump is guilty as sin, on many levels; but he pays to hide it; just like he did with Stormy Daniels.}

Here, in the Judiciary Committee, Democrats sent out letters demanding information from over 80 recipients; including the president's children, business partners, his employees, his campaign, his businesses, and his Foundation. {Castor makes it seem like it was completely inappropriate, to ask for financial information on Trump's whole family; but his family is complicit in his crooked business dealings;

-and he used the verbiage, that the Judiciary Committee had asked for information on from Trump's "children." I don't know if you can legally call an adult son or daughter somebody's "children." I don't think you can; so again, this is just another distortion that the Republicans are trying to float, to the American public. It's really pretty sad; but furthermore, the reason why it's appropriate for Congress to want to get information about Trump's sons and daughters is because they are in a family business together, as adults; and in fact, when the President first was elected, and had pledged to disavow himself of all business interests, his family who works with him every day in the White House, supposedly, technically took over that responsibility; but we can be pretty sure that Trump still call the shots, and has commanded his family to proceed with business transactions according to his wishes; so it is totally appropriate for Congress to want to look into the business records of a president who is very strongly suspected of enriching himself, as part of his presidency, which is absolutely prohibited for a President, of course.}

The main event for the new Judiciary Committee was a report from Mr. Mueller, that Democrats believed would serve as the evidentiary basis for impeaching the president. Despite interviewing 500 witnesses, issuing 2,800 subpoenas, executed almost 500 search warrants, and spending $25 million, the Special Counsel's 19 attorneys, 40 FBI agents, analysts, and staff found no conspiracy coordination between the Trump campaign and the Russian government. (Of course that's a complete prevarication; after Trump's Russia collusion accusations did not pan out, and of course we know that they really did, otherwise Mueller's team wouldn't have kept following hundreds of leads, on hundreds of individuals apparently involved in this vast, somewhat-traceable conspiracy; they just couldn't nail Trump, because of the concerted effort to withhold any conclusive information from falling into the hands of Mueller's team.}

Democrats focused their efforts on obstruction of justice to criticize the Attorney General bar for concluding that no crime of production having cured have Kurt that no crime of obstruction had occurred but in fact it was entirely appropriate no crime just had occurred in the special counsel investigation but in fact it was entirely appropriate that the Attorney General made that call because the special counsel declined to do so {But I should point out that the only reason that Mueller declined to do so; and he specifically wrote this into his report; was because of this OLC opinion written years ago, that a sitting president cannot be indicted. Mueller did say however, in his report, that he considered that Congress has the proper authority to take action against the President, if they deemed it necessary, after fully digesting Mueller's 400-page report. Then again, the report was highly redacted, and Congress also was not able to see a transcript of the testimony to the Grand Jury; which I'm pretty certain would've been additionally damning; and perhaps it would have led to a more successful confrontation of President Trump's ill conduct.}

The Democrats' Mueller hearing was underwhelming, to say the least, and the sequel, with Corey Lewandowski definitely did not move the impeachment needle either. {Trump and Barr successfully put a muzzle on Mueller. However, as more and more came out, about Trump's Ukraine scheme, pretty-much weekly, since the first week of

September, one by one, over 100 Congressmen announced they were now on board with impeachment}

The Intelligence Committee too, was heavily invested in the Russia collusion investigation. Committee Democrats hired former Federal Prosecutors, to prepare for their anticipated effort to impeach the president. {Those prosecutors may even have paid the Committee, just to be able to speak out against the odiousness of Trump!}

Now that the Russia collusion allegations did not work out, {They should have, but Barr foiled our plans, with his dastardly lies, and spins, and withholding of the report, for weeks, from the public; who should have seen it right away; it's very damning for Trump!}

Castor continues, Democrats had settled on the Ukraine phone; call 8 lines the President uttered on July 25th, with Ukrainian President Zelensky {-and of course, that's not what this is about; those 8 lines were merely the tip of the iceberg, which prompted an investigation that, along with the whistleblower complaint, indicated that Trump had seriously abused his power.}

Castor goes on, -but the Foreign Affairs Committee; the Committee of jurisdiction wasn't given the jurisdiction, to deal with the Ukraine scheme. {The Republicans had tried to say that this issue was most appropriately handled within that Committee; but this is only because they were suggesting that what President Trump had done was not that serious; and Democratic Congressmen were unanimous in denouncing that idea.}

Castor then says, -neither was the Oversight Committee; the House's chief investigative entity. The Judiciary Committee was only recently brought back into the mix, after testifying had been concluded. Instead, the impeachment inquiry was run by the House Intelligence Committee and these former Federal prosecutors.

Democrats on the Intelligence Committee ran the impeachment inquiry in a manifestly unfair way. {That may be Castor's version, however, the Intelligence Committee was very appropriately developing intelligence on all of the people that were involved; as well as regarding all the people who wanted to report what they knew about Trump's dirty little scheme; and then again, as I've said before, Bill Barr's Justice Department should have, by every measure, opened an investigation into this wrongdoing; but Bill Barr declined, because he is one of President Trump's strongest protectors; and that should never be; the Attorney General is designated as the people's lawyer, not the president's lawyer. This was totally inappropriate; and it will go down in history as an outrage, of course. Anyway, because Barr would not open an investigation, and an investigation was very much in order; the Democrats realized that, if they were being true to their oath, they were charged with confronting this abuse of power, and obstruction of justice. (Right from the start, All witnesses and documentation was not to be provided to Congress); but the Intelligence Committee saw that it would have to conduct the initial closed-door hearings; to get independent depositions from each of the witnesses; thus preventing any possibility that one witness would hear other witnesses' public testimony, and change their own account. And then once the initial closed-door depositions had been completed, the Intelligence Committee went to the next stage, which was public hearings; so, there was nothing at all improper about what happened. The Republicans are just trying to distract from the real issue at stake which is the presidents corrupt conduct.

Next, Castor claims that the secrecy of the Intelligence Committee's depositions "weaponized" the investigation; allowing misleading public narratives to form, including all the careful leaks of witness testimony; but what Castor and the Republicans are calling "leaks" were simply tidbits of unclassified information that came out of the initial depositions, disclosing significant details about the Trump Ukraine scheme; and the Republicans thought this was unfair; to broadcast what these officials and other credible witnesses that came forward, had honestly testified to and revealed.}

The Intelligence Committee refused to invite Republicans' selected witnesses; {but that was only because we know the Republicans would've called witnesses that would muddy the waters and dispute the credibility of these fine foreign service Officers. In fact, the few witnesses that were requested by the Republicans, that were also witnesses the Democrats wanted to hear, and so therefore they did have those witnesses appear, those few witnesses did in fact try to denounce the credibility of Col. Vindeman, most notably; but also other witnesses, such as Dr. Hill.}

In the public hearings, Democrats again refused to let Republicans invite their own witnesses, {for the same reason; that they would cast a distorted picture of what truly happened.}

Castor says that the Democrats interrupted Republican questioning; {but we know that the only interrupted questioning was merely heckling-trying-to-be-passed-off-as-questioning; and many, many times, heckling about wanting the whistleblower's identity to be revealed; and other such heckling, and out of order grandstanding, that certain Republican Committee members engaged in, liberally.

Castor says the Democrats never brought any of their subpoenas for a vote on whether they should be issued; {but do any of us doubt that, since the House Majority is Democratic, and there was very serious concern about what the President had been engaging in, every subpoena would have been voted a pass, I'm pretty sure.}

Castor says, Democrats are obsessed with impeaching the president; {and of course they are; because he's crooked as hell!} He says, the Democrats went searching for a set of facts in which to impeach the president; {but they didn't have to search very far! There were so many violations that kept popping up, almost every week! Trump inviting foreign diplomats to stay at his hotel in Washington, and other Emoluments Clause violations, such as Trump routing Military planes thousands of miles away from Military bases where US planes would normally refuel, in order to bring them to an airport very near to his resort property in Ireland. It should be noted that this airport was remote, and it was in danger of closing due to lack of business, which would have pretty certainly put Trump's resort out of business; and these refueling stops; which over a couple of years amounted to 11 million gallons of jet fuel sold, at that airport, certainly propped up the continuance of that airfield; and therefore the continuance of Trump's nearby resort; and I should also point out that Trump routed official business through that resort, including entourages of Secret Service people accompanying the officials; so these were all violations of the Emoluments Clause. Then, there was Mara Lago, where Trump had invited foreign diplomats to come and stay there when he was conducting meetings with them. Then there was the Doral Club, in Florida; where he had announced plans to have next year's G-7 summit held their, which would've created a huge amount of revenue for President Trump and his family once again.}

The impeachment effort is clearly an effort to upend our political system; {Yeah, the political system of corrupt Republicans!} According to Politico, the Speaker has tightly scripted every step of the impeachment inquiry. Democrats have reportedly convened focus groups, to test which allegations; whether it be quid pro quo, or bribery, or extortion, were most compelling, to the American public. {Of course, all 3 were true; they just were trying to connect with the American people, on which way that they most prevalently could identify with the same set of corrupt behaviors.

Castor says, Democrats must strike while the iron is hot. Castor tells us that the entire impeachment effort, from when Nancy Pelosi announced it, in September, has so far lasted 76 days.

As Professor Turley testified last Wednesday, this impeachment would stand out among modern impeachments, as the shortest proceeding with the thinnest evidentiary record, and the narrowest grounds ever used to impeach a president. {Well, that's a completely twisted statement; because there have only been two impeachments, in 200 years; so, the most recent was Bill Clinton; and before that, the last Presidential impeachment was 100 years ago! -and of course, we've never had such a strong reason to oust a president, with all of the horrendously terrible conduct that Trump has exhibited; but when Castor says it is the thinnest evidentiary record? I would certainly dispute that! The only basis that Castor could possibly have for saying this, is the fact that Trump prohibited everyone from testifying, and kept every document from being transferred; and yet still there were something like 17 witnesses who came forward, yet defying his lawless orders.

The artificial and arbitrary political deadline by which Democrats are determined to finish impeachment, by Christmas; leads to a rushed process, and missed opportunities to obtain relevant information. {We have all of the information we would ever need, already!} Democrats avoided the accommodations process required by federal court, in disputes between contractors and the Executive; {these things that Castor is now contending, are baseless process arguments; such as that it's inappropriate to rush the process; whereas, the aggregate of all of the witnesses clearly demonstrated the ill manner with which the President conducted himself and several other officials, so there was no need to go any further; and then, when witnesses were subpoenaed and would not come forward because of Trump's muzzling efforts, the Intelligence Committee took these matters to court and they won, and these witnesses were supposed to come and testify after that; but what happened was Trump appealed those decisions and kept appealing the next higher courts decisions that were decided in favor of the Intelligence Committee to, until they reached the Supreme Court; and at that point it might've taken years before these issues were resolved; so it is absolutely ridiculous for Castor to suggest that the Democrats did something improper. They are responsibly trying to impeach a lawless president as soon as possible; and the conventional pathway of the past has now become so jerry-rigged, to slow the process through the court system, that Trump's impeachment would be impossible, until maybe a couple of years down the road; if Trump was even still in Office, by then.

Castor says Democrats avoided the accommodation process required by federal courts; in disputes between Congress and the executive; Democrats declined to negotiate with the administration for the production of documents and witnesses; {I don't understand what he could possibly mean; if subpoenas for documents were presented, and the White House refused to comply, what is there to negotiate?}

Castor says sometimes the threat of a contempt proceeding gets you a different result; {but in this case, a contempt charge would trigger another worse result; being that Congress has very little power, compared to the command of a president in Office, to actually arrest and imprison those violating the subpoena, who are found to be in contempt.}

Sometimes the witnesses choose to appear, when contempt is on the table; {but I can only assume that Trump would have offered protection from any consequence that an official might be given; he has exhibited loud and clear, that he intends to use his full power, to disobey Congress.}

Castor brings up that, Democrats withdrew a subpoena; {at one point, when it was going to lead to a drawn-out court battle, which was pointless for the Democrats, who wanted to remove the President right away.}

Democrats told witnesses who refused to cooperate, that their actions would be held against them; {as is only reasonable, because by definition, the executive branch and the Congressional branch are co-equal in power; which means that, all else being equal, witnesses who know of Trump's wrongdoing, who won't come to testify, should properly have that held against them; and they will, throughout history.}

Democrats threatened federal employees that their salaries could be withheld for not meeting their demands. {In one breath, Castor criticizes the Democrats for not going through the process of trying to render uncooperative witnesses held in contempt of court; and in the next breath, he criticizes Democrats for threatening something of a much lesser magnitude, as inducement.}

These tactics are fundamentally unfair; {I can't believe he is saying that this is unfair, when Trump withheld every possible piece of evidence against him, which is the type of information, documentation, and witness testimony that has always been given to Congress, during an investigation of this type. Even in the Nixon era, where some of the same barring of documentation and testimony was a first-time precedent, there still was plenty of documentation and witness testimony that was forthcoming. Yet, the Trump administration, under Trump's personal order, has not delivered a single document, or cooperated in any way, with Congress's investigation. what other possible terminology could describe this, better than obstruction of Congress?!}

Castor says Congressional investigations take time; {so is he saying that there is a minimum duration that an impeachment investigation should stretch out to, even if conclusive evidence has been gathered? -Or is he saying that he wants Congress to take their time, in confronting a lawless crook of a president, who is endangering national security, and making terrible, rash decisions, that badly affect our country; and the world as a whole, even!

Castor suggests that Congress must take the information offered, even if they don't like the terms. {Yes, I would say that when the terms are, "We will give you nothing!" -that those are pretty unlikable terms.}

Castor accuses Congress of blocking information out; {that's a laugh! We're blocking information?!}

Castor points out that, even in recent Congressional investigations, there has been give-and-take between Congress and the executive; {but in this case, the executive has only taken; Trump is all take and no give.}

Castor suggests that Congress did not wait long enough for the White House to become willing to turn over documents; {however, we do note that when Congress did try to go through the courts, to try and overrule the White House's blanket refusal to provide anything that the Congress had asked for, they simply went through the motions to tie up those disputes, potentially for years; again, Republicans just wish to postpone the idea of impeaching Trump perpetually and endlessly; even though he should have been removed yesterday!}

Castor then contends that, contrary to talking points, the Trump administration has in fact cooperated with, and facilitated Congressional oversight and investigations. {Well, I suppose if you go far enough back, to a point before the Trump presidency started, this would hold true; but it certainly has does not hold true for the Trump administration; especially since the Mueller investigation began.}

Next, Castor tells the story of what happened when Democrats discovered that Trump was blithely giving White House security clearances to his family members, when the conventional channels for determining whether a clearance is appropriate were being usurped. For example, officials determined that Jared Kushner should not receive a security clearance; but Trump somehow circumvented the only process that has ever been used to make these determinations, and ordered that clearances be given anyway; which is just one other national security risk Trump put the nation at, in order to win his way; then doling out official responsibilities to merely inexperienced family members with no background in Government; yet another violation; nepotism.}

Castor explains that when the White House agreed to let the officials who go through the vetting process, to determine whether a security clearance is appropriate, for each individual that the President has requested; that when the Democrats wanted to investigate how these clearances were given anyway, the White House refused to let these people appear before Congress, without a staff lawyer to speak on their behalf. I'm sure the Democrats knew they wouldn't get any information, because the staff lawyer would strategically block the witnesses from giving any truthful testimony that would be incriminating; so, it wasn't worth pursuing nailing Trump for this foul behavior of his. {He has so many foul behaviors!}

Castor explains that eventually what happened, is that the Republicans on the Committee arranged to call the witnesses, with their attorneys; {and what a great surprise; that kangaroo court found that there was no wrongdoing! But in fact, we learned through news reports, that Jared Kushner should not have received a security clearance; and I think there were a few others too. I believe the news story was that, despite the fact that these security clearances were denied, Trump then forced the issue, and got some crooked official in his administration; no doubt an appointee of his; to issue the security clearance anyway. So, this is how the Republicans conduct business as usual in their lawmaker chambers; they just take matters into their own crooked hands, and make certain that no real wrongdoing is established, as long as it protects their fearless Leader, Mr. Trump.}

Castor says that the Democrats have denied having a negotiation in good faith with the White House, on the issue of documentation that should be turned over to Congress, for their investigation; {but if the White House is clearly unwilling to turn over a shred of documentation, I don't see what good any attempted negotiation would really do. Trump publicly announced, over the airwaves, that he would block every effort of Congress to investigate his wrongdoing; and we know that he could not afford to relax that standard, or he would be unequivocally, and indisputably found guilty of committing several crimes and coverups.}

Castor contends that the evidentiary record in this impeachment process is incomplete, and in many places incoherent. {I don't know how he could possibly come to this conclusion; anybody reading the transcripts, that I have transcribed here in this book, would certainly call the evidence against President Trump very clear and conclusive.}

Castor says that, since Congress failed to pursue all avenues available to it, to try and get documentation and witnesses' testimony, that makes the process somehow invalid. {Again, this is just a delaying tactic; why should the Congress go to any further lengths than it already has, to get valid testimony out of additional credible witnesses?}

Professor Turley had said in last week's hearing, that he's concerned about a paucity of evidence {i.e.- an insufficiency}, and an abundance of anger. I believe that this impeachment not only fails the standard of past impeachments; {we should understand that there is no appreciable record of past impeachments; you can't call one impeachment, decades ago, and another 100 years before that or whatever; you can't call that a record; and times have changed quite significantly, even since the Clinton impeachment; in terms of the political landscape.}

Castor thinks that these proceedings create a dangerous precedent for future proceedings; {that's a laugh! He doesn't think that it creates it dangerous precedent to allow Trump to blithely act in all of these lawless ways; defying any attempted restraint, defying Congress's oversight responsibility attempts, defying the Constitution's clearly stating, that foreign interference in elections poses an extreme risk to the very democracy that we have cherished for generations. Castor doesn't think that this is a risk; yet he thinks that Congress's circumventing the intentional endless red tape, that Republicans have hidden behind, in order to protect the President From successful confrontation regarding his lawless corruption. This, he thinks, would be setting a dangerous precedent; what an immoral idiot!}

Turley had said, that a lack of proof in this matter is so damaging; {but again, Trump has blocked any possibility of conclusive proof coming out; but that doesn't mean that we haven't seen very clear evidence, of a nature that should definitely warrant Congressional cooperation in impeaching this President.}

Castor contends that that Intelligence Committee's case relies heavily on ambiguous facts, presumptions, and speculation. The idiot continues, President Turley {he didn't even stop to realize this faux pas}, warned that impeachments have been based on proof; not presumption; {and again there's only been one impeachment, that anybody in the country can remember; and it was at a time where solid evidence was accessed because, unlike now, its provision was not blocked; so if he is trying to say that a president can act in corrupt ways, and then, as long as he can effectively cover it up, and prevent any first-hand evidence from becoming revealed, then that should entitle him to elude being impeached for his corrupt misconduct; that is so ridiculous!}

Castor preposterously says, contrary to Democrat allegations, President Trump was not asking for a favor that would help his reelection; he was asking for assistance in helping our country move forward, from the divisiveness of the Russia collusion investigation. {He thinks that, to investigate what was so evidently disturbing, to any lawmaker who cares about the fundamentals of our democracy, that it should not have been investigated like it was? Castor is so preposterous, and he represents the whole clan of crooked Republican lawmakers, that are just being ridiculous, and preposterous, and just trying to let this president get away with murder, murder of our Constitution, that is! Republicans should not be able to make, this whole spectrum of false contentions, right after the last witness, a lawyer who laid out the truth, in a very pragmatic way; who had just debunked all of those previously-stated false contentions. This whole hearing process is quite preposterous because of this allowance.}

Carefully crafted, Castor makes the comment that Zelensky did not vocalize that he felt any pressure; but we just heard Burke say that it was very definitely established in writing, in the emails that went back and forth between Sondland and the Ukrainian officials throughout the summer; establishing that they did, in fact, know what was going on; and that they felt pressured. They made it clear, that they didn't want to have to give-in, to that pressure. So again, we see Republican trickery and distortions; that's all they have!}

Castor claims that the Ukrainians did not know about the pause in the aid, until August 28th, when the Politico article came out, exposing it; but even if this was the case; which it wasn't, they knew weeks before that; still the aid was not released until September 12th, so that means there was a two-week period, when the Ukrainians did know that the aid was being withheld; and they were still being pressured to make these CNN-interview announcements; so, is Castor saying, that if the hold on the aid was only holding Ukrainians over a barrel for two weeks; and not since Trump first put the initial pressure on them, on July 25th, that this should render Trump excused?!}

Among the other bullshit that Castor is contending, he says that President Trump believes that other foreign allies should contribute more in aid to Ukraine; {but we learned, from testimony within the Intelligence Committee hearings, that the other European allies contributed something like 20 times as much as the US has, to Ukraine assistance, since 2014.}

Castor says that there were Ukrainian officials and journalists who spoke out against President Trump in 2016, when he was running for election; {but it has come out, in Dr. Hill's testimony, that there were many countries that made similar critical comments and assertions regarding Trump, during the same time period; and yet those countries still got their aid… -and Trump didn't mention any upset over what they had said… so this was not about Trump being upset or concerned about Ukraine; it was undoubtedly about the fact that Trump had connections in Ukraine, that would most easily enable a false narrative to be broadcast about Joe Biden, his political rival; and the promotion of this false conspiracy theory about Ukraine interference in our 2016 elections.}

Castor says that President Zelensky was an untried Leader, with a connection to a Ukrainian oligarch; {but he was elected, in a landslide victory, because his platform was that he was going to end the corruption that has been a political pandemic in Ukraine, for decades; and the Ukrainian oligarch that Castor is referring to, was Zelensky's greatest patron; and we find out that he was funding weapons and other Military aid to Ukrainians on the front lines of the war, against Russia; so how could the Trump administration be the least bit upset about that? Giuliani met personally with this oligarch, so he and Trump had to have known!}

Castor finally contends that the Republicans believe that there are legitimate explanations for these actions that are not nefarious, as the Democrats allege; {what a ridiculous joke!}

Castor contends, the evidence shows that President Trump has faithfully executed the duties of his Office, by delivering on what he promised the American voters he would do. Democrats may disagree with the president's policy decisions, or the matter in which he governs; but those disagreements are not enough to justify the clear revocable action of removing him from Office. Oh, we beg to differ!

Castor accuses the Democrats of hyperbole and histrionics; {I would say that the Republicans whole defense against what is being revealed about President Trump's conduct, and his malevolent thinking; now that is Republican hyperbola; and the ridiculous rants that Republican Committee members, like Jordan, and Stefanik, and Conaway, and Ratcliffe, would definitely be accurately described as histrionics!}

Another completely preposterous contention of Castor's here, is that this administration did not obstruct Congress; and this record also does not support the conclusion that President Trump obstructed Congress, during the impeachment inquiry. {God! I can't even believe it!!! This bastard has the gall to say that the Trump administration, and especially Trump himself, did not obstruct the shit out of this investigation?!!!! Castor, you are so full of shit!}

Castor falsely claims that President Trump released the two transcripts of his calls with President Zelensky. {He did not release the transcript of the July 25 call; he released a call summary, which I'm sure excluded some even-more-damning evidence; as if we would need any more damning evidence, to show his clear guilt; but I'm sure there was plenty more where that came from. The entire July 25th call transcript was ferreted away in the most top-secret server in Washington.}

Castor contends that President Trump has been forced to resist taking part in this process; {that is complete bullshit; he has forced Congress to pursue this entire investigation without any cooperation whatsoever from Trump.}

Castor says he thinks it's an abuse of power of Congress, for them to demand documents; and then when they are turned over, to impeach President Trump on that basis. {Well, I'm sorry if that's what the documents would indicate is called for; but still, not turning anything over, clearly constitutes obstruction of Congress; And that is an impeachable offense, is it not? How can Castor claim that impeaching Trump, at this point, would be undoing an election?! We are talking about someone who got elected, and has been in Office for three years!}

Castor stupidly refers to the fact, that during the Clinton impeachment in 1998, the Chairman said that, in the bare minimum, a president's accusers must go beyond hearsay and innuendo; and beyond the demands that the President produce evidence of his innocence; and he submits that those words ring true today too; {but in fact, that contention must not have actually rang true; because President Clinton did in fact get impeached!}

A parliamentary inquiry is then made: Nadler was asked why Burke and Castor were not sworn in, under oath? -and Nadler responds that they were not witnesses; that they were simply giving opening statements. Nadler says he will be swearing in the <u>witnesses</u>, who will now be questioned, {and in this case, it is Mr. Castor, and Mr. Goldman. However, I will not be transcribing anything further related to this hearing; the information revealed in the opening statements seems sufficient, to derive the gist of the Judiciary Committee arguments for, and against President Trump's impeachment.}

A summary of what Mark Sandy reported, regarding what happened at the Office of Management and Budget, related to the hold on Ukraine aid, within Trumps pressure scheme:

Mark Sandy heard from his boss, Mike Duffy, via an email he had received from Duffy on June 19th, that President Trump had seen a related news article, and had questions about the aid to Ukraine. The email stated that Trump was looking for more information on the background behind the news report, and additional information from the Department of Defense.

Sandy went on vacation on July 8, and by this point, he had not heard any more about this issue; and nothing more from the OMB either.

Sandy returned from vacation on July 19th, but he still had not heard anything further by July 22nd. At that point, Sandy asked Duffy if he had heard any reason why a hold had been placed on the Ukraine aid. Duffy had said he still hadn't heard. So, Sandy asked if Duffy was going to pursue more information on the matter; Sandy also indicated that others working on the aid situation within the department had concerns, too. These others were given that message, as well. Sandy apparently didn't hear anything more about it from Duffy, until he received an email in early September, explaining that Trump's concerns reportedly related to whether other EU countries were pulling their weight, contributing aid money to Ukraine.

The chairman of the House Intelligence, the Oversight, and the Foreign Affairs Committees, together made a joint statement in early September, to the effect that it appeared that hand-picked political appointees were "corrupting the official levers of US government power," citing the holding of the aid, presumably for a benefit of furthering Trump's political agenda, relating to himself personally. I assume this was just after information about Trump's scheme had just been learned via the whistleblower complaint.

At this point, Sandy heard from Mulvaney, that Trump had personally directed the hold. However, I think the hold was originally placed in July, so Mulvaney's message to keep the hold on, was just an update that there still was no reasoning behind why the hold on the aid was being ordered to continue.

At this point, Sandy contacted the OMB, and staff lawyers, raising his concern that holding up the Congressionally-Approved aid was in violation of the impoundment control act; which prohibits a President from holding up congressionally-approved foreign aid. This act was put into place in the Nixon era, when President Nixon was manipulating Congressionally-approved aid in like manner; so, there was a history of this prohibition, and the reasoning for it; yet Trump pushed that all aside, for his crooked ends.

In response to Sandy's outreach and complaint, his long-standing authority to approve security assistance was revoked, and instead transferred to hand-picked-Trump-appointee Mike Duffy. It was only after this, that the official word was spread around, that the hold was because Trump thought the EU countries were not paying their fair share of Ukraine assistance, However, around the same time, was when Mulvaney gave that press conference where he admitted that the hold was executed in order to pressure Ukraine to conduct the investigations Trump wanted. This constitutes evidence that the story about "concern over the EU countries possibly not pulling their weight," was simply concocted, after the fact. Further evidence, is that we found out the EU countries were contributing 4 times what the US was, since 2014; this we also learned from testimony given at these House Impeachment hearings.

It was on July 12th, that Mulvaney had originally contacted the OMB and said that Pres. Trump had directed the hold be put in place. Actually, apparently it was an email from Rob Blair, (Mulvaney's assistant, I think).

Duffy then emailed Blair on July 17th, to ask why. Sandy himself, didn't know the hold had been placed, until July 18th, when he returned from vacation.

At that point, Duffy told Sandy that they needed to create an apportionment that would implement the hold; to which Sandy replied that he wanted to contact the office of General Counsel, and get answers to some questions, which might better-direct him on how to proceed. A major concern was that if the money was not released to Ukraine by September 30th, the end of the government's fiscal year, the availability of these funds would expire.

What came out of Sandy's outreach, was a Defense Department opinion that placing a hold now, in July, would not impinge on the ability to provide the full funding before September 30th.

Sandy told interviewers that he had not ever been faced with a presidential order to hold funding, in the entirety of his tenure, which began in 2013. Interestingly, the OMB began the process for putting the hold on, the day of Trump's infamous call to President Zelensky, July 25th. The wording supporting the hold indicated that it would be put in place until August 5th, a 10-day period during which an interagency process would determine best use of the funds. Sandy informs us that this specifically meant the NSC would be making this determination.

The August 5th date was apparently the farthest date out, according to Sandy's contact at the Department of Defense, in conjunction with the staff lawyers' opinion, that there would definitely still be time, to release the funds prior to September 30th.

Then, on July 30th, Duffy told Sandy that he would now be taking on Sandy's former responsibilities to implement apportionments, to better track monies more closely. In other words, Duffy became the approver. Sandy told interviewers, that the amount of additional time and energy demanded, beyond all of Duffy's other responsibilities, as Associate Director, would be quite onerous. He knew that there were other ways Duffy could track monies more closely, that would be much more efficient, than taking on the entire task himself.

This change had also replaced Sandy, a career official, with Duffy who was a political official; and we know that politics is not supposed to enter into the aid apportionment process, according to officials testifying within the impeachment hearings.

At the end of July, a memo was sent to the acting director of OMB, jointly written by the NSC division that oversees US aid, and the office of legal counsel, recommending that the hold be lifted, based on arguments that releasing the aid was consistent with US national security policy, and that the funds were currently needed for Ukraine's defense against ongoing Russian aggression; and also that the allocation of the aid by Congress had strong bipartisan support.

The memo was received by Russell Vought. This information was provided in anticipation of an official discussion on the matter. Meanwhile, the hold stretching on, the Department of Defense indicated, in mid-August, that they could no longer hold the funds, and still be able to release them prior to September 30th.

Duffy made 6 more subsequent apportionments, (these are newly-attached footnotes), to continue the hold; on August 20, 27th, and 31st; and September 5, 6th, and 10th.

Apparently, as the hold stretched on throughout this extended time-period, one OMB budget attorney had even resigned. Ultimately the hold was released on September 12th; and this was so late, that $35 million of the funding could not be released by September 30th. Congress had to issue a continuing resolution to extend the expiration date, in order to provide the rest of the funding in September.

Assuming that President Trump had given the order, that Mark Sandy be removed from the apportionment responsibility, and Mike Duffy, a political appointee of Trump's, was instead to assume charge over apportionment; at least temporarily, until Trump's pressure scheme might ultimately result in President Zelensky announcing the opening of the Biden, Burisma, and 2016 Ukraine meddling investigations; this just reveals another instance of Trump's forsaking long-standing "abuse-of-office protection" protocols within government, in order to support his cockeyed vision of how things should work in US government.

This summary is just one last piece of the puzzle, that the House Intelligence Committee drew together, in the course of their investigation into Trump's wrongdoing.

Geoffrey Keane

The following, are some excerpts of the final debate of the Judiciary Committee, (just before they will cast their votes on whether to impeach President Trump:)

(2nd session, into the evening)
I wanted to capture some of the fine points, and the rationale put forth by the Democratic members of the House Judiciary Committee:

MR. JEFFRIES:
MY COLLEAGUES SUGGESTED THAT WE ARE HERE BECAUSE WE HAVE POLICY DISAGREEMENTS WITH THIS PRESIDENT. WE DO HAVE SOME POLICY DISAGREEMENTS WITH THIS PRESIDENT. WE DISAGREE WITH THE FACT THAT YOU PASSED, AS YOU'RE SIGNATURE LEGISLATIVE ACCOMPLISHMENT IN THE LAST CONGRESS, A GOP TAX SCAM OR 83% OF THE BENEFITS WENT TO THE WEALTHIEST 1% WHO EXPLODED THE DEFICIT AND THE DEBT. WE DISAGREE WITH THAT. WE DISAGREE WITH YOUR POLICY OF SEPARATING GOD'S CHILDREN FROM THEIR PARENTS, AND CAGING THOSE CHILDREN. THAT WAS UNACCEPTABLE, UNCONSCIONABLE, AND UN-AMERICAN. WE DISAGREE WITH THAT. WE DISAGREE WITH YOUR EFFORT, THAT IS ONGOING, TO STRIP AWAY HEALTH CARE PROTECTIONS FOR MORE THAN 100 MILLION AMERICANS WITH PRE-EXISTING CONDITIONS. WE DISAGREE WITH THAT AS WELL. BUT WE ARE NOT HERE AT THIS MOMENT, UNDERTAKING THIS SOLEMN RESPONSIBILITY BECAUSE WE DISAGREE WITH HIS POLICY POSITIONS. WE WILL DEAL WITH THAT IN NOVEMBER. WE ARE HERE BECAUSE THE PRESIDENT PRESSURED A FOREIGN GOVERNMENT TO TARGET AN AMERICAN CITIZEN FOR POLITICAL GAIN. THEREBY HE SOLICITED FOREIGN INTERFERENCE IN THE 2020 ELECTION BY WITHHOLDING $391 MILLION

DOLLARS IN MILITARY AID WITHOUT JUSTIFICATION. THE PRESIDENT SAYS THAT WAS "PERFECT." HERE IS WHAT OTHERS HAVE HAD TO SAY ABOUT THAT. AMBASSADOR SONDLAND WHO GAVE THE PRESIDENT $1 MILLION DOLLARS FOR THE INAUGURATION SAID, IT WAS A QUID PRO QUO. LIEUTENANT COLONEL VINDMAN, IRAQ WAR VETERAN, SAID IT WAS IMPROPER. DOCTOR FIONA HILL, TRUMP APPOINTEE, WHAT DID SHE SAY? A DOMESTIC POLITICAL ERRAND. AMBASSADOR TAYLOR, WEST POINT GRADUATE, APPOINTED BY REAGAN, BUSH AND, TRUMP; VIETNAM WAR HERO, HE SAID IT WAS CRAZY. JOHN BOLTON, A SUPERCONSERVATIVE, TRUMP NATIONAL SECURITY ADVISER, REFERRED TO IT AS A "DRUG DEAL." WHAT WOULD THE FRAMERS OF THE CONSTITUTION HAVE SAID? IMPEACHABLE! I YIELD TO MY COLLEAGUE FROM CALIFORNIA.

ERIC SWALWELL:
I THANK THE GENTLEMAN. (AS DIRECTED AT REPUBLICAN COMMITTEE MEMBERS) IN THE EFFORTS TO DEFEND THIS PRESIDENT, YOU WANT HIM TO BE SOMEONE HE IS NOT. YOU WANT HIM TO BE SOMEONE HE IS TELLING YOU HE IS NOT. YOU ARE TRYING TO DEFEND THE CALL IN SO MANY DIFFERENT WAYS, AND HE IS SAYING IT WAS A PERFECT CALL. HE IS NOT WHO YOU WANT HIM TO BE. RANKING MEMBER COLLINS, YOU CAN DENY THIS IS MUCH AS YOU WANT, BUT PEOPLE DIED IN UKRAINE, AT THE HANDS OF RUSSIA. UKRAINE, (SINCE SEPTEMBER 2018 WHEN IT WAS VOTED ON BY CONGRESS), WAS COUNTING ON OUR SUPPORT .. A YEAR PASSED, AND PEOPLE DIED. YOU MAY NOT WANT TO THINK ABOUT THAT, IT MAY BE HARD FOR YOU TO THINK ABOUT THAT. BUT PEOPLE DIED WHEN THIS SELFISH PRESIDENT WITHHELD

THE AID FOR HIS OWN PERSONAL GAIN. SINCE 2014, PRESIDENT OBAMA GAVE THEM MILITARY CAPABILITIES, MILITARY TRAINING, AND MEDICAL EQUIPMENT (ALL OF WHICH SUDDENLY WAS INTERRUPTED). SO DON'T TELL YOURSELF UKRAINIANS DIDN'T DIE. THEY DIED. AMBASSADOR TAYLOR SAID, THESE WERE WEAPONS AND ASSISTANCE THAT ALLOWED THE UKRAINIAN MILITARY TO DETER FURTHER INCURSIONS. IF THAT FURTHER INCURSION, AND FURTHER AGGRESSION WERE TO TAKE PLACE, MORE UKRAINIANS WOULD DIE. IT IS A DETERRENT OF FACT. YOU DIDN'T ONLY HURT UKRAINE, YOU HELPED RUSSIA. AND TO MY COLLEAGUES WHO BELIEVE THAT WE HAVE SUCH AN ANTI CORRUPTION PRESIDENT IN THE WHITE HOUSE, I ASK YOU THIS; HOW MANY TIMES DID THIS ANTI CORRUPTION PRESIDENT MEET WITH THE MOST CORRUPT LEADER IN THE WORLD, VLADIMIR PUTIN. HOW MANY TIMES DID HE TALK TO HIM? 16 TIMES! (BETWEEN MEETINGS AND PHONE CONVERSATIONS). HOW MANY CONDITIONS DID PUTIN HAVE TO MEET, IN ORDER TO GET A MEETING WITH THE U.S. PRESIDENT? ZERO CONDITIONS. THAT IS WHO YOU REPUBLICAN CONGRESSMEN ARE DEFENDING. SO KEEP DEFENDING HIM; WE DEMOMCRATS WILL DEFEND THE CONSTITUTION, OUR NATIONAL SECURITY, AND OUR ELECTIONS. I YIELD BACK..

00:33:28 MR. NEGUSE:
...THE PART OF THIS DEBATE THAT HAS BEEN SO FRUSTRATING FOR ME, AND I THINK FOR A LOT OF AMERICANS WHO ARE WATCHING TONIGHT, IS THE DIMINISHMENT OF THE PUBLIC SERVANTS; THE PATRIOTS, WHO STEPPED FORWARD AND PROVIDED THE EVIDENCE THAT DEMONSTRATES THAT THIS PRESIDENT ABUSED HIS POWER. PEOPLE LIKE LIEUTENANT COLONEL VINDMAN, WHO SERVED THIS COUNTRY BRAVELY

OVERSEAS. PEOPLE LIKE AMBASSADOR BILL TAYLOR, A WEST POINT GRADUATE, A VIETNAM VETERAN, PEOPLE LIKE DOCTOR FIONA HILL, PEOPLE LIKE LAURA COOPER. OFFICIAL AFTER OFFICIAL, AFTER OFFICIAL FROM THE TRUMP ADMINISTRATION. THESE INDIVIDUALS SERVE IN THE PRESIDENT'S ADMINISTRATION. AMBASSADOR TAYLOR WAS NOT APPOINTED BY PRESIDENT OBAMA. HE WAS APPOINTED BY PRESIDENT TRUMP. I WOULD HOPE THAT MY COLLEAGUES, AS WE PROCEED WITH THE SOLEMN DUTY THAT THIS COMMITTEE IS CHARGED WITH, THAT WE RESPECT THE PEOPLE WHO CAME FORWARD, WHO HAVE SERVED UNDER REPUBLICAN AND DEMOCRATIC ADMINISTRATIONS, TO TELL THE TRUTH, UNDER OATH, AND TO HELP THIS COMMITTEE, AS IT SEEKS TO HOLD THIS ADMINISTRATION ACCOUNTABLE. WITH THAT I YIELD.

1:31:22

…I TOTALLY DISAGREE WITH CHAIRMAN SENSENBRENNER IN HIS SUMMATION OF WHAT WE HAVE BEFORE US. I THINK THEY (REPUBLICAN COMMITTEEE MEMBERS) ARE DEAD WRONG IN THEIR THINKING ON THE ARTICLES OF IMPEACHMENT. THERE ARE TWO ARTICLES. THIS IS IN NO WAY STEALING THE ELECTION. IF DONALD TRUMP IS REMOVED FROM OFFICE, THE ELECTION OF 2016 IS NOT NULLIFIED. MIKE PENCE WILL BE THE PRESIDENT, AND THAT IS NO WALK IN THE PARK. IT IS THE SAME POLICIES, SOME OF THEM MAYBE EVEN WORSE, MAYBE A LITTLE BIT BETTER ETHICS AND MORALS, A LITTLE BIT MORE CIVILITY, BUT AS FAR AS POLICIES, THEY WOULD BE ABOUT THE SAME. THERE HAS BEEN A LOT OF DISCUSSION OF WHAT WE HAVE HAD HERE BUT BASICALLY THIS IS AN ISSUE ABOUT ABUSE OF POWER; BASED ON TESTIMONY OF LIEUTENANT COLONEL VINDMAN, AMBASSADOR YOVANOVITCH, AMBASSADOR TAYLOR,

AND DOCTOR HILL. THESE ARE FOUR INDEPENDENT
CLASSES; PEOPLE WE SHOULD ALL LOOK TO, AND WHO
WE ALL TALK ABOUT AS PATRIOTS, THEY ARE PATRIOTS
BUT THEY ARE CAREER FOREIGN SERVICE FOLK WHO
HAVE DONE A GREAT JOB FOR AMERICA, THEY ARE NOT
PARTISAN; THEY CAME FORTH OUT OF A SENSE OF DUTY
TO TESTIFY; AND WHAT THEY TESTIFIED TO IS WHAT
HAPPENED WITH THE UKRAINE ORDEAL, THAT THERE
WAS AN ABUSE OF POWER, AND THAT IS WHY THEY CAME
FORWARD. -AND TO SAY THAT THIS WHOLE PROCESS IS
CORRUPT, IS BASICALLY AN AFFRONT TO EACH OF THOSE
FOUR PATRIOTS WHO CAME FORWARD. FOR THOSE FOUR
CAREER FOREIGN SERVICE OFFICIALS, THOSE FOUR
PEOPLE WHO WERE NONPARTISAN. THEY DID A SERVICE
TO THIS COUNTRY. THE FACTS ARE UNDISPUTED. THE
PRESIDENT SAYING IT, "DO US A FAVOR, THOUGH;" AND
MULVANEY SAYING, GET OVER IT; GET USED TO IT. THAT
IS WHAT POLITICS IS. THAT'S WHAT HAPPENED! AND
THEN WE HAD SONDLAND SAYING, THEY WERE ALL IN
ON IT, IT WAS A REQUIREMENT, "TO GET THE MILITARY
AID, YOU'VE GOT TO ANNOUNCE THE INVESTIGATION."
THERE IS NOTHING OTHER THAN THAT,
...SOMEBODY ON THE OTHER SIDE TALKED ABOUT
HOW WE NEED TO BE UP HERE FIGHTING. THEY
(REPUBLICAN LAWMAKERS) HAVE EXPLODED THE DEBT.
THEY HAVE NO TRADITIONAL REPUBLICAN PHILOSOPHY
WHATSOEVER. THE KURDS? SIONORA. THEY RUINED US
IN THE MIDDLE EAST FOREVER! TRUMP JUST SOLD THEM
OUT FOR HIS FRIEND IN THE TERRITORY, ERDOGAN;
AND THE KURDS -- TO HELL WITH YOU. AND WE GAVE
SYRIA TO THE RUSSIANS; AND JUST YESTERDAY TRUMP
MET WITH THE RUSSIAN AMBASSADOR TO THE U.S. I
WANT TO TALK ABOUT WHAT THE WHITE HOUSE SAID
THEY TALKED ABOUT, NOT TO HAVE INFLUENCE IN THE
NEXT ELECTION, AND TRUMP HAD SAID THAT HE TOLD

THE RUSSIAN AMBASSADOR THAT THEY SHOULD NOT TRY TO INFLUENCE OUR NEXT ELECTIONS! YET WHEN REPORTERS ASKED, LAVROV SAID, WE DID NOT DISCUSS THE ELECTIONS! IT'S HARD TO FIGURE OUT WHICH ONE IS LYING, EVEN WHEN WE HAVE A VERY GOOD TRACK RECORD (TRUMP LIES CONSISTENTLY); SO I HOPE WE CAN GET IT FINISHED TODAY, AND PASS THESE TWO ARTICLES. DO IT. IT IS IMPORTANT TO PROTECT OUR DEMOCRACY...

(1 HOUR AND 40 MINUTES INTO THE EVENING DEBATE)
Mr. DEUTCH:
NOW, MY COLLEAGUES HAVE SUGGESTED THAT SOMEHOW ABUSE OF POWER IS NOT A SERIOUS OFFENSE; THAT WE SHOULD MAKE LIGHT OF THE PRESIDENT'S ACTIONS, AND NOT TREAT IT AS THE CONSTITUTIONAL VIOLATION THAT IT IS. YET IN FACT, ABUSE OF POWER WAS THE PRINCIPAL CONCERN OF THE FRAMERS OF THE CONSTITUTION; AND IT WAS CLEAR WHAT IT MEANT, THE EXERCISE OF OFFICIAL POWER, TO OBTAIN IMPROPER PERSONAL BENEFIT WHILE IGNORING OR INJURING THE NATIONAL INTEREST. THAT IS ABUSE OF POWER. IT IS ROOTED IN THE PRESIDENT'S DUTY, HIS CONSTITUTIONAL DUTY TO FAITHFULLY EXECUTE THE LAW, TO PUT SERVICE OVER SELF, TO PUT THE COUNTRY OVER HIS PERSONAL INTERESTS. I KNOW, AS WELL AS MY COLLEAGUES, THAT ALL FOUR OF THE CONSTITUTIONAL SCHOLARS WHO TESTIFIED, INCLUDING THE REPUBLICANS' OWN WITNESS, HAVE CONFIRMED THAT ABUSE OF POWER IS AN IMPEACHABLE OFFENSE. PRESIDENT TRUMP'S ACTIONS, IN FACT, EXEMPLIFY THE FRAMERS FEARS AND THE VERY REASON THAT ABUSE OF POWER IS A HIGH CRIME. WORSE, WORSE THAN

573

PRESIDENT NIXON, PRESIDENT TRUMP PRESSURED A <u>FOREIGN</u> <u>GOVERNMENT</u> TO AID IN HIS SCHEME. THAT IS THE ABUSE OF POWER ARTICLE, BUT THERE IS A SECOND ARTICLE, OBSTRUCTION OF CONGRESS. WE KNOW THAT NO PRESIDENT IN HISTORY, IN HISTORY HAS DIRECTED THE ENTIRE EXECUTIVE BRANCH NOT TO COOPERATE WITH AN IMPEACHMENT INQUIRY, HE HAS TOLD EVERY MEMBER OF THE EXECUTIVE BRANCH NOT TO SPEAK TO ANY OF THE IMPEACHMENT INQUIRY, TO ANY OF THE IMPEACHMENT INQUIRY ISSUES …

…AND FINALLY, JOHN EISENBERG, LIEUTENANT COLONEL VINDMAN COULD NOT BELIEVE WHAT HE HEARD ON THE CALL. HE REPORTED IT TO EISENBERG. NOW, EISENBERG CAN'T SPEAK? WHAT IS THE PRESIDENT IS AFRAID HE WILL SAY? THAT IS OBSTRUCTION OF CONGRESS, ABUSE OF POWER AND OBSTRUCTION OF CONGRESS, TO GET TO THAT IS WHAT THESE ARTICLES ARE ABOUT. WE ARE PROTECTING THE CONSTITUTION. WE ARE PROTECTING THE AMERICAN PEOPLE AND OUR ELECTIONS. THAT IS WHY WE NEED TO PROCEED WITH THESE ARTICLES OF IMPEACHMENT.

MS. JACKSON LEE:
…YOU KNOW, I WANT TO REITERATE, THIS IS NOT ABOUT DISAGREEMENT WITH THE PRESIDENT'S POLICIES OR PERSONALITY, OR EVEN HIS TWEETS. WE ARE NOT JUDGING THE PRESIDENT HIMSELF; OR JUDGING HIS OVERALL ACTIONS. AND I UNDERSTAND HE RAN TO DISRUPT THE GOVERNMENT. THE PROBLEM IS, HE WENT FURTHER. BY ABUSING HIS POWER, HE ENDANGERED OUR ELECTIONS AND OUR NATIONAL SECURITY; HE REMAINS AN ONGOING THREAT TO BOTH. HE HAS SHOWN A PATTERN OF INVITING FOREIGN INTERFERENCE IN OUR ELECTION AND TRYING TO COVER IT UP; TWICE! HE IS THREATENING TO DO IT AGAIN! SO, WE HAVE HEARD A

LOT OF LOOSE TALK ABOUT WHAT EVIDENCE WE HAVE OR DON'T HAVE. THERE IS PLENTY OF DIRECT EVIDENCE OF THE PRESIDENTS WRONGDOING...

...WE HAD DIRECT EVIDENCE ON THE MAY 23RD MEETING (IN THE OVAL OFFICE), AND SONDLAND HAS GIVEN DIRECT EVIDENCE; AND THE SECOND HAND ACCOUNTS ARE ALSO EXTENSIVELY CORROBORATED. FOR EXAMPLE, AMBASSADOR TAYLOR AND MR. MORRISON BOTH TESTIFIED THAT DURING THE PHONE CALL WITH AMBASSADOR SONDLAND, PRESIDENT TRUMP SAID THERE WAS NO QUID PRO QUO; BUT THAT PRESIDENT ZELENSKY HAD TO GO TO THE MICROPHONE AND ANNOUNCE INVESTIGATIONS. "GIVING WITH ONE HAND TAKING AWAY WITH THE OTHER!" -AMBASSADOR SONDLAND TESTIFIED HE HAD NO REASON TO DISPUTE AMBASSADOR TAYLOR AND MR. MORRISON'S TESTIMONY ABOUT THIS CONVERSATION. THERE IS ALSO CIRCUMSTANTIAL EVIDENCE: THERE WAS NO CONTEMPORANEOUS EXPLANATION GIVEN, TO THE PRESIDENT'S DECISION TO WITHHOLD MILITARY AID, THAT HAD BIPARTISAN SUPPORT FROM CONGRESS. THAT (PURPORTED EXPLANATION) DID NOT COME UNTIL AFTER THE ARTICLES OF IMPEACHMENT WERE FILED! -BUT THE UNIFORM CONSENSUS OF THE STATE DEPARTMENT, THE DEFENSE DEPARTMENT, AND WHITE HOUSE WITNESSES, IS THAT THE AID SHOULD HAVE BEEN RELEASED (SEVERAL MONTHS EARLIER). GIVEN THESE, FACTS THE ONLY LOGICAL EXPLANATION, AS AMBASSADOR SONDLAND CONCLUDED, WAS THAT, JUST LIKE THE WHITE HOUSE MEETING, THE AID WAS BEING USED TO LEVERAGE PRESSURE ON PRESIDENT ZELENSKY. AT THE END OF THE DAY, THE EVIDENCE IS OVERWHELMING AND INDISPUTABLE. PRESIDENT TRUMP'S PERSONAL LAWYER, RUDY GIULIANI, PUSHED UKRAINE TO INVESTIGATE HIS POLITICAL RIVAL AND

A DEBUNKED CONSPIRACY THEORY. HIS EFFORTS HAD NOTHING TO DO WITH U.S. POLICY. PRESIDENT TRUMP DIRECTED U.S. OFFICIALS AND PRESIDENT ZELENSKY HIMSELF, TO WORK WITH MR. GIULIANI. PRESIDENT TRUMP ORDERED THE CRITICAL MILITARY AID FOR UKRAINE BE WITHHELD. UKRAINIAN OFFICIALS WERE INFORMED THE AID WOULD NOT BE RELEASED UNLESS PRESIDENT ZELENSKY PUBLICLY ANNOUNCED AN INVESTIGATION; AND PRESIDENT TRUMP REFUSED TO RELEASE THE AID, ALL UNTIL HIS PRESSURE CAMPAIGN ON THE UKRAINE WAS EXPOSED. PRESIDENT TRUMP REFUSED TO ARRANGE A MEETING WITH PRESIDENT ZELENSKY. -AND PRESIDENT TRUMP'S AGENTS ADVISED UKRAINIAN OFFICIALS, THAT THE WHITE HOUSE MEETING WOULD BE SCHEDULED ONLY AFTER PRESIDENT ZELENSKY COMMITTED TO THE INVESTIGATIONS. PRESIDENT TRUMP ALSO IGNORED THE ANTI CORRUPTION TALKING POINTS PREPARED FOR HIS CALLS! PRESIDENT TRUMP ASKED PRESIDENT ZELENSKY DIRECTLY TO INVESTIGATE PRESIDENT TRUMP'S CHIEF POLITICAL RIVAL, AND PRESIDENT TRUMP STONEWALLED CONGRESS'S INVESTIGATION. YOU KNOW, I DON'T KNOW WHAT MORE YOU CAN ASK FOR HERE. WE'VE GOT ADMISSIONS FROM THE PRESIDENT. WE'VE GOT CORROBORATION FROM PEOPLE HE HAS APPOINTED, THE ONLY THING YOU CAN DO IS STICK YOUR HEAD IN THE SAND, IF YOU ARE NOT WILLING TO SEE WHAT HAPPENED HERE, AND WITH THAT I WOULD YIELD TO MY COLLEAGUE FROM FLORIDA. IS SHE HERE? OKAY....

MISS LOFGREN:
...THE CONTENT OF THE PHRASE, HIGH CRIMES AND MISDEMEANORS, FOR THE FRAMERS, IS TO BE RELATED TO WHAT THE FRAMERS KNEW, ON THE WHOLE, ABOUT THE ENGLISH PRACTICE;

IN THE BROAD SWEEP OF ENGLISH CONSTITUTIONAL HISTORY, AND IN THE VITAL ROLE IMPEACHMENT HAD PLAYED IN THE ELIMINATION OF ROYAL PREROGATIVES, AND THE CONTROL OF ABUSES OF MINISTERIAL AND JUDICIAL POWER. NOW, WHEN YOU'RE COMING TO PRIVATE AFFAIRS IN ORDINARY CRIMINAL LAW, IT IS POSSIBLE IN ADVANCE TO DEFINE WHAT IT IS YOU CANNOT DO. YOU CANNOT STEAL THAT MONEY. YOU CANNOT HIT THAT PERSON. BUT WHEN YOU ARE TALKING ABOUT THE ABUSE OF PRESIDENTIAL POWER, YOU CAN'T ALWAYS SPECIFICALLY DEFINE (THE ENTIRE SCOPE OF) WHAT A BAD ACTOR IN THE WHITE HOUSE MIGHT DO, AND THEREFORE, YOU HAVE THE TERM "HIGH CRIMES AND MISDEMEANORS," AND YOU HAVE "ABUSE OF PRESIDENTIAL POWER..."

...IT IS JUST INCONCEIVABLE THE THINGS I'VE HEARD TODAY, THEY ARE JUST STUNNING TO ME, THAT YOU COULD REACH A CONCLUSION AS DEFENSE COUNSEL HERE, DRASTIC -- GRASPING AT STRAWS. THE PRESIDENT HAS USED HIS PRESIDENTIAL POWER, TO GAIN A PERSONAL BENEFIT TO THE DETRIMENT OF THE INTERESTS OF THE UNITED STATES. IT WAS AN ABUSE OF POWER THAT HARMS US, AND IT IS ONGOING. IT IS A THREAT TO THE CONSTITUTIONAL ORDER. IT MEETS THE DEFINITION OF HIGH CRIMES AND MISDEMEANORS. IT IS ABUSE OF PRESIDENTIAL POWER AND IT IS OUR RESPONSIBILITY TO USE THE TOOL THAT OUR FOUNDERS GAVE US IN THE CONSTITUTION TO PRESERVE THAT CONSTITUTIONAL ORDER. WE MUST IMPEACH. I YIELD BACK.

MS. GARCIA:

... HE OFFERED OFFICIAL ACTS IN EXCHANGE FOR A POLITICAL FAVOR. HE IS A CLEAR AND PRESENT DANGER TO DO IT AGAIN. HE IGNORED THE POWER OF THE PEOPLE AND HE WILL DO IT AGAIN. IT IS REALLY JUST

THAT SIMPLE, THE PRESIDENT IS AN IMMINENT, AND HE SHOWS US A PATTERN OF CONDUCT, HE HAS MADE CLEAR THAT HE WILL CONTINUE TO ABUSE HIS POWER TO CORRUPT THE 2020 ELECTIONS. WE MUST ACT WITH A SENSE OF URGENCY, TO PROTECT OUR DEMOCRACY, AND DEFEND OUR CONSTITUTION. IN THE CLINTON CASE, THE HOUSE VOTED TO IMPEACH 72 DAYS AFTER HE AUTHORIZED AN INQUIRY. IT HAS BEEN 94 DAYS SINCE CONGRESS LAUNCHED ITS INVESTIGATION INTO THE PRESIDENT'S DEALINGS WITH UKRAINE. IMPEACHMENT IS A DECISION SUCH AS A GRAND JURY OR PROSECUTOR MAKES. WE HAVE SEEN MORE THAN ENOUGH EVIDENCE HERE TO CHARGE AND MOVE TO TRIAL IN THE SENATE. IT IS A PRESIDENT WHO IS ABUSING HIS POWER. WHAT IS NOT FAIR IS THE PRESIDENT'S REFUSAL TO PARTICIPATE IN THIS INQUIRY, FOR THE SOLE PURPOSE OF HIDING THE FACTS FROM THE AMERICAN PEOPLE. FEDERAL COURTS HAVE RULED THAT CONGRESS HAS A CONSTITUTIONAL RIGHT TO OBTAIN DOCUMENTS AND TESTIMONY FROM THE TRUMP ADMINISTRATION. ONE FEDERAL COURT SAID THAT THE PRESIDENT -- THE PRESIDENT'S OBSTRUCTION IS A FARCE AND HE IS OPENLY STONEWALLING CONGRESS. I AGREE. HE IS THE FIRST PRESIDENT TO ENGAGE IN WALL-TO-WALL STONEWALLING, AND IN SOME RESPECTS, HE IS ENGAGING IN AN OUTRIGHT COVER-UP OF HIS OWN BAD BEHAVIOR...

MS. JAYAPAL:
...ALL OF PRESIDENT TRUMP'S AGENCIES, ALL OF HIS ADVISERS, EVERYONE UNANIMOUSLY TOLD HIM THAT UKRAINE HAD PASSED ALL OF THE ANTI CORRUPTION BENCHMARKS. THE DEPARTMENT OF DEFENSE SAID THAT UKRAINE HAD PASSED ALL OF THE REQUIRED BENCHMARKS. PRESIDENT TRUMP'S ADMINISTRATION

HAD ACTUALLY <u>CUT</u> PROGRAMS DESIGNED TO FIGHT CORRUPTION IN UKRAINE! AND PRESIDENT TRUMP WAS GIVEN TALKING POINTS BY THE NATIONAL SECURITY COUNCIL THAT SPECIFICALLY SAID, SAY THESE THINGS ABOUT CORRUPTION, BUT GUESS WHAT HAPPENED ON THOSE CALLS IN APRIL AND JULY? PRESIDENT TRUMP DID NOT MENTION CORRUPTION. HE DID NOT USE THE TALKING POINTS THAT HE WAS GIVEN. THE ONLY TWO NAMES THAT HE MENTIONED ON THE JULY 25TH CALL, WERE JOE AND HUNTER BIDEN. SECOND, THE REPUBLICANS SUGGESTED THAT THIS WAS ALL ABOUT PRESIDENT TRUMP'S CONCERNS WITH BURDEN SHARING WITH OUR ALLIES. BUT THAT WAS NOT TRUE. MR. HOMES TESTIFIED THAT BURDEN SHARING WAS NOT A PROBLEM. EUROPE WAS ACTUALLY CONTRIBUTING FOUR TIMES AS MUCH MONEY AS THE UNITED STATES DID; AND AMBASSADOR SONDLAND TESTIFIED THAT HE WAS NEVER ASKED TO GO TO THE EUROPEAN UNION AND ASK FOR MORE MONEY. AND REMEMBER MR. SONDLAND IS PRESIDENT TRUMP'S AMBASSADOR TO THE EUROPEAN UNION. WHAT WAS AMBASSADOR SONDLAND TOLD TO COMMUNICATE TO UKRAINE BY PRESIDENT TRUMP? HE WAS TOLD TO SAY THAT RESUMPTION OF THE FINANCIAL AID WOULD LIKELY NOT OCCUR UNLESS PRESIDENT ZELENSKY ANNOUNCED THE INVESTIGATION, SPECIFICALLY, HE SAID THE QUOTE, UNLESS ZELENSKY WENT AND ANNOUNCED THIS INVESTIGATION, "THERE WOULD BE A STALEMATE OVER THE AID..."

...FINALLY, LEFT WITH NOTHING ELSE TO ARGUE IN DEFENSE OF THE PRESIDENT, THE REPUBLICANS HAVE RAISED ONE MORE THING WHICH IS THAT PRESIDENT TRUMP HAD A LEGITIMATE REASON, SOMEHOW A LEGITIMATE REASON TO INVESTIGATE VICE PRESIDENT BIDEN BUT ONCE AGAIN THAT MAKES NO SENSE. AND IT MAKES NO SENSE BECAUSE THE FACTS ARE THAT THAT

INVESTIGATION, THAT ISSUE OF BIDEN AND BURISMA
WENT BACK TO 2015 AND PRESIDENT TRUMP RELEASED
AID IN 2017 IN 2018, SO CLEARLY HE DID NOT HAVE A
PROBLEM BEFORE, WITH THESE ISSUES IN 2015, BECAUSE
HE HAD TWO OPPORTUNITIES TO RELEASE AID AND
HE DID; BUT SOMETHING CHANGED IN 2019, AND THE
ONLY THING THAT CHANGE WAS VICE PRESIDENT BIDEN
SUDDENLY STARTED BEATING PRESIDENT TRUMP IN THE
POLLS SO, THE EVIDENCE IS CLEAR, PRESIDENT TRUMP
SAID "DO US A FAVOR, THOUGH," AND WHO IS THE US?
WELL, HE TOLD US. HE TOLD US EXACTLY WHAT HE
MEANT BY "US." HE TOLD PRESIDENT ZELENSKY WHO
WAS THAT "US," HE SAID TO DEAL WITH RUDY GIULIANI.
PRESIDENT TRUMP'S PERSONAL ATTORNEY, WHO
KNOWS, AND THIS IS A QUOTE, "VERY MUCH KNOWS
WHAT IS GOING ON." PRESIDENT TRUMP COULD'VE GONE
THROUGH OFFICIAL CHANNELS IF THIS INVESTIGATION
WAS ACTUALLY LEGITIMATE. HE COULD'VE ASKED THE
DEPARTMENT TO INITIATE AN INVESTIGATION INTO
THE BIDENS AND BURISMA, BUT HE DID NOT DO THAT
. INSTEAD, PRESIDENT TRUMP ASKED HIS PERSONAL
ATTORNEY BECAUSE THIS WAS NOT ABOUT AMERICA.
THIS WAS NOT ABOUT OFFICIAL POLICY. THIS WAS NOT
ABOUT WHAT WAS RIGHT FOR OUR COUNTRY. THIS WAS
NOT ABOUT PUTTING AMERICA FIRST. EVERY WITNESS
TESTIFIED TO THAT, AS WELL. THIS WAS PERSONAL. IT
WAS ALL FOR PRESIDENT TRUMP'S PERSONAL POLITICAL
GAIN. ...
...HE ABUSED THE POWERS THAT THE PEOPLE
ENTRUSTED TO HIM. HE ABUSED THE OFFICE AND HE
PLACED OUR SAFETY, AND MILLIONS OF DOLLARS OF
TAXPAYER MONEY, ALL AT RISK FOR HIS OWN PERSONAL
POLITICAL RE-ELECTION CAMPAIGN;AND THAT IS THE
ONE THING THE PRESIDENT CANNOT DO. HE CANNOT
USE OUR MONEY, OR THE POWERS OF THE OFFICE THAT

"WE" ENTRUSTED TO HIM, WE THE PEOPLE," NOT FOR US, BUT FOR HIMSELF. THAT IS THE GREATEST ABUSE OF POWER, AND THIS PRESIDENT HAS LEFT US NO CHOICE BUT TO IMPEACH HIM.

02:28:17   THE GENTLELADY IS RECOGNIZED:

MS. BUTLER DEMINGS

A LITTLE WHILE AGO, ONE OF MY COLLEAGUES ON THE OTHER SIDE OF THE AISLE SAID THAT THE $391 MILLION IN AID WAS WITHHELD BECAUSE THE PRESIDENT WANTED TO INVESTIGATE CORRUPTION. THE IDEA THAT THE MOST CORRUPT PRESIDENT WE HAVE SEEN IN RECENT HISTORY WITHHELD MILITARY AID BECAUSE HE WAS CONCERNED ABOUT CORRUPTION, IS LUDICROUS! AS MY COLLEAGUES HAVE POINTED OUT, IN BOTH CALLS THAT PRESIDENT TRUMP HAD WITH PRESIDENT ZELENSKY, TRUMP NEVER MENTION CORRUPTION. THE DEPARTMENT OF DEFENSE VETTED GIVING UKRAINE THE AID, AND SAID THAT IT WAS OKAY. ONCE UPON A TIME PRESIDENT TRUMP LOVED HIS GENERALS. THIS TIME HE IGNORED THEM. MEMBERS OF CONGRESS AUTHORIZED THE AID, AND LOBBIED THE WHITE HOUSE TO RELEASE THE AID. STAFF FROM THE OFFICE OF MANAGEMENT AND BUDGET EVEN RESIGNED, BECAUSE THEY WERE WORRIED… ABOUT WHAT WAS GOING ON, AND WHY THE AID WAS WITHHELD (THEY BELIEVED IT WAS ILLEGAL TO HOLD UP THE AID); THEY WERE WORRIED ABOUT WHAT THE PRESIDENT WAS DOING, AND THEY BELIEVED THAT WITHHOLDING THE AID WAS WRONG.

…SO, FOR A MAN SUPPOSEDLY SO CONCERNED ABOUT CORRUPTION, HE ALSO HAS INTERESTING FRIENDS. HE HAS BROMANCES WITH SOME OF THE WORLD'S MOST CORRUPT LEADERS, THE LEADERS OF NORTH KOREA,

SAUDI ARABIA, AND TURKEY; HE HAD PRESIDENT ERDOGAN FROM TURKEY, JUST A FEW WEEKS AGO, AT THE WHITE HOUSE! BUT WE KNOW HIS NUMBER ONE MAN IS PRESIDENT PUTIN; SO ALL OF THE PRESIDENT'S MEN, ALL THE MEN AROUND HIM THAT WERE INDICTED, ARRESTED, INCARCERATED; MY MOTHER USED TO SAY THAT IF YOU LAY DOWN WITH DOGS, DON'T BE SURPRISED IF YOU GET UP WITH FLEAS. THE MAN WHO CLAIMED HE WANTED TO CLEAN UP THE SWAMP, INSTEAD CREATED HIS OWN SWAMP, AND HE IS DROWNING IN IT NOW…

…IT IS SO SAD TO SEE MY (REPUBLICAN) COLLEAGUES WHO I BELIEVE KNOW BETTER. THEY ARE NOT ABLE TO SAY IT. THEY KNOW THAT THE MAN IS CORRUPT. WHEN IT COMES TO IMPEACHMENT, THERE IS NO HIGHER CRIME THAN FOR THE PRESIDENT TO USE THE POWER OF HIS OFFICE, TO CORRUPT OUR ELECTIONS. WE WILL MOVE TO IMPEACH PRESIDENT TRUMP BECAUSE OF THE ABUSE OF POWER, SELF DEALING, THE BETRAYAL OF NATIONAL SECURITY IN THE SERVICE OF FOREIGN INTERESTS, AND THE CORRUPTION OF OUR ELECTIONS THAT UNDERMINES OUR DEMOCRATIC SYSTEM. SO, IF MY COLLEAGUES ON THE OTHER SIDE OF THE AISLE CANNOT BRING THEMSELVES TO DO WHAT IS RIGHT AND IMPEACH THE PRESIDENT, WHOM THEY KNOW IS A THREAT TO OUR ELECTIONS, THAT THEY KNOW IS A THREAT TO OUR STANDING IN THE WORLD, THEN WE WILL HAVE TO DO IT AND MAYBE DEMOCRATS ALONE, WILL HAVE TO MOVE TO IMPEACH…

MR SWALWELL:
FOOL ME ONCE, SHAME ON YOU; FOOL ME TWICE, SHAME ON ME! IF WE ALLOW THE PRESIDENT TO ABUSE HIS OFFICE, FOR HIS OWN PERSONAL GAIN, THEN SHAME ON ALL OF US! SHAME ON OUR CONSTITUTION! WE KNOW

HE'S GOING TO DO THIS AGAIN, BECAUSE ON JUNE 12TH THIS YEAR HE TOLD GEORGE STEPHANOPOULOS, IN THAT TELEVISED INTERVIEW, LONG BEFORE THE PHONE CALL WITH PRESIDENT ZELENSKY HAPPENED, HE SAID THAT IF HE COULD AGAIN RECEIVE AID FROM A FOREIGN POWER DURING AN ELECTION, HE WOULD WELCOME IT. THEN, AGAIN, ON JULY 24TH, BOB MUELLER TESTIFIED TO OUR COMMITTEE. HE SAID THAT THE PRESIDENT COULD BE CHARGED UP TO TEN TIMES FOR OBSTRUCTION OF JUSTICE, BUT THE DEPARTMENT OF JUSTICE PREVENTS HIM FROM DOING THAT. SO, THE VERY NEXT DAY, THE PRESIDENT DID IT AGAIN! THAT WAS THE DAY OF THE PHONE CALL WE ARE IMPEACHING HIM FOR! EVERY PROSECUTOR, WHEN THEY ARE ASSIGNED A CASE, WILL OPEN UP THE FILE, AND THE FIRST THING WE ALL DO, IS WE LOOK AT THE RAP SHEET. WAS THIS AN ABERRATION? OR WAS THIS A PATTERN OF CONDUCT THAT THE PERSON ENGAGES IN?

...THE PRESIDENT DOES NOT JUST HAVE BAD REVIEWS, HE HAS REALLY BAD PRIOR CONDUCT, SERIOUS PRIORS, HE IS A REPEAT OFFENDER, CRIMES AGAINST OUR CONSTITUTION; AND YES, CRIMES THAT ONE DAY MAY BE PROSECUTED STATUTORILY. HE HAS ABUSED HIS POWER IN THE PAST. HE IS ABUSING HIS POWER RIGHT NOW. AND HE WILL ABUSE IT TOMORROW. WE HAVE A DEPARTMENT OF JUSTICE WHO WILL CONTINUE TO PROTECT HIM. -BUT FORTUNATELY, THE AMERICAN PEOPLE HAVE A CONGRESS THAT CAN SAY HE IS NOT ABOVE THE LAW, AND WE ARE NOT HELPLESS IN HOLDING HIM ACCOUNTABLE. I NOW YIELD TO THE GENTLEMAN FROM OHIO.

...THE FOUNDERS TALKED ABOUT ABUSE OF POWER, BECAUSE THEY RECOGNIZED THAT THE POWER OF THE PRESIDENCY WAS ENORMOUS. THERE WAS A DANGER

THAT THE PRESIDENT WOULD USE THAT POWER, NOT FOR THE PUBLIC GOOD, BUT FOR HIS OWN PERSONAL, OR POLITICAL, OR FINANCIAL ADVANTAGE. SO, THEY CREATED ARTICLES OF IMPEACHMENT, A FINAL CHECK AGAINST ABUSE OF POWER, NO ONE IS HERE BECAUSE WE WANT TO DO THIS, WE ARE HERE BECAUSE WE HAVE NO CHOICE. WE ARE NOT ACTING OUT OF HATE, WE ARE ACTING OUT OF LOVE OF OUR COUNTRY, AND LOVE OF OUR DEMOCRACY. WHEN GENERATIONS LOOK BACK ON THIS MOMENT, THEY WILL, ASK WHAT DID WE DO TO PRESERVE OUR DEMOCRACY?

MR. JEFFRIES:
THE RECORD IS CLEAR, DONALD TRUMP ABUSED HIS POWER BY SOLICITING FOREIGN INTERFERENCE IN THE 2020 ELECTION, AND THEREBY UNDERMINING THE INTEGRITY OF THE DEMOCRACY AS WELL AS OUR NATIONAL SECURITY. MY REPUBLICAN COLLEAGUES WANT TO SPEND ALL DAY ARGUING "PROCESS." THAT IS WHAT YOU DO, WHEN YOU CANNOT DEFEND THE INDEFENSIBLE. YOU ARGUE PROCESS. WELL, HERE IS A PROCESS ARGUMENT YOU MIGHT REFLECT UPON. EARLIER TODAY, MITCH MCCONNELL GAVE SOME INDICATION AS TO HOW A POSSIBLE TRIAL IN THE SENATE MAY WORK. AND THIS IS WHAT SENATOR MCCONNELL SAID. I AM GOING TO COORDINATE WITH THE PRESIDENT'S LAWYERS, SO THERE WON'T BE ANY DIFFERENCES BETWEEN US ON HOW TO DO THIS. IN OTHER WORDS, THE JURY, SENATE REPUBLICANS, ARE GOING TO COORDINATE WITH THE DEFENDANT, DONALD TRUMP, ON HOW EXACTLY THE KANGAROO COURT IS GOING TO BE RUN.. I SUBMIT TO YOU RESPECTFULLY THAT THIS IS A "PROCESS" CONCERN; ONE THAT THE AMERICAN PEOPLE SHOULD BE WORRIED ABOUT. NOW, AMERICA IS A RESILIENT NATION; WE HAVE BEEN THROUGH TIMES OF TURMOIL BEFORE.

WE'VE ALWAYS COME THROUGH, WE ARE RESILIENT
NATION, AND LINCOLN SAID WE ARE IN THE HEART OF
THE CIVIL WAR. AMERICA IS THE LAST, VAST HOPE ON
EARTH. FDR, SAID ON THE EVE OF THE SECOND WORLD
WAR, DEMOCRACY IS NOT DYING. REAGAN SAID IN THE
MIDST OF THE COLD WAR, AMERICA IS A SHINING CITY
ON A HILL. WHAT EXACTLY WILL HISTORY SAY ABOUT
US? WILL WE PUT PRINCIPLE OVER PARTY? WILL WE PUT
THE CONSTITUTION ABOVE CORRUPTION? WILL WE PUT
DEMOCRACY OVER DEMAGOGUERY? WHAT EXACTLY
WILL HISTORY SAY ABOUT US?. I YIELD NOW TO MY
DISTINGUISHED COLLEAGUE FROM THE GREAT STATE
OF TEXAS, MS. ESCOBAR.

MS. ESCOBAR:
THANK, YOU MISTER CHAIRMAN, I'M GOING TO SPEAK
DIRECTLY TO THE AMERICAN PEOPLE ONCE AGAIN AND
I'M GOING TO ASK BUT THEY BYPASS THE REPUBLICAN
TALKING POINTS THAT WE'VE HEARD OVER AND OVER
AND OVER AGAIN, ESPECIALLY FOR THOSE AMERICANS
WHO HAVE BEEN LISTENING AND WATCHING ALL
DAY, AND INSTEAD GO DIRECTLY TO THE EVIDENCE
YOURSELF. OVER 100 HOURS OF TESTIMONY, TESTIMONY
BY SOME OF AMERICA'S GREATEST PATRIOTS, OVER 250
TEXT MESSAGES, MICK MULVANEY'S OWN WORDS, MR.
MULVANEY IS THE PRESIDENT'S CHIEF OF STAFF AND
FINALLY, THE PRESIDENTS OWN WORDS, HIS OWN
WORDS INVITING RUSSIA UKRAINE AND CHINA INTO
OUR ELECTION. THE REPUBLICAN COLLEAGUES THAT
WE HAVE ON THIS COMMITTEE CLAIM THERE IS NOT
ENOUGH EVIDENCE, REVIEW IT FOR YOURSELF; AND
AS TO OBSTRUCTION, WE HAVE GIVEN A NUMBER OF
EXAMPLES ABOUT OBSTRUCTION, BUT WE HAVE A
LIVING EXAMPLE THAT WAS RELEASED JUST TONIGHT.
ACTUALLY, BEFORE I TALK ABOUT THAT EXAMPLE, IF

MY COLLEAGUES, MY REPUBLICAN COLLEAGUES THINK THAT THE PRESIDENT IS SO FREE FROM WRONGDOING, I WOULD ASK THEM TO JOIN US IN CALLING ON PRESIDENT TRUMP TO RELEASE IT ALL. RELEASE THE WITNESSES, RELEASE DOCUMENTS, LET THE AMERICAN PUBLIC MAKE UP THEIR OWN MINDS, LET THEM SEE IT ALL. CALL ON TRANSPARENCY, JOIN US, BUT THEY WILL NOT, BECAUSE THE OBSTRUCTION IS CONVENIENT, TONIGHT, THERE WAS A VICTORY. THE CENTER FOR PUBLIC INTEGRITY SUED FEDERAL COURT FOR DOCUMENTS RELATED TO THE UKRAINE SCANDAL AND THIS IS WHAT THEY GOT. THEY WON IN COURT, BUT WHAT THEY GOT WERE HEAVILY REDACTED DOCUMENTS. WHY? BECAUSE, THE PRESIDENT DOES NOT WANT THESE DOCUMENTS TO SEE THE LIGHT OF DAY…

2:46:52 AFTER A YIELD BACK, ABOUT 30 LINES DOWN:

JUST A COUPLE OF THINGS I WANT TO CLEAR UP, RIGHT OFF THE BAT. I FEEL COMPELLED TO SAY THAT LIEUTENANT ALEXANDRA VINDMAN IS A HERO. BECAUSE HE RECEIVED THE PURPLE HEART FOR SUSTAINING INJURIES IN IRAQ. AND I AM EXTREMELY PROUD OF HIM FOR HIS COURAGE ON AND OFF THE BATTLEFIELD. SECONDLY YOU CAN SAY THIS ONE MORE TIME, THE INTELLIGENCE COMMITTEE DID NOT SUBPOENA THE PHONE RECORDS OF ANY MEMBER OF CONGRESS OR ANY MEMBER OF THE PRESS. ABUSE OF POWER HAS BEEN DEFINED AS OFFICIAL MISCONDUCT, COMMISSION OF AN UNLAWFUL ACTIVITY, DONE IN AN OFFICIAL CAPACITY WHICH AFFECTS THE PERFORMANCE OF OFFICIAL DUTIES. PRESIDENT TRUMP SOUGHT AN ANNOUNCEMENT OF POLITICAL INVESTIGATIONS, IN RETURN FOR PERFORMING TWO OFFICIAL ACTS: NUMBER ONE, HE CONDITIONED

RELEASE OF VITAL MILITARY ASSISTANCE IN UKRAINE ON PRESIDENT ZELENSKY'S PUBLIC ANNOUNCEMENT OF THE INVESTIGATIONS. NOW IMAGINE IF THERE WAS A MAYOR WHO WITHHELD CRITICAL DOLLARS FROM THE POLICE CHIEF TO FIGHT TERRORISM UNTIL THAT CHIEF WENT TO A MICROPHONE AND SIMPLY ANNOUNCED AN INVESTIGATION OF THE MAYOR'S POLITICAL OPPONENT. I DO NOT BELIEVE ANY COMMUNITY ANYWHERE WOULD ALLOW THAT. NUMBER TWO: THE PRESIDENT CONDITIONED A "HEAD OF STATE" MEETING AT THE WHITE HOUSE, ON UKRAINE PUBLICLY ANNOUNCING THE INVESTIGATIONS; AND FINALLY, PRESIDENT TRUMP ACTED CORRUPTLY THROUGHOUT THIS COURSE OF CONDUCT BECAUSE HE OFFERED TO PERFORM THESE OFFICIAL ACTS IN EXCHANGE FOR A PRIVATE POLITICAL BENEFIT, RATHER THAN BECAUSE IT WAS IN THE COUNTRY'S INTEREST. THIS LAST ELEMENT THE, PRESIDENT ACTING CORRUPTLY, IS PERHAPS IT'S THE MOST IMPORTANT ACT. IT BEARS REPEATING BECAUSE IT EXPLAINS WHY THIS ARTICLE IS STRUCTURED AS AN ABUSE OF POWER. IT HAS BEEN SUGGESTED THAT IT'S AS SIMPLE AS WE HATE THE PRESIDENT. I DON'T HATE THE PRESIDENT. I ATTENDED PRESIDENT TRUMP'S INAUGURATION. I WANTED TO BE THERE TO WATCH A PEACEFUL TRANSFER OF POWER. I FELT IT WAS MY DUTY BEFORE COMING TO CONGRESS. I HAVE PROVIDED DIGNITARY PROTECTION FOR REPUBLICAN AND DEMOCRATIC PRESIDENTS. AND I ALWAYS CONSIDERED IT AN HONOR. BUT PRESIDENT TRUMP, WITH ALL THAT HAS BEEN SAID, WITH ALL THE EXCUSES THAT WE HAVE HEARD TODAY, PRESIDENT TRUMP USED HIS OFFICE TO SERVE HIMSELF. TO SERVE HIS PRIVATE BENEFIT. AND BY DOING SO, HE JEOPARDIZED AMERICA'S NATIONAL SECURITY INTERESTS, AND THE INTEGRITY OF OUR PRECIOUS ELECTIONS, EVERY VOTE SHOULD COUNT.

AND HE WENT ALL OUT TO COMPLETELY OBSTRUCT ANY INVESTIGATION INTO HIS WRONGDOING. YES, WE'VE HEARD IT MANY TIMES. YES, THE PRESIDENT WAS DULY ELECTED BY THE AMERICAN PEOPLE. WE KNOW THAT. AND WE TAKE IT VERY SERIOUSLY. I WANT MY VOTE TO COUNT. AND EVERYBODY, I BELIEVE, WHO MAKES THEIR WAY TO THE POLLS, WANTS THEIR VOTE TO COUNT. BUT ARE YOU SUGGESTING THAT THE AMERICAN PEOPLE WILL ALLOW THE PRESIDENT TO DO ANYTHING THAT HE WANTS TO DO, ANYTIME, ANYPLACE, ANYWHERE?! TO MY REPUBLICAN COLLEAGUES, I REJECT WHAT YOU ARE WILLING TO SETTLE FOR. WE HAVE A RESPONSIBILITY TO HOLD THE PRESIDENT ACCOUNTABLE. AND I PLAN ON DOING MY CONSTITUTIONAL DUTY. HE SHALL BE HELD ACCOUNTABLE, AND WITH THAT MISTER CHAIRMAN, I YIELD BACK.

MR. NADLER
GENTLELADY YIELDS BACK. IF THERE ARE NO FURTHER AMENDMENTS WE HAVE CONCLUDED DEBATE. THE QUESTION OCCURS ON THE AMENDMENT TO THE SUBSTITUTE. ALL THOSE IN FAVOR RESPOND BY SAYING I. THOSE NO. IN THE OPINION OF THE CHAIR THE AYES HAVE IT. TO BE CLEAR, THE AYES HAVE IT; THE AMENDMENT THE NATURE OF THE SUBSTITUTE IS AGREED TO BE CLEAR, THE VOTE THE COMMITTEE JUST TOOK IS NOT A VOTE ON THE FINAL PASSAGE OF THE ARTICLE. IT IS A PROCEDURAL VOTE, WHICH PROCEEDS FOR FINAL PASSAGE OF EACH OF THE ARTICLES. IT HAS BEEN A LONG TWO DAYS OF CONSIDERATION OF THESE ARTICLES AND IT IS NOW VERY LATE AT NIGHT. I WANT TO ALLOW MEMBERS ON BOTH SIDES OF THE AISLE TO THINK ABOUT WHAT HAS HAPPENED OVER THESE PAST FEW DAYS, AND TO SEARCH THEIR CONSCIENCE, BEFORE CASTING THEIR FINAL VOTE. THEREFORE,

THE COMMITTEE WILL NOW STAND IN RECESS UNTIL TOMORROW MORNING AT 10 AM, AT WHICH POINT I WILL MOVE TO DIVIDE THE QUESTION SO THAT EACH OFFICE MAY HAVE THE OPPORTUNITY TO CAST AN UP OR DOWN VOTE ON EACH OF THE ARTICLES OF IMPEACHMENT.

My Comments Regarding the Impeachment Trial Itself:

I have decided not to transcribe any of the impeachment trial; as I found it very upsetting, to listen to such contrived Republican arguments, that Trump's removal wasn't warranted; in this case, it has never been more warranted!

I will make a few comments regarding my thoughts on what I saw and heard, of the actual Senate trial; and on the political situation in the US, in general, at this point:

I don't see why we have to sit listen to these silly arguments, of Republican Senators, and Trump's legal team. I would just go to exposing the real significant truth about this situation; which is that Republican legislators don't really have a problem with anything the Trump says or does, as long as their conservative agenda keeps moving along nicely, as it has for the past 3 years.

But the trouble with this viewpoint, is that it also means these Republican legislators don't give a rat's ass about things like, that we won't leave this planet too inhabitable for future generations; because the Trump administration is dead against owning any responsibility for our needing to deal effectively with global warming, which is causing so many disasters and challenges already; such as forest fires, and floods, and earthquakes; and for that matter, due partially to fracking, in order to remove oil and natural gas; which disturbs the deep layers under the

Earth's crust, destabilizing them and causing more earthquakes; even in places that have never had earthquakes before.

These Republican lawmakers don't give a rat's ass whether we put people in cages at the border, or separate children from their parents or anything else; or whether everybody in those hundred person pens has to eat nothing but bologna sandwiches once or twice a day, for months at a time. Then there's all the regulation rollbacks; like all of the changes allowing companies to pollute the air and water. These rollbacks, in aggregate, have probably hurt the masses in this country more than anything else, perhaps; and hardly anyone in the political sphere is even talking about all of these, at this point.

But the bottom line is that Republican lawmakers don't care about historic standards for doling out foreign aid, they may not even care much about Russia, militarily expanding its borders, and killing thousands of Ukrainians to do it; and this also sets a precedent that any country might emulate, thus causing warring factions all over the world, perhaps.

They don't care that Trump is playing dirty pool, by trying to fabricate, and spread around false contentions about his political rivals, in order to ensure his reelection. No other President has ever done this that I'm aware of; at least not on this huge scale. A Presidential race is supposed to be about how sensible each candidate is speaking, regarding the issues of the moment; and we should be judging candidates by how promising it might be to have them at the helm of government. Republican lawmakers simply seem to be a dirty gang, dead against the American citizen; all standing in solidarity behind an unconscionable administration with a lunatic as a Leader.

But even after their certain acquittal of this narcissistic sicko, this is not over; it is just the beginning of the next initiative for reasonable politicians and advocates. The good news, about what has been happening during the hearings and the trial that has occurred since the whistleblower came forward with this credible complaint, is that we have heard specific contentions and criticisms of the process, and of the witnesses, made by specific Republican members of Congress; so now it is time to broadcast the story behind each one of these politicians, to their constituent states; particularly those up for reelection, in November.

Maybe we should concentrate mainly on the 19 Republican Senators we stand to defeat, and their states; because if we simply lay out what these Senators have voiced, in terms of its implications for how the government will be run, as long as there is a Republican Majority in the Senate, we should be able to forge a democratic Majority in the Senate, as of November. This would be an important first step, toward getting back on a good path, as far as government leadership.

I think, that in the process of doing this, it would have good potential, for us each to try and point out, to as many of the voting public that we can reach with our entreaties, what the Republican Committee members' general attitude, and course of action has been; and how it has negatively affected many onlookers.

And, should Trump get reelected, by some stroke of bad luck, if we can at least elect a Democratic Majority in the Senate, let's not forget that there is still a lot of impeachable behavior, beyond what was talked about in the first 2 articles that the House brought; so we could conceivably have another impeachment process, next year; but this time governed by a body of Senators who apparently have some sensibility and integrity; not a group of unprincipled hellions who have simply sold out to the gun lobby, or big Pharma, or even more importantly, to the oil and gas industry, that has been able to ratchet up production of the very substance that pollutes our air with greenhouse gases, which has caused the global warming; but the Republicans don't care about any of this, as long as they get their tax cuts, and a deregulated environment that lets them pollute the water in order to make dirty money off of coal mining, and sales of it to coal-burners; and from strip-mining, and formerly-banned toxic chemical use. None of this seems to matter to Republican lawmakers.

Don't worry; we've got your number; we're going to Trumpet your unfitness for Office all over this land! We'll hammer out danger, and we'll hammer out warning; just like Peter, Paul, and Mary taught us! Unfortunately, these days, our votes are the only way we can hammer out justice, in this crazy modern age of "anything goes" politics.

If we make a mighty effort together, we can maybe render ineffective, Republicans' widespread ability to broadcast lies on a grand scale, via Facebook, for example, in order to convince people to vote a crooked, narcissistic lunatic into Office; and we <u>should</u> stamp out the massive broadcasting of lies and propaganda via the Internet, because we have recently learned that, once such a phony and a liar gets into Office through playing dirty pool, like Trump, they then proceed to forsake everyone who voted for them; with the exception of the top few percent of earners who the dirty scoundrel is beholden to; along with his personal impression of how he thinks America might be great again; which seems wildly askew, to say the least.

Trump's greatly-improved economy is really only slightly better than before; and it comes at the expense of completely upsetting the applecart, on so many levels, and causing major challenges for companies formerly supplied with inexpensive Chinese goods and parts, for example; which enabled US companies to sell their products for less, while making more of a profit. Perhaps, the GDP figure that Trump keeps touting, doesn't reflect how little profit is being made by US companies, in a Trump-impeded economy.

I can't believe so many people apparently think Trump has delivered something positive regarding the economy; just like on everything else, he cheats! Obama's economy did virtually as well, while responsibly addressing global warming and pollution, and while enforcing effective regulation of banks and investment companies, to prevent another purposely-manufactured market crash, which last time around, in 2008, benefitted the shrewdest of us, at everyone else's great expense; especially the middle class.

The tariff-wielding lunatic has caused US export sales to diminish, and his tariffs have resulted in raised prices for US citizens buying foreign-made goods. He thinks he's made an accomplishment, in having negotiated a partial truce with China, over trade; but all he has really received, is a promise that China will buy more agricultural products, and such. History indicates that they may well flout that commitment. Then again, this first step still keeps high tariffs in effect, on most other Chinese goods.

-And regarding the contended unjust stealing of US intellectual property, we could even ask ourselves, should we really be assuming that all good technological ideas are thought up and developed by Americans, and all China does is steal what we have innovated? From what I have seen, in terms of TV interview footage of Chinese technology and other invention-innovating centers, in provinces such a Schzen-Zhen, it seems pretty obvious that the Chinese have taken what they have learned from US innovators, and ran with it. Wouldn't we maybe get further, faster, if we developed Chinese/American cooperative companies; so that both countries get to take part in, and flourish from putting our heads together. We have obviously acknowledged that the tech developments of one country, can't be forever kept from being learned all about, in other countries.

Finally, regarding the recent impeachment effort; you know, just the fact that all of these State Department and Defense Department officials, Ambassadors, and Foreign Service officers have wanted to come forward, and reveal what they saw going on that was upsetting or concerning; this alone would suggest that these hearings were not, in any way, unwarranted; as the Republicans have feebly been trying to suggest.

Perhaps, we should also consider, regarding the team acting as counsel for Trump's defense, within this impeachment scandal, they don't really deserve any credit for his acquittal; the Senate would have voted to acquit, no matter what the defense team had argued or contended.

But it occurs to me that, had the trial been instead for murder, because Trump had shot someone in broad daylight on 5th avenue; if we project, based on the types of arguments they had put forth, at the Senate impeachment trial; perhaps these lawyers might have likely made arguments like, that sure, President Trump might have pulled the trigger, but surely we shouldn't convict a President for one act of a few seconds; or they might say something like, well, the victim really isn't actually dead, because he still lives on in our memory.

Trump has been a terrible pox on humanity; all around the world, really. We would all do well to become "Never-Trumpers!"

About the Author

Geoffrey Keane is a baby boomer who comes from a middle class family, and has not even ever really had any serious aspirations to become involved in politics; however, in recent decades, he has watched the very fiber of this country's leadership gradually erode; saved only by the incredibly competent and responsible leadership of Barack Obama for eight years. Then this crooked, maniacal phony cons half the country into believing he can help the common man even more; only proving to have absolutely no ability to deliver any of what he had promised while campaigning; it turns out he was just full of hot air. Okay, he could maybe swallow that; but then, Trump proceeded to do the most incredible amount of damage, way more than he could ever imagine a president would ever have the power to do; and Geoffrey was naturally driven to learn more and more about what was transpiring all around us, in these respects. He started reading the paper and watching cable news stations; it doesn't take a genius with a political degree, to educate themselves via the ample outlets of free US press, of course.

Geoffrey is a writer, and he has penned several books before this one. Most recently, he received a degree in psychology from Southern Connecticut State University, and wrote a self-help book, utilizing his lifetime experience combined with his newfound education in recent years. He merely felt called to this task.

www.ingramcontent.com/pod-product-compliance
Lightning Source LLC
Chambersburg PA
CBHW051707020426
42333CB00014B/875